D0516225

Bottom Line's
HOME BOOK

Better Ways to
Maintain, Improve and Enjoy
Your Home and Garden

John and Martha Storey

Bottom Line
Books

Bottom Line's Home Book: Better Ways to Maintain,
Improve and Enjoy Your Home and Garden

© 2002 by Boardroom Inc.
10 9 8 7 6 5 4 3 2
Published by arrangement with Storey Publishing LLC.

ISBN 0-88723-259-0
Bottom Line® Books is a registered trademark of
Boardroom® Inc.
281 Tresser Blvd.
Stamford, CT 06901

Edited by Deborah Burns
Additional editorial services provided by Greg Linder, Linder Creative Services, Mankato, Minnesota
Contributing Editors: Gwen Steege, Charles W.G. Smith, Dan Callahan, and Deborah Balmuth
Part opener and Foreword photographs by Martha Storey
Text design and production by Carol Jessop, Black Trout Design
Technical direction by Leslie Noyes
Additional text by Greg Linder, Nick Noyes, Jim Sherratt, and Gail Damerow
Production assistance by Elizabeth Collier, Susan Bernier, Jen Jepson, and Erin Lincourt
Illustrations edited by Ilona Sherratt
A list of illustrators appears on page 386.
Indexed by Susan Olason, Indexes & Knowledge Maps

Copyright © 1999 by Storey Publishing LLC.

Dedication

A number of our authors started writing about their passions forty or more years ago. Some of them are gone now, but many are still working and writing. Over the years others have joined us, offering new techniques and new solutions to the challenges of country life. Collectively, they have inspired millions of readers to do things for themselves, whether it's home building, animal husbandry, growing and preserving food, composting, soap making, or countless other practical skills.

This book is respectfully dedicated to this group of talented and inspiring authors.

Bottom Line's
HOME BOOK
Better Ways to Maintain, Improve and Enjoy Your Home and Garden

FOREWORD BY JOHN AND MARTHA STOREY

PART 1: YOUR PLACE IN THE COUNTRY

1. YOUR COUNTRY HOME 2
Finding Land • Buying Property • Country Dwelling • Inspecting a Home • Home Building in 25 Steps

2. OUTDOOR SPACES 16
Stonescaping • Walks and Paths • Decks • Patios • Outdoor Furniture

3. THE WATER SUPPLY 28
Water Sources • Water Supply Systems • Wells • Pumps • Natural Springs • Ponds • Water Distribution • Water Quality

4. PLUMBING 48
Plumbing Systems • Septic Systems • Leaky Faucets • Toilets • Clogged Drains • Repairing Pipes

5. HEATING YOUR HOME 60
Woodstoves and Fireplaces • Heating with Wood • Stacking and Seasoning Wood • Build an Old-Fashioned Woodshed • Heating with Coal • Heating with Gas • Heating by the Sun • Weatherproofing Your Home

6. ELECTRICITY 82
Understanding Electricity • Assessing Your System • Rewiring • Making Repairs • Solar and Wind Power • When the Power Fails

7. BASIC HOME IMPROVEMENTS .100
Hardwood Floors • Vinyl Flooring • Ceramic Tile • Carpeting • Painting • Wallpapering • Walls and Ceilings • Windows and Doors

8. THE HOME INTERIOR 124
Decorating Tips • Country Creativity • Renovating Furniture • Better Housekeeping • Soapmaking

PART 2: YOUR GARDEN, YARD & ORCHARD

9. THE VEGETABLE GARDEN 158
Planning Your Garden • Cool- and Warm-Season Vegetables • Extending the Season • Growing from Seed • Special Growing Techniques • Harvest and Storage • Seed Saving • Vegetables A to Z

10. THE HERB GARDEN 198
Herbal Theme Gardens • Harvesting and Storing Herbs • 32 Essential
Herbs • Herb Growth and Uses

11. THE FLOWER GARDEN 212
Annuals • Perennials • Bulbs • Flowering Shrubs • Roses •
Wildflowers • Art from the Garden • Flowers that Last

12. WATER AND ROCK GARDENS 252
Pool Gardens • Water in the Landscape • Plants for Water Gardens •
Rock Gardens

13. IMPROVING YOUR SOIL 266
Getting to Know Your Soil • Soil pH • Soil Nutrients • Composting •
Mulching • Green Manures

14. GARDEN PESTS AND DISEASES 284
Garden Management • Common Garden Insects • Pest Remedies •
Plant Diseases • Animal Deterrents

15. BIRDS AND BUTTERFLIES 300
Feeding the Birds • Gardening for the Birds • Hummingbird Gardens •
Building Nest Boxes • Butterfly Gardens

16. LAWN CARE 314
Installing a New Lawn • Tackling Weed Problems • Rejuvenating
Your Lawn • Lawn Alternatives

17. BERRIES AND FRUITS 326
Strawberries • Raspberries and Blackberries • Blueberries • Grapes •
Fruit Trees

18. ARBORS AND TRELLISES 348
Build a Lounging Arbor • Create a Rose Arbor • Trellising Vining
Crops • Build a Bentwood Trellis

19. GREENHOUSES 358
Greenhouse Choices • Setting Up a Greenhouse • Growing in a
Greenhouse • Troubleshooting

20. SHEDS AND MORE 366
Garden Shed • Storage Shed • Toolshed • Tree House

21. TOOLS AND TECHNIQUES 382
Basic Hand Tools • Power Equipment • Specialty Tools

ILLUSTRATION CREDITS 386

RESOURCES 388

INDEX 398

HARDINESS ZONE MAP 406

Foreword by country publishers and part-time farmers John and Martha Storey

Dear Reader,

Martha and I hope that you enjoy this book and that it helps you in your journey toward greater self-sufficiency and enjoyment of your home and garden.

Ours has been a gradual journey, under way since the 1950s when Martha's folks, cotton farmers from West Texas, found themselves in New Jersey, a few houses up the street from my parents' home.

Suburban life at that time was pleasant, to be sure, but only a few people like Martha's parents, Aulton and Elizabeth Mullendore, were "the real McCoys." While most of our neighbors had modest "victory gardens," they had a small-scale farm! They built their own home, raised meat, and grew crops for sale and for the table.

After Martha and I married, we were eager to have a vegetable garden in our small home. Armed with a six-pack of tomato seedlings and *Taylor's Garden Encyclopedia*, we began. We were hooked on gardening and on doing it all ourselves.

Soon I was working for a publisher in New York City, and when the possibility for a garden encyclopedia written by James Underwood Crockett emerged, I enthusiastically supported it. "Too narrow a subject," the old-timers said, but we found a surprisingly dedicated audience, eager for information on everything from lawns and landscapes to water gardens and ornamentals. I met Crockett and some other grand old pros of the gardening world, and my love affair with gardening deepened in the process.

Problem was, our home only had a 60' x 100' lot, mostly covered by patio and shade trees, providing just enough light for three tomato plants. We soon moved to still-rural Ridgefield, Connecticut, buying two acres of land and an old colonial house that needed just about everything. Here our occasional ecstasy, and regular agony, of life in the country really began.

The quaint old furnace, resembling Jules Verne's diving bell, collapsed first. We gleefully discovered a modest pond at the back of the property, which turned out to be an immodest septic system failure. Almost immediately our spick-and-span paint job began peeling, revealing a moisture condition that

required installation of a new drainage system. Was country life really all that it was cracked up to be?

John's garden in spring

At wit's end, we discovered a couple of life-savers—the *Popular Mechanics Do-It-Yourself Encyclopedia* and Carla Emery's *Encyclopedia of Country Living*. The former was long on specifics, the latter on kindred spirit. They helped us through these tougher times. And Martha's father visited often from New Jersey.

Becoming Entrepreneurs

Ever grateful for the help we received, Martha and I decided to start a publishing program to help others decipher country life and become self-reliant. We launched *The Practical Gardener's Newsletter* in the early 1970s. This led us to Lyman Wood, the founder of *Garden Way*, and to nearly a decade of entrepreneurial life with this venerable man. We learned about Ed and Carolyn Robinson and their *"Have-More" Plan*, which had offered "a little land, a lot of living" to GIs returning from World War II; nearly a half million copies of their book were sold.

In the early 1980s, we launched *Storey's Books for Country Living* in Vermont and the Berkshires of western Massachusetts.

Meet the Real Stars

The true joy of our journey has been in meeting and providing a forum for hundreds of authors from all over the United States, Canada and the world—all dedicated to bringing helpful, practical, step-by-step information to those who yearn to do more for themselves.

You'll meet many of these folks in this book. We've gathered together the best of their advice, providing a lifetime of wisdom in one volume.

We trust that you'll find this compendium motivating and inspiring. No matter where you live—whether you're still dreaming of life in the country or creating a suburban garden—this book will serve you for a lifetime.

A Farm of Our Own

Martha and I purchased an old farm in the Champlain Valley, where our large-scale gardening has become small-scale farming. When I asked my neighbor, a real farmer, to explain the business, he replied in a twinkle, "It's not a business; it's an illness!"

Martha and John's stone farmhouse in the Champlain Valley

To be sure, we've had our share of ups and downs. But we've also delighted in the opportunity to raise a family, grow a portion of our own food and create a life based on genuine American country values. We were recently reminded of the importance of community when a neighbor's barn, loaded with the summer's haying, caught fire and burned to the ground. Volunteers helped to raise a new barn in three weeks. Local farmers donated 10 percent of their hay crop. Our neighbor said it was as if the fire had never happened.

After owning a farm for several years, we're feeling progress. The barn has been saved, with a great drainage system surrounding it and a new roof overhead. We've uncovered the richest of black earth, where gardens now flourish. Three apple trees, hopelessly overgrown, have responded well to pruning and reshaping. Their clippings have added aroma and flavor to our barbecues. I've graduated from an early lawn and garden tractor to something a bit larger, and I dream of even grander machinery.

Each month still seems to deliver unexpected surprises. We know by now that the asparagus will be up in the Champlain Valley during early May, the rhubarb in June, the daylilies in July, and the corn in August, but it is still exciting. The fact that Martha still speaks to me after my delivery of thousands of Italian plum tomatoes each September is ever so reassuring. And I know, down deep, of her continuing joy in opening a jar of tomato sauce, paste, or ketchup on a cold winter evening, thinking contentedly, "We did it ourselves."

John making the most
of a fine summer day

Coming Full Circle

Our efforts don't necessarily impress our neighbors in this rural community of 1,800 people. After all, they're real farmers (or are related to one!). And if I figured out the cost per jar in our pantry, that wouldn't be impressive either. But none of that's important. To have been able to take care of and reinvigorate a dozen acres of our own, to develop and pass along knowledge and values to children and grandchildren makes it all worthwhile. We'd do it again in a minute.

Our journey, now in its fifth decade, has come full circle: We are now country parents whose suburban children strive to return to country ways. I'm sure somewhere our parents and grandparents are chuckling quietly to themselves.

So here's to the fun and pride of old-fashioned self-reliance, to the satisfaction of healthy living, and to the sheer joy of being able to say, "I did it myself!"

—*John Storey*

PART ONE

Your Place in the Country

For many people, the only place to live is in the country. They need to feel earth under their feet, to have the presence of wild nature in their lives, to experience the flow of seasons, to feel the freshness of a new morning and the peace of a quiet, starry night. But there's another key aspect of country life: self-reliance. Frequently you have to draw on your own skills and resources for solutions to problems large and small. Developing these skills is valuable, but even more important is having an attitude of confidence that you can solve your problems and learn from your mistakes.

YOUR COUNTRY HOME

FINDING LAND • BUYING PROPERTY
COUNTRY DWELLINGS • INSPECTING A HOME
HOME BUILDING IN 25 STEPS

Living in a Brooklyn apartment, we dreamed of owning a few acres, an old farmhouse, a garden, a stream, and a pond. We drove to the country on weekends, even took a seminar on "buying country property." We learned how to find properties and what to ask about water, sewage disposal, road maintenance, and utilities. We learned to return in different seasons, to see if the ecstasy of summer lasted through mud season. Our dream came true when we found a place in Ridgefield, Connecticut. Our journey into country living was under way.

—John & Martha Storey

For most people, country living implies a comfortable home with land, a healthful natural life, and a real chance to enjoy the outdoor world. The good news is that despite urban and suburban sprawl, there are thousands of places where it is still pleasant to live in the United States.

Everyone has an idea of the area where he or she would like to live. The choice is largely personal: the presence of friends, some knowledge of the area, or even an unfulfilled childhood longing. Some prefer a warm climate year-round; others feel restless without lots of snow in winter. Different states within the same region have a different "feel" to them. Only you can decide where you will be the most comfortable.

Once you have decided on the general region or area that you like, look carefully at the individual communities. Many factors will determine your final choice, such as the availability of jobs, schools, cultural centers, and markets for your skills.

Finding a Piece of Land

The best way to find a piece of land is to visit an area you like. Perhaps you have friends or spend vacations or summers there. Travel around on the back roads. Get acquainted with the local residents—go to local affairs, auctions, meetings. Get a feel for the area, the people, and the land market.

Occasionally a perfect opportunity will fall into your lap, but generally the following methods are most productive:

Land sale agencies. A number of companies deal in nationwide land sales. Their catalogs are generally free, and they have affiliated realtors in almost every area. Well-established land sale agencies have brought many people to the land they were seeking. At least, they will give you a feel for land prices.

Realtors. Even if you have lived in an area for quite a while, check with local real estate people. A good real estate agent will have years of experience listing and selling in the area. He or she may know the history of nearly every piece of property in town: the present owner, the past owners, what's wrong (or right) with it, and its present market value. The broker also knows the local development trends—tax rate, areas where land costs are inflated—and local attitudes about newcomers.

An agent wants to sell you a place, and the less time it takes, the higher the profit. He or she may suggest that you're hard to please. No matter. It's your money you're spending, so don't be hurried. No matter what else you do in buying land, take your time. Ask plenty of questions. You are under no obligation until you actually sign a purchase agreement.

Other sources. Other ways to locate property for sale include checking the local newspaper, which will carry personal as well as realtors' listings. Another good source, especially if you have lived or spent time in the area, is the grapevine. Through your friends, you may hear of someone who would like to sell land but has not gotten around to listing or advertising it.

How Much Land Do You Need?

Generally, it is a mistake to buy too much land. For one thing, land requires maintenance and use or it grows up with weeds, brush, or small trees. For another, land costs money and carries annual tax assessments. It's impossible to specify how large a homestead should be, but most people would not need more than a few acres, perhaps 15 at the outside. You can have a lovely and fairly self-sufficient homestead on five acres, if it is all good land. If you want to heat with wood, an additional five-acre woodlot will save you money, and it may be priced lower than your open homestead land.

—from *The Complete Homesteading Book* by David Robinson

Choosing a Community

Here's a list of important factors to consider when picking the location of your country home:

- Housing and land quality and availability
- Climate
- Air and water quality
- Cost of living
- Taxes
- Beauty of the area
- Economic health of the area
- Employment opportunities
- Gardening or farming suitability
- Quality of local schools
- Quality of government
- Proximity/quality of medical facilities
- Levels of crime and violence
- Community spirit
- Attitudes toward newcomers
- Cultural and educational opportunities
- Outdoor recreation opportunities
- Population trends and characteristics
- Churches and civic organizations
- Transportation convenience and traffic patterns
- Zoning and environmental factors
- Restaurants and markets

—from *How to Locate in the Country* by John Gourlie

BUYING PROPERTY

"A little land—a lot of living" was the slogan that went with Ed and Carolyn Robinson's The "Have-More" Plan, *first published in the 1940s and still in print.*

Tip: Investigate how the land was previously used. Could there be pollution or hazardous waste?

Zoning and Building Codes

It is essential to check into local zoning regulations and applicable building codes at an early stage in your inspection. It might turn out that the land is ideal, but that you would not be allowed to erect the sort of buildings you want or to keep animals. On the other hand, zoning that precludes industrial development near you could be valuable.

How to Evaluate Land

As you visit and inspect pieces of land, your excitement may distract you from practical considerations. Here, then, is a list to keep in mind.

Location. The best location for a practical homestead, assuming good soil and water, is on a gentle slope, neither in the valley nor on a hilltop, for the slope will provide good drainage. Look for southern exposures and protection from prevailing winds.

Water. Check carefully for springs or existing wells. If you find a year-round spring on a slope above your chosen house site, you need only install a gravity pipeline to your house. Next best is a good spring nearby, from which you can pump water. Make sure no one else owns the spring rights, and find out whether the spring goes dry in summer. If there's no spring, you may have to drill for water. When visiting properties, take a sterile-bottle water sample and have it tested for purity.

Drainage. Keep an eye open for drainage. Problems may come up. For example, your septic tank could start contaminating your well. Make sure the surface water drains somewhere besides your favored house site. If the soil is very clayey, think twice. Clay holds water and may cause a septic system to back up if the water table is too high. It's unstable to build on, too.

Fertility. Good soil is a primary concern. Scoop some up in your fingers. Does it harden into a lump of mud? It may have too much clay content. Is it too sandy? Or does it remain light and crumbly? The latter is one indication of good soil. Look at the plants already on the property. Are they earthy and lush? Are there plenty of dark green, sturdy weeds? If so, the land is probably good. Have a sample of the soil tested at your state or county agricultural office.

Woods. The ideal homestead is partly wooded, with enough open land and fairly even ground for a house, garden, and pastures. Most homesteaders in the northern states heat with wood, so a woodlot is often necessary. Sometimes land is available that is completely wooded or has been "clear-cut." In either instance, you will be able to buy the land more cheaply. However, clearing the land is expensive and time-consuming.

Access. Parcels of land are sometimes available cheaply because they have no road frontage or access, such as a farmer's back field. This may be a good buy, if there is an established and deeded access road somewhere on the property. If there is not, you have a serious problem.

Price and other costs. First, be wary of any land that is selling at a very low price out of line with similar parcels in the area. Find out what the going price for land is in the area and expect to pay it. Second, find out from the county or town clerk what you can expect to pay for taxes.

Title search. Have a local attorney or title insurance company confirm that the present owner has a clear title and that there are no old rights-of-way, easements, liens, or other rights that have been granted or retained by previous owners.

—from *The Complete Homesteading Book* by David Robinson

Setting Up a Productive Homestead

Even though no one layout will fit everybody's ideas and site, there are certain basic principles that ought to be kept in mind when setting up a productive country homestead:

1. Every bit of land should be used advantageously.
2. Garden rows should be of good length for easy cultivation, and should run north and south for equal sunlight.
3. Pasture should be fenced into plots for rotation. Pasture gates should be wide enough for entry for haying and plowing equipment.
4. Vegetable gardens should be handy to the kitchen.
5. Lawn and shrubbery arranged attractively, yet easily cared for.
6. Child's play area screened from street and located so it can be watched from house.
7. Compost heap should be placed between barn and garden.
8. Trees should be spaced so as not to be crowded at maturity.
9. Shower, bath, and dressing room should be accessible from outside.
10. Barn should be to lee of house, and close enough to make supervision of livestock easy.
11. Adequate closet and storage space in house.
12. Space for good home workshop.
13. Housing for garden tools, wheelbarrow, lawn mower, small tractor.
14. Cold storage room for vegetables and canned goods.
15. Fencing arranged so that livestock may be turned loose from barn.
16. Space for home freezer, laundry, fireplace wood.
17. Orchard should not shade garden.

—from *The "Have-More" Plan* by Ed and Carolyn Robinson

20-20 Hindsight

Below is a sketch of our homestead. It has been very productive and successful. However, some of the things we did wrong are errors anyone could make, and if we tell you about them, you can avoid them.

First, although lawn is pretty, we set up too much of it. Our house sits 90 feet back from the road and the front and back lawn take a good hour to mow each week. Second, our small barn is too close to our neighbor's property. Third, our quarter-acre hayfield isn't large enough. Fourth, there are too many trees in our pasture—good pasture grass needs sunlight.

Our total acreage is only about 2½. Three to five acres would give us enough pasture for our livestock and enough hay. We could then depend on our place to supply us with more than 75 percent of all our food requirements and a high percentage of the roughage and grains needed to feed our livestock.

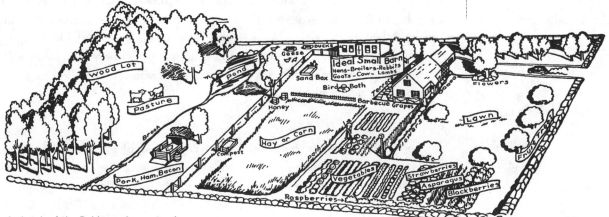

A sketch of the Robinson homestead

COUNTRY DWELLINGS

What kind of home will work best for you in your new environment? To help you answer this question, here's a look at six kinds of country homes:

Wood-Frame Homes

Most houses you see are of wood-frame construction. They have many advantages, among them the huge common fund of construction knowledge and the geometry involved in right angles and straight surfaces. They are easier to learn about, easier to build (in some ways), and easier to fit things into. Another advantage of the conventional frame is the availability of financing. Banks are more interested in financing a standard type of house—something they can sell if they are forced to foreclose—than an "oddball" house built for eccentric tastes. The disadvantage of conventional houses is cost. A small suburban house built by a contractor simply has to cost a lot, because of the price of lumber and the labor time involved.

Pole-Built Homes

Pole buildings are houses built not *of* poles but *on* poles. They can be built quite cheaply because they do not require a conventional foundation. The weight of the house is borne by the poles, which also serve as a frame. Another advantage of pole houses is their adaptability to steep hillsides and other terrain unsuitable for excavation. Installation of poles does not disturb much topsoil or create erosion problems. Beyond the weight limitation on the poles, the disadvantage of pole construction lies mainly in the need for extra insulating of the floor area, which is exposed. Pole houses might cost somewhat more to heat for this reason, and may be better suited to warmer climates.

Log Homes

The log cabin is one of the oldest kinds of pioneer houses in America. Logs were always free for the cutting in pioneer days, and the cost of the house consisted entirely of labor time and feeding the neighbors who came to lend a hand. Today a log cabin or log house may cost substantially more, but it can still be cheaply built. If you have your own source of conifers, you can cut your logs and haul them to the site in classic style. Many books explain the technique of log building, and you can probably find friends or neighbors who know a few tricks. The major cash outlays will be insulation, windows, roofing materials, flooring, and electrical wiring.

Stone Homes

The advantages of a stone house are partly intangible: a certain beauty and an impression of strength. In addition, stone is one of the cheapest building materials, since it can usually be gathered simply for the labor. The main disadvantage of stone is that it is heavy, and building by hand is a ponderous operation. Stone also suggests cold and rigidity, but cold can be cured with insulation and earthquakes are few except on the West Coast. Saving money on stone

The wood-frame house is uncomplicated to build, but materials are costly.

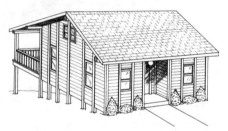

Pole-built homes are adaptable and relatively inexpensive.

Log homes are generally cheaper to build than wood-frame houses.

construction depends on getting the stones at the site and doing the building yourself—not the sort of home-fixing project one accomplishes in a few weeks. If you seriously want to build with stone, you had better have another house to live in meanwhile. In the end, though, a stone house may last hundreds of years and become almost an outgrowth of the rocky soil around it.

—from *The Complete Homesteading Book* by David Robinson

Stone can be one of the cheapest building materials, but building with it can be a slow process.

Brick Homes

Brick homes are both beautiful and solid. If a Victorian brick building is standing today and has no structural faults, it will probably stand for another hundred years. However, these buildings are most common in cities, and they are subject to the same problems that plague other older homes: poorly maintained exteriors, structural defects, roof malfunction, energy inefficiency, and so forth. If you find a brick home in the country, examine it closely. If it is free of major problems, you may have discovered an exceptional home.

—from *Renovating Brick Houses* by Phillip Decker and T. Newell Decker

If brick homes are carefully maintained they are both beautiful and solid.

Underground Homes

Many people envision problems with waterproofing, ventilation, roof structure, and natural lighting in underground homes. However, today's technology offers solutions for each of these problems. Underground homes offer energy conservation, minimal upkeep expenses, and best use of many building sites. They facilitate the use of solar heating. On the less desirable side, a properly built underground house may cost about 10 percent more than an equivalent conventional structure. Energy savings of more than 50 percent quickly offset the initial costs, however. In some areas, it can be difficult to find a knowledgeable contractor or consultant. Zoning ordinances and septic tank requirements can also present difficulties.

—from *The Underground House Book* by Stu Campbell

Underground houses can be expensive to build but are extremely energy-efficient to live in.

INSPECTING A HOME

Test for Health Hazards

- **Asbestos** is most often found in pipe insulation, siding shingles, and 9-inch square flooring tiles. Professional testing is the only way to determine whether asbestos is present. Professionals can also test if asbestos-tainted vermiculite was used in home insulation.
- **Lead.** Almost all houses built before 1960 used lead paint, which is now banned. Lead can also turn up in the water system where lead solder was used at pipe joints or from lead pipes in the water mains. Testing is best left to a professional, who can also recommend remediation procedures if needed.
- **Radon** is a naturally occurring radioactive gas that emanates from the soil. Radon-testing devices can be obtained at retail stores. Make sure the device is certified by the U.S. Environmental Protection Agency, which can also provide information on reducing home radon levels.

—from *Be Your Own Home Renovation Contractor* by Carl Heldmann

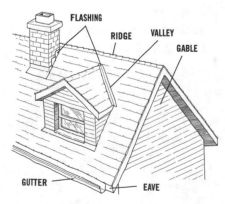

The roof and its parts should be carefully inspected.

Tip: Don't forget to check the chimney.

After your first guided tour through the house, you're interested in the place. You will want to know everything possible about it, and the best way to do this is to hire a professional home inspector. For the modest cost of a home inspector—a few hundred dollars—you add a big layer of protection to your investment. Lenders often require an inspection and an inspection clause is standard on purchase and sales agreements. Look for a trained and licensed inspector (if a license is required by law), and be sure that he or she carries errors and omissions (E & O) insurance.

The benefits of such an inspection are immediate. You will have confidence in whether to go for the house or forget it. And if you turn up an architectural scandal but you still want to buy the house, you not only can estimate the probable cost of renovation, but you also may be able to negotiate hundreds or even thousands of dollars off the purchase price.

The following inspection instructions can help you do a preliminary evaluation of a house and will provide a fuller understanding of what every new homeowner ought to know about a home. These instructions can also help in evaluating how thorough and accurate your inspector is. Always accompany the inspector whenever you have a home inspection performed—it is a learning experience whether or not you decide to buy the home.

Inspecting the Outside

The roof. Use binoculars—or a ladder, depending on the pitch and height of the roof.

- Look carefully at the shingles. Watch for torn shingles, patches, or unevenness due to curled shingles and missing pieces. Find out the age of the roof and how many layers of roofing are on the house.
- Check the flashing (sheet-metal protection) around the chimney and at places such as dormers, where a vertical wall adjoins the roof.
- Check the condition of roof valleys. Look for sags on the surface of the roof that might mean a broken rafter or rotted-out boards under the roofing.
- Look for sags and dips in the ridge of the roof. They could represent weakened foundations, termites in the walls, rotted places, or bowed exterior walls.
- A sag in the eave line might indicate a broken or rotted eave. If both the ridge and the eave sag at one end, you might suspect settling in the foundation, termite damage in the wall, a heavy chimney without sufficient foundation, or a drainage problem.
- Look at gutters and downspouts to check for deterioration.

Underneath the house. Look at the sills (the part of the structure that rests on the masonry foundation), the main supporting beams, and the posts that hold them up. You are looking for soundness, absence of rot, and termites.

Sewer lines. While you are under the house, look at the sewer lines. These are usually 3- to 4-inch cast-iron pipes, although you may find copper or plastic. Evaluate their quality, neatness, absence of leaks, and location. Watch for sewer lines wrapped with friction tape or duct tape—an indication of rotted-out or frost-cracked pipes.

Electrical system. Look at the wiring visible from under the house. What type is it? If you find a knob-and-tube or other cloth-sheathed, nongrounded system, you know the wiring is old. Open a junction box or two. Look for over-crowding and crumbling insulation. Examine the overall condition of the wiring.

Wood and siding. How is the siding and exterior wood? Are there bad areas that will need replacing? Look for any vertical area of the siding where the paint is peeling. This is usually a dead giveaway that there is water seeping in behind the wall. Poke any place that looks rotten with your knife or ice pick. Paint will never stick to rotten wood for very long. Watch for leaks in the eaves, manifested by missing or rotted boards or peeling paint. Check all windowsills for rotting or infestation.

Masonry. Your main concern is to assess the condition of masonry walls. Brick or stone houses usually have a crack or two running from bottom to top. This can be filled with caulk and forgotten. However, large cracks, bowed walls, or many fallen bricks may indicate that a whole wall or section of the house is falling. Watch for rotted mortar between the bricks or stones. Test with your ice pick at numerous places. If it is bad all over, you are in for a long project of tuck-pointing the mortar. If the house is constructed of stucco over wood lath, look for dark spots; these indicate that the lath is rotted under the stucco.

Outbuildings. Inspect the garage, barn, and other outbuildings. Are they in general disrepair? Are they big enough for your needs? Does the garage door operate easily? Is there any broken glass or broken wood panels? Is the roof of the garage in poor condition? Other features to look for are lights, adequate wiring, insulation or heating of work areas, and electrical outlets.

Water well pump. The water supply for the house may be furnished by a well. If the house is located near a chemical plant, heavy industry, farm fields that experience heavy use of pesticides, roads that are heavily salted, or areas where salt is stored, have a chemical analysis made of the water supply. If a water pump is the primary source of water to the house, you should be concerned with its age and its ability to deliver sufficient quantities of water.

Septic system. A septic system is a sewage collection and disposal system. Generally, a storage tank is buried in the ground at least 50 feet away from the house. A field bed of varying lengths is also buried in the ground. This bed accepts liquid waste that passes through the top of the septic tank. Solid wastes remain in the tank, where they decompose. Ask the seller when the tank and the field were last cleaned out and how old the system itself is. Have the septic system inspected. It can be a huge expense.

—from *Reviving Old Houses* by Alan Dan Orme

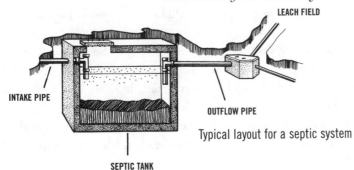

LEACH FIELD

INTAKE PIPE

OUTFLOW PIPE

Typical layout for a septic system

SEPTIC TANK

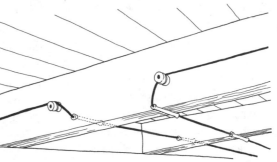

Knob-and-tube circuitry may go through joists, as shown at left, or be attached to them, as shown right.

Getting Ready to Inspect

For a thorough inspection, you'll find the following equipment valuable:

- Old clothes or coveralls
- Ladder
- Pair of binoculars
- Powerful flashlight
- Ball bearing or marble
- Ice pick or penknife
- Pad, pen, and clipboard

—from *Reviving Old Houses*

INSPECTING A HOME

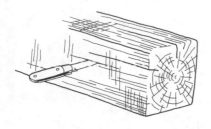

Underneath the house, use an ice pick or jackknife to test the soundness of the main supporting beams and posts. The outer portion (or sapwood) of old beams is often dry and crumbly, but on a sound beam a probe should hit hard wood about ½ inch below the surface.

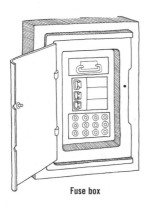

Fuse box

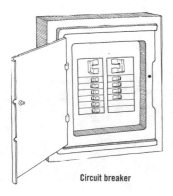

Circuit breaker

The service box can indicate whether the home has adequate electrical service.

Inspecting the Inside

Plumbing. Are bathrooms and sinks located in approximately the right places, or will you have to move everything? Do pipes that supply the upstairs run right up the surface of the walls, or is it a sensible installation? Check out all taps to see how fast the water runs and whether rust runs out. Be sure the hot-water taps are operable. A lot of rust indicates rusty pipes or a problem at the source of supply. Low pressure could mean pipes almost filled with mineral deposits. Look underneath sinks to see whether drainpipes show signs of leakage, indicated by greenish or white crystals around the joints.

Bathrooms. Consider whether you could improve the existing bathroom(s), or whether major remodeling must be done. If the floors are of ceramic tile, observe whether the tiles are tight, loose, or missing altogether. Inspect ceramic bathtubs, sinks, and toilets for cracks and breaks.

Heating system. If the house has radiators, note their location. Check them for leaks, especially at the valves. Turn the valves on and off to see if they work. You will need at least one radiator in every room, except perhaps the room directly over the furnace. If the owner is present, ask about the efficiency of the system—or better still, ask to see heating bills from the previous winter.

Kitchen. Notice whether the kitchen is modern, big enough, and conveniently located. Check the condition of cabinets, appliances, and countertops.

Living areas. Does the house provide enough space for your family? Does the layout offer enough privacy? Don't buy a house that is too small. But if you live in a part of the country where winters are long and cold, think about the amount of space you will have to heat.

Electrical system. Is the house served by a circuit breaker or a fuse box? What is the total amperage? A 200-amp service is more than adequate for a large family in a large house, but old houses may have only 60-amp service. If the service is this small, you will have to rewire. Look for the number and condition of electrical outlets and light fixtures in each room. Are they in working order? Loose switches and outlets are dangerous and must be replaced. If the house has only a minimum number of electrical outlets, you will probably have to rebuild or expand the system. Look for grounded outlets.

Ceilings. Give a light tap here and there on the ceilings. A hollow sound indicates that the plaster or lath has pulled away from joists underneath. Investigate sags. If you can lift the ceiling half an inch or more with a broom handle, the ceiling is obviously loose. Marginally adequate ceilings can be recovered with gypsum wallboard. If the plaster has pulled away from the ceiling above it, however, it must all be torn off and the wallboard nailed against the lath. All stains on ceiling plaster should be investigated for a source of leakage above.

Walls. Observe the walls as you move through the house. Rough, broken surfaces should be noted. At the least, any plaster pulled away from the lath on the walls will need to be removed and patched. In extremely bad cases, entire walls may need to be replaced.

Windows and doors. Watch for broken windows and rotted window sashes. Sash is apt to rot at the bottom where the water settles as it runs off the glass, especially at the joint between the bottom and the side piece of the sash. Gently test these areas with your ice pick and make a judgment. Check the fit of both windows and doors. Note the workability of door knobs and hinges.

Floors. Do the floors need nothing more than a fresh coat of shellac or polyurethane, or must they be sanded? Are they so bad as to require wall-to-wall carpeting? Watch for obvious dips, sags, and slopes. Roll your ball bearing to locate slopes. When you find one, check the baseboards at the floor line to see if there is a large crack. It may be as big as an inch or two. Floors will often slope toward a chimney, but the tell-tale crack should warn you of a recent problem. A room that shakes badly when you walk or jump on it may also have problems underneath. Give consideration to the floors in the kitchen and bathroom. Check for rot around the toilet and near the sink.

—from *The Home Inspection Manual* by Alfred H. Daniel

Things to Check in the Cellar

When you're in the basement, be sure to check for the following:

Moisture and leaks. Look carefully at the bottom of the first floor from underneath. Check for evidence of termite infestation, along with signs of leakage or rot. Watch for moisture and determine its apparent cause—generally surface water from outside or plumbing problems.

Water lines. Water lines are usually ½- to ¾-inch pipes. Those visible in the basement are a good measure of those in the walls that you can't see. Look for leaks. Powdery green stains indicate leaks that were never corrected. Scratch the pipes with your ice pick. If they are lead, the pick will sink into them, whereas the pick will scratch metallically against cast iron. Lead pipes must be replaced. Experts are also sounding the alarm about old copper pipes soldered with lead.

Hot-water heater. Look over the heater for an estimation of its age. The connecting pipes and fittings may give you a better clue than the enameled cover of the heater itself. Feel around the bottom for evidence of drip or rust, which usually means the tank has succumbed to old age. Note the capacity of the heater. Is the heater gas or electric? Although electric heaters are generally more expensive, many people prefer them.

Heating system. The heating system may originate in the basement. Various heating systems are now in use, most commonly wood, coal, oil, or natural gas used in a steam, hot-water, or hot-air system. Make a note of the furnace type and condition, as well as its age and efficiency rating when possible. Note the location and condition of the heat supply lines.

Sump pump. A sump pump must be present if there is not a deep-seal floor drain. Lift the rod going down into the sump pit until it activates the pump. Release the lift rod and listen. If the suction action operates quietly, that is good. If there is a metal rattling sound in the motor, a motor bearing is likely defective. When the pump has completed emptying the excess water, it should shut itself off. Water in the discharge pipe will drain back into the sump pit. If there is more than several quarts draining backward, the check valve is defective. Correcting sump pump defects can cost several hundred dollars or more.

—adapted from *Reviving Old Houses* and *The Home Inspection Manual*

Things to Check in the Attic

- **Insulation.** Is the house insulated? How deep is the insulation? A careful sweep with your flashlight will reveal a great deal. Blown-in insulation often settles, so you may be surprised how little is left. However, this kind of insulation is easy to supplement. Asbestos insulation is dangerous, and government standards call for its removal. If you suspect that old, fibrous insulation contains asbestos, have a professional test it.

- **Attic wildlife.** With your eyes and your nose, test for evidence of attic wildlife. The first step in eliminating such nonpaying visitors is to put screening over vents and repair any holes in the roof, eaves, or walls that allow them access.

- **Wiring.** Check out wiring in the attic and compare it with wiring in the rest of the house. Watch for damage by rodents. Squirrels are known to form a taste for old wire insulation.

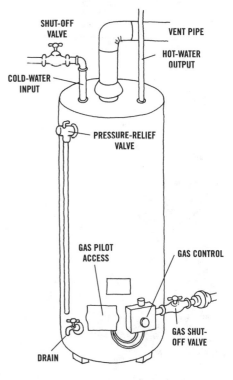

Gas hot-water heater

Carl Heldmann has helped thousands of readers learn contracting skills, both through workshops and through his books, Be Your Own House Contractor *and* Be Your Own Home Renovation Contractor.

25 Steps to a Home of Your Own

Here is a look at the steps necessary in building a house, including an estimate of how long each step will take:

1. Staking the lot and house (1–3 hours). I recommend that you have a registered surveyor/engineer do both. The least expensive one should be the one who surveyed the lot for purchase. When the lot is cleared and the basement — if you have one — is dug, you may want the surveyor to restake the house. If your lot slopes more than 3 or 4 feet, you may need a topographical plan so you can fit the house to the slope.

2. Clearing and excavation (1–3 days). Clearing the lot means clearing trees, brush, rocks, roots, and debris from where the house will sit and usually 10 feet around the site, allowing space for tractors, forklifts, and the like. The more area to be cleared, the more it will cost. Get a contract price for this work. It may cost a little more, but you will be assured of not having your first cost overrun.

3. Utilities hookup (1 hour). This involves making a few phone calls and/or a visit to each utility. Pay all fees and complete any necessary forms. Arrange for temporary electric service on your site. Wells and septic systems, if used, are best installed now. If no temporary source of water is available, you will have to have the well dug and temporarily wired for your brick masons.

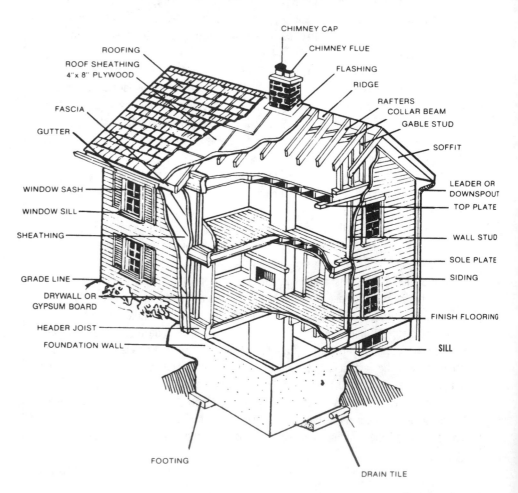

28 key elements involved in building a home, from footings to chimney caps.

Where to Site Your Home

First, position the house on a map of your property. Then you and your carpenter, surveyor, or footing contractor should stake that position on the site. The surveyor is best. Here are a few things to consider:

- Light. A north–south-facing house is darker than one on an east–west axis.
- Water flow
- Other houses on the street or nearby
- The street or road the house faces. Do you want it parallel with the road?
- Privacy on the front, back, and sides
- The potential to use solar energy
- Minimum setback and side-yard requirements

Subcontractors Wanted

Here is a list of the subcontractors you will probably be doing business with, listed generally in the order in which you will need them. Start by looking for your carpenter. Inquire at a lumber supply store. The carpenter sub will be able to recommend almost everyone else.

- House designer or architect
- Carpenter
- Surveyor
- Grading and excavation subcontractor
- Footing subcontractor
- Brick mason
- Concrete finisher
- Waterproofer
- Electrician
- Plumber (and well and septic system, if needed)
- Heating, air-conditioning, and vent (HVAC) specialist
- Roofer
- Insulation subcontractor
- Drywall subcontractor
- Painter
- Flooring, carpet, and Formica subcontractor
- Tile subcontractor
- Cleaning crew
- Landscaper

—from *Be Your Own House Contractor*
by Carl Heldmann

4. Footings (1 day). The footing is a mass of concrete supporting the foundation of the house. It can be poured into wooded forms or in trenches. It must be below the frost line, or it will heave when the ground thaws and freezes. I have a footing subcontractor who stakes, clears, excavates, digs, and pours footings. With a little effort, you can find the same. After your foundation walls are up, put in a footing drain, connected to a dry well, storm sewer, or any approved means of getting rid of the water. Building inspectors usually must check the footing locations before footings are poured.

5. Foundations (1 week). Foundations are made of concrete block or poured concrete. The foundation wall must be high enough so water will be diverted away from the house by the final grade of the soil around the house. The wood finish and framing of the house should be at least 8 inches above the finish grade, thus protected from soil moisture. A crawl space should be at least 18 inches high, so you can crawl beneath the house. If you are planning on a full basement, your foundation walls should give you at least 7 feet, 4 inches of headspace. A mason generally does the foundation work. The finished foundation should be waterproofed from the footing to the finish grade line. I recommend hiring a professional waterproofing company.

6. Rough-ins for plumbing (2–4 days). If you have a basement with plumbing, or if you are building the house on a concrete slab, once the foundation is in and the soil treated your plumber should install the sewer line and water pipes that will be under the concrete. Any wiring that has to be under the concrete should be placed in a conduit and roughed in. Your soil treatment company may want to wait until rough-ins are completed before treating the soil, so it won't be disturbed by digging in the plumbing lines.

7. Slabs for heated areas (1–2 days). Many locales require slab perimeter insulation, 1-inch Styrofoam that runs around the perimeter. I recommend it. Your contractor should put down a base for the slab, tamping down a layer of gravel or crushed stone 4 to 6 inches deep. A 4- to 6-mil-thickness vapor barrier of polyurethane goes on top of this. Any joints of the poly should overlap by four inches and be sealed. A 6- by 6-inch #10 wire mesh is laid on top of the poly to reinforce the concrete. Call for an inspection before pouring concrete if your code requires it.

BUILDING A HOME

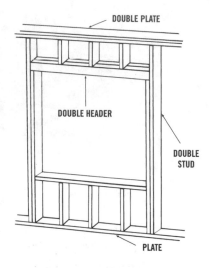

Framing around exterior wall opening using header and double studs

A TYPICAL FRAMING LIST

15	pieces	2 x 6 x 12 treated pine
10	pieces	2 x 4 x 12 treated pine
20	lineal ft.	2 x 2
250	lineal ft.	1 x 4
18	pieces	2 x 8 x 12
80	pieces	2 x 8 x 14
80	pieces	2 x 8 x 16
55	pieces	2 x 10 x 12
100	pieces	2 x 10 x 14
18	pieces	2 x 10 x 16
18	pieces	2 x 10 x 18
2	pieces	2 x 10 x 20
14	pieces	2 x 6 x 14
45	pieces	2 x 6 x 16
80	pieces	2 x 6 x 20
800	pieces	West Coast studs, 2 x 4 x 93
175	pieces	Half-inch CDX plywood
24	quarts	Plywood glue
10	rolls	#15 felt
60	pieces	Asphalt-impregnated sheathing ½ x 4 x 8
300	pounds	16d nails, coated
150	pounds	8d nails, coated
10	pounds	Steel-cut masonry 8d
25	pounds	⅞-inch galvanized roofing nails
50	pounds	1¾-inch galvanized roofing nails
10	pounds	16d galvanized finish nails
150	pieces	2 x 4 x 14
50	pieces	2 x 4 x 10

8. Framing (1–3 weeks). If you have a good carpenter, you need only order the lumber, the windows, and the exterior doors, and in two or three weeks you'll have something that looks like a house. I have included a typical order list for framing and drying-in, which means making the house secure from rain. When the framing is completed, order cabinets, bookcases, and bath vanity cabinets. Space for them can now be measured on the job.

9. Exterior siding, trim, veneer (1–3 weeks). This phase of construction is carried on while work progresses inside, and should be done before roof shingles are installed. Masonry chimneys are installed after siding or veneer. Veneers such as brick should be installed before final exterior trim is added. At the completion of this step, you are ready for exterior plumbing.

10. Chimneys and roofing (2 days–1 week). Chimneys should be built before the roof is shingled. This allows placement of sheet-metal flashing around the chimney and avoids damage to the shingles. A prefab fireplace and flue would also be installed at this time. Roofing follows completion of the chimneys.

11. Rough-ins (1–2 weeks). All electrical, plumbing, heating and air-conditioning, phone prewires, stereo and intercom, and burglar alarm systems should be roughed in at this time or any time after step 8 is completed. Inspections are needed when this step is completed.

12. Insulation (1 day). Consult with your local utility company on the insulation you need to qualify for its lowest rates. Some locales require an inspection of insulation by both the utility and the building inspection department when it is completed and before it is covered with drywall or paneling.

13. Drywall (2 weeks). Most residential walls are drywalled with ½" by 4' by 8' gypsum wallboard sheets called drywall or sheetrock. For baths and other moist areas, use a waterproof board, or paint it with an enamel paint, even before wallpapering. Figure on 3½ or 4 times the square footage of the floor area for the total square footage of wallboard.

14. Prime walls (2 days). After the drywall is finished and before interior trim is applied, I prime all walls and ceilings with a flat white latex paint. By priming first, the finish painting time is reduced considerably, thus saving you money. Priming the walls and ceilings will highlight any slight imperfections in the finishing drywall. You can have your drywall contractor touch up these places. This is called pointing up.

15. Hardwood flooring and underlayment (3 days–1 week). I find it easier to install hardwood flooring and carpet or vinyl underlayment before I have the drywall installed, but it can be done afterward.

16. Interior trim and cabinets (1–2 weeks). Doors, moldings, cabinets, and shelves are installed at this time. Cabinets that were ordered after step 8 should be ready for delivery and installation. Interior trim labor usually includes standard trim and moldings. Any special molding or trim work, or paneling, should be discussed beforehand with your carpenter.

17. Painting (2–3 weeks). You are ready for final painting inside. Your exterior painting can be delayed until this time, too. However, you don't want to leave the exterior trim unpainted or unstained too long, as it may warp or get moldy.

Eight Ways to Cut Construction Costs

1. Do the building yourself.
2. Instead of hiring an expensive architect to draw up your house plans, draw up your own design. Then find an architect or builder who will go over it with you.
3. Become a scavenger of materials.
4. Build only what you need or can afford.
5. Barter or swap services whenever possible, to avoid cash expenditures.
6. Plan ahead.
7. Buy in large lots and take advantage of special deals.
8. Read books on cheap building techniques for the amateur builder.

—from *The Complete Homesteading Book* by David Robinson

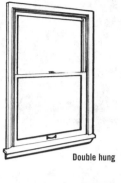
Double hung

Horizontal sliding

Fixed unit and awning

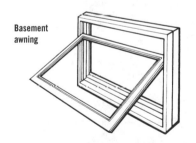
Basement awning

Casement

Five types of windows. Windows are installed during the framing phase.

18. Other trims (1 day–1week). It's time to install Formica, vinyl floors, and ceramic tiles. Wallpaper can be done at this time or delayed until after you move in. The others can't be delayed because plumbing cannot be completed until they are.

19. Trim out (1–2 weeks). Now the plumber finishes his or her work. This is called trimming out or setting fixtures. Some of the fixtures must be wired, so the plumber needs to finish before the electrician can finish. Also, your heating and air-conditioning must be completed before your electrician finishes up. The electrician installs switches, receptacles, light fixtures, and electrical appliances. He or she will also wire the electrical apparatus that has been installed by your plumber and heating and air-conditioning contractors.

20. Trash pickup. The bulk of the outside trash, and an incredible amount of inside trash can be picked up by truck and hauled away.

21. Carpet and hardwood floor finish (3 days–1 week). Hardwood floors should be finished before the carpet is installed, because of the sanding required before the floors are stained and sealed with polyurethane. Allow at least three days for hardwood finishing. No one else should be working in the house while this is done. Because of the dust, you may want to finish the floors before the cleaning up in step 20.

22. Driveway (1–3 days). Keep heavy trucks off newly laid concrete or asphalt drives for a period of time. Concrete can take a moving van on it a week after it is poured; not so with asphalt. If you use asphalt, wait until after you move in to pave. Put down a good stone base on the drive before moving in.

23. Landscaping (1–3 days). This is an item that can be put off until after you move in. Such a situation may be desirable due to weather, scheduling problems, or lack of money. You might get by with just grading and seeding, or mulching disturbed wooded areas.

24. Final inspections, surveys, loan closings (1–3 days). After completion of the house, all final inspections from the county or city, for building, electrical, mechanical, and plumbing, should be made. The lender will also make a final inspection, and may require drives and landscaping to be completed before disbursing the balance of the construction loan and closing it out to the permanent mortgage. Bring your insurance policy to the closing. It must be converted into a homeowner's policy.

25. Enjoy your home (a lifetime)!

2

OUTDOOR SPACES

STONESCAPING • WALKS AND PATHS
DECKS • PATIOS • OUTDOOR FURNITURE

A few years ago we became the happy owners of a stone farmhouse with 12 acres near Lake Champlain. Soon thereafter we learned, less happily, that the house needed "pointing"—the replacement of broken mortar with new. We found master stonemason Drew Vail, who proudly showed us the work he had done on local churches and homes. "It's all I do," he said simply. Drew arrived each morning at six and worked steadily until five. Under his skilled hands, our 185-year-old house was soon ready for another 185 years. Two other expert stone-masons and authors, Charles McRaven and John Vivian, start off this chapter with an overview of stone.

—John & Martha Storey

"Learning to build with natural stone," writes stone-mason Charles McRaven, "is less demanding than learning to build with most other materials —that is, if you proceed with liberal doses of common sense and care. Even your early efforts will afford you a great deal of satisfaction when you view the structures of plywood and plastic around you." *McRaven's classic book is titled* Building with Stone.

In the course of your building projects, you will sooner or later come to the use of stone, the oldest, most durable, and certainly one of the most beautiful materials. Stone is often misused, which probably means that it's misunderstood. It has certain design limitations and requirements, certain structural characteristics, certain overall uses. There are certainly some building applications for which stone is totally wrong.

Compared with other building materials, stone is expensive if you count your time, cheap if you don't. It's heavy, but also permanent. It's bad insulation, but it makes a tight wall that radiates stored heat for hours. It does not make a strong wall unless the wall is very thick, and it depends mostly on its weight for stability. The most natural of materials, stone can grace almost any monstrosity you want to build.

Stone weighs more than anything you will build with except steel and concrete. You'll handle each rock several times in gathering, hauling, stacking, shaping, and laying it. The weight will mean you need stronger footings and more carefully fitted arches and spans. But this weight will also keep what you build where you build it, against great odds.

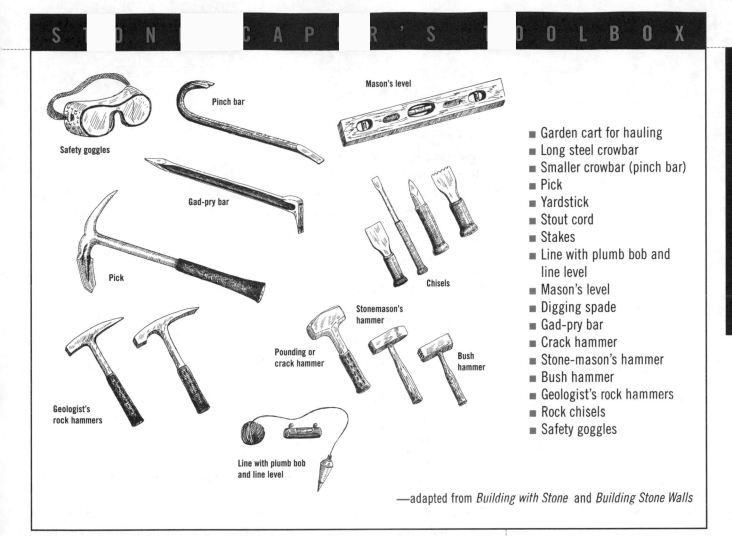

Safety goggles

Pinch bar

Mason's level

Gad-pry bar

Pick

Chisels

Stonemason's hammer

Pounding or crack hammer

Bush hammer

Geologist's rock hammers

Line with plumb bob and line level

- Garden cart for hauling
- Long steel crowbar
- Smaller crowbar (pinch bar)
- Pick
- Yardstick
- Stout cord
- Stakes
- Line with plumb bob and line level
- Mason's level
- Digging spade
- Gad-pry bar
- Crack hammer
- Stone-mason's hammer
- Bush hammer
- Geologist's rock hammers
- Rock chisels
- Safety goggles

—adapted from *Building with Stone* and *Building Stone Walls*

Finding Stone

Lacking a supply of stones in fields or creeks on your own place and not wanting to buy them, you can look in several places. Perhaps another landowner will let you haul off rocks from his walls or abandoned stone buildings. Rock ramps, cellars, and foundations left after an old house or barn has burned down provide one of the best "good" stone sources you can find. Often these old cellar holes are dangerous or an eyesore, and owners are glad to have part of the demolition or fill-in job done for free.

Construction sites often provide excellent flat-sided-rock picking, especially where new highways are being dynamited through hilly country. Streams, rivers, many lakes, and the seashore in some places are good sources for frost-split or water-rounded stones. And you'll find that stones only weigh half as much when moved under water.

If there are a good many old stone buildings or foundations in your area, you may find abandoned quarries or gravel pits scattered through the countryside that were dug by the original stone-builders. Ask around, or consult a U.S. Geological Survey topographical map. Abandoned and active quarries and gravel pits are shown on such maps. Operating quarries are often listed in the Yellow Pages, or you can consult the geology department of a nearby college or university.

—from *Building Stone Walls* by John Vivian

A Stone Wall Primer

Functional Terms

Freestanding walls stand alone.
Retaining walls hold earth in place vertically.
Veneer walls are walls made of concrete blocks or bricks faced in small flagstones or split stones. They can be either freestanding or retaining walls.

Materials Used

Ashlar is cut and shaped stone.
Rubble is uncut stone.

Methods of Construction

Wet walls are built with mortar.
Dry walls are built without mortar.

Anatomy of a Wall

Footings are the wall's foundation.
Wythes are vertical stacks of stones 1 stone wide.
Courses are the horizontal layers in which stones are laid.
Stretcher stones are long stones laid parallel with the face of the wall to add stability.
Tie stones are long stones laid parallel with the face of the wall to add stability.
Weep holes are through-wall drainage holes used in retaining walls to prevent water from backing up behind the wall.
Coping is the final layer of stones that caps the wall and prevents moisture from entering the wall.

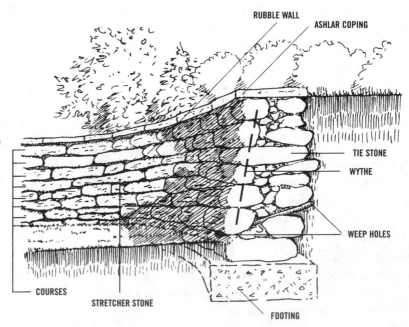

—from *Stonescaping* by Jan Kowalczewski Whitner

Building Your Own Stone Wall

Start with a wall of modest thickness, say 12 inches. It shouldn't go too high without angles, buttresses, or intersecting walls, but it's good for about a 4-foot height.

1. Dig a footing twice the width of the wall, to a depth below frost line. The idea is to keep water from getting between the rocks, freezing, and pushing them apart.

2. Reinforce the concrete footing with two ½-inch reinforcing rods floated midway in the footing. For a footing 6 inches deep, pour 3 inches of concrete, lay the rod quickly, then pour the remainder. Cover the fresh work with sheet plastic or wet burlap bags for five or six days.

3. You're ready to begin laying stones. The first stones will be belowground, so choose the least cosmetic large ones. Wet the cured footing, then spread on an inch or so of mortar.

4. Bed your first stones. Drop in whatever rock fits best, keeping in mind that you'll have to follow this act with another layer and another. Leaving a peak on top means you'll need a lot of mortar and possibly small stones to create a good surface to lay the next stone on. Bed the stone firmly by rocking it in place. Trim the excess mortar with a trowel, and use it in the space of about 1 inch between that stone and the one you laid next to it.

5. If necessary, use a small stone hammer to knock off offending protrusions. Use a chipping approach. Watch out for flying shards. Remember that a fresh cut or break will glare out from a surrounding of aged, lichened stones.

6. Lay a layer or two at a time, covering each day's work with sheet plastic or wet burlap. Uncover 4 to 12 hours later to brush the joints, then re-cover to hold the moisture in. Come back for another layer no sooner than two days later. This gives the mortar a chance to harden partially and gives you a solid wall to work on.

7. Aboveground, you will probably want to stretch strings for guidance for both sides of the 12-inch wall. If you let the stones touch the string, it'll get pushed off course. Use a level or plumb bob to stay vertical.

8. Even with a random stone wall, it's nicer to come out even on top. With this in mind, select capstones that have a more or less flat plane. Evening the top out with mortar is to be kept to a minimum for appearance and durability.

9. Brush out the excess crumbly mortar with a wire brush. Strike the joint deeper around jutting stones to the same depth as elsewhere.

—adapted from *Building with Stone* by Charles McRaven

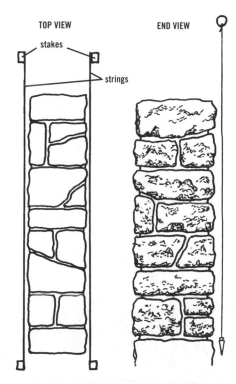

TOP VIEW   END VIEW

stakes

strings

Strings stretched between stakes will help keep your wall straight. Use a plumb bob to keep your stonework vertical.

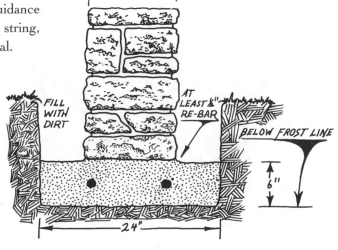

12"

FILL WITH DIRT

AT LEAST ½" RE-BAR

BELOW FROST LINE

6"

24"

WALKS AND PATHS

A straight-edged, formal flagstone path, above, and a "crazy paving" path, below

Building a Flagstone Path

Flagstone paths suit formal gardens, cottage gardens, and high-traffic areas adjacent to the house and terrace. To build one, follow these steps:

1. Choose flagstones whose colors and textures blend with the house and surrounding environment. They should be at least 5 inches wide and 1 to 2 inches thick.

2. Outline the run of the path and install any needed drainage.

3. A foundation of 4 inches of crushed rock topped by 2 inches of sand is usually sufficient. Calculate how deep to excavate the soil by adding the thickness of the stones to the 6-inch foundation.

4. Excavate the soil to the required depth and tamp it firmly.

5. Lay the foundation, making it approximately 1 inch higher on one side of the path so standing water will drain off the surface.

6. If you are using flagstones larger than 16 inches on a side and at least 1½ inches thick, position the flagstones directly on the sand, working from the sides of the path toward its center. Brush more sand between the cracks, leaving a gap ¼ inch deep from the surface.

If the ground is soggy or subject to frost heaving, or if your paving stones are smaller than 16 inches on a side, follow these steps instead of step 5:

1. Install edging on each side of the path. Edging can be made from various materials, including treated wood, bricks, railroad ties, and strips of cobblestones or Belgian blocks.

2. Dry-lay the flagstones first to create a pleasing pattern, working from the sides of the path toward its center.

3. After deciding on a pattern, move the flagstones to the side. Lay dollops of mortar on top of the sand and position the flagstones back onto the mortar, leaving gaps between individual stones ¼ inch to 1 inch wide, depending on your taste.

4. Brush a mixture of dry cement and sand into the gaps between the flagstones.

5. Gently hose the surface of the stones to clean them and to wash down all of the cement-sand mixture into the gaps.

6. Wait at least a week for the mixture to dry before using the path.

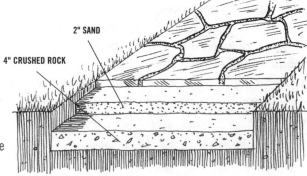

2" SAND

4" CRUSHED ROCK

Constructing a flagstone path in sand

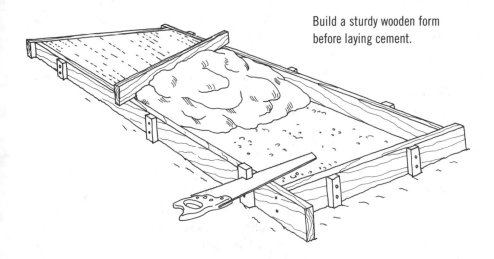

Build a sturdy wooden form before laying cement.

Making a Concrete Walk

Poured-concrete walks are safe, long-lasting, easy to keep clean of debris and snow, and fairly simple to install. When purchasing concrete, plan on 1 yard of concrete for every 80 square feet of surface.

1. Prepare wooden forms for the concrete. Make forms out of 1 x 4s or 2 x 4s. Place the forms on edge along the line of the walk and stake them with pegs driven into the ground outside of the forms at intervals frequent enough to hold them in place.

2. Cut off stakes level with the top of the forms before pouring the concrete.

3. Make any curves out of plywood, staked frequently to force the plywood to keep its shape.

4. In a wheelbarrow, mix concrete by using 3 parts gravel, 2 parts sand, and 1 part portland cement. Strive for a stiff but pourable consistency.

5. As a leveler, use a 2 x 4 that is a few inches wider than the form. Level the concrete to the top of the forms with a sawing motion.

6. Places where the vertical edge of the concrete will show after the form is removed (such as a step) require special treatment. Hammer on the face of the form with a big hammer to bring liquid to the surface and free it of any air pockets.

7. When the concrete is beginning to dry but is still wet enough to show a finger mark, smooth it with a rectangular trowel. For a mirror finish, trowel it a second time when it is almost dry, but soft enough to show a mark from a nail.

8. Leave the forms in place for two days to cure the concrete thoroughly. Otherwise, corners and edges may break when forms are removed.

—from *Reviving Old Houses* by Alan Dan Orme

Tips on Choosing Concrete

Type Bagged concrete mix (in 80-pound bags)

Use For small projects, such as setting a mailbox or a gate post

Type Gravel, sand, and portland cement

Use For medium-size projects, such as footings for two or three posts in the basement; transport it yourself from a gravel company in trash cans

Type Ready-mix concrete

Use For larger projects, such as walks; check to see if you can share a load with a neighbor—there is often a surcharge on less than 4 or 5 yards

DECKS

Monte Burch's first pole-building experience was helping his dad, a carpenter, build a pole barn, and it remains one of his favorite types of construction. Little site preparation is required, and pole-built structures offer increased fire safety and wind resistance. They are relatively fast and easy to build, and they are much less expensive than comparable conventional structures. New materials, like pressure-treated poles, and new techniques, like truss technology, have made pole building an even more attractive option for homesteader and suburbanite alike.

Designing Your Deck

If you decide you would like a deck added to your property, the first step is to look at magazines and books for design ideas. Next, carefully measure the space you have for a deck. Use graph paper and a scale rule to make a scale drawing of the deck. It doesn't have to be fancy, but the drawing can definitely help in designing and building your deck and preventing problems that may occur during construction. Make sure you also check local building codes and, most importantly, your property lines. Most building codes specify the distance any structure or construction must be from a property line.

In planning your deck, take care not to seal access to electric, gas, or drainage lines, and not to situate the deck over these lines. You must obtain information about the location of utility facilities from area utility companies. Make sure you get a building permit, if required.

Several things should be kept in mind when creating your deck design. When designing the deck height or railing, consider safety and plan for children and pets. Also plan for strength—what types of gatherings might there be, and how many people should the deck be built to support? Try to plan for the anticipated uses: Will the deck be used as a sundeck, dining area, bathing, or party area? How might this affect the design or shape of the deck, stairways, or railings? Local building supply dealers can also be of help in designing your deck. They know local frost depths, the best types of footings, decking material requirements, and other considerations. Often, these factors are based on the availability of materials in your area.

Building Your Deck

A deck consists of several specific parts, depending on how it is constructed. Naturally, a main part is the posts, normally 4 x 4, 4 x 6, or 6 x 6 posts, depending on load requirements. The posts sit on footings or piers. Beams, 4 x 6s or doubled 2 x 8s, 2 x 10s, or 2 x 12s, are fastened to or rest on the posts. A ledger

A deck can be a pleasant transition zone between your indoor and outdoor spaces. On this deck you can sit and sip iced tea while you keep an eye on your vegetable garden.

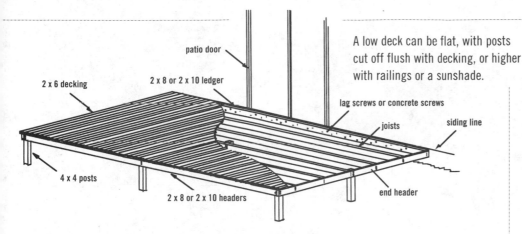

2 x 6 decking

patio door

2 x 8 or 2 x 10 ledger

A low deck can be flat, with posts cut off flush with decking, or higher with railings or a sunshade.

lag screws or concrete screws

joists

siding line

4 x 4 posts

2 x 8 or 2 x 10 headers

end header

is required (usually a 2 x 8) if the deck is to be fastened to the house or other building. Headers (usually 2 x 8s), which go around the outside of the deck edges, rest on the beams and anchor the joists, and the floor joists (usually 2 x 8s), which are fastened between the headers, rest on the beams and in turn support the deck flooring. Finally, there is the deck flooring, which is normally 2 x 6.

The sketches shown here are for the construction of a simple, on-ground deck fastened to a house that has a patio door opening onto the deck. This is a basic project.

The first step is to lay out your deck, making sure the outline is square and of the correct size. If you will be placing posts in concrete, make sure they are plumb. Use a carpenter's level to check the posts, then anchor them in place with stakes and braces until the concrete sets. Make sure all posts extend high enough, but don't worry now about having them level with each other.

Once the concrete sets and the posts are solid, use a long, straight 2 x 4 with a level on top of it to determine the level line with the posts and the ledger on the house. Use a small square to mark on their sides the correct height.

The beams can be anchored in place on the posts using a variety of methods. The end headers are anchored to the ledger and to the end posts, and extended the needed distance for the outside header. The outside header is fastened to the end headers. The joists are cut and positioned between the ledger and outside header and anchored in place.

Joists can be toenailed into the ledger and simply nailed on from the exterior of the outside header, but joist hangers make the job quicker and easier and the joint stronger. These are anchored in place on the ledger and outside header in the correct position, the joists cut to length, dropped in place, and anchored.

On most decks, diagonal bracing should also be added between the joists and headers to prevent the deck from shifting sideways or twisting.

Decking or deck boards are then fastened down on the joists, extending over the outside header and usually about an inch over the side headers. Don't worry about making sure all deck board ends are even on the outside edge. Once they are fastened in place, a chalk line is snapped and a portable electric saw can be used to cut them off smoothly and evenly.

Railings can be added, if desired, and steps can be installed. If the deck is low, steps may not be needed.

—from *Monte Burch's Pole Building Projects*

Posts and Piers

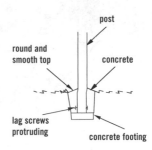

post

round and smooth top

concrete

lag screws protruding

concrete footing

When setting posts, you can install them on a concrete footing.

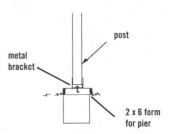

post

metal bracket

2 x 6 form for pier

Alternatively, pour the concrete into a 2 x 6 form.

Two Options for Deck Support

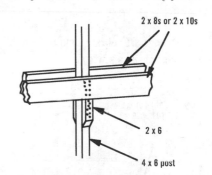

2 x 8s or 2 x 10s

2 x 6

4 x 6 post

Option 1. Brace headers with a 2 x 6.

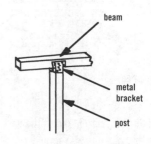

beam

metal bracket

post

Option 2. Hang beam from a bracket.

PATIOS

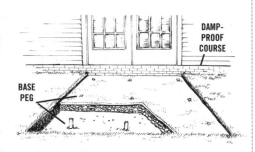

Base pegs are set into sand to keep the surface of the patio level.

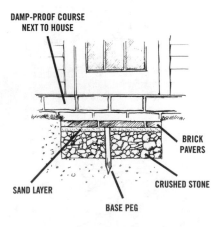

This cross-section shows the various layers of the completed patio.

Building Your Patio

A patio can be made of all sorts of materials, but concrete, brick, and flagstone are the usual choices. Here are the basic directions for constructing a patio with any of these materials:

Start by preparing a bed for the patio surface. Dig out the area to be covered to a depth of about 4 inches. Paved areas must be relatively flat, with a pitch to allow positive drainage and a minimum of water pooling. This pitch can be so slight as to be indiscernible to the eye (1 percent or a ⅛-inch drop per foot is adequate).

Concrete. If you are going to pour a concrete slab, make sure that the area is smooth and that there is a gentle slope of about ¼ inch per foot of patio. If the patio is not attached to the house, the slope should be from the middle of the area outward in all directions. This will ensure that water runs off the surface.

Brick. If you are going to use brick for the patio, set the bricks on a layer of sand. You can establish the border by setting the bricks on edge in trenches about 5¾ inches deep. The remainder of the bricks can be set in whatever pattern you wish, as long as you leave a uniform space between them. After all the bricks are down, set them in place by sweeping sand over them until all the cracks are filled. You can mix mortar in the sand for a slightly stronger structure. A good rain will take care of the rest.

Flagstone. Flagstones can be set down in much the same way, except that the depth of the cut in the ground needs to be only about 2 inches, or the thickness of the stone. After the stone is set where you want it, wet it down with a hose. Then mix 1 part portland cement with 3 parts sand and sweep that over the stone, filling all the cracks. Wet down the surface again to clean off the stone, and let the cement set. If you have large stones, you might consider setting the entire patio in cement.

Constructing the Patio Base

Unless you go below the frost line, there will be some movement of the paving material. You or your contractor should construct an adequate base to keep the area from heaving, whether it is laid dry or wet.

There are several ways to minimize heaving. We recommend using crushed stone to give water a place to go, and geotextile to keep the bed intact where the bricks or other stone will be set. Stone dust or concrete sand will compact for an excellent setting bed, so that the bricks and stones don't move around when people walk on them. One note about crushed stone: It must be sharp or have flat, not round, edges so it will compact.

You may wish to bind your stone or bluestone material with plants such as creeping thyme and grass. This method is best with loose-laid, loam-based patios or walks in informal settings using large pavers. Thyme actually prefers gravelly, well-drained soil. We don't recommend this method in heavy traffic areas, or areas likely to be shoveled in winter.

Edging Brick Patios

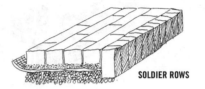
SOLDIER ROWS

SAILOR ROWS

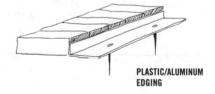
PLASTIC/ALUMINUM EDGING

To keep patios and walkways from migrating or separating, be sure the edges are finished with one of these methods (top to bottom): soldier rows (bricks placed vertically with the narrow side toward the pavement), sailor rows (bricks placed horizontally with the wider side toward the pavement), or plastic or aluminum edging.

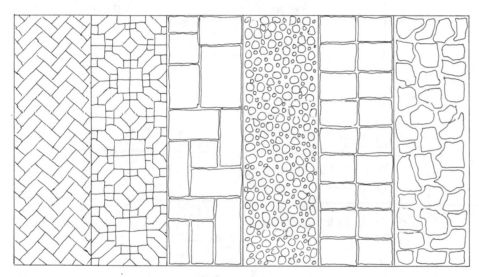

Patio Patterns. Options for paving materials include (left to right): brick, concrete pavers, bluestone, cobblestone, flat stone, and flagstone.

Tips for Working with Brick

Finding used brick. Look around for any demolition going on in your area or call a demolition company for information if you want to make a brick patio or walkway. The company may have bricks to sell or may be willing to let you pick your own from a site. Secondhand bricks will not last as long as new bricks, so consider this approach carefully.

Use water sealant. Sealing any brick or cement paver is a good idea. You can buy sealant from your local brick supplier or buy a nationally advertised brand. Use a roller or spray the sealant for best results.

—from *Landscaping Makes Cents* by Frederick C. Campbell and Richard L. Dubé

OUTDOOR FURNITURE

Build an Adirondack Chair

The classic symbol of summer, an Adirondack chair is easy to build. Before you start, cut all of your boards to the lengths specified. Then follow the step-by-step instructions below.

PARTS AND PIECES

QTY	PIECE	LENGTH
2	front legs	20" (1 x 4)
2	slanted legs	30" (1 x 4)
1	triangle	6" (2 x 4)
1	front brace	22" (1 x 4)
1	back brace	22" (1 x 3)
1	arm brace	22" (2 x 2)
2	arms	27" (1 x 6)
2	back pieces	26" (1 x 4)
3	back pieces	28" (1 x 4)
1	front seat piece	22" (1 x 6)
3	seat pieces	22" (1 x 4)
1	box of 1½" #8 flat-head screws	
1	box of 1½" #15 brads	

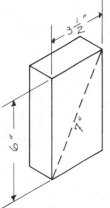

1. Make a diagonal cut across the 1½" x 3½" x 6" piece of stock so it forms two triangles.

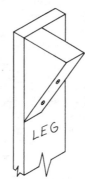

2. Put the 6" face of each triangle against the front outside corner of each front leg. Drill starter holes and screw the triangles in place.

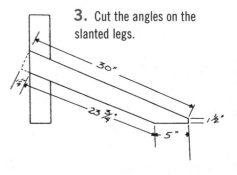

3. Cut the angles on the slanted legs.

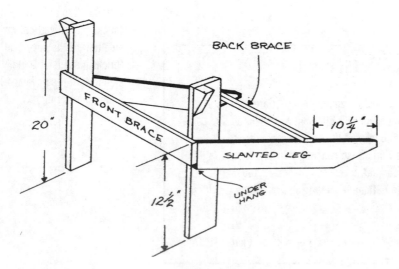

4. Drill starter holes and screw the slanted legs to the front legs. Drill starter holes and screw the front and back braces in place.

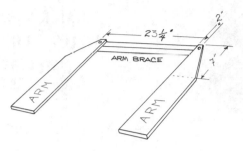

5. Plane the corner of the back brace as shown.

6. Cut the angles on the arms. Drill starter holes and screw the arm brace to the backs of the arms.

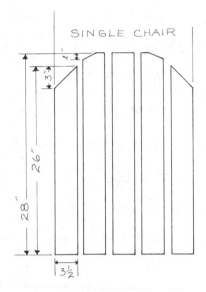

SINGLE CHAIR

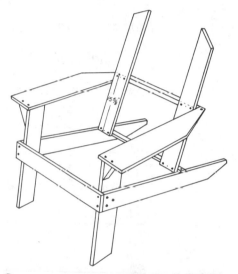

7. Cut the angles on the back pieces.

8. Have someone hold the arm brace while you tack the arms to the front legs with 1½" brads. Tack the two outside back pieces in place. Drill starter holes and screw the arm to the triangles attached to the front legs. Drill starter holes and fasten the two outside back pieces securely with the screws. Fasten the rest of the back pieces, spacing them evenly.

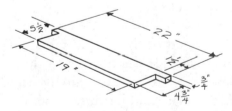

9. Cut the corner notches on the front seat piece. Drill starter holes and screw the piece in place. Screw the back seat piece in place, then the middle two.

10. Sand. This chair may be stained, varnished, or painted.

3

THE WATER SUPPLY

WATER SOURCES • WATER SUPPLY SYSTEMS
WELLS • PUMPS • NATURAL SPRINGS • PONDS
WATER DISTRIBUTION • WATER QUALITY

We started our publishing business in a converted motorcycle repair shop in Pownal, Vermont. One hot July morning, we ran out of water. We called Floyd Patterson, the builder, who explained that there was a reservoir in the hills and a pipeline that ran down a mile or so. "Could be a break anywhere on the line," he said. "We could dig it all up, but why don't we try a dowser first?" Skeptically, we watched the dowser use a forked stick made of hazel. Within 20 minutes he had found the break, allowing the backhoe to dig in just the right spot. We were quickly becoming converts to the arts, crafts, and skills of country life.

—John & Martha Storey

David Robinson's The Complete Homesteading Book, *first published in 1974, was a true classic of the back-to-the-land movement. You must have pure water, he wrote, as well as methods of heating and lighting your house and disposing of waste. These systems will affect your health and happiness as much as or more than any other factor. An ample and unfailing supply of good drinking water is one of the most significant resources your land could have.*

Good homesteading land must have an unfailing supply of good water. As you look at land, find out all you can about the amount—and quality—that is available. An ideal site will have a reliable spring, but if yours does not, it may have a well. As a last resort, you may have to develop a new well.

Spring. If you have a spring, be sure it has an ample flow of 4 to 6 gallons a minute. Does it flow year-round or dry up during summer? Is it reasonably near your home site? If the answer to these questions is "yes," you probably have a reliable water supply. But you'll need to have the water tested for purity and hardness, too.

Well. Dug wells are seen on old farms that were in operation before electricity became common. They were dug with hand tools, and the sides were rocked or bricked up to prevent cave-ins. Drilled wells are common today, primarily because of the availability of drilling equipment. To create a driven well, a pipe fitted with a well point is driven into water-bearing sand.

Town water. Many rural areas have established water districts. If you live close enough to the town water line, you may have a choice

Drawdown. The distance water in a well drops during pumping

Flow. Water supply, calculated in gallons per hour (gph) or per minute (gph)

Groundwater. Water within the earth that supplies wells and springs; in particular, water in ground that is completely saturated

Head. The source of a spring; also, the pressure of a mass of water

PSI. A measure of pressure: pounds per square inch

Sillcock. An outdoor water outlet

Water table. The uppermost surface of groundwater

of whether to dig a well or tap into town water. Figure the cost of both options over 10 or 20 years before deciding. Check with local officials, because sometimes you pay for town water anyway.

Non-drinking water. There are time-honored methods of gathering water for animals and for washing. One is the creation of the farm pond, usually the excavation of a low-lying, swampy area. Normal drainage should fill the pond to a consistent depth. Another method is catching rainwater from eave troughs in barrels. Some homesteaders in low-water areas provide most or all of their water needs from rainwater, which is naturally soft, by constructing home roof runoff systems that filter into very large storage cisterns.

Are You a Dowser?

Dowsing (water witching or water divining) is probably as old as man's need for water. It is a gift certain people seem to have that enables them to find underground sources of water. The dowser can determine where the water is, as well as its depth and volume. There is no trickery or chicanery involved.

Would you like to try dowsing? The rod you use can be as simple as a forked branch or as complex as electronic gear. Personally, I favor the forked willow branch.

Cut a branch and remove all small twigs. It should be pliable, so it bends rather than breaks when the end is pulled down. A branch of any tree that meets these requirements will do.

Grasp the branch by the tapering forks, palm up. Rest your clenched fists on your hips. Let the tip of the branch point straight out, slightly higher than level. Hold the forks firmly enough to prevent the tip from bending down as a result of gravity.

Holding the rod properly, walk slowly over the area to be dowsed. Keep your feet close to the ground, just avoiding a shuffle. If you are a dowser and you pass over an underground water supply, the end of the rod will suddenly be pulled downward to a vertical position. The pull can be so strong as to rupture the bark or even break the rod at the point where you are holding it.

—from *Sleeping with a Sunflower* by Louise Riotte

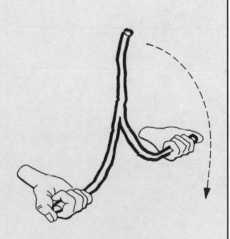

A dowser might hold a forked stick like this. Some advocate using thumbs on the stick ends, but the American Society of Dowsers says there is no single correct grip.

Five Kinds of Wells

Because groundwater moves in so many ways, at different speeds and different depths, the general term *well* is about as useful as the word *aircraft*. To say a well is any pit or hole in the ground used to extract water is a misleading oversimplification. Some shallow wells venture only a short distance from the ground surface. Elsewhere, wells penetrate deep into subterranean space.

Like groundwater, wells and well technology are complex and largely misunderstood by the public. Understanding begins with knowledge of the basic kinds of wells.

Dug Wells

Grandma's "wishing well," with its stone-wall top we could just see over, its little roof, and the bucket on a windlass, was almost certainly a dug well. Because it penetrated just a short distance into the water table, its water may

---

Tips for Working with a Well Contractor

A deep well, particularly one that's drilled or driven, should be left in the hands of a reputable well contractor—preferably one who is licensed by your state. Ask for a written contract.

A well-drilling contract should describe all the work to be done, prices, and terms, including:

- A statement that all work is to comply with all local and state codes.
- The size of the well hole and methods of eliminating surface contamination.
- Casing specifications. For instance: The casing is to be at least 4 inches in diameter and extend at least 20 feet below the ground. Discuss actual casing size so pump and casing are compatible.
- The type of well seal and grout seal around the casing, and the type of well development to be done, if necessary.
- The type of screen to be installed, where needed.
- A date for completion of the well, and delivery of the well log and test-pumping report.
- A guarantee of materials and workmanship.
- An itemized list of costs, including the cost of drilling per foot, charges for any other materials per unit (including casing), and any other charges for grouting, developing, and test pumping.
- Liability insurance for both owner and contractor.

Normally this is the time to select your pump. Ask your contractor for recommendations. Your contractor will also service the pump.

Keep in mind that some drilling companies have a minimum depth fee. In other words, they'll charge you for at least 100 feet (standard), even if they strike water at 50. Once water has been struck, it's normally part of the contractor's responsibility to pump the well free of sand and drilling particles and to disinfect it.

The well log describing depth and strata, aside from being a valuable record, is used to determine the size of the pump that will be installed. It's also in the owner's best interest to have the drilling company hook up to the well head and install piping that will bring water as far as the house.

—from *The Home Water Supply* by Stu Campbell

---

have been polluted—even in our grandparents' time. A very high percentage of today's dug wells are contaminated.

Dug wells are generally thought to be undependable as well as unclean. They're often known to fail during dry times. Still, in places where the water table remains pretty constant and groundwater quality is high, dug wells are common. They're rarely more than 50 feet deep, reaching just a few feet below the water table into soaked sand and gravel.

Digging the well hole, which may range from 3 to 20 feet in diameter, is normally a tedious, hand-excavated, pick-and-shovel operation. Dug-out material is hauled to the surface in a pail on a rope. A clam-shell bucket on a crane can be used if the earth is very soft. Digging a well can be very dangerous because of the potential for cave-in. Seek professional advice on constructing a structure within which to dig the well.

The stone wall around the top of Grandma's well was actually the upper end of the lining. Today, fieldstone is used to keep the well walls from caving in, but brick and mortar or concrete blocks are easier to work with. More often, dug wells are cased with sections of 3-foot-wide, precast well tile that fit together at tongue-and-groove joints. Whatever the material, the lining should be as well sealed and watertight as possible.

A modern dug well should have a sanitary seal at the ground surface, which effectively keeps rainwater out of water below. It will keep surface water from contaminating the water table. Space between the well liner and the surrounding earth should be plugged with a waterproof cement grout.

Country Wisdom

Rural Vermonters have learned something. It's lightning's usual habit to strike the tallest trees in a stand. But sometimes it picks on shorter ones—consistently. A tree that's particularly battered and charred may be standing on a spring or close to a water vein. Since water is a good ground, lightning may select that tree as the easiest route to earth. Look there for water.

—Stu Campbell,
The Home Water Supply

Which Well Is Right for You?

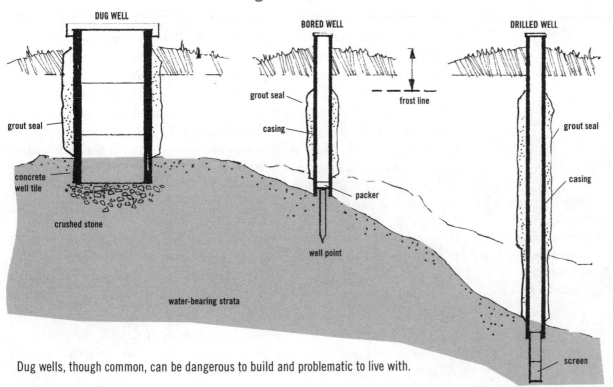

Dug wells, though common, can be dangerous to build and problematic to live with.

Tip: Newer, efficient water-saving toilets and dishwashers can reduce water needs by half.

DETERMINING WATER NEEDS

Needed by	Gallons Per Day	
Each person	75–100	
Each milk cow, drinking and sanitation	35	
Each horse, dry cow, or beef animal	6–12	
100 chickens	3–7	
100 turkeys	7–18	
Each hog	2–4	
Each sheep	2	

Home Fixtures	Gallons Needed	Rate of Flow (gals. per minute)
Filling ordinary washbowl	2	4
Filling average bathtub	30	5
Flushing toilet	6	4
Each shower or bath	up to 30	5
Automatic dishwasher, per load	20	2
Automatic clothes washer, per load	up to 40	5

Yard Fixtures		
½-inch hose with nozzle		3
¾-inch hose with nozzle		6
Lawn watering	600*	3–7

*Watering a lawn or garden with 1 inch of water on 1,000 square feet requires about 600 gallons of water.

—from *The Home Water Supply*

The Jetted Well

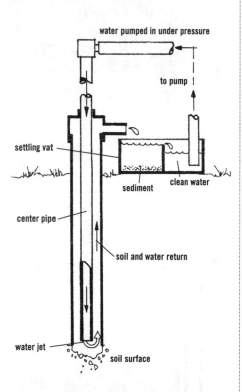

A jetted or washed well (above) can be dug in soft, consistent soil. Water is forced down a center pipe within a larger casing. Pressure at the jet loosens the sand or earth, forcing it back toward the surface. The soil particles are removed in the settling vat, and the cleansed water is recirculated through the system.

Bored Wells

A bored well is essentially a dug well made with an earth auger instead of a shovel. If the auger is turned by hand, the hole will be between 8 and 14 inches in diameter. Power-driven augers bore wider holes—up to 3 feet in diameter. A bored well might be somewhat deeper than an ordinary dug well, but rarely can it be expected to reach a water table lower than 100 feet in the ground.

Vitrified tile, steel, and plastic are the lining materials used most often. In some instances this casing is perforated where the pipe extends into water-bearing gravel and sand. These perforations receive water from the surrounding strata, and may need to be covered with screening to keep silt from entering the discharge line. Like all wells, a bored well head must be sealed and protected from surface drainage.

Jetted or Washed Wells

If conditions are right, a well can be jetted or washed. The two most important ingredients in this kind of operation—aside from soil with reasonably uniform texture—are a nearby water source and a pressure pump. A protective casing is driven into an augered hole and a riser pipe, fitted with a special washing point on its lower end, is inserted inside the casing. A stream of water is forced down this riser pipe and the jet from the wash point dislodges sand and

> ## Country Wisdom
>
> Complete independence, even with water, is simply impossible—no matter how far out of town we choose to live. The biggest lesson to be learned about water is that what's yours is mine and everybody else's.
>
> —Stu Campbell, *The Home Water Supply*

soil below. As the point is pushed deeper and deeper, the muddy mixture is carried back to the surface in the space between the center pipe and the casing, and is discharged into a settling vat. Later, when the wash point is removed, the riser pipe becomes the suction line for water being pumped out of the well from above, and the top few feet of space between the two pipes are grouted to make it watertight.

Driven Wells

A driven well is quick, relatively inexpensive, and, unless there's an unlimited water supply near the surface, relatively undependable compared to the drilled well. In places where well driving is easy but the water table fluctuates, homeowners hedge their bets by driving a number of wells and connecting them to one pump.

Driven wells can be 25 to 100 feet deep, though most draw water from 50 to 60 feet. A well point or sand point, made of cast steel, is connected to lengths of threaded pipe and forced into the ground by blows on the pipe from above. This is the simplest and most direct way to reach groundwater, as long as there are no rocks in the soil to damage the wire mesh jacket of the well point.

The well point itself is only 1¼ to 2 inches in diameter, so it has little resistance as it penetrates. The necessarily small riser pipe limits a driven well's yield to about 3 gallons a minute.

Drilled Wells

Maybe the best argument for a deep (and probably more expensive) drilled well is that it's less likely to be polluted. Second, it's more likely to produce greater yield, simply because of its immense draw-down potential.

In many districts, law demands that wells be drilled only by licensed drillers. There may be other regulations about well location, construction, capacity, disinfection methods, and water-quality standards. A drilling permit may or may not be needed. Rules vary from place to place. So do the per-foot drilling and casing costs.

Drilled wells are done in one of two ways: with a percussion-type cable tool that beats and punches its way into the ground, or with a rotary bit that grinds, bites, and crushes its way through rock. Both are mounted on portable derricks with self-contained hoists.

Rock cuttings are mixed with water trucked to the job site, and the resulting slurry is lifted to the surface in a bailer, a 10- to 20-foot length of pipe with a valve at its lower end. Bailing gives the drillers an indication of the formations the drill is breaking through.

When the Well Fails

A well may see decades of use without needing any attention. Sooner or later, though, like any machine, it will fail. When it does stop producing, it's almost surely for one of four reasons:

1. The pump quit.
2. The water level in the well got too low.
3. The screen got plugged up.
4. So much sand and silt has accumulated in the well hole that the water can't get there.

Any of these problems can be solved as long as there's good access through the top of the casing—a provision in almost any modern drilled well. Any time a well head is opened or work is to be done in a well, the water supply will be contaminated. It must be disinfected, just as it was when it was sealed for the first time. Calcium hypochlorite is perhaps the most common well disinfectant.

—from *The Home Water Supply*

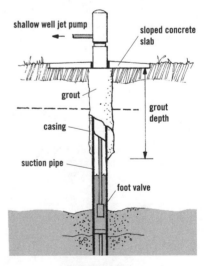

HAND-DRIVEN WELL

A hand-driven shallow well showing the well point packed within the casing. The jet pump sucks water from below.

PUMPS

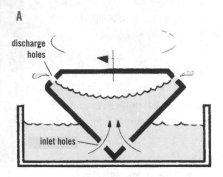

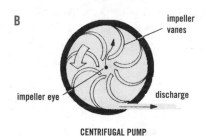

CENTRIFUGAL PUMP

A centrifugal pump works like a child's top filled with water (A). As it spins, water squirts out the sides and is sucked into the bottom holes. The impeller vanes (B) in a real centrifugal pump spin water outward, causing more water to be drawn into the impeller eye.

As everybody knows, pumps are machines for elevating water. Keep in mind that "pump" refers to both the water-moving mechanism and the power source that operates it—be it a windmill, motor, or the muscles in the arm that operate a hand pump. Remember, too, that pumps come in a variety of sizes and types. Proper selection and sizing are vital, and the range of choices is wide. It's worth spending the time to know a little about each.

Reciprocating (Piston) Pump

A reciprocating pump is a positive-displacement pump. It consists of a mechanical device that moves a plunger back and forth in a closely fitted cylinder. The plunger is driven by the power source, and the power motion is converted from a rotating action to a reciprocating motion by the combined work of a speed reducer, crank, and connecting rod. The cylinder should be located near or below the static water level to eliminate the need for priming. The pumping action begins when the water enters the cylinder through a check valve. When the piston moves, the check valve closes, forcing the water through a check valve in the plunger. With each subsequent stroke, the water is forced toward the surface through the discharge pipe.

Centrifugal Pump

If a child's hollow top had holes drilled around its greatest circumference, was filled with water to the height of these holes, and then was spun, it would shoot out water in all directions. As the top turned faster, water would be thrown farther and with more force, in proportion to the speed increase. Imagine that the top also had a hole in its base and could be spun as it sat in a

Measuring Yield

The numbers game approaches its moment of truth when we finally face up to the big question: Exactly how much water is available to you? There's little point in planning to move the water if there's not enough to begin with.

The yield of a particular groundwater or surface water source can be measured quite accurately. A well contractor will measure the approximate yield of the drilled or driven well before dismantling the rig, capping the well, and moving out.

Test pumping is probably the most accurate way to measure yield. Water is pumped from the well for several hours—sometimes as long as 24 hours—at a rate higher than the calculated daily needs of the family. This way the true story of the well can be written.

Every hour, pumped water is collected in containers, usually for 5 minutes. If 25 gallons are collected in that time (5 gpm), this number multiplied by 12 will be the well's per-hour yield. Averaging these numbers over many hours will give an accurate accounting of the well's capacity.

—from *The Home Water Supply* by Stu Campbell

pan of water. As water shot from the upper holes, an equal amount would be sucked into the bottom. A centrifugal pump works much the same way.

Within every centrifugal pump is at least one rotating impeller, which spins water outward across its curved vanes at ever-increasing speed. The water is accelerated enough to create a partial vacuum, causing more water to be drawn into the eye of the impeller. The impeller itself sits in a precisely machined wearing ring, which allows it to turn independent of the suction pipe.

A centrifugal pump does not displace a constant quantity of water. Increases in water pressure will slow it down, and it will pump less water as the water level in a well diminishes. A shallow-well centrifugal pump can't be called upon to lift water more than 15 to 20 feet. The centrifugal jet is the most common pump for domestic water systems. It requires little maintenance, is quiet, and because of its simple design, it's economical to own and operate.

Jet (Ejector) Pump

When water under pressure is jetting through a small opening like a garden hose nozzle, it accelerates and squirts. As it speeds up, a low-pressure zone is created at the very spot where the squirt begins. Any fluid near the squirt tends to get drawn into the jet stream. This additional fluid contributes to the overall flow. It's easy to see that a jet of water, blown into other water, could move a large volume of liquid.

If this happens in a confined space, such as a well pipe, all of the original water plus the extra can be slowed down again in a gradually widening venturi called a diffuser. Low-pressure water, diffused of its velocity, develops strong force that can be carried forward. In other words, high-speed water blown into the point of a hollow cone will slow down and be converted into pressure.

An ejector is a metal plumbing assembly that contains just such a nozzle and a diffuser. The combination of an ejector and a centrifugal pump—called a centrifugal jet pump—is a powerful one.

Submersible Pump

When a centrifugal pump is driven by a closely coupled electric motor constructed for submerged operation as a single unit, it is called a submersible pump. Today's units are slender enough to pass down a 6-inch, 4-inch, or even a 2-inch well casing, and are dependable enough to stay there for years without major servicing.

A typical submersible pump is operated by a ½-horsepower electric motor and has as many as 14 teams of impellers and diffusers, one above the other. It's suspended on a drop line attached to the well seal above. The pump's motor is filled with lubricating oil, but depends on the water that surrounds it for cooling.

Troubleshooting and servicing are usually easy and uncomplicated. The biggest danger to the pump is motor burnout, which can happen if the water level in the well gets too low or when the intake screen becomes clogged.

—adapted from *The Home Water Supply* by Stu Campbell and *Manual of Individual Water Supply Systems*, U.S. Environmental Protection Agency

About Water

When I was about nine my grandfather, a science teacher, taught me about the hand piston pump at his cabin in the Adirondacks. He had an old bathroom plunger that looked like a giant suction cup—nicknamed a plumber's helper —with a hole poked in it. The plunger fit tight in a tin can he just happened to have handy.

When he let me push the plunger into the can filled with water, water squirted up through the hole. The demonstration was so vivid that I've always remembered that water can't be squashed into a smaller space.

—from *The Home Water Supply* by Stu Campbell

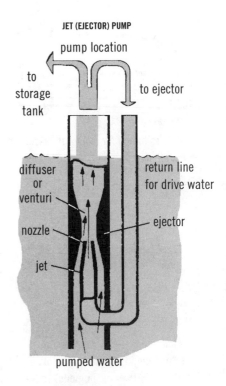

JET (EJECTOR) PUMP

pump location

to storage tank

to ejector

diffuser or venturi

return line for drive water

nozzle

ejector

jet

pumped water

The pump (at location of arrows, top of drawing) pushes part of the water into the return line. Flow of this water is speeded up at the jet, lifting water from the well into the stream and forcing it high enough so that the pump can lift it by suction.

PUMPS

The Submersible Pump

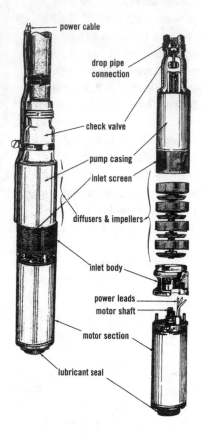

- power cable
- drop pipe connection
- check valve
- pump casing
- inlet screen
- diffusers & impellers
- inlet body
- power leads
- motor shaft
- motor section
- lubricant seal

A submersible pump is another variation on a centrifugal pump.

Warning

If yours is an older home, note that some submersible pumps contained polychlorinated bifenols (PCBs) in their cooling oils. These may have leaked into the groundwater, so it's essential that your well water be regularly tested.

Selecting a Pump

You've studied the basic operation of each type of pump. Now you're approaching another moment of truth—the selection of your pump. It's important to coordinate this with your well driller. You'll need to map out the yield of your water source, weigh it against your daily needs, and figure the total head and lift in your proposed system. A plumbing contractor or pump dealer can help you accomplish this.

If the lift from your source to the pressure tank is never greater than 15 to 25 feet—even when the well is at its lowest—a shallow-well pump offers the best bargain. All you do is drop a suction line down the well.

Don't forget that a shallow-well pump should have either a foot valve at the base of the suction line or a check valve in the suction line to keep it filled. This way the pump will always keep its prime. Obviously, a nonsubmersible pump should never freeze. So it must be sheltered in a warm, dry place where you can get at it easily.

If the lift is more than 25 feet, you'll have to explore the many deep-well pump possibilities. The size of the well casing will influence your decision, particularly if it's smaller than 4 inches in diameter. There are a number of deep-well piston pumps for casings as small as 2 inches. Jet pumps for 2-inch casings are also available.

Before you sign on the dotted line, get advice from plumbing contractors and several reputable dealers. Ask questions about reliability, initial cost, economy, efficiency, servicing, and availability of replacement parts. There's no reason for a good supplier to offer bad advice. A dealer who sells you the wrong product knows he or she is only going to end up with service and warranty problems later on.

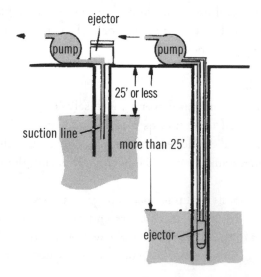

To pull water from a shallow water table (left), a centrifugal pump and ejector might work from above. Pushing water from an ejector below (right), even if the pump sits at the surface, lifts water to greater heights.

—from *The Home Water Supply* by Stu Campbell

Springs as Water Sources

Not all springs are enchantingly clean or beautiful. There's one behind my house that I didn't know about until the house was finished. I can depend on it only to erupt each November, do its best to flood my driveway all winter, then shut off automatically around May 15.

A spring is any opening where water flows out of the earth, either by gravity or artesian pressure. Unfortunately, many of these wounds in the earth's skin "bleed" erratically, and the irregularities are so dramatic that a spring may not always be considered a reliable water source. They are also easily contaminated, especially in places where there is a lot of contact water.

Tapping in. It pays to watch a spring for at least a year before you make up your mind to tap it. Observe the spring closely during dry spells. To be considered truly dependable, it should yield at least twice a family's maximum needs—24 hours a day, 365 days a year.

A spring on a hillside will provide water pressure to a home below. In fact, for every 2 feet of elevation, 1 pound of pressure will be developed. The pressure will always be there as long as the spring is productive enough to keep the intake pipe filled. The spring functions like an elevated reservoir.

If the spring's yield is inconsistent, a hydropneumatic system made up of a storage tank, pump, and pressure tank will be needed to pressurize the home's internal plumbing.

If the spring is located below the house, it's a whole different story. You will have to determine the distance water must be lifted and calculate head loss before designing a pump system that's sure to be adequate.

A developed spring will have at least five components: the spring box, a basin that's watertight above, yet open enough below grade to let groundwater flow into it freely; a cover or housing; cleanout access; an overflow; and an intake line that connects to the distribution system of the house.

Protection. Protecting the sanitary quality of any spring used as a potable water source is of paramount importance. A spring ought to have a removable cover, but the cover should be a heavy one and perhaps be locked in place. I've never known a child who could resist exploring a spring once he or she has found one. It's best to fence in a spring, to keep out both children and livestock.

Terrain above a spring should be bermed or swaled to divert surface drainage. If springwater looks turbid after a heavy rainstorm, runoff water is probably getting into the spring.

A contaminated spring should be disinfected, much like a well or cistern. A solution of water and bleach may be poured into the spring box. It should be allowed to run through the spring line to the house until its chlorine odor can be smelled at all fixtures. Disinfectant should sit in the system for as long as 24 hours if possible. Then it can be flushed out.

—from *The Home Water Supply* by Stu Campbell

The Underground World of a Spring Box

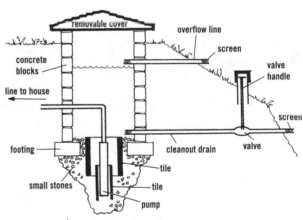

A typical spring box with removable cover. If the house is above the spring, there may be a submersible pump in the spring, or a suction pump in the house.

PONDS

Building an Excavated Pond

New ponds come in two categories: the excavated pond and the embankment pond. Excavated ponds are simpler and more economical to build on nearly level land. They eliminate the need for expensive and elaborate embankments, spillways, and drainage systems. Their maintenance cost is low, and they are relatively safe from floodwater damages. Their disadvantages may lie in limits on the size of the area that can be excavated.

Selecting the correct site is the most important part of any plan, and the water-holding capacity of the soil is especially critical. Test borings to the proposed depth of the pond, then filling the hole with water, will give some idea of the water-holding capacity of the lower soil strata. If there is some doubt that the test reflects the bottom strata, set a pipe the full depth of the hole, then fill the pipe with water. The result will reflect the water-holding capacity at your maximum proposed depth.

Excavated ponds may be fed by surface runoffs, groundwater aquifers, underground water from natural springs, or water pumped from man-made wells. If you have a good water table, the water-holding qualities of the soil at the pond site will not be a problem; if your water table is too low, include a supplementary water supply in your plans.

Bentonite is a volcanic clay that makes an excellent sealing compound. It is applied by mixing about 2 pounds per square foot of land surface, disking it into the top 6 inches of soil, then packing it tightly.

Rectangular ponds are the most popular, because they are simpler to build and can be adapted to most kinds of excavating equipment. The width will be dictated by the size of the equipment available; the length, by the square feet of water surface desired.

Some authorities recommend hauling away the excavated material. This is expensive. Instead, the excavated soil can be used to build embankments around the excavated area to raise the pond's water level.

Building an Embankment Pond

Embankment ponds are the most expensive and difficult to build. You will no doubt need an engineer or expert technical advice and assistance in both the planning and the construction phases.

The elevation of dams and spillways must be calculated precisely. The exact degrees of slope in the pond and the spillway must also be determined. Other important factors include the nature of the soil at the depth of excavation; the suitability of material for building the dam; and determining the best sealing agent for the particular conditions. A poorly planned or constructed embankment pond will be not only a sore disappointment, but also a waste of money.

Heavy equipment is needed to construct embankment ponds. The equipment may include a dragline excavator, bulldozer, tractor-pulled wheeled scraper, sheepsfoot roller, and a compaction roller. Renting this type of equipment can be expensive; hiring the operators adds to the cost.

An Excavated Pond

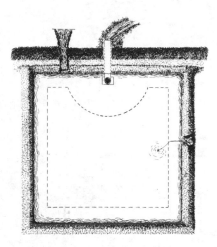

The diagram shows an excavated, square-shaped pond with a landfall adjacent to the pond. This situation is ideal, and will not occur often. In other than ideal situations, the drainage system will not apply and provisions must be made for pumping out the water when the need to drain the pond arises.

Tip: Be sure to check local and state regulations before you build a pond.

Before making even initial plans for an embankment pond, contact the people at the U.S. Soil Conservation Service. They provide many free services in the planning and construction phases.

Embankment ponds are usually built in valleys at the foot of a watershed, or at the foot of a small stream. Care must be taken about interrupting normal waterflows that affect other farms in the area. Check with your county and state authorities before altering streams, regardless of how small.

A solution might be to build your pond on the edge of a stream, then pump the water into the pond. However, such stream waters may be rife with trash fish that you will not want in your pond. To remove the wild fish and fish eggs from the stream water, you may have to pass the water through a screen filter.

First step

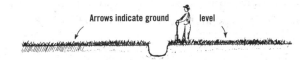

Arrows indicate ground level

Start building the embankment around your fishpond by excavating a trench deep enough to remove the topsoil and about 4 feet wide. Then fill with impervious material such as clay, compacting it by layers.

Second step

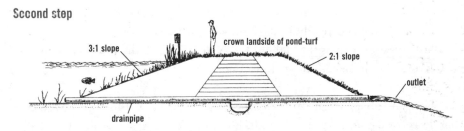

3:1 slope
crown landside of pond-turf
2:1 slope
outlet
drainpipe

Continue building the embankment core with clay up to the crown. Complete building sides with other soils, but not extremely sandy or gravelly soil. The soil removed in excavating should be sufficient to build the embankment. If clay is not available in your area, use bentonite to arrest seepage.

Third step

Turf spillway 2 feet below top of embankment, at least 10 feet wide

The spillway dimensions shown are considered minimum for an embankment pond of one to two acres. It should be level—true to the water level in the pond—so that more water will not spill over on one side than the other, triggering erosion. At the least, it should be well turfed, but concrete is strongly recommended to obviate danger of erosion.

What Fish Need

If you plan to stock your pond with fish, it should be deep. This is worthwhile, for a fish crop can be harvested regularly, just like any other crop on the farm. Better a smaller, deeper pond than a larger, shallower one. A flat, pancake-like pond loses immense volumes of water through evaporation, and may even turn into a swamp in summer.

Pond life in general needs clear water, not silt. This means land leading down to the banks should be planted with a good, deep-rooted cover crop like clover that will assure a runoff as clear as the rain itself, with only a few nutrients added through ground seepage.

Tip: Before you add fish to your pond, consult local conservation officials.

Caution

Impounded water is a hazard, and you are responsible if anything should go wrong, such as if the dam gives away. This kind of calamity may also be excluded from your homeowner's insurance. Water stored in normal pipes and tanks is not a problem, but the homeowner is responsible for all damages caused by water escaping from large tanks and impoundments.

WATER DISTRIBUTION

Planning Your System

Water distribution systems turn out best when they're thoughtfully planned, diagrammed, and tailored to circumstances rather than bound by traditions.

Long-term considerations for any plumbing machine (it is just that) must see beyond initial costs. Convenience and adequate supply to all corners of the system are not the least of your worries. Nor is energy use. Maintenance costs are another large factor. And noise in your system can become a big annoyance. Plumbing within the house itself may be part of your home's building plan. Outside sillcocks and hydrants are another story, and here you'll need to do your most careful thinking.

Start drafting your plan by making a sketch of your property, including all buildings and outbuildings. If you draw it to scale, the whole project will become that much easier to understand and estimate. Include in the drawing any known obstacles that would make a straight trench (between house and chicken coop, for instance) difficult.

Now you need to figure the demand at each outlet. Not only will you need to estimate a peak demand allowance for each building, but you should also determine which outlet will have the greatest fixture flow rate.

Draw a line from the source, such as the well, to the point of largest demand—probably the house. Draw a second line to the next closest major demand, and others to all locations. Pipes should be laid as straight as possible in trenches dug below the frost line, but there may be situations where a straight line is the shortest but not the easiest distance between two points.

Plan for cutoff valves throughout the system. Locate them so that when one part of the system needs to be shut down for repair, service everywhere else isn't interrupted.

Take your time figuring out what you want and need. Once you have your completed drawing, take it to a good plumber. It's worth investigating which plumbing contractor can do the best installation at the best price, as well as which will provide the best service.

Safety First

When building a water system, remember that trenches can be dangerous. The walls can collapse if they do not have boards supporting them during construction.

Also, trenches should never be left open when no one is around. They can fill up with rainwater and present a serious hazard.

Map Your System

Map out the water mains and branch lines needed on your property. If possible, draw them to scale. Then compute the water demands at each location and note them on the sketch.

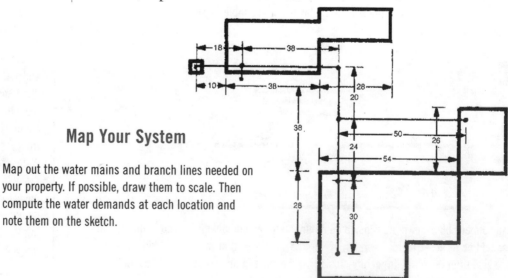

—from *The Home Water Supply* by Stu Campbell

Freeze Protection

When water is transformed from its liquid state to a solid, through the process we all know as freezing, its volume increases by 11 percent. This expansion is more than enough to shatter any pipe, container, or machine in which water is allowed to freeze. Freeze protection, then, is an important part of any water supply system.

Any storage tank, pressure tank, or pump located above the frost line must be kept in a place where it can't possibly become frozen during the winter. In most areas, a buried cistern can have its top above the frost line, so long as its outlet is below the freezing level.

Heat tapes wrapped around pipes, together with insulation, may prevent pipes from freezing wherever they're exposed to freezing temperatures. When pipes do freeze but don't burst, they can be thawed with a portable heat source such as a blow dryer. See the chart on this page for the proper depths at which to lay small water pipes.

DEPTHS AT WHICH TO LAY SMALL WATER PIPES

STATE	DEPTH (FEET)
Alabama	1½ to 2
Arizona	2 to 3
Arkansas	1½ to 3
California	2 to 4
Colorado	3 to 5
Connecticut	4 to 5
Delaware	2 to 3
Florida	1 to 2
Georgia	1½ to 2
Idaho	4 to 6
Illinois	3½ to 6
Indiana	3½ to 5½
Iowa	5 to 6
Kansas	2½ to 4½
Kentucky	2 to 3½
Louisiana	1½ to 2
Maine	4½ to 6
Maryland	2 to 3
Massachusetts	4 to 6
Michigan	4 to 7
Minnesota	5 to 9
Mississippi	1½ to 2½
Missouri	3 to 5
Montana	5 to 7
Nebraska	4 to 5½
Nevada	3 to 5
New Hampshire	4 to 6
New Jersey	3½ to 4½
New Mexico	2 to 3
New York	4 to 6
North Carolina	2 to 3
North Dakota	5 to 9
Ohio	3½ to 5½
Oklahoma	2 to 3
Oregon	4 to 6
Pennsylvania	3½ to 5½
Rhode Island	4 to 6
South Carolina	2 to 3
South Dakota	5 to 9
Tennessee	2 to 3
Texas	1½ to 3
Utah	3 to 5
Vermont	4 to 6
Virginia	2 to 3½
Washington	4 to 6
West Virginia	3 to 5
Wisconsin	5 to 7
Wyoming	5 to 6
District of Columbia	4

Water Reserves

Water reserves are an integral part of any water supply system for a home or farm. Water to be stored for later use can be collected in three primary ways.

Cisterns are ground-level or below-ground reservoirs. A cistern that collects and stores rainwater can be expected to gather as much as ⅔ to ¾ of the annual rainfall on the catchment. Some homes have cisterns just for emergency storage, but others use rainwater for garden water, cleaning, toilet flushing, and other nonpotable uses. Because rainwater is soft, water in a cistern can also be used for bathing, laundry, and dishwashing.

Constructing a good cistern is not a project to be taken lightly. Brick or stone masonry is sometimes used, but high-density concrete, vibrated as it's cast in place, is far better. The concrete should be allowed to wet-cure before the cistern is used.

Cisterns should be carefully covered, and their sidewalls should stick out of the ground at least 18 inches. Covers must be accessible, of course, but they should be locked to keep unwanted visitors and substances from getting in. Manhole covers make great cistern covers. Cisterns should be disinfected with a chlorine solution on a regular basis.

Elevated storage tanks, called gravity tanks, provide gravity-flow pressure to systems below. They're usually designed to hold enough to supply a family with at least two days' worth of water. Gravity tanks should have vents to allow air in as the water level within them is lowered, and to let air out as water is pumped in. Screening should cover these vents to keep out insects and small animals.

A gravity tank can provide pressure to a system without any need for a pressure tank if it's located high above the uppermost outlets in the house. As always, 2.3 feet of elevation will produce 1 pound of pressure. If the system needs 20 pounds per square inch (psi), the tank must be at least 46 feet above any faucet.

Pressure tanks and elastic storage cells constitute the third type of water storage. Although they generally have a small capacity, hydropneumatic tanks and storage cells are considered the most sanitary way to keep water on hand. Their additional function is to keep a steady push of water against the plumbing.

—from *The Home Water Supply*

WATER QUALITY

Routine Treatment of Your Water

Suspended matter found in water (particularly surface water) must be removed in order to provide safe drinking water. Various filtration systems are designed for this purpose.

The advantage of sand filters is that sand is usable indefinitely. Simply backwash or clean the sand bed to remove the accumulated matter. The disadvantages of sand filters are cost, requirements for chemical pretreatment with some units, and more intensive operating requirements.

Slow sand filters allow the slow passage of water through a sand bed. They are usually built outside within a concrete box. They require a larger filter area than do rapid sand filters, but they are ideal for gravity-flow surface sources. Slow sand filters are ideally suited for small individual systems.

Pressure sand filters have automatic controls, but they still require attention to operation and maintenance. They effectively remove oxidized iron and manganese, as well as large particles; however, they cannot remove fine suspended matter effectively. These relatively inexpensive filters can be installed by an amateur plumber.

Diatomaceous earth (DE) filters remove small particles, but they cannot remove very fine suspended matter. The filter medium cannot be reused and must be purchased new. DE filters are easily installed but require more extensive maintenance than do sand filters.

Carbon filters remove suspended matter and other contaminants through the process of absorption. They are the most effective means of removing a broad spectrum of organic compounds. Carbon filters are simple to maintain. If they become clogged, backwashing will clear them. However, they should be replaced routinely because they serve as an ideal environment for bacterial growth.

Slow Sand Filter

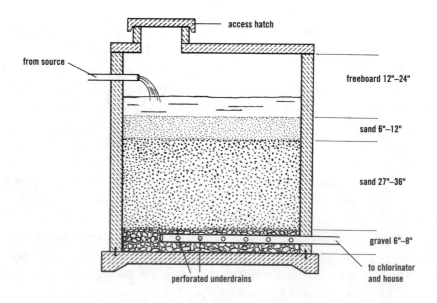

access hatch

from source

freeboard 12"–24"

sand 6"–12"

sand 27"–36"

gravel 6"–8"

perforated underdrains

to chlorinator and house

Slow sand filters work well with gravity-flow surface water systems.

CHOOSING A CHLORINATOR

TYPE OF WATER SYSTEM	TYPE OF CHLORINATOR REQUIRED
Pumped water	Positive displacement pump
Community water service	Water-flow activated
Gravity flow with 10 psi or more	Water-flow activated
Gravity flow with less than 10 psi	Erosion chlorinator
Multiple pumps	Water-flow activated or multiple positive displacement pumps
No electrical service to chlorinator	Water-flow activated or erosion chlorinator

—from How Safe Is Your Water?

Various cartridge, ceramic, and porous stone filters are installed at different points on the water system. Some attach directly to the faucet, others bypass the faucet; some attach to the main water line into the house. Cartridge filters are rated by micron size—that is, by the size particle the filter will remove. These units may remove coarser material, but they do not produce bacteriologically safe water. I do not recommend them. Continuous disinfection is necessary for water supplies drawn from lakes, ponds, streams, and cisterns. It is recommended also for shallow water sources such as dug wells and springs.

Chlorination or Disinfection

Continuous chlorination equipment feeds a chlorine solution into the water system, where it will have enough contact time to kill any microorganisms in the water. Different types of chlorinators work best with different water systems.

Positive displacement pumps. The most common type of chlorinator is a positive displacement pump, which is adjustable and can be synchronized to operate with a water pump. These chlorinators are widely available from plumbing and swimming pool suppliers, as well as from larger hardware stores. You can install one yourself in your basement if you have some basic pipe wrenches and a little plumbing and electrical experience.

Water-flow-activated chlorinators. These apportion the amount of chlorine added to the flow of water in the pipe. Such units are necessary where more than one pump may be used, or for gravity-flow systems. No electrical power is used, but a minimum water pressure of 10 psi (pounds per square inch) is needed to activate the drive mechanism. Because it needs no power, a flow-activated chlorinator can be installed on a long pipeline from a spring to the house, where chlorine contact time can be maximized. Alternately, an amateur plumber can easily install one in a basement.

Erosion chlorinators. As water passes through an erosion chlorinator, the proper amount of chlorine to disinfect the water erodes into the water. Generally, erosion chlorinators are not as accurate as positive displacement pumps, but they can be used where power is not available or where water pressure is low.

—from How Safe Is Your Water? by Kenneth M. Stone

Positive Displacement Chlorinator

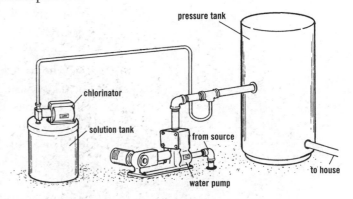

A positive displacement chlorinator is easy to install and available from hardware, plumbing, and pool supply stores.

WATER QUALITY

Clean Water for Poultry

A chicken needs access to fresh drinking water at all times for its body to function properly. Even when there's plenty of water, chickens can become water-deprived if they don't like the taste. If you suspect your water supply contains a high concentration of minerals, have the water tested.

—from *A Guide to Raising Chickens* by Gail Damerow

Content	Maximum Recommended Level
iron	2 parts per million
nitrates	45 ppm
sulfates	250 ppm
sodium chloride (salt)	500 ppm
total dissolved solids	1,000 ppm
total alkilinity	400 ppm
pH	8.0

Testing the Water

It is a good practice to have a complete analysis performed on a newly developed source of drinking water. Such an analysis will tell you if your water is safe, before you begin using it. It also serves as a baseline for all subsequent analyses.

If the purpose of the testing is to help diagnose a suspected problem and an earlier comprehensive test has been performed, testing can be limited. Discuss your problem with the testing laboratory to determine the degree of testing needed. Being specific can limit unnecessary costs for additional tests.

Proper sample collection is important to the accurate analysis of drinking water. Samples must usually be collected in properly prepared and pretreated bottles. Consult the testing lab.

If you are on a public water system, contact your water utility before having an analysis conducted. The utility may be willing to collect a sample from your home without charge.

Understanding Your Results

Lab reports provide an explanation of the results, including the maximum contaminant levels, and indicate which contaminants (if any) represent a problem.

The lab analysis should help determine if deficiencies exist in your water system and should suggest where the problems might lie. Some contaminants result from passage of the water through a piping system or treatment process; others are due to source contamination. See the chart on page 47 for general guidelines that indicate possible sources of contaminants.

Water-quality problems are solved either by correcting deficiencies in the existing supply or with a new source of supply. The basic public health principle of drinking water supply is to obtain the best possible source of uncontaminated water, then to protect its quality by proper development and construction. This solution is also the best financially, because wherever costly treatment equipment and operating costs (chemicals, electricity, repairs) can be avoided, you will save money. However, proper development and construction will correct only a limited number of problems, and additional treatment may be necessary. Your decision will depend on many factors, including:

- **The nature of the problem.** Is the contaminant easily removed or corrected? Is it causing a health risk?
- **The source of the problem.** Is the contaminant in the source of supply, due to poor construction, the piping, or the treatment system?
- **The availability of alternative sources.** Can you construct a new water supply on your lot? Does zoning allow individual water supplies? Is there a site available? Will the quality of a new source be any better?
- **The cost of the improvement.** Will the cost to treat the water source over a long period be more than the cost of a new source?

—from *How Safe Is Your Water?*

Short-Term Solutions

Water that has bacteriological contamination is not safe to drink. You must treat such water to prevent the possible onset of disease.

Boiling all the unsafe water to be consumed is the easiest treatment—at least for a short time. Bring the water to a rolling boil for at least 2 minutes. This will inactivate disease organisms that might be present.

Treat larger quantities of water by disinfecting with household bleach, which is 5.25 percent available chlorine. The water must be clear for effective chlorinization. If it is not, allow the water to stand until any suspended matter settles. Then draw off the clear water and disinfect it by adding 10 drops of household bleach per quart of water. Mix the solution thoroughly, and allow it to stand for 30 minutes before using. If there is no chlorine odor in the water after that time, repeat the process and allow it to stand another 15 minutes.

Chemicals other than volatile organics cannot be removed by boiling. In fact, boiling will further concentrate the chemical and should be avoided. Obtain drinking water from a neighbor with a safe source or use approved bottled water.

If elevated levels of the metal contaminants associated with home plumbing are detected, you can control them in the short term with a flushing program. When water sits in the pipes in your house overnight, or during the day when everyone is away, the leached metals may build up to unacceptable levels. Whenever water has been sitting for more than 6 hours, run the tap until the water becomes colder before using it. If a problem is apparent, it is also important not to cook with hot water, because it is more likely to have an elevated metals content.

—from *How Safe Is Your Water?* by Kenneth M. Stone

Emergency Water

When an emergency occurs, water might be held (and found) in bulk tanks, indoor pools, bathtubs, cisterns, hot-water tanks, toilet reservoirs, in canned or fresh fruit juices, and in fruits and vegetables themselves. Emergency water can be disinfected in 4 ways:

1. Boil it vigorously for at least 5 minutes.
2. Add 4 drops of chlorine bleach to 1 quart of water, then let the mixture stand for at least 30 minutes prior to use.
3. Add 5 drops of 2 percent iodine solution (usually found in a home medicine cabinet) to a quart of water. It should stand for at least half an hour before consumption.
4. Buy water purification tablets from a drug or sporting goods store. Add 1 tablet to a quart container filled with water before the container is tightly capped. After 3 minutes, shake the container thoroughly. The cap can then be tightened and the water allowed to disinfect for 10 minutes. Follow the manufacturer's directions, however, for maximum effectiveness.

Emergency water can be canned. Fill quart Mason jars, cover with regular jar lids, and process in a pressure cooker for 10 minutes at 15 pounds of pressure. Store these jars in a cool root cellar, or wherever other canned goods have been stored.

—from *The Home Water Supply* by Stu Campbell

Ten Simple Tips for Saving Water

- Insulate hot water pipes, so the hot water tap doesn't run so long while you wait for warm water.
- Use "gray water" for watering plants and in toilet tanks.
- Use water-saving shower heads.
- Install an aerator in your kitchen or bathroom sink faucet. The aerator reduces the water flow.
- Wait to use your dishwasher and washing machine until you have a full load.
- Scrape your dishes with a sponge or spatula instead of rinsing them under running water. Or hand-rinse them in a sink or dishpan.
- Double up in a shower or bath.
- Don't flush the toilet every time.
- Don't water lawns and gardens unnecessarily.
- Install "pistol grip" nozzles on hoses. They shut off water flow when released.

REMOVING CONTAMINANTS

Sewage Pollution

Unfortunately, clean, pleasant-tasting water isn't necessarily safe.

Contamination from sewers, cesspools, and septic tanks (if not yours maybe your neighbor's) should always be considered. Pollution has a knack of traveling great distances underground—often in lime-stone or in crevices between solid rock formations. Chlorides and nitrates found in your water are indicators of sewage pollution. The chart below gives mini-mum distances between wells and possi-ble sources of sewage contamination. While the minimum distance of 100 feet between a water source and any part of septic system is a good rule of thumb, consult your health department for local requirements.

—from *The Home Water Supply*

DISTANCE FROM WELLS

Source of Contamination	Minimum Distance (feet)
Waste disposal lagoons	300
Cesspools	150
Livestock and poultry yards	100
Privies, manure piles	100
Silo pits, seepage pits	150
Milkhouse drain outlets	100
Septic tanks and dis-posal fields	100
Gravity sewer or drain not pressure tight	50
Pressure-tight gravity sewer or drain	25

There are ways to treat most forms of water contamination. Expense and inconvenience will vary according to the nature of the contaminants.

Iron and manganese are often dissolved in groundwater. When exposed to air, they precipitate from water to form undesirable deposits. Filtration systems are available to remove these contaminants. Chlorine is a strong oxidizing agent that precipitates dissolved iron and man-ganese. When chlorination is followed by filtration, you have a very effective system. A greensand filter does the work of a chlorinator and filter in a single unit. Water softeners remove iron and manganese, as well as the more preva-lent calcium and magnesium. Aeration of water will oxidize dissolved iron and manganese.

Hard water is caused primarily by **calcium and magnesium,** which pro-duce scale deposits in piping and heating systems. Water softening removes divalent metal ions, including calcium and magnesium. Heating water acceler-ates the deposition of scale, so softening hot water is of primary concern. The best method of softening individual water systems is the ion-exchange method. However, this results in an increase in the sodium content of the drinking water. You can avoid adding sodium to drinking water by softening only the hot-water system.

Nitrates are a problem particularly for infants. Nitrate levels between 10 and 20 milligrams per liter can be managed by finding an alternative water supply for infants. Higher levels must be removed or reduced. Removal can be accomplished by several methods: reverse-osmosis, anion-exchange, and dis-tillation units. Both distillation and reverse-osmosis units remove many other contaminants, but they also remove beneficial minerals. Anion-exchange units are similar to water softeners.

Chlorides and sulfates can be removed in the same fashion as nitrates, except that chlorides must be removed with an acid-base-exchange unit rather than an anion-exchange unit.

Fluoride excess can be removed by reverse-osmosis units and distillation. Ion-exchange units using bone char or activated alumina are also effective.

Metals can be removed from drinking water using either reverse osmosis or distillation. Metals that enter drinking water from the piping system can

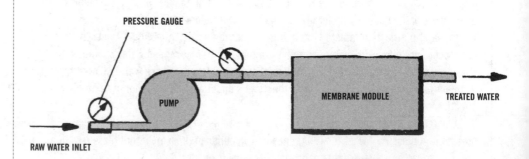

Basic reverse-osmosis unit. Because pressure is critical, it must be closely monitored, so gauges are placed before and after the pump.

also be maintained at safe levels by raising the pH of the water above corrosive acid levels. This can be done by feeding soda ash or by passing the water through a neutralizing tank that contains limestone chips. The pH of the treated water should be maintained above 7.0, or at even higher levels, depending on the metals being controlled.

The most common radionuclides in drinking water are **radium and radon**. Radium is a divalent ion that is easily removed by ion-exchange softening. However, in this case, all water to be consumed should be treated, not just the hot water. Reverse osmosis is also effective in removing radium. Both granular activated carbon and aeration are effective in removing radon gas. If radon is found in elevated levels in your water, check the radon levels of your home.

—from *How Safe Is Your Water?* by Kenneth M. Stone

SOURCES OF CONTAMINANTS

CONTAMINANT	POSSIBLE SOURCES
Contaminants of Source	
Bacteria	Inadequate sewage disposal, surface runoff, animals
Color	Leaves, organic matter, industrial pollutants, oxidized iron and manganese
Nitrate/nitrite	Sewage disposal systems, manure piles, fertilizer storage, heavily fertilized fields
Odor	Decomposition of organic matter, naturally occurring gases, industrial pollutants
Turbidity	Surface runoff, oxidized iron and manganese
Heavy Metals	
Arsenic	Natural occurrence, pesticides
Barium	Natural occurrence
Cadmium	Industrial wastes
Chromium	Natural occurrence, industrial pollutants
Fluoride	Natural occurrence
Lead	Industrial pollutant
Mercury	Industrial pollutant, pesticides
Selenium	Natural occurrence
Silver	Industrial pollutant
Contaminants of Piping	
Copper	Copper plumbing
Lead	Lead pipe, soldered copper plumbing
Zinc, cadmium, lead, iron	Galvanized iron pipe
Contaminants from Treatment	
Chlorides	Anion-exchange units
Copper	Treatment for algae with copper sulfate
Organics (trihalomethanes)	Disinfection with chlorine, reaction with organics
Sodium	Water softening
Miscellaneous	
Chlorides	Sewage, salt water intrusion, storage of road salt, salted roads, dirt roads treated with calcium chloride
Iron and manganese	Naturally occurring deposits
Pesticides and herbicides	Storage of chemicals, household and garden pest control, utility rights-of-way treatment, agricultural use
Radionuclides	Naturally occurring deposits Sodium Same as chlorides
Sulfates	Naturally occurring deposits
Volatile organics	Industrial waste disposal sites, septic tank cleaners, domestic waste disposal

YOUR PLACE IN THE COUNTRY

REMOVING CONTAMINANTS   47

4

PLUMBING

PLUMBING SYSTEMS • SEPTIC SYSTEMS • LEAKY FAUCETS
TOILETS • CLOGGED DRAINS • REPAIRING PIPES

Pipes and septic systems have a mind of their own, and a sense of timing to go with it. As we prepared last Easter's meal, the kitchen sink backed up. Plumbers enjoy holidays too, so we took on the job of unclogging, first with a plunger and then with a snake. Turned out that the roots of an oak tree had, over the years, put a lock grip on the line where it connected with a sewer. This ultimately proved costly. In fact, plumbing, and septic in particular, can be one of the larger expenses of owning an old house. We'll start the chapter with tips on how to do an inspection before you buy.

—John & Martha Storey

Even if you have no plumbing skills, say Phillip J. Decker and T. Newell Decker, you can still save a good deal of money by doing some of the less difficult plumbing tasks yourself. If you do decide to do your own plumbing, first hire a professional to inspect your system. You should then acquire some basic tools and learn about your local plumbing codes.

Water from a public utility or from your well enters your home through a large supply pipe. The supply pipe then splits into two lines, one of which goes to the water heater. Proceeding from the water heater is a hot-water line that runs parallel to the cold-water line to every plumbing fixture in your home. These supply lines move water through the house at a constant pressure, usually 50 to 60 pounds per square inch.

Your plumbing system also includes a waste system, consisting of a series of pipes that carry waste from your house to a city sewer or your septic tank. Another set of pipes vents gases and odors to the outside of the house. These pipes use gravity, rather than water pressure, to do their work. Drain traps located under your sinks prevent the gases from going back into your home. These U-shaped pipes allow running water to flow down through them, but when the faucet is turned off, the water that lies "trapped" at the bottom of these pipes acts as a barrier to prevent gases from reentering your home.

Inspecting the Plumbing

Before you buy a house, consider having a plumber make an inspection. Here are the main points to consider:

1. Water pressure. Check several faucets as high up in the house as you can get. Then go down low in the house and check again. Low pressure can have various causes. The supply line may be too small, or the pipes may have deposits of lime or some other material. At least a ¾-inch-diameter service line is required. Most new houses have a 1-inch copper line. Major distribution pipes should be ¾ inch, and most branch lines should be ½ inch. If you have cast-iron and lead lines in a house over 50 years old, you should replace them with copper and plastic.

2. Shutoff valve. Check the shutoff valve at the service entrance and make sure it is good. You may find a shutoff valve inside the house and a shutoff valve outside by the street. As long as one of them is in working order, you are okay.

3. Leaks. Be sure to check for leaks in the supply system. Rust or white or greenish crusting of pipes indicates leaks. If you have copper mixed with steel or iron lines, make sure that dialectic unions are in place.

4. Water hammer. Open up all the faucets in the house and listen for water hammer. This is a severe problem that occurs when you stop the water flowing in the pipe by abruptly closing the faucet. Air chambers are placed in the supply lines at the fixtures to absorb that shock and prevent water hammer. If you have water hammer, the chambers are waterlogged or not there. If you have to add them, it means going through the wall where the fixture is. That can be very costly.

5. Deteriorating pipes. Keep in mind that the fittings on steel or cast-iron pipes always last much longer than the pipes themselves. Everything may look fine, but the pipe may be extremely thin because of deterioration. There is no easy way to determine the condition of a pipe without sticking a screwdriver through it. You can tap it to see if it dents, but you obviously don't want to put a hole in the pipe.

—from *Renovating Brick Houses* by Philip J. Decker and T. Newell Decker

The Anatomy of a Plumbing System

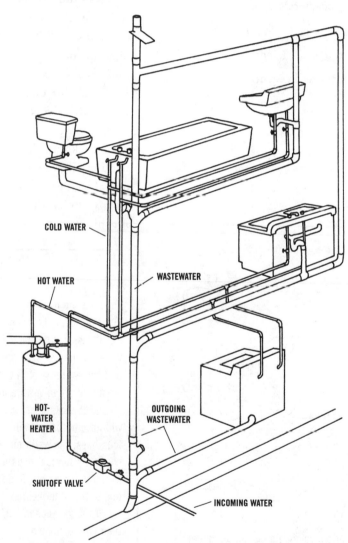

COLD WATER

HOT WATER

WASTEWATER

HOT-WATER HEATER

OUTGOING WASTEWATER

SHUTOFF VALVE

INCOMING WATER

The diagram shows a typical home plumbing system. The thinner pipes are the incoming hot- and cold-water pipes. The thick pipes are the drains and vents.

INSPECTING THE PLUMBING

Lyn Herrick credits her parents with encouraging her to learn how to fix everything in the home from appliances to broken windows. Now she writes a nationally syndicated column called "Ask Mrs. Fix-it" and is author of The Woman's Hands-On Home Repair Guide.

Here are four key steps in evaluating a plumbing system.

Scrutinize the waste system carefully for smell and leakage. If the house has a septic tank, determine when it was last emptied and the exact location of the septic tank cleanout. If the house doesn't have a septic tank, determine the location of the house vents for the waste line. Every house should have a minimum of one house vent, more if there is a long run to the sewer line. A house vent is a trap with a vent coming up to the surface of the ground. You can run augers down the vent to clean the line.

Examine the water heater. If you can open a drain valve, do it and see whether the water drains out clear or cloudy, and if any scale or rust comes out. Remove the cover of the burner, if any, and look for rust scaling.

Examine all fixtures in the house. They should be firmly mounted and drain quickly. Look for mineral stains, toilet bases that wobble, and water damage to floors. Fill the sinks and let them drain to see if there is gurgling in the adjacent toilet. If so, venting is probably inadequate. Upgrading venting in a house is very expensive, but poor ventilation results in septic smells.

Check for clogs. While inspecting the lateral sewer drainage outside the house, have someone flush every toilet in the house three or four times in a row to send a large volume of water down the sewage line. You can then see if anything backs up. You may find that the drainage system outside the house is made of vitreous bell tile, which may have been poorly installed or been broken, allowing tree roots to enter at the breaks or through the joints. These tree roots will clog the line. The roots can be removed mechanically with augers, but this operation will probably have to be repeated every few years.

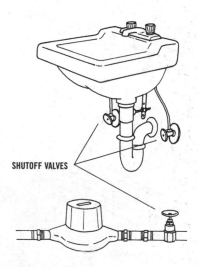

SHUTOFF VALVES

A shutoff valve should be located under each fixture (above); otherwise use the main shutoff valve where the water line enters the house.

How to Turn the Water Off

If you have a leak or are repairing a plumbing fixture, you must turn off the water going into that fixture before beginning your work.

Unless you have a very old house or a poorly planned one, you will find water shutoff valves under each of your plumbing fixtures. Bathroom and kitchen sinks have both hot- and cold-water shutoff valves, while toilets have only cold-water valves. In some cases these shutoff valves are in the basement or crawl space under the house.

If the sink, toilet, or shower you are working on does not have a shut-off valve, you will have to turn off all the water in the house at the main shut-off valve. This valve is found near the water meter or close to the wall where the main water line enters the house. If you must use the main shutoff valve, make sure that the power to your water heater is turned off. To do this, turn off the circuit breaker switch that regulates operation of the water heater.

If you get your water from the city or a source other than your own well or spring, there may also be a shutoff valve out in the yard near the street. You will often find this meter in a small hole in the yard, covered by a heavy metal lid. Remove the lid and use a large adjustable wrench to turn the valve. Sometimes a special wrench is required. If so, check with your water supplier about obtaining access to this wrench.

—from *The Woman's Hands-On Home Repair Guide* by Lyn Herrick

Septic systems come in a variety of designs, but all are designed to collect, treat, and purify home wastewater. Properly designed, constructed, and maintained septic systems can function well for decades. But a system that's too small for a household's needs, poorly built, or neglected can become the bane of your existence.

A typical home septic system begins with a sewage pipe that runs from the dwelling to a septic tank, usually a large concrete box. Wastewater containing floating and suspended solids enters the tank, where solids can begin to be broken down by bacterial action. Heavy solids settle to the tank bottom, forming a sludge layer. Floating solids, such as oil and grease, form a scum on the surface. Most of the tank's content is liquid, or effluent, which flows out of the tank through a separate outlet into a subsurface disposal area, often a system of buried perforated pipes, known as a leaching area. Alternatively, in areas with very good drainage, some systems use a seepage (or leaching) pit. Essentially a large porous concrete box, the pit allows effluent to seep out through its sides and bottom.

The leaching area or pit is surrounded with stone and covered with a layer of topsoil. Leaching spreads the effluent over a large area, where it is purified by flowing through the soil. A properly operating leaching system can remove up to 90 percent of the pollutants in household wastewater.

Instead of a septic tank and leaching system, some older homes use a cesspool. A cesspool is simply a large hole in the ground, lined with stone, bricks, or concrete blocks to create a porous tank, from which effluent can leach. Better cesspools consist of two tanks, the first a watertight one for solids and the second a leaching one to distribute effluent. While cesspools may perform perfectly adequately under the right conditions, septic tank systems are preferable.

The Anatomy of a Septic System

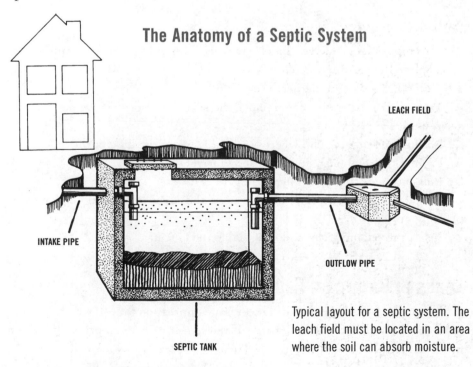

LEACH FIELD

INTAKE PIPE

OUTFLOW PIPE

SEPTIC TANK

Typical layout for a septic system. The leach field must be located in an area where the soil can absorb moisture.

Things to Know about Septic Systems

Septic waste systems may be subject to stringent regulations. In some states the system must be tested whenever a home is sold. If it fails to meet strict criteria for its design, distance from water sources, and performance, it must be replaced immediately.

Even if everything seems to be working fine, septic systems must be inspected on a regular basis and pumped out as needed. Failure to do so can ruin a leaching system—a costly oversight.

Your system must be located well away from wells and streams (typically 100 to 150 feet, depending on local codes). Leaching areas should not be paved over, and rainwater and snow melt should be directed away from them. Never drive on leaching areas, as it may damage the pipes.

You can help keep your system functioning better by reducing household water use; keeping oil, grease, bleach and other chemicals out of the drains; and eschewing the garbage disposal.
Signs of trouble include:
- Slowly draining toilet and sinks
- Water building up on top of leaching areas
- Foul odors near the septic system
- Snow melting (and bare ground appearing) in patches over the leaching area.

LEAKY FAUCETS

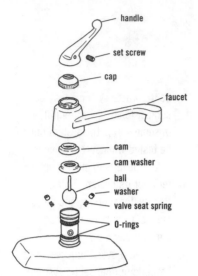

Use a replacement kit to fix a rotating ball faucet.

Labels: handle, set screw, cap, faucet, cam, cam washer, ball, washer, valve seat spring, O-rings

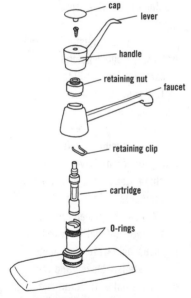

The cartridge faucet is simple to fix.

Labels: cap, lever, handle, retaining nut, faucet, retaining clip, cartridge, O-rings

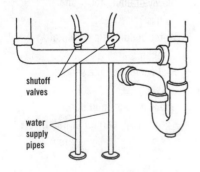

Turn off shutoff valve of hot or cold water.

Labels: shutoff valves, water supply pipes

Faulty Kitchen Faucets

A drip at the kitchen sink spout generally means one of the working parts needs replacing. The good news is that you can purchase prepackaged repair kits that contain replacement parts as well as directions for completing the repair yourself.

First determine the exact make and model of your faucet and purchase the appropriate kit at a hardware or plumbing supply store. A rotating ball faucet has a ball with three openings—one for hot water, one for cold water, and one for the spout. A cartridge faucet has a cartridge instead of a ball.

Rotating Ball Faucets

Over time, leaks may develop at the spigot or the base of the faucet. For leaks at the base of the faucet, replace the O-rings as described opposite. If your faucet drips at the spigot, first make sure the cap is tight. If it is, then, it is likely that the springs and small rubber seals need replacing.

1. Turn off the water under the sink.

2. Remove the set screw at the base of the handle with an Allen wrench or the small wrench that comes in the repair kit. Pull off the handle.

3. Wrap the serrated sleeve of the cap with tape to protect its finish and unscrew it with a plumber's wrench. This will expose the ball-and-cam assembly, which you can pull out with your fingers.

4. You will see two holes in the fixture. In each hole there is a spring and a small black rubber washer. Remove them with your fingers or with long-nosed pliers. Replace them with identical parts from the repair kit.

5. Check the ball for chips or scratches. If there are some, replace the ball.

6. To reassemble the faucet, line up the slot on the ball with a metal pin within the faucet body. The cam assembly should line up with the same slot.

Cartridge Faucets

This type of faucet is even simpler to work with. A leaky spigot requires that you replace the cartridge stem.

1. Shut off the water underneath the sink.

2. Take off the decorative cap, remove the screw, and pry off the handle with a screwdriver.

3. Locate the retaining clip where the handle meets the base of the faucet.

4. Pry out the retaining clip with a screwdriver.

5. Pull out the cartridge with your fingers.

6. Install the new cartridge, making sure the arrow or identifying mark is pointing up.

7. Insert the retaining clip and reassemble the faucet.

Leaks in Bathroom Faucets

The most common bathroom faucet is a compression faucet, which has separate handles for hot and cold water. If the faucet drips, you probably need a new washer. Another possibility is a damaged valve seat, which will need to be

Here is a list of the tools you're likely to need when working on your home plumbing system. Buy them on an as-needed basis to avoid unnecessary expense. Special jobs may require special tools. For instance, if you're repairing frozen pipes, you'll probably need a hair dryer!

- large and small adjustable wrenches
- large hex wrench
- Allen wrench
- pipe wrenches
- seat wrench
- stem wrench
- straight-slot screwdriver
- Phillips screwdriver
- long-nosed pliers
- seat grinding tool
- sink auger
- toilet auger
- vise grips
- hacksaw
- pipe cutter
- plunger
- kitchen knife

Leaks at the Base of a Faucet

If your leak occurs at the base of the faucet, you will need to replace the O-rings. First, turn off the water under the sink, and then disassemble the faucet as outlined on the page opposite. Remove the spout by pulling it up and working it from side to side, to expose one or more O-rings. Slip the old O-rings from the faucet with a knife or screwdriver. If O-rings are not included in the repair kit, purchase exact replacements. Insert the new O-rings and reassemble the faucet.

reground or replaced. Finally, if the leak is coming from the base of the handle, the O-rings are the problem (see instructions at right). If your bathroom sink has a cartridge faucet, see the section on cartridge faucets.

Replacing the Washer

1. Feel the temperature of the leaking water to determine which faucet—hot or cold—is the problem.

2. Turn off the water going to the faucet at the shutoff valve under the sink.

3. Pop or pry off the "H" or "C" cap on top of the handle, unscrew the handle, and pry the handle up and off.

4. Wrap a rag or tape around the packing nut to protect the fixture from being scratched. Unscrew the packing nut with an adjustable wrench by turning it counterclockwise.

5. Remove the stem by pulling it up.

6. With the stem removed, examine the washer that sits at the end of the stem. If the washer is damaged or worn, water can leak through the damaged area.

7. Remove the screw that holds the washer in place and take out the washer.

8. Replace the old washer with a new one exactly like it. Replace the screw also if it is badly worn or corroded.

9. Screw the stem and packing nut back in, and reassemble the handle.

10. Turn on the water valve under the sink.

—from *The Woman's Hands-On Home Repair Guide*

Pry off the screw cap, then unfasten the screw to remove the handle.

A leaky bathroom faucet probably means you need a new washer.

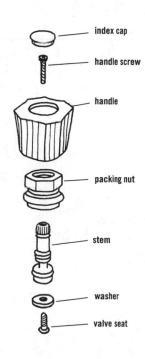

index cap

handle screw

handle

packing nut

stem

washer

valve seat

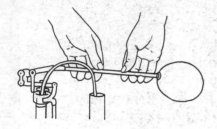

Gently bend the float arm to adjust the water level in the toilet tank.

The Toilet That Runs Constantly

Toilets that continually run between flushes waste a lot of water. You can tell if a toilet is doing this by the sound in the tank and the ripples of running water in the toilet bowl. Lift the tank cover to see what is going on. You will notice an overflow tube and water in the tank. If the water level is too high, the water spills into the tube, creating the problem.

Adjusting the Water Level

You can adjust the water level to just below the opening at the top of the overflow tube. The water level is regulated by the large ball that floats in the tank. A brass arm connects the ball to a shutoff valve. As the water in the tank rises and the ball floats upward, it creates downward pressure on the shutoff valve, which eventually closes. To make the shutoff valve close more quickly, increase the downward angle of the brass arm.

1. Screw in the ball a little on the connecting arm so the distance between the shutoff valve and ball is reduced.

2. If the ball is completely screwed in, gently bend the connecting arm so that the ball is lower in the water.

3. Flush the toilet and see how high the water rises. If it still rises above the mouth of the tube, gently bend the float arm so that the ball sits even lower.

Off the Grid: Consider an Earth-Friendlier Toilet

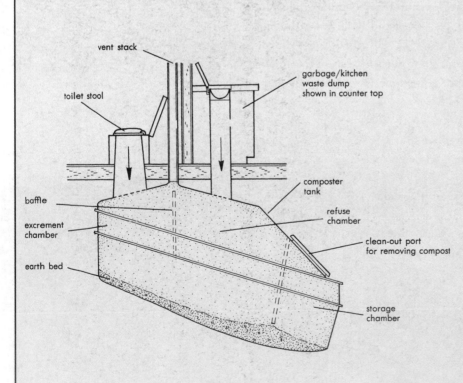

vent stack

toilet stool

garbage/kitchen waste dump shown in counter top

baffle

excrement chamber

earth bed

composter tank

refuse chamber

clean-out port for removing compost

storage chamber

Composting toilets are the most sensible, environmentally compatible method of human waste disposal. Composting toilets require air, heat, and damp (but not wet) conditions in order for aerobic organisms to decompose organic wastes. Good venting, a well-insulated tank, raising the pH, and maintaining a loose pile can eliminate problems with odor and excessive moisture. Higher costs and reports of occasional malfunctions are the potential disadvantages of these systems.

There are at least three different operating configurations for composting toilets: units that are relatively compact and require electricity to speed composting activity; units that are large and capable of holding wastes for a long period of time to ensure bacterial reduction; and units intermediate in size that are in some way solar-heated.

—from *The Waterless Toilet* by Ron Poitras

The Toilet That Won't Flush

When the tank does not fill with enough water, the toilet does not flush completely. The solution is to raise the water level in the tank. To adjust the water level, follow these steps:

1. For toilets with a plastic mechanism, turn the knob at the base of the regulator clockwise. For older toilets with a floating ball, slightly unscrew the ball on the connecting arm.

2. If the ball is unscrewed as far as it will go, gently bend the arm up.

3. Flush the toilet to check the new level of the water. You want the water to sit about ¾ inch from the top of the tube.

Replacing the Ball

If the toilet does not flush at all, it's likely that the water in the tank is leaking out as rapidly as it enters. A rubber ball sits on an opening at the bottom of the tank. When the toilet is flushed, the ball is forced up by the toilet handle, allowing water to flow out of the tank. When the tank empties, the ball falls back on the hole and forms a seal as the tank again fills with water. As the ball becomes worn, water leaks out of the tank. The solution is to replace the ball.

1. Shut off the water to the toilet by closing the valve underneath the tank.

2. Remove the old ball. The ball may be attached by a collar slipped over the overflow tube, a hook connected to two hooks on the side of the overflow tube, or, in older models, a chain linked to a lever, which is connected to the flush handle.

3. Take the old ball to the hardware store to replace it. If you have a ball with a chain, it is unlikely that you will be able to replace it exactly. Instead you can purchase a new flapper mechanism. The flapper slips onto the overflow tube and comes with a chain that connects to the flush handle. Adjust the chain so that the flapper rises and then sits snugly over the hole in the tank.

Unclogging the Toilet

When your toilet becomes stopped up and overflows, try using a plunger. Turn off the water to the toilet at the shutoff valve near the base. Place the plunger over the hole in the bottom of the toilet bowl. Push down hard and pull up several times. This action creates a partial vacuum, which should dislodge what is obstructing the flow of wastewater.

If the obstruction remains, use a toilet auger. This is a hollow, cylindrical tube with a handle on the top and a snake that proceeds from the bottom as the handle is turned. The bottom end of the auger curves in a J-like shape. You can also use a wire coat hanger. Straighten the hanger but keep the hook on the end.

1. Insert the auger into the bowl and aim it so the snake goes into the trap.

2. As you turn the auger handle, the snake will move toward the blockage.

3. When you reach the blockage, try to hook it and force it back into the toilet bowl by pulling down or turning the auger handle in the opposite direction. Avoid pushing the obstruction farther into the trap.

If after using the auger the blockage still remains, call a plumber. The only solution now is to disassemble the toilet, which is a difficult job.

—from *The Woman's Hands-On Home Repair Guide* by Lyn Herrick

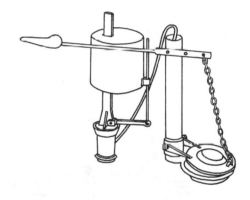

You may replace your old ball-and-chain mechanism with this flapper-and-chain version.

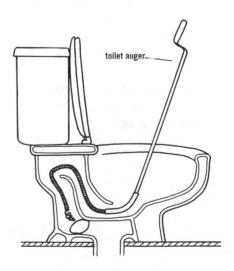

toilet auger

Hook the blockage with the auger. Do not push it farther into the drain.

CLOGGED DRAINS

Clearing Clogs

A clogged drain in the kitchen is frustrating and always seems to happen when the sink is full of dirty dishes. In the bathroom, sinks regularly become clogged with a combination of hair, grease, and soap that prevents water from draining properly. In either case, don't despair. You can solve the problem without calling a plumber.

Plunging the Drain

1. Run a little water into the sink.
2. Hold a plunger directly over the drain and plunge down, then pull up hard. Repeat several times until the water drains.

Flushing the Drain with a Hose

If the plunger method doesn't work, try using a garden hose.
1. Lead your garden hose from an outside spigot to the problem drain.
2. Insert the hose into the drain and stuff a towel around and inside the drain hole to make a tight seal.
3. Have a friend turn on the water at the outside faucet while you hold the hose in the drain. This may flush out the debris and clear the pipes.

Cleaning the Water Stopper

This approach can be helpful in the bathroom. Most bathroom sinks have a water stopper built into the fixture, except for older sinks that have removable rubber drain plugs. Underneath the sink and behind the drainpipe, there is a pivot arm that regulates the up-and-down motion of the water stopper. The arm is held in place by a retaining nut.
1. Unscrew the nut and push the arm toward the back of the sink. This lifts the stopper up from the drain hole.
2. Clean the stopper and the drain with a disassembled coat hanger or some other instrument that will reach into the drain.
3. Reassemble the arm, tighten the retaining nut, and check the drain.

Cleaning the Drain Trap

If the previously outlined methods fail, you may need to clean the drain trap—the U-shaped pipe under the sink. The drain trap is filled with water at all times to prevent sewer gas, pests, and other unpleasant contaminants from entering your house through the pipe. Drain traps perform an important function in your home. Unfortunately, they also become clogged.
1. Place a small bucket or pan under the trap to catch any water that remains in the sink drain.
2. Some traps have a plug at the bottom that can easily be removed for cleaning. Unfasten the plug using an adjustable wrench. If your pipe does not have a cleanout plug, remove the entire trap. Use a plumber's wrench to unfasten the two nuts that connect the trap to the drain pipe.
3. Once the plug or trap is removed, clean out the trap with your fingers or with a disassembled wire coat hanger.

Water Stopper Assembly

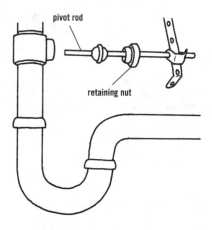

pivot rod

retaining nut

The first step in unclogging a sink that has a water stopper is the removal of the water stopper assembly.

Easy Ways to Avoid Clogged Drains

When you notice a drain becoming sluggish, take action. Try these methods:
- Use an environmentally friendly drain cleaner, available at hardware and building supply stores.
- Pour 2 or 3 gallons of boiling water down your drain once a month. This will help dissolve grease and soap.
- Avoid using commercial drain cleaners. The strong chemicals in these products can eat away at your pipes.

—from *The Woman's Hands-On Home Repair Guide*

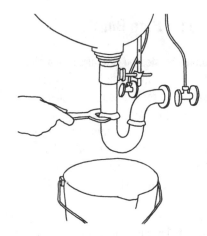

You can remove the drain trap to clean it.

4. Replace the plug or reattach the trap to the drainpipe, fastening the nuts tightly so the trap does not leak but not so tightly as to damage the threads.

5. Turn on the water to test the drain and check for leaks.

Using a Sink Auger

Occasionally the clog is farther down the pipe. In this case you will need to use a sink auger, also known as a plumber's snake. To assemble the auger, insert the end of the snakelike coil into the auger handle.

1. Place a bucket under the trap to catch any water remaining in the drain.

2. Remove the drain trap with a plumber's wrench by unfastening the two nuts that connect the trap to the drain pipe.

3. Insert the blade of the snake into the pipe that enters the kitchen wall. Allow the snake to run freely into the pipe. When the coil stops running into the pipe, you have reached the blockage or a bend in the pipe.

4. Tighten the screw handle and rotate the auger handle in a clockwise direction. This moves the snake coil around the bend in the pipe or enables it to cut through the blockage.

5. Reattach the drain pipe, turn on the water, and test the drain.

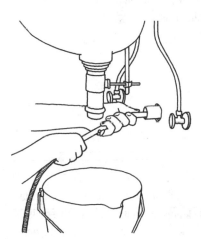

Run an auger into the drainpipe until it meets the stoppage.

Unclogging the Main Drain

The drainage system in your house consists of drains for each fixture leading into a main drain, which carries all of the waste out of the house. If two or more of your drains are clogged, the blockage may be in the main drain.

Before unclogging, be prepared with a mop, towels, and buckets, because several gallons of water may be backed up in the pipe.

1. In the basement, find a large cast-iron or plastic pipe that extends into the ground. Three or 4 feet from the ground there is a cleanout plug for the main drain, located on a small pipe that forms a Y-shape with the main pipe. Use a pipe or an adjustable wrench to remove the cap to the cleanout plug.

2. Thread a sink auger into the opening and move it toward the sewer. You may need to rent a long, powered auger to reach the blockage. If you succeed in removing the blockage, rinse out the pipe with fresh water from a garden hose. If the blockage remains, call a plumber.

—from *The Woman's Hands-On Home Repair Guide* by Lyn Herrick

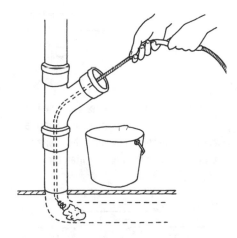

Thread a sink auger through the cleanout joint of the main drain.

REPAIRING AND PROTECTING PIPES

When a Pipe Bursts

If a pipe bursts, you can purchase a pipe cutter and a pipe repair kit at your local hardware store. This contains a plastic section of pipe with washers and pressure nuts on each side. Alternatively, you can purchase a length of snug-fitting heater tubing at your local car parts store, along with two clamps. Follow these steps:

1. Use a pipe cutter to cut away the broken section of pipe. Be careful not to bend or dent the pipe by tightening the cutter too quickly.

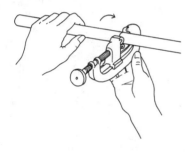

2. If you are using a repair kit, slip the two pressure nuts onto the pipe ends facing each other. Insert the washers onto the ends of each pipe, slip the repair piece onto each pipe end, and tighten the pressure nuts.

pressure nut

3. If using heater tubing, cut a piece to fit with 2 extra inches on each end. Slip the clamps onto the tubing and the overlapping ends onto the pipe. Tighten the clamps.

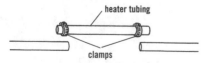

heater tubing

clamps

Insulating Pipes

If your pipes are exposed in the garage, in an uninsulated basement, under the house, or on the side of the house, they may freeze. Even in warmer climates, the temperature sometimes dips below freezing.

An easy preventive measure is to cover the pipes with an insulation material. You can purchase foam pipe insulation cut to the diameter of your pipe at a building supply store.

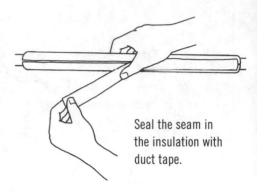

Seal the seam in the insulation with duct tape.

With a slit along the side, the insulation is easy to slip onto the pipe. Once the insulation is on the pipe, seal all the seams tightly with duct tape. Other forms of insulation such as pipe wrap and insulation tape may be less expensive, but they are are not quite as easy to install.

Winterizing Your Plumbing

To prepare an unwinterized house, such as a vacation home, for cold weather, you must winterize the plumbing.

1. Turn off the main water valve. If you receive your water from a public utility, the utility will need to shut off the main water valve outside your house.

2. Turn on all the spigots in the house, beginning on the top floor and working down. Make sure to get them all.

3. Flush all toilets and pour about 2 cups of household antifreeze into each toilet trap.

4. Pour antifreeze into the sink and bathtub traps. These traps should not be drained because they keep noxious odors and vermin from entering your home.

5. Put antifreeze in the main trap in the basement by unscrewing the cleanout plug and pouring in the antifreeze.

6. Turn off the power to the water heater at the circuit breaker box. Drain the water heater by attaching a garden hose to the drain valve. Make sure the hose is pointing downhill and outside the house.

7. Open the outdoor spigot, turn off the water, and take off the hose. It's a good idea to drain the water in your hose by hanging it downward to prevent the water from freezing and cracking the hose. If you want to be sure that water in the pipe leading to the spigot won't freeze, have a plumber install a shutoff valve in an appropriate place with a bleeder valve. Once installed, turn off the water to the pipe and open the bleeder valve. This forces air through the pipe, which cleans out any remaining water.

—from *The Woman's Hands-On Home Repair Guide* by Lyn Herrick

Thawing Frozen Pipes

If a pipe freezes, don't panic and call the plumber. First, listen to the weather forecast for the day. If the temperature rises above 32 degrees F, the pipes may thaw with no damage.

Usually pipes do not freeze their entire length; they freeze at points where they are exposed to the cold, especially near sills, exterior walls, and uninsulated spaces. To locate the freeze-up, turn on the water faucets. Follow the frozen pipe back to a juncture. Then test water taps off this second pipe to determine whether the pipe has frozen farther downstream.

Once you have located the culprit section of pipe, you probably can pinpoint the location of the freeze-up by looking for a bulge or feeling for where the pipe is coldest. Turn on all affected faucets so that when you heat the pipe, the frozen water can expand and the vapors from the melting ice can escape.

—from *What to Do When the Power Fails* by Mary Twitchell

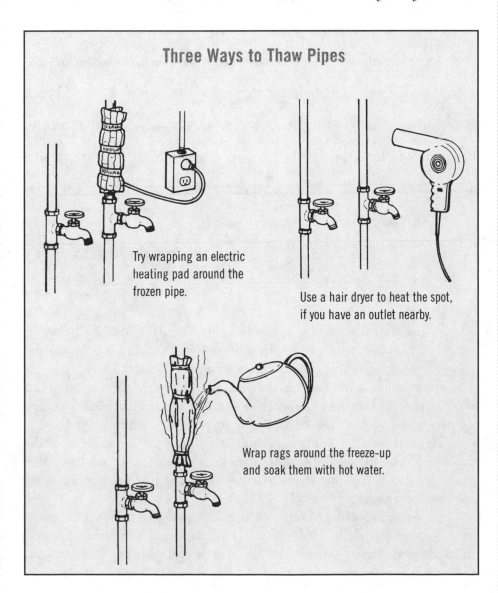

Three Ways to Thaw Pipes

Try wrapping an electric heating pad around the frozen pipe.

Use a hair dryer to heat the spot, if you have an outlet nearby.

Wrap rags around the freeze-up and soak them with hot water.

Using Plastic Pipes

Newer pipe materials are relatively inexpensive, easy to cut, and easy to install compared to those used in the past. You can use plastic soil pipe that glues together and flexible neoprene connectors that join new plastic to old cast-iron pipes. For water pipes, PVC and CPVC (polyvinyl chloride and commercial polyvinyl chloride) are the white or cream-colored materials that are most commonly used. They are cheap, easy to use, effective, safe (no lead problem here), and rust-free. These can be cut with a hacksaw and glued together. However, they can be broken, and will shatter if frozen with water pressure on. It is important to use CPVC, the more expensive of the two, for at least the hot-water lines.

The adapters that allow you to go from galvanized to plastic are the problematic aspect of plastic piping. They must be screwed on to the metal with the help of Teflon tape or some other sealer. Buy a couple of extra adapters so you can risk breaking them by screwing them on very tight. Then they won't leak when you turn the water back on.

—from *Reviving Old Houses* by Alan Dan Orme

5

HEATING YOUR HOME

WOODSTOVES AND FIREPLACES • HEATING WITH WOOD
STACKING AND SEASONING WOOD • BUILD AN
OLD-FASHIONED WOODSHED • HEATING WITH COAL
HEATING WITH GAS • HEATING BY THE SUN
WEATHERPROOFING YOUR HOME

Dr. Jay Shelton's books on wood heat, Wood Heat Safety *and* Solid Fuels Encyclopedia, *are considered two of the most invaluable reference works in the field of wood burning. His research into clean combustion and sound woodburning practices still stands as the ultimate wisdom on wood burning.*

Any of us who lived through the oil crisis of the '70s, complete with lines at the gas pumps and alternate-day-only fill-ups, developed discipline about heating our homes. We stopped chuckling over our parents' habit of turning the thermostat down to 64 degrees when home heating oil hit $1.75 a gallon. Our "homestead" in Connecticut had a substantial woodlot, so, equipped with a new chain saw and a rented splitter, we'd stack two cords of wood, enough to get us through the winter nicely. We learned the joys of a cast-iron stove and of lessening our dependence on oil while increasing our dependence on ourselves—a good trade!

—John & Martha Storey

When discussing methods of heating the country home, it makes sense to begin with wood. Wood fuel offers some outstanding advantages compared with other energy sources. Foremost, it is renewable in the time it takes to grow a tree. As long as the sun shines and the earth is a healthy place for life, wood will be available, if our forests are well managed.

All forms of solar energy, including wood, wind, and direct radiation, are renewable, unlike fossil fuels, which can be used up. But wood is special compared to other options because its energy is so conveniently stored.

In trees and other plants, nature has provided both collectors (the leaves with their chlorophyll) and storage. A pound of wood contains more than 50 times the amount of stored energy of a pound of hot water in a solar storage tank, and it needs no insulation.

Btu. British thermal unit; a unit of measure of heat. One Btu raises 1 pint of water 1 degree F

Cord. A stack of wood measuring 4 feet wide, 4 feet high, and 8 feet long. The cord represents 128 cubic feet of wood

Low-e glass. "Low-emissivity" window glass that reflects heat back into a building and is thus highly efficient in retaining heat

R-value. A measure of the thermal resistance of a material to heat transmission. The higher the R-value, the more effective the insulation

Solar gain. The absorption of the sun's energy by a structure

Thermal mass. A large, heat-absorbing element, usually made of stone or brick, that absorbs solar energy during the day and radiates it back at night

Vapor barrier. An impermeable material placed on the warm side of an exterior side of a wall to prevent moisture from migrating into the walls

In colonial New England, as much as 20 to 30 cords of wood per year were burned in open fireplaces, and even then not much of the house was warm. Today, because of tighter construction and insulation, the same size house in the same climate is heated more uniformly with only three to eight cords in a closed metal stove, wood furnace, or boiler—a big improvement over fireplaces.

Coal is popular as a residential heating fuel in parts of North America, especially where ship or barge transportation makes it cheaper than wood. A cubic foot of coal contains more Btu than a cubic foot of wood, which allows less frequent refueling. See page 72 for more on coal heat.

Wood Versus Coal

Advantages of Wood
- Wood fires are easier to start.
- Wood has much less ash.
- Wood ashes can be valuable for garden soils.
- Wood is cleaner to handle.
- The odor of wood smoke is pleasant.
- Wood flue gases are less corrosive; chimneys last longer.
- Because wood fires are easier to start, wood is the easier fuel to use in mild climates or in the spring and fall when only a little heat is needed once or twice a day.
- For many people, wood can be obtained from the effort of cutting and hauling it; one need not buy it.
- It is easier to learn how to burn wood.

Advantages of Coal
- Coal takes less space to store.
- Long-lasting, steady, and high-heat-output fires are easier to obtain.
- Flue deposits are less with anthracite, and easier to clean with bituminous.

—from *Solid Fuels Encyclopedia*
by Jay Shelton

How Wood Burns

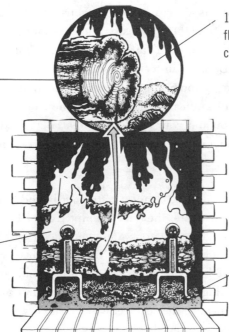

1. Radiation from flames and glowing charcoal heats wood.

2. Heated wood loses moisture, starts to char, and then decomposes into smoke and charcoal.

3. If heat is sufficient and oxygen is available, wood ignites.

4. Charcoal and air combine in glowing combustion.

WOODSTOVES AND FIREPLACES

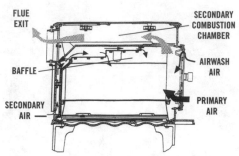

Noncatalytic stoves burn clean by pre-heating combustion air.

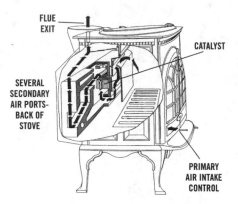

Catalytic stoves burn clean if operated correctly, in a chimney with sufficient draft, and inspected regularly.

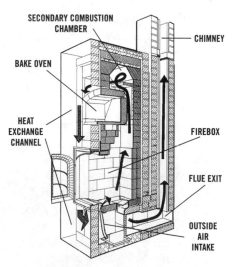

Masonry heaters need to vent on an interior chimney and work well when sited to act as a room divider. The quality of the gentle, radiant heat and the elimination of the risk of chimney fires make them truly the "heart (hearth) of the home."

Types of Woodstoves

When the Arab Oil Embargo began in 1973, woodstove use and production blossomed in the northern United States and Canada. Most of these stoves were designed without benefit of prior testing. Some worked quite well. Others smoked up the house and/or belched thick smoke out the chimney. Cast iron stoves imported from Scandinavia were prized as proven performers.

Air-tight stoves that achieved long burn times were the goal, but good combustion usually suffered. Once the Environmental Protection Agency found woodstoves to be the bearers of toxic air pollution, those manufactured after 1985 were required to burn within a limit of particulate emissions. This new generation of woodstoves has helped give woodburning the renewable resource "green" image it deserves.

Manufacturers have derived two models of firebox configurations to meet the EPA emissions requirements:

1. **Hi-tech or "noncatalytic" stoves** achieve clean burning by preheating combustion air and delivering it to the firebox where it will mix well with the volatile gases—much like the carburetor in gasoline engines. This is done with perforated stainless steel air tubes and channels. Firebrick is often used to help maintain the high firebox temperatures necessary for good combustion. "Non-cats" provide an elegant, user-friendly solution to clean wood burning.

2. Many of the early EPA-era woodstoves came with **catalytic combustors**. Catalytic stoves burn clean, but to work as designed, the following is needed:

■ **A "warm" chimney.** Most exterior chimneys don't maintain enough draft to keep a catalytic stove going.

■ **Attention to the temperature gauge.** The bypass that routes the smoke through the honeycomb should be engaged when 550 degrees has been maintained for at least 15 minutes.

■ **Semi-annual inspection of the combustor.** Fly ash accumulates and should be cleaned off or the combustor becomes inoperable.

Before you decide you can't afford a newer generation woodstove, consider the following: Because hi-tech and catalytic stoves burn wood more efficiently, you will save money (or time) each year in acquiring firewood. Also, because they burn significantly cleaner than their predecessors, you won't be polluting the air you and your neighbors breathe! You also reduce the risk of a chimney fire with a stove that produces far less creosote.

Masonry Heaters

Masonry heaters are the cleanest of the cordwood burners, but because of their weight and burn rate, they are exempt from EPA regulations. Built of firebrick and/or precast refractory units and faced with brick, stone, tile, or stucco, these heat-storing fireplaces are fired only once or twice a day. The 50- or 60-pound charge burns in an oxygen-rich environment for complete combustion. The resulting exhaust is routed through internal flue passages that store and conduct heat to the surface, which remains at a constant 150 to 170 degrees. Once the fire is out, the damper is shut.

—by Stephen Bushway, author of *The New Woodburner's Handbook*

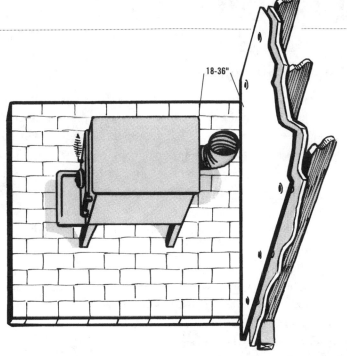

18-36"

When positioning a woodstove in a room, observe the following safety rules. The stove should be not less than 36 inches from any wall, unless sheet metal protects the wall, in which case 18 inches is adequate. The floorboard should extend 18 inches beyond the front of the stove and on any side where fuel is added or ashes are removed, and a minimum of 12 inches on the remaining sides. Distances may vary depending on the type of stove, and local building codes.

Installing a Woodstove

The most common installation involves linking the woodstove to an existing chimney. Follow these steps:

1. Check chimney linings and soot levels. If in doubt about their safety, seek guidance from a mason or fireman. While on the roof, check the chimney's height. It should be at least 2 feet above anything within a 10-foot radius. If your house has a flat roof, the chimney should rise 3 feet above it.

2. Select the woodstove's location before cutting holes. The center of the house is best. Choose a basement location if you're heating the whole house.

3. Older homes usually include flue entrances suitable for woodstoves. If there is no flue entrance, you'll have to cut one. Do not share flues with furnaces or any other heating appliance! The flue hole should be at least 18 inches below the ceiling, and it should be lined. Use a carbide-tipped drill to start the hole and cut the remainder with a masonry saw.

4. Position the woodstove at least 36 inches from a wall. If you place sheet metal on the wall stepped off from the wall with spacers, you may be able to reduce the distance. Stove legs should be at least 4 inches long, and the stove should sit on a stoveboard. Layers of brick, slate, stone, iron, or cement board less than 8 inches thick do not provide adequate protection for a wood floor and create a fire hazard.

5. Run the stovepipe from the stove to the flue. The pipe should be at least 24-gauge blued—not galvanized—steel, with no more than one elbow, and it should be as short as possible. Any horizontal section more than 6 feet long should be supported with wires. Join pipe sections with crimped end closer to stove. Your stove will need a damper if it is not airtight.

—from *Buying and Installing a Woodstove* by Charles Self

Floor Protection

Floors under and around stoves will need protection against two hazards —radiation from the bottom and sides of the stove, and sparks and hot coals that fall out of the stove during refueling, ash removal, or open-door operation of a fireplace stove.

If your stove has less than 2 inches of air space between the floor and the combustion chamber, do not install it on a combustible floor. It should be installed only on a cement slab or other noncombustible material.

Stoves with 2- to 6-inch legs should be placed on 4-inch hollow concrete blocks (with holes parallel for air circulation) atop a sheet of 24-gauge metal.

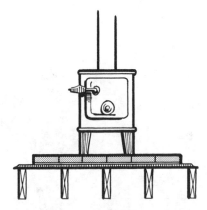

Stoves with legs longer than 6 inches should be placed on a 2- to 4-inch layer of bricks, concrete blocks, or stone, on a sheet of 24-gauge metal.

Stephen Bushway is a former C.S.I.A.-certified chimney sweep, certified masonry heater mason, and owner of Deer Hill Masonry Heat. He has spent his career lobbying for energy and environmental issues in Western Massachusetts where he is the owner of Village Chimney Services and author of The New Woodburner's Handbook.

Retrofitting a Fireplace with a Woodstove

Because the venting requirements for a woodstove are different than for a fireplace you need to retrofit a stainless steel chimney liner. A liner provides the draft necessary to ensure that the stove will operate safely and efficiently. First you should determine that the flue does not vent any other appliances (like the furnace or another fireplace). Next, try a fire in the fireplace. Smoke should not spill out into the room if you've used enough dry kindling and a couple of twisted-up newspapers. If it does, call in a professional chimney sweep. This indicates there may be a blockage or a construction defect, which may mean a liner will not go in.

A chimney liner is a flexible stainless pipe the same diameter as the stove collar. It will be listed by or to the applicable UL standard. It should be insulated with ceramic fiber blanket insulation when it is venting on an exterior chimney or any time it has been advised because of inadequate clearances between the chimney and the building.

The liner should be supported at the top of the chimney and the space sealed between the liner and the chimney with a plate and collar made for that purpose. The liner comes down through the smoke chamber and damper frame to a "T" which can sit on concrete blocks or be supported by heavy wire attached to fasteners in the upper firebox. In some cases you have to ovalize the liner or cut out part of the damper frame so the liner can pass through. Much of its weight will be supported on the bottom edge of the damper frame as the liner makes this bend. The stove will vent horizontally into the snout of the T.

Where space in the room or traffic patterns make it desirable, you can site the stove inside the firebox and vent it directly up into the liner pipe. Make sure the fireplace is large enough so that you can set a pan of water on the stove and operate a top-loading door if there is one.

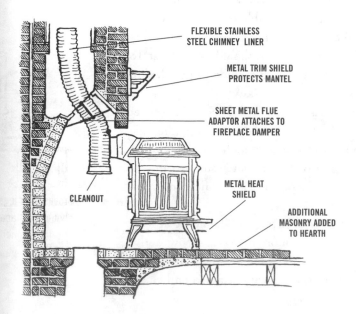

FLEXIBLE STAINLESS STEEL CHIMNEY LINER

METAL TRIM SHIELD PROTECTS MANTEL

SHEET METAL FLUE ADAPTOR ATTACHES TO FIREPLACE DAMPER

METAL HEAT SHIELD

ADDITIONAL MASONRY ADDED TO HEARTH

CLEANOUT

Be sure to meet the clearances to combustibles specified by the manufacturer. You will probably need to increase the depth of the hearth extension to at least 18 inches in front of the stove. Wood mantel surrounds usually require the fabrication of a heat shield attached with ceramic spacers that provide a 1-inch air space. This will allow a 50% clearance reduction.

Do not block off the fireplace opening. You will need access to the T for removal of the creosote and soot that will end up there when the chimney is cleaned. Paint liner parts, supporting blocks, and even the firebox flat black to keep them unobtrusive.

STACK CLEANER'S TOOLBOX

- dust mask and hat
- gloves
- screwdriver or small vise grips
- wire brush with attached paint scraper
- bucket and shovel
- mirror
- hammer or chisel
- powerful flashlight
- chimney brush
- screw-together fiberglass rods
- vacuum cleaner

Cleaning the Stack

Creosote buildup causes fires. Check your flue at the thimble. If you can scrape off ¼ inch or more of creosote, or if it's hard and difficult to scrape, it's time to clean the stack.

Cover the floor with a dropcloth or newspapers. If you don't have a clean-out door, have one installed. Remove creosote or debris from the bottom. If the chimney is straight, shine a mirror up the flue to see how coated it is. If you don't see a clean flue line outlining the sky, lower your bare rods down the flue and flail them against the inside to remove chunks. Wear a dust mask and hat.

The brush may cause falling creosote to form a plug partway down the chimney. If the rods don't band around inside the flue when flailing, leave them in the flue. Go to the clean-out and attach the brush to the rods. Return to the roof. Brush the chimney from the bottom up.

Proceed until your brush has done all it can. Remove and clean the connector pipe and thimble hole. Knock loose soot into a bucket and clean with a wire brush or scraper for gritty deposits.

Position your light so it illuminates the thimble hole while you work. Wearing gloves, reach through the hole into the flue above. Chip away deposits with a hammer, screwdriver, or wood chisel.

Clean soot accessible through the exposed stove collar according to your owner's manual. Vacuum fly ash from the combustor. Replace the cleaned thimble and connector, unless they obstruct access to the clean-out. Remove the debris; if it's more than 2 gallons, clean more often.

Woodstove Maintenance

Clean your stove each year. Use a flashlight to inspect for warped or cracked parts. Some stoves have interior parts that can be removed for access to air channels and smoke paths. These can fill up with ashes and should be cleaned.

If the stove and connector pipe are in a high-humidity environment, coat them with a rust inhibitor like WD-40. Doors that have gaskets should be checked. Insert a dollar bill between the door and stove. Close the door and try to pull out the bill. If you can, adjust the latch mechanism. Check to be sure the door is not warped. If it is, replace it. See your owner's manual for further maintenance instructions.

— from *The New Woodburner's Handbook* by Stephen Bushway

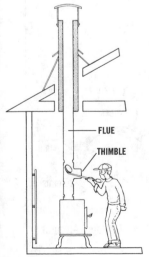

FLUE

THIMBLE

Use a mirror to peer up the chimney or stack and see how coated with creosote it is.

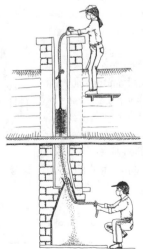

Another way to clean a chimney is to attach a rope to each end of a wire chimney brush. With a person on the rooftop and one near the hearth opening, the brush should be pulled back and forth at least five or six times in the chimney.

HEATING WITH WOOD

Before Lighting a Fire

- **Develop an escape plan.** Have at least two alternate routes out of the house. If you live in the country, stash flashlights, sweaters, sleeping bags, blankets, and an extra ignition key in your car, particularly in cold weather. Make sure your smoke alarms and fire extinguishers are in working order.
- **Have fire drills.** Set off one of your smoke alarms to trigger a practice fire drill. Hang a referee's whistle on your doorknob to be used in an emergency. Practice getting out fast.
- **Use alarms.** Battery-operated smoke alarms should be tested once a month. A chirping sound tells you to replace batteries. Chimney alarms monitor flue gas temperatures and sound an alarm when a specified temperature is exceeded.

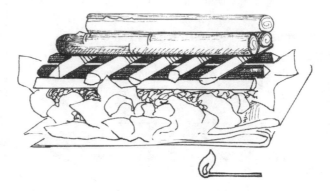

This fuel load is ready for ignition. Lay the logs with enough space so that air and flames can penetrate between them.

Building a Roaring Wood Fire in Seven Steps

1. Lay the fire with four or five pieces of newspaper. Ball them up in the firebox near the air supply.
2. Lay finger-sized sticks over the paper.
3. Add three or four wrist-sized pieces of wood. Arrange to permit air circulation; curvy, gnarly ones that won't roll work best.
4. Construct a cross-hatched cribbing across the shorter dimension of the firebox with shorter lengths of wood. Light the fire.
5. Open air intake holes or leave the door cracked open.
6. After 3 or 4 minutes, open the door and rearrange the wood. Add two larger sticks. Close door.
7. In 15 minutes or so, when the two larger sticks are resting on the fire, add a full charge of well-seasoned wood.

—from *The New Woodburner's Handbook* by Stephen Bushway

Fireplace Efficiency

A typical fireplace steals more heat than it delivers. The chimney draft pulls warm air from the room, resulting in a net heat loss. Here's how you can increase the efficiency of your fireplace:

- Reduce the damper opening as soon as the fire is no longer smoking.
- Glass doors permit you to see the fire while minimizing heat loss.
- If you're building an open fireplace, include a sheet-metal Heatilator box. It will draw in cool air from the floor, warm it, and send it into the room through vents. Combine it with a glass screen for improved efficiency.
- Consider a hollow-tube grate—a set of metal pipes open at both ends that are shaped with their lower ends facing the room near floor level. The pipes direct heat into the room, and some models come with an electric blower.

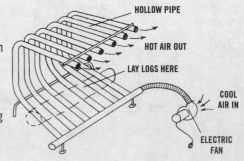

HOLLOW PIPE
HOT AIR OUT
LAY LOGS HERE
COOL AIR IN
ELECTRIC FAN

— from *547 Easy Ways to Save Energy in Your Home* by Roger Albright

Wood Pellets as Fuel

Yearning for the warmth and cozy atmosphere of a woodstove, without the work and maintenance involved? A wood-pellet stove could provide an environmentally sensible, convenient, and practical alternative. These low-emission stoves burn manufactured pellets, formed from compressed white wood (no bark) sawdust, a by-product of the wood industry.

Available as freestanding models, fireplace inserts, and even furnaces, the stoves use a hopper system, from which the pellets are fed into the fire by an electrically powered auger or other feed device. Compared to woodstoves, pellet stoves burn much cleaner and heat more evenly for a longer period of time untended (as much as 36 or more hours, depending upon the hopper size and burn rate).

Most pellet stoves have two electrical blowers, one for venting the exhaust and a convection fan that circulates the room air over a heat exchanger. The blowers typically consume approximately 60 watts of power each. Twelve-volt DC models are available, as are models with a battery backup for power failures.

Pellets are manufactured in a standardized size, approximately 1½ inches long by ¼ inch around. Pellets are typically packaged in 40-pound bags—an average day's worth of heat—and sold by the bag or by the ton (50 bags).

What to Look for in a Pellet Stove

Hopper capacity. May range from 40 to 100 or more pounds. Choose a heater with at least a full day's capacity for the space you are heating.

Maintenance. Pellet stoves need periodic maintenance and occasional professional service and repair. Ash from the stove must be removed at least every two weeks to maintain proper airflow for combustion.

Ignition. Firing up manual ignition stoves requires the use of a starter material, which is lit with a match, while automatic ignition stoves ignite with the push of a button. Automatic ignition may not be such a big deal if you plan to run your stove more or less continuously.

Venting. A variety of venting options are available, from using an existing chimney (which could require a lining) to installing a natural draft chimney through a wall or ceiling to terminate above the roofline. Mechanical exhausts that go directly out the side wall behind the stove are the cheapest to install, but beware—they'll leave you with a smoke-filled abode if the power fails. A stovepipe with a minimum vertical rise of 4 feet should provide sufficient natural draft to overcome this.

Off the Grid

Because of their electrical requirements, pellet stoves have been impractical for locations without power. However, solar panels are now being used to operate some stoves.

Pellet Stoves and Woodstoves—Facts and Figures

- One ton of pellets can produce as much heat as 1½ cords of wood, while taking up only one third the space.
- The relative costs of cordwood and pellets, generally comparable, will depend on local conditions such as firewood type and availability and proximity to pellet mills.
- Pellets produce far less ash than do woodstoves and virtually no chimney fire–causing creosote.
- Pellet stoves cost 10 to 20 percent more than a comparable woodstove, but installation is cheaper, because of the smaller, often shorter flue used by pellet stoves.
- Pellet baskets—basically a vented metal box to contain the pellets—are available to fit most woodstoves. While not as efficient as a pellet stove, a basket-equipped airtight stove won't build up creosote.

HEATING WITH WOOD

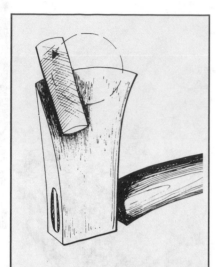

Sharpening an Ax

The how-to of sharpening begins with a "don't." Don't use a high-speed, motor-driven bench grinder. It will heat the edge and ruin the temper of your ax. There are fine-cut files and carborundum files, but you'll get best results with an oval sharpening stone—fine grained on one side, coarse on the other. Use with a light oil.

Rest the ax on a plank or workbench with the head projecting a little toward you; hold down the handle with a carriage clamp. Make straight strokes at a uniform angle if using a file; use a rotary motion with an oval hand stone. Go easy. Don't take off any more metal than necessary and don't try to get out all the little nicks. They don't matter much.

—from *Axes and Chainsaws*
by Rockwell Stephens

The Wood Supply

People familiar with firewood know when it is dry. The first clue is the wood's appearance. Are there cracks? If so, it is dry. Sound is also important. When you hit two sticks together, do you hear the high-pitched ring of the bowling alley (dry) or a low-pitched thud (green)? Smell and weight also tell you about the moisture content of the wood. If in doubt, the safest thing is to split a sample log and try burning the sticks. If they smoke excessively, they still contain a lot of moisture.

Water in wood does not lower the fuel value of a cord. But water does reduce the overall heating efficiency, because it takes energy to vaporize water and heat it to the temperature of the flue gases. Wet wood's cooling effect is often just enough to prevent complete combustion. Therefore, burn green wood on a hot fire if you have to burn it at all. To keep it burning, split it up into small sticks.

CHOOSING FUELWOOD

When purchasing fuelwood, the densest wood is the best. This table shows species arranged with the densest at the top of each group. Remember that density varies somewhat within a species.

HARDWOODS			SOFTWOODS		
Best Choice	**Good Choice**	**Acceptable**	**Best Choice**	**Good Choice**	**Acceptable**
Live oak	Sugar maple	Red alder	Slash Pine	Yew	Ponderosa
Eucalyptus	American	Large-toothed	Pond Pine	Tamarack	pine
Hop horn-	beech	aspen	Western	Nut pines	Red fir
beam	Honey locust	Basswood	larch	(Piñon)	Noble fir
Dogwood	Yellow birch	Chestnut	Longleaf	Shortleaf	Black spruce
Hickory	White ash	Catalpa	pine	pine	Bald cypress
Shadbush	Elm	Black willow		Juniper	Redwood
Persimmon	Black gum	Box elder		Loblolly pine	Hemlock
White oak	Red maple	Tulip poplar		Douglas fir	Sitka spruce
Black birch	Black walnut	Butternut		Pitch pine	Yellow cedar
Black locust	Paper birch	Quaking		Red cedar	White spruce
Apple	Red gum	aspen		Norway pine	White pine
Blue beech	Cherry	Cottonwood			Balsam fir
Crabs	Holly	Willow			Western red
Red oak	Gray birch	Balsam			cedar
	Sycamore	Poplar			Sugar pine
	Oregon ash				
	Sassafras				
	Magnolia				

—from *Heating with Wood* by Larry Gay

Stacking and Seasoning Wood

To start with, get the wood off the ground and piled on rocks or unwanted logs so that air can circulate. There is one exception: If you cut down trees still in leaf, leave them there for a few weeks. Until the leaves dry up, the tree will continue to lose water through them.

Wood dries fastest when it's "penned" or "chimneyed." In other words, stack two sticks, then two more at right angles, and so on. The best drying time is during windy spring months before the hardwoods leaf out. Spring-cut wood can be burned the following winter, but it's best to dry the wood outside the first summer and in the barn the next. Try to have some of your dry wood under cover at all times. Polyethylene, old planks, and metal sheets do nicely. Half a cord or so tucked away in the house is good insurance against sieges of inclement weather.

Wood dries best when arranged for maximum air circulation.

What's in a Cord?

Wood is usually sold by the cord—a stack 4 feet wide, 4 feet high, and 8 feet long. The cord represents 128 cubic feet of wood. If it's split, the actual volume of wood varies between 77 and 96 cubic feet. Often "cord" is applied to a 4 x 8 pile of wood cut 12, 16, or 24 inches long. This is legal in most states so long as it is identified as a "face cord."

In many areas, consumer-protection laws do not extend to fuelwood, so it is up to the buyer to find out just how much wood is offered in what are called stove cords, pick-up cords, and fireplace cords. Definitions vary from place to place.

—from *Heating with Wood* by Larry Gay

To measure your own woodpile, neatly stack your wood with the pieces parallel and the ends aligned. With a tape measure, measure the height and length of the pile and the average length of the pieces. Then multiply the three figures together to get the volume in cubic feet.

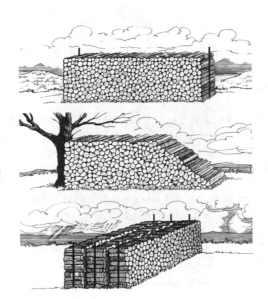

Tips on Splitting Wood

- Buy your firewood unsplit; it's less expensive and splitting is good exercise.
- Some woods don't split worth a darn. Birch and maple split beautifully. Gnarled cherry is tough. Choose firewood with this in mind.
- Cut long sections of wood into shorter ones before splitting. It's easier.
- Use a somewhat dull ax rather than a razor-edge. It's safer.
- Hold ax handles as near to the end as you can and take a full swing. The momentum and weight of the ax head does all the work.
- Use an ax whose head tapers out to a flat wedge. A slender head gets stuck more easily. Do not use a double-bitted ax.
- To split big, knotty lengths of wood, use a maul or sledgehammer and wedges.
- If you're splitting a year's supply of wood, consider renting a power log-splitter.

—from *547 Easy Ways to Save Energy in Your Home*

HEATING WITH WOOD

Felling Trees

The best way to learn to fell trees is to volunteer with a woods-wise neighbor. It is a job that requires skill, concentration, and common sense. It can be very dangerous and should not be done when you are tired or when the light is poor or the footing slippery.

A "harvest-size" tree is usually 8 to 12 inches in diameter on the stump. The time to harvest is before the growth rate slows down and the wood begins to deteriorate. It is better to cut it down and let a new seedling grow in its place. It is difficult to make wise decisions when the chain saw is running, so mark all the trees you want to cut before harvesting.

A straight, well-balanced tree can be felled in any direction. First, undercut it in the direction you want it to go—preferably away from other good lumber trees. The undercut is a wedge-shaped notch made with two cuts about one-third of the way through the trunk.

Make the felling cut horizontally from the opposite side of the tree, slightly above the undercut. End the felling cut an inch or two short of the undercut to leave a hinge.

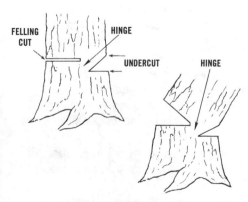

Make the wedge-shaped undercut first, on the side where you want the tree to fall. Make the felling cut opposite and slightly above the undercut.

Build an Old-Fashioned Woodshed

Here are instructions for building a versatile woodshed for storage of wood and equipment.

1. Lay out the shed and locate positions for the 4 x 4 posts. Then dig the holes, pour concrete piers, and erect, plumb, and brace the posts.

2. Nail the bottom girders in place all around the sides, front, and back. Be sure they are level.

3. Nail the top girders in place, then nail the back nailing girts. Nail the side girts on the inside and outside walls. Next, nail the front plates across the front of the sheds and the extended porch.

4. Frame in the door in the center section using 2 x 4s, then add the blocking on the side posts for nailing siding to the front of the posts.

5. Install knee bracing on all corners. Nail knee bracing on the front into the surface of the posts, then to the back of the top girder.

6. Cut the upper 2 x 4 rafters and the 1 x 6 ridge board to length. Install the ridge board and end rafters. The ridge board should extend 8 inches past the

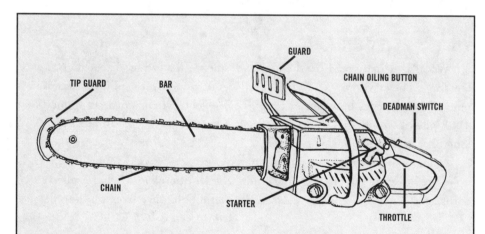

Maintaining a Chain Saw

Never operate a chain saw that is damaged, improperly adjusted, or not securely assembled. Follow manufacturer's maintenance and repair instructions in the owner's manual. In addition:

- Keep the chain, bar, and sprocket clean; replace worn sprockets or chains.
- Keep the chain sharp. A chain is dull when easy-to-cut wood becomes hard to cut and burn marks appear on the wood.
- Keep the chain at proper tension. Tighten all nuts, bolts, and screws except the carburetor adjustment screws after each use.
- Keep spark plug and wire connection tight and clean.
- Store saw in a high or locked place, away from children.

—from *Axes and Chainsaws* by Rockwell Stephens

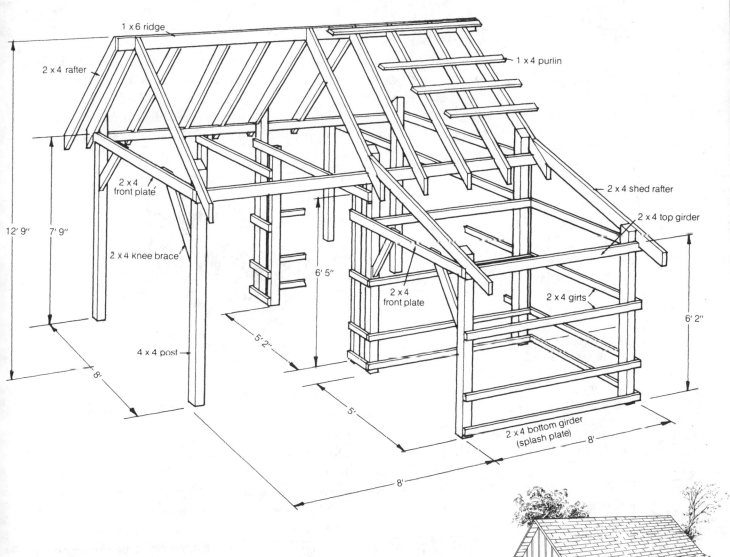

1 x 6 ridge

2 x 4 rafter

1 x 4 purlin

2 x 4 front plate

2 x 4 shed rafter

2 x 4 top girder

12' 9"

7' 9"

2 x 4 knee brace

6' 5"

2 x 4 front plate

2 x 4 girts

6' 2"

4 x 4 post

5' 2"

2 x 4 bottom girder (splash plate)

5'

8'

8'

8'

outside edge of the shed. End rafters are nailed to the outside edges of the posts and sit on the top girders. Install upper rafters at the center posts and follow with the rest of the rafters, spacing them about 24 inches on center. Cut off the tops of the posts flush with the top edges of the rafters.

7. Cut the shed rafters. The end shed rafters must fit down flush on the upper rafters. The remaining rafters can simply be extended past and nailed to the upper rafters.

8. Nail 1 x 4 collar ties (not shown) to the upper rafters.

9. Use the siding and sheathing of your choice. One option is to cover the main shed while leaving the sides of the two smaller sheds open for better air-drying. If you use wood shingles for the roof, apply a sheathing of plywood or 1 x 4s, spaced about 2 inches apart.

10. Cut 2 x 4s for lookouts and nail them between the end rafters and fly rafters.

11. Make doors using a Z-frame and 1 x 12s. The best option is two doors for the main shed that swing out into the porch area.

—from *Building Small Barns, Sheds, and Shelters* by Monte Burch

This woodshed features an enclosed area for storing tools and equipment. The extended roof provides a dry place for splitting kindling. The side sheds are for wood storage. The exterior is covered with rough-sawn siding or native materials, over which 1 x 2 battens are added. The roof is shingled.

HEATING WITH COAL

Coal-Burning Tips

- Burn coal only in a coal-burning appliance. There are distinct differences between wood- and coal-burning stoves, because the two fuels burn differently.
- For new stoves, burn wood fires for the first week to break in the stove.
- Do not use charcoal starter or any flammable liquids to start a coal fire. Charcoal is not recommended either, because it gives off toxic fumes.
- Because coal burns hotter and puts out steadier heat than wood, save it for the coldest months. Burn wood in the coal stove during spring and fall.
- Clean the stove, connector pipe, and chimney in the off-season. Coal soot is acidic and corrosive. Use care when cleaning pipes. Wear leather gloves and a mask. Check for pinhole leaks and replace any suspect parts. Clean and check the stove, especially the grates; replace warped parts. A light coating of lubricant such as WD-40 inhibits rust.

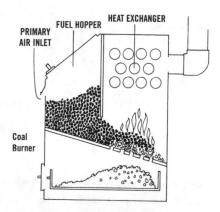

Coal fires are generally started with wood fires. Add coal a little at a time with the primary air inlet wide open. Add small amounts of coal every 5 or 10 minutes. Once a vigorously burning coal bed is established, you can fill up the stove to the recommended level; a few minutes after that, set the primary air control to the desired position.

Burning Coal in Your Home

In some parts of the country, coal is the most abundant and cheapest fuel for home heating. Because of its sulfur content, coal emissions are blamed for the serious environmental threat of acid rain. However, coal has some endearing qualities. It takes less space to store and, because of its density, it burns slower and hotter than wood. It doesn't have to be cut, split, or seasoned.

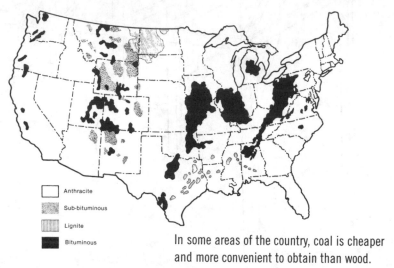

In some areas of the country, coal is cheaper and more convenient to obtain than wood.

Building a Coal Fire

Coal's ignition temperature is 200 to 400 degrees higher than wood's, so it's more difficult to start than a wood fire. Open the air supply ashpit door (primary air intake), then loosely arrange newspaper, kindling, and small pieces of wood. After a few minutes, add larger pieces of wood. When fully ignited, add a thin layer of coal. Don't add coal too soon or it will smother the fire.

When the coal is burning, add a thicker layer. Depending on the depth of the firebox, you may need to add a third load of coal. Once the stove is hot, partially close the pipe damper and the primary air supply. This keeps the draft from exceeding the needs of the fire, yet is sufficient to maintain combustion. Leave the secondary air supply, located above the fire, slightly open.

When the load burns down halfway, it's time to refuel. Open the pipe damper and air intakes before loading the door. This increases draft and ensures that gases go up the chimney. Gently pull the coal bed toward the front, creating a pocket for the new fuel.

Shaking Ashes

Most stoves have a mechanical means of moving or shaking the grate so the ashes fall into an ashpit. If there is no provision for this, use a fiddle stick or rod to poke the ashes through. Do this when you sense that the fire is not getting enough air. A few short shakes should be all it needs. Overshaking or overpoking can form clinkers, which are very hot pieces of coal that were extinguished by the ash layer. They won't burn or be shaken through the grate, but must be removed before the next refueling.

—from *The New Woodburner's Handbook* by Stephen Bushway

Depending on the accessibility of your dwelling, propane—also called liquefied-petroleum gas (LP gas)—may be the most convenient fuel for heating a home or cabin not served by electric power. Propane exists either as a nontoxic, colorless, and odorless gas or, at moderate pressure, as a liquid. For home use the liquid is stored in an above- or below-ground outdoor container and withdrawn as gas as it is used. LP gas is given an identifying odor to make leakage detectable. Clean-burning propane is cost competitive with other fuels and with electric power for many applications.

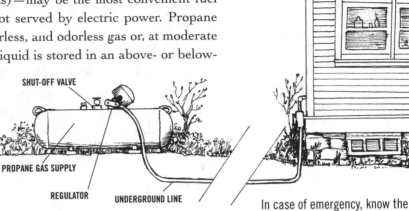

SHUT-OFF VALVE

PROPANE GAS SUPPLY

REGULATOR   UNDERGROUND LINE

In case of emergency, know the location of the shut-off valve on your propane tank or cylinder. The regulator controls the gas pressure.

Vented heaters and systems use either a conventional metal or masonry chimney or a vent installed directly through an outside wall. Gas heating systems distribute their heat via traditional hot-water baseboard or hot air forced through ductwork and require electricity to power their pumps or fans. Locations without electricity can use room heaters, freestanding vented or (if allowed by local building codes) vent-free space heaters that circulate heated air by convection. With an efficiency rating of nearly 100 percent, vent-free room heaters use inside air for combustion and vent directly into the room. An oxygen-depletion sensor on the unit automatically shuts it down if oxygen levels in the room begin to get too low.

Storage-tank size is an important consideration, because fuel consumption can vary widely depending on climate, equipment, and use. Home heating tanks are either DOT cylinders (meeting U.S. Department of Transportation specs) that hold 100 to 420 pounds of propane (1 gallon equals 4.24 pounds) or American Society of Mechanical Engineers (ASME) spec tanks that hold 80 to 800 gallons. ASME tanks must be filled on site from a bulk delivery truck. DOT cylinders are usually installed empty and filled on-site but may be filled off-site and transported as specified in the LP-Gas Code of the National Fire Protection Association.

Off the Grid

While fuel oil, coal, or wood can provide heat, propane can serve all of your cooking, lighting, hot water, and refrigeration needs as well. Most natural gas appliances can be converted to run on LP gas, and vice versa. For cooking, traditional gas ranges with an oven are available. Propane gas lights use a tie-on mantle—similar to a camping lantern—and are quite bright. Instantaneous (tankless) water heaters are available that will provide plenty of hot water for everything from a small cabin to a busy household. Propane-powered refrigerators are available that use less than 1½ gallons of propane a week. Propane is also an ideal choice for fueling backup electrical power generators.

Gas appliances should be professionally installed. Have all gas appliances and systems inspected at least once a year.

Gas Safety

Most appliances must be vented to prevent the buildup of deadly carbon monoxide. Be sure vents do not become blocked, especially after a heavy snowfall or when units are used only intermittently.

If you smell gas, or think you might have a leak, extinguish smoking materials and all sources of ignition (don't use light switches or the phone). Evacuate the house immediately. Call your propane supplier or the fire department. Remain outside until the problem has been found and corrected.

If your propane tank runs out, a potentially hazardous situation exists. Turn off all control valves on all appliances, and turn off the main shutoff. Call your propane supplier and advise him of the situation. Let him refill the tank, relight, and check all appliances.

Passive Solar Design

If you've ever enjoyed basking in the warmth of the winter sun coming through your window on a January day, you already understand the advantages of passive solar design. The radiation produced by the sun passes through the glass and warms every surface it strikes. Even in homes built without any consciousness of solar "gain" (the absorption of the sun's energy by a structure), the sun will shine through eastern, southern, and western windows, and will heat the outside walls and the roof, warming the interior spaces somewhat on sunny days. The aim of passive solar house design is to take maximum advantage of this solar gain: collecting and storing the sun's radiation during the day and distributing it at night.

Basic Elements of Passive Solar Design

When designing your country home, incorporate as many elements of passive solar design into the plans as possible. Start by providing excellent insulation in the walls and roof (see page 78). Look at floor plans, especially open floor plans, where the main living areas can be located on the south side of the house. Open floor plans let air circulate freely. Plan for the maximum amount of windows on the south-facing walls. Adding a sunroom is one way to accomplish this. Many people enjoy morning sun in the kitchen and bathroom. These rooms can be located on the east side of the house, and can also have larger windows. Avoid lots of windows on the west side, as the afternoon sun will

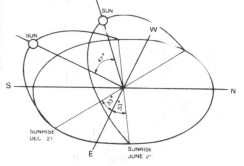

The diagram above shows the positions of the sun at the winter and summer solstices, for a location at 40 degrees latitude. A house oriented on an east–west axis with the largest amount of wall area facing south will receive the most sun in winter, when the sun is lowest on the horizon.

Local climate will also affect siting. Refer to this chart to determine your objectives, and how you can use your land to its best advantage when building.

	COOL	TEMPERATE	HOT ARID	HOT HUMID
OBJECTIVES:	Maximize warming effects of solar radiation. Reduce impact of winter wind. Avoid local climatic cold pockets.	Maximize warming effects of sun in winter. Provide shade in summer. Reduce impact of winter wind but allow air circulation in summer.	Maximize shade late morning and all afternoon. Maximize humidity. Provide air movement in summer.	Maximize shade. Maximize air movement.
Position on slope	Low for wind shelter	Middle-upper for solar radiation exposure	Low for cool air flow	High for wind
Orientation on slope	South to southeast	South to southeast	East-southeast for P.M. shade	South
Relation to water	Near large body of water	Close to water, but avoid coastal fog	On lee side of water	Near any water
Preferred winds	Sheltered from north and west	Avoid continental cold winds	Exposed to prevailing winds	Exposed to prevailing winds
Clustering	Around sun pockets	Around a common, sunny terrace	Along E–W axis, for shade & wind	Open to wind
Building orientation*	South to southeast	South to southeast	South	South, toward prevailing wind
Tree forms*	Deciduous trees near bldg. Evergreens for windbreaks	Deciduous trees nearby on west. No evergreens near on south	Trees overhanging roof if possible	High canopy trees. Use deciduous trees near building
Road orientation	Crosswise to winter wind	Crosswise to winter wind	Narrow; E–W axis	Broad channel. E–W axis
Materials coloration	Medium to dark	Medium	Light on exposed surfaces; dark to avoid reflection	Light, especially for roof.

* Must be evaluated in terms of impact on solar system.

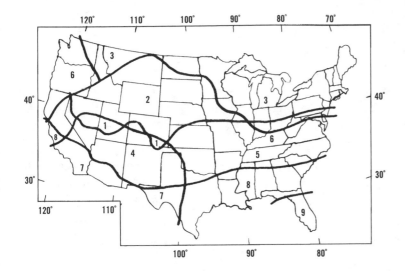

Your location by region is important to consider when determining if solar heating will be practical. This map indicates that the upper Midwest, Northeast, Great Plains, Rocky Mountains, and Southwest are good areas for solar heating. 1 = High Heat Demand, with excellent sunshine. 2 = High Heat Demand, with good sunshine. 3 = High Heat Demand, with fair sunshine. 4 = Moderate Heat Demand, with excellent sunshine. 5 = Moderate Heat Demand, with good sunshine. 6 = Moderate Heat Demand, with fair sunshine. 7 = Low Heat Demand, with excellent sunshine. 8 = Low Heat Demand, with good sunshine. 9 = Low Heat Demand, with fair sunshine.

overheat the house. The fewest windows should face north. Choose double-glazed, low-e windows to cut down on heat loss and to minimize damage to furnishings from ultraviolet rays.

Thermal Mass

Although many south-facing windows make very efficient solar collectors during the winter months, the temperature in the house can fluctuate uncomfortably without some method of absorbing the solar energy during the day and radiating it back at night. Wood, furniture, and carpeting don't absorb enough of the solar energy to do this. A thermal mass is a large, heat-absorbing element, usually made of stone or brick, added to the house design to perform this function. Often, the floors on the south side of the house are poured concrete and paved with stone, brick, or tile. Solar greenhouses and sunrooms often have gravel or crushed-stone floors. A large stone or brick partition wall placed where the sun will shine on it is another type of thermal mass.

In addition, you will want to install insulated drapes, window shades, or shutters to cover large expanses of glass. Covering the windows at night keeps heat in, and in the hottest weather the glass can be covered during the day to keep the house from overheating.

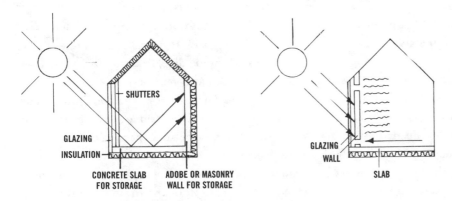

An insulated concrete floor (left) can act as a thermal mass, as can a masonry wall (right) placed behind a window.

What You Need to Build a Passive Solar House

- Southern exposure
- Lack of obstructions on the southern horizon
- Axis of house oriented east–west
- Maximum insulation
- Open floor plan
- Most windows on the south and east sides of the house
- Large thermal mass integrated into the design
- Insulated shades, drapes, or shutters

—contributed by Jim Sherratt, owner, Sun Energy

HEATING BY THE SUN

A cutaway sketch of a typical flat plate solar collector. Water running through the channels in the collector plate is heated by the sun and returned to the storage tank elsewhere. The glass on top traps radiation and holds heat inside the panel.

Backup Heat

If you already have a hot-water tank in your home, leave it in place. The solar storage tank can be used as a preheater. Or you can install a bypass valve and switch to 100 percent solar hot water during the peak months, then use the conventional hot-water tank when the solar heating system isn't working.

Solar Domestic Hot Water Heating

Even in the northern United States, a solar system can provide all the hot water required by an average family from mid-spring to mid-autumn. Another method of hot water heating will be needed during the coldest winter months, and to supplement the solar heating system during extended cloudy periods.

Collectors

All solar domestic hot water systems use solar panels, or collectors, to absorb the sun's energy and transfer its heat to a fluid, either water or antifreeze (see drawing). Solar collectors are mounted on rooftops or on racks on the ground. For the average family, two 4 x 8 solar panels are usually sufficient for heating water. To take full advantage of the sun's rays, the collectors should be sited and mounted properly.

Once the requirements of the location have been determined, the manufacturer will provide a customized mounting system with the collectors. Wooden racks can also be built, and the solar panels bolted to them.

It is important to consult your local building inspector before installing a solar hot water system. Most building codes require a licensed plumber to perform any work involving tying in to the domestic water supply.

Three Basic Systems

Opposite you will find diagrams for the three basic systems. For areas where freezing occurs, a **Closed Loop Hot Water System** is recommended. Heat from the collector is transferred to storage water through a water-to-water heat exchanger in the storage tank. Antifreeze circulates through the closed loop, eliminating the need to drain the solar panels when a freeze occurs. It works during the winter months and requires little electricity to run the small pump that circulates pressurized heat transfer fluid through the collectors. The collectors can be mounted anywhere. The main disadvantages are high cost, possible overheating, and the required professional installation and servicing.

For backup heating you can drill two holes in a woodstove and run a water line from the solar hot water storage tank through it, then back into the tank as shown in the drawing. This arrangement works well in cold weather when the solar collectors aren't working, but the woodstove is being used the most.

In the **Forced Drain-Down Hot Water System,** a pump circulates water from the storage tank through the collector back to storage. During a freeze, an automatic sensing device activates a solenoid valve, draining the water from the collector. You'll need a nonfreezing automatic vent on top of the collector.

The simplest system to operate is the **Gravity (or Thermosiphon) Hot Water System.** Where freezing rarely occurs, this system is recommended. No pump is needed to circulate the water through the solar panels; ordinary head pressure and gravity do the work. The main drawback is that the tank for storing the hot water must be located higher than the collectors. Also, you must manually shut off the flow of water to the collectors and drain them thoroughly whenever a freeze threatens. A plumbing and heating contractor, rather than a professional solar technician, should be able to install this system.

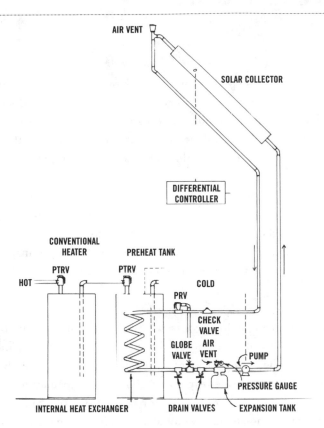

In the **Closed Loop Hot Water System,** heat from the collector is transferred to storage water through a heat exchanger.

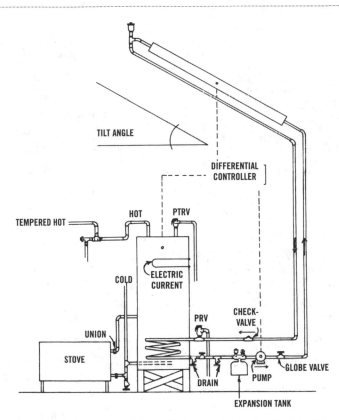

Above, both the stove and the collector can feed hot water into this single-tank **Closed Loop Hot Water System.**

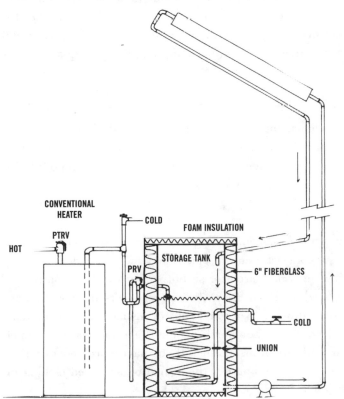

In the **Forced Drain-Down Hot Water System,** a pump circulates water from the tank through the collector and back to storage.

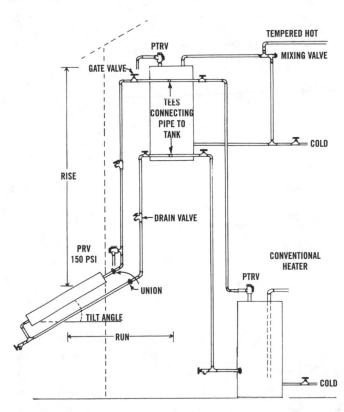

In the **Gravity Hot Water System,** water heated in the collector becomes lighter and rises; colder (heavier) water will flow from the bottom of the storage tank to the bottom of the collector.

WEATHERPROOFING YOUR HOME

Fiberglass insulation is available in batts, rolls (above), and loose and rigid forms. Roll insulation is the most widely used and often comes with a built-in vapor barrier.

R-VALUES

Because different insulators have different insulation values, they are rated by their R-values. The higher the R-rating, the greater the insulator's resistance to heat loss. Use this chart to determine how one kind of insulation stacks up against another, and to calculate how many inches you'll need.

R-VALUES PER INCH OF THICKNESS

Material	Value
Fiberglass	3.33
Rock wool	3.33
Cellulose	3.70
Vermiculite	2.08
Perlite	2.70
Urea formaldehyde	4.48
Urethane board	7.00
Polystyrene	3.45
Isocyanurate	7.00

—from *Weatherize Your Home*
by Steve Sherman

Simple Steps for Efficient Insulation

By insulating, you want to keep the coldest air from getting into your house at the bottom and stop warm air from getting out through the walls or the top. The best insulators include expanded glass and mineral fibers sold as fiberglass, newspaper products like cellulose, and rigid foam boards. A thorough job of insulating your attic, walls, and floor can save up to 50 percent on winter fuel bills.

Check Building Codes

To begin planning for insulation, check the insulation codes in your area. Be sure you understand whether the figures are for the R-value of the insulation or for an average R-value for the wall, ceiling, and other places.

Attics

Many attic insulation jobs can be do-it-yourself tasks. How much insulation you need depends on the severity of your winters, how you heat your home, and how much you can get into the area you want to insulate. You will probably want at least R-30 in your attic, equivalent to about 10 inches of insulation.

Before you begin, check exposed roof areas for moisture stains and discolorations. Find the source of moisture. Wet insulation is ineffective and may damage your home by causing rot. This is the purpose of ventilation. A combination of high vents and low vents is best for adequate airflow, and vents can be installed in the gables, eaves, or roof. The rule of thumb is that for every 150 square feet of attic space without a vapor barrier, or every 300 square feet *with* a vapor barrier, you will need approximately 1 square foot of ventilation.

Walls

If yours is an older house that has never been insulated, find out whether the walls can be insulated. If you need insulation, cellulose can be blown into the walls from the outside by drilling a hole through the wall or clapboard. For a remodeling job, install insulation from the interior.

Floors

Consider insulating the basement ceiling. Your first floor will feel warm and comfortable, but by contrast, your basement may feel somewhat colder.

Batts or blankets of fiberglass are easiest, but measure before you buy. If the floor joists are spaced on 16- or 24-inch centers, you're in luck, because those are the standard widths for batts and rolls of insulation. The standard length for batts is 6 feet. The vapor barrier should face the warmth, which means it faces up in an under-floor installation. If you have a problem of fitting, you may be able to solve it by rolling out the insulation and then tacking up lengths of wire mesh or chicken wire.

—from *547 Easy Ways to Save Energy in Your Home* by Roger Albright

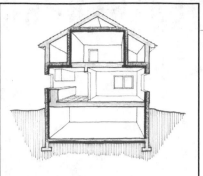

Stopping Window Heat Loss

Weatherstripping and Caulking

If your storm windows aren't weatherstripped or caulked, they may not reduce heat loss. Caulking comes in squeeze tubes. Apply it with a gun around outside window frames between the frame and the siding, and between the frames of combination storm/screen units and siding. Make sure all cracks are filled. Caulking also comes in puttylike strands that can be pushed into cracks for a temporary seal.

Weatherstripping is inexpensive, and is used to fill the gaps between window and frame. It is available in felt fiber or adhesive-backed foam. Attaching these strips can reduce the infiltration of outside air by 50 percent.

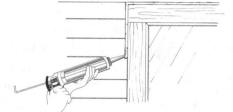

Apply caulking between the window frame and the siding.

Plastic Storm Windows

Plastic storms can be as simple as fastening plastic over the window, or you can build wooden frames. Plastic storms can be installed on the outside or inside. Either way, they are economical and efficient.

You'll need:

- 4-mil or 6-mil polyethylene plastic or heavy-gauge plastic vinyl film caulk and caulking gun
- Furring strips (for exterior plastic)
- Masking tape (for interior plastic)

Measure the width of your largest window to determine the width of the plastic you'll buy. Then measure the length of your windows to determine how many linear feet you'll need. Cut the plastic to the area of the window plus 2 inches on each side. If the plastic is going on the outside, mount with furring strips. Nail them over the plastic around the window, making sure the plastic is taut. Caulk all sides.

If the plastic is going on the inside, seal tightly with masking tape.

Plastic Window Kits

Ready-made windows of clear, rigid plastic are available at hardware stores. They mount on inside windows with self-sticking frames that lie flat to ensure an airtight seal. They can be mounted against the window casings or on a flat lip of the casement molding. You can also use the plastic by itself, cutting it to the desired dimensions and weatherstripping the edges.

Glass Storm Windows

You can make these with wooden or aluminum frames. Both are available at hardware stores in varying lengths. They can be installed inside or outside. Use window glass for its durability.

—from *Window Heat Loss* by Mary Twitchell

Don't Forget the Vapor Barrier

Standard insulation rolls and batts have a vapor barrier on one side. It should face the heated living space. A vapor barrier has a layer of impermeable material and is placed between the interior wall sheathing and the insulation. It prevents moisture vaporized in the warm air inside a house from traveling through the wall, condensing, and freezing on the inside of the outer wall covering.

Plastic window kits are the fastest way to insulate a window.

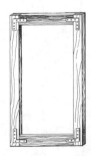

Wooden window frames hold heat in a room better than aluminum frames do.

WEATHERPROOFING YOUR HOME

Snow lingering on a roof (above) indicates that the house is well insulated. If snow melts quickly, it often means the attic heat is warming the roof—and wasting your money.

Weatherizing Doors

Think of the 1/16-inch cracks around an ordinary door this way: Totaled, this space equals an open hole of 4 square inches! Here's what you can do to seal out the cold and keep in the heat.

Sweeps and thresholds. A variety of door sweeps are available. The easiest ones to install are self-adhesive stick-on types. These come with vinyl, felt, or brush bottoms that extend to the carpet or floor. Unfortunately, they don't stick around long enough, especially with the constant opening and closing of a door.

A more permanent sweep is one that is nailed solid to the door bottom. These also come in vinyl, felt, and brush. An aluminum and vinyl combination sweep provides a solid barrier to air. Unlike the felt or brush, it will not bunch up or tear easily. Sweeps are easy to install.

Installing a new threshold is a more expensive option. The threshold is the cross section of wood along the bottom of the doorway. Before installing one, be sure your door is hanging straight. If not, tighten the screws in the hinges. Replace a threshold with hardwood (if wood is your choice)—never with pine or spruce, which will wear out in short order. Plan to remove the door for easier installation.

Weatherstripping. Apply weatherstripping at the junction of the doorstop next to the hinges, against where the door closes tight. Weaker weatherstripping materials may deteriorate faster than you want. In general, tacking rather than sticking is a more permanent way to install weatherstripping.

Storm doors. Storm doors are installed in front of your permanent exterior doors to block the cold air and create dead air space. Like storm windows, they require a moderate expenditure. However, they also add immeasurably to weatherizing your home. To be effective, storm doors should be weatherstripped.

Don't Forget the Foundation

Over the years, the juncture between the foundation and the sill (the bottom horizontal beam of your house) develops gaps. These should be filled. Large cracks can be filled with mortar. Even if you cannot see a gap all the way through the foundation, cement what you do see.

Stuff smaller gaps (down to 1/4 inch) with dry insulation such as oakum, which can be pressed into the holes. Hold the material in place by caulking the edges to the foundation or sill. For even smaller gaps, use caulking compound. In fact, a wise move is to completely reseal the sill and foundation joint with caulk.

Skirting the foundation with plastic is a worthwhile yearly job. Measure the entire perimeter of your foundation, then buy a large roll of 4- to 6-mil plastic and enough flat pine molding to reach around the house. Wrap the edge of the plastic around the pine bracing and tack it to the house clapboard. Weight the bottom of the plastic with earth or rocks.

—from *Weatherize Your Home* by Steve Sherman

Keeping a House Cool in Summer

In summer, keep an eye peeled for extra lights burning, particularly incandescent bulbs. They furnish heat as well as light and cause your air conditioner to work harder.

An air conditioner operates most efficiently when placed on the shady (usually north) side of the house. Set the thermostat no lower than 78°F, and shut it off and open the windows on breezy days.

A large window fan costs one-fifth as much as an air conditioner, and uses one-fourth as much power. Place one in an attic window to push hot air out of the house.

In summer you want low humidity. Keep kitchen, bathroom, and laundry areas closed off from the rest of the house as much as possible. And when you take a shower, open the bathroom window to let out the moisture.

Because heat rises, in summer open upstairs and attic windows to let the warm air escape. In the cool of the evening, open windows to admit cool air, and close the windows in the early morning to keep that cool air inside.

Six Easy Ways to Cut Heating Costs

1. For many people, home heating bills can be cut 10 percent or more with one simple move: Have the furnace cleaned and adjusted properly. If yours is an oil burner, that means at least an annual inspection by a qualified technician.

2. While your oil burner is under discussion, check and see whether a smaller fuel nozzle can be installed. The burner may operate just as well with a smaller fuel nozzle, and save as much as 15 percent on your fuel bill.

3. Forced warm air furnaces need to have their air filters cleaned or replaced at least twice each winter. A clogged filter chokes off the necessary breathing of the furnace and makes it work harder.

4. When you're rearranging furniture, be sure that radiators, warm-air registers, or heating units aren't blocked from their proper functioning. If there's an arrangement you "must" have that blocks heat flow, let it wait till summer, when it won't affect heating efficiency.

5. Many kitchens and bathrooms have exhaust fans to take away unwanted odors, and in some bathrooms they turn on automatically with the light switch. Convenient, but expensive. In winter, those exhaust fans not only take out odors, but they're also blowing away warm air as fast as they can. That's expensive. Use them sparingly and save money.

6. A little extra humidity permits a lower thermostat setting without discomfort. Some furnaces will accept a humidifying system easily and inexpensively. If that's not the case with you, place pans of water on radiators or heat registers to put a little moisture in the air. Houseplants, particularly broad-leafed and ivy types, can also provide significant extra humidity during the winter.

—from *547 Easy Ways to Save Energy in Your Home* by Roger Albright

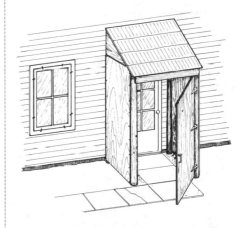

Simply constructing a shelter around your door will save heating costs every time you enter or leave the house in winter.

ELECTRICITY

6

UNDERSTANDING ELECTRICITY • ASSESSING YOUR
SYSTEM • REWIRING • MAKING REPAIRS
SOLAR AND WIND POWER • WHEN THE POWER FAILS

Like most of our city friends, we took electricity for granted. Then a major ice storm hit our area and left us without power for a week. The fun of "camping out" by the woodstove and barbecuing in 15-degree weather faded as stoves, toilets, and refrigerators all failed. We updated our checklist of emergency supplies and invested in a two-burner Coleman stove and a generator. We also upgraded our first-aid kit and manual, realizing that help might not be easy to summon with the lines down. The restoration of power was a cause for celebration, but as a result of this experience we were better prepared for future outages. In this chapter we'll hear first from Phillip and Newell Decker with an overview of electrical systems.

—John & Martha Storey

I f you take a few precautions and learn some fundamental procedures, you can wire a house and do many types of electrical projects without incident. Some basic knowledge is required, however, because mistakes can be lethal.

Most modern electrical wire consists of two conductors, one white and one black, and a third uninsulated or green wire that acts as a ground. The black wire is the hot wire; the white is the neutral wire. In a general sense, electricity flows to your house from the black wire and returns to a power station through the white wire. The green wire does not conduct any electricity unless there is a failure in the circuit. If that happens, electricity is shunted through the ground wire to the earth.

Think of the flow of electricity as if it were water flowing through a garden hose. The voltage is like the pressure of the water in the hose. The amperage is the speed at which the water flows. The wattage is the total amount of water that flows past a certain point in the hose in a given time.

AC. Alternating electric current, the type provided by utility companies

Amperage. The strength of a current of electricity, expressed in amperes (amps)

DC. Direct electric current, the type provided by home generators

Fuse. An electrical safety device that melts and interrupts the circuit when the current exceeds a particular amperage

Circuit Breaker. A switch that automatically interrupts an electric circuit

Rotor. The spinning wheel of a wind turbine, also known as windwheel

Swept area. The area inside the perimeter of a rotor's spinning blades

Watt. The standard unit of electrical power. 746 watts make 1 horsepower

Electrical Systems

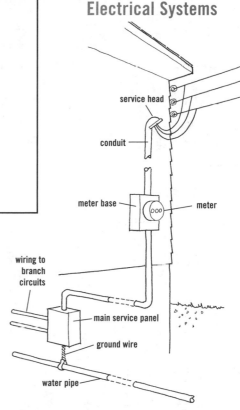

The drawing above shows a typical electrical system from the outside of a house. The drawing below shows how power travels through individual circuits inside.

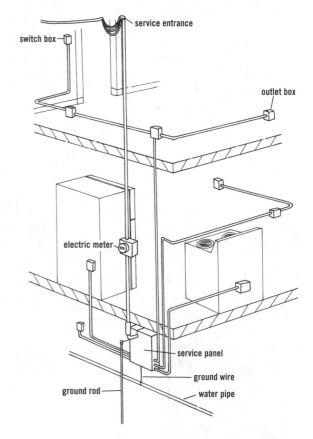

Service to your house is through a two-line (one hot and one neutral) or three-line (two hot and one neutral) system. The two-line system carries 120 volts, while the three-line system carries 240 volts. The former is found primarily in old homes and is usually inadequate for modern usage.

The wires enter your house through the service head and go into the service box. Inside the service box is the fuse box or circuit-breaker panel. Running down the inside of the service box are the bus bars, containing all the branch circuits in your house. In almost all 120-volt installations and hookups, it is important to attach the wires black to black and white to white. Never mix them. In 240-volt installations, there will be two hot wires (one red and one black) and one neutral wire (white).

Fuses come in two types—screw-in and cartridge. Both types utilize a metal strip that is made to handle the heat caused by a certain amperage rating. If the circuit overloads, the heat increases and the metal strip melts, causing the circuit to be open. The open circuit prevents the flow of current.

A circuit breaker has a thin strip of metal that bends when the circuit overloads. This causes the breaker to trip and the circuit to open up. Fuses and breakers should be installed with caution, and should never be larger than the amperage rating of the circuit.

Another type of circuit breaker is the ground fault circuit interrupter. This type senses tiny leakages in a wiring circuit, and can be more effective in preventing damage and shocks. For this reason, most codes require that all circuits in bathrooms and outside the house be ground-faulted. Ground Fault Circuit Interrupters are easily installed, and we highly recommend their use.

Inside every modern service box, you will find the grounding bus, and all circuits should have a ground wire running to the bus. Never ignore this part of your circuit, and never break off the round ground lug on an electrical plug. One final word of caution: Never attempt to complete the outside wiring hookup to your box, or to set up the box itself. These tasks should be left to a licensed electrician.

ASSESSING YOUR SYSTEM

Circuit Breakers and Fuse Boxes

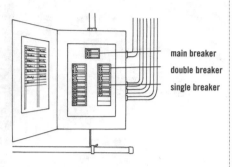

main breaker
double breaker
single breaker

A circuit-breaker service panel (above) or a fuse box (below) should have a rating of at least 100 to 200 amps to power a home.

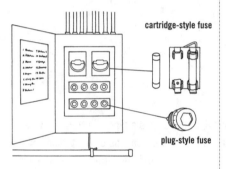

cartridge-style fuse

plug-style fuse

Safety Tip

A ground fault circuit interrupter (GFCI) is a device that senses tiny leaks of current and then immediately turns off the power. Standard electrical code requires GFCIs for bathrooms, garages, and outdoor receptacles. Left, a permanent receptacle type GFCI; right, a portable plug-in type.

—from *The Woman's Hands-On Home Repair Guide* by Lyn Herrick

Can Your System Handle the Load?

The first step in assessing your system is to find the electrical service box and look inside. Do you see fuses? Are there lots of them or just a few? If you see just a few, you probably ought to replace them with a multi-circuit breaker box. With this type of box, you simply add circuit breakers when needed.

While looking into the service box, note whether there are two or three large wires entering the house from the street. If there are only two, you have 120-volt service, which will not be enough for an electric range, dryer, or air conditioner. Note the amperage of the service box. In most old boxes, the service rating will be 30 to 60 amps, which is not enough to power a newer home. You will need a box with a rating of at least 100 to 200 amps.

Wiring. The next thing to observe is the type of wire that leads away from your service box. If your house is old, chances are it will have knob-and-tube wiring, in which the wires run through ceramic tubes and around ceramic knob insulators (see drawing in chapter 1). Notice the state of the insulation on the wire. Is it frayed? Does it crack when you bend it? If so, think about replacing the wiring. Also check the state of the wire insulation in the attic.

Restructuring. Before beginning to restructure your wiring and electrical service, decide how much power you will need on each circuit and how many circuits you will need. The electrical code will help you determine this. For example, the code indicates that you should have separate lighting and appliance circuits. Lighting circuits should be rated at 15 amps and there should be one 15-amp circuit for about every 500 feet of floor space. The small-appliance circuits should be 20-amp, and no more than 1,500 watts should be connected to any one circuit.

Most local codes require that there be a wall receptacle every 12 feet, and that no space along the wall be more than 6 feet from a receptacle. The number of outlets per circuit is fixed by your local code but probably will be limited to 9 or 10 outlets per 15-amp circuit and 12 per 20-amp circuit. Each stationary appliance should have its own circuit. The kitchen should have three circuits. Remember that the bathroom circuits, as well as those in other wet areas, should be ground-faulted.

How much power? To decide what the total capacity of your system should be, add up the wattage of (1) the lighting and general-use circuits; (2) the small-appliance circuits; (3) the laundry circuit; (4) the major-appliance circuits; and (5) the heating and air-conditioning system. You can calculate the wattage of the general-use circuits by estimating the total square footage of the house. Multiply the square footage by 3 watts. Next, give each small-appliance circuit and the laundry circuit 1,500 watts apiece. The wattage values of the major appliances will be listed on the nameplate of each. This will also be true of the air conditioner and furnace. Once you have totaled up this wattage, divide the sum by 240 volts to determine the size (in amps) of the service box you need.

—from *Renovating Brick Houses* by Phillip J. Decker and T. Newell Decker

- wire stripper
- electrician's pliers
- needle-nosed pliers
- straight-slot screwdriver
- Phillips screwdriver
- voltage tester
- circuit tester
- neon tester
- volt-ohm meter
- wire fishing tape
- electrical tape
- wire nuts
- wood saw
- drill and drill bits
- flashlight

WIRE STRIPPER

NEEDLE-NOSED PLIERS

ELECTRICIAN'S PLIERS

WIRE FISHING TAPE

Installing New Work

The term *new work* generally refers to work that is done when the walls are not in place. If you have gutted your dwelling and are redoing the wiring, you are doing new work. If the walls are still in place and you are doing wiring, you are doing old work.

Choosing wire. The most common sizes of wire are, from smallest to largest, numbers 14, 12, and 10. These are used in circuits that have amperage ratings of 15, 20, and 30, respectively. Larger wire sizes, such as number 8 for 40 amp circuits and number 6 for 50-amp circuits, will be used for items such as stoves, ovens, and dryers.

Plastic-sheathed solid wire is the most commonly used wire. There are three principal types: NM, used in most indoor installations; NMC, used indoors where moisture is likely to exist; and UF, used in underground applications.

Another type of wire is called BX. This wire is armor-wrapped cable with a flexible outer covering of galvanized steel and either two or three conductors on the inside wrapped in paper. BX has no ground wire, as the metal of the cable armor is connected to the metal of the outlet boxes to provide the continuity to ground. BX is usually used in dry indoor applications where it is important to protect the wire from nails and other carpentry projects. In addition, individual wire can be run in conduits for areas where the wire must be protected (for example, basement walls).

Inside an Electrical Wire

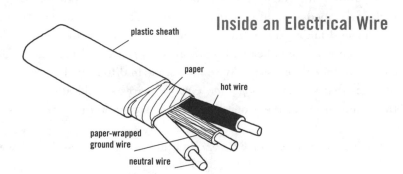

plastic sheath

paper

hot wire

paper-wrapped ground wire

neutral wire

So Obvious, But So Important!

Remember to turn off the power before doing any electrical work.

Wiring ... by the Numbers

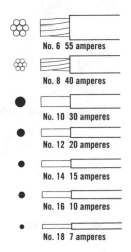

No. 6   55 amperes

No. 8   40 amperes

No. 10   30 amperes

No. 12   20 amperes

No. 14   15 amperes

No. 16   10 amperes

No. 18   7 amperes

The smaller the wire number, the greater the diameter and ampacity. Most work will be done with number 12 or 14 wire. This wire has two conductors (one white and one black) and also an uninsulated ground wire. Some of the work you do will involve three-way switches, which require three conductors plus a ground wire, but most wiring can be done with two-conductor wire. Always use copper wire.

REWIRING

Making the Connection

OUTLET BOX

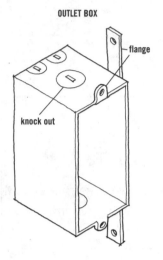

flange

knock out

An outlet box like this, or the octagonal junction box pictured below, may be nailed to a stud by its flange.

flange

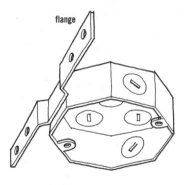

OCTAGONAL JUNCTION BOX

Running the Wire

Begin by locating the positions of all the outlet boxes and ceiling fixtures. Drill holes through all the studs and run wire through the holes, starting at the outlet box that is farthest away from the service panel. Staple down the wire every 2 feet or so (check the code in your area). Usually the wire must be stapled within 12 inches of each box. Wire that will be run to ceiling boxes can be run under the floor joists if a suspended ceiling will eventually be used. If the ceiling will be attached directly to the underside of the joists, the wire will have to be run through drilled holes. Pull about a foot of wire out of each junction box so you have plenty to work with when you begin to attach receptacles and switches. As you run wire, leave a surplus loop once in a while in case you have misjudged the distance.

Placing wall boxes. Wall boxes are usually placed about 12 inches above the finished floor, and switch boxes are usually about 4 feet up the wall. When you place switch boxes near doors, be sure they are on the side opposite the hinges. Whether you place a switch for a room on the outside of the wall or the inside is a matter of preference, but it is sometimes easier if the switch is outside the room. You need special receptacles for 220-volt circuit outlets, and the wire size will be much larger than that used for typical 110-volt circuits.

Placing ceiling boxes. Boxes for ceiling lights are usually set in the center of the area to be lighted. If the area is large, you should install several fixtures. Divide the room evenly, with the boxes at equal distances from one another. If there is no ceiling fixture, tie one wall plug into a switch near the door.

The type of ceiling or wall box you should use is dictated in part by the local code. Boxes are made of metal or plastic. Most have a tab through which you can drive a nail to attach the box to a stud. Some even have nails preattached or a mounting depth gauge etched onto the box, so you can see how far the box should stick out from the wall. If you intend to hang heavy light fixtures or fans from a ceiling box, you should purchase a special box that hangs across two ceiling joists. However, you can hang these fixtures from a standard metal box if it is secured with screws to a block nailed between two joists.

Attaching wire. Attaching wire to a switch or receptacle is pretty straightforward. First strip off about 6 to 8 inches of the outside insulation, so that the individual wires are exposed. Make sure the outside insulation is still intact where the wire exits the box to prevent wearing or breaking of the individual inside wires. Then strip off 1 to 1½ inches of insulation so you can make a loop to go around the attaching screws on the switch or receptacle. You can stick ⅜ inch of stripped wire into the back of modern switches and receptacles, but we recommend taking the extra attaching time to fasten the wire to the screws. Splice the wires together with wire nuts, as these will provide a tight fit that can be undone if necessary. Wire nuts come in different sizes to fit the number of wires that are joined together. Ground wires should always be attached to the switches and to the grounding (green) screw on the receptacles.

—from *Renovating Brick Houses* by Phillip J. Decker and T. Newell Decker

Common Connections

These illustrations show some of the more common types of connections. They should provide you with the information you need to wire many two-way switches, three-way switches, and other types of switches, lights, and outlets.

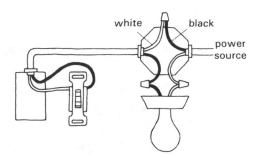

Wall switch controlling ceiling fixture at end of run

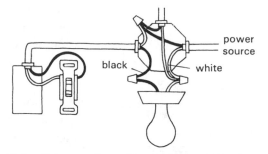

Wall switch controlling ceiling fixture in middle of run

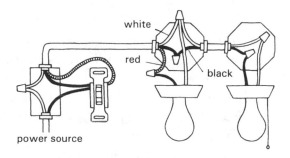

Two fixtures on same line controlled by different switches

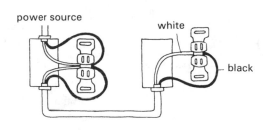

Adding a supplementary outlet

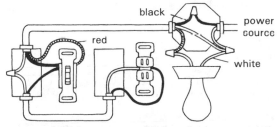

Adding a new switch and outlet to an existing fixture

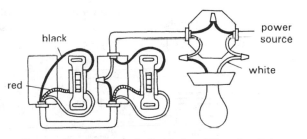

Same ceiling fixture controlled by two different switches

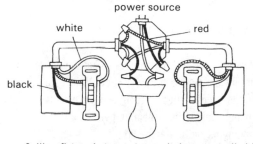

Ceiling fixture between two switches, controlled by either

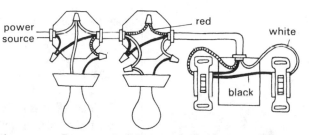

Two separate fixtures controlled by two switches

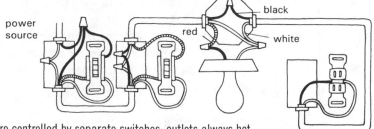

Fixture controlled by separate switches; outlets always hot

—from *Renovating Brick Houses*

REWIRING

Tricks of the Trade

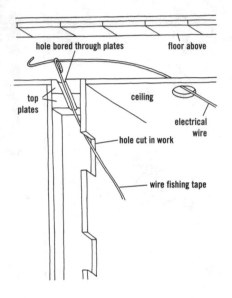

hole bored through plates

floor above

top plates

ceiling

hole cut in work

electrical wire

wire fishing tape

Use wire fishing tape to hook an electrical wire (above) and guide it to the right location (below).

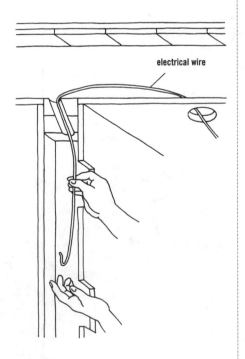

electrical wire

Boosting Your System

Perhaps the easiest method to determine where an old circuit goes and how much power is on it is to throw all the circuit breakers or unscrew all of the fuses except for the circuit in question. Then it's a simple matter of going around the house with a lamp, plugging it into each receptacle that you come across, and throwing each switch that you see. By doing this and keeping notes of watts and amperes, you can determine where the circuit goes and what it does.

Installation of additional wall outlets, switches, and lights is usually a matter of deciding where you want them to be and then figuring out where you are going to tap into the power supply to add onto the circuit. The most convenient place to tap into the circuit is at a wall outlet. Sometimes this will not be possible, and you will have to go into the attic or the basement to find a circuit you can use.

The rest of the problem is figuring out how to run the wire for the addition and cause the least disturbance of existing wall structures. Any empty space in the wall is fair game. If the run of the new wire is of any length, you will often have to "fish" the wire from one spot to another. This is done with wire fishing tape and a helper. One person feeds the tape through the space where the wire will run, and the other person looks for it to appear. Once he or she sees it, the tape can be pulled out of the space, the new wire can be attached to it, and it can be pulled back in the opposite direction with the wire attached. While this sounds easy, it is often a very frustrating experience and requires great patience.

Replacing Electrical Switches

To replace a defective switch, proceed as follows:

1. Turn off the power to the switch at the circuit breaker.

Nine Safety Tips When Working with Electricity

Here are some safety tips aimed at protecting you and making your work easier:

- Before working on anything electrical, turn off the circuit breaker or remove the fuse for that area of the house, or turn off the main electrical switch. Make sure the power is off by testing a receptacle on the circuit with a voltage tester or neon test light.
- Don't attach wires to service panels before disconnecting power.
- Don't wire buildings while standing on wet or damp surfaces.
- Be sure to check with local codes before beginning any wiring projects.
- Make a wiring diagram before unfastening any wires. It will help you reattach the wires correctly.
- Be sure all equipment and wiring is properly grounded.
- Use pliers and other electrical tools with insulated handles.
- Purchase plug-in GFCIs and plug them into receptacles where you are using power tools and other types of electrical equipment. Then plug your tools into these receptacles to protect yourself from shock.
- Never replace a fuse with a fuse of a different amperage.

In the Dark?

If you flip a light switch and nothing happens, one of the following could be wrong:

- The circuit breaker may be off for that part of the house. Check to see if other electrical units in the room are working.
- If the light you switched on is the only thing not working, the bulb may be burned out. Replace the bulb.
- The switch may be defective. If the light still does not work after replacing the bulb, test the switch with a neon tester. Take off the switch cover with a screwdriver. Touch the probes of your neon tester to the terminal screws with the switch in the ON position. Be careful not to let the probes touch the box sides. If the tester lights, the switch needs replacing.

2. Remove the switch cover with a screwdriver. You will see two screws holding the switch in place.

3. Remove these screws and pull the switch out of the wall. You will now see two wires connected to the switch. They will either be attached to two screws on the sides of the switch or inserted into the back of the switch.

4. Loosen the screws and disconnect the wires or gently pull the wires out of the back of the switch. The switch will now be free. Note or mark where the wires were attached, because you will repeat this procedure in reverse order when you connect the new switch.

5. Take the switch to a hardware or electrical supply store and replace it with a similar one.

6. Reconnect the new switch to the wires in the wall, screw it back onto the wall, replace the cover, and turn the power back on.

Three-way switches. If you are dealing with a three-way switch, the same principles apply. The basic principle is that the common or hot wire (the dark-colored one) proceeds from the power source to the first switch. Two lighter-colored traveler wires link the two switches together. The common wire then runs from the second switch to the light fixture. A white wire runs from the power source to the light fixture, which completes the circuit. Simply remember to make a wire diagram before unfastening the wires to a damaged switch. Install the new three-way switch with the same wiring pattern you found in the damaged switch.

Installing dimmer switches. A dimmer switch allows you to control the amount of illumination a light puts out, conserves energy, and increases the life of your lightbulb. An incandescent dimmer switch is installed like any other lighting switch (see above). If you are dealing with a three-way switch, it is best to install only one dimming switch and to leave the other switch alone. Make sure you attach the black wire from the box (the common wire) to the black switch wire. Then connect the two red wires from the switch (the traveler wires) to the traveler wires in the box—one will likely be red and the other white. Fluorescent dimmer switches are installed the same way, with one exception. You must install a special ballast for the fluorescent fixture, which can be purchased at an electrical supply store.

—from *The Woman's Hands-On Home Repair Guide* by Lyn Herrick

Neon Testers

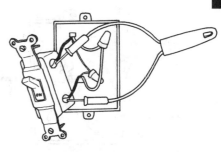

Use a neon tester to determine whether the switch is defective. Unscrew the switch cover and then, with the switch in the ON position, touch the terminal screws with the probes of the neon tester. Be careful not to let the probes touch the box sides. If the tester lights, the switch needs replacing.

Dimmer Switches

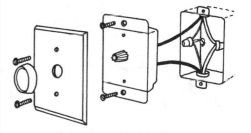

Turn off the power before installing a dimmer switch. Unscrew the switch cover and then the plate holding the switch to the wall. Disconnect the two wires, replace the switch, and reconnect the wires in the same position. Screw the switch back into the wall, replace the cover, and turn the power back on.

MAKING REPAIRS

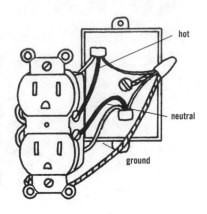

The outlet above is at the middle of the circuit; the one below is at the end.

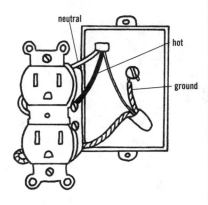

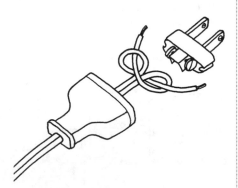

Connect a wire to a new plug by first unplugging the appliance and cutting off the old plug.

Replacing an Outlet

Replacing an outlet is similar to replacing a switch. The obvious test for an outlet is to plug in an electrical appliance that you know works. If there's a problem, follow these steps:

1. Turn off the power to the outlet at the circuit breaker box. Test the circuit with a voltage tester to be sure the power is off.

2. Remove the outlet cover with a screwdriver. Take the two screws out of the outlet to remove it from the wall and notice how the wires are connected. These wires will be connected to two screws on the sides of the outlet, or will be fastened on the back of the receptacle.

3. Loosen the screws and remove the wires, or depress the release slot in the outlet to free up the wires.

4. Take the old outlet to the hardware store and replace it with an identical new one.

5. Install the new outlet by reversing the above steps. Put the cover back on and turn on the power. Retest the appliance.

Replacing Plugs

If you encounter a problem with a plug, you have several options:

Molded rubber plugs. For molded rubber plugs, unplug the light, cut off the plug, and bring it to the hardware store to be replaced. Purchase the type of plug that can simply be clamped back onto the cord.

Two-pronged plugs. Follow these steps:

1. Unplug the appliance and cut off the plug. Purchase a plug that can be attached to the two wire strands with screws.

2. Thread the wire into the plug, separate the two strands, and strip the insulation material.

3. Tie the two strands into a loop before connecting them to the screws. Loosen the screws and wind a small part of the wire around the screw.

4. Tighten the screws and cover them with the insulating material that comes with the plug.

Three-wire extension cords. For these cords, replace the three-pronged plug the same way as you would replace a two-pronged plug (see above).

Repairing Light Fixtures

Repair of light fixtures is another job that can be handled without calling an electrician. Follow these steps:

1. Turn off the power to the fixture at the circuit breaker and test the circuit with a voltage tester. It is not enough merely to turn off the wall switch.

2. Remove the cover and plate that hold the fixture to the ceiling or wall. Disassemble the fixture. Be careful not to drop the cover, and note how the parts fit together so that you can reassemble them later.

3. Once you have uncovered the electrical box, you will see three (sometimes two) wires attached to the socket mechanism. The black one is the hot wire

TROUBLESHOOTING LIGHTS

PROBLEM	CAUSE	REMEDY
Light doesn't work	Lightbulb burned out	Replace bulb
	Loose or broken wires	Repair and tighten wires
	Light switch broken	Replace light switch
	Blown fuse	Repair wires
	Socket defective	Replace socket
Light flickers	Light bulb loose	Tighten bulb
	Wire coating melted	Tape wire
	Socket defective	Replace socket
	Dimmer switch	Replace dimmer switch

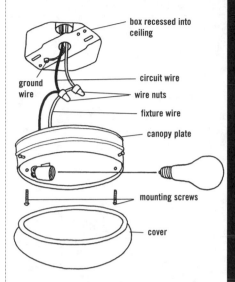

Note the arrangement of parts of an incandescent ceiling fixture, so you can reassemble it correctly. Be sure to turn off the power at the circuit breaker.

that carries the current from the circuit breaker to the fixture. The white wire takes the used current back to the breaker, where it is safely guided into the earth outside your house.

Trouble can arise, however, when a short circuit causes current to leak to adjacent metal parts. These parts become "hot" and will shock you if touched because your body serves as the path the current travels to the ground. For safety reasons, most fixtures provide a third wire, either green or bare, which grounds the equipment.

4. Check for loose or broken wires connected to the socket and tighten all connections. If you find a damaged wire, peel back the insulation and resplice the wire by twisting the ends together. Cover them carefully with electrical tape.

Repairing Cords

Many electrical shocks are caused by faulty cords. Rabbits, puppies, and mice love to chew cords, which exposes the wire and interrupts the flow of electricity. It is important to fix these problems, because in addition to causing shocks, they pose fire hazards. If you discover a frayed cord, follow these steps:

1. Unplug the cord and find a sharp kitchen knife.

2. Cut the cord on either side of the damaged wire. Next cut each of the two sections of cord down the middle about 2 inches.

3. You now have four strands of wire. Strip off about 1 inch of the plastic coating that insulates each of the four strands of wire. To do this, take a knife (or use a wire stripper) and gently go around the coating of the wire, making sure you don't cut through the wire.

4. Slip off the coating, leaving the wire exposed.

5. To reconnect the two sections of cord, splice the wires. Take a strand of wire from each section of the cord and twist them together. Do this again to reconnect the remaining wires.

6. Completely cover each set of spliced wires individually with shiny electrical tape. Then cover the entire section with tape.

7. Another solution is to connect the wires with wire nuts. This is often the simplest method. Twist the wires together, then insert them into the nut. It is important to make sure that the nut is securely fastened.

—from *The Woman's Hands-On Home Repair Guide* by Lyn Herrick

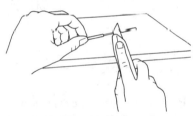

To repair a broken wire, first peel back the insulation, without cutting the wire itself.

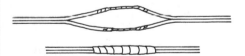

Then twist each pair of wires together and cover with electrical tape; then cover the entire splice with tape as shown above. Alternatively, you can reconnect spliced wires with wire nuts.

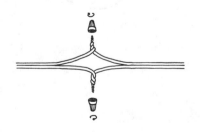

SOLAR ELECTRICITY

Photovoltaics: Generate Your Own Power from the Sun

The technology of solar electricity, or photovoltaics, begins with one of the most common elements on earth, silicon. Silicon crystals, when exposed to sunlight, become semiconductive: that is, they produce an electrical charge. Solar cells contain the electrical charge and direct it from one cell to the next. A number of cells are connected together to form a solar module, which in turn connects with others to form a panel, and the panels in turn connect to form an array.

Solar modules are extremely sensitive to light. A shadow falling on them will lessen their effectiveness. So will placing them at a less-than-optimal angle. For this reason, large solar arrays are often mounted on motorized racks that track the sun across the sky. With a small system, placing the collectors on a south-facing roof free of shading from trees and buildings, with a tilt angle equal to the local latitude, will be sufficient for good performance.

Batteries

Photovoltaic cells produce DC, or direct current. DC electricity can easily be stored in batteries for later use. Most PV modules are designed to charge 12-volt batteries, so the typical module will produce between 15.5 and 17 VDC under average conditions. In photovoltaic systems for the home, deep-cycle 12-volt lead-acid batteries, very similar to car batteries, are most often used. If they are kept well charged and not exposed to extremes of heat and cold, they will typically last three to five years. A voltage regulator installed between the solar array and the battery bank controls the flow of current and keeps the batteries from overcharging or undercharging.

Using the Power

Although direct current is a more efficient type of electrical power, the utility grid supplies alternating current, or AC, through its lines. Appliances large and small, electronic equipment, power tools, and lighting—just about everything we buy today that runs on electricity—runs on AC. There are very few electrical products available in DC versions, and they are more expensive than their mass-produced AC counterparts.

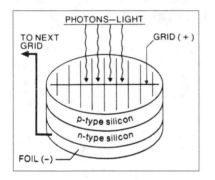

Solar Cell. This schematic diagram of a single solar cell shows silicon wafer between the upper and lower contact. This causes electron flow when light strikes the surface. The bottom of the cell is coated with foil to collect current for the next cell.

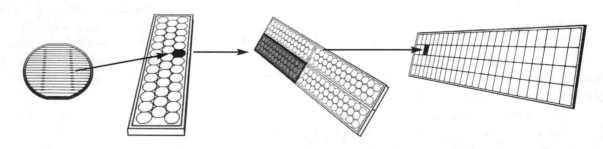

This diagram shows how a photovoltaic cell fits into a module, a panel, and an array.

The solution is to convert the DC power from the batteries to AC using an inverter. Inverters are designed not only to sustain a constant low-level demand for power, but also to respond quickly to a "surge load," which can occur when a large AC motor starts up, or when several appliances are turned on at the same time. Certain inverters can sometimes cause interference with electronic equipment, such as computers, televisions, and telephones. Sine wave inverters, though usually more expensive, produce AC power most compatible with these devices.

Photovoltaic Systems

One of the most attractive reasons for considering adding a photovoltaic system to your home is the ease of adding more solar modules and batteries whenever you want them. A system can have a single application, such as powering a well pump, or it can power an entire home with every convenience, depending on your needs and your budget. Photovoltaic systems for entire homes are still very expensive, but for a remote location where connecting to the utility grid would be impossible, undesirable, or too costly, a photovoltaic system would be an excellent choice. Smaller systems have worthwhile applications as well. Here and on the next pages are three possible systems to consider.

Battery Care and Maintenance

1. Always protect your eyes with goggles, your hands with rubber gloves, and wear old clothing when working on batteries.
2. Check the water level regularly and refill with distilled water only.
3. Clean the battery tops and terminals.
4. Monitor the batteries closely with a voltmeter to avoid letting the batteries run down completely.
5. Protect the batteries from freezing.
6. Keep the batteries charged, even when not used for long periods.

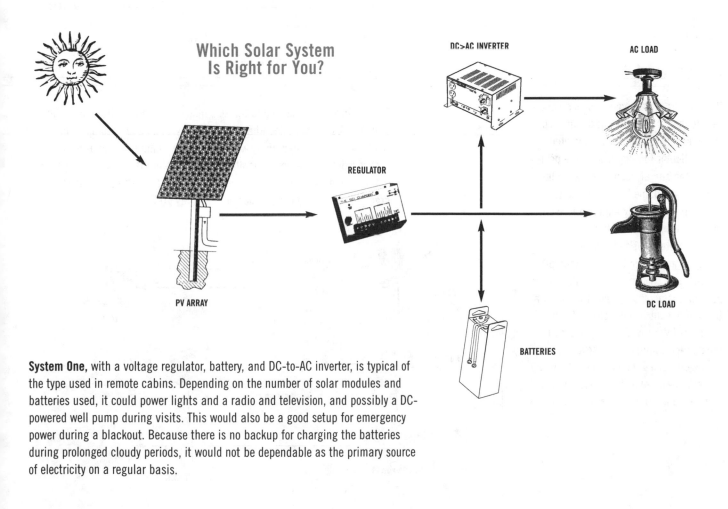

Which Solar System Is Right for You?

DC>AC INVERTER

AC LOAD

REGULATOR

PV ARRAY

BATTERIES

DC LOAD

System One, with a voltage regulator, battery, and DC-to-AC inverter, is typical of the type used in remote cabins. Depending on the number of solar modules and batteries used, it could power lights and a radio and television, and possibly a DC-powered well pump during visits. This would also be a good setup for emergency power during a blackout. Because there is no backup for charging the batteries during prolonged cloudy periods, it would not be dependable as the primary source of electricity on a regular basis.

SOLAR ELECTRICITY

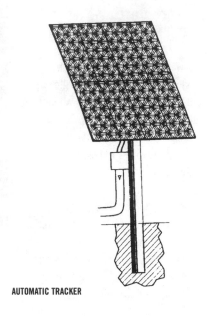

AUTOMATIC TRACKER

Getting the Best Performance from PV Modules

PV modules are expensive, so it's important to mount them for maximum electrical output. When they are oriented perpendicular (90 degrees) to the position of the sun at noon, they can collect the most available light. This angle should be seasonally adjusted for summer and winter sun positions.

For systems of eight modules or more, an automatic tracker, pictured above, turns the array to face the sun as it moves across the sky. The use of a tracking mount is most cost-effective when the PV array has clear access to the sun for a minimum of seven hours per day. Tracking mounts will add 35-50 percent power input to the system in summer, and 10-15 percent in winter.

System Two adds a generator and battery charger to the system. A propane generator is highly recommended. In the peak months for solar gain, or insolation, the generator would only be used to assist the PV system in charging the batteries during periods of cloudy weather and high demand. During times when little sun is available, the generator would do the majority of battery charging, with some assistance from the solar modules. If a large array is used, with many batteries (and you have a high tolerance for generator noise), this system can power a house entirely "off the grid."

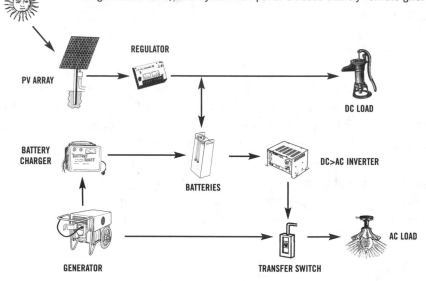

System Three remains tied to the electric company. Power from the utility grid charges the batteries whenever the PV system can't keep up. This would be a good system to try when completely going to a stand-alone system would not be economically feasible. The primary investment would initially be in batteries and an inverter. Solar modules could be added gradually, lessening dependence on the utility grid over time.

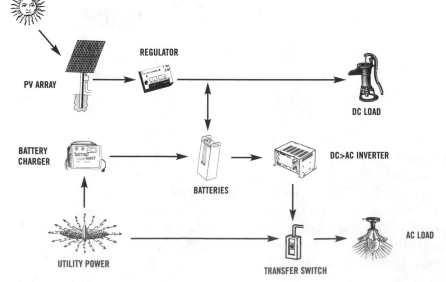

Determining Your Electrical Needs

Using electricity wisely is the key to success with a photovoltaic system. The average home squanders electricity. Look at your electric bill and see how many kilowatt-hours you use each month. As you begin considering the feasibility of generating your own power, you will become painfully aware of how expensive it will be to try to produce all the electricity you currently use yourself. The answer to reducing the cost of a photovoltaic system is to seek out ways to consume less electricity without giving up the necessities (and some of the luxuries) of life. The following chart gives some possible alternatives for the most energy-guzzling appliances in the home.

Many books and catalogs with technical information about system sizing are available. If a solar contractor specializing in photovoltaics is located in your general area, request a site evaluation. He or she will be able to help you decide if solar electricity is feasible for your home.

Combining Sun and Wind

Both photovoltaic and wind-power systems store excess power in a bank of batteries for use when the wind is calm and the sky is gray. For those seeking true energy independence, the best option may be a "hybrid" system that uses both wind and sun to generate power. In most of the United States, summer sun is bright while wind speeds are low; winter brings more wind and less light. A wind- and solar-power combination produces power throughout the widest range of conditions.

Energy-Conserving Alternatives

Switching to off-the-grid power requires a dedication to conserving electricity wherever possible. Most appliances that run on AC are designed for convenience and performance, not efficiency. To prolong battery power, replace a few or all of the power guzzlers listed below with an energy-efficient alternative.

Current Appliance	Energy-Efficient Replacement
Electric baseboard heat	Passive solar design; new gas or oil furnace
Space heating	Woodstove
Large, inefficient refrigerator	Propane refrigerator
Electric stove	Propane or natural gas range
Electric hot-water heater	Solar hot-water heating, gas hot-water heater
Electric clothes dryer	Gas dryer, or hang clothes outside
Dishwasher	Hand-wash or select energy-efficient model
Air conditioner	DC fans or select energy-efficient model
Shop equipment	Replace AC motors with DC
Water pump	A variety of DC pumps are available
Incandescent lighting	Run house lights on DC or choose fluorescent lighting

---

—contributed by Jim Sherratt, owner, Sun Energy

WIND POWER

Will Wind Work for You?

To be suitable for a wind turbine, your location should have average annual wind speeds of nine or more miles per hour. U.S. Department of Energy (DOE) wind resource maps will show you whether wind speeds in your region are generally sufficient. Actual wind resources, however, can vary within your site, so monitor the wind and choose your location with care.

Different uses will require different types of systems. Pumping water from a deep well, for example, demands very high starting torque from the rotor in order to lift the heavy load. A solid, multibladed farm windmill is designed for this. A system that is meant to supply electric power requires a fast-turning, three-bladed windwheel.

In addition to considering initial cost, installation, and maintenance, remember that local ordinances may restrict what you build. Be sure to talk to your insurer about what you should have for liability coverage to put up and own a wind turbine.

n the 1920s and '30s thousands of small wind turbines dotted the midwestern landscape, providing homes and farms with the only power available for lights and electric motors. Wind power faded as the government's Rural Electrification Administration brought electric power nationwide. The winds of change have shifted again, however, as rural homeowners and others with environmental concerns and a self-reliant bent are discovering the advantages of providing their own electrical power.

Wind energy systems don't deplete fossil fuels, and they don't pollute. While they represent a significant up-front outlay, well-planned, properly sited wind systems can stack up favorably against conventional power sources when the payback is amortized over the life of the system. Ultimately, your payoff depends upon wind availability, local electricity costs, and the system itself and how it's used.

The Wind Turbine

Home wind turbines consist of a three-blade rotor (or windwheel) and a frame-mounted generator with, in most cases, a tail to keep the rotor properly oriented. The rotor diameter determines its "swept area," or how much wind the turbine intercepts. Most turbines are equipped with automatic speed-governing systems to keep rotors from reaching excessive speeds in high wind conditions. Turbines are mounted on a tower and, in general, the higher the tower the greater the wind and the greater the turbine's power output. Towers also overcome turbulent conditions that may occur near the ground.

The accepted rule of thumb for wind turbine installation is to keep the bottom of the rotor blades at least 30 feet above any obstacle within 300 feet of the tower. Towers are either freestanding or guyed to the earth with cables. Guyed towers are cheaper but need plenty of room, as cables may extend out up to three-quarters of the tower height. Wind generators require routine maintenance, which in most cases must be performed by climbing (or convincing someone else to climb) 40 to 100 or more feet up a tower.

Like photovoltaic systems, wind turbines produce DC (direct current). If you want to run a standard AC appliance like a refrigerator, you will need a device called a synchronous inverter to transform the current.

Though many who are off the grid are loath to use fossil fuels, the addition of a gas, diesel, or propane engine generator can enhance wind- or sun-only and hybrid systems. Battery banks are usually sized to handle one to three days of power consumption without substantial recharging. A generator, which can take over when you're in darkness and/or becalmed, will recharge low batteries and can reduce the wind generator output or the number of photovoltaic modules and batteries a system requires. Depending upon your location and system, a fossil fuel generator can bridge an energy gap that might be quite expensive to fill using renewable resources.

FOSSIL-FUEL GENERATORS

Choosing a Generator

Because of their noise and exhaust fumes, generators should be located outdoors in a shelter. Generators are available that monitor battery power and start and stop automatically as needed. Other features to weigh are durability, reliability, power output (those rated in the 4- to 6-kilowatt range are suitable for most off-the-grid applications), and noisiness. A sturdy, well-made generator that does its work (relatively) quietly with minimal intervention on your part will bring years of comfort and joy.

Gasoline generators. Although they are the most common generators in use, gas generators have a couple of noteworthy disadvantages: Gasoline is a hassle to transport and use, and gasoline engines as a rule need more maintenance than do your other choices.

Diesel generators. Diesel engines sip fuel and enjoy a reputation for long life and low maintenance costs. On the other hand, they are very loud and may spew nasty pollutants. Diesel fuel is only marginally more fun to transport and handle than gasoline, and in some areas can be more difficult to obtain.

Propane generators. Propane may be the most logical generator fuel choice for off-the-gridders, especially for those who may already be heating, cooking, and keeping food cold with propane appliances. Most gasoline generators can be converted to run on propane, and though they may cost you a little in power output, propane-fueled engines burn cleaner and last significantly longer than gasoline-powered engines. Natural gas is another excellent option.

Getting Going with a Generator

- Buy a product made by a reputable manufacturer, and be sure there is an authorized service facility in your area.
- A generator is only as reliable as its engine. A cast-iron engine block will usually last longer than one made of aluminum.
- Be sure you can start the engine easily. Some units have electric starting, some have recoil, and some have both.
- Your unit should be protected by a circuit breaker to prevent overloading.
- Most units hold 1 to 5 gallons of fuel and will run 2 to 5 hours on a tank.
- If the generator will serve as a home emergency power system, you will need a transfer switch so you can switch from utility to generator power.
- Let the engine run for an hour once a month to keep the unit in good condition.
- Follow the manufacturer's instructions for regular changing of oil, fuel, and water.
- Wipe dust and dirt off the generator periodically to prevent overheating during use.

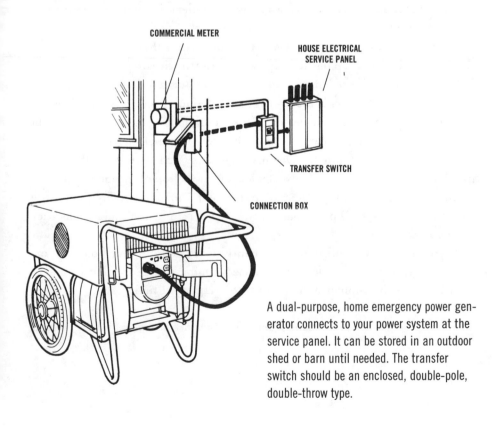

A dual-purpose, home emergency power generator connects to your power system at the service panel. It can be stored in an outdoor shed or barn until needed. The transfer switch should be an enclosed, double-pole, double-throw type.

WHAT TO DO WHEN THE POWER FAILS

Light Up Your Life!

If you take these suggestions, the light you save could be your own:

- Clean bulbs and fixtures. Dirt and grime obstruct light, so keep bulbs, fixtures, and shades clean.
- Position your lamps. Make sure lamps are placed to make the most efficient use of their light.
- Check your lamp shades. Many decorative shades bottle up light or direct it where you don't need it. Light-colored, translucent shades are best for releasing light.
- Use fewer bulbs. You can often replace a number of low-wattage bulbs with one high-wattage bulb.
- Reduce wattage. Use lower-wattage bulbs in halls, vestibules, and other places where no close-up work or reading occurs.
- Use fluorescent lighting. These lights consume one-quarter to one-fifth the amount of electricity as their incandescent counterparts.
- Change habits. When leaving a room even for a short time, turn off the lights.
- Use daylight. Schedule activities requiring good lighting for the daytime whenever possible.

—adapted from *547 Easy Ways to Save Energy in Your Home* by Roger Albright

A Blown Circuit

Sometimes a fuse blows or a circuit turns off automatically, causing loss of electrical power in your home. This happens to prevent fire from occurring. When it happens, you must determine whether the problem is caused by an overloaded circuit or a short circuit. The general rule is that an overloaded circuit will take several seconds or a minute to blow, while a short circuit will trip the circuit immediately.

Overloaded circuit. If you plug in too many appliances in one area, the circuit breaker or fuse box will automatically shut off the electric current to that area. To locate and restore an overloaded circuit, follow these steps:

1. Look inside the service panel. If you have a circuit breaker system, check to see if the switch to the relevant area of the house is between the ON and OFF positions. If so, go back and unplug all appliances in that area. If you have a fuse box, you will see glass-topped fuses. A blown fuse will have a broken wire or blackened top. Unplug all appliances in the area of the house serviced by the blown fuse.

2. When you are certain that the circuit is not overloaded, flip the circuit breaker to the OFF position and then to the ON position. Replace a blown fuse by unscrewing the broken one and inserting a fuse of equal amperage. (The number is printed on the top of the fuse.)

3. When you have returned power to the particular area of your home, plug in each appliance one at a time. This will enable you to determine the load capacity of the circuit. If the first appliance you turn on triggers the circuit breaker or blows the fuse, you have a serious problem that will require the services of an electrician.

Short circuit. If you suspect a short circuit, follow these steps:

1. Check all cords and plugs for exposed or frayed wires.

2. If you discover a problem, try the circuit again or replace the fuse, leaving the lamp or appliance with the damaged cord unplugged. If that solves the problem, repair or replace the device. If the circuit fails again, the short may be in the house wiring, a problem that must be fixed by an electrician.

Turning power off and on. One main power switch controls all the electricity in the house. This switch is usually located at the top of the circuit breaker. If you are fixing something electrical and do not know which circuit controls that area of the house, flip the main switch to OFF to turn off all the electricity in your house.

If you need to shut off power frequently to an area of your home to conserve energy, it is a good idea to purchase a timing switch for that area. The water heater is the appliance that most often requires a timing switch.

—from *The Woman's Hands-On Home Repair Guide* by Lyn Herrick

In an Emergency

It may be romantic to eat by candlelight, but the romance quickly dies when the power fails and stays off, especially when it includes frozen pipes, a flooded basement, and the loss of a freezerful of food. Such catastrophes can cost thousands of dollars. If electric service to your home was interrupted, would it be a calamity or an adventure for your family?

The best way to prevent a power outage from becoming a catastrophe is to plan ahead. Locate your main electrical box and be sure everything is clearly labeled. Know which appliances should be unplugged during an outage to prevent damage. Keep a list. Choose a lamp to be your "tell-tale" and label the switch so you will know which position is ON and which is OFF. When a power outage occurs, you may not remember which lights and appliances were on. During an outage, leave this lamp on at all times. It will tell you when power is restored.

Power outages due to snowstorms, sleet, hurricanes, and other natural disasters are often preceded by a warning. In such cases, heat stews, soups, beans, spaghetti, and other one-pot meals and pour them into insulated Thermos bottles, where they will keep warm for up to 12 hours.

Two- and three-burner Coleman stoves that burn white gas and stoves that use disposable propane cylinders are available for a modest investment. Make sure you have pots that will fit the stove. All of these stoves should be used in a well-ventilated space because they consume oxygen.

Sterno stoves or canned-heat burners can be used safely indoors. Pry off the cover and touch the contents with a lighted match. Extinguish the flame by sliding the cover on top of the flame. Once the can has cooled, secure the cover.

Charcoal grills and hibachi stoves must be used outside the house. The fuel gives off carbon monoxide, which can be fatal in a closed room. Three or four briquettes in a small grill will generate enough heat to cook a simple meal.

Always keep a flashlight handy, perhaps one per family member, in each bedroom, and a large four-battery flashlight in the kitchen. Have spare batteries and bulbs available.

Kerosene lamps yield better light than flashlights or candles, but they can be dangerous because kerosene is highly flammable. Keep wicks trimmed and chimneys cleaned. On 1 quart of fuel, a kerosene lamp will burn 10 to 12 hours.

Safety Tips

- Unplug all major appliances to prevent them from becoming damaged when the power is restored. Unplug all lights except one so you know when the power returns.
- Have emergency telephone numbers listed and kept in an accessible location near the telephone.
- Review emergency plans with everyone living in your house.
- Be sure your supplies of fuel and medication are out of reach of children.

—from *What to Do When the Power Fails* by Mary Twitchell

Preparing to Evacuate

If you must evacuate your house during a natural disaster, follow these steps:

- Turn off power at the circuit breaker box.
- Drain water pipes and heater.
- Pour antifreeze into all water traps.
- Store canned and bottled foods on inside walls to prevent freezing.
- Take pets, plants, essential medications, and valuables with you.
- If possible, check your house daily.

—from *What to Do When the Power Fails*

7

BASIC HOME IMPROVEMENTS

HARDWOOD FLOORS • VINYL FLOORING • CERAMIC TILE • CARPETING • PAINTING • WALLPAPERING WALLS AND CEILINGS • WINDOWS AND DOORS

Often people assume that they are incapable of solving a problem, writes Lyn Herrick, nationally known as Mrs. Fix-It, author of The Woman's Hands-On Home Repair Guide. *But once they see a friend fix something, they want to learn to do it themselves. Go into each project knowing you can do it, she advises, laugh at your mistakes, and you'll be amazed at what you can accomplish.*

Martha's father, Aulton, was raised on a small cotton farm in West Texas, far enough from town to make it easier to fix it yourself than to hire help. For fun on rainy days he taught Martha to take apart radios and then reassemble them. As a result we've saved a good deal over the years by substituting (her!) time for money. When you figure hourly rates can reach $50 for skilled help, it's always worth a try! She's shown us that wallpapering could be fun, leaky faucets could be tamed, and frozen pipes could be thawed. As a result, our children have all become do-it-yourselfers. A premiere do-it-yourselfer, Lyn Herrick, starts off this chapter from the ground up—with flooring.

—John Storey

Whether you plan to refinish a wood floor, install tile, or lay vinyl, it's important to understand floor construction. Most home floors have three layers—a subfloor attached to the floor joists, an underlayment laid over the subfloor, and the finished flooring.

It helps to have the subfloor as solid as possible. Concrete is the best surface. A wood subfloor is also fine, but it should be covered with an underlayment of plywood. Unpadded vinyl works well, too, if it is glued firmly in place. If you want to add new flooring to a room, you can often put it directly over the old flooring if the latter is in good shape. The old flooring or subfloor must be free of dirt, because dirt weakens the adhesive bond. It is also necessary to fill in all cracks and holes and to nail down loose boards.

It is easier and faster to keep the old flooring, but this does add height to the new floor. If the old flooring has badly deteriorated, either remove it or place a new underlayment over it. Either way, you will need to add a new underlayment. The two most common types

Gasket. An elastic strip forming a seal between two parts

Jamb. The top and sides of a door or window

Joists. The horizontal beams that make up floor framing, usually 2 x 6s, 2 x 8s, or 2 x 10s, laid edgewise at 16-inch intervals. They are supported by the house foundation at one end and by a carrying beam on the other

Shoe molding. A molding placed around the perimeter of a room where the floor and baseboard meet

Subflooring. The bottom layer of flooring, laid over the floor joists

Underlayment. A layer of flooring placed over subflooring to strengthen it

of underlayment are plywood and hardboard, which come in both 4 x 4- and 4 x 8-foot sheets.

The secret to a good job is to arrange the wood sheets in a staggered pattern, so the joints of adjacent sheets are not perfectly aligned. Leave a ⅟₃₂- to ⅛-inch crack between each sheet to allow for expansion. Use resin-coated 4d nails to fasten the sheets to the subfloor. Space the nails about 6 inches apart throughout the entire surface.

Four Kinds of Wooden Flooring

There are four primary kinds of wooden flooring. **Strip flooring** is by far the most common. It is available in widths of 1½ inches to 2¼ inches and thicknesses of ⅜ inch, ½ inch, and ²⁵⁄₃₂ inch. The lumber has been milled so there is a tongue along one edge and a groove along the other; the boards are laid in a random pattern of end joints, and the strips interlock as they are laid tongue to groove. The interlocking prevents the floor from moving or squeaking. The strips, 2 feet to 16 feet in length, are nailed every 10 to 12 inches through the tongue at a 50-degree angle; the nail heads are countersunk and are invisible in the finished floor because they are covered by the groove of the next board.

Plank flooring is also tongue and groove; the lumber comes in random widths of 3 to 9 inches. Originally, the planks were pegged into the subfloor; today, the pieces are bored, the screws countersunk, and the holes plugged to simulate the wooden pegs.

Block flooring, which looks like parquet, is made up of short strips of hardwood that have been glued together in a rectangle or square. It is sold in tongue-and-groove squares of 6 x 6 inches, 9 x 9 inches, or 11¼ x 11¼ inches. The strips are usually oak and are fastened together. Then the blocks are glued with the grains at right angles to the surrounding ones.

Softwood flooring is less costly to install and less wear resistant than hardwood flooring. Softwoods are easily marred and will show scratches wherever furniture is carelessly moved. They are best used in bedrooms or closets where the traffic is light. Softwood floors can be sanded, but because the wood is less dense than hardwood, they soon become too thin to resand.

—from *Restoring Hardwood Floors* by Mary Twitchell

Inside a Floor

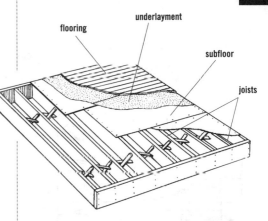

A typical floor has the structure shown above.

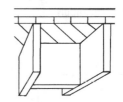 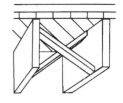

Today solid bridging, as shown at left, is used to brace and strengthen weak or twisted floor joists, although older homes often have the crisscross bridging shown at right.

Tongue-and-groove flooring has an interlocking pattern.

HARDWOOD FLOORS

Removing Molding

To prepare the floor for refinishing, remove the shoe molding around the perimeter of the room. If you intend to reuse the molding, follow the steps below. First, run the blade of a matt knife between the molding and the baseboard to separate the paint and make removal easier. Number the pieces as you go so you can renail in the same spot.

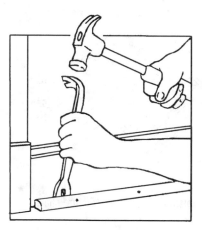

Use a pry bar to remove shoe molding. Work slowly along the edge, applying pressure at each nail site.

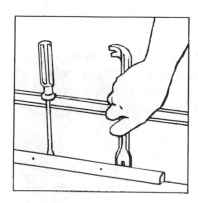

A screwdriver holds the loosened piece away from the baseboard.

Sanding Wood Floors

Unless your floor is too thin to withstand sanding, you'll need to sand before refinishing. If the floor is painted but carries only a thin coat, you can sand right through the paint.

Prepare for sanding your floor by first removing all furniture and cleaning the floor. Countersink all nail heads, remove shoe molding, open windows for ventilation, and close adjoining doors. Seal off hallways with plastic, and remove curtains or protect them with plastic bags. Also remove floor registers and any radiators in the room. If they are difficult to disconnect, you can work around them.

You will need an upright sander for the open spaces and an edger (or disk sander) for cutting in along baseboards. These are available at rental centers, which will also supply you with ample sandpaper. Before leaving the store, be sure the sanders are in working order and ask the clerk to show you how to mount the sandpaper. Other tools you may need include a hammer, chisel, paint scraper, and a hand-held finish sander.

The drum sander. Drum sanders are heavy, noisy, and create a mini dust bowl. You will want ear protectors and a face mask. After mounting the sander with medium or coarse sandpaper, begin in one corner of the room. For parquet floors, use only a fine grade of sandpaper, because the coarser grades are too abrasive.

Position the sander to go in the direction of the grain. Rock the sander then turn it on and let the motor rev up. Slowly bring the drum into contact with the floor. It will pull you forward; hold it in check so you move at a slow, steady pace throughout the process.

As you reach the other side of the room, tilt the sander back from the floor. Move the electric cord so you won't trip on it when you walk backward. As you retrace your steps, lower the drum and pass over what you have already sanded. Be sure to rock the sander back at the beginning and end of each pass. The sandpaper will gouge the floor if you lower the sander too quickly or raise it too slowly.

Keep the sander in constant motion; otherwise, it will dig troughs that will be visible once the floor is sealed. As you move to an unsanded area, overlap the previous pass by 2 or 3 inches. If you are making no progress with the coarse sandpaper because the floor is badly cupped, make diagonal passes.

Continue until the entire floor is done. You won't get closer to the baseboards than 6 inches. This border must be done with the edger. When you want to stop sanding, turn off the machine but keep the drum tilted away from the floor until the belt stops turning.

The edger. Edgers are used to sand edges, corners, doorways, closets, around radiators, and other places you cannot reach with a drum sander.

Grasp the edger firmly with two hands before turning it on. Then move the edger in a semicircular pattern. It will be sanding across the grain, and the circular action will tend to leave ring marks on the floor. Therefore, don't press down on the machine or let it linger; otherwise the swirl marks will show once the floor is sealed.

- drum sander (upright sander)
- edger (disk sander)
- hand-held or electric hand sander
- natural-bristle paintbrush
- long-handled roller
- putty knife
- floor polisher
- hammer
- chisel
- paint scraper
- vacuum cleaner
- drill (if needed for loose boards)

Wear a face mask and ear protectors when using a sander.

When you're finished, repeat the process with both the edger and the drum sander, using a medium- and then a fine-grit sandpaper. Empty the dust bags as necessary. The dust is very combustible and should be disposed of carefully.

Sand hard-to-get areas by hand. A paint scraper should remove most of the old finish. Sand with a hand-held sandpaper block or an electric hand sander.

Vacuum the floor thoroughly with the brush attachment. Then wipe it down with a rag moistened with turpentine. The floor is now ready to be stained, varnished, shellacked, or urethaned.

Stripping Wood Floors

Floors that are too thin to be sanded must be stripped. Regular household ammonia and steel wool work best, although the fumes may irritate your eyes and sinuses. Be sure to open all windows. You may want to use an electric fan set to vent out.

Wear gloves when using the ammonia. Pour a cupful directly on the floor and let it stand for a few minutes. Then rub the ammonia with the grain of the wood. Once the old finish begins to dissolve, wipe off the residue with rags. After you have finished, let the floor dry for a few days. If the first application of ammonia doesn't completely dissolve the old finish, you may have to repeat the process.

Bleach stains out of the wood with laundry bleach. Mix 1 part bleach to 10 parts water. Apply to the entire floor with a mop. Wait 5 minutes, then neutralize with white vinegar or ammonia. Mop dry. If there is fuzz from the wood fibers, scrub the floor with steel wool. Let dry, then vacuum.

Wood flooring with a heavy accumulation of paint also needs stripping. Apply a paint remover first. This liquid is painted on with a brush. The remover softens the paint, which you can then remove with a scraper. This is a very messy and time-consuming process. After it is completed, you will probably need to sand the floor to remove any paint that remains.

—from *Restoring Hardwood Floors* by Mary Twitchell
and *The Woman's Hands-On Home Repair Guide* by Lyn Herrick

Edgers are used to sand places you cannot reach with the drum sander.

Fixing Loose Boards

Nails may work loose when floorboards shrink or the edges cup. Resecure these boards by predrilling holes with a bit that is slightly smaller than the diameter of the annular-ring flooring nails. Nail through the warped area into the sub-flooring below. This forces the high points back into position.

Drive the nails in pairs. Angle the nails and drive them in opposite directions for the best grip. Sink the nail heads with a nail set and fill the holes with wood putty matched to the wood of the floor. Space the nails at least ½ inch in from the edges of the floorboard, so you don't crack the wood.

—from *Restoring Hardwood Floors*

HARDWOOD FLOORS

Repairing Squeaky Floors

Squeaky floors result from two boards rubbing against each other or a board moving against a nail. If you have a basement with exposed floor joists, you can probably fix the problem.

1. Begin by examining the floor from above for any loose nails. Pound them in.
2. Locate the squeak. Have a friend walk over your floor while you listen in the basement. Mark the spot where you hear the noise, then check for gaps between the floor joists and subflooring.
3. If you find a small gap, hammer a wedgelike wooden shim that is covered with glue into the gap.
4. For longer gaps, take a 2 x 4 about twice as long as the gap and glue the top edge against the subflooring. Force the 2 x 4 tightly against the subflooring and nail the 2 x 4 to the floor joist.

If you find long gaps in one or more joists, you should consult a building contractor. It may be that you need additional support for your flooring system.

—from *The Woman's Hands-On Home Repair Guide* by Lyn Herrick

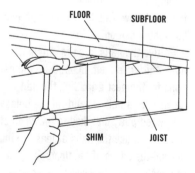

To alleviate squeaking, tap a wood shim, covered with glue, between the subfloor and the joist.

Refinishing Hardwood Floors

If your floor has been stripped, wait until it is thoroughly dry before applying a finish. If the floor is freshly sanded, apply the finish as soon as possible. An untreated surface begins to absorb moisture immediately.

You can apply a surface finish or a penetrating finish. Penetrating finishes seal the wood fibers and produce a velvety sheen. They are wear resistant, easy to apply, and easy to repair. The finish resists stains and does not chip or crack. A surface finish (varnish, shellac, or polyurethane) creates a durable surface film on top of the wood. It protects the floor from moisture and scratches.

Choose your finish depending on the use of the room. Floors that carry heavy traffic or are exposed to frequent spills (kitchens, for example) should be sealed with a surface film. Of the floor finishes, polyurethane provides the hardest and most durable protective film.

Penetrating Finishes

Stain. Light stains emphasize the beauty of the wood's grain. Oil stains give the most natural finish, although most dry darker than the original wood color. Experiment on a sample of your flooring. You can control the color by the length of time you let the stain penetrate the floor.

Stain should be applied only over itself or on raw wood. Apply liberally with a brush, cloth, or roller; remove excess with a clean cloth and let dry before applying a second coat. Make sure the stain you choose is compatible with the protective finish you plan to apply. You can apply polyurethane, shellac, varnish, or lacquer after 8 hours.

Sealer. A penetrating sealer is applied with a rag or brush (squeegee or lamb's-wool applicator). Wear rubber gloves. Use a rag to spread the sealer along the grain with long, sweeping strokes.

Apply generously over a strip 2 to 3 feet wide. Allow the sealer to penetrate the wood for 10 to 15 minutes. A helper can follow you with a couple of rags to mop up the excess. You can simultaneously apply the second strip of sealer. Always keep your knees on untreated wood.

Let the sealer dry for 8 hours, then apply matching wood putty to cracks and small holes with a putty knife. To ensure a color match, make your own putty by mixing a paste of sawdust from the final sanding with enough sealer to create a thick paste. Remove excess putty, let dry, and hand-sand with fine sandpaper.

Buff the sealed wood with a floor polisher fitted with a steel wool pad. This will eliminate puddles in the sealer coat. Hand-scour hard-to-reach areas with steel wool pads. Vacuum the room carefully and go over it with a tack cloth (a rag moistened with turpentine).

Surface Finishes

Polyurethane. Polyurethane seals the floor with plastic. It provides a rugged, clear, water-resistant surface. However, it should not be used on softwood floors. Polyurethane comes in dull, satin, and high-gloss finishes. High gloss is generally used in offices where there is constant daily traffic. It offers the greatest resistance to wear.

A room must be free of sawdust particles before the urethane is applied. Ensure that there is plenty of cross-ventilation during application and drying times. Apply at temperatures between 60° and 90°F. You may have to turn on the house heat to hasten the drying process.

Stir the urethane, but don't shake it. Use a natural-bristle brush to apply it on corners, edges, and hard-to-reach areas. For the main part of the floor, use a long-handled roller. Work along the grain, applying the finish slowly and carefully. It is easy to miss spots in the floor or leave bubbles in the urethane.

Wait 8 hours, or until the finish has dried. To test for dryness, press your thumb down on the surface. If it leaves a thumbprint, the first primer/sealer coat isn't ready. Once it has dried, buff the floor with steel wool or sand lightly. Apply a second finish coat of urethane and let it dry.

If the room is a heavily trafficked area, apply a third coat. Let the final coat dry. Then replace the shoe molding, pipe collars for plumbing and radiators, floor registers, and furniture.

Varnish. Varnishes produce a deep luster and are glossier than other finishes. They are less expensive than urethane, but darken with age and show scratches easily. Before applying a varnish, vacuum the floor thoroughly. During application, close any forced-air furnace ducts. Apply two or three coats with a brush, allowing each coat to dry for 24 hours. If bubbles appear as the varnish is spread, apply more varnish and continue to brush until the bubbles are worked out.

Shellac. Shellac will not darken the color of wood. It provides only light protection and should not be used where moisture or stains are a problem. However, shellac is economical and durable.

Apply two or three coats; let dry for 2 hours between coats and sand lightly before applying the next coat.

Wax. Wax can be applied over varnish or shellac once the finish is thoroughly dry. It can also be used alone if you want the floors to look as natural as possible. Do not use wax on polyurethaned floors—it will preclude adding an additional coat of polyurethane after the finish begins to wear.

Apply a thin coat of wax with a soft cloth. Let dry before applying a second coat. Polish by hand with a soft cloth or with an electric polisher.

—from *Restoring Hardwood Floors* by Mary Twitchell

Hardwood Floor Care Tips

- Sweep or vacuum frequently to remove dust, crumbs, and grit that can get ground into the finish.
- Check the soles of your shoes for stones and pebbles before walking on hardwood floors—or better yet, leave shoes at the door.
- Wipe up spills immediately, wash with cool water, and dry with a soft cloth. Do not allow water spots to air-dry.
- Clean floors weekly if possible. Start by vacuuming, then follow with a bucket of cool water and a mop. Hot water should be avoided, as it will make the top layer of finish just tacky enough to set the dirt.
- If a stronger solution is needed, use a very small amount of a mild detergent. For very dirty floors, gradually strengthen the cleaning solution. Avoid cleaners with ammonia.
- If you are uncertain about the effect a cleaner will have on the floor's finish, test it first in an inconspicuous location.

—from *Restoring Hardwood Floors*

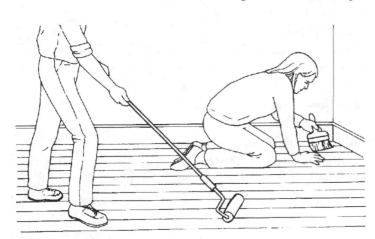

The Fine Points of Poly

Before a polyurethane finish can be applied, the room must be free of sawdust particles. For example, do not sweep the floor just before applying the urethane: The sawdust particles will settle back down and show up in the finished floor. Apply polyurethane with a bristle brush for edges and a roller for open areas.

VINYL FLOORING

Tips for Success

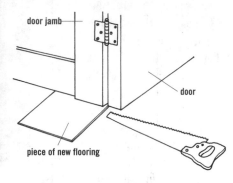

Slide a piece of the new flooring under the door jamb. If necessary, trim the door jamb so the flooring fits underneath.

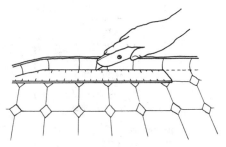

Trim the overlap with a sharp utility knife and a straightedge for a guide.

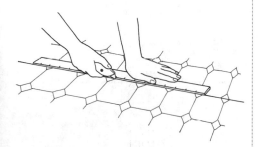

Align the pattern carefully where two sheets create a seam.

Laying Vinyl Flooring

Vinyl flooring is made of polyvinyl chloride and comes in both tile and sheet forms. It is sometimes confused with linoleum, a product no longer manufactured in the United States. Although some vinyl floors look like linoleum, they are much improved in terms of durability and resistance to wear.

In its sheet form, the flooring comes in three types. Sheet vinyl is solid vinyl. It is durable, and because it is made from pure vinyl, it tends to be the most expensive type. Unfortunately, it is difficult to lay. Cushioned sheet vinyl comes with foam backing. Several grades are available. Roto sheet vinyl is made from a cellulose felt or mineral fiber base with a thin coat of vinyl for its cover. Although easy to lay and relatively inexpensive, it tends to be less durable.

Solid vinyl tiles have the same characteristics and composition as sheet vinyl. Vinyl composition tile is the most popular. It is durable, resistant to wear, and easy to install if you select the adhesive-backed variety.

When you've selected your flooring, follow these steps:

1. Prepare the subfloor by filling in all cracks and holes, nailing down loose boards, and cleaning it thoroughly.
2. Gently pry up the baseboard so you do not damage it.
3. Try sliding a piece of the new flooring under the door jamb. If it doesn't fit, trim the door jamb so the new flooring fits under it.
4. Cut and trim the vinyl sheets to fit your floor. The initial cut should leave each sheet with an additional 3 inches on all sides. The overlap will curl up along each wall when the sheet is laid out on the floor. Put a piece of plywood under the vinyl when cutting to protect the floor underneath.
5. To trim the overlap, create a crease along the wall. Using a sharp utility knife and a straightedge for a guide, cut the vinyl sheet along the crease. When trimming, leave a small gap (about ⅛ inch) between the flooring and the wall to allow for expansion.
6. Roll up half of your fitted sheet and apply glue according to the manufacturer's directions. Apply the adhesive with a notched trowel, and leave the edge(s) that will be along the seam unglued.

VINYL FLOOR TOOLBOX

- hammer
- crosscut or power saw
- pry bar
- utility knife

- notched trowel
- metal straightedge
- putty knife
- iron

7. Press the sheet into place and make sure that the flooring fits evenly up to the edge of the wall. Repeat this process for the other half of the sheet.

8. Once the flooring is glued in place, take a 2 x 4 about a yard in length. With a towel underneath it to protect your new flooring, move the 2 x 4 up and down the entire floor while applying downward pressure. This will ensure that the vinyl is properly bonded to the subfloor.

9. If your floor is wider than the vinyl sheet, align two sheets together by creating a seam. As you glue the first sheet to the subfloor, leave several inches of space without glue where the seam will be located. Slide the new sheet under the one you have just glued and match the patterns exactly. Place a metal straightedge along the edge of the top sheet. Using the straightedge as a guide, cut the bottom sheet with a sharp utility knife. Fold back the top sheet, remove the bottom strip, apply glue to the subfloor, and press the two sheets into place.

10. Wash any excess glue from your new flooring with warm water.

11. When reattaching the baseboard, leave a small space between it and the floor to allow the vinyl to expand and contract.

12. Follow the manufacturer's instructions regarding drying time for the glue, and save the excess vinyl for later repairs.

Repairing Vinyl Flooring

Over time, vinyl flooring can become damaged by holes, tears, and blisters. Large holes should be patched.

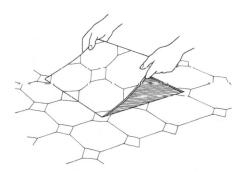

Use a utility knife to cut out the damaged area, then replace it with a clean new piece.

1. Select a replacement patch that closely matches the pattern of the damaged piece.

2. Take a pencil and draw a square around the damaged area.

3. Using a straightedge to guide you, cut along the line with a sharp utility knife.

4. If the vinyl is not glued to the subfloor, lift out the damaged section, spread glue onto the subfloor, and press the patch into place. Wipe off any excess glue and weight down the patch evenly for at least 24 hours.

5. If the vinyl is glued, you can often peel it up by shoving a putty knife underneath the flooring. If that doesn't work, use an iron to weaken the glue. Place the iron on a damp cloth rather than placing it directly on the vinyl. Lift out the vinyl, spread glue on the subfloor, and press the patch into place.

6. For vinyl that is torn, lift the torn section, spread new glue, and press the torn section back into place. Cover the damaged area with a weighted board for a minimum of 24 hours.

7. For a blister, flatten it by cutting through its center. You now have a tear, which can be fixed as just outlined.

—From *The Woman's Hands-On Home Repair Guide* by Lyn Herrick

CERAMIC TILE

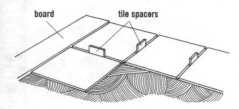

Align tiles against a board, and place tile spacers between the pieces as you lay them.

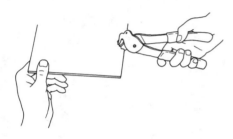

Use tile-cutting pliers to trim out small pieces in tile to fit around doors and pipes.

Laying Ceramic Tile

Ceramic tile is attractive, moisture resistant, tough, and easily cleaned. Laying the floor yourself is time-consuming, but you will save lots of money. Tile comes in many styles, colors, and sizes. The most common sizes are 4-, 6-, 8-, and 12-inch squares. The larger the tile, the easier the installation, but you will have to live with it, so choose what looks best.

Tile also comes in two surfaces. Unglazed tile is hardened clay with the color and texture of natural clay. Glazed tile has a smooth, shiny coating. It is easier to clean but slippery when wet, which means it may not be the best choice for your bathroom. When purchasing tile, give the dimensions of your room to a salesperson. Remember to purchase extra tile for later repairs and in case you end up breaking a few.

In addition, purchase plastic spacers, glue, and grout. You will also need rubber gloves and safety glasses.

Begin laying tile by dividing the room into four equal sections.
1. Find the midpoint for each wall and mark off the room into four quadrants using a chalk line.
2. Begin laying the tile, without gluing it, at the midpoint of the room (the point where the lines intersect) and work within one quadrant from the midpoint to the outer walls.
3. Place plastic spacers between each tile so the amount of space between them is the same. You can also use a board to make sure the tiles are aligned.
4. Do this for all four sections of the room.

There are advantages to laying out the tiles before gluing them. If the space along the wall for the last tile is an inch or less, it will be very difficult to cut the tile without splitting it. You can correct this problem by moving the chalk line dividing the room 3 inches closer to the wall.

Cutting tile. The best way to cut floor tile is with a wet saw, which is an expensive tool. If all your tiles are laid out, you can mark the tiles that need to be cut and take them to a building supply store. If they have a wet saw, they will usually cut them for free. If that doesn't work, find out where you can rent such a saw. Wear safety glasses when using it.

To cut around a door frame, pencil out the area on the tile that needs to be cut. Use tile-cutting pliers to slowly chip away at the section to be removed. Again, wear safety goggles. For fitting around a pipe, plan to have the tile come up to the edge of the pipe. Mark the area along the edge to be removed with a pencil, then chip away small bits of tile with the tile-cutting pliers.

Gluing tile. When you're ready to glue the tile, follow these steps:
1. Pick up the tile in one quadrant of the room.
2. Apply glue to the subfloor with a notched spreader in an area of about 1 square yard at a time.
3. Starting at the midpoint of the room, press the tile into the adhesive and insert the spacers. Keep the tiles in a straight row and at the same height.

FOR LAYING TILE
- chalk line
- straightedge
- wet saw (rent if possible)
- tile-cutting pliers
- notched spreader
- plastic spreader
- level (if needed)

FOR REPAIRING TILE
- straight-slot screwdriver
- ice pick
- hair dryer or iron
- pry bar
- putty knife

4. After completing each square-yard section, balance a 2 x 4 on the tiles or use a level to check for height. Push down any tiles that are too high.

5. Check the adhesive manufacturer's instructions for drying time. Drying time is usually a minimum of 24 hours.

6. Once the adhesive has dried, fill the cracks with grout. Pour a generous amount of grout onto the tiles and spread it with a special plastic spreader. Make sure to work it into all the seams.

7. Remove the excess grout as you go, then clean the entire surface with a damp sponge. Thoroughly sponge the tiles again the next day.

8. Grout creates a stronger bond if it is kept damp for two or three days. Cover the floor with plastic while your tile is drying to seal in the moisture.

—from *The Woman's Hands-On Home Repair Guide* by Lyn Herrick

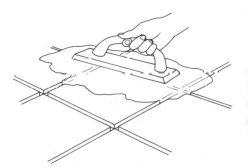

Pour a generous amount of grout onto the tiles, then spread it with a plastic spreader, working the grout into all seams.

Repairing Tile

If the problem is a small crack, it can easily be fixed with a ceramic tile repair kit from a hardware store. Read the directions to make sure the kit contains the right mix of paints to match your tile. Using the same directions, mix the epoxy to fill in the cracks.

If the tile must be removed, your project becomes more difficult, because tile is generally glued to the subfloor.

1. Begin by removing the grout with a screwdriver or ice pick. Be careful not to cut yourself or damage adjacent tiles.

2. Soften the glue with heat. You can do this with your hair dryer or by working the tile with a medium-hot iron. Protect the tile with a damp cloth and avoid heating adjacent tiles.

3. Slip a putty knife under the tile and pry up. If that does not do the job, lift up with a pry bar. It is a good idea to use a 2 x 4 for leverage and to protect the adjacent tile.

4. Once the tile is removed, use a putty knife to scrape away as much of the old glue as possible.

5. Apply a new coat of adhesive and insert a new tile that matches your pattern. If the new tile is a little too large, sand the edges. Cover the new tile with a board and a light weight while the glue dries. If you are gluing the new tile to a vertical wall, hold it in place with strips of masking tape.

6. Complete the project by applying grout to the seams after the specified drying time.

CARPETING

Tips for Success

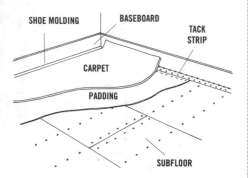

Place tack strips around the entire perimeter of the room, about ½" from the wall.

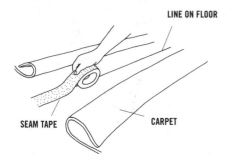

Run seam tape between pieces of carpet.

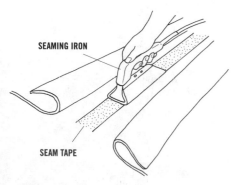

Melt glue with a seaming iron.

Installing Carpet

You can install carpets with only a few tools, but carpets are heavy, so it helps to do this project with at least one friend. In addition, without expensive tools it is difficult to stretch the carpet tightly to the wall. You may have to settle for good, rather than perfect, results.

Carpets can be bonded to a subfloor with glue, double-sided tape, or tack strips. Glue is not necessary for most residential situations. Double-sided tape often does not provide an adequate bond. This leaves tack strips.

Tack strips are narrow wood slats with tacks sticking up from them. They are placed alongside each wall about ½ inch from the wall. If you have a wooden subfloor, it is easy to nail these strips into place. If you are working with a concrete subfloor, the job is more difficult. You can nail the strips into the concrete with masonry nails or glue them in place.

In addition to the carpeting, you will need tack strips to fit the dimensions of your room, seam tape and access to a seaming iron if the room is wider than the carpet width, and a utility knife with sharp blades.

First, obtain an accurate measurement of the room. This will require measurements from several places, because the room may not be square. Next, purchase enough carpet so that there is an overlap of 4 inches for each wall. Depending on the type of carpet you're installing and the subfloor, you may also need to purchase padding to go underneath the carpet.

1. Before laying out the carpet, prepare the subfloor by getting rid of all dust, repairing any cracks, and securing loose tiles and/or floorboards.
2. Nail or glue the tack strips into place alongside each wall about ½ inch from the wall.
3. To lay out the carpet, start from the middle of the room and work toward each wall. Press the carpet against each wall and allow it to settle for a few hours. Gravity will take care of some of the wrinkles and folds. To further straighten the carpet, raise one of the corners, stand on the subfloor, and gently kick the carpet.
4. Once in place, the carpet can be cut with the utility knife. Leave 4 inches of overlap on each side for trimming.
5. If the width of the carpet is smaller than the width of the room, attach two pieces of carpet with seam tape. Keep the seam away from high-traffic areas such as doorways. Cut the seam tape to the length of the seam.
6. With your two large pieces of carpet in their approximate places, align the carpet naps so they face in the same direction. The nap is the fibers that make up the carpet surface. Determine whether the naps are aligned by rubbing your hand along the carpet fibers. Rubbing in one direction will smooth down the fibers, while rubbing in the other direction will raise them.
7. Fold back one carpet section and draw a line on the subfloor along the edge of the carpet that remains in place.

CARPETER'S TOOLBOX

- steel tape measure
- hammer
- utility knife and razor blades
- masonry nails (if needed)
- seaming iron
- straightedge

8. Fold back the other piece of carpet and place the seam tape on the subfloor, with the line serving as the midpoint.

9. Run the seaming iron across the tape to melt the glue. Place one section of the carpet firmly on the tape and lay the second carpet section as close to it as possible. Use your hands on both sides of the seam to press the two sections of carpet together.

10. The next step is to trim the carpet overlap along each wall. If you have baseboards, cut the carpet again so the overlap is reduced to 1 inch. If you don't have baseboards, push the carpet firmly against the wall and trim as close to the edge as you can.

11. To trim a bunched-up corner, fold back the carpet toward you. On the back side of the carpet, use a straightedge to draw two lines that continue the earlier cuts. Place a protective board between the folded carpet and the carpeted floor and cut along the lines.

12. To trim around a door frame, cut along both sides of the frame, cutting down from the edge of the overlap piece toward the floor. Fold back the carpet and cut away the strip at the base of the door frame. Then create a crease at the door opening and cut along the crease. If the carpet ends there, purchase a metal doorstrip to help hold the carpet in place.

13. Secure the carpet by pushing the carpet edge into the tacks on the tack strips and close to the wall. If you have a baseboard, push the carpet into the tacks and then slip the excess carpet under the baseboard. This should complete the project.

Patching Carpet

Cut out the damaged section of carpet with a sharp utility knife. From a piece of surplus carpet, cut an identical replacement piece. If you do not have surplus carpet, cut your patch from carpet that is hidden from view, such as in a closet. Apply several strips of double-sided tape to secure the patch to the subfloor, although you can also use an appropriate glue from a carpet supply store. That should patch things up nicely.

—from *The Woman's Hands-On Home Repair Guide* by Lyn Herrick

Fitting Carpet

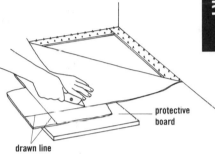

To trim a corner, fold back the carpet toward you and use a protective board when you cut.

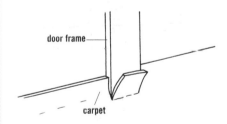

Cut along both sides of the door frame, from the edge to the floor.

PAINTING

- putty knife or paint scraper
- sandpaper
- paintbrushes
- 2-inch brush (for molding, trim, windows)
- straight-slot screwdriver

- Phillips screwdriver
- steel tape measure
- roller and roller pan
- roller extension (if needed)
- razor blades
- masking tape

Choosing Paint

When ordering paint, you must make two basic decisions. The first relates to the level of gloss in the paint. Gloss is a measure of the resins that bind the paint to the surface. Paint ranges from high gloss to flat. Higher-gloss paints are shinier, more durable, and moisture-resistant.

The other decision is choosing between latex and oil-based paint. Latex paint is water soluble, which means that everything (except for clothing) can be cleaned with warm, soapy water. It also dries quickly, has excellent color retention, and is practically free of noxious odors and dangerous fumes. Latex can be used over wallboard, bare masonry, and flat oil-based paint. However, it does not adhere well to high-gloss, oil-based finishes. To use latex over a high-gloss oil paint, prime the surface first.

Oil-based paints require turpentine or mineral spirits for cleaning. The paint chemically bonds with the surface it is covering. High-gloss, oil-based paints are therefore resistant to water. They provide an excellent finish for areas that need frequent washing.

Save on paint by measuring the area you're planning to paint. A general rule is that 1 gallon of paint covers about 400 square feet. Measure the length, width, and height and discuss these dimensions with a knowledgeable sales clerk. Request that the paint be thoroughly mixed before you bring it home. Try to purchase all the paint you need at one time. Purchasing more of a custom color later may lead to an imperfect match.

Getting Started with Painting

A good paint finish depends on proper wall preparation.

1. Dust the walls and remove any spots so your paint will adhere properly. Wash each wall with water mixed with a household detergent. Allow time for the walls to dry thoroughly before you start to paint.

2. You may see signs of mildew, a tiny organism that grows on warm, moist, dark surfaces. The mildew you washed off in step 1 could quickly reappear if conditions are right. To prevent this, clean your walls with a mixture of 1 part bleach to 4 parts water. For heavy stains, use 1 part bleach and 3 parts water. Wear gloves to protect your hands. Allow the wall to dry for 32 hours. It is then advisable to use paint containing a mildewcide.

3. Chipped paint must be scraped and the wall surface sanded smooth. Sand any splinters on a wood wall. Painting over knotholes with shellac will help prevent the sap from seeping out and ruining your new paint.

4. Finally, remove all switch and outlet plates.

Painting Tips

Now that you are ready to paint, here are a few tips to make the job go smoothly:

- Cover the floor and furniture with an old sheet, newspapers, or a plastic tarp, and be sure to wear old clothes. Paint—even latex—is difficult to remove from clothing.
- Paint bare surfaces with a primer first. The primer seals and protects the wall surface. It also helps bond the finish coat to your walls. When the primer dries, begin painting.
- Do not load the roller or brush with too much paint. If the paint drips, you have too much paint.
- It is not a good idea to paint over hard-to-remove wall stains like rust, lipstick, and crayon marks. Such stains will often bleed through the paint. Instead, wash away as much of the stain as possible. Then seal the stain with white shellac. When the shellac dries, paint over it.
- Wait for wall surfaces to dry completely before applying a second coat.
- If you get paint on the glass in a window, carefully scrape it off with a razor blade.
- For painting the bottom of a baseboard in a room with wall-to-wall carpeting, use a protective shield as you go. Firm cardboard or plywood is perfectly adequate.
- If you fail to complete the job in one day, you can wrap your roller and brush in plastic and place them in the freezer for overnight storage.
- Once the job is completed, clean your roller and brushes thoroughly so they can be used again.

—from *The Woman's Hands-On Home Repair Guide* by Lyn Herrick

Textured Paint

Applying textured paint is one of the least expensive options for covering uneven wall surfaces. It can also create drama in your room. I've covered several layers of wallpaper by applying this thick, grainy paint with a brush.

Before beginning to paint, be sure that any wallpaper is fastened securely to the wall so it doesn't pull away. Tear off loose paper or refasten it with wallpaper glue.

If you are applying textured paint to a previously painted surface, try to find out what type of paint you are covering. Many oil paints are incompatible with latex-based textured paint. Before applying latex over oil, always apply a primer. I learned this lesson the hard way.

In one of my houses, the dining room walls and ceiling were in terrible condition. I decided to hide the imperfections. I had no way of knowing what was on the walls and ceiling, so I painted the ceiling the first day. It went on easily and looked great.

The next morning I peeked in and was shocked! The paint was dripping off the ceiling in long strings. It looked like a scene out of a horror movie. Those extra minutes of priming would have saved me two days of scraping and several hours of cleanup.

—from *Be Your Own Home Decorator* by Pauline B. Guntlow

Protect carpeting with a stiff shield as you paint baseboards.

WALLPAPERING

Choosing Wallpaper

Here is a list of the various types of wallpaper available, as well as possible uses and tips for hanging:

Vinyl. Vinyl paper is the most popular and easy to apply. It is relatively inexpensive and durable. Vinyl coverings arc backed with either cloth or paper. Vinyl-coated paper has been sprayed with a thin coat of plastic, which means it should be cleaned only with mild soap and water. Vinyl is good for high-traffic areas such as hallways, kitchens, and baths. However, thick, heavy vinyls are difficult to hang in small areas.

Paper. Paper wallpaper is made of plain paper with no coatings or special treatments. It usually requires paste, and cannot be handled as much as vinyl because it rips and tears.

Fiber cloths. The most popular fiber cloths used in home decorating are grass cloth, burlap, hemp, and jute. The fibers are woven and laminated on a paper or cloth backing. They contain natural irregularities. As a result, seams will show when the cloths are hung.

Flock. Flock is two-dimensional paper that resembles damask or cut velvet. It is usually used in formal rooms. Due to its texture, it is excellent for hiding imperfections on the walls. Flock can be tricky to hang, because glue cannot be washed off easily on the front side and it can easily become crushed while hanging.

Foils. Foil wallpaper is made by laminating a thin metallic sheet to paper or fabric backing. Many foils are coated with mylar, which gives a mirrorlike finish. The reflective qualities of foil can open up a space and brighten a room. However, this kind of paper does not "breathe," making air bubbles hard to remove. Foils also wrinkle easily and show imperfections on the wall's surface.

Murals. Murals are used as "eye catchers," giving the illusion of a larger space. Murals are available on foil, paper, and vinyl, and need thorough surface preparation to look their best. To ensure a smooth surface, hang murals over lining paper.

—from *Wallpapering Step-by-Step* by Marian Lee Klenk

Wallpaper Psychology

- The larger the room (height and wall space), the bigger the print design.
- Dark colors make a room seem smaller and warmer.
- Stripes make a room seem higher and larger.
- Geometric prints give a greater impression of space.
- Miniprints create a sense of space in a small room.
- Large prints cover imperfections in the walls better than small prints.
- Textured paper gives heaviness and warmth to a room.
- Consider continuity. If a hallway opens onto your living room, the papers in each room should complement one another.

- plumb line and chalk (to guide placement of first strip)
- chalk line
- large, sharp scissors
- trimming knife with extra razor blades
- smoothing brush, smoothing blade, or large sponge
- steel tape measure
- wallpaper paste, paste bucket, and brush (for paper that is not prepasted)
- water tray (for prepasted paper)
- clean rags to remove excess paste
- table or other flat work surface
- thumb tacks

- seam roller
- straight-slot or Phillips screwdriver
- putty knife
- wallpaper steamer (rent if needed)
- large paintbrush
- scaffold (if papering ceilings)

FOR REMOVING OLD WALLPAPER
- sponge
- bucket
- paint scraper (6-inch width)
- steamer (as needed)
- medium sandpaper
- goggles and gloves

Removing Old Wallpaper

Removing wallpaper is a messy job. The trick is to soften the glue on the back side of the paper, so the paper can be scraped off.

Begin with a sponge, a pail of hot water, and a 6-inch-wide scraper.

1. Use the sponge to thoroughly soak the old paper. If the glue has softened, the paper will slide along the wall.

2. Remove loosened sections of the paper with the scraper.

3. If the paper resists your scraper, try soaking it more. You can also purchase wallpaper-removal products that help soften the glue.

4. If nothing works, rent a wallpaper steamer and steam off the paper. Steamers are often necessary for walls covered with several layers of paper.

5. Once you have removed the old paper, use medium-grade sandpaper to sand off the remaining scraps of paper.

6. Before hanging new wallpaper, wash the wall with a household cleaner to remove any glue residue.

Preparing the Wall for New Paper

Prepare the walls as you would for painting. If you are papering over old wallpaper, remove all loose wallpaper with a scraper. Remove all old paper if there are large sections of loose paper or if you discover several layers. For small areas, use a chemical solution to remove the old paper. For large areas, rent a wallpaper steamer.

When papering new plaster or sheetrock walls, apply a coat of flat primer-sealer to the walls, then size them. You can purchase sizing powder from the hardware store. Mix it with water according to the directions and brush or roll it on the walls. Allow it to dry overnight.

Wallpaper Tools

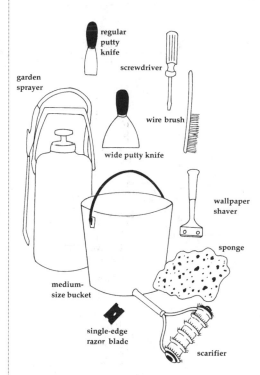

Gather tools for wallpaper removal after covering floor and furniture with drop cloths.

WALLPAPERING

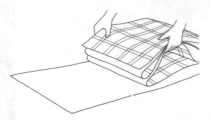

Step 6: Fold glued paper accordion-style, glued sides together.

Step 7: Roll paper up backwards and place in lukewarm water tray.

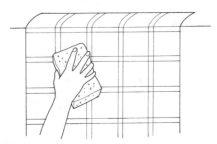

Steps 8 & 9: Place top edge just above ceiling level. Use a sweeping motion to smooth from top to bottom with a large sponge or smoothing brush.

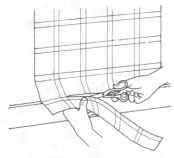

Step 10: Use the dull edge of your scissors to make a crease along the baseboard edge, then pull paper back to trim with trimming knife. Gently press paper back into place.

Hanging Wallpaper

You're ready to start the project. Follow these steps:

1. Cut paper strips 4 to 6 inches longer than the length of the wall. The extra amount can vary depending on the pattern selected. This overlap is necessary for proper matching. If you are cutting the paper by yourself, use thumb tacks at the top to hold the piece in place before cutting.

2. Hang the first strip of paper perfectly straight. Because few walls are square, this is a problem. Use a plumb line. Put a piece of chalk at the end of the line, so you will be able to mark on the wall where the line has fallen. It is best to start alongside a door.

3. Measure the width of the paper. Then measure from the top of the door and mark the wall at a distance equal to the paper's width less 1 inch.

4. Attach your plumb line at the top of the wall where you marked it. Let it drop, and mark the spot where it stays. This will ensure a straight line.

5. Take your chalk line and hold it or attach it at the top of the plumb line and at the spot where it landed. Pull the chalk line tight and snap it. This will leave a straight chalk line on the wall to use as a guide.

6. For paper requiring paste, place the cut paper on a table, pattern-side down. Apply paste generously with a brush. Spread it evenly throughout, and make sure the edges receive extra paste. Fold the paper, glued sides facing, accordion-style, to make it easier to handle.

7. For prepasted paper, roll the paper up backwards so the glued side faces out when placed in the lukewarm-water tray. When you roll it up backwards, you will start with the bottom of the piece in order to have the top of the wallpaper pull out of the tray first. Immerse the roll in the tray and hold it so it does not unravel for the length of time specified on the instructions. It is now ready to hang.

8. Place the water tray below the area where you are working and pull the paper up slowly, letting the excess water run off—or carry folded, prepasted paper to the wall and lightly place the top edge just above ceiling level. Press the paper onto the wall at the ceiling joint and in alignment with the plumb line. Leave a 2- to 3-inch overlap at the ceiling joint. Now align the lower portion with the baseboard and plumb line.

9. When the entire strip is placed properly on the wall, smooth from top to bottom with the smoothing brush or a large, wet sponge. Smooth from the center outward to the seams. Use a sweeping motion to prevent stretching.

10. Trim the paper at the ceiling joint, baseboard, and along the door frame. Remember that you established the plumb line 1 inch narrower than the width of the wallpaper. This was done because door frames are never quite straight. Trim by creating a crease in the paper by pushing it into the joint and then running a trimming knife along the crease. After trimming, wipe away any excess paste with a clean sponge.

11. Hang the second strip exactly the same way, using the first strip as the guiding line. Match the the pattern as closely as possible. When cutting the paper, match at eye level and allow extra paper at top and bottom. When applying the paper to the wall, either make a butt seam by bringing the two

edges of the paper together with no overlap or create a ⅟₁₆-inch overlap. The first method is neater, but be aware that the paper tends to shrink as it dries. If you have cut the strip long enough, you will have leeway to slide the strip up or down the wall until it matches. Be sure to press along each seam with a seam roller or a firm fingernail.

Papering around Windows

Hanging wallpaper around windows can be a problem. I prefer to do it without making extra cuts. Start the process as if the window were not there.

1. Align the paper with the strip beside it and place it 2 inches above the ceiling joint. Attach the paper with your smoothing brush.

2. When you reach the window, make a crease along the entire window frame. Take special care to mark the corners. Trim away the paper that would otherwise cover over the window, cutting first at angles toward the corner marks and checking the vertical and horizontal marks once again.

3. When the paper is glued into place, go over it with a clean, wet sponge to remove any excess paste.

Papering Ceilings

When wallpapering a ceiling, you will be working overhead, standing on a scaffold. Prep the ceiling as you would a wall. To mark off the first plumb line, measure ½ inch less than the width of the paper to create a ½-inch overhang on the wall. This prevents gaps. Cut each strip of paper 4 inches longer than needed, so it will overlap onto the walls.

Mark plumb lines as you go. Using a chalk line may be easier than holding a level upside down and drawing a pencil line along it. However, you will need a yardstick to make sure the line is plumb.

Apply paste and fold the paper accordion style. Line up the first strip with the plumb line and smooth down the first section along the line, gently pushing paper into the corner and edges of the ceiling. Have another person hold the remaining folds of paper up with a broom while you work your way across the ceiling.

—from *Wallpapering Step-by-Step* Marian Lee Klenk

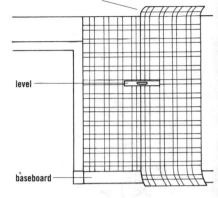

Step 11: Leave excess paper at top and bottom to allow for the match.

Working around Windows

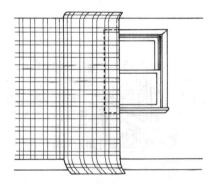

Hang the paper over the window as though it weren't there, then crease the paper where it should be trimmed, taking special care to mark the corners. When trimming, cut first into the corners, cutting at an angle.

Smoothing Out Bubbles

If a large bubble appears, peel back your wallpaper off the wall to the point where the bubble appears. Smooth it out by brushing the bubble toward the seams. Next, move the paper slowly back onto the wall, smoothing as you go. If you end up with a bubble and the paper has started to dry, take the point of your razor's edge or utility knife or trimming knife and poke a hole in it, then smooth it out from the outside toward the hole.

—from *The Woman's Hands-On Home Repair Guide* by Lyn Herrick

WALLS AND CEILINGS

Repairing a Hole in a Plaster Wall

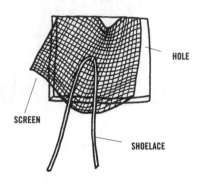

To fix a hole in a plaster wall, thread a shoelace through a wire screen, and push the screen through the hole.

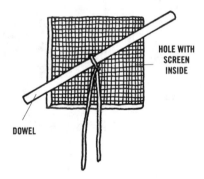

Tie a dowel to the screen with the shoelace.

Fixing Holes

For plaster walls without lath, you will need plaster, a wire screen, a thin shoelace or wire, and a wooden dowel, thin stick, or pencil that is longer than the width of the hole.

1. Remove all loose plaster from around the hole.

2. Construct a supporting device within the hole to hold the plaster used for the repair. A good solution is to cut a section of wire screen considerably larger than the hole.

3. Take the shoelace or wire and thread it through the screen.

4. Insert the screen into the hole, pull the shoelace so the screen fits tightly against the hole, and tie the shoelace to the dowel, which you will place across the hole. This will hold the screen in place while you put the first coat of plaster into the hole.

5. To apply the plaster, first moisten the hole and screen with water using a paintbrush. Insert enough plaster into the hole so that it oozes into the screen and covers the sides of the hole.

6. When the plaster is thoroughly dry, remove the dowel and the shoelace.

7. Now apply several coats of plaster to the hole.

8. When the hole is fully covered and dry, sand the area smooth.

9. Apply a priming coat of paint before rolling on the finishing coat.

Applying New Wallboard

Walls. Some walls are so badly deteriorated that you need to replace them with a new surface. To prep the walls, remove all loose plaster, including everything that is not tight to the lath. Fill all resulting holes with lath or shingle to bring the area up to the level of the original plaster. If large areas are loose or the surface is very uneven, remove all the plaster.

For best results installing the wallboard, use a cordless screwdriver and long, self-tapping screws called sheetrock screws. These screws will pierce even soft tin without a starter hole. They don't have to be driven into studs, so you don't have to place your wallboard joints over studs.

After the wallboard is in place, cover the joint where the new wall and existing plaster meet with joint compound and tape.

Ceilings. For both ceilings and human beings, just hanging around for 50 or 75 years is hard on the ability to hold together. Badly deteriorated ceilings should also be covered with wallboard.

Remove loose plaster before applying wallboard. For small problem areas, remove the plaster, shim the area to bring it to level, and cover the entire ceiling with wallboard.

To apply the wallboard, construct two big Ts, making the horizontal members 3-foot-long 1 x 4s and the vertical members 2 x 4s about 1 inch longer than the ceiling height. Put the wallboard in place, at the same time forcing these Ts up against the wallboard to keep it in position until you get it nailed or screwed permanently to the ceiling. Screw the ceiling into the lath and, wherever you can, into the joists.

— from *Reviving Old Houses* by Alan Dan Orme

Holes in Sheetrock

There are two ways to fix a large hole in sheetrock. The first method requires enlarging the hole so it extends to a stud on each side. The other method involves gluing a sheetrock patch against a plywood backing. In either case, you must first purchase a piece of sheetrock from a building supply store.

Method I

1. Take a small saw or large knife and cut out a rectangle around the hole. Make sure the rectangle extends to a stud on either side.
2. Measure the rectangular hole and cut a new piece of sheetrock with the same dimensions.
3. Nail the patch into the hole by securing it to both studs.

Method II

1. Using a small saw, cut a new piece of sheetrock into a rectangular shape larger than the hole in the wall.
2. Place the patch over the hole and outline the patch with a pencil. With the saw, cut an opening in the wall along the penciled line.
3. Construct the backing by first cutting a piece of plywood that is larger than the patch but can be diagonally inserted into the hole.
4. Insert a small screw into the middle of the plywood, leaving enough space on the screw head to attach a string.
5. Place rubber-based or plastic glue along the border of the plywood, then insert it diagonally into the hole.
6. Attach a string to the small screw so the plywood can be pulled flush against the wall.
7. While holding the string, drill three or four screws through the sheetrock and into the plywood. Black, all-purpose drywall screws are the best ones for this. Use screws at least 1¼ inches long.
8. Allow the glue about an hour to dry, then insert the patch. Apply joint compound to sides and back of the patch and gently fit it up against the plywood.
9. Use a putty knife to fill the outline cracks with joint compound and then cover the entire surface with it.
10. When the repaired area is dry, lightly sand it.

— from *The Woman's Hands-On Home Repair Guide* by Lyn Herrick

---

Sealing Cracks

To repair a crack or small hole in the wall, purchase a can of spackling compound and a putty knife about an inch in width.

1. Scrape away any loose plaster along the crack. A good way to handle this is to gently run a beer bottle opener (church key) along the crack.
2. Scoop the spackling compound onto a putty knife and run the knife over the crack.
3. Allow the compound to harden, then apply another layer to the crack.
4. Apply layers until the crack is completely filled.
5. When the final layer is dry, gently sand the repaired surface using fine sandpaper.

—from *The Woman's Hands-On Home Repair Guide*

Repairing a Hole in Sheetrock

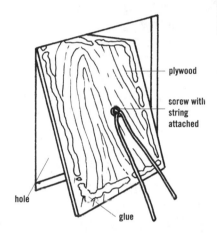

plywood

screw with string attached

hole

glue

Cut a piece of plywood larger than the hole, place a screw at the center, and attach a piece of string to the screw.

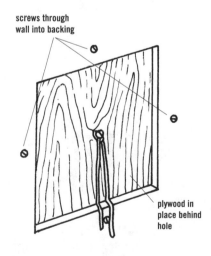

screws through wall into backing

plywood in place behind hole

Use the string to pull the glued piece of plywood against the hole.

Fixing Broken Windowpanes

Replacing a broken pane of glass is not a difficult task, and it can save you lots of money. The project varies slightly with each type of window, but you should be able to follow these steps:

1. In a wooden window, broken glass is often held in place by a layer of putty and glazier's points (small metal triangles with sharp points). Scrape away the old putty with a kitchen knife or putty knife.

2. Next, carefully pull away the broken pieces of glass. Wear protective gloves.

3. You will probably see three or four glazier's points inserted into the wood. These can be pulled out with pliers. Some windowpanes are held in place by small wooden slats that are nailed into place. Pry out these slats.

4. Clean around the lip of the wooden frame, then take an exact measurement of the frame. Write down the length and width. Purchase a new glass pane at a hardware store or glass company. Have it cut to fit ⅛ inch smaller than each dimension of your frame. Buy a small can of putty and some glazier's points.

5. Thinly layer the window frame with putty.

6. Gently push the new glass into place. It should fit snugly against the lip of the frame.

7. To hold the glass in place, insert a glazier's point along each side of the window frame. Hold the glazier's point next to the glass and push it into the frame with a straight-slot screwdriver or a putty knife.

8. Seal the window with an additional layer of putty. Take a handful of putty and shape it into a ball. Rub the putty ball between your hands until the putty takes the shape of a snake. Press the snake along the edges of the glass to form the seal. Finally, smooth over the putty with your putty knife, removing excess.

Aluminum windows. In aluminum windows, the panes are usually held in place by a rubber gasket.

1. Pull out the gasket and remove the pieces of glass.

2. Have a piece of glass cut ¹⁄₃₂ inch smaller than the frame.

3. Lay the new pane in the frame and replace the gasket by pushing it in place with your thumb.

Replacing Glazing Compound

Glazing compound holds your windowpanes in place and seals out moisture. It becomes brittle and cracks with age. This leads to air drafts entering the house and to moisture, which can damage the window sash. Here's how you can solve the problem:

1. Remove all the old, loose compound with a putty knife. Be careful not to disturb the triangular glazier's points that hold the pane in place.

2. Roll new glazing compound or putty in your hands to form a long snake and press it against the windowpane.

3. Take a putty knife and run it along the snake at a 45-degree angle, pressing it against the pane as you proceed.

4. Paint over the glazing compound to complete your seal.

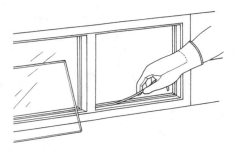

Scrape away the old putty and carefully remove the broken glass.

Run a bead of putty all the way around the frame.

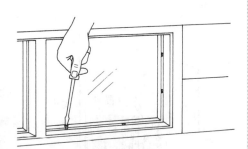

Push glazier point in with a screwdriver.

- putty knife or kitchen knife
- pliers
- paintbrush (if needed)
- straight-slot screwdriver
- protective gloves
- duct tape

Repairing Screens

Screens are attached to window and door frames in many different ways. Some are hooked onto the sill, some have spring-loaded plugs, others slide in and out.

1. To repair a torn screen, determine which type you have and remove it accordingly.

2. Once this task is accomplished, take the screen away from the window or door and lay it on a table or flat work area.

If the window frame or door is wooden, the screen will be held in place by a narrow molding. Pry off this molding gently with a straight-slot screwdriver so the screen can be taken out. The small nails or staples holding the molding in place should yield to your gentle prying. Try not to split or break the molding. However, the molding can be inexpensively replaced if it breaks. Take out the screen and remove as many tacks or staples from the molding as you can.

If you have a metal window or door frame, the molding that fastens the screen to the frame is actually a thin rubber hose or gasket. To remove the damaged screen, pry up the gasket with your screwdriver and pull it out.

3. Measure the frame and take the dimensions to a hardware store. Ask for a cut section of screen to fit your frame. Consult with a salesperson to determine the type of screen that best suits your needs. You may have to buy a roll of screen and cut the piece yourself. Scissors will cut the screen easily. Leave 1½ to 2 inches extra on each side.

4. Fold over this excess screen to form a reinforced edge on each side.

5. With a wooden window or door frame, place the new screen into the frame and attach it with carpet tacks or by using a staple gun. Make sure you stretch the screen tightly. Now replace the old molding and the job is finished.

With a metal window or door frame, install the new screen by placing it on the frame. Next, take the gasket and put it back into place while pushing the screen into the indented track. An inexpensive tool is available from hardware stores for pushing the gasket back into the track.

Taking a Screen Apart

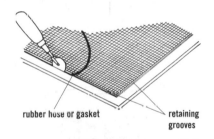

rubber hose or gasket • retaining grooves

With a metal frame, the gasket is pushed back into place with a special tool, available from a hardware store.

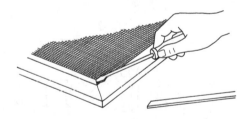

With a wooden frame, pry off the molding strip to expose the screen edge.

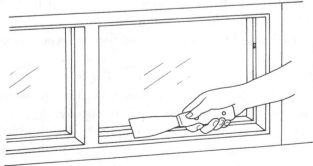

Press glazing compound against the pane with a putty knife.

WINDOWS AND DOORS

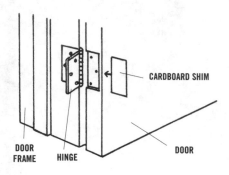

Place a cardboard shim in the recessed space of the door jamb.

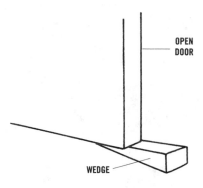

Put a wedge under the outer edge of the door to hold it up while you repair the hinge.

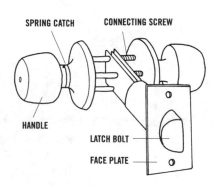

Cutaway of doorknob and face plate mechanism

Unsticking Wooden Doors

Doors become difficult to open and close when the hinges are out of alignment. Wooden doors are also sensitive to the amount of moisture in the air. When it rains a lot, wooden doors may become difficult to open and close. When the rain subsides, they may or may not return to their previous size.

Adjusting hinges. Tighten any loose screws, which will prevent the door from sagging. If you cannot tighten the screws because the holes have enlarged, drive a wedge under the outside edge of the door to support it. Take out the hinge screws, fill the holes with glue, then insert scrap wood or wooden matchsticks into the holes. After the glue has dried, drive the screws into the old holes. You may need to drill a small hole to accomplish this task.

If the door sticks at the top or bottom, place a cardboard shim (a thin piece of cardboard about the size of a credit card) behind the hinge leaf in the door jamb. Shim the top hinge for a door that sticks at the top and the bottom hinge for one that sticks at the bottom. With the weight of the door supported by a wedge under the outside edge, unscrew the hinge leaf in the door jamb, place the shim in the recessed space of the door jamb, replace the hinge leaf, and screw it back into the door jamb.

Sanding or planing the door. Another way to solve the problem is by sanding or planing the door.

1. Close the door and see how it fits by sliding a business card between the door and the jamb. Wherever the card sticks, mark the door with a pencil.

2. Sand or plane the door in the places marked by the pencil. Use sandpaper if the problem area is a small one. Remove the door only if you're working on the side where the hinges are located or working on the bottom of the door.

Replacing a Doorknob

A door that is difficult to lock or refuses to stay shut may have a faulty doorknob. It may have either of the following kinds of doorknobs:

Type 1. Two screws on the inside knob hold the entire mechanism in place. Unfasten these screws and slip off the knob that is not fastened to the mechanism. You will see the doorknob mechanism on the inside. Slip the entire mechanism out.

Type 2. A stem with a latch within the knob holds the doorknob in place. You will notice a small hole in the stem. Push a sharp tool into the hole while pulling off the doorknob. The rest of the mechanism will slide out from the other side. Unscrew the latch mechanism and slide it out.

1. Take the old doorknob to the hardware store and purchase the type of doorknob you want.

2. Read the directions for the new doorknob before installing it.

3. The first thing to install is the latch mechanism. This will screw into the end of the door. Make sure the rounded part is toward the door opening.

4. Take both sides of the doorknob and insert them into the latch mechanism. You will have to depress the latch for the doorknob to fit into the slot in the middle. Screw in the two screws that fasten the doorknob to the door.

- straight-slot screwdriver
- Phillips screwdriver
- chisel
- hammer

- electric drill
- sander
- plane
- specialty drill bits (if needed)

Installing Dead-Bolt Locks

Dead-bolt locks are an inexpensive way to add security to your home. They are not difficult to install if you have the necessary equipment. The most important item is a set of specialty drill bits for drilling large holes. Before purchasing the lock, measure the thickness of the door so that you buy the right size lock.

1. The lock comes with a template, which indicates where to drill two large holes. Tape the template onto the door in the place where you want to position the lock.

2. Drill the two holes in the door as indicated by the template.

3. Using a specialty drill bit for drilling large holes (the directions that come with the lock will specify the correct drill-bit size), drill a hole through your door as indicated on the template. To avoid splintering the door frame, stop drilling as soon as the bit breaks through to the other side. Finish the job from the other side.

4. Drill a smaller hole starting from the door's edge into the larger hole. The exact location of the hole will be marked on the template. This smaller hole is the one that the bolt will travel through.

5. You are ready to insert the dead bolt and its latch plate. The latch plate must be recessed into the edge of the door frame with a mortise cut. With the lock in place, draw an outline of the latch plate with a pencil on the door's edge. You now need to chisel out the mortise cut.

6. Take a hammer and tap the chisel along the outside edges of your outline. Be careful not to cut deeper than the thickness of your strike plate.

7. While holding the chisel at a 45-degree angle, make a series of cuts that run from the top of the plate to the bottom.

8. Work out the chips by tapping your chisel from the side of the door frame. Lay the latch plate into the mortise cut to see if it fits. You may need to fine-tune your cut to ensure that it lies flush.

9. Once you are satisfied with the position of the plate, screw it in.

10. Finish assembling the lock by following the directions that come with it.

11. Install the strike plate on the door jamb. This will involve making another mortise cut into which the strike plate fits, as well as drilling a hole for the dead bolt. In some cases, the drilling of this last hole is all that is required.

—from *The Woman's Hands-On Home Repair Guide* by Lyn Herrick

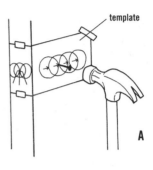

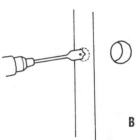

Use a template to determine where to drill for a new dead bolt (A and B above).

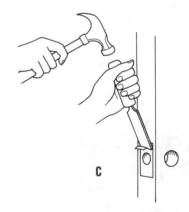

Chisel out the mortise cut for the latch plate (C).

8

THE HOME INTERIOR

DECORATING TIPS • COUNTRY CREATIVITY • RENOVATING FURNITURE • BETTER HOUSEKEEPING • SOAPMAKING

Pauline Guntlow, author of Be Your Own Home Decorator, *has been designing and renovating single-family homes professionally for more than a decade. Known for her creative ideas, she has appeared numerous times on television programs. She is a licensed contractor and owner of a construction company in Massachusetts, where she lives.*

Our homes have always had a country feel, even in our urban and suburban days. When you walk in the door there's a lot going on—kids working on a nature craft project at the kitchen counter; fresh pies baking, filling the house with good smells; new curtains being sewn at the dining room table. We take pride in creating a welcoming atmosphere for family and friends, and many of the decorative touches are handmade by someone in our family. As my mother, Mimi, puts it, "Homemade beats store-bought every time." Author and home decorator Pauline Guntlow starts off this chapter with tips on how to make your house a home.

—Martha Storey

Thinking about all your decorating options can be overwhelming. It helps to take a step-by-step approach, beginning by deciding what look you want to achieve in your home. Here are some suggestions:

Collect Examples

How do you find your look? Visit furniture stores and model homes. Make design research a part of your daily routine. Every week, invest in one decorating magazine.

For a couple of months, cut out pictures that appeal to you and keep them in a scrapbook. Then organize the pictures according to what room they illustrate. When you have at least five examples for each room, analyze the pictures to determine what common denominator makes them appealing. You may discover that you prefer:

- Certain color families
- The unadorned, uncluttered look
- The rustic country look
- Glass and chrome, with contemporary art

Distilled white vinegar. Made from grains, petroleum by-products, or wood pulp. Colorless, coarse-flavored. Used in pickling and for household chores

Essential oil. Oil that is a concentrated extract of a plant or food

Lye. Chemical (sodium hydroxide) used in soapmaking; can burn skin and eyes

Stencil. Flat sheet with a cut design used for decorating walls and furniture. Made of oiled cardboard or precut polyester (Mylar)

Swag. A curtain made from one continuous length of fabric and draped around a window

Identify Key Elements

Identify specific features that you want to duplicate in your house. Analyze furniture, fabric, and accessories, and write down your emerging choices.

Select a Color Scheme

Color is the most important factor in decorating. To begin putting a color scheme together, take an inventory of the colors of furniture, walls, carpet, and so on within each room. Decide whether each item is worth keeping, could be renovated, or needs to be replaced.

Now bring out that scrapbook and look at the pictures. Note the predominant colors in the style you selected. Think of ways you could adopt these colors in each room.

Develop a Whole-House Plan

Think about repeating one or more design elements throughout your living space. Rooms shouldn't necessarily mimic each other, but they should share at least one or two design coordinators.

To blend elements and create a unified, harmonious environment, I suggest repeating at least two of the following five design coordinators throughout most of your living space:

- Wall colors
- Flooring materials
- Window treatments
- Color-coordinated furniture and small items
- Architectural features (door styles, ceiling moldings, baseboards, etc.)

Establish a Budget and a Schedule

To calculate how much you'll need to spend, begin by listing everything you need to buy to accomplish the desired look. Then research how much each item costs at several different stores. If you're really on a tight budget, concentrate on just one room at a time and develop a plan for purchasing items over several months.

Exchanging leisure time for a decorating hour or two can yield long-term payoffs. The hardest part is getting started, but you'll be surprised how much you can accomplish by devoting just one hour a day to decorating work.

Tips on Color

- Light colors recede and make spaces look larger.
- Dark colors make spaces look smaller.
- Natural light affects color. Any color will look lighter with lots of natural light and darker with a limited amount.
- Incandescent bulbs "warm" any surface; colors look different at night.
- Using at least two strong colors in different areas of a home adds interest.
- Cream is a warm, neutral color that combines with most other colors.
- When using a light color for walls, make the trim color a little darker. This will make doors, moldings, and windows stand out just enough.
- Contrasting woodwork will usually make a room seem smaller but cozy.

—from *Be Your Own Home Decorator* by Pauline B. Guntlow

DECORATING TIPS

Decorating Made Cheap(er)

Author and antiques dealer James McKenzie knows how to find treasures for the home at bargain prices. Here's where he suggests looking.

Antiques Shops

The first and most obvious source for antiques is multiple-dealer antiques centers and antiques shops. Invariably, if you visit enough shops, you'll find things that are underpriced. The pickings are much better at large antiques centers, or malls. The very best time to get bargains is when a new mall first opens.

Auctions

There are two types of auctions at which you can purchase antiques and collectibles: estate sales and consignment sales. Most estate sales are held at the home and include everything from the furniture to the contents of the kitchen cabinets. Consignment sales usually take place at an auction house that holds sales on a regular basis.

I don't recommend one type of auction over the other; I regularly attend both. For the most part, everything is sold with no reserve at estate sales. Regardless of how low the bid is, the item will be sold to the highest bidder. This is often not the case at a consignment sale.

Classified Ads

I buy newspapers from several surrounding towns and peruse the classified ads almost daily. Although I look at the antiques category, I rarely find anything of interest. The ads that yield the best results for me are under "Furniture" and "Miscellaneous." I try to scan these ads thoroughly, but that doesn't mean I read every word. What I'm looking for are key words. Words that cause me to pause include *old, oak, mahogany, marble, brass,* and *unusual.*

Yard Sales

This is such an obvious source of merchandise that it barely warrants mentioning. But for the uninitiated, you could be overlooking an opportunity to find surprising bargains. Remember, rock-bottom prices are the lure of yard sales. The people holding them are clearing out things they no longer want. They don't want to carry it all back into the house. Almost every yard sale I stop at yields something.

Vintage Buildings

Keep your eye out for vintage houses and buildings that are being renovated or demolished. Many architectural antiques can be had for the asking. The first thing you need, though, is permission. Don't ever go into a house, even one that's being torn down, without permission from the owner. Once that's settled, look for lighting fixtures, fireplace mantels, claw-foot bathtubs and pedestal sinks, and ornate hardware such as doorknobs, hinges, window latches, and switch plates.

Sold Homes

People always seem to have more possessions than they have room for in the moving van. If they have the time or the inclination, they might have a yard sale prior to moving day. But it's the people who didn't have the moving sale whom you should approach. People contemplating loading and unloading all of their possessions to and from a truck might welcome an opportunity to leave some behind.

Paint Stores

Paint stores make mistakes, the most common being to mix "custom" paint color incorrectly. If it doesn't match what the customer ordered, it's practically worthless. Erroneously blended colors typically end up in some inconspicuous spot like a stockroom. You'll usually have to ask to see them. Don't hesitate to dicker on the price for this paint.

Wallpaper Shops

The next time you go to the wallpaper store, ask what they have in discontinued patterns. There's a good chance that you can pick these patterns up at a drastically reduced price. Check out the borders, too. You may be able to find an inexpensive border that matches the wallpaper.

—adapted from *Antiques on the Cheap* by James W. McKenzie

Decorating with Plants

If you love plants, decorate with them to your heart's content. They make great fillers for spots needing a bit of color or balance. The only potential problem is that if you overwater them, the water may mark a piece of furniture or the floor. But you can avoid this by using deep saucers and a small plastic mat under the saucer. Effective ways to use plants include:

- Massing them to create a dramatic and beautiful focal point. Combine a birdbath, birdhouse, and hanging plants for a charming vignette. Install a recirculating pump in a fountain for real drama.
- Creating a natural screen in large open windows
- As a "furnishing" in a large built-in planter. A six-foot-long planter in front of a picture window is gorgeous.
- Arranging plants in clay or decorated pots up a staircase
- Grouping hanging plants in the bathroom
- Creating a minigarden on the floor in front of a south-facing window

—from *Be Your Own Home Decorator* by Pauline B. Guntlow

COUNTRY CREATIVITY

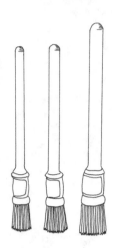

Available in several sizes, stencil brushes have blunt-cut bristles.

Spread a small amount of stencil paint on a plate, keeping a paper towel nearby for a blotter. Always work with a nearly dry brush.

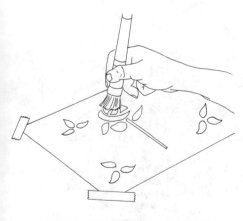

Tape your stencil to the surface. Hold your brush at a right angle to the surface and apply paint with a scrubbing motion.

Stenciling Your Walls

When stenciling, you apply color through a hole cut in a piece of stencil material that is held against a surface being decorated. A cut-out image may be printed repeatedly. To keep the stencil stable, break large areas into small segments separated by "bridges." The way in which a design is segmented is what gives it the distinctive stenciled look.

Supplies and Materials

Many craft and art supply stores carry ready-cut stencils. Or you can create your own design with polyester stencil sheets (Mylar) and a stencil-cutting pen. Stencil sheets are long-lasting and easy to clean.

Brushes. The nature and size of the project dictates brush size. For stenciling large areas, 1-inch brushes provide more even coverage. For narrow, dainty borders or designs with small figures, use a ½-inch brush. Experiment to determine whether you prefer stencil brushes with blunt-cut bristles or soft bristles.

Sponges. Use sponges to achieve interesting textural effects. Cut new sponges to desired sizes. To apply paint, either blot or scrub it through the stencil opening.

Other supplies. You will need a piece of glass, a paint tray, or a non-absorbent surface on which to pour a few drops of paint. Paper towels or scrap paper will rub excess paint from brushes. If you are mixing colors, have several small containers. Other items may include a tape measure or yardstick to determine placement of designs; chalk to keep lines straight; a level to create exact horizontal or vertical lines; and adhesive stencil spray to temporarily hold the stencil. If you stencil on a painted surface, it must be dry so the adhesive won't pull up the paint.

Choosing Paint

Most paints sold for stenciling are acrylic, which are easy to remove when mistakes occur. You can also use crayons, pastels, or marking pens, but take care to avoid getting dark-colored ridges on the outside of a stencil's pattern.

Placing the Design

In older houses, ceiling lines may not be straight. Before applying a stencil border, place a level in several spots along the wall where it meets the ceiling and use it as a guide to draw a straight line.

Designs with a large repeating pattern need careful planning. Mark the center of the wall, then measure backward from the design to find where to place the first print. For small running designs, lay one design against the other all the way around the room, making smooth turns at corners.

Applying Paint

Too much paint smears and drips. A couple of tablespoons of paint is enough to stencil a border for an entire room.

1. Position the stencil with tape or spray adhesive. Dribble a small amount of paint on a paint tray.

2. In a circular motion, dab the stencil brush into the paint, taking up a small amount. On a piece of scrap paper or paper towel, blot the brush until only a faint shade shows.

3. Holding the brush upright, apply paint through the stencil in a circular, scrubbing motion. Work from the edge of the stencil toward the center. Remove the stencil. If the print smears or runs, you have too much paint or the paint is too runny.

—from *The Woman's Hands-On Home Repair Guide* by Lyn Herrick

Fixing Mistakes

Stenciling mistakes are repairable. Put paint thinner on a clean cloth and rub off the design. Allow the paint thinner to evaporate until you can no longer see it — only a minute or two. Look at the spot where the design was. If the background paint shows a shiny spot, blot on some of the background color with a rag and let it dry. Then reapply the design. If you find a mistake after the stencil paint is thoroughly dry, sand the spot lightly, reapply the background paint, and proceed with your painting.

—from *Stenciling* by Judy Tuttle

Picking Proper Fabric

- On your first attempt, use relatively inexpensive fabric. Remnants are ideal if you can get enough yards for your curtains. Muslins and cotton/polyester blends are another cost-effective alternative.
- For best results, the fabric should be of medium weight with medium body. If the fabric is too stiff or bulky, the curtain won't hang nicely. If it's too limp or flimsy, the curtain will be droopy.
- I recommend staying away from plaids and one-directional patterns. All-over prints or solids are much easier to work with and much more forgiving of imperfections.
- Avoid loosely woven or very sheer fabric. The raw edges unravel easily. Cutting and sewing very sheer fabric is tricky business.
- As a general rule, avoid washing the fabric before making your curtains. The fabric will lose a lot of its body, and your curtains won't look as crisp or new.
- If you have the luxury, bring home swatches of fabric you're considering and live with them for a couple of days before making a final decision.

—from *Making Country-Style Curtains*
by Barbara Farkas Casey

Tab Curtains

If you like a country look, tab curtains may be just right for many of your rooms. Hang tab curtains on curtain rods made from wooden dowels. The only sewing involved is turning under hems on the side, top, and bottom, and attaching the tab loops.

You'll need approximately 5 yards of fabric, with 1 of those yards allocated for the tabs. The curtain panel should be only slightly wider than the area to be covered. If the inside width of the window is 32 inches, each panel will be 16 inches wide. Add 4 inches for a little fullness and 1 inch on each side to allow for hemming, for a total of 22 inches.

Measure for length by installing the curtain rod first. Measure from ½ inch below the rod to the bottom of the inside frame of the window. Add 1½ inches for the top hem and 2 inches for the bottom hem.

1. To hem the sides of each curtain panel, fold ½ inch of fabric along each side to the wrong side and press. Fold over ½ inch again (to enclose raw edge) and press. Stitch ¼ inch from the edge.

2. To make a hem at the top of the panel, fold ½ inch of fabric to the wrong side and press. Now fold that edge down 1 inch and press. Stitch along the edge. Do not hem the bottom panel until after step 10.

3. To make the tab self-tape, cut strips of fabric measuring 3½ inches wide and 1 yard long. One yard of 45-inch fabric will produce about 60 tab strips 7 inches long. You will need about 16 tabs for each window.

4. Press the long raw edges of each strip inside ⅜ inch. Fold each strip in half lengthwise, wrong sides together, and pin the folded edges together evenly to make strips about 1 inch wide. Machine-stitch a ⅜-inch seam along the length of each strip, ¼ inch from the folded edges.

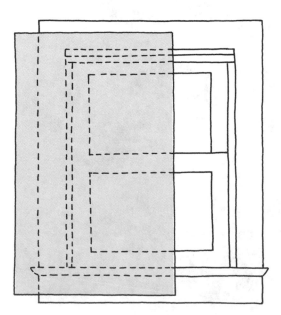

Your tab curtains should hang from near the top of the window frame to below the sill. Allow fullness in the width (about 25 percent more than the window width).

5. Cut each long strip into 7-inch tab strips. Test a strip to be sure it fits comfortably around your dowel.

6. Decide how far apart you want to space your tabs. The optimal space depends on the fabric. Try 4 inches and see if that works with your fabric. Use dressmaker's chalk to mark spots (on the wrong side) for each tab, beginning with a spot at each edge of the panel, in the middle, and between the middle and sides. Then add marks in between as needed.

7. Fold each tab strip in half and position loop-side down on the marked places on the wrong side of the curtain. Raw edges of the tab should be about ¼ inch below the top of the curtain. Push one end of each tab ¼ inch forward of the other to eliminate as much bulk as possible. Pin all the tabs in place.

8. Stitch in a straight line across all tabs, crossing about ¼ inch down from the raw edges.

9. Press each tab up with your fingers, pin, and stitch close to the top edge of the curtain, across all the turned-up tabs.

10. Slip the tabs on the dowel and hang. Pin up the hem so the bottom of the curtain is just ⅛ inch from the inside bottom window casing.

11. Remove curtain from rod and stitch up hem.

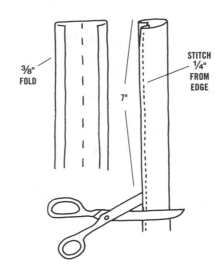

After you fold and stitch the tab strip, cut into 7-inch lengths.

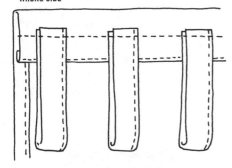

Stitch the evenly spaced tabs to the curtain panel with the loops pointing down on the wrong side. Place ends of tabs ¼ inch from top fold of curtain. Stitch across entire top, ¼ inch from ends of tabs.

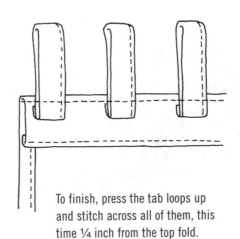

To finish, press the tab loops up and stitch across all of them, this time ¼ inch from the top fold.

—from *Be Your Own Home Decorator* by Pauline B. Guntlow

A Rule to Measure By

For all drapes and curtains, remember this golden rule: Measure once, measure twice, and measure again for good measure.

If time permits, I like to measure fabric on one day, write down the measurements, then measure again the next day and compare my notes. Sometimes the darndest revelations occur overnight!

—from *Be Your Own Home Decorator*

COUNTRY CREATIVITY

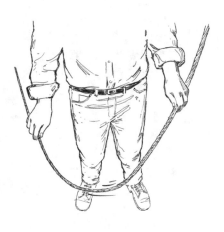

Harvesting equipment is simple: a pruning saw, pruning shears, and a tape measure.

Benders are green, flexible, ½ to ¾ inch in diameter, and 6 to 8 feet long.

Bent Willow Furniture

Harvesting Willow

Careful harvesting promotes healthier growth of willow thickets and has a low environmental impact, since willow propagates very quickly. Always use sharp cutting tools to harvest willow. Make clean cuts: Never rip or tear the branches or pull out the roots. Get permission before harvesting on someone else's property or on public lands.

You will use a pruning saw to harvest the larger limbs for frame material. Use pruning shears to trim small branches and cut the long thin shoots for flexible benders and back and seat rails. Ratchet-action shears will help you cut larger branches as easily as smaller ones. A tape measure will help you cut the right lengths of willow.

Harvest in fall and winter if you intend to leave the bark on your furniture. Harvest in spring and summer if you intend to remove the bark. You will need both seasoned (dry) pieces of willow and green, flexible, "bender" pieces, depending on your project design. The seasoned branches are required for frames and support pieces, while the benders are used to create arched pieces.

Frame pieces. The willow branches for the frame should be 1 to 3 inches in diameter, and as tall and straight as possible. These pieces need to be seasoned for about 7 days before they can be used. To season, stand the pieces against a sunny wall or lay them out in the sunshine. Provide good ventilation, and keep the pieces off the ground.

Bender pieces. The green, bender pieces of willow should be ½ to ¾ inch in diameter, 6 to 8 feet long, and as straight as possible. Place these pieces cut-end down in a bucket of water to keep them flexible. Leave your bucket of benders in a cool, shady spot.

—adapted from *Making Bent Willow Furniture*
by Brenda and Brian Cameron

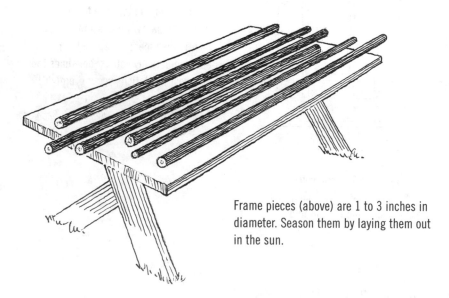

Frame pieces (above) are 1 to 3 inches in diameter. Season them by laying them out in the sun.

To keep benders flexible, stand them, cut-ends down, in a bucket of water in a shady spot until needed.

- hammer
- marker pencil
- tape measure
- safety glasses and gloves
- pruning saw or bow saw
- pruning shears
- side-cutting pliers
- rasp or utility knife
- flat double-cut steel file
- ⅜ inch variable speed drill and bits

Rustic Quilt Ladder

I first saw this simple, very functional rustic ladder in Arizona. It leaned against the side of a stucco fireplace. A very colorful quilt hung from the top rung and herbs were tied to dry on the two bottom rungs.

This quilt ladder is an ideal project for a beginner.

MATERIALS

Part	Quantity	Diameter	Length	Type of Wood
rails	2	2"	72"	seasoned
top rung	1	1½"	16"	seasoned
center rung	1	1½"	cut to fit	seasoned
bottom rung	1	1½"	24"	seasoned

1. Starting from the small (top) end of each rail, measure and mark points along the side of the rail at 12 inches, 28 inches, and 44 inches. Keep the paired marks in line with each other and in the center of the limbs. Drill ⅛-inch pilot holes straight through the center of the rail at each point.

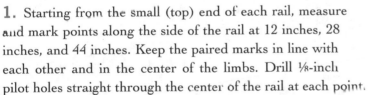

2. Drill a ⅛-inch pilot hole in the center of each end of the top and bottom rung pieces. Place the top rung between the rails at the 12-inch marks and nail with 16d nails. At the 44-inch marks, do the same with the bottom rung.

Measure between the rails at the 28-inch mark and cut the center rung to fit. Drill a ⅛-inch pilot hole in the center of each end of this rung. Secure it as you did the other rungs.

3. Round the top and bottom edges of the rails with a rasp.

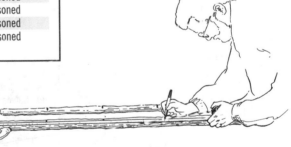

Step 1 (above). Mark and drill points for rungs along side rails.

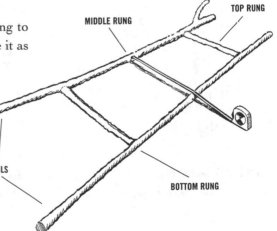

MIDDLE RUNG

TOP RUNG

RAILS

BOTTOM RUNG

Step 2 (right). Custom-fit the middle rung after the top and bottom rungs are in place.

Children's Ladder-Back Chair

Here's a simple, sturdy, and functional chair you can build yourself in three hours. The design was inspired by the old ladder-back chairs we use in our kitchen. The dimensions are just right for our two-year-old and five-year-old grandchildren.

MATERIALS				
Part	Quantity	Diameter	Length	Type of Wood
back legs	2	1½"	20" (straight)	seasoned
bottom back rungs	2	1½"	10"	seasoned
top back rungs	3	1"	10"	seasoned
side rungs	4	1½"	10"	seasoned
front legs	2	1½"	9"	seasoned
front rungs	2	1½"	12"	seasoned
front trim	1	¾"	13½"	seasoned
seat rails	approx. 13	½"	approx. 13"	seasoned

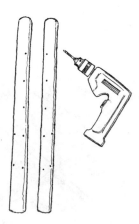

Step 1. Drill starter holes in the back legs for top and bottom back rungs.

1. Lay the back legs next to each other on a flat surface with the thick (bottom) end toward you. Hold them together and look at the way they fit against each other. Roll one of the legs against the other until you get the tightest fit from top to bottom. Through the center of each back leg, drill two ⅛-inch in-line holes, one 4 inches from the bottom and the other 7½ inches from the bottom. Mark these pieces L (left) and R (right) at the top hole. You will attach the side rungs here in step 2.

Rotate the back legs 90 degrees so that the holes you drilled are on the side. On what is now the upward side, measure up from the bottom of each back leg and mark these locations: 3¾ inches, 7¼ inches, 10½ inches, 13½ inches, and 16½ inches. Drill ⅛-inch pilot holes in line with each other in the center of the limb on these marks.

Rotate the back legs until the L and R marks touch each other. Start 16d nails through the series of five holes you just drilled in each back leg. Drive the nails through the limb until they slightly stick out on the other side.

2. Drill a ⅛-inch pilot hole in the center of both ends of all five back rung pieces. Drill these holes about 2 inches deep. Starting at the bottom, nail the two 1½-inch bottom back rungs to the back legs with 16d nails. Continuing up the legs, nail the three top back rungs to the back legs with 16d nails. You may have to trim some of the rung pieces.

Drill a ⅛-inch pilot hole in both ends of the side rung pieces. Place the side rungs on the back leg holes you marked R and L, and then nail them in place with 16d nails.

3. Through the center of each front leg, drill two ⅛-inch pilot holes, one 4 inches from the bottom and the other 7½ inches from the bottom. Mark an X on the top holes with a felt-tip marker.

Rotate the front legs 90 degrees so that the holes are on the side. On what is now the upward side, measure up from the bottom and mark at 3¾ inches and 7¼ inches. Drill ⅛-inch pilot holes in line with each other through the center of the limb on these marks.

Rotate the front legs until the X marks touch each other. Start 16d nails through the two holes you just drilled. Drive the nails through the limb until they stick out slightly on the other side.

Drill a ⅛-inch pilot hole in the center of both ends of the front rung pieces. Then nail the front rungs between the two front legs using 16d nails.

Fit the front leg section to the front ends of the side rungs with the X marks against the ends of the top side rung. Nail them together with 16d nails.

4. Center the front trim piece between the front legs with the top edge about ½ inch above the top edge of the top front rung. Drill a 1/16-inch pilot hole angled down through the center of the front trim piece into the top front rung. Nail with a 1⅝-inch paneling nail.

Adjust the trim piece across the front rung and then drill 1/16-inch pilot holes through the trim and angled into the front of both front legs. Nail with 1⅝-inch paneling nails.

Set the chair on a flat surface and adjust the frame until it does not tip. Check to make sure the front legs are square with the back legs. Adjust as necessary.

Place the first seat rail in the center of the seat section. Butt it against the front trim piece. Drill 1/16-inch pilot holes through the center of the trim and into the top center of both the top front rung and parallel back rung. Nail the trim in place with 1⅝-inch paneling nails.

Space the next seat rail about ½ inch from the first, drill as before, and nail it in place. Continue in this manner in both directions across the seat. Alternate thick and thin seat rail ends to keep the spacing fairly even. The chair is 2 inches wider in the front, so the spaces between the seat rails will be slightly wider at the front.

—from *Making Bent Willow Furniture* by Brenda and Brian Cameron

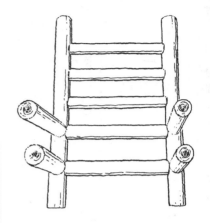

Step 2. Attach side rungs with 16d nails at pilot holes.

Step 3. Attach front rungs to front legs, then attach entire front to side rungs.

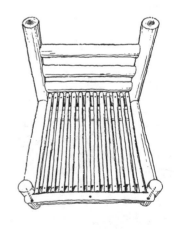

Step 4. Attach front trim, then butt each seat rail against the trim, starting at the center and working out to both sides.

CROSSPIECES

Attach crosspieces at top and bottom and over the middle shelf.

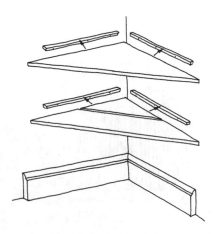

Triangular shelves should fit snugly into the corner. Piece wide shelves, if necessary, as described in step 7.

Mock Corner Cupboard

If you have a free corner in the dining room and would like to show off your good dishes or a treasured collection, here's a cupboard you can display them in.

A mock corner cupboard is a number of simple corner shelves with molding surrounding the shelves and two doors on a base. You'll need:

- five (#2) pine boards (1" deep X 12" wide and 6' in length)
- 20' of ½" pine molding
- 2" finishing nails
- jigsaw and punch
- yardstick
- hammer
- level
- string
- five 1 X 4 boards to form the sides and three crosspieces
- pair of premade doors
- 4 hinges
- 2 knobs

To make corner shelves:

1. Determine desired height of the shelf and mark on the corner of the wall.

2. Determine desired width (where the edges of the shelf will extend to on the corner walls) and mark on wall.

3. Use a level to draw a horizontal line to the point of the desired width. Do this for both sides of the shelf.

4. Cut two strips of pine molding, each 2½ inches shorter than the length of the final shelf width as drawn on the wall.

5. Place one strip of molding about 1½ inches from the inner corner, with the top of the molding lined up with the level line drawn on the wall. Nail it in place. Repeat.

6. Place one end of a piece of string on the outer left side of the shelf line; holding that end in place, stretch the other end to the outer right side and mark this place on the string. This is the finished front-edge length measurement of the shelf.

7. Cut a rectangular piece of shelf board the same length. Cut the sides at a 45 degree angle to fit the corner. The shelf should fit snugly in the corner of the wall, resting on the molding strips. If you need to piece the board, you can cut a triangular piece for the rear of the shelf.

8. Repeat for each shelf.

To finish the cupboard:

1. Measure the finished height of the cupboard and cut two lengths of 1 X 4 board, each equal to this measurement.

2. Place each board perpendicular to one side of the shelves, with the edge of the board against the wall edge. Nail the boards to the shelves. Countersink the holes so you can fill them in.

3. Measure the width between the two side boards at the top, bottom, and middle, where the crosspieces will go. Mark this length with a T square along a 1 x 4 board three times. Cut precisely, so the crosspieces will butt up against the side pieces.

4. Place each crosspiece level across the front of the shelves and attach by nailing through to the shelves.

5. Attach the premade door to the bottom. Use hinges that are face-mounted with screws.

6. Add the knobs by drilling a hole slightly larger than the screw and twisting the knob on. You can also install a door or window on the top section of the cupboard.

Architectural Molding

Moldings are relatively inexpensive, quick to install, and helpful in providing style and flow throughout your home. Adding or decorating moldings is one of the best values you can get for your decorating dollars. Although most commonly placed where the ceiling meets the walls, it can also be used over fireplaces, around plain cupboard doors, around hollow doors for a Shaker look, around mirrors, above kitchen cabinets, and on shelves and bookcases.

It takes a little practice, but you can learn to install molding yourself. You'll need a coping saw to cut off excess wood on the end cuts on the back side of the molding, when joining the miter cut with the adjoining corner. You'll also need a miter box, a nail set, a small hammer, a countersink punch, and a good tape measure.

Before cutting your actual molding pieces, practice cutting corner angles on scraps and see how they fit together. Cut off excess back material, place in position, and presto, you have molding.

Prime and paint all molding before installation. Later, you will need to do a little touching up around nail holes and corners on the installed molding.

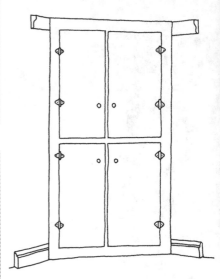

You can leave the shelves for the top half of the cupboard open, or you can enclose them with doors to match those at the bottom.

Apply molding to a plain wall to create a totally new look. A chair railing combined with square frames (below) simulates the look of raised paneling.

You can customize molding for a distinctive, personal look. Combine two strips of molding with a border print or stenciling in between (left). Or combine two strips of molding (above) and apply to the top perimeter of a room, painting the two strips and the wall area in between the same color.

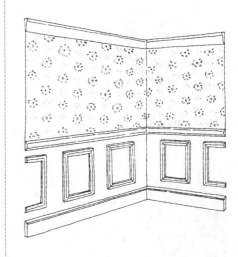

—from *Be Your Own Home Decorator* by Pauline B. Guntlow

James McKenzie prides himself on being "The World's Cheapest Antiques Dealer." He has spent more than 25 years buying, restoring, and selling antiques in and around his home in West Virginia, where he wrote his book Antiques on the Cheap.

Furniture Repair for People with Few Tools

Some of us don't have unlimited budgets for tools, don't have big workshops, and can't spend all day fooling around with a wobbly leg. Fortunately, a lot of common furniture problems have a quick-and-easy fix.

Loose Stretchers

If a chair's legs sprawl out when you sit in it, the chair probably has loose stretchers—the pieces of wood that connect all the legs and brace the chair.

1. Remove the stretcher. If it's really loose, you can spread apart the legs and pull out the stretcher. If one side is still stuck, place a padded block of wood against the leg and strike it lightly with a hammer.

2. Clean the glued ends (and the holes in the legs) with coarse sandpaper and apply new wood glue.

3. Reinsert the ends of the stretcher into the legs and apply a tourniquet. Loop a length of nylon rope around the legs and tie a knot. Insert a stick in the knot and twist, drawing the legs together. To prevent untwisting, allow the end of the stick to wedge itself under the bottom of the chair. Leave in place until the glue dries.

4. Drive a small finishing nail into the leg and through the end of the stretcher. Drive in the nail from the back of the leg, where it's less visible. Sink the head with a nail set and fill the small hole with matching wood putty.

Sticky Drawers

In a lot of older pieces, the drawers don't fit well anymore. When you shove them in, they don't stop where they should, they tip down in the back, and they don't slide easily. These problems are easily fixed.

1. Examine the drawer guides for wear. These are the strips of wood on each side of the chest that the sides of the drawers rest on. If they're badly worn, it's a simple procedure to turn them over.

2. If you can get the claw of your hammer in there and force it between the strip of wood and the side of the chest, you'll be able to pop off the guide.

3. Knock the nails flush with the guides, and turn the guides over so what was the bottom is now the top. Run a bead of glue along the guides and nail them back in place. Rub a candle, some paraffin, or a bar of soap on the drawer where it makes contact.

Pry out worn drawer guides and replace, turned over, as described in step 3.

4. Check the stops—little wooden blocks that stop the drawer from going in too far or keep the drawer from being pulled all the way out. Replace any missing ones. Measure one and make new ones approximately the same size.

5. Normally you can see where the old stops were, or you can estimate appropriate placement from those still there. A drop of glue and a short nail are all

- claw hammer
- package of single-edge razor blades
- flexible rule (tape measure)
- inexpensive ¼-inch electric drill
- four drill bits: ⅛-inch, 3⁄16-inch, ¼-inch, and ½-inch (with ¼-inch shaft)
- medium-sized standard and Phillips screwdrivers
- sandpaper
- wood glue
- nylon rope
- wood-color "putty" sticks
- nail set
- tack puller

you need to secure them. Drive a nail all the way through each block before nailing them in place inside the chest.

Bubbled Veneer

When small areas of veneer have raised, forming little humps, they can usually be reglued.

1. Using a single-edge razor blade and following the grain, make a cut through the veneer, spanning the entire length of the blister.

2. With the tip of a knife or other flat instrument, force some glue into each side of the cut. Press down the veneer with the heel of your hand, squeezing out the excess. Remove it with a damp rag, place a piece of waxed paper over the repair, and weight or clamp it. Let it dry overnight.

Missing Veneer

Replacing small areas of missing veneer is also quite simple. You can use a bit of veneer you've salvaged from some other piece of furniture, a piece from a less noticeable area of the same furniture, or a piece from a sample or starter kit, available from a woodworker's supplier.

1. Lay the veneer "patch" on top of the area to be repaired, matching the grain pattern as closely as possible. Cut through the new and old veneer, slightly beyond the edges of the missing material. This will ensure that your patch is exactly the same size as the area to be patched. Remove the old veneer.

2. Replace the missing material. Spread a small amount of glue on the underside of the veneer patch, position the piece and press it down, squeezing out the excess glue. Remove the excess with a damp rag, place a piece of waxed paper over the repair, and weight or clamp it. Let it dry overnight.

Making an Invisible Patch

Gouges, missing wood, and nail and screw holes from previous botched repair jobs can be fixed and the patch neatly hidden.

1. Fill the hole. Use a wood filler that can be stained, to improve your chances of getting a good color match.

2. Since you're not going to get a perfect color match, you need to do something to minimize the contrast. If the wood's grain continues right through the patched area, your eyes won't be drawn immediately to that spot. Draw lines to match the wood grain with a soft lead or colored pencil.

—from *Antiques on the Cheap* by James W. McKenzie

Surface Solutions

Fixing bubbled veneer. Cut through blistered area and fill with glue, then press.

Replacing veneer. Place veneer patch over hole, and cut through both layers with a utility knife to ensure a perfect match.

Patching furniture. Draw grain on filler patch with a pencil.

RENOVATING FURNITURE

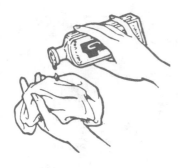

Furniture Juice

The formula for this wonderful wood cleaner and finish rejuvenator is simplicity itself:

- 1 part white vinegar. Apple cider vinegar might also work, but I've never tried it.
- 1 part boiled linseed oil. Don't use raw linseed oil.
- 1 part turpentine. This paint thinner is available at paint and hardware stores.

To use furniture juice, put the three ingredients into a jar with a tight lid and shake like crazy. Then use very fine (000 or 0000) steel wool to scrub the furniture. Don't be afraid to apply some pressure.

Work on one area at a time. Don't apply it all over the piece and then rub, but rub as you apply it. When the surface is smooth, wipe it off with a soft rag. You'll be pleased with how the years of grime melt away and how you're left with a smooth, clean surface.

—from *Antiques on the Cheap*

Stripping Furniture

I'm not a fan of stripping. I consider it a last resort. But there are times when cleaning just won't do the trick. Sometimes a really nice piece can be had reasonably, precisely because it needs to be refinished. Follow these steps:

1. Work outdoors. Wear a long-sleeved shirt and protective gloves.
2. Place the piece to be stripped on a large pan or tray (if possible), and pour the stripper into a container like a large coffee can.
3. Apply the stripper liberally with a bristle brush. The biggest mistake people make is not using enough stripper. Working from the container and the runoff that collects in the tray, keep the surface wet. Continue putting on the stripper until the finish begins to wrinkle (if it's paint) or dissolve (if it's a varnish or lacquer).
4. Scrape off as much of the mess as you can. Use a plastic drywall "joint" knife for flat surfaces, and your stripping brush, which has soft plastic and copper bristles, for the nooks and crannies. (If you're using wash-off stripper, you're not ready to wash it off yet.)
5. Apply more stripper with the bristle brush. With this coat, you'll need to work it in and scrub the surface with steel wool or a stripping pad saturated with the stripper. Use the stiff-bristle brush for those crevices. Don't rub too hard or you'll damage the surface.

Step 4. Apply plenty of stripper, and remove finish with a plastic scraper.

PROS AND CONS OF FURNITURE STRIPPERS

	PROS	CONS
WASH-OFF STRIPPERS	Remove finish thoroughly, including most of the underlying stain	Water can damage wood, raising the grain and loosening veneer and glue
	Do most of the work for you	Can remove the grain "filler" that gave a porous wood its smooth finish
SCRAPE-OFF STRIPPERS	Remove the old finish, but allow more control: retain stain and grain filler	Require a long drying time before finish can be applied
	Don't raise grain	Take a bit longer to remove old finish
	Usually won't loosen glue joints or veneer	Require several applications and more stripper

- long-sleeve shirt or arm protectors
- chemical-resistant gloves (PVC-coated is best)
- large pan or tray (optional)
- stripper
- container for stripper
- "real bristle" brush

- scraper
- stripping brush for scrubbing
- coarse, medium, and fine steel wool or stripping pads
- rags
- denatured alcohol, lacquer thinner, or paint thinner

6. If you're using wash-off stripping, you're ready to wash everything off. Use a bucket of soapy water and coarse steel wool for this task. Scrub down the piece, rinsing your steel wool in the bucket occasionally. Spray the piece with a water hose and scrub with clean, medium steel wool or a stripping pad. Wipe it down with dry rags and allow it to dry.

If you're using scrape-off stripper, keep repeating step 5, wiping off the piece between coats with clean rags, until the old finish is gone but the underlying stain and filler are still intact.

Step 6. Scrub off remaining stripper with soapy water and steel wool.

7. When the piece is dry, use lacquer thinner, denatured alcohol, or paint thinner with fine steel wool or a rag to remove the final traces of finish. Put used rags in a container that contains water. Contact your local waste collector for approved disposal procedures.

Save Money on Reupholstery

Most people have upholstered furniture that needs re-covering. If you and an upholsterer can reach an agreement, you can save considerable money by doing the unskilled work yourself.

- Cut the fabric away from the frame with a sharp razor blade. Don't remove the material that covers the padding and the springs unless the upholsterer has agreed to this.

- Remove the tacks or staples. No matter how much of the stuffing the upholsterer wants to remove, you can bet you'll get a gold star for removing all the tacks or staples. It's a slow, nasty job, but with pliers and a tack puller, you can do it. This is also the time to clean or refinish any exposed wood. You can't do it after the re-covering.

A Calendar Lampshade

Have you been saving attractive calendars, thinking someday you might frame the prints? Here's another use for them. Replace the cover on a flat-sided, hexagonal shade with the calendar prints. Each panel will be complementary and unique.

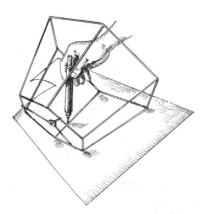

1. Cut and rip off the old shade, without bending the frame. Then trace one of the sections on the paper you wish to use as the new cover, allowing a little extra room on the edges.

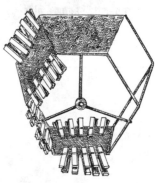

2. Run a bead of craft glue along the frame, then attach the paper with clothespins and let dry. Attach other sections the same way, weighting the top section with a bag or two of beans.

—from *Antiques on the Cheap* by James W. McKenzie

Refinishing Furniture

If you're interested in obtaining a "nice" finish that you'll be proud of but you don't want to make refinishing a career, stick with me. I'll get you through it without spending a heap of money on equipment or materials.

Preparation of the surface prior to application of the finish is one of the most important steps, so let's start there.

Sanding Tools and Methods

Few occasions in refinishing antiques require the use of sandpaper. If you've stripped the furniture properly, only light sanding is needed after using wash-off strippers and between coats of finish.

Electric sanders. The fact that power sanders aren't necessary to refinish furniture should be good news. But if you absolutely must own an electric sander, make it a "finishing" or oscillating type, not an orbital sander. The two sanders look the same, so you've got to read the description of their action. The working surface of an oscillating sander moves in a straight, back-and-forth motion—the proper motion for sanding with, or in the direction of, the grain.

Detail sanders. This tool has a small, triangular head that can get into hard-to-reach places that other sanders can't. I wouldn't recommend this machine if it didn't have another useful function: The sanding head can be removed and replaced with a scraper head. Although you won't use this feature often, there will be times when you'll find an electric paint scraper useful.

Hand sanding. Hand sanding should be adequate for 99 percent of refinishing work. But even when sanding by hand, there are decisions to be made.

To sand flat surfaces, make a sanding block. You'll need a block of wood that's 3 inches by 5 inches, and 1 to 1¼ inches thick. Glue a piece of felt to the bottom of the block to act as a cushion. Cut a standard 9- x 11-inch sheet of sandpaper into quarters, then fold the sandpaper around the block and hold it in place.

If you're not familiar with sanding sponges, they're made from a dense foam material and have abrasive on all four sides—usually a medium grit on one side and edge and fine grit on the other. They're firm enough to act as a sanding block, but flexible enough to get into contours. Sanding sponges are nearly indestructible. They're also washable, so when they become clogged with wood dust, simply rinse them out.

Sandpaper itself can be confusing: flint, aluminum oxide, silicon carbide, 150 grit, 220, 400. Let's keep it simple. Make or buy a sanding block for most work, and get some 220 and 400 wet-or-dry paper.

Either by hand or with an oscillating sander, sand bare wood with fine paper (using it dry) before applying finish. After that, between coats, use very fine sandpaper wet (or use fine again if there are noticeable brush marks).

Sanding Dos & Don'ts

- Sand lightly between coats of finish.
- Never sand wood against the grain if you plan to use a stain or varnish on it, since all scratches across the grain will be visible.
- Keep sandpaper dry by storing in a plastic bag or a plastic or metal toolbox.

Staining

Almost anything you've stripped is going to need some staining. Wax stains are your best bet. They penetrate well and are easy to apply. Sometimes you can even get by without applying a finish coat.

Applying stain. Applying stain is easy: Just dip a disposable foam brush or a rag in the stain and apply it over all the surface. As you work, go back and wipe off any excess before it begins to dry. You can apply additional coats if you want a darker finish. After that, you're ready to topcoat with varnish or simply buff up the surface with a soft rag. In many cases, especially with oak, that's the entire process. No finish coat is needed, and you're left with a nice, hand-rubbed effect.

Finishes. If you're just starting out, stick to one of a couple of finishes: water-based acrylic varnish or oil-based vinyl sealer/finish. You can't beat acrylic varnish for most jobs. It dries fast, allowing you to apply several coats a day, and it rubs to a nice finish. Its only disadvantage is that you can't apply it directly over a mahogany stain. If you've used a mahogany stain, you must coat the piece with an oil-based sealer or use the vinyl sealer and finish before applying acrylic varnish.

Oil-based vinyl sealer and finish dries faster and can be sanded even sooner than the acrylic varnish. It also rubs to a nice finish. Because it's an oil varnish and sealer, it can be used over any type or color of stain. Unlike the acrylic product, it thins and cleans up with paint thinner rather than water.

Applying finish. You can use throwaway, foam rubber brushes. Buy brushes that have wooden handles and dense foam if you can find them.

Before you tackle your first project, practice on a piece of scrap. The recommended finishes don't take too well to being brushed over once applied. If you try "brushing out" (i.e., the applying of pressure and repeated strokes of the brush), which is recommended for the application of slow-drying oil finishes, you're bound to mess up the surface.

Lay a good coat of finish on the piece, brushing with the grain and bringing the brush back over the same area only once. You need to work rather quickly, because it dries fast. Any imperfections in the stroke can be smoothed out in the sanding and rubbing stages.

Between-Coat Sanding and Final Rubbing

Between coats of varnish, sand lightly. Use the fine wet-or-dry paper with a little water. Wipe it off occasionally with a damp rag, and check for smoothness.

After you've applied the last coat, which might be the second or third coat, do not sand. Using very fine (0000 grade) steel wool and a lubricant, rub down the varnished surface until it's velvety smooth to the touch. Rub with the grain. A little diluted oil soap or some saddle soap works fine. If the surface needs a bit more leveling, common automobile rubbing compounds will do the trick. If you're happy with a "satin" sheen, you're finished. If you want a higher gloss, apply a coat of paste wax and buff.

—from *Antiques on the Cheap* by James W. McKenzie

Applying Stain and Varnish

Use a disposable foam brush to apply stain over the entire surface.

Brush on varnish along the grain. Work quickly, because it dries fast.

After you've applied the last (second or third) coat of varnish, do not sand. Instead, use very fine steel wool and a lubricant such as oil soap or saddle soap.

Patti Barrett, author of Too Busy to Clean?, *is a newspaper columnist and editor. She lives in Massachusetts with her husband and two daughters and is pursuing her master's degree in divinity.*

Cleaning the Gruesome Twosome

Kitchens and bathrooms somehow always need to be cleaned, and because people who visit usually have to use the bathroom or want a cup of tea, the rooms demand extra attention. Here are some ways to make cleaning them easier.

The Kitchen

Kitchens are more than just kitchens nowadays. They are family rooms where everyone gathers, so they get messy.

Oven. There are oven-cleaning products on the market that are hazardous, so wear rubber gloves and read instructions.

- Wipe up spills inside self-cleaning or continuous-cleaning ovens so they won't burn and stain surfaces.
- Sprinkle recent spills with salt. When the oven is cool, brush off and wipe with a damp sponge.
- Sprinkle the bottom of the oven with automatic dishwasher soap and cover with wet paper towels. Let stand a few hours, then wipe.
- Remove burned food from broiler pan: While hot, sprinkle with dry laundry detergent. Cover with a dampened paper towel and let sit for a while.

Dishwasher. Dip a damp rag in baking soda and wipe spots inside and outside. Use a glass cleaner on chrome trim.

- If the inside smells, sprinkle baking soda in the bottom; leave overnight.
- To remove film from dishes and the dishwasher, put a bowl in the bottom of the washer and add 1 cup of bleach. Run through the wash cycle but do not dry. Refill bowl with 1 cup of white vinegar and run through entire cycle.

WHAT TO DUST IT WITH

Item	Dust with
blinds	feather duster followed by soft cloth
CDs	soft cloth
computer	soft cloth
couch	vacuum
glass-framed pictures	cloth, liquid glass cleaner
lampshades	feather duster, brush attachment of vacuum cleaner
oil paintings	feather duster, very soft cloth
radiator	vacuum, feather duster
records	soft cloth
screen	sponge with dish-washing soap, rinse, buff dry
shutters	vacuum, wipe with a damp sponge
stereo	soft cloth
telephone	cloth, rag with liquid cleaner
television	soft cloth, vacuum with small brush attachment
woodstove	enamel: wipe clean and wash when cool black: reblack occasionally

Sink. For a whiter sink, place paper towels across the bottom and saturate with bleach. Let stand half an hour. Rinse.

- If drain is clogged with grease, pour 1 cup of salt and 1 cup of baking soda down the drain, followed by boiling water.
- Remove rust marks on stainless-steel sinks by rubbing with lighter fluid. Wipe with liquid cleaner.
- Remove water spots by dampening a cloth with rubbing alcohol or white vinegar. Wipe.

The Bathroom

Towels, makeup bottles, and toothpaste tubes often get thrown around. It helps to have a place for everything, but you'll still end up with soap scum to clean.

Super solutions. Use a solution of white vinegar and water to remove hard-water deposits.

- For bathtubs, mix ½ cup of vinegar with 1 cup of clear ammonia and ¼ cup of baking soda in a gallon of hot water. Wear rubber gloves and make sure the room is well ventilated. Works on fixtures, fiberglass, and porcelain.
- Use lemon oil on bathroom tiles to keep the shine longer.
- Rubbing alcohol shines chrome faucets.
- Clogged shower head? Boil for 15 minutes in ½ cup of white vinegar mixed in 1 quart of water. Soak plastic shower heads in a hot vinegar-and-water solution of the same ratio.
- Clean grout between tiles with a toothbrush. Mix 3 cups of baking soda with 1 cup of warm water into a paste. Scrub and rinse. Dip the brush in bleach to get at mildew. Cover spots with white shoe polish.
- Pour ½ cup of chlorine bleach in your toilet bowl and let stand for 10 minutes. Scrub with a brush. Not recommended for septic tanks.

Kitchen Tricks and Tips

- **Rid a cutting board of garlic or onion smell.** Rub surface with the cut side of a lime or lemon, or make a paste with baking soda and water. Apply. Rinse.
- **Broken egg on the floor.** Sprinkle egg heavily with salt, wait 5 minutes, sweep dried egg into dustpan.
- **Clean outside of cast-iron pans.** Use commercial oven cleaner. Let sit for 2 hours; remove stains with vinegar and water.
- **Clean copper pots.** Fill spray bottle with vinegar, add 3 tablespoons of salt. Spray liberally on copper surface, let sit, and rub clean. To remove tarnish, rub with toothpaste, Worcestershire sauce, or ketchup.

—from *Too Busy to Clean?*
by Patti Barrett

COUNTRY HOUSEKEEPING

Cleaning Wallpaper

Wallpaper in high-traffic areas often becomes spotted from dirty hand marks. If the room accumulates large amounts of smoke from fireplaces, woodstoves, or cigarettes, it is likely to acquire a grayish black tinge.

You can wash dirt and stains from washable or vinyl wallpaper by using a solution of mild soap and water. It is not a good idea to use strong chemical cleaners.

Nonwashable paper presents more of a problem. Gum erasers and some commercial spot removers will lighten stains. Real problem stains will have to be patched. That is why it is always a good idea to keep scrap pieces of wallpaper.

—from *The Woman's Hands-On Home Repair Guide* by Lyn Herrick

A Sampler of Housekeeping Tips

Gail's No-Buff Furniture Polish

4 ounces linseed oil

4 ounces malt vinegar

40 sweet cicely seeds, chopped and crushed,
    or 1 teaspoon each lemon oil and lime oil,
    or 1½ teaspoons lavender oil and 4 drops peppermint oil

Pour the oil and vinegar into a jar and seal tightly. Shake well. Add the sweet cicely or essential oils, and shake again. If you use the sweet cicely mixture, leave it for two weeks in a warm place and shake it daily; if you use essential oils, you may polish with it immediately.

Dampen a duster with the mixture and rub it hard on furniture or paneling. It will polish and dust at the same time, with no need to buff.

—from *Herbal Treasures* by Phyllis V. Shaudys;
recipe contributed by Gail Duff

Mirror Reflections

■ Use window cleaner on mirrors. Spray lightly, then wipe evenly with a dry cloth.
■ To remove hair spray, wipe with rubbing alcohol.
■ To defog a mirror quickly, blow hot air from a hair dryer at it.

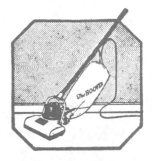

Wise Window Washing

- Use vertical strokes when washing outside and horizontal strokes when washing inside (or vice versa). Then you'll know which side the streaks are on.
- Wash windows from top to bottom, so you won't have drips messing up what you have already done.
- Use a long-handled squeegee on big windows. These are fun to use and don't leave many streaks.
- If you want a real shine, rub a clean blackboard eraser over a just-washed window and stand back!
- Don't let window cleaner get on woodwork, as it can damage it. Never use steel wool on glass.
- Try not to wash windows on a sunny day, as the glass may streak.
- What to use? Some say use newspaper. Others say use anything but newspaper. One friend says newspaper crumbled up and dipped into a bowl filled with vinegar works wonders. She dips the paper, puts it on the window, and wipes the glass with the same paper until it's almost dry. Then she shines it with a cloth or a piece of dry newspaper.

Super Solutions for Windows

- Mix ⅓ cup of ammonia in 1 gallon of warm water. Apply with a sponge or pour into a spray bottle.
- On cold days add ½ cup of rubbing alcohol to each quart of water and you won't have ice.
- Another solution: Add ½ cup of ammonia, 1 cup of white vinegar, and 2 tablespoons of cornstarch to a bucket of warm water.
- Spotted sills: Pour diluted rubbing alcohol on a cloth and rub entire sill. They'll look newly painted.
- Grease spots: Use leftover cola.
- Screen windows: Rub a brush-type roller over the screen and it will pick up dust.
- Use cream silver polish on aluminum window frames.
- Wear rubber gloves when using strong window cleaners.

—from *Too Busy to Clean?* by Patti Barrett

Cleaning Rugs

- **Natural fiber rugs.** Vacuum rugs made of sisal or grass and then treat with a damp cloth to keep in moisture.
- **Fur rugs.** Work cornmeal through the pile until the cornmeal shakes out clean. Vacuum up all that is left.
- **Washable rugs.** Air-dry small rugs to keep their shape, or dry flat. Don't hang them to dry or their shape may change.
- Vacuum top and bottom of rugs to keep dirt from wearing out fibers.

—from *Too Busy to Clean?*

Patti Barrett on Cleaning Fabrics Right

It's often a mystery how to clean certain fabrics, especially when you've lost the label or you've received a handmade item as a gift. Here are some guidelines.

Chiffon. Hand-wash in lukewarm, soapy water. Squeeze gently until clean; rinse well. Lay garment flat on a large towel and pull into shape. Place another towel on top and roll up. When almost dry, press with a warm iron.

Chintz. Hand-wash in lukewarm, soapy water and rinse well. Completely dissolve 2 teaspoons powdered size in 1 cup boiling water and strain. Dip garment into solution and squeeze out excess. Roll garment in a towel to dry partially; press lightly with a warm iron. Use stiff, hot starch if size is not available. Never use washing soda to wash chintz.

Comforters. Wash down-filled comforters individually in washing machine with hot water and soap. Rinse well and tumble dry. When dry, shake vigorously to fluff out feathers. Do not dry-clean.

Cotton. Wash white cotton in hot, soapy water. Add mild chlorine bleach to wash if needed. Rinse in clean water. Press with hot iron while damp.

Wash colored cottons together so long as the colors are fast. Add salt to the water to prevent colors from running; wash as above.

Wash drip-dry cottons in plenty of hot water. Do not squeeze. Hang up and pull the garment into shape and let drip dry.

Lace. Squeeze lace when washing, never rub it. Wash white lace in pure soap flakes and hot water mixed to a thick lather. Pour soap solution into a jar and add lace, then cover jar and shake it for 5 minutes. Change soap and repeat the process until lace is clean. Rinse in warm, then cold, water.

Next dissolve 1 teaspoon gum arabic starch in 2 cups water and dip lace into it. Squeeze out excess water and roll in a towel. Lay lace flat, face down, on a damp ironing board. Cover with a damp cloth and press with cool iron.

Linen. Wash white linen sheets, napkins, and cloths like white cotton. Natural-colored linen needs gentler treatment: Wash in cool water and do not bleach. Wash dyed linen carefully, squeezing the fabric as little as possible. Press all linens while damp with a fairly hot iron.

Satin. Add ½ tablespoon kerosene per quart of warm, soapy water, then immerse the article. Lift garment up and down until clean. Rinse several times in warm water and add a little borax to the rinse to restore gloss. Squeeze out excess water and partially dry, then press on the "wrong" side with a warm iron.

Wool. Avoid temperature extremes, as woolens will shrink. Do not soak woolens; leave them wet, or rub, twist, or wring them. Use a little soap, and rinse well. Don't machine-wash unless specified on the tag. Wash wool in hand-hot water in pure soap flakes. Dissolve soap completely before adding garment. Agitate gently; rinse in warm water. You may wash woolens in cold water with Woolite.

Patti Barrett is the author of Too Busy to Clean? *She much prefers gardening to cleaning, so she has discovered and developed many strategies for how to clean quickly and effectively.*

Stains and Spills

Here are a few points to keep in mind:

- Most stains are easy to remove if treated while fresh.
- Always remove as much of a spill as possible before you start treating a stain. Wringing or rubbing causes a stain to penetrate. Lift spilled material with a spoon or butter knife.
- Start at the outer edges and work toward the center to avoid spreading a stain. Always blot; never scrub.
- To avoid staining other parts of a garment, stretch the stained section over an old towel folded over several times.
- Always test a stain-removal agent in an inconspicuous place such as the tail of a shirt or blouse or an inside seam or hem.
- Try the simplest approach first. Cold water can remove many stains quickly, easily, and safely. (But even water can damage some textiles. Check garment tag.)
- Air-dry items you treated to be sure that a stain is completely gone. Some stains are not easily seen when a fabric is wet, and a hot dryer could set a stain, making it difficult to remove.

Greasy Stains

Greasy stains include butter and margarine, oily foods, and automotive oil. Pretreat washable fabrics by rubbing a little liquid detergent or dry-cleaning fluid directly on the spot. Treat an old oil stain that has yellowed with bleach. For nonwashable fabrics, apply dry-cleaning fluid from the edges to the center of a stain. Allow the spot to dry before repeating. Or dust an absorbent substance, such as cornstarch, cornmeal, or chalk, directly on a greasy stain, wait until it looks caked, then brush off gently.

Nongreasy Stains

Nongreasy stains include fruit juice, coffee, tea, and ink. Sponge nongreasy stains on washable fabrics with cool water as soon as possible. Soak the fabric in cool water for a few hours or overnight. If a stain persists, rub liquid detergent directly into it, then rinse with cool water. As a last resort, try color-safe bleach, but always check the tag.

Sponge nongreasy stains on nonwashable fabrics with cool water. Flush stain: Place clean, absorbent cloth behind the stain and apply cool water with an eyedropper or spray bottle. This works best when the stain is fresh.

Combination Stains

When you have a combination of greasy and nongreasy stains (e.g., coffee with cream, lipstick), first deal with the nongreasy stain. For washable fabrics, sponge stain with cool water, then apply liquid detergent and rinse well. Let fabric air dry, then deal with the greasy stain: Apply dry-cleaning fluid to the stain and allow it to dry. If the stain is not gone, reapply dry-cleaning fluid.

—from *The Stain and Spot Remover Handbook* by Jean Cooper

Laundry List

- Get white socks white again by boiling them in water with a slice of lemon.
- Rub suede lightly with an emery board to remove rain spots.
- A white vinegar solution will remove a permanent crease. Sponge the material with vinegar and press with a warm iron.
- Scorched whites? Sponge with a piece of cotton that has been soaked in peroxide. Or bleach with water and lay the item in the sun to dry.
- To remove chewing gum, apply ice to harden gum and then scrape it off. Soften with egg white before laundering. Or sponge with dry-cleaning solvent.
- Remove knots from a sweater with a fine piece of sandpaper. Or shave the sweater with a razor.

—from *Too Busy to Clean?*

A freelance author, photographer, and horticulturist, Maggie Oster has written more than a dozen books, including Herbal Vinegar.

An herbalist for fifteen years, Colleen Dodt grows many of the plants she uses in her work. She is the owner of Herbal Endeavors, Ltd., in Michigan and the author of numerous articles on herbs and aromatherapy. She has written two books: Essential Oils *and* Natural BabyCare.

Vinegar Solutions

Laboratories develop all manner of complex chemicals, yet for many of the same uses, vinegar, a substance that has been around for thousands of years, is a safer alternative. A gallon of distilled white vinegar or apple cider vinegar can replace a number of chemical household cleaning products.

Remove water rings on wooden furniture. Combine vinegar and olive oil in equal parts. On a clean soft cloth, work mixture with the grain.

Remove stains on wood floors or furniture. Clean the area with coarse steel wool dipped in mineral spirits. Scrub stain with vinegar, allowing it to penetrate for several minutes. Repeat, if necessary, rinse with water, then wax.

Remove stickers, decals, glue. Apply vinegar directly or with a clean cloth.

Make plastic antistatic. Vinegar decreases static and attraction of dust on plastic and vinyl. Wipe upholstery with a cloth dampened with a vinegar-water solution. Add a pour of vinegar to rinse water when laundering plastic curtains or tablecloths.

Clean up pet or people accidents. Combine a small amount of liquid detergent and 3 tablespoons vinegar in 1 quart warm water. Sponge on soiled area until clean, rinse with warm water, and blot dry.

Remove perspiration odors. Wipe or rinse article with vinegar.

Remove cooking odors. Prevent odor of boiling cabbage by adding a little vinegar to the cooking water. To remove fish or onion odors from hands, wipe them with vinegar. Pour vinegar into the hot skillet after cooking fish or onions and simmer briefly.

Wash dishes. To cut grease, add a capful of vinegar to dishwater.

Rinse crystal and glassware. They will sparkle when rinsed in a solution of 1 part vinegar to 3 parts warm water.

Clean bottles, jars, and vases. Remove chalky film by pouring in vinegar. Let stand several minutes or longer, then shake or brush vigorously.

Clean coffee and tea stains from glass and china. Boil vinegar in glass coffeepots once a week, wash, and rinse. Equal parts vinegar and salt removes stains from cups.

Freshen lunch boxes. Dampen a piece of bread with vinegar and leave inside overnight.

Remove lime deposits. To clean tea kettles, coffee brewers, and irons, fill with vinegar and heat or run through one cycle. Run through another cycle with plain water.

Loosen rusted, corroded screws and hinges. Pour vinegar over the head of a rusty screw or a hinge to loosen. Soak screws, bolts, and nuts in vinegar and scrub with a brush.

Improve light from propane lamps. Remove mantle, place in container, and cover with vinegar. Soak several hours. Dry thoroughly.

Dye Easter eggs. For bright colors, combine ½ cup boiling water, 1 teaspoon vinegar, and 1 teaspoon food coloring. Dip eggs until colored as desired.

Keep hiking water fresh. Add several drops of vinegar to an insulated water container to keep the water fresh longer and make it a better thirst-quencher.

Make windshields frost-free. Wipe windshields with a sponge soaked in a solution of 3 parts vinegar to 1 part water.

Clean stiff, caked paintbrushes. Soak mildly caked brushes in vinegar until clean. For worse cases, gently simmer in vinegar for 5 to 10 minutes. Wash in warm, soapy water, then rinse.

Remove fruit stains from hands. Rub hands with vinegar.

Clean salt marks on leather. Wipe salt-stained boots or shoes with a cloth moistened with vinegar.

Iron without shine. To keep wool or other fabrics from becoming shiny when ironing, place a cloth dampened with 1 part vinegar to 2 parts water over the fabric.

Remove crayon stains. Moisten a soft toothbrush with vinegar and rub out crayon from fabric or other surfaces.

—from *Herbal Vinegar* by Maggie Oster

Cleaning with Essential Oils

Adding pure essential oils to your cleaning routines can bring new meaning to this necessary but often boring task. Many of the cleaning products available on the market today are full of chemicals. Essential oils offer a natural alternative.

Washing Dishes

I finish up a sinkful of dirty dishes much more quickly when I add 5 to 7 drops of lemon essential oil to the dishwater and dish soap. The steam fills my nostrils with tart, sassy lemon; my hands benefit from the lemon oil; and it cuts grease.

I add ½ ounce to the dishwater to help glasses and dishes come out squeaky clean. Add lemon essential oil directly to vinegar, then add this mixture to the dishwater. I recommend 10 drops of lemon for 1 ounce of vinegar.

Washing Floors

For mopping the floors, try a combination of Murphy's oil soap and pure essential oils, in a ratio of 20 drops of essential oils to 2 gallons of water. When guests enter my home they ask, "What smells so good in here?"

Freshening Carpets

Carpeting can hold pet smells and smoking odors. I treat my carpets to a homemade carpet freshener. Start with a box of borax, available at the grocery store. To 2 cups of borax, add 25 drops of pure essential oil. Make sure the drops of oil are crushed well and evenly distributed in the borax. Apply it to the carpet or rug by shaking it off a large spoon or out of a large can with a shaker lid. An old powder bottle works well.

I have two cats and I never have a problem with fleas. I attribute this to the consistent use of the borax mixture on my rugs and carpets.

—from *The Essential Oils Book* by Colleen K. Dodt

Essential Oils for Cleaning Floors

eucalyptus
lavender
lemon
patchouli
pine
rosemary
sweet orange

—from *The Essential Oils Book*

COUNTRY HOUSEKEEPING

Using Herbs for Moth Control

Place cloth or paper packets of herbal mixtures in each bureau drawer, in the knitting basket, and in quantity in closets and chests, replacing them yearly. The following herbs are insecticidal and useful for moth control.

Camphor Basil, Mint Family. Harvest leaves during the growing season, or the whole plant before frost. Place in a brown paper bag; hang to dry.

Eucalyptus, Myrtle Family. Use silver-dollar tree and blue gum. Lemon-scented gum does well as a houseplant in a sunny window.

Pennyroyal, Mint Family. Use either the European or the American variety as an insecticide. Harvest upright stems when in full bloom; hang to dry.

Pyrethrum, Composite Family. Painted daisy and Dalmatian insect flower produce insecticidal ingredients in the center yellow disk flowers. For maximum concentration, harvest flowers on the day that buds open, dry on screens, and store in jars in a dark place. Grind flowers to a fine powder and add to herbal moth-repellent mixture.

Red Cedar. Renew cedar chests periodically by sanding interior or treat wood with cedar oil.

Southernwood, Composite Family. A wood-moth repellent. Harvest early to midsummer. Effective 6 to 12 months.

Tansy, Composite Family. Contains the insecticidal compound thujone. Harvest leaves in summer or fall; hang to dry.

Rita Buchanan's Moth-Repellent Mixtures

- For a distinctive scent, use camphor basil, pennyroyal, eucalyptus, southernwood, or rosemary leaves. Combine equal parts of the dried fragrant plant with ground pyrethrum flowers.
- Mix equal parts southernwood, wormwood, and tansy for a sweet mix.
- Mix equal parts camphor basil, lavender, and rosemary for a tangy aroma. Optional: Add camphor or cinnamon.
- Mix 2 parts lavender, 2 parts southernwood, 1 part rosemary, 1 part pennyroyal, and 1 part wormwood. Add 1 tablespoon of powdered cloves to each 2 cups of herbs and mix well.

—from *Herbal Treasures* by Phyllis V. Shaudys; contributed by Rita Buchanan

Bug Bulletin

Pets and fleas. Feed your pet yeast powder or tablets with its food every day, starting in February and continuing through flea season. It's available at health food stores. Fleas don't like to bite dogs or cats that smell of yeast.

Ants. They don't like tansy, so if you have some, spread it where they are entering the house.

Silverfish. Sprinkle boric acid mixed with sugar on affected areas.

Trouble with Roaches

It can be very difficult to get rid of roaches They come inside for food and water, so remove the source and half the war is won. You also must destroy any and all roach eggs. They are brown and about the size of a grain of rice.

Roaches like dark places, so vacuum under the refrigerator, the heater, all furniture, the sink (pipes, too), the washing machine, and stove burners; go behind the toilet, books, the piano, the heavy dresser, and in the folds of drapes.

After roach eggs are destroyed, spray with a roach spray or try turpentine. Or use a mixture of 2 parts borax and 1 part sugar. Spread this wherever roaches might be. If any water, food, or garbage is available to them, the roaches won't feed on the borax, so put all foods in sealed containers. Also, be sure to put away the pet dish.

—from *Too Busy to Clean?* by Patti Barrett

TANSY

Controlling Pests with Essential Oils

- To make a natural insect repellent that is safe to apply to your skin, combine ⅛ ounce each of citronella, patchouli, and vetiver oils with 3 ounces of sweet almond oil.

- To use pennyroyal as a flea repellent, do not apply it directly to the animal's fur. Instead, use a few drops in the pet's bathwater or put a few drops on a bandanna or rope collar around the animal's neck for a constantly effective and safe flea retardant.

- For a repellent effective against a variety of insects, mix 10 drops of pennyroyal, 10 drops of eucalyptus, 30 drops of citronella, and 10 drops of cedarwood oil with 4 ounces of sweet almond oil.

- For a flea repellent for carpets, combine 3 drops of pennyroyal, 3 drops of eucalyptus, 9 drops of citronella, and 3 drops of cedarwood oil with 1 pound of baking soda. Sprinkle on carpet, let stand 1 hour, and then vacuum.

—from *Herbal Treasures* by Phyllis V. Shaudys; contributed by Jen and Mike Mescher

Bugging the Bugs

Grandmother didn't have much in the way of household sprays, but she knew that planting tansy around doorways would keep out ants. And strips of cucumber laid here and there would offend them enough to make them go away if they found some other way of getting in.

When outdoors, she dabbed chamomile tea on exposed skin as an insect repellent. For keeping moths out of clothes closets, she hung them with sprigs of rosemary or wormwood. These also were put in storage chests for clothes. She used sage, tansy, and spearmint to chase flies, rue to repel flies, fleas, and other insects. Pennyroyal discouraged flies, fleas, and mosquitoes. Try putting pennyroyal on your cat's collar to keep her free of fleas.

—from *Sleeping with a Sunflower* by Louise Riotte

SOAPMAKING

Getting Started with Soapmaking

The tools needed to make basic soap are minimal and probably already available in your kitchen. Remember to dedicate your equipment for soapmaking only—do not use it for food preparation. You will need:

- 16-ounce glass measuring cup
- 2 plastic or stainless-steel spoons
- 2-quart stainless-steel saucepan
- 8-quart stainless-steel pot
- plastic spatula
- plastic ladle
- paring knife
- scale
- plastic wrap and newspaper
- glass candy thermometer
- molds
- spray-on corn oil, mineral oil, or petroleum jelly

Never attempt to make soap in aluminum containers—you will ruin both your containers and your soap. Strong plastic spoons are preferable to wood because lye will eat away at wood fibers.

You can obtain molds from many sources. Candy and candle molds also work well as soap molds, giving you a variety of shapes and sizes. Make sure the molds are clear, because soap is inclined to absorb colors. You can also make an easy mold out of wood with dimensions of 20 inches by 14 inches and a depth of at least 2 inches. A cardboard box of this size will work well also.

—from *Milk-Based Soaps*

Basic Recipe for Milk-Based Soap

3	pounds pure vegetable shortening
17	ounces extra-light olive oil
12	ounces safflower oil
8	ounces canola oil
3	pounds goat's or cow's milk, prepared for soapmaking (see below)
12	ounces pure sodium hydroxide (lye)
1	ounce borax
½	ounce white sugar
½	ounce glycerine

1. Cover work surfaces with plastic or newspaper, prepare mold(s), and lay out equipment.

2. Melt vegetable shortening in an 8-quart pot over low heat.

3. Weigh liquid oils on a digital scale; add them to the pan with the shortening. Heat only until vegetable shortening is completely melted; immediately remove from heat. Do not overheat. Set aside until step 9.

4. Fill sink with cold water. Add 4 to 6 trays of ice cubes.

5. Put 3 pounds of cold, pasteurized milk (it first must be frozen, then thawed) into a 3- or 4-quart stainless-steel pot. Place saucepan into ice water and stabilize it by placing plastic cups filled with water around it.

6. Gloves on: Measure 12 ounces of lye into a 16-ounce glass measuring cup.

7. Very slowly pour lye into the cold milk in the ice-water bath, stirring all the while with a plastic spoon. It should take no less than 15 minutes. This slow process prevents the lye from scorching the milk and is one of the keys to success. The milk/lye mixture is corrosive, so you must not let it contact your bare skin.

8. Gauge the temperature of the lye/milk mixture so it does not drop below 80°F. The two mistakes you might make at this point are allowing the lye/milk mixture to get too cool and letting it sit too long before combining it with oils. This causes the mixture to congeal into a useless mass. Keep stirring. Remove mixture from the cold-water bath when the milk turns a bright yellowish color, which means that the lye combined with it successfully.

9. Reheat the oils to 125°F over low heat, then remove.

10. Slowly pour the lye/milk mixture into this oil. Add borax, sugar, and glycerin. Stir constantly, but do not splash on your skin. It will get very warm. Keep stirring gently or the lye/milk mixture may refuse to join with the oils. Be patient.

11. With a plastic ladle, scoop evenly mixed amounts of the oil/lye mixture into a blender, filling it halfway. Secure the lid before switching it on! Run blender for 1 minute on medium speed, remembering to stir the contents of the pan in the sink. The liquid in the blender will turn a pale cream color. After 1 minute, pour from the blender into a second 8-quart saucepan. Now you have two pans to stir and a blender to run—a partner is helpful! Repeat this procedure until all the mixture is blended.

12. Quickly wash the first (now empty) saucepan, dry well, and repeat the whole process, going from the second pan to the blender for 1 minute and then to the first pan, stirring both pans all the while. It is during the second blending that you add fragrance, herbs, or grains. There is now little or no separation of the oils from the rest of the mixture; after the second blending, the mixture is ready to pour. It will thicken, but if it seems thin, it is still ready for a mold. If it is too thin, repeat the blending procedure a third time.

13. Pour the mixture into the prepared mold and screed the top surface by pulling the flat edge of a putty knife or spatula across from one end to the other.

14. Allow the mixture to sit uncovered and undisturbed in a draft-free, low-humidity area. In 12 hours, you may notice sweatlike, tan-colored beads on the surface. Most will evaporate after 24 hours. Gently wipe off beads that don't with a paper towel before cutting into bars.

15. Cut into bars after 24 hours, but allow the cut soap to remain in the mold for another 24 hours, until it is hard enough to hold its shape when removed. If too soft, check every 4 hours until ready. Do not wait more than 24 hours to cut, or the soap becomes too brittle.

16. Allow the bars to cure for 6 weeks in a dry, cool room. Cover lightly with plastic wrap to protect from dust.

Shepherd's Pride

Makes 32 (4-ounce) bars

This soap is enriched with pure lanolin and aloe vera, both renowned for their healing and moisturizing qualities. It is scented with jasmine and is excellent for dry skin.

3	pounds pure vegetable shortening
17	ounces extra-light olive oil
12	ounces safflower oil
4	ounces canola oil
4	ounces lanolin
3	pounds goat's or cow's milk, prepared for soapmaking
12	ounces pure sodium hydroxide (lye)
1	ounce borax
¼	ounce white sugar
¼	ounce glycerin
½	ounce jasmine fragrance oil
½	ounce aloe vera

Special instructions: Melt lanolin with oils; add the fragrance oil and aloe vera when you run the liquid mixture through the blender the second time.

—from *Milk-Based Soaps* by Casey Makela

Working with Lye

The lye used in soapmaking is a chemical called sodium hydroxide. You can purchase it from your grocery store in 12-ounce containers. Be absolutely sure that the product you purchase contains only sodium hydroxide.

Never forget that lye is a powerful and dangerous chemical that must be handled with care. Strictly observe these safe practices:

- Read and observe the precautionary statements on your lye container.
- Do not undertake soapmaking when tired or rushed, or while caring for young children. Making soap requires your undivided attention.
- Always wear safety glasses. Don't risk exposing your eyesight to the perils of a lye burn.
- Always wear rubber gloves. If you do get any lye on your skin, run cold water on the area.
- Work in a well-ventilated room, preferably near an open window.
- Set aside utensils, pans, and any other soap-making equipment for soap-making use only.
- Thoroughly clean every utensil, container, counter, and tabletop that was used for soapmaking.

PART TWO

Your Garden, Yard & Orchard

Growing things is at the center of country life. Whether you want a fruit orchard, an herb garden, a large vegetable garden, or a lush perennial bed, the first priority is to choose the right location. Find a sunny spot for your garden that is fertile, well drained, and close enough to the house that you visit it frequently. The ideal site is a southern slope that is easily worked and harvested. Your next consideration is to build the soil so it is fertile, well balanced, and easy to work with, using compost and other organic matter. This is a lifelong process. As your garden matures you will find its productivity improves every year.

THE VEGETABLE GARDEN

9

PLANNING YOUR GARDEN • COOL- AND WARM-SEASON VEGETABLES • EXTENDING THE SEASON • GROWING FROM SEED • SPECIAL GROWING TECHNIQUES • HARVEST AND STORAGE • SEED SAVING • VEGETABLES A TO Z

Our family's World War II victory garden was a source of fresh vegetables during a time of scarcity, but also of pride in doing our part. It brought neighbors together, swapping tales over the fence. Every neighborhood has a green thumb. When I was a boy in New Jersey it was Mr. Koeffel, who grew the biggest and earliest tomatoes. When Martha and I bought our small farm, it was Roger Smith, whose northern garden yielded perpetually from spring to fall. I asked Roger where to plant my new garden. We walked the grounds together, and this man of few words said simply, "Here." I did as he said, uncovering some of the richest black soil I'd ever seen. Quiet men make great gardeners.

—John Storey

Start your vegetable garden with a plan, just as if you were designing a flower bed. Lay it out on paper, using tracing pads of graph paper. You'll have a choice of several grid sizes; four squares to the inch is most practical for laying out a garden to scale.

Tracing paper allows you to overlay this year's garden plan on last year's (and even that of two years ago) to plan crop rotations easily. Note each vegetable variety in the layout and, after you plant, the date of planting. It's important to ensure proper spacing so you can calculate how much seed to purchase.

You will also want to keep in mind the best combinations of companion plants, trap crops, and insect-deterrent plants to ensure a healthy garden. You'll find most of that information in this chapter.

To get maximum sun, plant the tallest crops on the garden's north side so they won't shade shorter ones, or run your rows north and south. Plant vegetable families together so you can plan the rotation of crops in subsequent years.

Garden Planning Chart

VEGETABLE	SEEDS OR PLANTS FOR A 50' ROW	DISTANCE BETWEEN ROWS IN INCHES	FEET OF ROW PER PERSON	SPACING BETWEEN PLANTS IN INCHES
Beans, dry	4 oz.	18	20–30	6–8
Beans, shell	4 oz.	18	30	8–10
Beans, snap	4 oz.	18	30	2–4
Beets	½ oz.	12	10–15	2–4
Broccoli	25 plants	24	5 plants	12–24
Brussels sprouts	25 plants	24	5 plants	12–24
Cabbage	25 plants	24	10 plants	12–18
Carrots	⅛ oz.	12	10	1–3
Cauliflower	25 plants	24	5 plants	14–24
Corn	1 oz.	24	25	9–15
Cucumbers	¼ oz.	48	10–15	12
Eggplant	25 plants	24	5 plants	18–36
Endive	⅛ oz.	18	10	8–12
Kale	⅛ oz.	18	12	18–24
Kohlrabi	⅛ oz.	18	10	3–6
Lettuce, head	⅛ oz.	15	5–10	10–15
Lettuce, leaf	⅛ oz.	12	5–10	10–12
Muskmelons	12 plants	48	3 plants	12
Onion sets	1 lb.	12	10–20	2–4
Parsnips	¼ oz.	18	5–10	3–6
Peas	8 oz.	24	50–100	1–3
Peppers	33 plants	18	5 plants	12–24
Potatoes	33 plants	30	50	9–12
Pumpkins	¼ oz.	60	1 hill	36–60
Radishes	½ oz.	12	5	1–2
Salsify	½ oz.	18	5	2–4
Spinach	½ oz.	15	20	2–6
Squash, summer	¼ oz.	60	1 hill	24–48
Squash, winter	½ oz.	60	3–5 hills	24–40
Swiss chard	¼ oz.	18	5	3–6
Tomatoes	12–15 plants	30	5 plants	12–24
Turnips	¼ oz.	15	10	2–6
Watermelon	30 plants	72	2–3 hills	72–96
Zucchini	¼ oz.	60	1 hill	24–48

Know Your Vegetable Families!

- **Brassicas:** cabbage, kale, broccoli, collards, cauliflower, kohlrabi, Brussels sprouts
- **Corn**
- **Leafy greens:** spinach, chard, lettuce
- **Legumes:** peas, beans, limas
- **Nightshade family:** peppers, tomatoes, potatoes, eggplant
- **Root vegetables:** beets, carrots, turnips, salsify, parsnips, radishes, rutabagas, onions, garlic, leeks
- **Vine crops:** cucumber, melons, squash

—from *The Big Book of Gardening Skills*

PLANNING YOUR GARDEN

Louise Riotte lived a remarkable life, until her death in 1998 at age 88. Living on her productive Oklahoma homestead, she was a creative and talented gardener, a passionate amateur naturalist, a farmer, a dowser, a bee-keeper, and a grandmother, as well as a beloved and best-selling writer. She was perhaps best known for her books Carrots Love Tomatoes *and* Roses Love Garlic, *which presented the secrets of companion planting to hundreds of thousands of eager readers.*

Louise Riotte on the Secrets of Companion Planting

The magic and mystery of companion planting has intrigued and fascinated humans for centuries, yet it is a part of the gardening world that has never been fully explored. Even today, we are just on the threshold.

Vegetable growers find that companion planting provides many benefits, one of which is protection from pests. A major enemy of the carrot is the carrot fly, whereas the leek suffers from onion fly and leek moth. Yet when leek and carrot live together in companionship, the strong and strangely different smell of the partner plant repels the insects so much that they do not even attempt to lay their eggs on the neighbor plant. This is why mixed plantings give better insect control than a monoculture, where many plants of the same type are placed together row after row. Even when plants are affected by disease, a mixed plant culture can usually alleviate the situation.

Vegetable Companion Guide

	Beans, bush	Beans, pole	Beets	Cabbage	Carrots	Celery	Corn	Cucumbers	Eggplant	Lettuce	Melon	Onion	Peas	Pepper	Radish	Spinach	Squash	Strawberry	Tomato	Special
Basil														X					X	
Beans, bush			X	X	X	X	X	X	X	X		O	X		X			X		1
Beans, pole			O		X		X	X	X	X		O	X		X					2
Beets	X			X								X								
Cabbage family	X		X				X					X						O	X	3
Carrots	X	X								X		X	X		X				X	4
Celery	X			X								X				X			X	
Corn	X	X						X			X		X				X		O	
Cucumbers	X	X					X			X		X	X		X					5
Eggplant	X	X													X					
Lettuce	X	X			X			X				X			X			X		
Marigold	X	X		X				X										X	X	
Melon							X								X					
Nasturtium				X				X			X				X		X		X	
Onion	O	O	X	X	X	X		X		X			O	X			X	X	X	6
Parsley																			X	
Peas	X	X			X			X	X			O			X					7
Pepper												X								
Radish	X	X			X			X			X	X						X		8
Sage			X	X	X			O												
Spinach						X			X									X		9
Squash							X					X			X					
Strawberry	X			O						X		X				X				
Tomato				X	X	X	O					X								10

X Good Companions   **O** Bad Companions

SPECIAL COMPANIONS

1. Savory, tansy
2. Savory, tansy
3. All strong herbs
4. Sage, no dill
5. No strong herbs
6. Savory
7. Turnips
8. No hyssop
9. Cauliflower
10. Mint, no fennel

Succession Planting for Greater Yield

There's no need to have a bare spot in your garden after you harvest early crops like lettuce and onions. Letting the sun hit bare soil during the growing season is a waste of solar energy. Here's how to plant a succession crop for a late-summer or fall harvest.

YOUR GARDEN, YARD & ORCHARD

1. Harvest your early crop and then turn over the soil, turning in any remaining plant material. Add a little fertilizer, such as dehydrated manure, to the row.

2. After leveling off the soil, pull your garden rake straight down the row. It will leave a mark that will become the row.

3. Sprinkle the seeds in the row and then pat down the soil by hand. Bury the seeds with about four times their diameter of soil, then pat it down again.

SUCCESSFUL CROP ROTATION PRACTICES

PLANT	FOLLOW WITH	DO NOT FOLLOW WITH
Beans	cauliflower, carrots, broccoli, cabbage, corn	onions, garlic
Beets	spinach	—
Cole crops	beans, onions	tomatoes
Carrots	lettuce, tomatoes	dill
Cucumbers	peas, radishes	potatoes
Kale	beans, peas	cole crops
Lettuce	carrots, cucumbers, radishes	—
Onions	radishes, lettuce, cole crops	beans
Peas	cole crops, carrots, beans, corn	—
Potatoes	beans, cabbage, corn, turnips	tomatoes, squash, pumpkins
Radishes	beans	cole crops
Tomatoes	carrots, onions	cole crops

4. Water the seeds, and watch how fast they come up during the warm summer months.

—from *Down-to-Earth Gardening Know-How for the '90s* by Dick Raymond

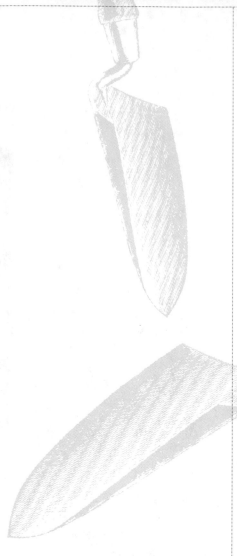

Dirt-Cheap Gardening Tips

Don't think for a minute that an inexpensive garden has to look cheap. If you expend a little time, energy, and creativity—without a lot of money—you will have a garden others envy. Here are some of the many ways to accomplish this:

$ Invest in longer-living plants and perennials that come back year after year.

$ Choose disease-resistant varieties for longer-lived plants.

$ Don't waste money or time growing crops that are cheaper to buy.

$ To find great deals on plants, join your local garden club and participate in its plant swaps and sales.

$ To save money on seeds and plants, and to increase your selection, join a seed-savers exchange club or plant association.

$ Find out when a nursery is expecting a new shipment so you can shop for the healthiest plants.

$ Use stem cuttings or leaf cuttings to propagate plants.

$ Start with healthy soil for healthier, longer-lived plants.

$ Don't waste money giving plants more nutrient supplements (fertilizer) than they can absorb.

$ Use readily available, free, or low-cost soil amendments such as compost, animal manure, sewage sludge, green manures, coffee grounds, and sawdust.

$ Maximize your harvest in limited spaces by planting in raised beds.

$ Watch for signs of insect or disease damage so you can take steps early and save more plants.

$ Group together plants that need heavier watering so you can concentrate extra water in a few locations.

—from *Tips for Dirt-Cheap Gardening* by Rhonda Massingham Hart

Mix Your Own Soil

A standard formula is:

- 1 part soil
- 1 part peat moss
- 1 part perlite, vermiculite, or sharp, clean sand
- 1 part compost (optional)

Stir until thoroughly mixed.

—from *Tips for Dirt-Cheap Gardening*

Raised Beds: Easier Gardening, Healthier Crops

A raised bed is a mound of loose, well-prepared soil, 6 to 8 inches high. The beds can be permanent, with edgings of stone, blocks, timbers, or railway ties, or they can be re-formed each time the garden is planted.

Raised beds are particularly helpful if you are working with heavy soils that drain poorly. In the long run, easy maintenance and the use of hand tools make this method extremely appropriate for the home garden.

What are the other benefits? First, no one actually steps into the raised beds, so the soil always stays porous and loose and never compacts. This loose soil provides good drainage, allowing water, air, and fertilizer to penetrate easily to the roots of your plants.

If you make permanent raised beds, the garden path next to the raised bed is never used for growing vegetables. Because it is constantly being walked on and packed down, it stays dry, clean, and relatively weed-free.

Since the beds are isolated by the paths between them, you can rotate the varieties of vegetables you plant in each bed each year. This allows you to keep one particular family of vegetables from consuming all the same kind of soil

Raised beds can be supported with boards (as shown at left) or other materials, or they can simply be raked into hills (as shown in the box below).

nutrients. It also discourages insect pests and pathogens from remaining in the soil over the winter and infecting the next season's crop.

Finally, the raised-bed gardening system makes a beautiful garden that is always orderly and organized because it is so easy to maintain. You can easily reach into every corner to cultivate the beds, and to pull young weeds as they appear. Succession planting will keep the garden constantly filled with vegetables and pleasing to the eye.

—from *The Big Book of Gardening Skills*

Getting Started with Raised Beds

Using Hand Tools

1. To make a raised bed, mark the bed with stakes and strings. Sixteen inches is a good width, but some gardeners prefer beds 3 or 4 feet wide. Make your bed any convenient length. Walkways can be up to 20 inches wide.

2. Using a rake, pull the soil from the walkway to the top of the bed. Stand in one walkway and draw soil toward you from the opposite walkway. Do the same on the other side.

3. Enrich the bed with compost, manure, or other organic materials. Then level the top of the bed with the back of the rake. Sides should slope at a 45-degree angle. A lip of soil around the top edge of a new bed helps reduce erosion.

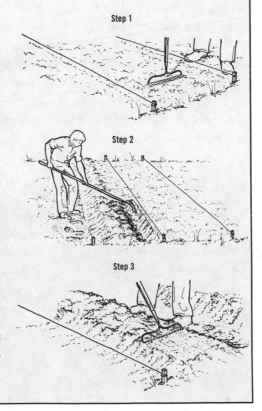

Step 1

Step 2

Step 3

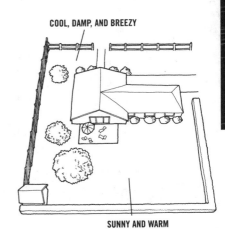

COOL, DAMP, AND BREEZY

SUNNY AND WARM

Know Your Microclimates

Even the smallest yard has a variety of growing areas within it, known as microclimates. As you will learn from nurseries, garden centers, or the instructions on your seed packets, plants all have their own unique growing requirements. Some plants thrive in the shade, while others falter there for a lack of sun. When assessing your chosen garden area, note your microclimates. They will help you decide what plants to grow and where to put them.

—from *Tips for Dirt-Cheap Gardening*

PLANNING YOUR GARDEN

Crops That Thrive in Wide Rows

anise
beans of all kinds
beets
cabbage
caraway
carrots
chard
chives
collards
cress
dill
endive
garlic
kale
kohlrabi
leeks
lettuce
mustard
onions (seeds and sets)
oregano
parsley
parsnips
peas (English, crowder, field, southern)
peppermint
radishes
rutabagas
salsify
shallots
spearmint
spinach
summer savory
sweet marjoram
turnips

—from *Wide-Row Planting*

Planting in Rows: Wide or Narrow, Short or Long?

Some vegetables resent transplanting, so it's best to start their seeds right in the garden plot where they will mature. Depending on the plants, they'll do better if you determine whether to plant them in single rows or wide rows. The row width depends on the crop (see chart earlier in chapter). For some plants, if rows are too narrow, they won't have room to grow. For others, if rows are too wide, you'll waste space, allowing weeds to intrude and preventing the cross-pollination necessary for producing fruits or vegetables.

It is best to fertilize below or between the rows, rather than enriching the soil immediately surrounding the seeds. Very rich soil will stimulate early leaf development, but plants will do better if they start with a good root structure.

When planting tall crops, orient the rows from north to south so each plant gets the most sunlight possible. It is also better to plant several short rows rather than a few long ones, to ensure cross-pollination. On a small scale, you can form single rows by raking loose soil into narrow furrows and rows with a garden rake. On a larger scale, a motorized tiller may be necessary. Consider setting out stakes and strings as guides to help keep the rows straight.

Once your rows are formed, plant seeds in a straight line at the center of the row. Spacing will depend on the crop, but it is always better to plant extra and thin later than be disappointed by a poor germination rate.

Always firm the soil over the seeds to bring them in contact with moisture held in the soil. Water thoroughly after planting and regularly until the plants are established. Mulch applied between the rows will help cut down on weeds and hold moisture in the soil.

Nine Reasons to Plant Wide Rows

1. Increases yields. Just about anyone can grow two to four times as much produce by using wide rows. More square feet of garden space is producing food, and less is wasted on cultivated areas between rows.

2. Saves time. You'll spend less time weeding and harvesting. When you bend over a wide row, you'll have far more growing area at your fingertips.

3. Saves space. By planting shorter, wider rows, you leave yourself space to plant more varieties of vegetables.

4. Saves mulching. Wide rows shade the soil beneath them, keeping the soil cool and moist. This reduces your need for mulch.

5. Makes harvesting easier. Since the rows produce so much more food per foot of row, you pick more from a single location, while sitting on a stool!

How to Plant a Wide Row in 4 Easy Steps

A

B

C

D

(A) Use two lengths of string to mark off a row at least 16 inches wide, or about the width of a steel rake. You can make the bed wider if you choose. (B) Rake the seed bed smooth. (C) Broadcast the seeds over the area, aiming for good coverage over the entire bed. (D) Depending on the type of seed being planted, you may need to cover seeds by sprinkling compost over them, or rake soil over them from outside the row.

If you are setting out transplants, stagger their positions. A pattern of 2-1-2-1 is effective.

6. **Permits cool-weather crops in heat.** Since shading the ground keeps it cooler, these plants grow for a longer period in wide rows.

7. **Improves quality of crops.** The texture and consistency of produce are greatly improved because of the more even environment in wider plantings. For example, the rows are less susceptible to drying winds.

8. **Reduces insect damage.** Non-isolated plants are less attractive to hordes of chewing insects and worms.

9. **Makes companion planting easier.** You can spread more than one type of seed. It is not complicated to plant radishes with just about anything else, or to sow beet or carrot seeds among onions.

—from *Wide-Row Planting* by Dick Raymond

Tips for Planting Wide Rows

Follow these basic steps and you'll grow more food with less work and far less weeding.

- Prepare a seed bed 6 to 8 inches deep and quite loose.
- Never step on the seed bed or compact it in any way.
- Don't be stingy with the seeds. Sow thickly.
- Sow a few radishes in every wide row.
- Pull soil with a rake from beyond your rows to cover seeds. Smooth soil with a rake upside down, covering seeds with the same amount of soil.
- Use a garden rake to thin plants when they are ½ inch. Drag rake across the row with the teeth going down in the soil about ¼ inch.
- Start harvesting as soon as something is big enough to eat.

—from *The Joy of Gardening* by Dick Raymond

The gardener's biggest challenge is to keep plants with different needs healthy and happy.

Cool-Season Crops

arugula, roquette
broad beans
beets
broccoli
broccoli raab
Brussels sprouts
cabbage
Chinese cabbage
cauliflower
collards
corn salad
endive
Florence fennel
kale
kohlrabi
lettuce
parsley
parsnip
peas
radicchio
radish
red mustard
spinach
turnip

Cool-Season Vegetables

The cool season is that time of year when night temperatures stay above about 25°F and below 60°F. The length of time cool weather lingers differs every year, but a typical cool season ranges from less than 60 days in the far North and Deep South to more than 100 days elsewhere.

Many cool-season crops are planted in staggered sowings to ensure a constant supply of vegetables. A safe general rule is to plant seeds every 10 to14 days. This rule doesn't always work, however, because conditions in the garden change over the course of the season. As temperatures warm or cool and moisture concentrations change, the growth rates of the plants increase or decrease.

To time your staggered crops more exactly, sow your second plantings of root crops and greens, such as radishes and spinach, when the first seedlings show their first set of true leaves. For crops such as peas, make successive plantings when the seedlings are as tall as your index finger.

Warm-Season Vegetables

Planting the warm-season vegetable garden marks the end of the long transition between winter and summer, and from indoor to outdoor gardening. The soil is warm enough to foster the growth of tender seeds, and the corn, tomatoes, and pepper plants explode with life.

Some of the plants of the warm-season garden are holdovers from spring. Carrots, potatoes, and Swiss chard can all stand cool weather, but unlike other cool-season plants they can also tolerate or even thrive in the warm days of summer. Other warm-season crops, such as tomatoes, corn, and snap beans, evolved in the semitropical regions of the world, where cool nights alternate with warm days for most of the year. This is still the best environment for their cultivated relatives; the best crops are grown where the summer nights are at least 15 degrees cooler than the days.

Keeping so many plants with such different likes and dislikes happy in one garden is a bit of a challenge, but it doesn't have to be a daunting one. Even though these plants are a varied group, they still have much in common. All of them thrive in evenly moist soil rich in organic matter bathed in sunshine. There are some subtleties to master, but they make the resulting accomplishments that much sweeter.

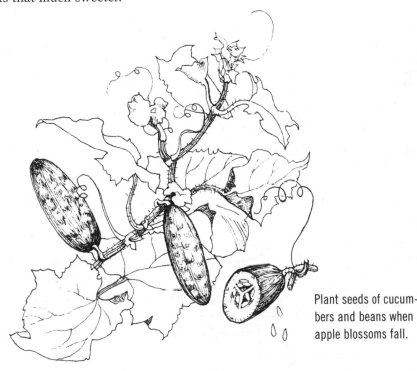

Plant seeds of cucumbers and beans when apple blossoms fall.

Warm-Season Crops

artichokes
asparagus
bush beans
carrots
celery
corn (sweet)
cucumber
eggplant
garlic (*Allium sativum*)
leek
melon
okra
onion (bulb)
peanuts
pepper (sweet)
pole beans
popcorn
potato
pumpkin
rhubarb
squash (summer and winter)
sweet potato
Swiss chard
tomato
watermelon

—from *The Big Book of Gardening Secrets*

Warm-Season Phenology

Phenology is the science of using indicator plants to determine when certain weather conditions will prevail and certain insect pests will be active. Here's how you might use phenology to guide your plantings:

- Plant Swiss chard, spinach, beets, and onions when your daffodils bloom.
- Plant peas when the maple trees flower.
- Plant potatoes when the leaves of white oaks are the size of a cat's ear.
- Sow bush beans, pole beans, and cucumbers when apple trees drop their petals.
- Transplant tomatoes, melons, and eggplants when black locust trees and peony bushes flower.
- Transplant when you see swallows swooping close to the ground over fields. The insects they eat fly closer to the ground before it rains.

—from *The Big Book of Gardening Secrets* by Charles W.G. Smith

EXTENDING THE SEASON

Favorite Season Extenders

Floating row cover

Black polyethylene mulch

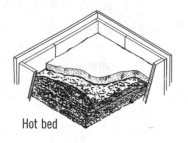

Hot bed

The Old-Fashioned Hot Bed

The old-fashioned hot bed is a wonderful invention that can keep fresh lettuce on the table just about all winter long. To build a hot bed, simply remove all the soil to a depth of 2 feet inside the cold frame. Line the earthen sides with 1- or 2-inch-thick panels of Styrofoam insulation. Add a wooden frame around the insulation to brace it, if desired. Add an 18-inch layer of fresh horse manure and firm well. Spread 6 inches of sand on top of the manure. Use a soil thermometer to track the temperature of the sand. As the manure composts, it will heat the sand to over 100°F. Place flats and pots of plants in the hot bed when the sand temperature drops below 90°F. The manure will heat the bed for many weeks. When the manure is composted, the hot bed can once again be used as a cold frame.

—from *The Big Book of Gardening Secrets*

Plant Protectors: Extending Your Growing Season

In some respects, the term *extenders* is a misnomer. More than adding a few weeks to the start or end of a season, extenders actually modify the climate. They protect from not just frost but also wind, pests, rain, and snow. Low-cost, old-fashioned season extenders that remain popular include cold frames, plastic cones, hot caps, plastic milk jugs with bottoms cut away, hay bales, newspaper, blankets, plastic-wrapped wire frames, and even grocery bags with their edges turned down and weighted with soil. All work well in certain situations. We'll examine a few in some detail.

Row Covers

Row covers are extenders that protect your plants. There are two main kinds—floating and plastic.

Floating row covers are soft, white "garden blankets" made of light-

Plastic row cover supported by hoops

weight, permeable material. They require no supports and are available in numerous weights, sizes, and thicknesses. The lighter they are, the more light transmission they allow, but the lighter ones also offer less frost protection. The thicker they are, the more frost protection they provide. But the thicker covers also generate more heat—something to watch for when the sun intensifies.

Use floating row covers immediately after transplanting tomatoes, eggplants, broccoli, melons, cucumbers, cauliflower, strawberries, and other heat-loving plants. Remove them when blossoms are ready for pollination or temperatures exceed 85°F. In the fall, keep covers on longer to maintain soil heat on cool evenings.

Plastic row covers are often perforated or slitted to let rain or moisture through. They protect plants from pests, but they do not keep out all insects. The covers are laid in the form of a tunnel supported by wire hoops. Most offer only a few degrees of frost protection, significantly less than the thicker-fabric row covers. They also tend to generate more heat than floating row covers, making them well suited for heat-loving plants such as cucumbers, melons, and eggplants.

Install plastic row covers as soon as the soil can be worked in the spring. They can increase vegetable germination and yields by as much as three weeks and 50 percent.

Mulches, Cool and Warm

Cool mulches control weeds by blocking visible light from reaching the soil. Many differ from warming mulches in that they reflect most of the sun's energy instead of absorbing it. Cooling mulches include white plastic (used rarely), straw, pine needles, and black-and-white newspaper. As they inhibit weeds, they allow water to penetrate readily. The mulch then acts as a water conservator, allowing moisture to percolate down through the soil but inhibiting evaporation. Temperatures beneath a cooling mulch can be several degrees lower than the ambient air temperature.

There are three types of warm mulches. **Black polyethylene mulch** is made of 1.25-mil black plastic sheeting. It has been used for decades, but it has some disadvantages. It is not biodegradable and is often difficult to remove from the garden. **Black paper mulch** works similarly. It does not warm the soil as efficiently as black poly, but the difference is slight. Unlike black poly, black paper mulch allows water to seep into the soil. **IRT-100** is a dark-colored plastic that allows a good deal of energy from the sun to warm the soil directly. It then helps retain the accumulated warmth. It is the most effective soil-warming mulch to date, but it is not biodegradable. See Chapter 13 for more on mulch.

Hot Caps

Hot caps are simple devices to protect individual small plants from frost. One option is the plastic milk container. Simply cut the bottom from a 1-gallon container and set it over the plant. Leave off the cap for ventilation. Seedlings can be protected by setting paper cups over individual plants.

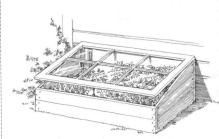

Homemade hot cap

Wall-O-Water hot cap

The best device for frost protection is the Wall-O-Water hot cap, which consists of several plastic cylinders joined into the shape of a tepee. When you place it around the plant, fill the cylinders with water. In tests among paper cups, milk jugs, row covers, and Wall-O-Waters tepees, the tepees were most effective in providing frost protection.

Hot caps give plants a head start on growth. However, if plants are not weaned from them by blossom time, the plants' yields will be smaller than those gathered from plants grown without the caps.

Cold Frames

The cold frame is a small, easily built structure used to lengthen the growing season. Traditional cold frames are most often made of wood such as redwood, white cedar, or cypress. The headboard is about 18 inches high, with a footboard 12 inches tall. Sloping, 6-foot-long boards connect the two and serve as support structures for the window sash used as glazing. The entire structure is then set so the footboard faces south.

The cold frame becomes a small greenhouse, letting solar energy pass through to warm the soil, then trapping the heat that radiates back. This is a boon to northern gardeners who wish to grow cool-season crops such as lettuce into the winter. For maximum heat retention, line the floor with black plastic. A thermometer in the frame helps you gauge when it's warm enough in spring to plant or hot enough to ventilate.

You can also purchase precut cold frames made with tubular polycarbonate sheets and aluminum joiners. This kind of glazing is almost as clear as glass.

—from *Row Covers and Mulches* by Fred Stetson
and *The Big Book of Gardening Secrets*

Cold Frames

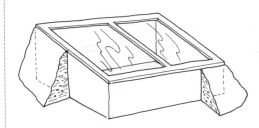

Small wood-sided cold frame

Cold frame with insulated sides

Cold frame with stone sides

EXTENDING THE SEASON

Planting Dates in Relation to Frost

Hardy
Plant as soon as ground can be prepared

asparagus
beets
broccoli
cabbage
carrots
chard
kale
lettuce
onions
parsnip
peas
radishes
spinach
turnip

Semi-Hardy
Plant 1 to 2 weeks before average date of last frost

cauliflower
potatoes

Tender
Plant on or just after average date of last frost

New Zealand spinach
snap beans
sweet corn
tomatoes

Very Tender
Plant 2 weeks after average date of last frost

cucumber
eggplant
lima beans
muskmelon
peppers
pumpkins
squash
watermelon

Average Frost Dates

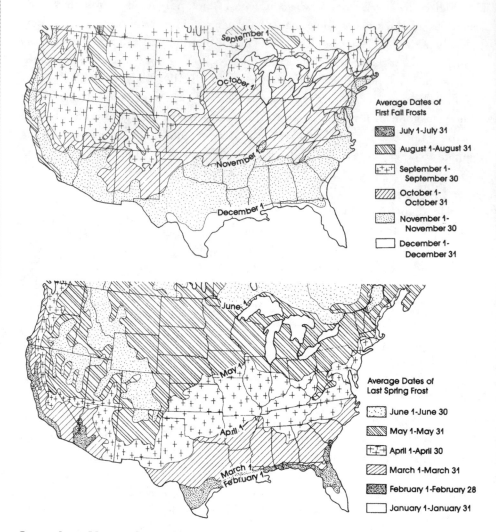

Average Dates of First Fall Frosts

	July 1-July 31
	August 1-August 31
	September 1-September 30
	October 1-October 31
	November 1-November 30
	December 1-December 31

Average Dates of Last Spring Frost

	June 1-June 30
	May 1-May 31
	April 1-April 30
	March 1-March 31
	February 1-February 28
	January 1-January 31

Starting Your Own Plants from Seeds

You'll need seeds, of course, but you'll also need a few more supplies to be successful at starting plants from seeds.

Containers

Basically, anything that can hold a germinating medium and is the right size will do. Seed-sowing flats should be 3 to 3½ inches deep and can be of any size, depending on how many seeds you intend to germinate. Generally the ones you buy are made of plastic or fiber.

Peat pots are good for seeds that resent transplanting and for larger seeds. These pots are usually 2½ to 3 inches across, and are a combined germinating-growing-transplanting unit.

Peat pellets are made of compressed peat. When placed in water, they expand into a unit similar in function to a peat pot. They are best for larger, reliably germinating seeds and seeds that resent transplanting.

Plugs are cone- or cylinder-shaped transplants. You can buy plug trays, which have up to 200 plug holes. One seed is sown into each plug hole.

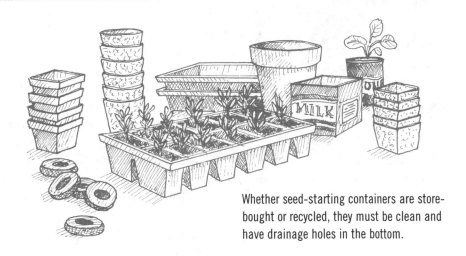

Whether seed-starting containers are store-bought or recycled, they must be clean and have drainage holes in the bottom.

You can also use things lying about the kitchen, such as coffee cans, paper cups, aluminum baking trays, milk or juice containers, and plastic food storage containers. Before using them, wash them in soap and water and rinse in a bleach solution (1 ounce bleach per 2 gallons water). This prevents diseases that might kill your seedlings.

Containers must have excellent drainage. If you make your own, be sure to punch out some drainage holes in the bottom.

Growing Media

There is no one perfect germinating medium, but here is a look at some of the available choices.

Baled or bagged peat moss comes from decomposed aquatic plants. Its composition varies greatly. It is rarely used by itself for propagating or growing, because water may not penetrate it easily or evenly. However, it is widely used in sowing and growing mixtures.

Sphagnum moss is relatively sterile, lightweight, and able to absorb 10 to 20 times its weight in water. It is generally milled (shredded) for use as a seed-sowing medium.

Vermiculite is expanded mica. It holds tremendous amounts of water for long periods of time and contains a high percentage of magnesium and potassium, two elements necessary for good root growth. Although it is not usually used alone for seed germination, it is an excellent addition to a mix.

Perlite is a volcanic ash that stays cool and is therefore good in mixes used for germinating seeds that prefer lower temperatures. However, it will float to the surface when the seed bed is watered. Use the finest grade for seed germinating.

Soil from the garden should not be used to germinate seeds, unless it is first sterilized to kill weed seeds and fungi. To sterilize it, bake in a shallow pan at 180°F for 30 minutes. Be prepared for an unpleasant odor.

Mixtures of peat or sphagnum moss with vermiculite and/or perlite are the best media for germinating seeds. You can buy these ready-made or make them yourself, using ⅓ to ½ sphagnum or peat moss and vermiculite, perlite, or a combination of the two for the rest.

—from *Starting Seed Indoors* by Ann Reilly

Double-Dig Your Garden

About the same time that you are starting seeds, you might also start thinking about one of the best treatments for your garden: double digging.

Dig a trench about a foot wide and as deep as your shovel. Place soil on a tarp or in a cart.

Drive the tines of a garden fork or a broadfork as deep as you can into the bottom of the trench. Rock the handle back and forth to loosen the subsoil. Spread a little compost over the loosened soil.

Dig another trench alongside the first, turning the removed soil into the first trench. Continue to the far end of the bed, and fill the last trench with the soil from the first trench.

STARTING WITH SEEDS

Five Easy Steps to Sowing Seeds Indoors

Step 1. Fill flat with soil and level.

Step 2. Spread seeds evenly.

Step 3. Cover seeds.

Step 4. Firm the soil and water.

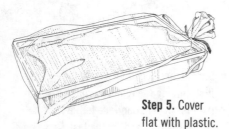

Step 5. Cover flat with plastic.

Sowing Seeds Indoors

Here's how to start seeds indoors in early spring (see drawings at left):

1. Fill a flat to within ¼ inch of the top with potting mixture and level the surface with a piece of wood.

2. If you are going to plant the seed in rows, use the edge of the wood to make ¼-inch troughs in the soil. Otherwise, spread the seeds over the soil, evenly and not too thickly, then press them in with the flat side of the wood.

3. Cover them, remembering that they should be buried to a depth of about four times their own diameter. Try to make sure that you spread an equal amount of soil over the whole area.

4. Use a flat piece of wood to firm the soil a second time. Newly planted seeds should be watered liberally but gently—preferably with a fine spray.

5. Last, the flats or pots should be put in plastic bags or covered with plastic to seal in moisture. You should not have to do more watering until the seedlings come up.

Helping Your Seeds Germinate and Grow

Provide your seeds with the following environmental conditions:

- **Light.** Place them near a sunny window with a southern exposure or under cool-white fluorescent bulbs. If they are by a windowsill, turn newly sprouted seedlings regularly so they will grow straight and evenly.

- **Warmth.** Most seeds germinate and grow best in a spot where the temperature remains 70 to 75°F. Most seedlings prefer normal room temperatures of 60 to 70°F.

- **Moisture and humidity.** Keep the germinating medium moist, but never soaking wet. Slip your seed flats into plastic bags or cover them with glass until the seeds germinate. Remove the cover as soon as seeds sprout. Check new seedlings every day to see if the medium is lighter in color, indicating it is drying out. Water from the bottom until seedlings are fairly large.

Suspend standard fluorescent lights over seedling trays.

The first sprouts you will see are seed leaves, which are food storage cells. Once the first true leaves develop, start fertilizing. Use a soluble plant food at one-fourth the label strength when seedlings are small. Increase to half strength as the plants mature. When bottom-watering young seedlings, mix the fertilizer into the water; later, the seedlings can be fertilized from above.

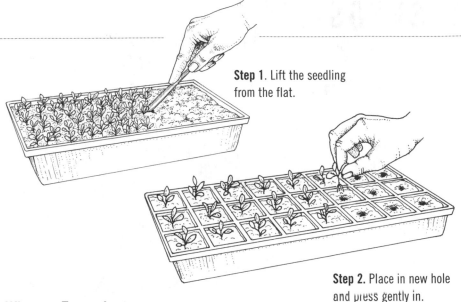

Step 1. Lift the seedling from the flat.

Step 2. Place in new hole and press gently in.

When to Transplant

Seedlings started in flats should be transplanted to a larger container before going into the garden, or at least be thinned so they won't become crowded, leggy, or weak. Seedlings started in individual pots do not need transplanting.

Transplant or thin when seedlings have developed four true leaves. If thinning, leave at least 1 inch between seedlings. Larger seedlings need more space. When transplanting, water the seedlings thoroughly first. If they're going into peat pots or peat pellets, wet the peat as well. Premoisten any media that seedlings are going into. Fill the container with the medium, then open a hole in the center deep and wide enough to fit the seedling's roots.

1. Using a spoon handle or fork, gently lift the seedling from the flat . Separate it carefully so as not to break any more roots than necessary. Always handle a seedling by its leaves, never by the stem.

2. Lower the seedling into the new hole, placing it slightly deeper than it was growing in the flat, and press gently on the medium.

Transplants may droop or wilt, but they will recover if properly cared for. Some plants benefit from pinching while in the transplant stage. Simply reach into the center of the plant and nip out the growing tip.

Special Seed Treatments

Many seeds require special handling to ensure that they will sprout. Check the package or ask your nursery whether your selections require any of the following techniques.

Scarification. Nick the outer shell with a file or knife to make it easier for the plant to start growing.

Soaking. Pour hot water over the seed and let it cool overnight before sowing.

Stratification. Plants often need a re-creation of natural cycles for seeds to grow. Place the seed in a sealed container or plastic bag with four or five times its volume of moist peat moss or vermiculite. Place the container in a warm spot for warm stratification, or in the refrigerator for cold stratification (in the freezer if 32°F is required). After the first month or so, examine the seed every few weeks. When small, white primary roots appear, sow the seed in soil or potting mixture immediately.

—from *The Big Book of Gardening Skills*

Special Seed Treatments

Scarifying seeds by nicking with a file

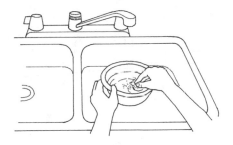

Soaking seeds

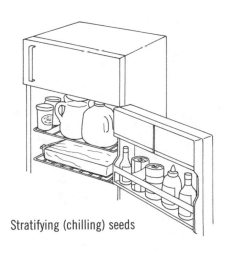

Stratifying (chilling) seeds

STARTING WITH SEEDS

Four Easy Steps to Sowing Seeds Outdoors

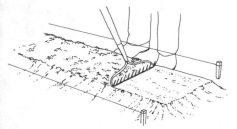

Step 1. Use a string to mark straight rows, and then drag your rake down the bed.

Step 2. Sprinkle seeds over the bed.

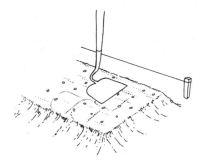

Step 3. Firm them with the back of a hoe.

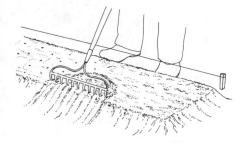

Step 4. Cover the seeds with soil.

Harden off plants by putting them outdoors in a sheltered spot for a week or two before they go into the garden.

Getting Plants Ready for the Garden

Hardening off is a process that acclimates plants to new environments. It gradually toughens their tissues so they can adjust to a more challenging environment. One to two weeks before transplanting to the garden, place the young plants outdoors on a patio or step, first on a cloudy day, then on sunny days. (Bring them in at night.) Mild breezes will help strengthen their stems. If a frost is expected, bring them indoors and place them back outside the next day.

Sowing Seeds Outdoors

To start an outdoor seedbed, create a loose bed 6 to 8 inches deep. Use a rototiller to make it easy and fast. Excellent seedbeds can be readied with hand tools, also.

1. Use a string to establish the edge of the row. It tells you where your first walkway will be. Stay right there in the walkway to plant, as well as to perform your other garden chores.

Use a rake to mark the exact width of beds, making them at least 15 to16 inches. Drag your rake down the bed, keeping the edge of the rake close to the string. Rake only the areas where you're going to broadcast seeds. Smooth the soil with the back of the rake until the seedbed is smooth and level. Remove large stones, clumps of soil, and large pieces of organic matter.

2. Sprinkle or broadcast the seeds over the bed like grass seed.

3. Firm them in for good germination, using the back of a regular hoe. To germinate well, seeds should come in good contact with warm, moist soil on all sides. Tamping them down gives them this contact.

4. Now comes the important step—covering the seeds with just the right amount of soil. Small seeds like carrots and most annuals usually need about ¼ to ½ inch of soil to cover them. Larger seeds such as peas and beans need about 1 inch. A rule of thumb for seeds is to cover them with enough moist soil to equal four times their own diameter.

The easy way to cover seeds is to use a rake and pull soil from 1 to 2 feet beyond the row up onto the seedbed. The important thing is to lift up the soil onto the bed and not to rake into the seedbed. Once you have little mounds of soil sitting on the entire seedbed, smooth them out with the back of the rake.

Tips for Setting Out Plants in the Garden

Double-check planting dates before you start moving plants to the garden. Most annuals and vegetable must wait until the danger of frost is past; some can go out earlier. Tomatoes, eggplants, and peppers must wait until the ground has completely warmed up.

- Prepare garden soil with organic materials to get the most from your plants.
- Water both the ground and the transplants to cut down on transplanting shock. Do your transplanting on a cloudy day or late in the afternoon, so the heat of the sun won't cause excess wilting.
- Dig a hole about twice the size of the root ball. Set the transplant into the hole deeply enough so the root ball will be covered by ¼ inch of soil. Press the soil firmly about its roots.
- If seedlings are growing in peat pots, plant them as they are. Peel back peat pots slightly so the walls will not confine roots, and cover them completely with soil.
- Use a knife or trowel to cut out transplants growing in flats that are not compartmentalized.
- Transplants in individual pots can be turned upside down and tapped out.
- Water immediately after transplanting and again every day for a week, until the plants are established. If some of them wilt, misting or shading them will help them revive quickly.

Dig a hole about twice the size of the root ball.

Gently put the plant in place and press soil about its roots.

—from *Starting Seeds Indoors* by Ann Reilly

Outdoor Seedling Care

- If the soil is dry on planting day, use a sprinkler on your rows after planting.
- Keep the soil slightly moist until the seedlings come up. Once the seeds germinate, don't let them dry out.
- Watering is usually unnecessary early in the spring, when most garden soils have quite a bit of moisture.
- After a rain or watering, a clay-type soil may become so hard that young seedlings can't burst through. Here's how to beat crusty soil: Drag a garden rake carefully over the seedbed with just enough force to break up the crust. The tines should penetrate the soil only about ¼ inch. You may have to water hard-packed seedbeds before loosening your soil.

—from *The Big Book of Gardening Skills*

STARTING WITH SEEDS

Plant a Scarecrow with Your Seeds!

Experienced gardeners know that spring is the best time to erect a scarecrow, when birds go after tender young sprouts.

The classic scarecrow is made of a simple T, pounded into the ground and then dressed and stuffed with straw.

This scarecrow is a little more ambitious and fanciful and can hang in a nearby tree.

—from *Scarecrows* by Felder Rushing

IMPROVE YOUR TIMING, INCREASE YOUR YIELDS!

Here are some sowing and setting-out dates for a few vegetables and flowers that are commonly started indoors. Use them as approximate guides; the best planting time will vary depending on your locale and gardening practices.

Plant	Sowing Date (weeks before last frost date)	Days to Germination	Transplant Date (weeks before (-) or after (+) last frost date)
Vegetables			
Broccoli	10	5 – 10	-3
Cabbage	10	5 – 8	-3
Cauliflower	10	5 – 10	-3
Collards or Kale	10	5 – 8	-3
Leeks	10	5 – 10	-2
Onions	10	5 – 8	-2
Parsley	10	10 – 15	-3
Celery	8	14 – 21	+2
Lettuce	8	2 – 3	-4
Chives	6 – 10	7 – 14	3
Basil	6 – 8	7 – 10	+2
Marjoram	6 – 8	8 – 14	3
Dill	6	21 – 28	+2
Eggplant	6	10 – 14	-2
Peppers	6	10 – 15	+2
Tomatoes	6	7 – 10	+2
Summer Squash	3 – 4	7 – 10	+2
Flowers			
Lobelia	10	14 – 21	+2
Petunias	10	7 – 10	+2
Calendulas	8	7 – 10	-2
Snapdragons	8	7 – 10	-2
Four-O'Clocks	6	7 – 12	+2
Nicotiana	6	14 – 21	+2
Stock	6	7 – 10	+2
Strawflowers	6	3 – 5	+2
Cosmos	4	3 – 5	+2
Marigolds	4	3 – 5	+4
Zinnias	4	3 – 5	+2

—from *Easy Gardening 101* by Pat Stone

CHARLES SMITH ON HIGH-YIELD GARDENING

People who have acres and acres of corn don't worry too much about a few straggly stalks here and there. But those who have only a 20-foot-square garden must use that small space wisely. Many factors—from spacing to weeding—have a profound effect on garden yields.

Proper Spacing

Certain plants, such as root crops (carrots, radishes, beets), are less sensitive to close spacing than others. Leaf crops, such as spinach, celery, and lettuce, can also grow closely together. Fruit-bearing upright plants such as peppers and tomatoes give highest yields when their foliage is almost overlapping. If they are spaced so the foliage of mature plants is separated by 3 to 4 inches, the total yield declines but the size of the individual fruits increases. Vining crops such as melons, cucumbers, and pumpkins need more space and more light.

Pinch out suckers on tomato plants so more energy goes into main stems.

Light

Fruits such as melons and storage parts such as potato tubers are reservoirs that hold accumulated energy gathered from sunlight by the leaves. These plants should be in a spot where sunlight falls on the entire plant. Leaf crops such as lettuce and Swiss chard, on the other hand, do not need as much light.

Hoe out weeds regularly so crops don't have to compete.

Watering

To produce the best crops, plants should have uninterrupted growth—which translates to an even, constant supply of water. Under most conditions, this means about an inch per week; however, this may depend on the stage of growth. Ripening strawberries that receive slightly less than an inch of water per week produce smaller but sweeter fruits. A little less water while fruits are ripening will reduce the yield but increase quality. Potatoes and onions need much less water just before harvest. This helps the crop last longer after the harvest.

If seeds fail to germinate, fill gaps in row with additional seeds.

Weeds

It comes as no surprise that an unweeded garden produces smaller yields. What is a surprise is just how much a difference weeding makes. Studies show that regularly weeded fields produced six times as many tomatoes as did unweeded ones. Potato yields increased threefold, onions more than tenfold, carrots more than fifteen-fold. But the timing of cultivation is critical. Do not weed after a rain of less than half an inch, or you will lose soil moisture. Weed during dry times or after a heavy rain. Vegetables are most susceptible to competition from weeds from the seedling stage through the time fruits begin to enlarge and mature.

—Charles Smith is the author of *The Big Book of Gardening Secrets*

Water regularly to foster uninterrupted growth.

SPECIAL TECHNIQUES

Growing Plants Vertically

If your garden feels cramped and crowded, take advantage of vertical space. It is healthier for vining plants to climb upward into the air and sunlight than to sprawl on the damp earth. (See Chapter 18 for more on trellising.)

Stakes

The simplest of all plant supports are stakes or poles. Drive them into the soil near the base of a plant and the vines instinctively latch onto them. Tie tall or heavy plants to the stakes to support them. Then prune the excess growth at the top. Garden centers offer a variety of wooden, bamboo, and manufactured stakes, or you can make your own from scrap lumber, pieces of metal or PVC pipe, or other rigid materials.

Tepee Trellises

Tepees make excellent supports for beans, peas, and tomatoes, and for heavily fruited crops such as melon and squash. To build one, you will need three to six poles—thin ones for flowers or lightweight plants, stouter ones for heavily fruited crops. Cut the poles 10 to 12 feet long so you can sink them 1 to 2 feet into the ground. Use twine, raffia, or strips of rawhide or cloth to lash poles together near the top. Pull the poles into a tight bundle, wrap the twine around the bundle a few times, and tie it snugly. Prop the bundles over the planting area, positioning the bottom ends so each pole will support one or two vines. Thicker poles are heavy enough to be freestanding.

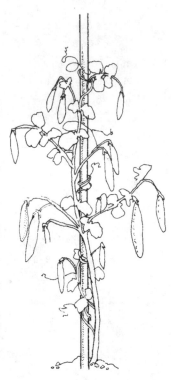

Simple stakes are excellent for twining vines.

Try Vertical Growing to Expand Your Gardens

- Fruit is cleaner and less susceptible to damage from rotting, insects, and slugs.
- More air and sunlight reach the plants.
- Cultivating and harvesting are easier.
- Requires less space.
- Yields are generally higher.
- Creates a shady garden spot.
- Provides a framework for plant coverings.
- Allows more efficient watering.
- Makes monitoring and managing pests easier.
- Earliest, cleanest, and longest-lasting harvests.

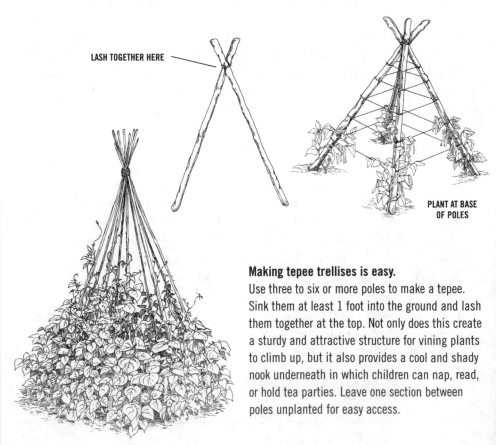

LASH TOGETHER HERE

PLANT AT BASE OF POLES

Making tepee trellises is easy.
Use three to six or more poles to make a tepee. Sink them at least 1 foot into the ground and lash them together at the top. Not only does this create a sturdy and attractive structure for vining plants to climb up, but it also provides a cool and shady nook underneath in which children can nap, read, or hold tea parties. Leave one section between poles unplanted for easy access.

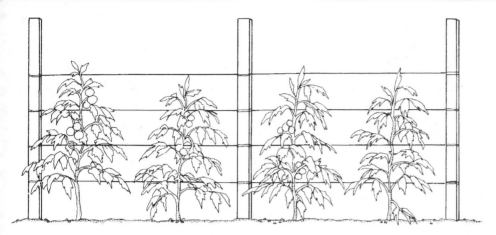

Fence trellises provide sturdy support for vining tomatoes.

Fence Trellises

Drive a post at each end of a row and place other posts in between where needed. String with twine, wire, netting, or wire mesh and you have a fence-type trellis. Fences over 20 feet long should have an extra post installed every 10 to 12 feet. By attaching cross arms to the end posts and running wires between them, you can convert the simple fence trellis into a double fence or clothesline trellis that can support two or four lines instead of just one.

Cages

Another simple and efficient method of containing sprawlers is with a cage. Cages can be nailed together from scrap 1 x 2 lumber or made with sturdy wire mesh. Bend the mesh into shape and arrange it over transplants such as tomatoes and cucumbers. Round or square cages, 2 to 3 feet in diameter and 3 to 4 feet high, will both contain and support a variety of vines.

A-Frames

Construct an A-frame trellis of lightweight lumber—1 x 2s or 2 x 4s. Wire mesh fencing, garden netting, or vertically or horizontally strung wire or twine will serve as the plant support. You can design an A-frame in any dimensions, but it must be of manageable size if it is to be portable. Both sides of this versatile trellis are used, and it can be made sturdy enough to support heavy crops such as gourds and pumpkins.

—from *The Big Book of Gardening Skills*

Cages are another favorite technique for supporting tomatoes.

Use **A-frame trellises** for vines with heavy fruits, such as melons, gourds, and pumpkins.

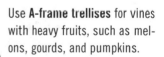

HARVEST AND STORAGE

Harvesting Tips

Pick berries when they slide easily from the plant.

Cut asparagus when the tips are still tightly budded.

Pinch off the tops of basil to prevent flowering and prolong the harvest.

Storing Root Vegetables

The term *root cellar* includes a whole range of ingenious vegetable-saving techniques, from hillside caves to garden trenches. The traditional root cellar is an underground storage space for vegetables and fruits. Root-cellar storage helps you eat better, saves money, conserves energy, and rewards with a good sense of providing for yourself.

When heavy frost sparkles and crunches in the grass each morning, it's time to begin thinking about bringing in the root vegetables. There's a lot to be

DICK RAYMOND ON HARVESTING VEGETABLES

The home gardener has an advantage over the commercial vegetable grower, and does not have to harvest crops before they are ripe. We can pick our vegetables just as they reach their prime.

In general, bring things in from the garden just before you are going to eat them or prepare them for storage. With every minute that passes from the time the produce is picked, the vegetables lose quality and food value. Never leave fresh vegetables sitting around for a long time. Keep them in a refrigerator or a cool, dark cellar. This will slow down the deterioration process.

Some vegetables can be picked before they are completely mature. Young onions, beets, carrots, cabbages, and the leaves from head lettuce plants that have not formed heads are all delicious. Most of the early crops in your garden will mature quite suddenly, so there is an all-too-short period of time to harvest them. Later varieties are not apt to mature quite so quickly.

If you want your plants to continue to bear vegetables, keep them harvested. Pick everything as soon as it is ready, even if you know it is impossible for you to use it all. Throw any surplus on the compost pile. Or better still, make plans to share with friends, neighbors, and needy folks. Giving fresh vegetables away is one of the friendliest gestures I know.

The crops you harvest later in the season are the easiest and best ones to store. If you have a root cellar, it will have cooled off by this time. Potatoes, cabbages, and turnips should be ready just in time to go into the root cellar. Eat your first plantings of beets and carrots throughout the summer months and plan to use later plantings for canning and freezing.

Big, big vegetables have passed the point of being ripe, tender, and flavorful. I like to grow vegetables that I call "table size." This means harvesting beets, for example, when they are slightly larger than a lemon. Carrots shouldn't be much bigger around than your thumb.

The more you harvest, the more you grow. If you don't pick your lettuce, it will go to seed. Chard and other heat-tolerant greens can be cut continuously all summer long.

—Dick Raymond is the author of *The Joy of Gardening, Gardening Know-How for the '90s,* and many other books.

done—digging, trimming, rounding up containers, gathering sawdust, sand, and leaves, and packing the vegetables away.

Timing of the harvest is important. It is a good idea to leave root vegetables in the ground as long as you can, so that when you do harvest them the temperature in your storage area will stay low enough for good keeping.

There are two things to watch out for. One is the tendency of some root crops—especially beets, rutabagas, and sometimes turnips—to shoulder their way above ground. Mulch them to prevent severe frost damage. Second, don't put off harvest too long—until the ground is frozen. Once November has gotten a foothold, winter's on its way. In the upper northern states, make that October. In the upper South, you can wait until December.

—from *Root Cellaring* by Mike and Nancy Bubel

The Dos and Don'ts of Root Vegetables

DO

- Keep fruits and vegetables in small piles, not heaped in large mounds.
- Handle produce carefully.
- Check stored food often and weed out questionable specimens.
- Store only your best—sound, unbruised, mature.
- Keep vegetables as cool as possible.
- Provide for ventilation in your storage space.
- Use frozen onions and cabbage, but don't let them thaw and refreeze.
- Make use of leafy tops of vegetables when you harvest them.
- Plant your root crops in deeply worked soil.
- Cut back leafy tops of root vegetables to within 1 inch of the crown before packing them away.
- Harvest storage produce in cold weather when soil is dry.
- Keep a record or simple map of what you stored and where.
- Keep containers of vegetables raised several inches above the floor.
- Pack root vegetables in sand or sawdust that's damp but not soggy. If your cellar is dry, you may need to add a bit of moisture to packing materials once or twice during the winter.
- Eat up what you've stored. It's there to be used.

DON'T

- Wash root vegetables before storing them.
- Put vegetables right on a bare concrete floor.
- Store insect-damaged, bruised, or immature produce.
- Keep onions, garlic, squash, pumpkins, or sweet potatoes in a damp place.
- Store stemless squash or pumpkins.
- Give root crops or storage fruits large doses of high-nitrogen fertilizer.
- Seal incompletely dried nuts and grains in tightly closed containers.
- Feel bad if a small percentage of your store produce spoils. You're still way ahead when you grow and keep your own food.

More Harvesting Tips

Cut the main head of broccoli while buds are tight.

Broccoli plants will continue to grow after the main harvest. Side shoots will develop and you will be able to harvest for several more weeks.

Mike and Nancy Bubel, authors of Root Cellaring, *have written a number of practical books about their life in rural Pennsylvania. There is something about a root cellar, they say, that calls up associations of "home" and "security." They have designed and built not only traditional root cellars but also all kinds of improvised and ingenious systems that work equally well.*

STORAGE REQUIREMENTS OF VEGETABLES AND FRUITS

COLD AND VERY MOIST
(32–40°F and 90–95 percent relative humidity)
Carrots
Beets
Parsnips
Rutabagas
Turnips
Celery
Chinese cabbage
Celeriac
Salsify
Scorzonera
Winter radishes
Kohlrabi
Leeks
Collards
Broccoli (short term)
Brussels sprouts (short term)
Horseradish
Jerusalem artichokes
Hamburg-rooted parsley

COLD AND MOIST
(32–40°F and 80–90 percent relative humidity)
Potatoes
Cabbage
Cauliflower (short term)
Apples
Grapes (40°F)
Oranges
Pears
Quince
Endive, escarole
Grapefruit

COOL AND MOIST
(40–50°F and 85–90 percent relative humidity)
Cucumbers
Sweet peppers (45–55°F)
Cantaloupe
Muskmelon
Watermelon

Eggplant (50–60°F)
Ripe tomatoes

COOL AND DRY
(32–50°F and 60–70 percent relative humidity)
Garlic (keeps better in even lower humidity, around 50 percent)
Onions
Green soybeans in the pod (short term)

MODERATELY WARM AND DRY
(50–60°F and 60–70 percent relative humidity)
Dry hot peppers
Pumpkins
Winter squash
Sweet potatoes
Green tomatoes (up to 70°F is OK)

—from Root Cellaring

The Basement Root Cellar

Basement root cellars are convenient to use and relatively inexpensive to build. If you live in an old house, you may already have a dirt-floored room or corner in the basement. If it has a window, you can cool and ventilate the room. If yours is a finished basement that stays pretty warm, consider partitioning off one corner on the north side to enclose a root cellar. Try to include one outside window.

All you need for a basement root cellar is a 3½- by 7-foot space. It will hold 28 half-bushel baskets of produce. You can vary it to suit your space and needs.

If you can't spare even this much space, you can build a vegetable hideaway closet rather than a room, simply by putting up shelves, enclosing them with studs and insulation, and putting two insulated doors on the front for easy access to all corners of the root closet. Use Aspenite (wood chips pressed together with exterior glue) to line the closet; it's durable in damp places and inexpensive. Or use even less expensive liner materials such as aluminum offset press plates, linoleum rugs, scraps of Formica, or scrap paneling. Here's how to build your vegetable closet:

1. Attach a sill of 2 x 4 lumber to the floor. To fasten the 2 x 4 to a concrete floor, drill holes through the wood every 2 to 3 feet, using a wood drill bit. Place the sill in position on the floor and, using the predrilled holes as a template, drill holes in the concrete with a masonry drill. Sweep away the fine concrete dust. Run a bead of construction cement around the edges of the 2 x 4. Place the 2 x 4 over the predrilled holes. Insert the sleeve and screw in lag bolts, taking care not to strip the threads. Your sill should run around the perimeter of the root cellar, leaving a 30-inch rough opening for a door.

2. Toenail 2 x 4 studs to the plate every 16 inches on center.

3. Nail a 2 x 4 header on top of the studs.

4. Fasten a vapor barrier (tar paper or 6-mil polyethylene sheets) to the studs. The vapor barrier should face the warmer area.

5. Attach insulation to the studs. Styrofoam or urethane panels are less likely than fiberglass to become waterlogged in a very damp cellar.

6. Hang an insulated door in the door frame. Use a standard door with 2 x 2 lumber nailed all around the edge on the inside. Fit 2-inch Styrofoam inside this frame of 2 x 2s. Cover the Styrofoam with Aspenite or improvised paneling.

7. Install plastic vent pipes (or use what you have). Carry the intake pipe across the wall to the opposite side of the room to ensure air circulation. If the intake pipe is too close to the exhaust pipe, it's almost a closed loop and the air doesn't go anywhere in the cellar. The exhaust pipe is carried above the outlet level before opening into daylight. This forces stale air up and out.

If you live in a very cold place where the temperature of the outside wall is quite low, you may want to insulate the upper 12 to 24 inches of the wall to prevent loss of humidity through condensation on the wall. If the door does not fit tightly at the bottom, use weatherstripping and shove an old rug tight against the crack to prevent warm basement air from entering the root cellar.

—from *Root Cellaring* by Mike and Nancy Bubel

Build Your Own Root Cellar

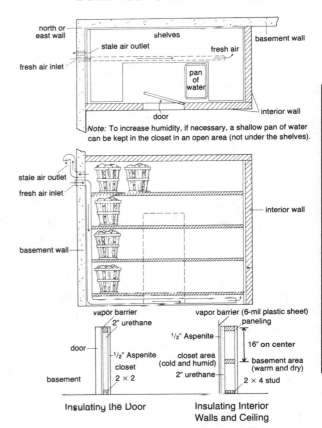

Locating your root cellar in a corner with a window will keep your produce cool and well ventilated.

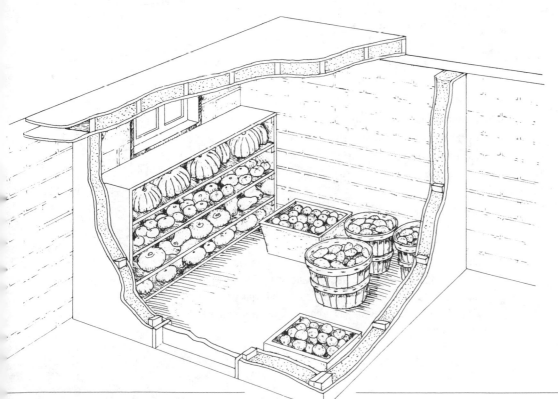

The diagram at left shows a root cellar just 3½ by 7 feet. That's about the minimum for a room you can enter, and doesn't leave much room for closing the door behind you. Nevertheless, it can hold 28 half-bushel baskets of produce.

SEED SAVING

1. When seeds are thoroughly dry and seem about to scatter, cut off the seed heads with shears.

2. Lay them out on a light-colored surface in a warm, dry place for a week or so, or place them upside-down in a bag and tie the bag shut until the seeds have released themselves. Leave a few small air holes in the bag.

3. When the seed heads are dry, separate out the individual seeds and remove any plant debris or chaff, especially green leaves and stems. The debris may be big enough to pick out by hand, or you can sift it. For small seeds, a kitchen strainer is useful.

4. When the seeds are clean, spread them out indoors to continue drying for a week or so before being stored. (Seeds with beards or tufts should not be given this extra drying time.) Pick out and discard seeds that are lighter than the rest. These have usually lost viability.

Harvesting and Cleaning Seeds

Timing is important when harvesting seed. Observe your plants carefully and note the time and method of their seed dispersal. You'll soon get a good sense of when to collect seeds from each plant.

Methods for collecting seed vary, determined in part by the type of plant you are working with. Some seeds can be removed from their pods by hand. With others, the entire plant must be cut down and threshed (beaten or flailed). Many seeds can simply be shaken free of their pods into a container.

Storing Seeds

Most seeds can be stored for at least a year and still germinate, as long as the storage conditions are right. Temperature is critical. Try to keep seeds consistently cold, or at least cool; fluctuating temperatures can be fatal. The refrigerator, or any other place that stays just above freezing, is ideal for storing most seeds. They can also be stored in the freezer, but they must be completely ripe and very dry.

Moisture may be an even more important factor. Since seeds begin to germinate when they absorb water, moisture is the death of seeds in storage. Always dry seeds thoroughly before placing them in storage containers. Make sure the containers themselves have no trace of moisture inside, and that moisture cannot enter them.

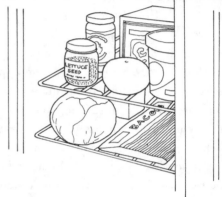

Label it!

Don't forget to label everything throughout the seed-collecting process. You don't want to confuse your cherry tomatoes with your beefsteaks. Mark each batch of seeds with the variety name and date collected, and any other information you might want to include.

Store seeds in a variety of small containers: screw-top glass jars, such as baby-food jars; paper or glassine envelopes (labeled and sealed inside glass jars); plastic or metal film containers; prescription medicine containers; and cans with metal lids. The container shouldn't be airtight (this would prevent gas exchange), but it should be securely closed to keep out moisture and pests.

—from *Seed Sowing and Saving* by Carole B. Turner

CHARACTERISTICS OF COMMON VEGETABLES SAVED FOR SEED

Crop	Plant Type	Seed Viability* (Years)	How Pollinated	Need Isolation If You Are Collecting And Saving Seed
Beans	Annual	3	Self	Limited
Beets	Biennial	4	Wind	Yes
Broccoli	Annual	5	Insects	Yes
Brussels sprouts	Biennial	5	Insects	Yes
Cabbage	Biennial	5	Insects	Yes
Carrots	Biennial	3	Insects	Yes
Cauliflower	Biennial	5	Insects	Yes
Celery	Biennial	5	Insects	Yes
Chinese cabbage	Annual	5	Insects	Yes
Corn, sweet and pop	Annual	2	Wind	Yes
Cucumber	Annual	5	Insects	Yes
Eggplant	Annual	5	Self	Limited
Kale	Biennial	5	Insects	Yes
Kohlrabi	Biennial	5	Insects	Yes
Leek	Biennial	3	Insects	Yes
Lettuce	Annual	5	Self	Limited
Melons (all)	Annual	5	Insects	Yes
New Zealand spinach	Annual	5	Wind	Yes
Okra	Annual	2	Self	Limited
Onions	Biennial	1–2	Insects	Yes
Parsley	Biennial	1–2	Insects	Yes
Parsnip	Biennial	1–2	Insects	Yes
Peas	Annual	3	Self	Limited
Peanut	Annual	1–2	Self	Limited
Pepper	Annual	2	Self	Limited
Potato	Annual	NA	Self	No
Pumpkin	Annual	5	Insects	Yes
Radish	Annual	5	Insects	Yes
Rutabaga	Biennial	5	Insects	Yes
Soybeans	Annual	3	Self	Limited
Spinach	Annual	5	Wind	Yes
Squash, summer and winter	Annual	4	Insects	Yes
Squash, winter	Annual	4	Insects	Yes
Swiss chard	Biennial	4	Wind	Yes
Tomato	Annual	4	Self	Limited
Turnip	Annual	5	Insects	Yes

* As reported by various authorities. Ideal storage techniques can significantly prolong seed viability.

Source: *Saving Seeds* by Marc Rogers (Garden Way Publishing)

Growing Asparagus Successfully

Step 1. Set 1-year-old asparagus roots in a deep trench on a mound of enriched soil.

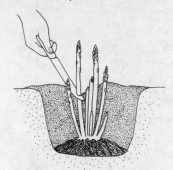

Step 2. Fill the trench with soil as stalks develop.

Step 3. Cut spears with a knife, just below soil level.

Lima beans are warm-weather vegetables.

Asparagus

Asparagus is a perennial that can be grown from seed, but is usually started with one-year-old crowns planted in late spring. From first planting to harvest, asparagus takes about three years to mature. You can also purchase two-year-old crowns or roots. These are more expensive, but they save you a year of waiting.

Planting. If you live in a cold region, set out asparagus roots in early spring. In warm regions, set them out in the fall when temperatures begin to cool. It grows in most types of soil, but it does best in soil with good drainage.

- Dig a trench 12 to 18 inches deep and add 6 to 7 inches of aged manure, compost, or a little peat moss.
- Sprinkle on a dusting of 10-10-10 fertilizer, add 1 to 2 inches of soil from beside the trench, and mix everything together.
- Create mounds at the bottom of the trench about 12 inches apart.
- Set each crown, roots down, on top of a mound and drape its roots down around the mound (Step 1).
- Place the top of the crowns at least 4 inches below the soil surface. Fill up the trench to cover them with a couple of inches of soil. The soil level will be a little below the rest of the garden. When the shoots grow up, fill in the trench with a little more soil to give the stalks support (Step 2).

Care. The first year, mulch small spears after they emerge. Let plants grow though the summer and fall without cutting shoots or ferns. Let tops die down in late fall. Simply put, let them be.

In spring of the second year, cut and clear out old ferns. Remove mulch and fertilize with a capful of 10-10-10 for each 3 feet of row. Don't harvest, just mulch, weed, and wait.

In the third year, cut away the old ferns, pull back mulch, and fertilize. When spears reach 6 to 8 inches or as thick as your finger, harvest. If they're skinny, let them grow to ferns.

Harvest. Carefully cut spears a hair below the soil surface (Step 3) with a knife. As they get older and stronger, you'll be able to harvest for five to eight weeks each spring before letting the remaining stalks grow ferns. After the last harvest each spring, pull weeds, fertilize, and mulch.

Beans

Beans are warm-weather vegetables. Plant seeds into soil directly when the danger of frost is past and the soil is warm. They will grow in any soil (except very wet ones) and don't require much fertilizer. Beans can be divided into three types:

Green and yellow snap beans. These come in bush and pole varieties. Harvest them when pods are young and tender—when they "snap."

Shell beans. Lima beans, southern peas, and horticultural beans are the best examples. To harvest, open the pods or shells and collect the beans.

Dry beans. These beans come from plants that have completed their growth and have produced hard, dry seeds inside pods. When mature, they are packed with protein. To harvest, separate the beans from their hulls and store.

Beets

Beets are cool-weather vegetables. Plant in spring about two weeks before last frost, sowing them in succession every two weeks until June. Make a large planting about 90 days before the first fall frost.

Sow about 2 inches apart in square-foot blocks, about ½ inch deep. Seedlings sprout in two weeks if soil temperature is below 50°F, or in one week at 75°F. Thin the beets to 3 to 4 inches apart, then mulch with clean straw. Keep steady moisture levels to avoid fibrous roots. Mulch lightly to retain moisture and retard weeds. Beets like a pH of 6.5 to 8.0. Sweeten the soil with about a pound of lime for each square yard of bed before planting.

Golfball-sized beets are the tastiest (unless they're long-season beets). Storage beets can be pulled when a frost threatens in fall, preferably after a dry spell. In mild-winter areas, store the roots right in the ground under 8 to 12 inches of straw. Otherwise, pull them out and allow them to cure in the sun for a few hours. Top the roots, leaving half of the stem above the crowns, and pack in moist sand.

Beets are best when golfball-size.

Broccoli

Broccoli is a cool-weather vegetable. In hot weather, or if deprived of water, it will attempt to send up flowers and make seed. The center head must be cut out before it blossoms, even if it's on the small side. When the head is young, its individual buds are packed very tightly. As long as the buds stay tight, let the head grow. When they loosen up and spread out, they are about to produce yellow flowers. After you cut the center head, smaller heads or side shoots will form; though small, they can be eaten, so keep them picked.

Cut the center head of broccoli before it flowers.

Brussels Sprouts

The sprouts form where a leaf grows out of the thick stalk, starting at the bottom. To encourage early sprouts to grow big, break off all the branches, starting from the lowest and continuing up 6 to 8 inches as soon as you see tiny sprouts begin to form. Stripping the stalk stimulates the plant to grow taller and directs energy to the tiny sprouts at the bottom of the stalk. These are ready for picking five to seven days later. As you harvest, snap off more branches higher up on the stalk.

Encourage bigger Brussels sprouts by removing all leaves.

Cabbage

For a continual harvest of cabbages, set out the plants in wide rows three to four weeks before the last spring frost date. Sow more cabbage seeds in early summer, some in the garden and some in flats in partial shade outdoors. In mid-summer, set the seedlings in the garden; these will produce eating-size heads from late summer until the ground freezes.

If cabbage heads start to crack, they are probably growing too fast in the center (often caused by heavy-handed fertilizing). If you see a cracked head, hold it and twist the whole plant halfway around, like turning a faucet. This breaks off some of the roots and slows the inner top growth of the plant. Give the plant another quarter turn in a few days if the cracking continues.

Stagger cabbage plants in wide rows.

Well-shaped carrots need stone-free, deeply worked soil.

Carrots

Carrots are cool-weather plants that need a stone-free, deeply worked soil that drains well. The plant's taproot must meet no resistance in the soil if it is to grow straight.

Carrots produce best in raised beds of tilled soil at least 8 inches deep. They like compost, but no manure, unless it's well rotted. For potassium, till wood ashes into the top 4 inches. Start sowing carrots two weeks before the last spring frost. Make successive plantings every three weeks until July. Space ¾-inch-deep furrows about 4 inches apart. When sowing the seeds, try to place them ½ inch apart—not an easy task. Because carrots are slow to germinate, gardeners often mix radish seeds with carrot seeds to mark the rows.

Add a ½-inch layer of sifted peat moss to the bottom of each furrow, place seeds sparingly on top, then cover with ¼ inch of peat moss. To help germination, cover the bed with burlap bags, soak them, and keep the bed moist until the carrots sprout. Remove burlap, and water daily until seedlings are well established.

Because they grow slowly, seedlings can't compete with weeds. Hand-weed until the plants are 2 inches tall. Thin to 3-inch spacings, then mulch with chopped leaves, pine needles, and compost.

Blanch cauliflower by tying leaves over its head.

Cauliflower

Cauliflower is less tolerant of hot weather than its relatives are, so set out your plants very early or plan on a fall crop. Heads that mature in high heat are apt to have a bitter taste or go by very quickly.

For your first crop, set out some plants three or four weeks before last spring frost. Pinch off a couple of the lower leaves.

When heads are 4 to 5 inches across, blanch them by preventing sunlight from reaching the heads. This keeps the heads creamy white and sweet-tasting. Blanch by tying the plant's leaves around its head. Blanching normally takes four to eight days, but it may take a little longer in the fall.

Begin harvesting when heads are about 6 inches across. Depending on the variety, you can let them get as large as 12 inches across. Be sure to cut the heads before the tight flower buds start to open. Unlike broccoli, cauliflower does not produce side shoots.

Pick lower leaves of collards to prolong harvest.

Collards

This perennial is one of the oldest members of the cabbage family. Unlike kale, collards can withstand considerable heat, yet they tolerate cold better than cabbage. Collards grow in a large rosette of blue-green leaves.

Use one of two planting methods: (1) in spring, sow seed or set out plants to stand 10 to 15 inches apart; or (2) in summer, sow seed thinly and let seedlings grow until large enough for greens, then harvest seedlings to give 10 to 15 inches of spacing.

Collards require little fertilizing. Successive plantings are not necessary for a continuous supply. Harvest seedlings or entire plants, or gradually pick the lower leaves.

Corn

Corn is a member of the grass family. To support its heavy appetite, corn needs a ready supply of food. Enrich the soil well in advance of planting. If possible, plow under a 1-inch layer of manure the preceding fall or grow a green-manure crop. Turn this crop under in spring before planting corn.

If you want fresh corn week after week, plant early- and mid-season varieties the same day. The result will be five or six weeks of steady eating. Or you can stagger planting dates by sowing a block of corn every 10 to 14 days for about a month. Corn does best in a full day of sun. Because of its height, plant it on the north side of a garden, where it won't shade other sun-loving plants.

For sturdy corn, plant seeds 10 inches apart in a furrow or trench, then hill the plants as they grow. Plant sweet corn in blocks of at least four rows to ensure good pollination. If you're planting popcorn, keep it at least 100 feet away from other corn.

Thin the seedlings to 8 to 12 inches apart. Leave the tillers (those extra-long stalks growing from the base) on the plants. When the plants are small, keep weeds under control so corn doesn't have to compete for nutrients. Watering is most effective at the time of tasseling, and when kernels are forming. Soak the soil at least 4 inches deep. For spectacular corn, side-dress twice during the growing season with liquid plant food such as diluted fish emulsion or manure tea.

Sweet corn is at its best for only a few days, 18 to 20 days after the silks have been pollinated. Its juice is milky. Test by puncturing a kernel with your fingernail to see if it squirts out. If you're too early, the juice will be watery; too late, and the kernels are doughy. Look for dark green husks, brown but not brittle stalks, and well-filled ears.

Cucumbers

Cucumbers are warm-weather plants that belong to the squash family. They are generally grown in mounds and send out vines. Cucumbers do well on trellises and resent transplanting, so it's best to sow them in the ground. Since trellised plants dry out more quickly, watch their water supply.

Side-dress with a 5-10-10 fertilizer in a band around the plants when they blossom. Cover the fertilizer with soil so the leaves don't flop down on it and get burned. Mulch with hay between mounds for weed control.

Eggplant

Eggplant is a warm-weather plant. It can't stand frost. Set out a few transplants before your last frost date and surround them with plastic or cover with hot caps. Put others in later, when the soil is warm. Set plants in the soil just slightly deeper than they were in the flat or pot.

Eggplants prefer sun and lots of heat, and are drought tolerant. They don't need a lot of fertilizer. Fertilize them lightly with 5-10-10 at planting time and again when blossoms set.

They taste best when they're young. Pick eggplants when the fruits reach one third of their full growth, or any time after their skins appear glossy.

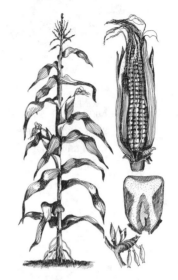

Sweet corn is ready to pick when the juice in the kernels is milky, not watery.

Cucumbers thrive when trained up a trellis, but they must be watered frequently.

Eggplants prefer hot, dry weather.

Horseradish is invasive; plant it where it won't crowd out other plants.

Jerusalem artichokes also spread and are very easy to grow.

Give kale extra nitrogen for more vigorous leaf growth.

Blanch leeks by planting them in a trench and filling soil around them as they grow.

Horseradish

To start a bed, get some roots from a friend. A horseradish grower won't mind, because the plants expand quickly. In fact, unless you till around it several times a year, horseradish will try to invade neighboring crops.

You'll need only six root pieces. Plant them in early spring. Till or spade the area to 6 to 8 inches deep. Dig a hole or furrow 4 to 6 inches deep, add a handful of compost or fertilizer, and top with 2 inches of soil. Push each root piece in at a 45-degree angle. The top of the root should be 2 inches below the soil surface. If you buy roots at a store, one end will be cut on a slant. Be sure to place that end downward.

Jerusalem Artichokes

Jerusalem artichokes are closely related to sunflowers. Their underground tubers are delicious and low in calories. They will grow anywhere in the United States, and you can plant them either in the fall or as soon as the ground can be worked in spring. They are almost completely free of diseases and pests. They are so prolific that they may take over the whole garden if you don't watch them closely. Any tuber left in the soil will sprout the next year.

Cut six tubers, each with an eye, into quarters for a 25-foot row. Plant them 4 inches deep, spaced 1 foot apart. Leave 3 to 4 feet between rows for tilling. They are mature when they reach 6 feet tall.

They need a long growing season of about 126 days. Harvest them after frost has killed the tops or in the spring before they resprout.

Kale

Kale is a member of the cabbage family. Much like collards and mustard, it is grown for its greens. Kale doesn't like heat. In fact, it is at its best after fall frost. Fertilize it with nitrogen for healthy leaves. Prepare the soil with added compost and animal manure, and boost during the growing season with a side-dressing of manure tea, blood meal, or diluted fish emulsion. Kale can be bothered by the cabbage worm. Routine sprayings with *Bacillus thuringiensis* (Bt) after you spot the white cabbage moth should prevent problems.

Leeks

Start leeks indoors early along with onions, and set them out in the garden as transplants. Set them in the bottom of a narrow furrow 4 to 6 inches deep. Place them an inch deeper than they were in their flat. As the plants grow, gradually fill the furrow with soil to keep the growing stem white. The tastiest harvest is in the spring, when they are small and mild. Leave some in the ground and fertilize. They will go to seed in early summer and produce new plants.

Lettuce

Like most greens, lettuce thrives in cool weather. The key to a continuous harvest is succession planting. Put lettuce in the rows where peas have finished. Tuck quick-maturing leaf lettuce in the wide spaces between tomatoes, melons, or squash transplants before they spread. Lettuce likes nitrogen. The plant's shallow roots must be well supplied with water (1 inch per week) to maintain a mild flavor. If the weather isn't too hot, lettuce will come back when cut down to an inch above the ground. Sprinkle with fertilizer and enjoy a second crop.

Melons

Melon refers to cantaloupe, muskmelon, winter melon, and watermelon. Their culture is similar to other members of the squash family. Plants are generally grown in mounds 6 inches apart, and are thinned to two or three plants per mound.

Work the soil, then warm it with black plastic mulch. You can direct-sow or transplant melons. Sow in shallow rows or hills. If planting in rows, place the seeds 1½ to 2 inches deep in groups of three, spacing the groups 18 inches apart. Thin to about 2½ feet by cutting the stems at the soil line. Avoid planting until the soil warms to 65° to 70°F in the daytime.

Make sure the fruits are supported by a sturdy trellis. Melons thrive in a well-drained, rich, light soil and full sun, and they are sensitive to frost. Their seasons are long, which can be a limiting factor in northern climates. To get them off to a good start, use hot caps or plastic tunnels in the spring to trap heat. Water them deeply at least once a week; side-dress when they blossom with a tablespoon of 5-10-10 fertilizer in a band 3 to 4 inches from the plant's stem. Keep leaves from touching the fertilizer by covering it with soil.

Mustard

Mustard is a cool-weather plant. This tasty green is a member of the cabbage family. Mustard greens are peppery with greenish purple leaves.

Direct-sow mustard seeds 1 inch apart in shallow rows. Sow them in early spring and late summer, or during winter in warm areas of the South. Thin them to about 6 inches apart, separating the rows by 18 to 24 inches. If you want a constant supply, sow them every 10 days. Mustard needs even, steady moisture.

Harvest the outside leaves when they are 3 to 4 inches long and still tender, leaving the inner leaves to develop, Or you can harvest the entire plant when warm weather sets in. Use leaves 3 to 5 inches long for flavorful salads.

Okra

Okra is a warm-weather plant that likes heat. Soak the seeds 24 hours before sowing to speed germination. Plant them 8 to 10 inches apart in rows 3 to 4 feet apart. In northern areas, start the seed indoors in pots about five weeks before you plant corn or beans. To keep the plant producing, no pods should be allowed to ripen on the stalk. Young pods are more tender and more nutritious than older pods. Handle the pods with care; bruised or broken pods may become slimy or pasty during cooking.

Cut side leaves of leaf lettuce to prolong harvest.

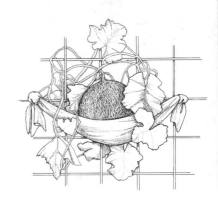

Support developing melons with a nylon-stocking "sling."

Harvest outer leaves of mustard, and inner leaves will continue to develop.

Keep okra producing by picking all pods before they ripen.

Braid onion stems while still soft and hang to dry.

For the sweetest parsnips, leave them in the ground over winter and harvest the next spring.

Onions

The key to growing onions successfully is to start early in the season. The cold won't hurt onions, and they need a long time to grow lush, green tops. Warm temperatures and the number of daylight hours signal onions to stop growing, sending their energy down to make bulbs. If you plant late, you may get smaller bulbs.

You can sow seeds indoors, buy started plants, or plant sets. You get the widest choice of varieties if you start your own from seed, but it takes 100 to 120 days to get mature bulbs. Begin in early March if you live in a cold climate. Buying plants limits your choices, but you get an edible crop more quickly.

Onions prefer a well-worked soil with a pH of 6.0. The fall before planting, compost and/or manure the area and till it in. Also incorporate a 5-10-10 fertilizer at a rate of 3 to 4 ounces per square yard.

Onions can go outside as much as a month before the last frost date. Be sure to harden them off first. Plants should be set out at about the same level they were growing. Press sets into the soil so they are not more than 1 inch below the surface, and 4 to 6 inches apart. You will need about 4 pounds of sets per 100 feet.

For seeds, allow ½ ounce of seed for every 100 feet of row to be sown. Seeds should be placed at a rate of two per inch, in a row to be covered with 1 inch of soil. Use the greater depth for soil that may dry out quickly.

Scallions, or bunching onions, don't form bulbs. Plant them thickly in early spring. Thin them with a small rake when they come up, then let them grow.

Keep onions weed-free. Water them regularly until tops start to yellow, then withhold water and ease them partially out of the ground. Bend the tops away from the sun, so bulbs get sunlight. For maximum-sized onions, pull the soil away from the upper two thirds of the bulb. Take care when weeding around their shallow roots.

When the tops are dry, lift the bulbs and leave them in the sun to dry, long enough so the dirt on them is dry. Prepare for storage by braiding the long tops or hanging them; or cut off the tops, leaving an inch of stem for each bulb. Curing takes several weeks. Keep onions in a shed or under cover where air circulates freely.

Harvest scallions when they are pencil-thick, but leave some to grow. They will winter over and come back in spring.

Parsnips

Plant parsnips in early spring, at about the same time as peas and radishes. Like carrots, they require a deeply tilled, well-prepared soil, raked smooth of rocks and clods. They thrive in a soil rich in potassium and phosphorus, so work in a dusting of wood ashes (potash).

Seeds germinate slowly (up to three weeks), even in the best garden conditions. Some gardeners soak them overnight or treat the seeds with boiling water before planting. You can start seeds indoors between moist paper towels. Presprouted seeds have a better chance of survival.

Plant parsnips in conical holes. Drive a crowbar into the soil 2 feet deep and rotate it in a circle until the hole is 6 inches across. Fill the hole with sand, peat moss, and sifted soil, leaving a slight depression at the top of the hole. Place two or three sprouted seeds in the depression, then cover with ½ inch of sifted sphagnum moss and water. Space the holes 8 inches apart each way in a bed.

Keep beds evenly moist, but not saturated. Thin to one strong plant when each plant has three or four leaves. Parsnips grow slowly, and mulching with straw is the best way to pamper them. If they receive inadequate moisture during the summer, they'll be tough and likely to split and rot with the fall rains. During dry spells, water the beds deeply once a week.

Peas

For an extended pea season, plant early, midseason, and late varieties at the same time—as soon as the soil can be worked. These are cool-weather plants that can withstand many freezes.

In warm climates, plant peas in wide rows, using a dwarf variety. Snow peas also do well in wide rows without fencing.

Because peas are legumes, they don't need much fertilizer—especially nitrogen. If you do fertilize, mix 5-10-10 fertilizer in the soil a day or two before planting. Treat the seeds with an inoculant unless they come pretreated, and sow them in 16-inch-wide rows. Tamp them down and cover them with soil or simply rototill them in a few inches.

Peas quickly screen out the sun from hitting weeds, so you never have to weed a good wide row of peas. The shade also keeps the soil moist and cool. Peas don't need much staking. You can prop them with piles of hay or plant dwarf varieties that grow to only 15 to 18 inches. You can also stick twigs into the soil so peas can grow on them, or use chicken wire fencing stretched on metal fence posts.

Harvest any time after pods form. You can pick shell peas as soon as the pod is full. Waiting until it begins to bulge is not necessary.

Peppers

Peppers—both hot and sweet—like sunny areas and soil that is warm, dry, fertile, and slightly acidic. Don't plant them where you have used a lot of lime.

Start pepper seeds indoors in a warm place. They need more heat than other crops to get going. Use fertilizer, but in small doses, and put compost or manure under them when you transplant them. Side-dress them with rich, organic fertilizer when they blossom.

When they start to blossom, spray the leaves with a weak mix of warm water and epsom salts—a form of magnesium. The leaves turn dark green, and you will soon have an abundance of peppers. Most peppers start out green, so for red peppers, wait till the peppers turn color.

Hot Pepper Jelly

I can't think of a nicer appetizer than good crackers topped with cream cheese and a blob of hot pepper jelly. The jelly is also a terrific accompaniment to meat or poultry. Use all green peppers or all red ones, so the jelly has a soft color.

- ¼ cup chopped jalapeños
- ¾ cup chopped sweet peppers
- 6 cups sugar
- 2½ cups cider vinegar
- 2 3-ounce pouches liquid pectin
  A few drops red or green food coloring (optional)

Run the jalapeños and sweet peppers in a blender or food processor until finely ground. Combine with sugar and vinegar in a large saucepan. Bring to a full boil over high heat, stirring constantly, then turn down heat and simmer for 10 minutes.

Strain, then return the liquid to saucepan. Add about 2 tablespoons of the pepper mixture from the strainer. Bring back to a boil. Add pectin and food coloring if you're using it. Bring back to a boil one more time and boil for 1 minute. Ladle into freshly sterilized jelly glasses with two-part canning lids, leaving ⅛ inch headroom, and seal. Process in boiling-water bath for 10 minutes.

Makes about 6 (8-ounce) glasses

—from *Growing Hot Peppers*
by Glenn Andrews

To plant potatoes, cut large ones into chunks with two or three buds each. Then allow to dry.

Kid Stuff

Children love to watch their own personal pumpkins grow. When pumpkins start turning yellow on the vine, let a child choose one. Invite him or her to scratch initials into the outer skin with a nail. As the shell hardens, the lettering clearly shows in the form of a raised scar.

A face or design scratched into the shell helps children learn how pumpkins stretch while they grow. To take advantage of the twisted effect that develops as the pumpkin matures, work on designs a little at a time, adding to them once a week.

—from *The Perfect Pumpkin*
by Gail Damerow

Potatoes

A good potato crop starts with good seed potatoes. Garden stores have certified, disease-free seed potatoes. Old potatoes from your root cellar may have disease organisms without showing it.

When you buy seed potatoes, some will be small. Plant these whole. Cut bigger ones into two or three blocky pieces that have two or three buds, or "eyes." Do this one or two days before planting and leave them in a warm place so the cut pieces have time to heal over and dry out a little. You can douse cut pieces with sulfur immediately after cutting; it helps protect potatoes from rotting. Two ounces protects 10 pounds of potatoes. Put both the cut and whole potatoes in a paper bag, add 1 to 2 tablespoons of sulfur, and shake the bag.

Plant an early crop five or six weeks before last frost. A frost before the plants come up is no problem. The soil will insulate them. But if leaves have popped up and there's a frost warning, cover them with soil. The leaves will grow back in a few days.

Plant your main crop of potatoes after the average last frost day. This planting can go into the root cellar just before the first fall frost.

Potatoes prefer silt or sandy loam that has good drainage and is high in organic matter. Their preferred pH level is 6.0 to 6.5; a higher level may promote potato scab. Avoid using lime. Get a soil test to find out what you have. If your soil is deficient in phosphorus and potash, add rock phosphate and greensand or granite dust. Apply according to package directions.

For bed planting, plant the potatoes under straw, hay, leaves, or other mulch to minimize weeding after sowing. Set the bed up in a rectangle about 6 feet wide and as long as you wish. If heavy rains are a problem in your area, slope the bed to permit drainage. Place potato chunks, cut-side down, 12 inches from the bed's sides and ends, spacing them 12 inches apart in each direction. Press them firmly into the soil and top them with a thick layer of straw, hay, or shredded leaves. Weight the mulch down if there is a chance that it might blow away.

For row planting, hoe or dig 12-inch-wide trenches to about 6 inches deep. The rows should be 2 to 3 feet apart. If needed, add 2 inches of compost and work it into the soil. Place potato chunks, cut-side down, 12 inches apart and 3 inches deep. As plants emerge, hoe the soil up to them, gradually filling the trench and building a row-long hill about 8 inches high. Mulch the mounds to keep soil moist and discourage weeds.

Harvest in dry periods after the vines are dead and dry. Use a potato hook and work carefully to avoid puncturing the potatoes. Let them dry for 1 to 2 hours before moving them into dark storage. Keep them at 60° to 70°F if you're using them within a month, at 40°F if you want to store them for months.

Pumpkins

Pumpkins are easier to grow than to classify. At least three different species are called pumpkins, and all can also correctly be called squash.

Pumpkins dislike being transplanted, so it's best to direct-sow them in hills one to two weeks before the last frost. Plant three seeds per hill, leaving about 4 feet between hills. Keep the area well weeded until the plants begin to vine.

When your thumbnail doesn't easily cut the skin, cut the vine a few inches from the fruit, leaving a good handle. The fruit must be cured, which allows the skin to harden. Field-curing is done by leaving the pumpkins in a bright, sunny, dry spot in the garden for 7 to 10 days. Cover them if frost threatens. Store them indoors.

Giant pumpkins require special coddling. Choose a variety such as 'Dill's Atlantic Giant', a proven prizewinner. In the fall, select a sunny spot 30 feet in diameter, and dig manure into the soil. In spring, prepare a hill 8 to 10 feet in diameter and plant four seeds in the center, watering well. When the seedlings have four to six true leaves, pinch off all but the best plant. Alternatively, you can start seeds indoors or in a cold frame and bring them outside when the soil warms up. Protect the large leaves and vines against wind, and water deeply once or twice a week.

Radishes

Radishes like cool weather, constant moisture, and uninterrupted growth. For a steady supply, make small weekly plantings in April and May, then again in August and September. For succession plantings, keep in mind that the longer the radish, the better it tolerates heat.

Till the radish bed to a depth of 8 inches, mixing in organic matter. Make furrows with a yardstick, spacing them about 3 inches apart, and sow the seeds at a depth of ½ inch. Space the seeds about 1 inch apart; when 2 inches tall, thin to 3-inch spacing. Most radishes are ready to harvest in less than a month. If mulched with straw, the fall varieties can remain in the garden through the winter to be harvested as you need them.

Rhubarb

Three or four root crowns will produce all the rhubarb you can eat.

In the spring, dig planting holes several inches deep and 18 inches apart. Add compost or fertilizer and place a single piece of root in each hole, covering it with about 1 inch of soil. Do not harvest these plants the first year. Add a few side-dressings during the season, so they'll grow lots of tops.

The next season, harvest some stalks when they're 8 to 10 inches tall. Gently pull out and up on the ones you want to tear away from the plant. Don't eat the leaves, which are toxic. During the second year, the plant may put out tall seedpods. Remove them so the roots will produce tasty stalks all season. The more stalks you harvest, the more the plant will produce. Divide the plant every four to five years in the fall or in spring before growth starts. Do this by driving a shovel into the middle of the plant and digging up half the root. Fill the hole with compost. This forces the plant to produce younger, better crowns.

Giant Pumpkin Growing Tips

- Since it takes a big vine to grow a big pumpkin, don't let your plant set fruit until it has at least 300 leaves, when runners are about 10 feet long. Until then, remove any female blossoms or baby pumpkins that appear.
- When the plant is large enough in midsummer, many growers let one fruit set on each main runner. Remove any other fruits that develop.
- When the pumpkins reach volleyball size, cut off all but the best one or two on each vine.
- Place a bed of straw or sand or a sheet of plywood beneath each pumpkin to protect it from insects and moisture.
- Feed the plant with manure tea or other liquid fertilizer every 10 days.
- When the plant is 20 to 25 feet in diameter, start pinching off the tips of all runners. Continue removing new growth until your pumpkin is ready for harvest.

—from *The Perfect Pumpkin*
by Gail Damerow

Remove tall seedpods from rhubarb to prolong harvest.

Harvest rutabaga after a few frosts.

Spinach is one of the earliest cool-weather crops and can also be planted in late summer for fall harvest.

Squash loves plenty of heat and evenly moist soil.

Sweet potatoes need a long (4- to 5-month) growing season.

Rutabagas

Plant rutabagas in mid-June or about 90 days before planned harvest shortly after the first frost. Sow the seeds about ¼ inch deep at 8-inch spacings. Provide plenty of moisture until the seedlings are growing strong, then mulch well and water deeply once a week.

Harvest rutabagas after a few frosts, but before the ground freezes. Cut the tops and store them like carrots in a root cellar or basement. Good roots will keep for up to six months if you store them just above freezing with 90 percent humidity.

Spinach

Spinach is a cool-weather plant and should be direct-sown about one month before the last spring frost; direct-sow fall crops about one month before the first autumn frost. Set the seeds about 2 inches apart (1 inch in fall), in shallow rows about 18 inches apart. Thin the seedlings to about 4 inches apart. Repeat sowings every 10 to 14 days to ensure a continual supply. Spinach responds well to fertilizers. Try regular applications of fish emulsion.

Pick the outer leaves as needed or cut the entire plant. Harvest in the cool of the morning and store spinach in the refrigerator until you're ready to use it.

Squash

The seeds of summer squash germinate best when soil temperatures are above 65°F. It grows best in raised beds warmed with black plastic mulch for a few weeks before planting. Direct-sow them one or two weeks after the last frost, planting the seeds about 4 inches apart and 1 inch deep in rows 3 to 4 feet apart. For winter squash, direct-sow pairs of seeds about 1 inch deep, spacing them every 18 inches. Keep them evenly moist, especially after the fruit has begun to set.

Harvest most summer squash when the fruit is 3 to 5 inches long. Snip the vine with scissors and handle the fruit carefully to prevent bruising. It will keep for up to two weeks in the refrigerator.

To harvest winter squash, wait until your thumbnail easily cuts the skin. Cut the vine a few inches from the fruit, then let the fruit cure for 7 to 10 days. Cover it if frost threatens. Stored winter squash can last all winter long.

Sweet Potatoes

Ideally, sweet potatoes should have 130 to 150 frost-free days, with most of them up to 80° to 85°F, and with moderate to high humidity. Plant them well after the last frost, when the soil is about 70°F.

Purchase sweet potatoes from a market seven to eight weeks before the last spring frost. Cut them in half lengthwise and lay the pieces cut-side down in aluminum pie plates filled with moist peat moss. Put a shallow covering of the peat moss over the pieces and wrap the works in a plastic bag.

When the slips (tiny sprouts) appear, remove the plastic and put the plants in a sunny window. After the last frost date, pull each slip and plant it separately. It will grow into a full-sized sweet potato plant.

Plant the slips in raised beds 5 to 6 inches deep and 12 to 15 inches apart. Fertilize them lightly with 5-10-10.

Water young plants generously for the first few days, then infrequently. Just as the vines begin to run along the ground, side-dress once with fertilizer—1 tablespoon of 5-10-10 per plant.

Dig them up on a dry day before cold weather. Dry them for 1 hour. To cure, place in a warm, dark, ventilated place for 10 to 14 days.

Tomatoes

Tomatoes don't do well until the soil warms to 65°F or more and nighttime temperatures get up into the 50s. They thrive in rich soil with a pH of about 6.5 (see chapter 13, Soil Improvement).

To start plants indoors, begin six to seven weeks before the last spring frost. Harden them off before setting them out. Spacing in the garden depends on your method of growing. If you're going to let them sprawl on the ground, each plant needs 4 square feet. For those that will be staked, 3 square feet is adequate. If your soil is wet, set each plant on a mound 4 to 6 inches high. If your soil is dry, create a depression for the plant. Water plants well an hour before transplanting.

Set the plants about 2 inches deeper than they are in the pot. Pick off a couple of the lower leaves. If plants are leggy (much stem and few leaves), lay the plant down on its side and bury part of the stem along with the roots. Prune the lower leaves off, leaving just the top leaves exposed. Roots will later form on the stem.

Immediately after transplanting, water the plants well. Mulch four to six weeks later, when the soil is nice and warm. If you let the tomato sprawl on the ground, a mulch is not necessary.

Pruning is generally not necessary, but staked and trellised plants will be easier to train if they have only one or two main stems. Pruning means pinching off the shoots or suckers that grow out from the stems at their branching points. This encourages larger fruits.

A general yellowing or pale green indicates nitrogen need. Avoid side-dressing with nitrogen until after flowering is well under way. You can then side-dress with an ounce or so of 5-10-10 or a quart of manure tea around the base of the plant.

Turnips

Direct-sow the seeds about 1 inch apart in single rows spaced 12 to 15 inches apart.

Thin to 4 inches when the seedlings emerge. Fertilize regularly with fish emulsion and water. Cover with fabric row covers to inhibit pests.

Begin to harvest the greens and bottoms when the roots are about 1½ inches across. Pull the entire plant and snip off the top. For best flavor, the roots should be gathered before they exceed 3 inches in diameter.

Secrets of Tomato Staking

If you stake your tomatoes, place the stake before you transplant, so you don't disturb the roots.

Tie tomato vines loosely to the stake as they grow.

Pinch suckers to encourage strong growth of the main stem.

When the vine reaches the size you want, pinch back the growing tip.

THE HERB GARDEN

**HERBAL THEME GARDENS • HARVESTING AND STORING HERBS
32 ESSENTIAL HERBS • HERB GROWTH AND USES**

We once spent a year living outside Bologna, Italy, where 95 percent of homes have gardens. Herbs were a heady part of our lives. The path to our apartment was bordered with a huge hedge of rosemary. In the garden was not just sweet 'Genovese' basil, but also purple, lemon, cinnamon, leaf, and licorice varieties. Our house had a kitchen garden with oregano, sage, thyme, parsley, mint, chives, lavender, and cilantro, which we harvested nightly and used fresh in everything. Teaching grandchildren about the smells and flavors of herbs, making teas that soothe and calm, creating unique recipes, all make the herb garden an important part of our lives.

—John & Martha Storey

Thousands of years ago, long before science began its attempt to provide rational explanations for everything, plants were seen as repositories of mysterious powers or conveyors of valuable gifts. The chamomile flower relaxed the sleepless mind, for example, and the olive tree provided sustenance for the body. The ancient cultures of Egypt, China, India, Europe, and elsewhere did not cultivate plants for their beauty; they grew plants because they saw them as useful and spiritual additions to their lives.

Now we are finding our way back to the wisdom of the ages. There is always room in the garden for the lovely perennial that contributes beautiful flowers to a sunny summer day. But save a place as well for the herbs that provide the warm seasoning in a winter meal or add a cooling touch to the lotion that eases our sore muscles at the end of the day.

Gardening with Herbs

You can find most of the basic herbs you want already started as transplants at your garden center. Starting your own is much like starting other seeds, with a few changes. First, herb seeds are usually tiny. After leveling off your soil mix, sprinkle the herb seeds on the surface and just tamp them down. You don't have to bury the tiny ones. Be sure to keep them moist and in a warm spot. The other big difference is that they seem to take forever to germinate. Two or three weeks is not uncommon.

Another way to get perennial herbs like chives, oregano, and tarragon is to divide an existing plant. In early spring, or after the growing season in fall, drive a trowel or spade through the plant and remove a chunk for your garden. Keep the roots moist as you move them, and transplant them immediately.

You can grow a good collection of the basic herbs in one or two hanging baskets, in a corner of your vegetable garden, in pots or window boxes, or mixed in a flower bed. My advice is to put your herbs as close to the kitchen as you can. You'll use them more if you don't have to make a special trip to the garden for a few leaves of basil or chives.

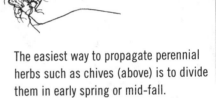

The easiest way to propagate perennial herbs such as chives (above) is to divide them in early spring or mid-fall.

A large pot of herbs is easy to move if you set it on a dolly.

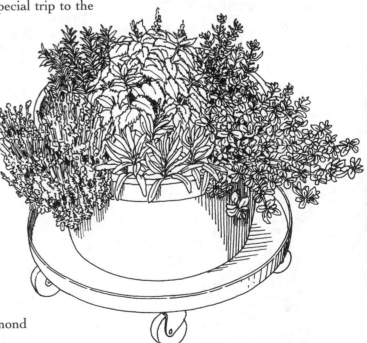

Caring for Herbs

Herbs like 5 to 8 hours of sunshine every day and well-drained soil that is rich in organic matter. The exception is mint, which likes damp, partly shady areas.

If you have fertilized the soil at planting time, you shouldn't need more during the growing season. Too much fertilizing makes herbs big and rangy, when what you're after is compact, bushy plants with greater concentrations of flavorful oils.

Most herbs are at their best as they begin to flower. Pick the tender leaves and pick off the flowers to encourage continued growth. Herbs grow best if they are not allowed to set seeds. Prune them to control their size and shape as you harvest them for your own use.

—from *Gardening Know-How for the '90s* by Dick Raymond

HERBAL THEME GARDENS

Dorie Byers, author of Herbal Remedy Gardens, believes that the act of gardening itself is as therapeutic as any medicine. It offers exercise, teaches patience, fosters creativity, and gives you an opportunity to spend time in the natural world. Growing your own herbs is a wonderfully sensory experience, and you know your plants will be at the peak of freshness when you harvest.

An Easy and Fragrant Kitchen Border

Plant this herb garden near your kitchen door for easy access. The number in parentheses refers to the number of plants required.

1. Sage (2 plants)
2. Peppermint (1—will spread)
3. Spearmint (1—will spread)
4. Oregano (1)
5. Marjoram (1)
6. Tarragon (1)
7. Lemon balm (1)
8. Rosemary (1)
9. Chives (2)
10. Upright thyme (1)
11. Lemon thyme (1)
12. Burnet (1)
13. French thyme (1)

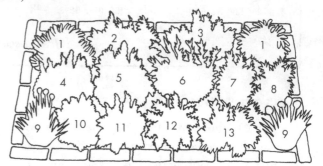

—from *Herbal Treasures* by Phyllis V. Shaudys;
design by Kate and Fairman Jayne

A Cold and Flu Garden

When cooler winter weather arrives, colds and flus often arrive, too. You can plant a garden that provides an herbal harvest to treat your cold or flu. This plan can take up quite a large space. Peppermint becomes invasive, so plant it in a large tub or container with drainage holes in the bottom and sink it into the ground. Butterflies are drawn to echinacea and yarrow.

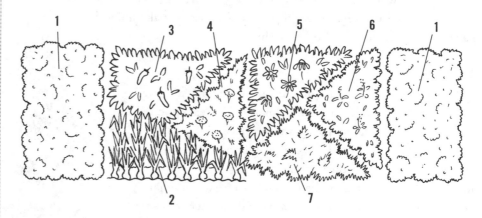

Plants for the Cold and Flu Garden

1. Thyme (4)
2. Garlic cloves (9)
3. Cayenne pepper (3)
4. Yarrow (1)

5. Echinacea (2)
6. Peppermint (1)
7. Rosemary (2)

—all healing gardens from *Herbal Remedy Gardens* by Dorie Byers

A First-Aid Garden

If you have wild plants on your property, you may need to plant only calendula and add a pot of aloe to create this First-Aid Garden. Yarrow, plantain, and chickweed are wild plants that you can frequently find growing on their own. Plant your First-Aid Garden near any other gardens or near the door of your house for quick first aid. Stagger the heights of the plants; yarrow is the tallest, and should be in back. Plant the yarrow, calendula, and aloe in containers, and let the plantain and chickweed grow in the ground in front of them.

Plants for the First-Aid Garden

1. Yarrow (1)
2. Calendula (4)
3. Aloe (1)
4. Plantain (4 to 6)
5. Chickweed (4 to 6)

An Infusion for Cuts and Scrapes

The antibacterial properties in calendula make it an appropriate treatment for minor cuts and scrapes. As an alternative, apply fresh aloe vera gel.

- 1 tablespoon dried or 2 tablespoons fresh calendula blossoms
- 1 cup boiling water

Add the calendula blossoms to boiling water. Cover and let steep 15 minutes, then cool to lukewarm. Apply to minor cuts and scrapes to clean them and promote healing.

---

15 Herbs That Make Delicious Tea

anise hyssop	lemon balm	pineapple sage
basil	'Lemon Gem' and 'Orange	rosemary
calendula	Gem' marigolds	sage
catnip or catmint	lemon verbena	scented geraniums
chamomile	mints	
lavender	monarda	

—from *15 Herbs for Tea* by Marian Sebastiano

Herbal Broth

Most people have trouble avoiding a cold or flu at some time during the winter. This broth will provide you with herbal comfort when you're ill. It is flavorful, warming, and packed with vitamins.

6 minced garlic cloves
1 tablespoon olive oil
2 cups water or vegetable broth
1 teaspoon fine-chopped fresh cayenne pepper, or ½ teaspoon dried powdered cayenne
1 teaspoon fine-chopped fresh or ½ teaspoon dried rosemary
½ teaspoon fresh or ¼ teaspoon dried thyme
Pinch to ¼ teaspoon salt to taste if the vegetable broth is unsalted

Add the garlic to the olive oil and sauté over high heat briefly, until the garlic starts to change color. Add the water, turn down heat to medium-low, and simmer for 20 minutes. Add all of the herbs and salt to taste. Simmer for 5 more minutes. Sip slowly.

—from *Herbal Remedy Gardens*

HARVESTING AND STORING HERBS

Hang small bundles of herbs to dry in an airy, dark place.

Store completely dried herbs in labeled, tightly sealed jars.

Harvesting Herbs

When you are ready to harvest, choose a dry day and pick after the dew has evaporated. The essential oil concentration is said to be highest in the morning. Remember, essential oils give a plant its fragrance, flavor, and any health benefits attributed to the herb. Because the oil content is higher in a plant before flowering, many herb gardeners recommend picking before the plant flowers. But I've harvested at all stages of growth. The best way is to experiment with different times. You might prefer the more delicate flavor of small, new leaves, especially for the more pungent herbs.

The easiest way to clean herbs for harvesting is to rinse them with a garden hose. Set the hose to a light spray or mist. Soak the plants well and let them dry in the sun before you harvest. If you choose instead to rinse them after cutting, use a salad spinner to remove excess water.

Drying

After harvest, dry your herbs quickly but with gentle, even heat to preserve their delicate flavors. If you're using a food dehydrator, place 4- to 6-inch sprigs in a single layer on each tray. You can dry all the trays in several hours. When they are "chip dry," strip off the leaves and store them in airtight tins or jars. Check the containers for moisture (condensation) and redry if any moisture is visible.

Another way to dry herbs is in a 100° to 125°F oven for several hours. Keep the door slightly ajar to allow moisture to escape. Check the progress often to determine when the leaves are dry; different herbs dry at different rates. To preserve flavor, it might be better to dry one type of herb at a time. If your oven doesn't have a setting this low, heat it to 150°F, turn it off, then put in the herbs.

You can also bunch herbs with rubber bands and hang-dry them. Be sure to hang them in a dry place—never in a garage. Make sure you label each bunch you hang. Check for dryness in two weeks. Once the herbs are dry, strip off the leaves and place in airtight, clearly labeled containers.

Storing

The secret of preserving herb quality is to keep the dried herbs away from moisture, sunlight, and extreme heat.

Many sources sell glass jars with lids that seal tightly. Baby-food jars are a good size for preserving small quantities. For bigger bunches, try canning jars or mayonnaise jars—just be sure they are well washed and completely dry. Zipper-locking plastic bags are another good choice. Store them away from light. I store mine in a cookie tin.

Another way to preserve and store your harvest is to freeze some or all of it. Freezing herb sprigs in zipper-locking bags can preserve delicate flavors lost in drying. To use the frozen herbs, take out a few sprigs and mince them with a sharp knife.

—from *15 Herbs for Tea* by Marian Sebastiano

Create an Herbal Wreath

Even if you have only a mint patch, you can make a lovely fragrant wreath. If your garden also contains lemon balm, sage, southernwood, tansy, or any of the silvery artemisias, you are in business. If you need additional material, use cedar, boxwood, arborvitae tips, or evergreens. Cut a large basket full of snippets 6 inches long.

The supplies you'll need are a box-type 4-ring wreath frame (10 or 12 inches or larger) and a spool of sturdy carpet thread in a neutral color.

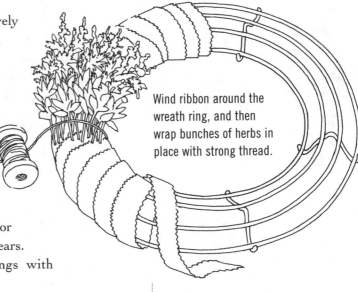

Wind ribbon around the wreath ring, and then wrap bunches of herbs in place with strong thread.

1. Wrap the wreath ring with leftover scraps of ribbon or strips of leftover fabric cut on the bias with pinking shears.

2. Secure the beginning and end of the wrappings with straight pins or staples.

3. Start anywhere and lay a small handful of assorted herbs (6 to 10 stems) against the ring. Attach a length of thread to the frame without cutting the thread from the spool. Hold the spool firmly and secure the herbs in place by bringing the thread through the center of the wreath form several times.

4. Place a second, similar bunch so it covers the stems of the preceding bunch. Wrap them in place by pulling the thread tightly around. Continue around the ring in this manner until it is covered. Lay the bunches on thickly, covering the base as much as possible. Vary them as much as you like.

5. When the herbs begin to dry and shrivel, snip off drooping tips or heavy protruding stems. Tuck in additional material.

6. Allow the wreath to dry for several days lying flat in a warm, dry place, preferably out of strong light. When dry, hang it on the wall and enjoy it.

7. Embellish the wreath by attaching "favorite things" or a bow.

—from *Herbs for Weddings and Other Celebrations*
by Bertha Reppert

Try These Combinations

- Southernwood dries to a unique olive green color that is nicely complemented by bunches of dried silver mound artemisia and red bergamot flowers. Use fresh southernwood when shaping your wreath as the herb is more pliable and less fragile before it dries.

- Silver King Artemisia is a good choice for wreaths because its silver-gray color blends with any color scheme. Try attaching sprigs of culinary herbs along with a pine green candle and some green ribbon, or create a very colorful wreath by adding whole spices, dried fruits, nuts, and tiny pinecones.

- Make a grapevine wreath by attaching Concord grapes, wild grasses, and the tops of large peacock feathers to a wire base.

—from *The Pleasure of Herbs*
by Phyllis V. Shaudys

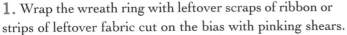

32 ESSENTIAL HERBS

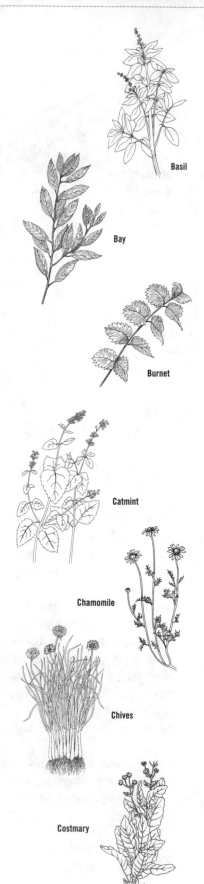

Basil

Bay

Burnet

Catmint

Chamomile

Chives

Costmary

Basil

Basil is a tender annual very sensitive to frost. Sow seed directly into the garden after soil is warm, with an extra dose of compost. Plant it in full sun and water it weekly in dry weather.

This fast-growing plant grows to 2 feet. To keep the plant bushy, pinch out the blooms or the tips of each stem before they flower. Harvest the leaves throughout the summer.

To dry basil, harvest just before it blooms. Hang, screen-dry, or freeze.

Bay (Bay Laurel)

Bay is a slow-growing evergreen shrub with aromatic leaves. Sun-loving, it is a tender perennial that must go indoors during winters in cold climates. It is difficult to propagate. Bay can grow to a height of 10 feet.

Burnet

Burnet's cucumber-flavored leaves are used in drinks, soups, and salads. It is easily grown from seed. Burnet grows 1 to 2 feet tall in sun or light shade and slightly alkaline soil.

Catmint (Catnip)

Beloved by felines, catmint is used in tea by humans as a cough remedy and an aid to digestion. The plants are 2 to 3 feet high. Easily grown in sun or light shade, catmint tolerates most soils.

Chamomile

Tea made from chamomile blossoms is used as a soothing tranquilizer; it is also used as a tonic. Chamomile grows easily from seed or divisions. It grows up to 10 inches with a spreading growth habit.

Chives

These are small, onionlike plants, useful in salads, soups, and egg dishes. They are a hardy perennial, reaching 12 to 18 inches. Cut off the mauve-blue flower heads to keep the plant growing, but leave them on later in the season for foraging bees.

Chives prefer full sun, rich soil, and plentiful water. Mulch around the plants to keep out weeds and grasses.

Harvest chives as soon as the spears are a few inches long. Snipping out entire spears encourages tender new growth. Chives do not dry well. Freeze them for winter use.

Costmary (Bible Leaf)

Its fragrant leaves with a minty flavor were pressed and used as bookmarks in Bibles during colonial days. Today, costmary is used as a garnish, in tea, and for potpourri. Propagate by root division. The plants grow 2 to 3 feet high. Costmary likes sun and ordinary garden soil.

Dill

Dill is a hardy annual that grows 2 to 3 feet tall; plant in groupings to keep them supported in windy weather.

Sow seed directly in the garden. Dill does best in full sun in sandy or loamy, well-drained soil that is slightly acid (pH 5.8 to 6.5). Enrich soil with compost or well-rotted manure for best growth. Dill reseeds itself easily.

Both dillweed and dill seed are used in cooking; the weed is mild, but the seeds are pungent. Harvest dillweed any time, but its volatile oils are highest just before flowering. Cut seed heads when the majority of seeds are formed, even though some flowers are still blooming. Thresh the seeds after drying.

Echinacea

Echinacea is widely used to stimulate or support the body's immune system. A perennial that loves full sun, echinacea grows to about 3 feet, spreading gradually. Butterflies love this plant. When the blooms are finished, they dry out and reseed themselves; remove the spent blooms if you don't want this to occur. To harvest, dig the roots after blooming, usually in early fall. Harvest only two- to four-year-old roots, making sure that you leave enough plants for future use. Wash and dry, then chop coarsely. Store thoroughly dried roots in a tightly covered glass container away from heat and light.

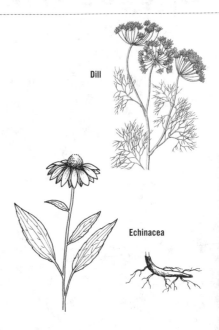

Dill

Echinacea

Make an Echinacea Tincture

Tinctures are a simple and useful way to make the healing properties of herbs available to you. Use the instructions below to make a basic echinacea tincture. At the first sign of cold or flu's onset, herbal experts recommend 30 drops of tincture every 3 hours for the first two days only. You will need pure grain alcohol, also known as Everclear. If your state does not sell it, look for the highest-proof brand of vodka or brandy. If you do not want to ingest alcohol, place drops of tincture in a small amount of warm water and stir to evaporate the alcohol.

1. Combine ¾ cup alcohol with ¾ cup distilled water in a jar with a tight-fitting lid.
2. Add 1½ ounces dried echinacea.
3. Replace lid and place jar in a cool, dark spot.
4. Shake the mixture daily for two weeks.
5. Strain the mixture to remove the herb. Do it quickly, or the alcohol will evaporate. I pour the mixture into a strainer lined with an unbleached coffee filter and place it in the refrigerator to slow alcohol evaporation. Then squeeze the filter to remove as much liquid as possible. Store in a dark-colored glass bottle with an eyedropper fitted into the lid. Label, including the type of tincture and the date.

Cautions. Echinacea can cause adverse reactions in people who are allergic to sunflowers. Do not use it if you have a severe systemic immune disorder or a collagen disease such as lupus or scleroderma. Echinacea should be used with caution by pregnant women. Always always make a positive identification of any plant before using it.

—from *Herbal Remedy Gardens* by Dorie Byers

Making Herbal Vinegars

Herbal vinegars are incredibly easy and inexpensive to make. Use a delicate rice wine vinegar with a subtle herb like chervil for a gentle hint of summer's glory. Combine a robust red wine vinegar with garlic, rosemary, marjoram, and black peppercorns, and enjoy extra gusto in a hearty bean soup.

The biggest mistake people make when creating herbal vinegars is not using enough herbs. To achieve the best effect, use about 1 cup of loosely packed fresh herb leaves to 2 cups of vinegar. For dried herbs, use ½ of cup leaves to 2 cups of vinegar.

After cleaning the herbs, place them in a clean, sterilized jar and bruise them slightly with a spoon. Pour vinegar over the herbs and cover the jar tightly. Do not heat. Let the mixture steep in a dark place at room temperature. Shake the jar every couple of days an, after a week, taste it. If the flavor is not strong enough, let it stand for another one to three weeks, checking the flavor weekly. If a stronger flavor is desired, repeat the steeping process with fresh herbs. When the flavor is right, strain, fill clean sterilized bottles, cap tightly, and label.

—from *Herbal Vinegar* by Maggie Oster

32 ESSENTIAL HERBS

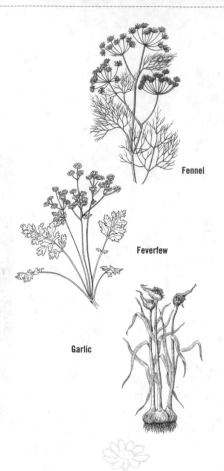

Fennel

Feverfew

Garlic

Fennel

Herb fennel is a hardy biennial that becomes a perennial in favorable climates. It reaches 3 to 5 feet. Fennel prefers a rich, well-drained soil in full sun. Add lime if your soil pH is below 6.0. Harvest leaves just before the plant flowers. Fennel adversely affects the growth of other plants nearby. It is related to dill, and the two should not be interplanted because they may cross-pollinate, resulting in dilly fennel or fennelly dill!

Feverfew

Biennial or perennial. As the name implies, this hardy medicinal herb is credited with many beneficial properties. It is easily grown from seed or division, and the plant reaches 2 to 3 feet. It does best in sun or light shade and a well-drained soil.

Garlic

This pungent herb is grown for the flavor of its corms, or cloves. Garlic needs full sun, rich soil, a pH between 6.0 and 6.8, and even moisture. Plant it in fall at about the time of first frost for a summer harvest or in spring to harvest a fall crop. Harvest before flowering, when the stalks start to turn brown. Dig the plant up carefully, brush off dirt, and spread the heads on soil or a screen to dry.

Braiding Garlic

Braiding garlic heads is the best way to preserve them, because air can circulate around the hung braid.

The soft-necked variety works best. Start making the braids as soon as you pull the heads from the ground, so the stems are still pliable. Brush off soil rather than rinsing off the heads. Be sure to use heads that have their leaves attached.

Beginning braid

On a flat surface, start with three fat heads and braid their leaves together. Then add other heads (like French-braiding hair). For braids you plan to give away, or if you care a lot about the appearance of the braid, put the heads so closely together that the leaves don't show. You can use light wire to reinforce the braids. When you've done as many heads as you want, braid the last of the leaves and tie off with raffia or twine, forming a loop for hanging. Hang in a well-ventilated area.

—from *Growing and Using Garlic* by Glenn Andrews

Finished braid

Horehound

The leaves are dried for tea and used fresh in candy and cough syrup. Grown from seed, cuttings, or division, the plants reach 1 to 2 feet. Horehound needs full sun and dry, sandy soil.

Hyssop

A hardy, ancient herb used as a purifying tea and for medicine, hyssop is said to cure all manner of ailments from head lice to shortness of breath. Start by seed or division. The plant grows to 3 feet. Hyssop prefers full sun and well-drained, alkaline soil.

Lavender

An aromatic herb used fresh or dried in sachets and pillows lavender grows from seeds, cuttings, or divisions. Plant it in a protected location in northern areas. It prefers lime soil. English lavender produces the loveliest blossoms and fragrant oil. Plants grow 1 to 2 feet.

Lemon Balm

The lemon-scented leaves are used dried or fresh for tea, jelly, and flavoring. The plant attracts bees. Start from cuttings or division. Plants grow 1 to 3 feet high. Plant lemon balm in sun or light shade and well-drained soil.

Lemon Verbena

Lemon verbena is a tender, aromatic perennial that cannot stand frost, so it must be used as a houseplant during winters in northern climates. Its leaves drop in fall, but they return promptly. It is fragrant and grows to 10 inches.

Lovage

The celery-flavored leaves and stalks are used in soups, salads, and similar dishes. Lovage grows well from seed in partial shade and moist, fertile soil. Mature plants may be 4 to 6 feet high.

Marjoram

Marjoram is a tender perennial. In cold climates, it is grown as an annual. The plant reaches 8 to 12 inches and thrives in a light, rich soil with neutral pH in full sun. It has a shallow root system, so mulching around the plant helps retain soil moisture and keep down the weeds. Marjoram is highly aromatic, and its flavor improves with drying. Harvest just before the flowers open.

Mint

Mints are hardy perennials that often attain 3 feet. They are notorious spreaders. They prefer a moist, rich soil and thrive in full sun to partial shade. Harvest throughout the summer by cutting stalks just above the first set of leaves, as soon as the flower buds appear. Hang to dry for 10 to 14 days.

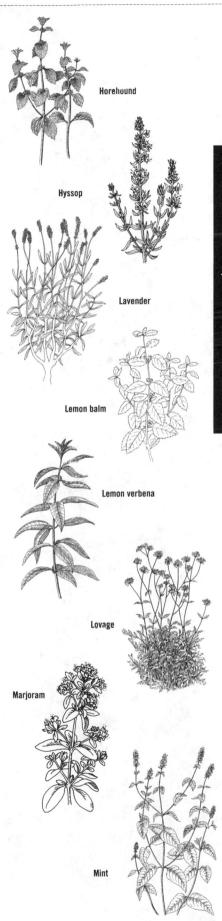

Horehound

Hyssop

Lavender

Lemon balm

Lemon verbena

Lovage

Marjoram

Mint

32 ESSENTIAL HERBS

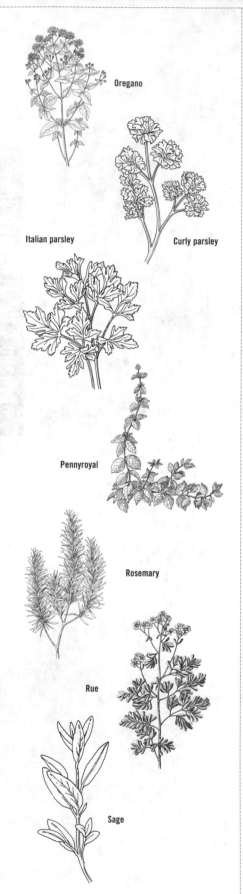

Oregano

Italian parsley

Curly parsley

Pennyroyal

Rosemary

Rue

Sage

Oregano

Oregano, or wild marjoram, is a hardy perennial growing 18 to 30 inches. The plant grows in ordinary soil but prefers well-drained, sandy loam. If the pH is below 6.0, add lime and calcium. Oregano likes full sun away from winds. Mulch if winters are severe. Propagate by seed, divisions, or cuttings. The seeds are slow to germinate; it's best to set out young plants. Space them 15 inches apart. Cut the stems an inch from the ground in fall, just before the flowers open, and hang to dry.

Parsley

There are two main types—Italian parsley and French or curly parsley. This herb is a hardy biennial, often grown as an annual. The plant reaches 12 to 18 inches and thrives in moist, rich soil. It prefers full sun but survives in part shade. Seeds take three to four weeks to germinate, so it is best to set out young plants, spacing them 8 to 10 inches apart. Pick parsley fresh all season. Cut the leaves in the fall and dry or freeze them.

Pennyroyal

This old-time medicinal herb was used for flavoring and to cure a variety of illnesses. Native Americans and early settlers also used it as an insect repellent. Grow pennyroyal from seed, cuttings, or root divisions. The plants grow 1 foot high, and prefer shade and moist soil.

Rosemary

Rosemary is used as both an aromatic and a flavoring herb in sauces, soups, and teas. It is a tender perennial evergreen shrub that grows 2 to 6 feet, depending on climate. Rosemary must be sheltered or grown in containers and taken indoors in winter in cold areas. It thrives best in warm climates and prefers moist, well-drained, alkaline soil. Apply lime or wood ashes to acid soil below pH 6.5. Grow rosemary from cuttings, root divisions, or layering, since seed germination is poor. Harvest all season or hang to dry for winter supply.

Rue

Rue is a bitter medicinal herb used for centuries as an antidote to many poisons. It is easily grown from seed, but the ancient Greeks believed that a plant stolen from a neighbor's garden had more power than one acquired honestly. Plants grow 2 to 3 feet high and thrive in an alkaline soil, in sun or partial shade.

Sage

Sage is a hardy but short-lived perennial growing to about 2 feet. The mature stems become woody and should be pruned. Because the plant takes a long time to mature, transplants are usually set out. Space them 2 feet apart, in a well-drained, rich soil and full sun. Add lime if pH is below 5.8. Water sage well while it is young. Harvest sparingly the first season; increase yearly. Pick leaves any time, but harvest two crops a year—one in June and another in the fall—to keep the plants less woody. Hang in small bunches to dry.

Scented Geraniums

The leaves of rose geraniums are used in jelly and to make tea. Most varieties are grown primarily as scented houseplants. These geraniums are not frost-hardy. Started from cuttings. They prefer full sun and well-drained soil.

Sorrel

Sorrel leaves have a sour, acidic, citrus flavor and are used in soups and salads. Sorrel grows easily from seeds or division, prefers acidic soil, and often becomes a weed. Plants grow to 2 feet in sun to partial shade.

Sweet Woodruff

Used in Germany for many centuries to flavor May wine, it has also been used as an ointment, in perfume, and as an internal medicine. Placed in drawers, it repels insects and gives sheets and towels a pleasant scent. Sweet woodruff likes acid soil. It is difficult to grow from seed, so buy plants instead. The top may be cut and dried anytime; the fragrance appears only after drying. Plants grow to 8 inches high.

Tarragon

Tarragon is a perennial. The French variety has the best flavor and is preferred to Russian tarragon, which is weedy and lacks essential oils. Tarragon grows 2 to 3 feet tall and tends to sprawl. Because it rarely sets seed, propagate by cuttings or divisions. Tarragon prospers in fertile soil, sun, and moisture. Mulch the roots in late fall and divide every three to four years. Harvest throughout the summer. To dry, cut the stalks a few inches from the ground in early fall. Hang or screen-dry.

Thyme

The many varieties of this perennial include lemon thyme, creeping thyme, and garden or common thyme. Most have ornamental, culinary, and aromatic qualities. Thyme is a short plant, growing only 8 to 12 inches tall, and is used as a ground cover or in rock gardens. It flourishes in sandy, dry soils in full sun. Propagate by seeds, divisions, or cuttings, but the seeds are slow to germinate. Space thyme 15 inches apart. Rejuvenate an older plant by digging it up in early spring and dividing it. Fertilize with compost or seaweed. Harvest the leaves throughout summer. To dry, cut stems just as flowers start to open. Hang in small bunches. Harvest sparingly the first year.

Watercress

Watercress is used for garnish and flavoring. If you have a shallow, slow-moving pond or stream where there is no threat of flood, you can try growing this flavorful herb. It can easily be transplanted from one stream to another. Propagated by division. Low-growing.

—from *The Big Book of Gardening Skills*

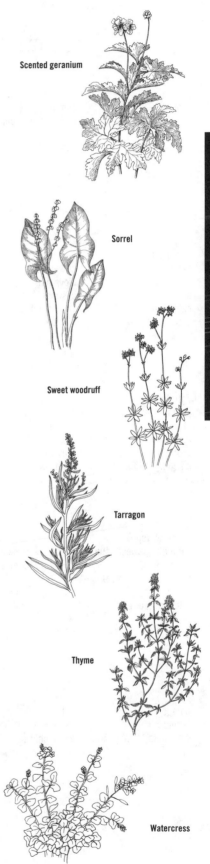

Scented geranium

Sorrel

Sweet woodruff

Tarragon

Thyme

Watercress

YOUR GARDEN, YARD & ORCHARD

HERB GROWTH AND USES

CLEVER HERBAL THEME GARDENS YOU CAN CREATE

PARTIAL SHADE GARDENS

aconite	comfrey	French tarragon	lungwort	snakeroot	wormwood
angelica	common or sweet vio-	Good-King-Henry	mints (not catnip)	sweet cicely	yarrow
bee balm	let	lady's-mantle	mother-of-thyme	sweet flag	
borage	coneflower	lemon balm	parsley	sweet woodruff	
carpet bugleweed	costmary	liatris	Roman chamomile	valerian	
chervil	English pennyroyal	lily of the valley	running myrtle	wild ginger	
chives	fennel	lovage	St.-John's-wort	wintergreen	

ROCK GARDENS

artemisia	chamomiles	garlic chives	hyssop	parsley	scented geraniums
basils	chives	germander	lady's-mantle	pennyroyal	sweet marjoram
bedstraw	clove pink	golden oregano	lavender	rosemary	thymes
burnet	costmary	golden, red, and silver	lavender cotton	saffron	violet
calendula	curry plant	sage	mints	santolina	wild ginger
catmint	dittany	horehound	pansy	southernwood	

FRAGRANCE GARDENS

catmint	curry plant	lemon balm	patchouli	scented geraniums	tansy
chamomiles	dill	lemon verbena	pennyroyal	southernwood	thymes
clove pink	fennel	lime balm	rosemary	sweet cicely	valerian
coriander	hyssop	mignonette	sages	sweet flag	violets
costmary	lady's-mantle	mints	savory	sweet marjoram	
creeping santolina	lavender	oregano	scented basils	sweet woodruff	

GROUND COVERS

bedstraw (sun)	common violet (part shade)	mints (sun or shade)	wild ginger (part shade)
carpet bugleweed (sun or partial shade)	dead nettle (sun)	oregano (sun)	wintergreen (shade)
	ground ivy (sun or part shade)	pennyroyal (part shade)	woolly betony (sun)
catmint (part shade)	lady's-mantle (shade)	Roman chamomile (sun)	wormwood (part shade)
catnip (sun)	lavender cotton (sun)	running myrtle (shade)	
coltsfoot (sun)	lily of the valley (shade)	sweet woodruff (part shade)	

SALAD GARDENS

anise	chicory or witloof	lamb's-quarters	marjoram	rose	thyme
basil	chives	leek	mints	savory	watercress
borage	dill	lemon balm	mustard	shallots	
burnet	fennel	lemon catnip	nasturtium	sorrel	
calendula	garlic chives	lime balm	oregano	sweet violet	
chervil	Good-King-Henry	lovage	parsley	tarragon	

BIBLICAL HERBS

aloe	costmary	hyssop	mint	pasqueflower	rue
anise	cumin	lady's bedstraw	mustard	rose	saffron
coriander	garlic	mandrake	nigella	rosemary	sesame
					wormwood

POTPOURRI GARDENS

ambrosia	clove pink	lemon verbena	scented basils	sweet woodruff
anise hyssop	fennel	lime balm	scented geraniums	vetiver root
bay	Florentine iris	orange bergamot mint	southernwood	
bergamot	lavender	patchouli	spearmint	
chamomiles	lemon balm	peppermint	sweet flag	
clary sage	lemongrass	pineapple sage	sweet marjoram	
Clevelandii sage	lemon thyme	roses	sweet violet	

TEA GARDENS

agrimony	calendula	dill	lemon-scented	pennyroyal (do not use	scented geraniums
angelica	caraway	fennel	marigold	if you are pregnant)	(rose and lemon)
anise	catmint	garden sage	lemon verbena	rose hips	sweet marjoram
anise hyssop	catnip	horehound	lime balm	rosemary	thymes
basils	chamomile	lemon balm	lovage	saffron	wintergreen
bergamot	costmary		mints		yarrow

CONTAINER GARDENS

alliums	chives	hyssop	marjoram	pennyroyal	thymes
artemisia (silver	clove pink	lavender	marigold	rosemary	violet
mound)	curry plant	lavender cotton	mignonette	rue	wormwood
basils	dill	lemon balm	mints	saffron	
bay	dittany	lemon catnip	oregano	sage	
calendula	garlic	lemon verbena	pansy	savory	
chamomiles	garlic chives	lime balm	parsley	scented geraniums	

SHAKESPEARE GARDENS

bay	calendula	lemon balm	poppy	rue
beebalm	garlic	pansy	rosemary	violet

BEE GARDENS

anise hyssop	creeping santolina	hyssop	pennyroyal	winter savory
bee balm	fenugreek	lemon balm	sage	woolly betony
borage	German chamomile	mints	sweet basil	
comfrey	horehound	oregano	thymes	

—from *Just the Facts!*

11

THE FLOWER GARDEN

**ANNUALS • PERENNIALS • BULBS • FLOWERING SHRUBS
ROSES • WILDFLOWERS • ART FROM THE GARDEN
FLOWERS THAT LAST**

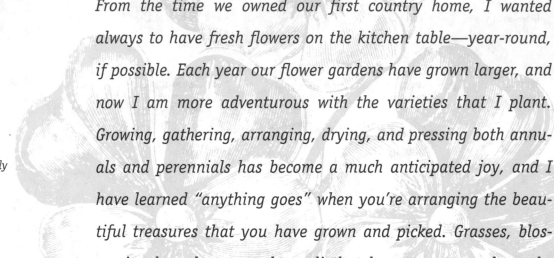

*Hardie Newton ran a highly
successful flower design
business in Washington,
D.C., for many years and
dreamed of moving to the
Virginia countryside. She
finally found her place in
the Blue Ridge Mountains
by accident, when she and
her realtor got lost. It was
just what she wanted—a
beautiful combination of
woodland and meadow.
Hardie's designs have been
commissioned for many
public and private spaces.
She gives flower design
workshops at her home, and
especially loves working
with children. Her book
is* Hardie Newton's
Celebration of Flowers.

*From the time we owned our first country home, I wanted
always to have fresh flowers on the kitchen table—year-round,
if possible. Each year our flower gardens have grown larger, and
now I am more adventurous with the varieties that I plant.
Growing, gathering, arranging, drying, and pressing both annuals and perennials has become a much anticipated joy, and I
have learned "anything goes" when you're arranging the beautiful treasures that you have grown and picked. Grasses, blossoming branches, even broccoli that has gone to seed can be
lovely additions to a natural arrangement.*

—Martha Storey

Flowers heal our spirits. They feed our souls with subtle ener-
gies, providing visual nourishment and irresistible scent.
Whether we are kneeling to plant seeds in the warm spring soil,
nurturing the seedlings as they emerge, or arranging flowers in
a chosen container, I believe that at their core and ours, flowers speak
to us in a unique way.

Flowers are a way of life. As a language, they and their cousins—
vines, shrubs, and trees—awaken our consciousness on an elementary
level. I like to think of flowers as the first creative art form, believing
that they were used by our ancestors to decorate caves and castles.

Wherever you live—farmhouse or high-rise, city or small town—
rejoice in the world of flowers. Celebrate with them. Allow them to
touch you. Call them into your life.

Annuals. Plants that bloom, produce seeds, and die in one year

Compost. Rich, porous soil made of decomposed organic matter

Deadheading. Clipping or pinching off fading flowers

Desiccant. A substance that absorbs moisture

Ground cover. Low-growing plants that spread by seed, underground stems, or horizontal top growth

Perennials. Plants that live for more than two years, often referred to as herbaceous (nonwoody) perennials

Species. A group of individual plants belonging to the same genus (similar characteristics)

Cut flowers at an angle (above) and then condition overnight in a bucket of warm water (right).

Annuals

The easiest and most rewarding way to achieve color in your landscape is with annual flowers. They create a mood, add another dimension, and enhance the beauty of the home.

Wherever space permits, include annual flower beds or borders in your overall landscape design. Plant annuals to unite a stand of evergreens and flowering trees or shrubs; to highlight or camouflage certain areas; or even to direct foot traffic. If you want to draw attention to your front door, frame it with color. If you want to conceal your trash cans, let an annual vine climb on a trellis in front of them. If you don't want the children cutting across the front lawn, plant a border of annuals to make them walk around the lawn to the path.

In addition to their primary use in beds and borders, bedding plants can be called upon for a variety of special uses. Flowering vines are unequaled as temporary screens on fences, trellises, and arbors. Select from morning glory, black-eyed Susan vine, cardinal climber, moonflower, sweet pea, scarlet runner bean, or nasturtium.

In newly planted landscapes, annuals can be used as a "quick cover" while you wait for the shrubs and permanent ground covers to mature. In hot climates, choose vinca, portulaca, petunia, or sweet alyssum. In cool areas, select phlox or lobelia.

You may want to bring the beauty of your garden indoors and have cut flowers for the living room. Your flowering annuals can do double duty if you choose types that can be cut and used in arrangements. Frequent cutting of flowers encourages new growth as well as increased bloom.

—from *Landscaping with Annuals* by Ann Reilly

Filling your house with fresh bouquets not only refreshes the spirit but also is good for the garden. Cutting flowers promotes vigorous new growth in most plants.

Tips for Arranging Flowers

- Invest in a good, heavy-duty pair of pruners for cutting woody branches.
- Keep knives and clippers sharp to prevent mashing the stems.
- Cut flowers after sunset, if possible.
- Cut stems on an angle to provide more surface for water absorption.
- To condition flowers for arrangements, place cut flowers and other materials in a plastic bucket filled with warm water overnight.
- Remove all foliage (leaves) below water level to prevent bacterial growth.
- When conditioning roses, remove only the thorns below water level.
- Flowers maintain their stamina longer in fresh water (with preservative) than when placed in floral foam.
- Change the water in glass containers every two to four days, adding fresh preservative.
- "Standard-grade" floral foam is the best type for general use.
- Hay, straw, dried leaves, mosses, rocks, and lichen are great disguisers for floral foam.
- Keep flowers away from heat outlets, air intake vents, and fans.
- Cut off spent flowers in bouquets, rather than pulling them out.

—from *Hardie Newton's Celebration of Flowers*

ANNUALS

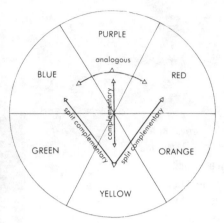

Use a color wheel to guide your garden design.

Use varied shapes, such as (left to right) spired snapdragons, globe-shaped marigolds, and ruffled petunias.

Place tall plants in the back of the garden bed and ground-hugging annuals in front.

Painting with Annuals

Color is usually the most striking aspect of flower bed design. Warm tones of yellow, gold, orange, and red attract attention to those sections of the garden where they are used. Blue and violet, on the other hand, create a quieter, more tranquil mood. Warm colors make a planting appear smaller than it actually is, while cool colors make it appear larger.

You can select from a number of color harmonies. Choose *complementary* (opposite) colors such as orange and blue, or violet with yellow. *Split complementary* color combines one color with the color to either side of its opposite. Examples would be red with blue, and red with yellow. Treat pink, a tint of red, the same way as red when designing. Treat violet the same way as purple.

Analogous color harmony is three colors in a row on the wheel, such as yellow, yellow-orange or gold, and orange. Monochromatic design is different tones of the same color. Select one harmony and stay with it throughout the bed or border for best effect.

Designing with Annuals

Design is the next step in creating your colorful world. Here are a few basic considerations.

Size. Use low-growing plants in small beds or as edgings. In large areas, vary the height to make the effect more interesting, especially if the ground is flat. In a freestanding bed, place tall plants in the center, stepping down to an intermediate-sized plant and then to a ground-hugging annual in front. For a mixed bed or border, choose three sizes of plants. This can be done by combining three varieties of the same plant or by combining three different plants.

Shapes. Plants grow in many different shapes, and a mixture of shapes is very attractive in a mixed bed. However, a mass planting of one variety in one shape or color is just as appealing. The decision depends on the effect you want to achieve.

Garden spaces. If space is tight, plant in areas that are most visible. For example, plant annual beds or borders along the walkway or driveway to greet you when you come home, or place them in the backyard where you will be relaxing on weekends. The shape of your planting area may be influenced by your home. A stately Georgian or very modern house demands a formal, straight-lined bed. A Colonial home calls for a closely packed, cottage-garden style. Most of today's architecture is complemented by semiformal, contoured flower beds or borders.

Planting Annuals

If you purchase bedding plants instead of growing annuals from seeds, look for deep green, healthy plants that are neither too compact nor too spindly. It is better if they are not yet in bloom.

An old-fashioned cottage garden can provide fresh cut flowers much of the year.

Most bedding plants are grown in individual "cell packs." If you can't plant them right away, keep them in a lightly shaded spot and water them as needed and again just before planting.

Tender annuals cannot be planted until after all danger of frost has passed and the soil is warm. *Half-hardy* annuals can be safely planted if nights are still cool, as long as there will be no more frost. *Hardy* and *very hardy* plants can be planted in early spring as soon as the soil can be worked. Plant in a cloudy or overcast late afternoon.

When planting, lift plants from cell packs or pots, keeping the root ball intact. Gently squeeze or push up the bottom of the container if it is pliable enough, or turn it upside down to have the plant fall into your hand.

Occasionally, you will find plants in a flat without individual cells. Just before planting, separate the plants gently by hand or with a knife. Other times, plants may be growing in individual peat pots. In this case, either peel away most of the pot or be sure that the top of the pot is below soil level after planting.

Dig a hole slightly larger than the root ball, set the plant in place at the same level at which it was growing, and firm the soil around the roots. Water well soon after planting, and again frequently until the plants are established.

Invert pot and tap on bottom to let plant fall into your hand.

Dig a hole larger than the root ball. Firm soil after planting.

—from *Landscaping with Annuals* by Ann Reilly

Keeping the Garden Colorful, Every Day

The first steps to a beautiful flower garden are good soil preparation and proper planting. After that, keeping color at its peak is up to you and Mother Nature.

Mulching. After planting, add a 2- to 3-inch layer of mulch to reduce weeds and conserve soil moisture. The best mulches are organic, and include bark chips, pine needles, shredded leaves, peat moss, and hulls.

Watering. Heavy but infrequent watering encourages deep root growth. Keep foliage dry during watering by using soaker hoses. If overhead sprinklers must be used, water early in the day.

Fertilizing. Most annuals do not require high levels of fertilizer. Once or twice during the growing season, use 5-10-5 fertilizer or a similar ratio at the rate of 1 to 2 pounds per 100 square feet. Or use a soluble fertilizer such as 20-20-20 and apply it every four to six weeks.

Weeding. Remove weeds as soon as possible so they do not compete for nutrients and water. Remove them carefully, so you do not disturb the annuals' roots.

Deadheading. Some annuals need to have faded flowers removed. This is known as deadheading, and it keeps the plants attractive and in full bloom. Deadheading can be performed with pruning shears or sometimes by pinching flowers off with the fingers.

Pruning. Use hedge clippers to clip back plants that sprawl, to encourage heavier blooming.

Clip back plants to encourage bloom.

ANNUALS

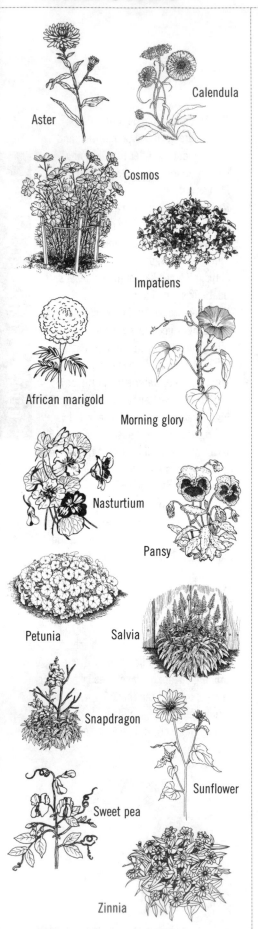

Aster

Calendula

Cosmos

Impatiens

African marigold

Morning glory

Nasturtium

Pansy

Petunia

Salvia

Snapdragon

Sunflower

Sweet pea

Zinnia

14 Favorite Flowering Annuals

Aster. Single or double blooms in many forms, including pompon, chrysanthemum, peony, cactus, and plumed. Blue, white, lavender, purple, yellow, pink, or red flowers. Uses include cutting gardens, beds, and borders. Prefers fertile, moist soil.

Calendula, pot marigold. Bright 3- to 4-inch blooms. Orange or yellow flowers. Uses include mass plantings, containers, petals as garnish for food. Prefers rich, moist soil.

Cosmos. *C. bipinnatus* has lacy foliage and daisylike flowers of pink, white, or lavender. *C. sulphureus* has broader leaves and semi-double blooms in red, yellow, gold, or orange. Uses include borders and mass plantings. Grows in dry, infertile soil.

Impatiens. The most popular flower for shady areas. White, pink, salmon, orange, scarlet, red, and violet flowers. Used under trees, in containers, and in shaded borders. Grows in rich, moist, infertile soil.

Marigold, African. Medium to tall, formal plants. Yellow, gold, or orange flowers. Uses include tall borders, edgings, and backgrounds. Grows in average soil.

Morning glory. Vining plant with flowers of heavenly blue, magenta, and deep purple. Some hybrids are multicolored. Soak or notch its hard seed before planting. Place in moist soil low in nitrogen to get more blooms.

Nasturtium. Bushy or vining plant; easy to grow from seed. Red, yellow, or orange flowers. The flowers, leaves, and buds are edible. Grows in dry, infertile soil.

Pansy. White, blue, bronze, yellow, purple, lavender, or orange flowers, solid or two-toned. In warm areas, plant in fall for spring bloom. Prefers cooler weather and rich, moist, fertile soil.

Petunia. Blooms are in every color, sometimes several. Grandifloras have large flowers and are best in containers. Multifloras have many small flowers and are used in mass plantings. Grows in dry, sandy soil.

Salvia. Red, white, coral, or purple-blue flowers. Uses include beds, borders, edgings, and containers. Grows in rich, average-to-moist soil.

Snapdragon. Showy, erect spikes. Red, bronze, pink, white, rose, yellow, scarlet, primrose, apricot, orange, crimson, magenta, or lilac flowers with a light, spicy fragrance. Uses include borders, beds, rock gardens, and cut flowers. Grows in rich, fertile soil.

Sunflower. Dwarf varieties are available for garden borders and low hedges. Yellow, bronze, gold, brown, mahogany, cream, or crimson flowers. Grows in dry, infertile soil.

Sweet pea. A vining or bushy plant with blooms of purple, rose, red, white, pink, or blue, solid or two-toned. Uses: trellises (vines) and borders (bushy). Grows in soil that is rich, alkaline, fertile, and moist.

Zinnia. A diverse group of annuals in all colors except true blue. Available in many flower shapes and forms. Can be used for any purpose in the garden, and makes a good cut flower. Grows in average to dry soil.

—from *Landscaping with Annuals*

SPECIAL PLANTS FOR SPECIAL PLACES

Most annuals are happiest when bathed in sunlight, rooted in average soil, and receiving moderate temperatures. Here are the notable exceptions:

HEAVY SHADE
begonia
browallia
coleus
fuchsia
impatiens
monkey flower
wishbone flower

PART SHADE
ageratum
aster
balsam
dianthus
dusty miller
forget-me-not
lobelia
nicotiana
pansy
salvia
sweet alyssum
vinca

DRIEST CONDITIONS
African daisy
amaranthus
celosia
dusty miller
petunia
portulaca
statice
strawflower

MOIST AREAS
aster
balsam
tuberous begonia
calendula
forget-me-not
fuchsia
impatiens
lobelia
nicotiana
pansy
phlox

HOTTEST SPOTS
amaranthus
balsam
celosia
coleus
dusty miller
nicotiana
petunia
portulaca
salvia
statice
vinca
zinnia

COOL CLIMATES
African daisy
tuberous begonia
browallia
calendula
dianthus
flowering cabbage
  and kale
forget-me-not
lobelia

pansy
phlox
snapdragon
sweet pea

ALKALINE SOIL
aster
dianthus
scabiosa
strawflower
sweet pea

HANGING BASKETS
begonia
browallia
coleus
fuchsia
impatiens
ivy geranium
lobelia
petunia
portulaca
sweet alyssum
vinca vine

Container Basics

By planting annuals in containers, you can locate color wherever you want it—and take it away if you change your mind. Here are some tips:

- Select annuals that are compact, long-blooming, and proportioned to the container.
- Use any container that will hold plant media, as long as it has good drainage (or use a thick layer of gravel in the bottom of the container).
- Use a soilless medium of peat moss or bark with perlite and/or vermiculite. Real soil attracts more insects and diseases.
- Reserve ½ inch of space from the top so water won't spill over.
- For a fuller effect, plant closer than you would in the ground.
- Check for dryness every day; containers are prone to drying out.
- Fertilize lightly but frequently.
- Rotate the planter toward your light source to make growth symmetrical.

—from *Landscaping with Annuals*

A Child's Garden of Annuals

A garden designed just for children is a garden where kids can play and learn. Here are some basic rules to keep in mind when creating a garden for children.

- Keep flower beds narrow, so little arms can reach across. Any furnishings, such as tables and pergolas, should be small as well. Tools should be kid-sized and sturdy.
- Plants with interesting textures can keep a child's attention for hours.
- Children like to see things happen. Choose plants that grow quickly: petunias, marigolds, nasturtiums, hollyhocks, zinnias.
- Plants that smell good are always a hit with kids. Flowers with rich fragrances include blue petunias, sweet alyssum, snapdragons, four-o'clocks, stocks, and spider flowers.
- With a little string and some wooden poles, it's easy to make a tepee-shaped trellis, perfect for a hideaway. Plant scarlet runner beans at the base of the strings and watch the vines transform the trellis into a leafy fort.

—from *The Big Book of Gardening Secrets* by Charles W.G. Smith

PERENNIALS

Choosing Perennials

It may be tempting to choose perennial species for your garden by looks alone. But, as in choosing a spouse, you need to be aware of what is unseen before you take the plunge. The thousands of different perennials vary widely in their growth and blooming habits, and each has different needs that must be met in order to thrive. Read about the plants you'd like to grow, find out if other local gardeners have had success with them, and try to see them bloom at a nursery or neighbor's garden before allotting them space in your own backyard.

A small flowering tree forms a striking focal point in this garden.

Shade-loving hostas make a serene ground cover in a wooded area.

LEWIS AND NANCY HILL ON THE JOYS OF PERENNIALS

From studying the new garden catalogs in mid-January to tucking in the plants with mulch just before the winter snows arrive, we derive enormous pleasure from our perennial flowers. As soon as the snow melts in the spring, we hurry to the gardens to discover which plants are peeping through the wet earth after their long hibernation. With the first spring shower, many that had seemed dead on first inspection suddenly sprout green buds, and we know that more surprises will appear each day until the cycle of seasons brings winter once again.

It is this quality of metamorphosis that attracts us to perennials. The annual flowers that grow, bloom, produce seed, and die the same year are lovely, colorful, and predictable throughout the summer. Herbaceous perennials, on the other hand, are fascinating because most bloom for only short periods and seldom look the same two days in a row, or two years in succession. They reward us with an endless variation of plant textures, heights, and fragrances.

Sometimes we wonder, nevertheless, why we spend our summers digging, planting, moving plants from place to place, feeding, and spraying while others swim, boat, play tennis and golf, or relax in a hammock. Perennial gardening isn't always fun. In fact, one gardener has described the struggle with soil, weeds, bugs, and diseases as a "war of the (prim)roses."

Our desire to garden, and the pleasure it gives us, no doubt has something to do with the challenge of winning that war, and creating beauty in a spot where only grass and weeds would otherwise be found. It also provides exercise, lovely bouquets, and a good excuse to be outdoors. But the root of our motivation goes deeper, to the peace that subtly creeps over our minds when we are absorbed with our plants. In working with the soil, we join a long procession of humanity tied to the cycle of planting and harvest since the beginning of time.

—Lewis and Nancy Hill have written many books on gardening from their northern Vermont nursery, including *Successful Perennial Gardening*.

Starting a Perennial Garden

Some famous gardens include huge beds of perennials, but a few strategically placed plants can do wonders for a small-scale landscape. A perennial garden, like a vegetable plot, is more beautiful, productive, and satisfying when kept to a manageable size. The Chinese have a saying to which all gardeners should pay heed: "Praise large gardens, plant small ones."

Choosing a Site

Most flowering perennials prefer full sun. Ideally, a perennial garden grows for many years in the same location, so make a note not only of present light conditions, but also of future possibilities. If you or your close neighbors have young trees growing nearby, the amount of shade will increase as they grow, and some pruning or perhaps complete removal of trees will be necessary to ensure adequate sunlight for your perennials.

Soil

Most common perennials like soils similar to that of vegetable gardens. However, some perennials prefer dry soil, others like it moist. Most thrive in soil with a pH of 5.5 to 6.5, but there are exceptions. Wild orchids need very acidic soil; delphiniums prefer it alkaline. Read descriptions of each perennial to learn about any special light and soil requirements it may have.

Plant Positioning

The concept of clumping is basic to good garden design. To create the masses of color and the shapes that make perennial borders so attractive, plant clumps of the same variety at intervals throughout the garden.

When spacing plants, allow plenty of room for the expansion of each clump. Each grows differently, but as a rule allow at least 1 foot between every plant in a clump, and 2 or more feet between each clump. However, even with generous spacing, most perennials will need to be divided from time to time and the clumps reduced to a manageable size.

A Note on Weedy Plants

Some fast growers can crowd out less aggressive plants and cause no end of frustration and work. We've learned to limit the more vigorous plants, watch them carefully, and don't hesitate to cut them back whenever our flower beds become threatened with unfriendly takeover.

—from *Successful Perennial Gardening* by Lewis and Nancy Hill
and *The Big Book of Gardening Skills*

Varying heights and textures provide interest whether plants are in bloom or not.

Informal beds can be any shape that pleases you and fits your space.

PERENNIALS

Plan your garden so that different heights and colors appear natural. Planting in masses is one way to achieve this.

EARLY SPRING

LATE SPRING

SUMMER

Consider the bloom time of plants when you place them in your garden.

Remove dead flowers with sharp pruning shears.

Designing Your Perennial Garden

There is no one "right" way to design a planting. Still, if you want your garden's overall appearance to appeal to most onlookers, it is essential to follow a few basic guidelines of good design.

Plant Size

Common sense dictates that plants must be arranged according to height, so that plants such as sweet William and pansies will not be completely hidden behind a tall clump of foxglove. However, inflexible arrangements may seem artificial. A garden is more pleasing to the eye if plants of different heights, colors, and varieties are arranged as if they're growing naturally throughout the garden. Remember that identical varieties may grow to different sizes, depending on the soil, light conditions, and climate.

Flowering Times

Most perennials bloom for only a limited period in their growing cycles, so both new gardeners and longtime horticulturists complain of "gaps" when the garden produces few if any flowers.

Although charts are useful as broad guidelines, the expertise of neighboring gardeners will be more precise. After a season or two of observing perennial plants in your area, you will better understand how they are likely to behave in your garden.

—from *Successful Perennial Gardening*

Pruning Perennials

To many, the word *pruning* conjures up visions of cutting branches from trees with loppers and sharp-toothed saws. In a practical sense, though, pruning is simply the removal of part of a plant. Whether you cut off a branch or snip off a dead flower, you are pruning.

The types of pruning required for the aboveground portions of herbaceous perennials fall into these categories: deadheading, pinching, disbudding, and cutting back.

Deadheading

Deadheading, or removing dead or spent flowers, encourages the formation of additional flower buds by inhibiting seed production, thus prolonging the plant's blooming season. Old flowers are also excellent places for diseases to find a home, so regular deadheading keeps your plants healthier.

To deadhead, use a pair of scissors or small pruning shears. For such plants as daylilies, with many buds clustered at the end of a stalk, carefully nip out individual flowers as they go by. For such plants as phlox, whose flower heads consist of many smaller flowers, or peonies with solitary large blossoms, wait for most of the flowers in the flower head or most of the petals in the large flowers to go by. Then snip back the flower stalk to the first leaf.

Pinching

Pinching, or removing the growing tip of a plant, causes the buds along the stem to break and grow into new branches.

Pinching of perennials is usually done in spring, when the plants first begin to grow actively. To pinch, simply remove the section of plant above the topmost set of leaves. Perennials that benefit from pinching include aster, boltonia, chrysanthemum, and any others that you want to form rounded, bushy plants.

Disbudding

Disbudding is the removal of a flower bud. Some perennials, such as peonies, produce a large terminal flower bud with two axillary buds on either side. In many plants the terminal bud is female and the axillary buds are male. The terminal female flowers are often larger and much showier than the axillary males. However, if the male flowers are disbudded, the terminal female bud often responds by producing an even bigger and more beautiful flower than it normally would have.

Cutting Back

Cutting back is the horticultural equivalent of a haircut. It's the uniform cutting of a plant to reduce its height. Cutting back improves the appearance of straggly plants and, in some plants, encourages flowering. Plants that are frequently cut back include lavender, yarrow, and geranium.

—from *The Big Book of Gardening Secrets* by Charles W.G. Smith

Pinch back the growing tip to encourage branching.

Remove small side buds to promote showier main flowers.

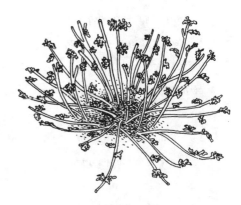

Cut back straggly plants for better appearance and more blooms.

ACCENT PERENNIALS FOR FOUR SEASONS

A garden is easier to plan if you first select a few basic or accent plants for each of the four blooming seasons. Accent plants are prominent perennials that form the backbone of your display—strong growers that are durable, have attractive blooms, and furnish interesting foliage for most of the season. If you are unsure of the best choices for accent plants, the following list may help.

SPRING	EARLY SUMMER	SUMMER	LATE SUMMER AND FALL
Tall	**Tall**	**Tall**	**Tall**
columbine	delphinium	globe thistle	Japanese anemone
common bleeding	German iris	baby's breath	aster
heart	lupine	daylily	rose mallow
leopard's-bane	peony	hosta	sage
Siberian iris	**Medium**	liatris	**Medium**
Medium	golden marguerite	lythrum	turtlehead
fernleaf bleeding	bellflower	bee balm	chrysanthemum
heart	cornflower	phlox	**Short**
sweet William	pyrethrum	**Medium**	aster (dwarf
daylily (early	daylily	spirea	varieties)
varieties)	lily	Shasta daisy	chrysanthemum
Short	beardtongue	campion	(dwarf varieties)
moss pink	**Short**	tritoma	betony
violet	English daisy	coneflower	
	Carpathian bellflower	**Short**	
	coralbells	cranesbill	
		sea lavender	
		balloonflower	
		Stokes' aster	

PERENNIALS

Janet Macunovich is owner of Perennial Favorites, a landscape design company in Michigan, and she teaches popular classes in garden design and maintenance techniques. She knows from experience that successful gardeners must "hustle in spring" in order to "coast in summer." In other words, time spent in early to mid-spring preparing beds, weeding, edging, and so on, will pay off with relaxed days in midsummer. This reflects plants' own cycles, in which their most rapid growth occurs in spring. Janet is author of Caring for Perennials *and* Easy Garden Design.

Caring for Your Perennials

Edgings: Barriers and Beautifiers

Edgings are needed to protect the perennial bed from weeds, which can invade the garden by sneaking their roots in from the sides. An edging serves other worthwhile purposes. It defines exactly what is garden and what is not, and gives a bed a finished appearance, often making the difference between a fine garden and a mediocre one.

Install an edging when you first prepare the bed. If you want a straight-edged border, use a taut string tied to stakes at each end as a guide. An irregular or curved bed can be created by using a rope, clothesline, or garden hose to define the area.

In many gardens, the edging is simply a narrow strip of bare earth about 8 inches wide between the flowers and lawn. These were once very popular, and the edging tool used to create them—a sharp blade on a straight handle—

Three Ways to Support Your Plants

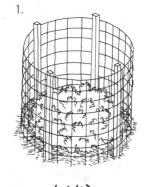

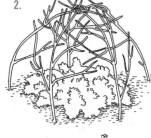

1. Stakes and hoops like this one of fencing wire (left) are not usually long-term eyesores. Plants soon grow over them.

2. Staking with twigs is less expensive but more time-consuming than other methods.

3. My favorite staking arrangement (below) is stakes and string. Start with five stakes around the crown. Link them together around the perimeter, then across the top of the plant. Make the first loop at least a hand's breadth above the soil to allow weeding room.

As the plant grows, the string web provides support for the central stems, and the whole structure is gradually covered by foliage.

—from *Caring for Perennials* by Janet Macunovich

Garden beds with graceful S-shaped curves are not only easy on the eye, but they are also much easier to mow than beds with corners. Use a hose or a rope as a guide when laying out the bed.

Dividing Perennials

Division is a simple form of pruning. It is as essential to good perennial gardening as the pruning of a fruit tree is to a productive orchard.

Propagate shallow-rooted perennials by gently pulling apart the clump.

Keep clump plants healthy by occasionally cutting away sections of the exterior and replanting them elsewhere.

Bulbs can be propagated by separating and replanting them, or by removing bulblets and setting them out in a transplant bed.

was an indispensable piece of equipment for the serious gardener. Such a cut-out edging is attractive, but it is used less often today because it must be recut frequently.

Plastic, steel, or aluminum edgings take longer to install initially, but they make effective, long-lasting barriers. They are available at most hardware and garden stores, and can be bent easily to fit beds of any shape, which makes them useful for an island garden or pathway as well as for a straight border.

The depth of the edging you need depends on the type of growth that surrounds your garden. A 4-inch depth will keep out shallow-rooted weeds and most lawn grasses, but 8 inches will do the job even better. Edgings that are 2 feet or more in depth are necessary to halt the deep-roving roots of shrubs and hedges. To install one—after marking the edge of the border—dig a ditch straight down to the necessary depth. Sink the edging vertically, but make sure the top edge is level with the soil, so it won't be visible or interfere with mowing the lawn.

Many perennial beds are delineated with visible edgings, which are intended to add beauty to the garden. Bricks (placed either horizontally or at an angle), flagstones, paving blocks, tiles, concrete, wooden timbers, stone chips, and similar products are used. If you decide to use a wood edging, choose cypress, redwood, or another long-lasting type. Treat less durable woods with a nontoxic preservative. Avoid using timbers such as railroad ties that have been soaked in creosote or other chemicals that are toxic to plants.

Brick (above) and aluminum (below) edgings are effective and long lasting.

Attractive edgings can also be made with living plants, such as a low, tight hedge of dwarf shrubs, perennials, or annuals. Boxwood, barberry, ivy, lavender, Pachysandra, candytuft, thyme, thrift, alyssum, and alpine strawberry are often used as edgings, especially in large formal gardens. Though beautiful, they require more maintenance than an inanimate edging, and they are not effective in keeping out weed roots.

—from *The Big Book of Gardening Skills*

When plants have carrotlike roots, it is necessary to dig up the entire plant and use a knife to cut it into a number of smaller plants.

—from *Successful Perennial Gardening* by Lewis and Nancy Hill

PERENNIALS

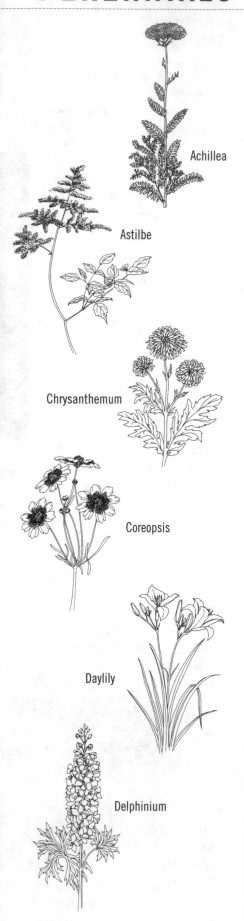

Achillea

Astilbe

Chrysanthemum

Coreopsis

Daylily

Delphinium

A Dozen Favorite Perennials

Achillea. This easy-to-grow group includes yarrows and sneezeworts and ranges in size from tiny, creeping rock garden plants to 4-foot giants. Drought- and heat-tolerant. Thrives in full sun and poor, dry soils with a pH of 5.5 to 7.0. Three reliable species are fernleaf yarrow, sneezewort, and common yarrow.
Zones: 3 to 9, depending on species.
Propagation: Easily propagated by division in spring or fall. Common varieties can also be started from seed and root cuttings.

Astilbe. A group of feathery-plumed flowers, ranging in height from a few inches to several feet. Pink, red, cream, and white flowers. Likes full sun or light shade; ordinary garden soil. They are heavy feeders, so additional fertilizer is needed if the plants are to thrive.
Zones: 2 to 8, depending on species.
Propagation: By division in early spring.

Chrysanthemum. Mums like full sun and rich soil. Pinch back young plants several times in late spring and early summer, and keep faded blooms picked for best appearance and longer flowering.
Zones: 3 to 9, depending on species.
Propagation: Divide the plants or root the tops you pinch off in spring and early summer in moist, sandy soil.

Coreopsis. These plants, with their bright, daisylike, yellow-toned flowers, reach heights of 1 to 3 feet. Prefers sun and moist garden soil. Pick the fading blooms to maintain blossoms over a long time. Mulch in northern zones.
Zones: 4 to 8, depending on species.
Propagation: New plants are easily started by division. Seeds planted early will often bloom the first year.

Daylily. The daylily grows easily, multiplies well, is easy to care for, and is not susceptible to insects or disease. Each flower lasts only a day. Daylilies prefer full sun but tolerate some light afternoon shade, and they thrive in soil that is fertile, well drained, and slightly acid to neutral in pH.
Zones: 4 to 9, depending on species.
Propagation: Divide the roots in early spring, or in late summer after they finish blooming. Slips can also be rooted in moist sand or sandy soil.

Delphinium. Delphiniums like sun but tolerate light afternoon shade. They need rich garden soil with a little lime. Give the plants plenty of space to allow the good air circulation necessary to prevent mildew. The stalks should be cut down after blooming. In some areas , they will bloom again in September.
Zones: 3 to 7; most species prefer a cooler climate.
Propagation: Easily grown from seed; plant in spring (North) or fall (South); or take stem cuttings in early summer.

Echinacea. Echinacea, or purple coneflower, offers a large, daisy-type, cone-shaped flower in late summer. The plants like a sunny spot but will tolerate light shade, and grow in ordinary good garden soil. The plants grow to a height of 3 to 4 feet. (See chapter 10 for more information on echinacea.)

Zones: 3 to 8.

Propagation: Divide them when the clumps get too large, or every 3 to 4 years.

Hosta. The hardy hostas are low-maintenance plants that often thrive where other plants refuse to grow. They prefer light shade, but they will grow in full sun if the soil is moist, deep, and well supplied with humus and nutrients.

Zones: 3 to 9.

Propagation: Divide the clumps in early spring.

Iris. All species of iris prefer full sun, but each variety has its own soil and moisture specifications. Of the many spectacular bearded species, the German iris is the most popular because it grows well in ordinary soil with no unusual moisture requirements. Cut off any diseased foliage or borer damage as soon as it appears, and spray with a garden fungicide once or twice early in the season.

Zones: 3 to 9.

Propagation: Divide the root clumps in late summer. Divisions with three or more sprouts should bloom the following year.

Peony. Peonies are hardy, fragrant, and long-lived, and make superior cut flowers. The shrublike foliage grows up to 3 feet in height and width, and the blooms can be 10 inches or more across. They like full sun but also grow well on the southeast side of a building, where they will get light afternoon shade but plenty of sky light. Allow 3 feet in diameter for each plant. Stake the plant as soon as buds begin to develop.

Zones: 3 to 8, depending on species.

Propagation: Peonies need only infrequent dividing—usually every 8 to 10 years.

Phlox. Garden phlox thrives in rich, deep garden soil and prefers full sun. It needs adequate moisture, plus a little extra fertilizer and lime. Good air circulation is essential to prevent the onset of powdery mildew, so space the plants at least 2 feet apart. Thin out the phlox stems while they are still small.

Zones: 2 to 9, depending on species.

Propagation: Divide the clumps in fall or early spring, or by taking stem cuttings in early summer.

Sedum. Sedums like dry, infertile soil, and they grow in sun or light shade. One of the best for the border is showy stonecrop, 18 to 24 inches high, and its cultivars. Some varieties are well suited to rock gardens and ground covers.

Zones: 3 to 8.

Propagation: Take cuttings. Nearly every piece will root and grow into a new plant in practically no time.

—adapted from *The Big Book of Gardening Secrets* by Charles W.G. Smith and *Successful Perennial Gardening* by Lewis and Nancy Hill

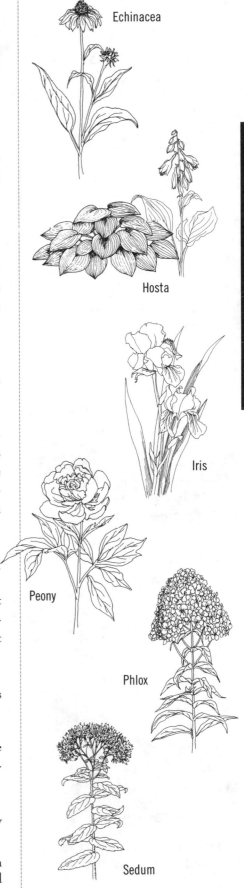

Echinacea

Hosta

Iris

Peony

Phlox

Sedum

BULBS

Informal plantings of narcissus will spread freely in a meadow.

Mass tulips along a fence.

For a large planting, dig the entire area to the depth recommended.

Using Bulbs in the Landscape

Spring and summer bulbs are among the most beloved of flowers. They are easy to care for yet sublimely beautiful, from the first snowdrop in late winter to the final daylily in fall.

Planning Your Bulb Planting

Before making a decision about what bulbs to plant, consider the effect you want to achieve:

- **Formal or informal look.** A formal design is a more symmetrical garden with regular borders. It is a suitable site for tulips and hyacinths in blocks of one to two colors. An informal look is pretty, with bulbs planted in natural-looking drifts and a rainbow of colors.
- **Color.** Bright red, yellow, and orange are warm, exciting colors. Blue, pink, white, and lavender are cooling and soothing to the eye. Buy a color wheel from an art store to help you choose the color harmony you want.
- **Succession of bloom.** When choosing bulbs for the garden design, select a number of types so you will have color from late winter until early summer.
- **Geometric patterns.** These are very effective in bulb plantings. Think in terms of circles, arcs, swales, or any pattern that you find pleasing.
- **Perennials.** Perennials make excellent companions to bulbs. They start to come into bloom at about the time the bulbs are fading.
- **Clumps.** Almost without exception, bulbs look better when planted in clumps of at least three. The smaller the bulb, the more flowers you need in the clump.

How to Plant Spring-Flowering Bulbs

Plant spring flowering bulbs any time in fall until the soil freezes. If you can't plant them all at once, start with the smaller, earlier-flowering bulbs. Begin with crocus, squills, glory-of-the-snow, winter aconite, and other tiny bulbs; then plant tulips and daffodils.

Bulbs generally prefer full sun to light shade. You may note that bulbs planted under a large deciduous tree seem to be in heavy shade. Since most bulbs bloom before trees leaf out, this type of shade is not a problem.

Good soil preparation is critical. Because bulb roots reach deep, spade and prepare the bed to a depth of 12 inches. Before you plant, add organic matter equal to 25 percent of the soil volume. This matter can be peat moss, compost, leaf mold, or something similar.

When it's time to plant, prepare holes by one of two methods: Either dig individual holes for each bulb or dig out a larger area. The latter is better if you are planting a large number of bulbs.

Plant bulb with pointed end up.

Although bulbs contain their first season's food supply, fertilizing fosters future growth. To encourage root growth, add phosphorus-rich bonemeal to the bottom of each planting hole and place the bulb (pointed-end up) on top of it. Then return the soil to the hole and tamp down gently.

—from *Landscaping with Bulbs* by Ann Reilly

Add organic matter and bonemeal to the area when planting.

SPRING-FLOWERING BULBS

FLOWER	HEIGHT	BLOOMING TIME	DEPTH
Snowdrop	4–6"	Early spring	4"
Crocus	3–5"	Early spring	3–4"
Anemone blanda (Wildflower)	5"	Early spring	2"
Grape hyacinth (Muscari)	6–10"	Early spring	3"
Early tulips	10–13"	Early spring	6"
Hyacinth	12"	Early spring	6"
Daffodil	12"	Midspring	6"
Darwin hybrid tulips	28"	Midspring	6"
Crown imperial (*Fritillaria imperialis*)	30–48"	Midspring	5"
Late tulips	36"	Late spring	6"
Dutch iris	24"	Late spring	4"
Allium giganteum	48"	Late spring	10"

Easy Care for Spring Bulbs

Spring-flowering bulbs are about the easiest of garden plants to care for. A few chores in spring will keep bulbs at their blooming best.

- **Fertilizing.** When foliage emerges in spring, sprinkle 5-10-5 fertilizer or bulb food on the ground and water in. For maximum results, feed again as the foliage starts to yellow.
- **Watering.** Water bulbs deeply if spring rain does not fall.
- **After-bloom care.** When tulips, daffodils, hyacinths, and other large bulbs have finished blooming, cut off the flowers to prevent seed formation and to direct energy to the bulb. Smaller bulbs can be left to go to seed, which will scatter and increase the colony. Maturing of foliage is an important part of providing strength to the bulb. Never remove leaves until they have completely browned and pull away from the plant easily.
- **Mulch.** Mulching helps keep smaller bulbs from heaving out of the ground during winter. Use an organic mulch such as leaf mold, compost, bean hulls, wood chips, or pine needles to enrich the soil.
- **Dividing and replanting.** Daffodils and crocuses should be dug and divided every 5 to 6 years when the clumps get too large and bloom size and number decline. Do this in the spring, right after the foliage starts to yellow. Replant them immediately.
- **Replacing bulbs.** Tulips and hyacinths usually diminish in size rather than multiplying, so they should be replaced every several years.

BULBS

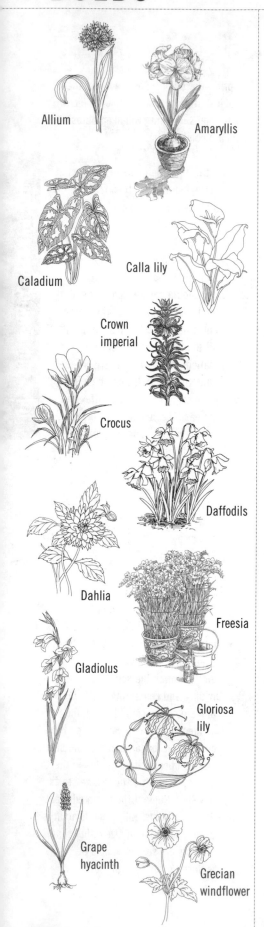

Allium

Amaryllis

Caladium

Calla lily

Crown imperial

Crocus

Daffodils

Dahlia

Freesia

Gladiolus

Gloriosa lily

Grape hyacinth

Grecian windflower

26 Popular Bulbs

Allium
Summer bulb
Height: 1 to 5 feet
Soil: rich, well drained, moist
Light: full sun
Planting depth: 3 inches for small; 10 inches for large
Planting distance: 4 inches for small; 12 inches for large

Amaryllis
Blooms indoors in winter
Height: 18 inches
Soil: rich, moist
Light: indoors, near window
Planting depth: top ⅓ of bulb should be above soil
Planting distance: 6 inches

Caladium
Does especially well in the South
Summer bulb
Soil: rich, moist
Light: full to part shade
Planting depth: 1 inch
Planting distance: 12 inches

Calla lily
Summer bulb
Height: 12 to 60 inches, depending on species
Soil: rich, moist
Light: sun or part shade
Planting depth: 3 inches
Planting distance: 12 to 24 inches

Crocus
Very hardy spring bulb
Soil: rich, well drained
Light: full or part sun
Planting depth: 3 to 4 inches
Planting distance: 3 inches

Crown imperial
Spring bulb
Height: 30- to 48-inch stems
Soil: average
Light: part sun
Planting depth: 5 inches
Planting distance: 18 inches

Daffodils and jonquils
Spring bulb
Height: 6 to 12 inch stems
Soil: rich, well drained
Light: full sun or part shade
Planting depth: 6 inches
Planting distance: 6 to 12 inches

Dahlia
Summer bulb
Height: 12 to 48 inches
Soil: rich, moist
Light: full or part sun
Planting depth: 4 inches
Planting distance: 6 to 24 inches

Freesia
Summer bulb
Height: 12- to 18-inch stems
Soil: average
Light: full sun
Planting depth: 2 inches
Planting distance: 2 inches

Gladiolus
Summer bulb
Height: 36 inches
Soil: well drained
Light: full sun
Planting depth: 4 inches
Planting distance: 6 inches

Gloriosa lily
Summer bulb
Height: 6 feet (needs trellis support)
Soil: rich, well drained
Light: full sun
Planting depth: 4 inches
Planting distance: 6 to 8 inches

Grape hyacinth
Spring bulb
Soil: average
Light: full to part sun
Planting depth: 3 inches
Planting distance: 4 inches

Grecian windflower
Spring bulb
Soil: fast draining
Light: full sun
Planting depth: 3 inches
Planting distance: 6 inches

Hyacinth
Spring bulb
Soil: rich, well drained
Light: full to part sun
Planting depth: 6 inches
Planting distance: 6 inches

Iris
Spring bulb
Height: 4 to 8 inches
Soil: well drained
Light: full sun
Planting depth: 4 inches
Planting distance: 3 to 4 inches

Lily
Height: 3- to 7-inch stem
Soil: deep, rich, moist
Light: full sun
Planting depth: 8 inches
Planting distance: 6 to 8 inches

Lily of the Nile
*Water and feed liberally, blooms heavily
when root-bound*
Summer bulb
Height: 18- to 36-inch stalks
Soil: rich, moist
Light: full or part sun
Planting depth: 1 inch
Planting distance: 18 to 24 inches

Peruvian lily
Summer bulb
Height: 12- to 48-inch stems
Soil: rich, moist
Light: full sun
Planting depth: 6 inches
Planting distance: 15 to 18 inches

Ranunculus
*Soak tubers before planting,
prefers cool climates*
Summer bulb
Height: 12- to 18-inch plants
Soil: rich, moist, well drained
Light: sun
Planting depth: 2 inches
Planting distance: 8 inches

Snowdrops
Spring bulb
Height: 4- to 6-inch stems
Soil: average

Light: full sun or part shade
Planting depth: 4 inches
Planting distance: 2 inches

Star of Bethlehem
Thrives in poor condition.
Spring bulb
Height: 6-inch stems
Soil: average to poor
Light: full to part sun
Planting depth: 4 inches
Planting distance: 3 to 4 inches

Sweet-scented gladiolus
Plant in groups of 10
Summer bulb
Height: 20-inch plants
Soil: well drained, coarse
Light: full sun
Planting depth: 2 inches
Planting distance: 5 inches

Trout lily (dogtooth violet)
Spring bulb
Height: 6- to 12-inch stems
Soil: rich, moist
Light: shade
Planting depth: 3 inches
Planting distance: 4 inches

Tuberous begonia
Summer bulb
Soil: rich, moist
Light: part shade
Planting depth: 2 inches
Planting distance: 8 inches

Tulip
Spring bulb
Height: to 30 inches
Soil: rich, fast draining
Light: full sun
Planting depth: 6 inches
Planting distance: 4 to 6 inches

Winter aconite
Do not let tuber dry out
Spring bulb
Soil: rich, moist
Light: full or part sun
Planting depth: 2 inches
Planting distance: 3 to 4 inches

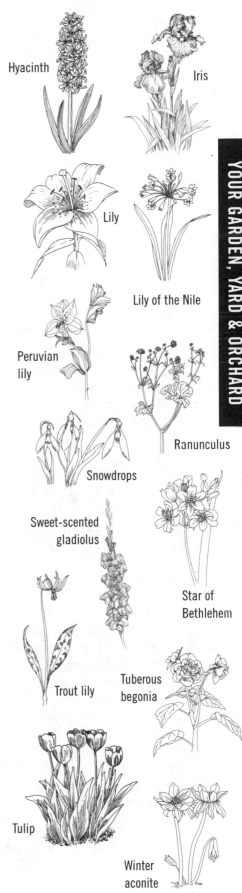

Hyacinth

Iris

Lily

Lily of the Nile

Peruvian lily

Ranunculus

Snowdrops

Sweet-scented gladiolus

Star of Bethlehem

Trout lily

Tuberous begonia

Tulip

Winter aconite

YOUR GARDEN, YARD & ORCHARD

BULReiLBS

Caring for Summer Bulbs

- **Watering.** Water soil deeply and often. Apply a mulch of organic matter 2 to 3 inches thick to conserve moisture and keep roots cool.
- **Fertilizing.** Summer bulbs benefit from heavy feeding with a balanced fertilizer.
- **Winter care.** Lift bulbs from the ground and store them over winter. Dig up tuberous begonias before the first fall frost. Leave others until the foliage is blackened by frost.

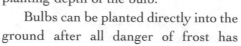

Tuberous begonia

Wash off as much soil as possible with a gentle spray of water, and dry them in a sunny spot for several days. Store bulbs in a dark, dry area at 40° to 50°F. A good method of storage is in dry sphagnum peat moss in a plastic bag.
- **Dividing.** If your summer bulbs need dividing, do it in spring just prior to planting. Cut roots and tubers with a sharp knife. Each division must contain at least one growing shoot or eye.

Dividing tubers

- **Disbudding.** Some summer bulbs, primarily dahlias, benefit from disbudding. As flower buds develop, pinch out the side buds and allow only the center bud to develop.
- **Staking.** For taller-growing summer bulbs, set stakes into the ground at planting time, so the bulbs will not be injured later on. Large plants or clumps of smaller plants can be staked with a hoop or cage.

—from *Landscaping with Bulbs* by Ann Reilly

How to Plant Summer-Flowering Bulbs

Summer-flowering bulbs require soil with excellent drainage. Before planting each spring, be sure the soil is rich in organic matter and well prepared. Work the soil several inches deeper than the planting depth of the bulb.

Bulbs can be planted directly into the ground after all danger of frost has passed in the spring, but it is better to give some a head start indoors about four to six weeks before planting time outside. The ones most in need of this are tuberous begonias, caladiums, and calla. Start them in a flat with a growing medium of 50-50 sphagnum peat moss and perlite. Set them in a warm spot with bright light but not direct sun, and keep them moist.

Plant large bulbs individually. Plant smaller bulbs in clumps for a massed effect. Summer bulbs combine perfectly with annuals and perennials.

—from *Landscaping with Bulbs*

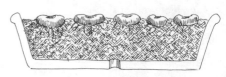

Start tuberous begonias, caladiums, and calla in flats indoors 4 to 6 weeks before planting outdoors.

SUMMER-FLOWERING BULBS

FLOWER	HEIGHT	PLANTING TIME	DEPTH	SPACING
Acidanthera	20"	early Spring	2"	5"
Anemones de Caen, St. Brigid	18"	South—Sept.-Jan. North—early Spring	2"	3"
Dahlia large varieties dwarf varieties	48" 12"	after last frost	4" 4"	24" 6"
Galtonia	40"	April — May	5"	10"
Gladiolus large flowering small flowering	60" 30"	April-mid June	3-4" 3-4"	6" 6"
Lily	3-7'	Fall or early Spring	8"	8"
Montbretia	24"	April-end of May	4"	4"
Ranunculus	12"	South—Sept.-Jan.	2"	8"
Tigridia	16"	early Spring	3"	6"

Getting Started with Shrubs

If you are new to gardening, learn something about the different shrubs before you purchase plants for your garden. Walk around a well-planted neighborhood in early spring. Look at the shrubs that are in bloom. Most gardeners love to talk about their plants and can give you lots of information. Other good places to see mature shrubs are in arboretums, parks, college campuses, and cemeteries.

Shrubs tend to grow in different shapes that can be used singly or in combination to create a variety of effects in the home garden. These shapes are: rounded, spreading, prostrate, low spreading, open spreading, globular, columnar, weeping, and pyramidal.

Designing with Shrubs

Think about how you plan to use your shrubs. Would you like a hedge of shrubs to separate your home from your neighbors? Do you need a windbreak on the north side of the house? Would you like a low hedge running along your entrance path, or perhaps a few shrubs to accent your doorway? Before you plan or plant any shrub, keep the following factors in mind:

Shrub size and shape. Consider the plant's ultimate height, shape, and growing habit. Some plants that grow in neat, compact shapes give a more formal look, while those that run rampant give a more informal feel to a landscape. One rule that landscapers go by, at least for an informal planting, is that you can combine two shapes in a single planting, but almost never three.

Color. Flowering shrubs come in an amazing array of colors with subtle differences in blossoms as well as foliage. There are many shades of green from which to choose—from a pale mint green to a dark, almost black green.

Texture. Texture is found in the shrub's foliage. Some shrubs have large leaves, while others have very small leaves. The large-leafed plants tend to give a lush effect in the garden, while the smaller-leafed plants give a more formal look.

—from *Flowering Shrubs* by Patricia R. Barrett

Shrewd Questions for Shrub Shoppers

Before you choose a shrub, review these questions:

- Will it grow well in the location chosen?
- Will it fit into the allotted space?
- Will it receive the right amount of light?
- Is it hardy for the area?
- Will it bloom or produce fruit at the right time?

—from *Flowering Shrubs*

Spreading

Low spreading

Open spreading

Prostrate

Shapes of Shrubs

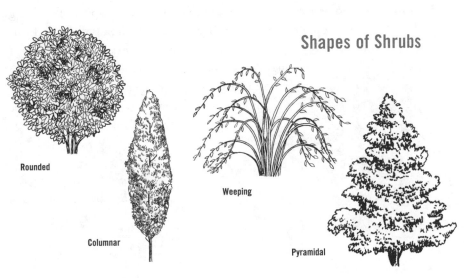

Rounded

Columnar

Weeping

Pyramidal

FLOWERING SHRUBS

1. Remove dead and crossing branches.

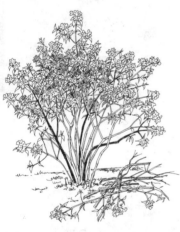

2. Remove one fifth to one third of oldest stems.

3. Deadhead faded flowers just above side shoots.

4. Water fertilizer into soil.

Pruning Spring-Flowering Shrubs

Many deciduous shrubs flower in spring, providing a beautiful and often fragrant backdrop for the early-season garden. Among those is mock orange, shown here. These shrubs are easy to care for, requiring only basic watering, fertilizing, and pruning. It is important, however, to prune them soon after their flowers fade, since this is when they begin to develop the new growth that will mature over summer and fall and produce flowers next spring.

1. **Remove dead and crossing branches.** When pruning, aim to retain and enhance the shrub's naturally graceful habit, taking care not to cut it into a boxy or unnatural shape. Before starting, clear out leaves and other debris from the plant's crown and the area beneath its branches, so you can see the whole plant. Use pruning shears or heavy-duty loppers to prune out dead branches, cutting them flush to the ground. Also remove branches that seem diseased or abnormal, and those that cross each other or rub together.

2. **Renewal pruning.** The branches of old vigorous-growing shrubs tend to become overcrowded, preventing the oldest stems from producing sturdy new side shoots. To give shrubs renewed strength, let light and air into the center of the plant, and provide growing space for new flowering stems, cut one-fifth to one-third of the oldest canes back to the ground. Repeat the process next year if the shrub needs further thinning.

If some overly long stems remain, consider shortening them, but keep in mind that branches cut back partway often give rise to a profusion of new shoots, making the shrub appear overgrown. Cut back these stems to just above a side branch that is growing in the direction you want, usually away from the center of the plant.

3. **Deadhead flowering stems.** You can begin while the plant is still blooming by cutting a few branches for fragrant bouquets. Immediately after the flowers have faded, selectively remove the dead blossoms, cutting each stem back to a pair of young laterals, or side shoots. These shoots will grow over the summer, forming buds for next year's blossoms.

4. **Routine care.** Some routine maintenance will keep your spring-flowering shrub healthy and blooming prolifically. If you haven't already fertilized this spring, do so after pruning. Use an all-purpose organic fertilizer, spreading it lightly in a circle around the outer edges of the branches. Thoroughly water it into the soil. A mulch of aged compost, shredded leaves, or straw will conserve moisture and prevent most weed growth.

—from *Year-Round Gardening Projects;* illustrations by Elayne Sears

TEN FAVORITE SHRUBS

SHRUB	COMMENTS	SIZE	FLOWER	BLOOM TIME
Buddleia ○	The buddleias or butterfly bushes like well-drained soil rich in loam.	10 to 20 feet tall and 15 feet wide, depending on variety	Lilac, orange, other colors in clusters	Early summer
Chaenomeles ○	All members of the Chaenomeles family—the flowering quinces—are popular shrubs.	3 to 6 feet	1- to 2-inch flowers pink, red, and white	Late spring
Cornus ○	The dogwoods are easy to grow in any good soil.	Many sizes, depending on variety	Small, white or yellow	Mid- to late spring
Daphne ○	Daphnes grow in any good soil but prefer a loose sandy soil that is neutral or even slightly alkaline. They also like full sun and cool roots.	3 feet	Pinkish white, fragrant, some with red berries	Spring
Hydrangeas ○ ◐	Hydrangeas do well in a moist, well-drained soil.	Large clusters	Most have white flowers, but can be blue, pink, or purple	Summer
Potentilla ○ ◐	The potentilla, or bush cinquefoil, likes ordinary garden soil with good drainage.	2 to 4 feet high	Bright yellow, white, and red	All summer
Rhododendron ◐	Rhododendrons need moist, acid soil. Many are not hardy in northern areas.	3 to 6 feet high, depending on variety	Pink, orange, rose, red, cream, yellow	Late spring to midsummer
Spirea ◐	Spireas thrive in almost any garden soil. They are easy to move around and have no pests. You can revitalize an old spirea fairly easily by cutting it back to the ground.	4 to 8 feet	White, pink, red	Late spring, early summer
Syringa (Lilac) ○ ◐	Lilacs like a neutral soil or one with peat moss or leaf mold added to it. Cut off the flower heads each year as soon as they fade.	Range from miniatures up to 20 to 30 feet	Purple, white, pink, yellow	Spring
Viburnum ◐	Viburnums are tolerant of most soils.	Wide variation	White, cream, bright red foliage in fall	Most in mid-spring, but varies

○ SUN
◐ PART SUN

—from *Flowering Shrubs*

ROSES

A Rose Is a Many-Splendored Thing

Rare is the person who doesn't know and love roses. Rare, also, is the person who thinks they are easy to grow. An entire mythology has sprung up about the diverse problems of insects, diseases, winterkill, special fertilizers, and complicated pruning techniques.

In reality, roses are no more difficult to grow than any other shrub or flower. A basic understanding of proper rose selection and care will reward you with the glorious blooms we all prize so highly.

Roses can certainly be a valuable addition to the landscape. No other shrub can bloom almost continuously from early summer until frost. No other shrub comes in such a wide range of growing habits. And no other plant produces the quantity or quality of blooms each year, even the same year of planting.

Roses in the Landscape

The traditional way to use roses in the landscape is in beds. These can be any shape and are an attractive, albeit conservative, choice for a formal garden. But there are many other exciting ways to grow roses. Here are a few ideas to try:

- Plant several floribundas or miniatures on either side of your doorstep, or massed in front of the traditional foundation planting of evergreens for a bold color statement.
- Surround a patio or terrace with roses. Planting roses around the mailbox or lamppost and along walks and drives also makes your home inviting.
- Don't forget to include hybrid tea, grandiflora, floribunda, shrub, and heritage roses as part of a shrub border. Miniatures can be used as an edging to plantings of roses or other plants. Any of the roses can also be planted in flower borders.
- Climbing roses provide a romantic touch to arbors, trellises, and gazebos. Let them frame a door, cover walls, or screen an unsightly view. They also soften the lines of a fence.
- Shrub roses create broad, informal hedges. Grandifloras make tall, narrow ones, while floribundas are best for low hedges. Prune them heavily after planting to encourage branching.
- Any of the roses are also good in container plantings. These are great placed around decks or entranceways. Miniatures can grow in pots as small as 6 x 8 inches.

Tie climbing roses loosely to a trellis.

Try miniature roses in 6- to 8-inch pots.

—from *10 Steps to Beautiful Roses* by Maggie Oster

Bush Roses

Usually upright-growing, bush roses need no support and grow from less than 6 inches to over 6 feet tall, depending on the variety and climate. Here are some common bush varieties:

Hybrid tea roses are long-stemmed, with narrow buds that open into large blooms. They flower throughout the growing season in a wide range of colors, and they are generally 3 feet or more tall.

Floribunda roses are hardy, compact plants 2 to 3 feet tall. They produce abundant medium-size flowers in short-stemmed clusters all summer long. These are considered among the easiest roses to grow.

Grandiflora roses grow 5 to 6 feet tall and bear large flowers in clusters on long stems throughout the growing season. They're excellent plants for accent or for a background planting.

Miniature roses are a small version of almost every other category, but they usually grow less than 2 feet tall. Blooms and foliage are proportionately smaller as well. They are hardy and vigorous, and are usually grown as edgings, mass plantings, accents, or container plantings.

Heritage, or old, roses are a diverse lot of plants developed before 1867. Most are direct descendants of species roses, with varying plant and flower forms, hardiness, and characteristics.

Climbing Roses

Roses do not actually climb like beans or peas, but some kinds have such long, flexible canes that they can readily be attached to arbors, trellises, posts, or fences. *Large-flowered climbers* have thick, sturdy canes that grow about 10 feet long. They bloom continuously or off and on throughout the summer. *Ramblers* have longer, thinner canes and bear clusters of small flowers once in late spring or early summer.

Shrub and Ground Cover Roses

Growing upright with slightly arching canes, most shrub roses are hardy, low-maintenance plants. Size ranges from 4 to 12 feet tall. They are a good choice for hedges as well as background and mass plantings. Shrub roses often produce seedpods called rose hips after blooming. These are high in vitamin C and can be used in teas and cooking.

Ground cover roses have limber, arching canes that trail along the ground, producing slightly mounded plants. There are spring-blooming and repeat-blooming varieties.

Tree Roses

Any rose that is bud-grafted onto a straight, sturdy trunk is a tree rose. The trunk may be 1 to 2 feet tall for miniature and floribunda roses, or 3 to 4 feet tall for hybrid teas. To create a weeping effect, climbers are budded onto 6-foot trunks. Tree roses require winter protection in all but the mildest areas.

Floribunda

Hybrid tea

Grandiflora

ROSES

Planting Bare-Root Roses in Five Easy Steps

When you purchase a rosebush, you hold in your hand the potential for many years of satisfaction and pleasure. To ensure that this potential is realized, you must plant the rose properly.

The first order of business is to be sure that your rose does not dry up while you prepare the planting hole. Immediately soak the root ball in water for up to 12 hours, allowing the plant to absorb as much water as it can hold. Then take the bush out for planting. If you cannot plant it immediately, bury the roots in a trench in your garden or in damp bark or sawdust until you are ready. Remember that even a few minutes in a dry spot can mean disaster.

Soak rose root ball before planting.

1. To prepare the planting hole, first remove any weeds and their roots from in and around the site. Dig a hole 15 to 18 inches wide and deep. Mix a quart of peat moss, compost, or other organic material with the soil removed from the hole. Form a blunt pyramid of some of this soil mixture in the planting hole.

2. Remove any broken or injured roots or canes from the plant, as well as canes less than pencil-size in thickness. Position the rose on the soil pyramid so the bud union (the swelling at the stem base) is just above the ground if you live in a mild climate. If you live where winter temperatures fall below freezing, place it so the bud union is 1 to 2 inches below the surface. Spread the roots in a natural manner down the slope of the pyramid.

3. Work the soil mixture around the roots to eliminate any air pockets. Firm the soil around roots and add more soil until the hole is three-fourths full.

4. Fill the hole with water, allow it to soak in, then refill with water. After the water drains the second time, check to see whether the bud union remains at the proper level. If not, add soil as necessary. Fill the remainder of the hole with soil and tamp lightly. Trim the canes back to 8 inches, making cuts ¼ inch above an outward-facing bud at a 45-degree angle.

5. Mound soil around and over the plant to 6 inches deep. This protects canes from drying out. When buds sprout, gradually and gently remove the soil mound—probably within two weeks.

Position rose so that the bud union is above ground in warm regions, and 1 to 2 inches below ground in cool regions.

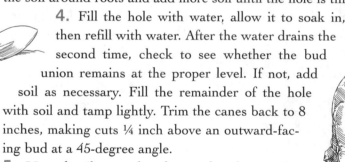

Mound soil over plant.

Fill the planting hole with water.

—from *10 Steps to Beautiful Roses* by Maggie Oster and *Hardy Roses* by Robert Osborne

Pruning a Hybrid Tea Rose

Hybrid teas are the most common roses in the United States. Hundreds of named varieties are offered every spring in catalogs, garden centers, and supermarkets. You must prune them each year to keep them blooming well. The flowers bloom on new shoots sprouting from canes that grew the previous year.

1. Thin out the old, weak, and winter-damaged canes and those that are crossed or too close together. If you prefer tall-growing roses, you may not want to shorten them except to make drooping canes a bit stiffer. If short, bushy plants fit better in your garden, cut all the ends of the canes farther back.
2. Remove all suckers originating from below the bud union.
3. Cut older main stems back to strong new shoots. Cut across the stems, not at an angle.
4. Cut back to five or so strong canes, each about 8 to 10 inches high. As spring arrives, the plant will burst into vigorous new growth and will regain its former height come summer.

Fertilizing Roses

To produce and maintain lush, healthy foliage and gorgeous flowers, plenty of fertilizer is needed. A basic fertilizer program for roses that bloom repeatedly throughout the summer includes three feedings:

- in early spring, just as buds begin to break
- when flower buds have developed
- about six weeks before the first fall frost in your area

If your soil is sandy, or if you live in a warm climate with an extended growing season, feed more often.

For the first two feedings, use ½ cup of general-purpose, dry granular fertilizer for each rosebush. Use 10-10-10 if the plant is mulched; 5-10-10 if it's not. For the last feeding, use a formulation without nitrogen such as 0-10-10. Scratch fertilizer into the soil around the plant, then water well.

—from *10 Steps to Beautiful Roses*

Step 1. Thin out the old and weak canes.

Step 2. Remove suckers below the bud union.

Step 3. Cut back older main stems.

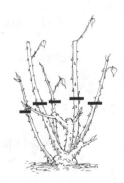

Step 4. Choose about 5 main strong stems and cut back to 8–10 inches.

Pruning Floribundas

Floribundas resemble hybrid teas; however, they have several flowers in a cluster and are generally shorter-growing plants. Prune them the way you would prune hybrid teas. When they are dormant, cut out nearly all the wood that is more than one year old. Slightly cut back younger wood and remove weak branches.

ROSES

Winterizing Roses

The amount of protection a frost-sensitive hybrid tea rose needs depends on the climate. Roses grown in USDA Zones 8 to 10 generally need no protection. Those in Zones 6 and 7 will probably require covering, and those in Zone 5 and below most surely will.

The time-honored method of protection is to pile up dirt around the base of the bush just before the ground is likely to freeze solid. The hill should reach a height of 6 to 8 inches if you are in a moderate zone but at least 12 inches in colder areas. Here are the steps for winterizing your roses:

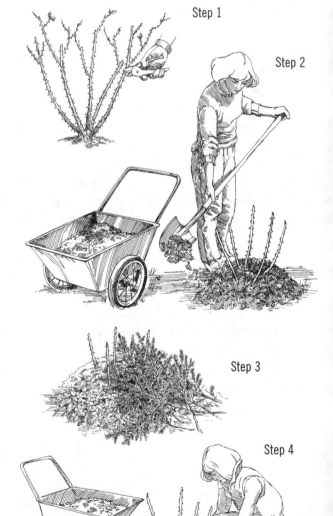

Step 1

Step 2

Step 3

Step 4

1. Prune back. A couple of weeks after the first frost, prune your rosebushes by trimming long canes by half and shorter ones by about a third. Don't worry about buds during this pruning. The aim is to reduce each bush's overall bulk, so it can be protected most efficiently.

2. Cover with soil. Whenever you sense that the ground is about to freeze, bring soil from elsewhere in the garden and pack it loosely around the base of your plants.

3. Add a mulch. In colder zones add salt hay, bark chips, pine needles or leaves over soil, holding them in place with evergreen boughs or branches.

4. Be cautious about removal. In spring, wait until the ground has thawed and remove soil promptly, so that new growth is not damaged. Keep some extra mulch on hand to pile temporarily around your plants in the event of a late frost.

—from *Gardening Techniques Illustrated*, text by Oliver E. Allen; illustrations by Elayne Sears

Six Wonderful Old Roses

Here are some rose varieties that can thrive in the Northern United States and Canada but are also exceptionally fragrant:

- **White**: *Rosa alba* 'Jeanne d'Arc'
- **Yellow to rich orange**: *R. foetida* 'Soleil d'Or'
- **Light pink**: *R. alba* 'Celestial'
- **Medium pink**: *R. centifolia* 'Common Moss'
- **Dark pink**: *R. gallica officinalis* 'Apothecary's Rose'
- **Mauve**: *R. rugosa* 'Hansa'
- **Dark red**: *R. rugosa* 'Roseraie de l'Hay'

—from *Hardy Roses* by Robert Osborne

DISEASE AND PEST CONTROL GUIDELINES FOR ROSES

Disease/Pest	Visual Signs	Solutions
Disease		
Blackspot	Round black circles on yellowing leaves that eventually drop off; prevalent during rainy or hot, humid weather; fungus over-winters on leaves or in lesions on canes.	Remove and destroy damaged leaves and canes; keep foliage dry when watering; treat with fungicidal soap, copper sulfate, or sulfur regularly throughout the season.
Powdery mildew	Leaves, shoots, and buds covered with white powder; deformed, stunted growth; prevalent during hot, dry weather with cool, humid nights.	Avoid damp, shady conditions or over-crowding plants; remove and destroy dam-aged parts; apply lime sulfur to dormant plants; treat with fungicidal soap or sulfur.
Rust	Small, orange to red-orange spots on leaf undersides, spreading to yellow blotches on leaf surface, leaves eventually drop; most prevalent in western and southwestern states.	Remove and destroy damaged plant parts; treat with fungicidal soap, sulfur.
Pest		
Aphids	Stunted, deformed leaves and flowers; clusters of 1/8-inch green, red, brown, or black insects in new growth, flower buds, and undersides of leaves.	Ladybugs, insecticidal soap, pyrethrin.
Beetles	Holes chewed in leaves or flowers; beetles include Japanese, rose chafer, rose curculio, and Fuller.	Pick off by hand (early morning is best) and destroy; where Japanese beetles are a problem, treat turf with milky spore disease (Bacillus popilliae) or treat plants with pyrethrin or rotenone.
Borers	Sudden wilting of new growth; puncture holes in stems or canes; caused by rose stem girdler, rose stem sawfly, or carpenter bees.	Cut off damaged shoot, being sure to include larvae, and cutting just above an outward-facing bud; seal end of stem or cane with putty, paraffin, or nail polish.
Caterpillars and worms	Holes chewed in leaves and flowers by larvae of butterflies and moths.	Hand-pick and destroy; treat with Bt (Bacillus thuringiensis).
Leafhoppers	Leaves turn pale with tiny white or yellow spots; 1/4-inch-long, greenish yellow insects that hop.	Insecticidal soap, pyrethrin, rotenone.
Rose midges	Blackened, deformed flower buds and leaves.	Remove and destroy damaged parts.
Spider mites	Leaves turn yellowish or spotted; webs and microscopic mites on undersides of leaves.	Spray leaf surfaces in early morning with streams of water, repeating for 3 days; treat with insecticidal soap or sulfur.
Thrips	Uneven coloring on flowers, deformed flow-ers, brown edges on petals or unopened flowers; tiny yellow, black, or brown insects.	Remove and destroy damaged flowers; treat with insecticidal soap, pyrethrin, or rotenone; predators include predatory mites, lacewings, ladybugs, and beneficial nematodes.

—from *10 Steps to Beautiful Roses* by Maggie Oster

Blackspot

Aphid

Beetles

Borer

Leafhopper

Spider mite

Thrips

WILDFLOWERS

Native Grasses Add Beauty to the Landscape

Natural meadows are a combination of wildflowers and grasses. The grasses provide support and the ideal amount of competition for the wildflowers, encouraging them to grow straight and tall. In northern regions, the dead remains of the grasses provide additional insulation, protecting the overwintering roots of the wildflowers.

Some grasses form sod, which is ideal where a continuous, tight cover is required, but is not much of an environment for growing wildflowers. Other grasses form distinct clumps or bunches when they grow, allowing space for wildflowers to coexist. When establishing your wildflower meadow, the grasses you interplant should be bunch grasses.

Native wildflower seeds should be combined with a mixture of native grasses suited to your region. Grasses should comprise about 60 to 90 percent of the seed mixture. The wildflower and grass seed mixture should be sown at a rate of 5 to 20 pounds of live seeds per acre, depending on the species composition. If you purchase wildflower and grass seed in bulk, the supplier can make specific seeding-rate recommendations.

A. Leadplant
B. Rattlesnake master
C. Purple prairie clover
D. Gayfeather
E. Nodding wild onion
F. Big bluestem
G. Little bluestem

A meadow garden of wildflowers and grasses in summer

HENRY ART ON WILDFLOWER MEADOWS

Whether your backyard is the size of a postage stamp or "the back 40," wildflowers can enhance its beauty. You may want to convert a portion of the lawn into a beautiful natural landscape. Wildflower meadows cost less than lawns to maintain, and they consume much less water, gasoline, fertilizer, and time.

Choosing Wildflowers

For best results, choose wildflowers that are compatible with your climate and environmental conditions. Some wildflowers are hardy, while others are killed by frosts. Remember that sunny southern slopes are usually warmer than the average climate of a region, and you may be able to grow more southerly wildflowers there.

Obtaining Wildflowers

Wildflowers should never be dug from the wild except as part of a rescue operation to save plants that would otherwise be destroyed. Propagate them either by making cuttings and divisions or by planting seeds.

The quickest way to obtain seeds is to purchase them from a reputable supplier. Seeds are generally available year-round and can be sent through the mail. If you are planning to plant large areas, inquire about wholesale prices for wildflower and native grass seeds.

Use prepared wildflower seed mixtures cautiously. Some suppliers carefully formulate mixes especially for your region using high-quality native species; others simply add the cheapest, most readily available seeds. If you are going to spend your money on wildflower seeds, you might as well purchase species that will survive well in your region.

The most pleasant way to obtain wildflower seeds is to collect them from the wild. Follow commonsense conservation guidelines. Collect only a few seeds or fruits from common species that are locally abundant. Do not collect fruits and seeds from plants growing in public places, and obtain permission before collecting on private property.

—Henry W. Art is author of *A Garden of Wildflowers* and *The Wildflower Gardener's Guide.*

WILDFLOWERS BY REGION

Common Name	Scientific Name	NE	MW	SE	GP	RM	SW	NW
Annual phlox	Phlox drummondii	X	X	X	X	X	X	X
Baby blue-eyes	Nemophila menziesii	X	X	X	X	X	X	X
*Black-eyed Susan	Rudbeckia hirta	X	X	X	X	X	X	X
Blanketflower	Gaillardia aristata	X	X	X	X	X	X	X
Blue flax	Linum lewisii	X	X	X	X	X	X	X
Blue-eyed grass	Sisyrinchium bellum						X	X
Butterfly weed	Asclepias tuberosa	X	X	X	X		X	X
California poppy	Eschscholzia californica	X	X	X	X	X	X	X
Chinese houses	Collinsia heterophylla		X	X		X	X	X
Colorado columbine	Aquilegia caerulea					X	X	X
Cosmos	Cosmos bipinnatus	X	X	X	X	X	X	X
*Eastern columbine	Aquilegia canadensis	X	X	X	X	X		X
Farewell-to-spring	Clarkia amoena				X	X	X	X
*Gayfeather	Liatris pycnostachya	X	X	X	X	X	X	
Lance-leaved coreopsis	Coreopsis lanceolata	X	X	X	X	X	X	X
Linanthus	Linanthus grandiflorus					X	X	X
Mexican hat	Ratibida columnifera		X	X	X	X	X	
*New England aster	Aster novae-angliae	X	X	X	X	X		X
Pasqueflower	Anemone patens	X	X		X	X		X
*Purple coneflower	Echinacea purpurea	X	X	X	X	X		X
Scarlet sage	Salvia coccinea			X	X		X	X
Spiderwort	Tradescantia virginiana	X	X	X		X		X
Standing cypress	Ipomopsis rubra	X	X	X	X		X	X
Tidy tips	Layia platyglossa					X	X	X
Wild bergamot	Monarda fistulosa	X	X	X	X	X		
Wind poppy	Stylomecon heterophylla						X	X
		NE	MW	SE	GP	RM	SW	NW

*requires cold treatment
for germination of seeds

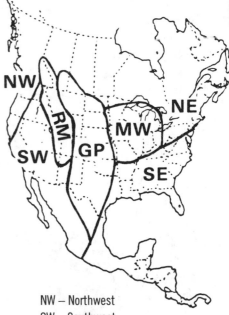

Wildflower and Grass Region Map

NW – Northwest
SW – Southwest
RM – Rocky Mountain
GP – Great plains
MW – Midwest
NE – Northeast
SE – Southeast

—from *A Garden of Wildflowers* by Henry W. Art

WILDFLOWERS

Five Wildflower Gardens

Cultivating native wildflowers opens new horizons in low-maintenance, all-terrain gardening. The drawings show five kinds of successful wildflower plantings. Note that the wildflowers depicted may not bloom simultaneously.

Early-Spring Woodland Garden

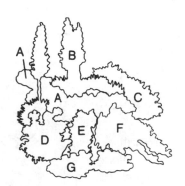

A. Eastern columbine
B. Mayapple
C. Bloodroot
D. Common blue violet
E. Purple trillium
F. Sharp-lobed hepatica
G. Eastern trout lily
H. Foam flower
I. Wild ginger
J. Dutchman's-breeches

These wildflowers will bloom in early spring before forest trees have fully leafed out.

Xeriscape Garden

Xeriscaping means establishing a landscape adapted to an arid environment, rather than importing water-loving species from the humid East or tropics.

Southwestern (pictured)
A. Sagebrush
B. Our Lord's candle
C. Ceanothus
D. Prickly poppy
E. Eaton's firecracker
F. California fuchsia
G. Desert marigold

Butterfly, Hummingbird, and Cut-Flower Garden

This wildflower garden will provide a long season of winged guests.

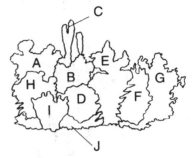

A. Wild bergamot
B. Purple coneflower
C. Gayfeather
D. Prairie phlox
E. Butterfly weed
F. Leadplant
G. Wild columbine
H. New England aster
I. Purple prairie clover
J. Silky aster

Rock Garden

No rock garden is truly complete without representative native species. (See chapter 12 for more on rock gardens.)

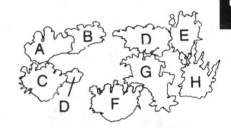

A. Douglas's wallflower
B. Desert marigold
C. Farewell-to-spring
D. Indian pink
E. Chinese-houses
F. Blue-eyed grass
G. Shooting star
H. Checker bloom

Ground Covers

Native plants make excellent ground covers. The species shown below will thrive in acid soils.

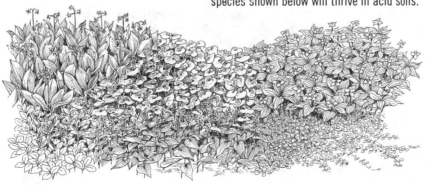

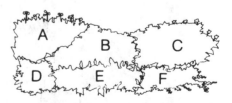

A. Yellow clintonia
B. Wild ginger
C. Bunchberry
D. Wintergreen
E. Wild lily of the valley
F. Partridgeberry

—from *The Wildflower Gardener's Guide* by Henry W. Art

WILDFLOWERS

19 Favorite Wildflowers

Annual phlox
Color: pink, red, purple
Flowering: spring
Fruiting: summer
Height: 6 to 20 inches
Growth cycle: annual

Baby blue-eyes
Color: blue and white
Flowering: late winter to early spring
Fruiting: spring to early summer
Height: 10 to 20 inches
Growth cycle: annual

Black-eyed Susan
Color: yellow and orange
Flowering: summer
Fruiting: summer to early fall
Height: 1 to 3 feet
Growth cycle: annual, biennial, or
   perennial

Blanketflower
Color: yellow and red
Flowering: summer to frost
Fruiting: late summer to fall
Height: 2 to 4 feet
Growth cycle: hardy perennial

Blue flax
Color: blue
Flowering: summer
Fruiting: midsummer to fall
Height: 1 to 4 feet
Growth cycle: hardy perennial

Blue-eyed grass
Color: purple-blue to lilac
Flowering: early to mid-spring
Fruiting: late spring
Height: 6 to 12 inches
Growth cycle: tender perennial

Butterfly weed
Color: orange
Flowering: late spring to summer
Fruiting: early to mid-fall
Height: 1 to 2½ feet
Growth cycle: hardy perennial

California poppy
Color: golden-orange
Flowering: spring to fall
Fruiting: late spring to fall
Height: 1 to 2 feet
Growth cycle: tender perennial, self-
   seeding; grown as annual in
   northern regions

Colorado columbine
Color: blue and white
Flowering: late spring to mid-
   summer
Fruiting: summer
Height: 1 to 2½ feet
Growth cycle: hardy perennial

Cosmos
Color: red, pink, white
Flowering: late spring to early fall
Fruiting: summer to fall
Height: 3 to 5 feet
Growth cycle: annual, but self-seeds
   in all areas

Eastern columbine
Color: scarlet, yellow
Flowering: mid-spring to early
   summer
Fruiting: summer
Height: 1 to 2 feet
Growth cycle: hardy perennial

Gayfeather

Color: lavender
Flowering: midsummer to mid-fall
Fruiting: fall
Height: 1 to 5 feet
Growth cycle: hardy perennial

Lance-leaved coreopsis

Color: yellow
Flowering: late spring to summer
Fruiting: mid- to late summer
Height: 8 to 24 inches
Growth cycle: hardy perennial

Mexican hat

Color: yellow, yellow and red
Flowering: late spring to early fall
Fruiting: late summer to fall
Height: 1 to 3 feet
Growth cycle: hardy perennial

New England aster

Color: violet-purple with yellow
Flowering: early to mid-fall
Fruiting: fall
Height: 1 to 3 feet
Growth cycle: hardy perennial

Pasqueflower

Color: lavender to blue to white
Flowering: early spring
Fruiting: mid- to late spring
Height: 6 to 9 inches
Growth cycle: hardy perennial

Purple coneflower (Echinacea)

Color: dull purple to crimson
Flowering: late spring to early fall
Fruiting: fall
Height: 2 to 4 feet
Growth cycle: hardy perennial

Spiderwort

Color: light blue to lavender to rose
Flowering: mid-spring to midsummer
Fruiting: summer
Height: 6 to 18 inches
Growth cycle: hardy perennial

Wild bergamot

Color: lilac to pink
Flowering: early to midsummer
Fruiting: summer to early fall
Height: 2 to 4 feet
Growth cycle: hardy perennial

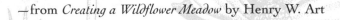

—from *Creating a Wildflower Meadow* by Henry W. Art

ART FROM THE GARDEN

Favorites for an Arranger's Garden

Trees
Birch
Crab apple
Cherry
Dogwood
Japanese maple
Magnolia
Threadleaf
  Japanese maple

Shrubs
Azalea
Barberry
Box or boxwood
Broom
Butterfly bush
Cypress
Eucalyptus
Euonymus
Forsythia
Holly
Lilac
Mock orange
Rhododendron
Viburnum
Witch hazel

Flowers (Annuals)
Calendula
Calliopsis, or
  annual Coreopsis
Cosmos
Flowering Tobacco
Marigold
Snapdragon
Zinnia

Flowers (Perennials)
Artemisia
Astilbe
Baby's breath
Bee balm
Bellflower
Chrysanthemum
Columbine
Coralbells
Coreopsis
Delphinium
Gaillardia
Hosta
Iris
Lady's-mantle
Lily
Monkshood
Peony
Phlox
Pincushion flower
Salvia
Veronica
Yarrow

The Flower Arranger's Garden

The flower arranger is an artist whose materials are those things that grow around him or her. Choosing and growing your own materials can be as creative an experience as making the finished arrangement. With some forethought, you can grow certain flowers for a special event such as a wedding, have enough foliage for larger arrangements, and decorate your home year-round with bouquets of homegrown flowers.

A flower arranger's garden does not, however, have to be large. A garden can be created on a small scale that will give you flowers and foliage throughout the year. Trees, shrubs, edging plants, and even herb and vegetable gardens can be planted with flower arrangements in mind. Consider what you already have growing around your home. Make a list of the kind of plant material you already have, and another list of what you would like to have. The listing on this page includes a few of the many, many plants you might consider for your flower arranger's garden.

Planning the Arranger's Garden

From the choices provided or other favorites, choose the flowers you like best. A small arranger's garden might include a euonymus, a small juniper, a peony, three yarrows, three astilbes, two coral bells, three Heliopsis, three veronicas, a dozen daffodils, and as many zinnias and cosmos in between as possible. These, and things gathered from nearby fields and lots, would give you many delightful bouquets throughout the year.

A. *Achillea* (yarrow), B. *Anthemis tinctoria* (golden marguerite), C. *Campanula* (bellflower), D. *Chrysanthemum maximum* and *C. x superbum* hybrid (Shasta daisy), E. *Gypsophila paniculata* (baby's breath), F. *Papaver* (poppy)

Pick a spot for the garden and sketch the area to scale on graph paper. If you already have garden space, amend the soil for new plantings by adding organic materials. If you're creating a new garden over sod, try the following:

- In early spring or in fall, outline the garden on the sod, using stakes or string or a long garden hose, or "paint" the borders with lime.
- Dig up the sod. If it's fall, turn over the sod and layer organic materials on top of it, creating a mini compost pile. If it's spring, remove the sod and replace it with peat moss, lime (if needed), rock phosphate, rotted manure, and compost.

—from The Flower Arranger's Garden *by Patricia R. Barrett*

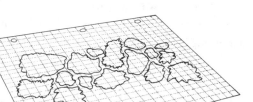

Sketch your plan on graph paper.

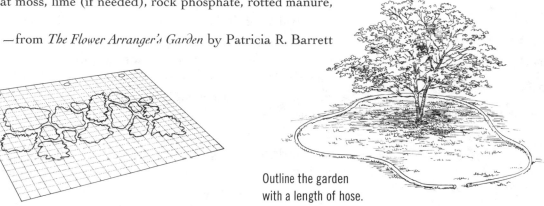

Outline the garden with a length of hose.

HARVESTING AND CONDITIONING FLOWERS FOR ARRANGEMENTS

Flower	When to Cut	HOW TO CONDITION
Anemone	½ to fully open	Scrape stems
Aster	¾ to fully open	Scrape stems
Azalea	bud to fully open	Scrape and crush stems
Bachelor's button	¾ to fully open	Scrape stems
Bleeding heart	4 or 5 florets open	Scrape stems
Calendula	fully open	Scrape stems
Carnation	fully open; snap or break from plant	Scrape stems
Chrysanthemum	fully open; break off	Scrape or crush stems
Daffodil	as color shows in bud	Cut foliage sparingly and scrape stems
Dahlia	fully open	Sear stems in flame
Daisy	½ to fully open	Scrape stems or sear in flame
Dephinium	¾ to fully open	Scrape stems, break off top buds
Gladiolus	as second floret opens	scrape stems
Iris	as first bud opens	Leave foliage, scrape stems
Lilac	½ to fully open	Scrape and crush stems; put wilted branches in very hot water for 1 hour
Lily	as first bud opens	Cut no more than ⅓ of stem
Marigold	fully open	Scrape stems
Peony	bud in color or fully open	Scrape or split stems
Poppy	night before opening	Sear stems; a drop of wax in heart of flower keeps it open
Rose	as second petal unfurls; cut stem just above a 5-petal leaf	Scrape stems; cut stems again while holding under water
Tulip	bud to ½ open	Cut foliage sparingly; scrape stems; stand in deep water overnight
Zinnia	fully open	Sear stems in flame

FLOWERS THAT LAST

Betty E. M. Jacobs and her husband had an herb farm on Vancouver Island, British Columbia, for many years and developed a love for everlasting flowers. Be sure, she cautions, that your plant material is of perfect quality and absolutely dry. Choose an area in your home that is dry, well ventilated, and dim or dark. A spare bedroom, an attic, a basement, and a clothes cupboard are all suitable.

Air-Drying Plants

Before you start, be sure that all the material you dry is in perfect condition when picked. It is a waste of time to use odd bits and pieces, overmature flowers, or material that is faded and droopy. Plant materials should be quite dry when you gather them, also. Pick them in the late morning or early afternoon, after they've had a few hours of sunshine—preferably two or three consecutive sunny days.

Remove some of the foliage before drying. If the leaves are thick or there are too many of them, it slows the drying process.

Air-drying by hanging. Gather material into small bunches with the flower heads at different levels, securing stems with rubber bands. Hang large flower heads individually for more air circulation. Slip a plastic-covered twist tie through the rubber band and twist it to create a loop from which to hang the bunch. If you use string, tie with a slip knot. Attach bunches to hooks, clothes hangers, or rails.

Air-drying upright without water. Weight a tall juice can with stones or sand, and stretch chicken wire over the mouth. Insert plant stem or stems through the holes. Don't crowd the plants. Place in a warm, dark, well-ventilated place. Most grasses dry well using this method.

Air-drying upright with water. If you are air-drying baby's breath, bells-of-Ireland, cockscomb, fernleaf yarrow, any of the *Hydrangea* species, or mimosa in an upright position, they need 1 inch of water in the bottom of the container: They will wilt without it. Allow the water to evaporate, then dry in the now waterless container.

Air-dry bells-of-Ireland in water.

Air-dry yarrow in sand.

31 Classic Everlasting Plants

Acroclinium	Feather grass, European	Pearly everlasting
African daisy	Globe amaranth	Pink pokers
Baby's breath	Globe thistle, small	Safflower
Bells-of-Ireland	Hare's-tail grass	Squirreltail grass
Cardoon	Heather	Statice
Carline thistle	Honesty	Starflower
Chinese-lantern plant	Immortelle	Strawflower
Cockscomb	Job's-tears	Teasel
Cupid's-dart	Love-lies-bleeding	Yarrow, fernleaf
Eryngo	Pampas grass	
Everlasting sand flower	Pearl grass	

Betty Jacobs on Preserving Flowers

Some years ago, when my husband and I still had our herb farm on Vancouver Island, we grew a lot of everlasting flowers and plants. Recently there has been renewed interest in these useful plants. The best plants for drying are the True Everlastings, because they have naturally papery petals or seedpods, and the Perpetuelles, which are easily dried by hanging and last a long time. A few of the attractive ornamental grasses also dry well.

If you never grow anything else, the True Everlastings will give you an excellent variety of dried material to work with. All of them can be preserved with a minimum of trouble, and when dried will retain good color and form. You will have access to flowers at all seasons of the year, even if you live in a climate where winters are severe and fresh flowers expensive, or in a hot climate where summer flowers are hard to come by. You can make arrangements ahead of time for special occasions, and if you keep them airtight under glass, they could actually last forever. Dried flowers are economical and versatile. Without need of water, they can be used in ways that wouldn't be possible with fresh flowers.

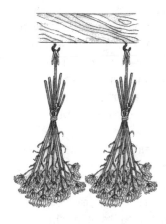

Dos and Don'ts of Air-Drying

Do
- Store material in a warm, dry, dark place.
- Leave space for air to circulate around and through hanging bunches.
- Store glass containers of material in a dark cupboard.
- Put silica gel with dried plant material stored in plastic bags, or condensation may form on the inside of the bag.

Don't
- Store materials where there is no warmth.
- Store materials near any heat source; greater fragility and brittleness will result.
- Store materials in an outside shed, greenhouse, or damp garage.
- Store material with different scents in the same container.
- Store glass containers where any light can fall upon them.

Plants That Air-Dry Well

Ageratum	Heather	Pussy willow
Bear's-breech	Hop, common	Queen Anne's lace
Bird-of-paradise	Hydrangea	Ravenna grass
Blanketflower	Hydrangea, French	Rocket larkspur
Blazing star	Lady's-mantle	Rosemary
Blue lace flower	Lamb's ears	Rue, common
Box, common	Larkspur	Rush
Broom	Lavender	Sage, blue; mealy-cup
Broom, Scotch	Lavender cotton	sage
Candle larkspur	Mimosa	Sedge
Chrysanthemum	Montebretia	Silver-dollar gum
Clary sage	Oats	Silver king artemisia
Coneflower	Onions, leeks, chives,	Silver-leaved mountain
Dusty miller	garlic	gum
False dragonhead	Peony	Sweet corn; Indian corn
False goatsbeard	Pincushions	Tansy, common
Goldenrod	Plantain lily	Wheat, common
Heath	Protea, king	Zinnia

—from *Flowers That Last Forever* by Betty E.M. Jacobs

FLOWERS THAT LAST

Pressing in a Hurry

If your need for pressed leaves or flowers is immediate, prepare them as you would for long-term pressing. After they have been pressed for a few hours, lay them in a container with 1 inch of silica gel directly under and on top of them, put weights on top, cover, and leave overnight.

If you can't wait until the next day, pop the container with silica gel (without the weights) in the microwave oven for 1 minute on high. Let it cool for half an hour, then pour off the silica gel.

Set your flowers or leaves on a 1-inch bed of silica gel, and pour another inch of silica gel over them.

Testing for Dryness

Be gentle when you check to see if the flowers are dry. Tip the container and feel some of the petals. If they are still soft, they need more time. If they feel like dry tissue paper, they are ready. If they are brittle and crumble, they have been in too long and will be a total loss!

Press flowers or leaves between layers of silica gel

Drying with Desiccants

Flowers that do not dry well by any air-drying method can often be preserved by using a desiccant. Desiccants are drying agents that absorb moisture. Even plants that can be air-dried successfully will retain a more natural color when a desiccant is used, and almost any flower will retain its shape better.

General Procedures

Dry or cut off any wet part of the stems before putting plants into a desiccant, and strip off all the foliage. It is important to give the drying flowers plenty of room. Be sure there is space between each flower head, and that petals from different flowers do not touch.

It is difficult to give the exact times that any specific flower must remain in a desiccant. This will depend on the amount of moisture in the material being dried and the desiccant being used. It can vary from two days to as much as three weeks—just check the material regularly until it is quite dry.

When you take the flowers out, some of the desiccant may stick to the petals. To remove it, hold the flower upside down by its stem and tap or flick the stem with your finger. Any desiccant that still sticks should be brushed off with a soft camel-hair brush.

Drying with Silica Gel

Flowers dried with silica gel retain their color better than those dried by any other method, and they dry faster. Silica gel can be bought as rough crystals, fine crystals, and in a sandy form. You will need the fine ground, sandy form. It is not toxic, but avoid inhaling it because it can irritate your sinuses.

If silica gel is white or pale pink, it is moist and needs drying. To reactivate its properties, heat it in a 250°F oven for 20 to 30 minutes or in a microwave oven on high for about 2 minutes. When it's blue, it's ready to use again. Store it in airtight containers.

To use silica gel for drying flowers, follow the general procedures for desiccants. Flowers will take two to six days to dry. To speed up the process, use the silica gel when it is still warm from the oven, but take care to remove the flowers before they become brittle.

Drying with Sand, Borax, and Cornmeal

To dry flowers with these substances, buy a grade of washed, fine sand. Because it is heavy, it is suitable by itself only for a few heavy-petaled flowers such as peonies and large-flowered dahlias. To dry more delicate flowers, mix 1 cup of sand with 2 cups of borax *or* cornmeal *or* silica gel. Materials may take as long as three weeks to dry using sand and sand mixes.

Pressing Flowers

As always, be sure that any plant material you want to press is quite dry when it is gathered. Press it immediately.

Pressing in a Book

Open the book a few pages from one end, and lay a tissue or folded piece of blotting paper on the page. Gently crush the center of each flower between your thumb and first finger. If it has a hard calyx, cut it out or press it between sheets of wax paper with a cold iron.

Lay the flowers on the tissue or blotting paper so they do not touch. Cover them with another tissue or close them between the folded sheet of blotting paper. Turn over about 10 pages and repeat the procedure until the book is full or you are out of flowers.

Pile heavy weights on top. Bricks, cans of sand, and heavy books are suitable. In one to two days, open the book carefully. If the tissues or blotting paper look damp, lift the flowers with tweezers and place them on fresh paper in the book. Repress the flowers. They should be dry in about two weeks. To store them, simply leave them in the book.

Press flowers in a book along with a tissue to absorb moisture.

Make Your Own Flower Press

To make a press for flowers and leaves, you will need two pieces of plywood, four bolts with wing nuts and washers, some newspaper, and sheets of blotting paper. A small press would measure about 10 by 14 inches, which is the size the two pieces of plywood should be.

1. Bore a hole in each corner of the plywood, about ½ inch from the edges. Make the holes large enough to accept the bolts. The length of the bolts depends on the thickness you want your press to be.
2. Place the 4 bolts—B, C, D, E—through the holes in plywood piece A.
3. Put a few sheets of newspaper on A, cut smaller than the plywood.
4. Put a piece of blotting paper, folded in half, on the newspaper.
5. Place the material to be pressed between the folded blotting paper. Keep materials of similar thickness in the same layer.
6. Cover with a few more newspapers and continue making a "sandwich" of plant materials, blotting paper, and newspapers.
7. Top the whole thing with the lid, plywood piece F.
8. Screw down the wing nuts securely.
9. Keep the press in a warm, dry room away from sun and fluorescent lights.
10. Check the tightness of the wing nuts daily. Check the material after a few days, but unless the blotting paper is damp, do not disturb it. If it is damp, change it with the greatest care.
11. Drying should be complete in two to three weeks, depending on the moisture content of the plant material.

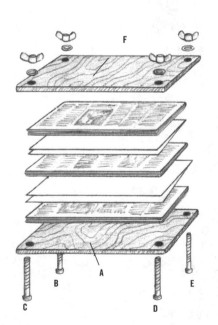

This 10 x 14 flower press can hold large flowers such as daylilies, Queen Anne's lace, and cosmos, as well as grasses and leaves.

—from *Flowers That Last Forever*

12

WATER AND ROCK GARDENS

POOL GARDENS • WATER IN THE LANDSCAPE
PLANTS FOR WATER GARDENS • ROCK GARDENS

My relationship with author and friend Louise Riotte had a rocky start when I referred to her, in print, as "my favorite 80-year-old author." My phone crackled. Louise chided, "Get your facts straight—I'm only 79!" Anything Louise took on she was passionate about, including her pond. Living in landlocked Ardmore, Oklahoma, made the thought of a pond all consuming. The pond her son built became the focus of Louise's passions for fishing, gardening, natural science, and cooking. Her Cajun catfish, Texhoma hush puppies, stewed turtle, and barbecued rattlesnake will not soon be forgotten. This chapter starts with Louise's advice on a small backyard lily pool.

—John Storey

Friends snickered, wrote the late Louise Riotte, when her son, Eugene, bought a piece of property containing a big ravine—until he turned that ravine into a beautiful pond. In her 80s at the time, Louise took on the task of landscaping the pond with trees, shrubs, and wildflowers. She then wrote her twelfth and last book, Catfish Ponds and Lily Pads, *about the experience.*

One of the nice things about gardening with water is that minimal work is required after the initial construction and planting. As long as the ecological balance of the area is maintained, there is no hoeing or cultivating, little weeding, and, of course, no watering!

For several years, we had a small pool in our backyard planted with red and white water lilies. It was much enjoyed both by us and by a friendly green frog who spent a lot of time sitting on the pads, catching insects, and being photographed by visitors. We made our garden by sinking a child's plastic wading pool into the ground and filling it with water. We then placed several pots in it, each containing one lily planted in soil. Water trickled in slowly through a camouflaged inlet pipe, and the small amount of overflow spilled out onto the lawn. It could not have been more simple or carefree, which was its undoing. We became so accustomed to ignoring it that during a dry spell one summer we forgot to check the water inflow. It had stopped, and we lost all the plants.

If you already have a naturally wet area, you can scoop out part of it to create a pond about 2 feet deep. Plant water lilies directly in

Aquatic plants. Plants that live in water; they may be free-floating or rooted in soil, with submerged or floating leaves

Native plants. Plants that originated in the area where they are found growing

Bog. A wetland with a high water table and little flow of water into or out of the area

Rill. A channel created by a small stream

Rock garden. A garden of low-growing, spreading perennials grown among rocks, often on slopes

the muddy soil, provided the water isn't more than 2 feet in depth. If you raise water plants in your pond, don't try to keep ducks or geese there, because they'll wreck the plantings.

—from *Catfish Ponds and Lily Pads* by Louise Riotte

The Garden Pool

Water lilies need at least five hours of full sunlight each day, and their location must be away from trees that might drop leaves or needles into the water. The pool should be 2 to 2½ feet deep for best results. At one time, most were built of reinforced concrete, but now fiberglass and heavy polyvinyl plastic are more often used because they are easier to install and less likely to crack in freezing temperatures. Nurseries that sell water plants frequently stock preformed pools and liners in many sizes.

Although a pool does not need fresh water running through it all the time, plumbing should be installed so that water can be added whenever evaporation makes it necessary. The pool needs cleaning occasionally; a drain and plug at the lowest end of the pool will save you the trouble of pumping out the water.

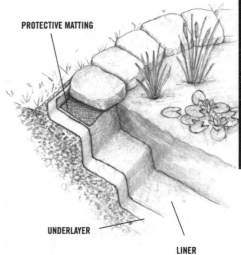

Edge your pool with flat stones placed on a shallow shelf just below water level.

Caring for the Pool

Although a water garden requires less care than one planted in soil, it cannot be completely neglected. Remove any unsightly yellow foliage and seedpods as they appear. If the plants are not thriving, place soluble fertilizer tablets around their roots every two weeks.

Water lilies growing in the soil bottom of a shallow pond can be left undisturbed, but those in containers should be divided every two to five years. If the plants get too large, the flowers will become fewer and smaller, but if they are given proper care, the plants may live for 50 years or more.

Like their soil counterparts, aquatic plants are affected by pests. Never use insecticides as pest control in ponds or pools, however, especially if you have fish or frogs there.

Examples of types of water plants (from left to right): aquatic (water lilies), submerged, and floating.

—from *Successful Perennial Gardening* by Lewis and Nancy Hill

POOL GARDENS

Installing a Preformed Pool

A great way to take the plunge into water gardening is to start with a pre-formed pool, available from catalogs and some garden centers. This is less daunting than digging your own free-form hole and cutting a large piece of plastic sheeting to size. A person can install one of these alone in just a single afternoon.

Pools sold for this purpose come in a variety of shapes and sizes and are durable and puncture resistant. Those made of ¼-inch-thick fiberglass will last up to 50 years. If you want to grow water lilies in your pool, choose a form that is at least 18 inches deep. The 4-foot by-6-foot, kidney-shaped pool shown here holds about 150 gallons of water and can provide a home for one or two water lilies, three or four marginal plants such as rushes and aquatic irises, some oxygenating plants to keep algae at bay, and perhaps a few goldfish or koi.

1. Mark the pool's outline with a trowel.

1. **Site the pool.** Choose a spot out in the open, or at least away from the shadow of overhanging trees and shrubs. This also ensures that you won't encounter tree roots when you dig or have to clean the pool of fallen leaves. A water garden tends to look more natural when sited in a low, level area. Avoid putting it in the lowest part of the yard, however, because it may overflow during rainy spells or be vulnerable to runoff contaminated by fertilizers, herbicides, or insecticides used elsewhere. Station the pool within reach of a hose as well. This will make it easier to fill the pool initially, and to top off the water level when necessary.

Set the pool on the chosen spot. The sides are slightly angled to prevent them from caving in, so your hole will need to reflect this shape. Use a trowel, rope, or a couple of hoses to mark an outline of the pool's bottom and of its top edge. The result should be a circle-within-a-circle design.

2. Make the hole slightly larger than the pool.

2. **Dig the hole.** Make the hole an inch or two bigger than the pool, excavating from the outer boundary down to the inner one, and trying to match the angle of the pool. Remove all sod, rocks, and debris as you work. The bottom of the hole must be level so the surface of the water will be level when the pool is filled. Once the hole is deep enough, stomp on the bottom or tamp it down with

the back of the shovel blade. Smooth it further with a piece of lumber.

The top of the hole should also be level. To determine this, lay a board across the hole at various points and set a carpenter's level on the board. If the top isn't level, it's better to adjust the soil on the ground's surface than to change the depth of the hole.

3. Pour a 1-inch layer of sand in the bottom of the hole.

3. Set in the pool. The pool will sit more easily in the hole and respond better to fine-tuning if you set it on a base of sand. The sand also forms a protective cushion and provides a smooth surface for the pool to rest on. Empty enough builder's sand into the hole to make a layer an inch or more deep. Then set in the pool and wiggle it into position. Remove it temporarily to see if it made a level impression. Add sand until it does. Add even more sand if you want the pool to be slightly elevated above the hole. This is a good idea if you're concerned about runoff.

Return the pool to the hole and maneuver it into its final position. Use the board and carpenter's level to make sure the pool is even all along the rim.

4. Fill the pool. To equalize the pressure from the water and the soil and to prevent bulges, it is important to fill the pool with water and surround the liner with soil simultaneously.

4. Fill the pool with water while you fill the outer gap with soil.

Set the end of a hose in the bottom of the pool and start filling it slowly with water. Begin filling the gap between the ground and the pool with the excavated soil. Tamp in the soil with a trowel or board. Work your way around a few times, until the gap is filled evenly on all sides.

To hide the pool's edge and give it a more natural look, lay bricks, rocks, or stone slabs around and slightly over the edges. Wedge them in well or set them in with mortar so that you and other kneeling admirers won't dislodge them.

Once the pool is finished, wait 24 hours before adding plants and fish to give the chlorine in the water a chance to evaporate. If your water also contains chloramine, treat the pool with liquid-concentrate chemicals sold for this purpose by water garden suppliers.

—from *Year-Round Gardening Projects,* text by Teri Dunn;
illustrations by Elayne Sears

Best Plants for Bog Gardens

- Plant iris, horsetail, bulrush, cattail, and pickerel weed in natural-looking groups throughout the area.

- Include surface-floating plants such as the four-leaf water clover and the white snowflake, whose foliage floats like lily pads on the water's surface but adds a different texture. You will need at least 4 inches of water over the soil for these floating plants.

- Tropical bog plants add an exotic flavor to your garden. Plant them as you would their hardy relatives. They will die off when cold weather hits in late fall. For this reason, tropical bog plants are treated as annuals—beautiful while they last.

—from *Creating Your Own Water Garden* by Charles B. Thomas

BLUE-FLAG IRIS

Bog Gardening

Is there a poorly drained or swampy area of your lawn that you just don't know what to do with? That problem area, too wet for most terrestrial plants, is the natural place to create a water garden. If the area is always wet, even throughout the hot summer months, you can plant the bog plants directly in the soil without any previous construction effort. Keep in mind that bog plants generally like to spread, so there will be conflict among various inhabitants of the bog.

If your naturally low spot does not retain water, it is still easy to create a bog garden with a PVC liner. Dig out the area to a depth of 8 to 12 inches and put the liner in the excavation. Place the removed soil back on top and thoroughly saturate the soil with water. Plant the bog plants directly in the soil. Keep the bog area slightly below the surrounding ground level to catch runoff.

Bog plants like to keep their feet wet in soggy soil or in water 1 to 6 inches deep. They can be planted in a container of almost any size, but if you are dealing with a single plant, a 5- or 10-quart pail will do nicely.

When the first hard frost comes, trim back the foliage and lower the plant in its container to the bottom of the pond to weather the winter. The roots of

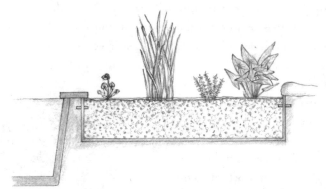

This bog garden is located next to a small man-made pool. A drainage hole is kept open with a short length of tubing.

IRIS: ROYALTY OF THE BOG

Plant Name	Mature Height	Water Depth	Blooming Season	Flower Color	Hardiness
Bayou comus	24"	0–6"	mid- to late spring	tan	Zones 7–9
'Black Gamecock'	24"	0–4"	spring	blue	Zones 6–9
Blue iris	24"	0–6"	early to mid-spring	blue	Zones 4–9
'Clyde Redmond'	24"	0–6"	mid-spring	blue	Zones 4–9
'Eolian'	42"	0–6"	mid- to late spring	blue	Zones 7–9
'Her Highness'	36"	0–6"	early to late spring	white	Zones 7–9
Kaempferi varieties	30"	0"	early to midsummer	blue, purple, white	Zones 4–9
'Marie Caillet'	36"	0–6"	mid- to late spring	purple	Zones 7–9
Red iris	24"	0–6"	early to late spring	red	Zones 5–9
Yellow water iris	48"	0–10"	early spring	yellow	Zones 4–9

—from *Creating Your Own Water Garden*

surface-floating plants must not freeze or the plant will probably die. If this is a possibility, bring the plants inside in their soil containers for winter storage. Keep the plant moist (cover with a plastic bag) and cool, about 40°F.

Creating a Backyard Waterfall

If a pond, a small stream, and a waterfall suit your waterscaping plans, the streambed must be poured at the same time as the pond. Here are some points to attend to when you pour these additions.

A pond/rill/spring combination requires flexible PVC tubing (I.D. ¾-inch is suggested), attached at the pond end to a submersible pump. Water is pumped uphill to the location of the waterfall or spring. Hide the tubing's upper side for a natural look.

The flow of the water must be deposited in a catch basin before it moves down the rill to the lower pond. The rill should be a meandering stream that will slow the water down, looking more natural than if the water were shooting in a straight line toward the pond.

Dig the streambed deep enough to bury the flexible plastic water pipe beneath concrete work, and install the pipe before you pour. The concrete need be only 2 to 3 inches thick, but it must be reinforced. You can use chicken wire.

Dig a trench 12 inches deep and 12 inches wide on both sides of the watercourse and fill it with pea gravel and sand. The trenches will take up any overflow during heavy rains, and will provide a foothold for ferns, crested iris, and other moisture-loving plants.

Pumps

A submersible pump that can handle 1,380 gallons of water per hour at 1 foot of elevation is just about right for operating a pond/rill/spring combination. With a 6-amp motor, it can lift 5 gallons of water a minute to a height of 20 feet. A pump that is too powerful will be a better buy than one that is too small.

Before installing the ¾-inch tubing under the rill, adapt the end at the lower pond to standard male garden hose threads and add a short length of flexible garden hose between the tubing and the pump, which also takes standard garden hose threads. It is then simple to connect the system by laying the pump on its side above a flat rock. (See chapter 3 for more on choosing pumps and building ponds.)
—from *Catfish Ponds and Lily Pads* by Louise Riotte

A backyard waterfall. A rill of water meanders about 20 feet downslope from the catch basin, over a small ledge, and into a lower pond. Occasional overflow provides a boggy area for water-loving plants. The rill is about a foot wide. The lower pond is 14 to 16 inches deep, 5 to 10 feet in diameter, with a surrounding border of rocks.

Add Ornamental Fish to Your Pond

If you want ornamental fish in your pond, the general rule of thumb is 1 inch of fish per 3 gallons of water.

To increase your pond's oxygen content, recirculate the water with a fountain or waterfall, and grow plants in the pond.

Keep pH between 6.7 and 7.3, especially in newly concreted ponds; the concrete can turn the water very alkaline.

Do not overfeed your fish. Give them 48 hours to adjust to the pond before feeding them. Excessive feeding may cloud the water, as will feeding your fish bread or crackers. Use only the high-quality foods formulated for the type of fish you have chosen, and discontinue feeding the fish whenever water temperature is below 45°F.

—from *Catfish Ponds and Lily Pads*

WATER IN THE LANDSCAPE

Planting a Water Lily

A tub or pool of water lilies brings all sorts of pleasures to a garden, among them constant, colorful blossoms; fragrance; and a parade of admirers ranging from your neighbors to bees and frogs. Once you choose a lily that suits you in terms of size and color, you'll find that it is easy to plant and care for. All it requires is a pot to put it in, a tub or pool that is at least a foot and a half deep, and a spot that receives at least five hours of sun a day.

There are two kinds of water lilies: those that are cold-hardy and those that are not, called tropicals. The simplest way to tell them apart is to remember that the blossoms of hardy water lilies usually float on the water's surface, while those of tropicals are raised several inches above.

Hardy water lilies grow from a rhizome and can be set in water as cool as 50°F. You can plant them early in the season and enjoy their flowers into the fall. Tropical water lilies, on the other hand, grow from tubers and require water temperatures of at least 65°F. Tropicals have a shorter bloom season than hardy water lilies, but they better endure the heat of summer.

1. Prepare the rhizome or tuber. Water lilies are sold bareroot, usually with a few leaves intact. Keep the rhizome or tuber moist by placing it in a bowl of water as soon as you get it home. Keep it moist until you are ready to plant.

Carefully inspect the rhizome or tuber for viable roots, which are white and crisp. Use a small, sharp knife to trim off any brown, black, or limp ones. You may also notice some tiny lime green or bronze leaves emerging from the plant's growing point.

2. Get ready to pot. In nature, water lilies grow in soil at the bottom of ponds, but garden hybrids do fine in containers. The size of the pot you use depends on the size of your tub or pool. The more room you give the roots, the more robust the plant will be. A 4-quart pot is fine for a half barrel; for a pool, you may use a larger pot or a small laundry tub. Either way, be sure the container has a drainage hole, even though plant and pot will be immersed in water. This prevents gases from building up inside the pot.

Fill the container one-third full with heavy topsoil or garden loam. This soil is closest to pond muck and won't float off the way a peat-based soil mix will. In addition, heavy soil helps hold the rhizome or tuber firmly in place.

Next, insert a water lily–fertilizing tablet (available from mail-order nurseries) or a handful of a low-analysis granular fertilizer such as 5-10-5 or 6-10-4. Then fill the container to the top with soil and drench it until water runs out the drainage hole.

3. Pot the plant. To pot the rhizome or tuber, remove a third of the saturated soil and set it aside. (You may want to wear rubber gloves, as this can be a muddy operation.) If you are planting a hardy water lily, set the rhizome roots-down in the pot at a 45-degree angle. Aim the rhizome so the plant has room to elongate across the pot and the crown is pointed upward. It's okay to place

Step 1. Trim off dark or limp roots, and then place rhizome in water.

Step 2. Fill tub with topsoil, add fertilizing tablet, then water thoroughly.

the opposite end flush against the pot. If you are planting a tropical water lily, look for a white line on the tuber. This indicates where the soil level should be once you fill the pot. Set the tuber lengthwise in the center of the pot, roots down.

Gently top off the pot with the reserved soil, filling it to within an inch or two of the rim. Be sure to leave the growing point of the rhizome or tuber free of soil. To avoid air pockets, firm the soil with your thumbs as you work. Water the pot once more, taking care not to wash soil away from the root. Top off the pot with pea gravel (again, making sure to leave the growing point exposed) to prevent soil from washing away once it is in the tub or pool.

Step 3. Set rhizome so its roots are down, then replace soil.

4. **Set the pot in water.** Most water lilies prefer to be a foot or so beneath the water's surface. If your pool is deeper than that, place some bricks or an empty, overturned pot on the bottom to elevate the plant. Lower the pot in slowly at an angle to allow air bubbles to escape, then set the pot on its base. If the plant has a few leaves, gently position them so they float on the surface of the water.

Within a few weeks, your water lily will adjust to its new home. New leaves will soon begin to appear, and shortly thereafter the first blossoms should make their debut.

Step 4. Set container in water.

—from *Year-Round Gardening Projects*, text by Teri Dunn;
illustrations by Elayne Sears

PLANTS FOR WATER GARDENS

Hardy Bog Plants

Arrowhead
Water arum
Dwarf bamboo
Cattail
Graceful cattail
Narrow-leaved cattail
Variegated cattail
Chinese water chestnut
Floating heart
Golden club
Horsetail
Lizard's-tail
Parrot's-feather
Pickerelweed
White pickerel rush
Spike rush
Sagittaria
Yellow snowflake
White snowflake
Sweet flag
Variegated sweet flag
Thalia
Water clover

NATIVE PLANTS FOR WATER GARDENS

Grassy Plants for Wet Soils

Native Grasses
rattlesnake grass
fowl meadow grass
reed meadow grass
Eastern gamma grass

Cultivated Grasses
perennial quaking grass
feather reed grass
tufted hair grass/fairy
  wand grass
variegated manna grass

maiden grass
eulalia grass
Japanese silver grass
Formosa maiden grass
purple moor grass
gardener's-garters

Native Ornamental Flowering Plants

Spring
camassia or wild hyacinth
shootingstar
water avens or purple
  avens
Quaker-ladies or bluets
copper iris
blue flag iris or fleur-de-lis
yellow flag iris
blue-eyed grass
violets
flower of the west wind,
  zephyr lily
golden Alexanders

Summer
wild celery, angelica, or
  Alexanders
swamp milkweed
queen of the prairie
oxeye
slender blue flag
lilies

mints
monkey flower
bee balm or Oswego-tea
meadow phlox or wild
  sweet William
obedient plant or false
  dragonhead
meadowsweet
tall meadow rue
Virginia spiderwort
Culver's root

Late Summer/Autumn
New England aster
swamp aster
tickseed sunflower
boltonia
swamp sunflower
sawtooth sunflower
sunchoke or Jerusalem
  artichoke
cut-leaf coneflower
cup plant or rosinweed

marsh or bog goldenrod
blue boneset or mist flower
Joe-Pye weed
boneset
spiked gayfeather
common ironweed
white turtlehead
closed gentian, blind
  gentian, or bottle
  gentian
biennial fringed gentian
grass-of-Parnassus
meadow beauty
Canadian or American
  burnet
blue vervain

Non-Native Ornamental Flowering Plants

astilbe
canna
Siberian meadowsweet
Siberian iris

Japanese iris
big-leaf ligularia
narrow-spiked ligularia
rhubarb

shield-leaf rodgersia
guinea-hen flower
daffodils

ROCK GARDENS

Plant a Rockery

If your property is sloped and dotted with interesting or weathered rock formations, it may be an ideal spot for a rock garden—or rockery, as it is sometimes called. But any garden that features rocks prominently can be called a rock garden. It is not even necessary to have a slope—one can be created on a flat location with just a few loads of topsoil and a pile of rocks.

Some purists feel that a rock garden should contain only those plants that grow naturally on rocky slopes in poor soil, but most rock gardeners use a wide variety of low-growing perennials, annuals, bulbs, and shrubbery. If you want the overall effect to be beautiful, a rock garden must be carefully designed rather than aimlessly constructed. Yet even though it may have been weeks in the planning, it should look as if it evolved naturally.

Because rockeries must be planted and cared for by hand, it is best to start with a small area unless you have lots of time, interest, and skill. If you have the perfect spot, you may simply have to choose plants, locate paths, and create level outcroppings as kneeling places. But if you must bring in rocks and soil, you'll have planning and work ahead.

Choose rocks that are compatible with the landscape, if they are available, rather than those that are quarried, highly colored, or polished. If excavating is necessary, dump the topsoil in piles close by while the work is being done, so you can replace it later.

Set the rocks in the lowest, front part of the garden first and work upward, burying more than half of each rock firmly so it's well anchored. After the rocks are in place, let the soil settle around them for a few days before planting. Check your construction frequently in the early stages by viewing it from a distance as well as close up, to be sure the positioning is aesthetically pleasing.

—from *Successful Perennial Gardening* by Lewis and Nancy Hill

Grow a Footpath Garden

You can plant herbs among paving stones on a path to create a fragrant miniature rock garden. Best plants to use are creeping thyme, catmint, and dwarf chamomile. When crushed by footsteps, they will release their scents but not be damaged. In a shady area, mosses will thrive among paving stones.

These plants thrive in many rock gardens.

(A) bellflowers
(B) rock candytuft
(C) Crimean iris or crested iris
(D) mother-of-thyme

ROCK GARDENS

Jan Kowalczewski Whitner is a professional writer and garden designer living in the Pacific Northwest. She has always been intrigued with the contrast of the garden's "living" elements, such as plants, water, sunlight, shadows, and the use and placement of stone. She is author of Stonescaping: A Guide to Using Stone in Your Garden.

A Rocky Outcrop on a Slope

If your garden has no natural stone outcrop but does contain banks, hillocks, or areas with a significant grade change, these are the best spots in which to design and construct a rocky outcrop.

Your major concern is to make the feature look as natural as possible. Study rock outcrops in the natural landscape. They invariably look like the worn, exposed tips of a huge mass of buried rock. To replicate the effect, grade your site to a gentle slope of no greater than 45 degrees. Leave space for a relatively flat area several feet wide at the bottom, which will tie the outcrop to the rest of the garden when mulched and then planted as the last step in construction.

Excavate the contours of the slope at least 18 inches deep. Then lay a drainage layer of 6 inches of crushed rock topped by 2 inches of fine gravel or coarse sand. Bury a few large rocks beneath this layer as a stable foundation for the major exposed stones or boulders.

Most natural outcrops feature one or two large boulders set among smaller stones that have fallen away from the main mass. When constructing your outcrop, cant the major boulders slightly upward and inward, so rain will run along their surfaces to the plant roots nearby. Then carefully set a few stones around them, preferably at their bases. Fill the crevices between the stones with an appropriate soil mix, tamping it firmly. If you use a stratified stone such as limestone or sandstone, position all the rocks so their strata lie on the same angle, as though an earthquake had heaved them into place simultaneously.

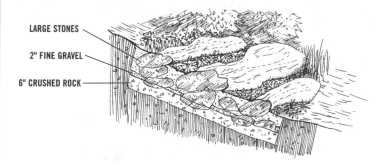

LARGE STONES

2" FINE GRAVEL

6" CRUSHED ROCK

Large, buried rocks on a bed of fine gravel form a stable foundation for the rock garden.

A Rock Garden on a Level Site

If you wish to build a rock garden on a flat site, you can use a construction technique first developed by ancient Chinese gardeners to introduce different levels. Dig out low areas, then mound the excavated earth into ridges and plateaus above. Use half-buried, weathered stones to replicate outcrops, and work from the bottom of the rock garden toward the top.

A few large boulders with a litter of smaller stones and gravel at their base will look more natural and more restful than a hodgepodge of smaller stones or, even worse, rocks evenly spaced like gravestones. As an alternative, you might use flat sedimentary stones to establish a restful horizontal or tiered effect, varying the height from outcrop to outcrop for a natural look.

Some gardeners who are starting with a flat site eliminate large-scale excavation and rock moving by using old tires as the foundation for their rock gardens. They form the base of their mound on level soil with the tires, then fill the tires with gravel, sand, or crushed rock. After building up several layers of tires in a rough mound, they cover the entire construction with a good, porous soil, then bury the rocks in it.

—from *Stonescaping* by Jan Kowalczewski Whitner

Plants for the Rock Garden

The best plants for rock gardens are compact, low-growing perennials. To achieve pleasing combinations, consider not only plant color and mature height but also form: Are they rounded (cranesbill), spiky (iris), or prostrate and spreading (thyme and ground phlox)?

The size of the plants should be on the same scale as the garden itself. Tiny plants look best in a small space; taller perennials, dwarf evergreens, and low-growing shrubs are appropriate for a long, wide hillside. And because so many of the plants best suited to rock gardens bloom only in the spring, consider strategic placement of summer-blooming heaths, heathers, and perhaps annuals to add color during the rest of the growing season.

Select plants suitable for your climate and exposure. If you live where winters are long and the growing season short, you may be able to establish a true alpine garden of plants that are native to the European mountain ranges, the Rockies, the White Mountains, or other high elevations. Most of these are small or compact, with rugged root systems that enable them to live in poor soil and under severe weather conditions. They need cool weather and perfect drainage to do well.

Rock Garden Care

Your rock garden could be compared to a collection of potted plants, and each will grow best if you tend it accordingly. Be sure each "pot" is well drained so water will not collect there and drown the plant. Loosen the soil in each pocket occasionally with a small garden fork. Although most rock plants do well in poor soil, add dry manure or liquid fertilizer if the plants seem weak.

Housekeeping chores for a rock garden include:
- cutting back leggy plants after flowering
- clipping off dead portion
- dividing plants that become rootbound or too large for their space
- checking for insects (especially slugs) and diseases
- weeding unwanted plants out of the nooks and crannies

Winter can be hard on tender plant varieties in rock gardens, because they are more exposed to cold winds and dehydration than are plants growing in level beds. If you don't get much snow, a mulch will help protect both hardy and more tender plants. In particularly exposed regions, cover the entire bed with evergreen branches or straw, as well, just after the ground starts to freeze.

—from *Successful Perennial Gardening* by Lewis and Nancy Hill

A rock garden with a foundation of tires. Secondary outcrops tie the rockery to the rest of the garden.

Common Alpine Plants

alpine anemone
alpine columbine
alpine rockcress
alpine aster
alpine pink
alpine sunflower
edelweiss
alpine forget-me-not
alpine poppy
savory
alpine catchfly

ROCK GARDENS

These rocks have been placed harmoniously in the landscape.

Adapting Japanese Traditions to Western Rock Gardens

The Japanese believe that stone is a magical, evocative garden material. Western gardeners can follow that approach as well, using the following principles as guidelines:

- Respect the conditions and appearance of the site and its surrounding landscape. Use stone and rock native to the area, or choose nonnative stone that harmonizes with the site.
- Use nature as a guide when positioning rocks in the garden.
- Whenever possible, avoid mixing different types of stone and rock in the same feature.
- When piling rocks together, make sure the striations and furrows of each rock point in the same direction.
- Set stones and stone features with broad, horizontal lines to create a sense of tranquillity and serenity. Use low, flat-headed rocks; large, rounded rocks; and reclining rocks as the major stones, with a few tall, vertical stones for accent.
- Keep a pleasing balance between rock features and plants. Too much rock in a garden makes it heavy and overwhelming; too little makes it seem frivolous and unconvincing.

—from *Stonescaping* by Jan Kowalczewski Whitner

A Rock, Gravel, and Thyme Garden

The main features of Zen dry landscapes are rocks and gravel, which never need a drink of water from one year to the next. In traditional Japanese gardens, dry landscapes are often surrounded by whitewashed walls that highlight the shapes and colors of the stone features.

Some Western gardeners would undoubtedly enjoy importing some of the atmosphere and all of the water-conserving qualities of a Japanese dry landscape. They might well consider tearing out areas of their (thirsty) lawns, particularly where those areas are bordered by relatively subdued plantings of the kinds of shrubs and trees typically found in Japanese gardens, such as azaleas, rhododendrons, camellias, and pines.

Such a garden can feature gently curving boundary lines between the shrubs and the graveled area, with stones and thyme acting as a substory to the shrubs. An island composed of a drought-tolerant shrub such as *Elaeagnus pungens,* natural stones, and thyme softens the effect of the graveled area and ties it to the surrounding vegetation. Islands of thyme, shaped to resemble gourds or sake bottles, add interest to the composition. The thyme islands are raised about 1½ inches from the surface of the gravel and are contained by a boundary of ½-inch dowels that stand ¾ inch above the surface of the gravel.

—from *Stonescaping*

35 Traditional Rock Garden Plants

Artemisia. Usually planted for its silvery gray foliage rather than its bloom.

Baby's breath. Dwarf varieties can be excellent for the rock garden.

Basket-of-gold. Excellent for edging perennial borders and rock gardens.

Bellflower. Dwarf bellflowers make good rock garden plants. They do best when mulched over the winter.

Betony. Lavender flowers appear in summer.

Blanketflower. One of the best varieties is known as 'Goblin'. It grows only 12 inches tall and has red and yellow blooms from July until frost.

Blue fescue. A silvery blue, tufted grass that grows to a height of 10 inches.

Bugleweed. Fast-growing, dwarf ground cover.

Cactus. The hardy cacti are good rock garden plants. They need light soil with lots of leaf mold, loam, sand, and enough lime so the soil is not acidic.

Columbine. Native wild varieties are best for rock gardens.

Coralbells. Small and dainty flowers that bloom all summer in pink, red, and white.

Cranesbill. Low-growing plant that likes moist, cool places.

Cupid's-dart. Attractive blue or white flowers, excellent for drying.

Daylily. Dwarf kinds add summer bloom when the flowering season is over for most rock plants.

Edelweiss. One of the most beloved of all alpine plants, easily grown in the rock garden.

English daisy. Free-flowering dwarf plant with daisylike blooms.

Fernleaf bleeding heart. This neat little plant blooms for most of the summer.

Flax. These blue-flowering perennials make ideal rock plants.

Forget-me-not. Allow them to go to seed, which will keep new plants coming.

Garden pinks. Many species of *Dianthus* add color when little else is in bloom. Among the best are sweet William, the grass pink, and maiden pink.

Iris. Dwarf irises are ideal for rock gardens. They like sun and need little care.

Lady's-mantle. Good ground cover that spreads rapidly from seed.

Moss campion. Summer-blossoming dwarf plant with pink blooms.

Pasqueflower. Grows 8 to 12 inches tall with finely cut grayish leaves and purple flowers.

Phlox. Dwarf, creeping kinds are best as rock garden plants.

Saxifrage. Ideal for the rock garden because they grow easily in tough places.

Sedum. Old reliables of the rock garden.

Siberian dragonhead. Purple flowers in spikes that grow about 12 inches tall.

Soapwort. Fast-spreading, creeping plant with pink flowers.

Sunrose. Shrubby plant, good for hot, dry places.

Sweet woodruff. Good ground cover, grows well in the tiny crevices between rocks.

Thyme. Some thymes make a thick mat with a heavy bloom of pink or lavender flowers, ideal for the rock garden.

Violet. An easy-to-grow perennial. Choose varieties carefully.

Wild ginger. Low-growing plant with fragrant rootstocks and attractive foliage.

Wooly yarrow. Yellow, flowering dwarf plant about 12 inches high.

—from *The Big Book of Gardening Skills*

This rock garden is planted with woodland wildflowers.

A rock, gravel, and thyme garden is a drought-tolerant landscape that blends into many garden styles.

13

IMPROVING YOUR SOIL

**GETTING TO KNOW YOUR SOIL • SOIL pH • SOIL NUTRIENTS
COMPOSTING • MULCHING • GREEN MANURES**

During the 1960s I responded to a one-inch magazine ad with the improbable headline "Let an Earthworm Be Your Garbage Man!" I soon discovered that there were more than 3,000 different species of earthworms, but that only a few contribute to soil productivity. We built a compost pile, introduced a few night crawlers, and soon had hundreds, enough to put in the garden and sell to passing fishermen. The worms seemed to "manufacture" soil out of compost overnight. Each year our garden became more porous and productive. Those squirming worms created channels, allowing the easy distribution of water through the top- and subsoils, rather than losing it through runoff.

—John Storey

Liz Stell has never outgrown a child's simple love of dirt since those early days of mud pies and simple earthworks. After studying it at the university level, she learned to respect its complexity and call it soil, and years of gardening have taught her how resilient it is. She shares her enthusiasm about soil in her book Secrets to Great Soil: A Grower's Guide to Composting, Mulching, and Creating Healthy, Fertile Soil for Your Garden and Lawn.

The easiest, most dramatic way for any gardener to improve a garden is to improve its soil. As you build up your soil, it will become crumbly and easy to dig. You'll be rewarded with healthy plants that look better and produce better, even when subjected to weather quirks such as droughts and cold spells. You can also significantly reduce your pest problems and your use of pesticides by building up your soil. Healthy soil just does a better job of producing healthy plants.

Though the earth beneath our feet seems solid, only half the soil consists of hard particles. The other half is a combination of air and water. In good soils, about half of this "empty" half is filled with water. Dissolved in this water are lots of chemicals, including the nutrients essential for plant growth. The remaining air is also important. It supplies oxygen to plant roots and soil organisms.

Humus. Organic matter in its final stage of decomposition, processed so completely that it is unrecognizable as plant material

Legume. Edible member of the pea family whose seeds grow in pods

Loam. Ideal soil, made up of a balanced mix of sand, silt, and clay

Nitrogen fixation. The process of converting inorganic nitrogen from the air to organic nitrogen held in the soil

Organic matter. Decomposed plant materials

Subsoil. The deeper layer of soil, usually lighter in color, where water is stored

Topsoil. The top layer of soil, usually darker and more crumbly than deeper layers, where most nutrients, roots, and soil organisms exist

Vermicompost. A highly concentrated substance made of compost and earthworm castings; an excellent soil amendment

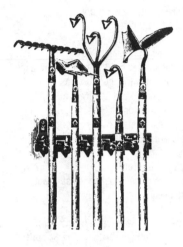

YOUR GARDEN, YARD & ORCHARD

WHAT YOUR SUBSOIL TELLS YOU

Dig a hole 2 to 3 feet deep and look at the layers of soil. Different colors show how well the subsoil drains, which in turn affects the drainage of the overlying topsoil.

What You See	What It Tells You
Red or yellow subsoil	Indicates lots of iron oxides from weathering of parent materials; usually indicates good drainage; often indicates acidic soil; common in warm climates
Blue or blue-gray subsoil	Indicates lack of oxygen and therefore poor drainage; common in thick layers of clay
White to ash gray subsoil	Indicates that nutrients and humus have been leached away; usually sits above a darker area where the leached nutrients and humus have deposited; often indicates acidic and/or sandy soil; common under pines and similar trees
Even, medium brown subsoil	Adequate drainage
Pale subsoil little different from topsoil	Very young or poorly developed soil; original topsoil may have eroded or been removed (as by bulldozing during house construction)
Dark brown subsoil	Indicates abundant (usually decomposed) organic matter; usually occurs only with peat or muck soils, or where former wetlands have been drained
Patches or streaks of different colors	Indicates pockets of poor drainage or different soils (see specific colors); plant roots may have trouble moving from one pocket into the next
Roots all end at same depth	Indicates layer of compacted soil (hardpan) or, in dry climates, a cemented layer (caliche); usually causes poor drainage and hampers plant growth

Six Good Things to Do for Your Soil

Here are six things that can do more for your soil than all the fertilizer you could buy.

- Keep levels of organic matter high by adding compost, composted manure, or plant residues regularly, or by plowing in green-manure crops. This will encourage abundant, healthy soil organisms.
- Do not cultivate your soil when it is wet or overly dry.
- Make sure soil contains a good balance of calcium and magnesium, but avoid overliming.
- Cover bare soil; mulch areas that aren't covered by plant leaves to minimize pounding from heavy rains.
- Keep soil in use as much as possible; plant a green-manure or cover crop if an area will be bare for a couple of months.
- Minimize rototilling and other forms of cultivation, as these break up desirable soil crumbs and channels.

—from *Secrets to Great Soil*
by Elizabeth P. Stell

GETTING TO KNOW YOUR SOIL

Rub a small handful of soil between your fingers. This will help you "read" your soil.

Texture: Sand, Silt, or Clay?

Texture describes soil ingredients. Too much clay results in a "heavy" soil with plenty of nutrients but poor aeration and slow drainage. Too much silt can also cause drainage problems. Too much sand ("light" soil) means there's never a drainage problem, but you have to keep adding fertilizer because most of it washes away. The best soil texture is loam, made up of a balanced mix of ingredients.

Structure: Crumbs or Clods?

Structure describes how soil hangs together, whether soil particles clump into crumbs or clods. Loose crumbs and clods ensure ample pore space. Soil with good structure absorbs more rainfall more quickly, and excess water drains away quickly. Roots and soil organisms push through more easily, and gardeners dig with ease. Good structure makes good gardens.

The Simple Soil Fix

There's a simple fix for soils with less-than-ideal texture and structure: Add organic matter, such as compost. Abundant amounts of organic matter increase the ability of sandy soils to stay moist and retain nutrients and also improve the aeration and drainage of clay soils.

If the soil is compacted—crusted on the surface or forming a dense layer below the surface—adding organic matter isn't enough. You'll also need to double-dig (see page 171) or loosen the soil with a broadfork.

When to Work Your Soil

Grab a handful of soil and squeeze it. If it turns to loose powder, your soil is too dry. Water the soil and wait several hours (ideally, overnight) before digging. If water runs out when you squeeze, or you see a solid, sticky lump in your hand, your soil's too wet. Wait a day or so and test another handful before digging. If you see a mostly solid lump that easily breaks apart when you poke it, dig away! Your soil is slightly moist, just right for cultivating.

Too wet

Just right for cultivating

Too dry

SOIL ORGANISMS

Though you may not realize it, good soils are teeming with a variety of life. Most soil creatures are microscopic, though some, such as worms and ants, are easy to see. Plants (and gardeners) depend on soil organisms to convert nutrients into forms they can use, and to recycle nutrients from organic matter. The different forms of life present in soil interact to create a complex ecosystem.

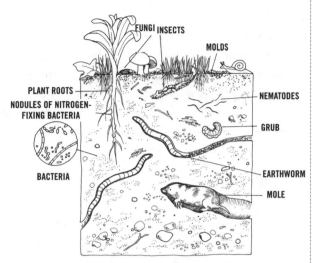

FUNGI INSECTS
MOLDS
PLANT ROOTS
NODULES OF NITROGEN-FIXING BACTERIA
NEMATODES
GRUB
BACTERIA
EARTHWORM
MOLE

The best way to build super soil is to keep its complex ecosystem in balance.

Six Ways to Encourage Soil Life

1. Add organic matter such as compost to improve soil texture and structure and ensure good drainage.
2. Correct extreme acidity or alkalinity and keep your soil pH between 6.0 and 7.5.
3. Make sure your soil is well supplied with calcium, as this nutrient is needed by both soil organisms and plants.
4. Minimize the use of pesticides.
5. Avoid overfertilizing, because an excess of some nutrients will upset the soil's chemical balance.
6. Test your soil periodically to see which nutrients are actually needed, and whether any have built up to excess.

The Mighty Earthworm

Earthworms are the best soil improvers. Studies have shown that an increasing number of earthworms in soil is directly related to increased productivity of the plants grown in that soil.

Earthworms dig as deep as 3 to 6 feet in good soils. By doing this, they open up channels to increase soil aeration and drainage. They are powerful composting machines, swallowing and processing 20 to over 200 tons of soil per acre. Their digestive systems break down organic matter into pure humus.

Earthworm activity increases both size and stability of soil crumbs. As a result, these small creatures do more to improve soil structure than any other burrowing organisms.

—from *Secrets to Great Soil* by Elizabeth P. Stell

An Earthworm Census

You can measure earthworm activity in your soil. Counting the number of earthworms present in a sample of your soil gives a pretty good idea of its organic matter and overall health.

1. Choose a 12- by 12-inch site that is a good average of your garden. Dig out the top 6 inches of soil and place it in a shallow pan.

2. Count the number of earthworms in the removed soil. Start by pushing all the soil to one end of the pan. Go through it bit by bit, moving soil to the other side of the pan as you count.

3. If you find only one or two earthworms, your soil needs help in the form of organic matter. Five to nine earthworms means you're getting there but still need more organic matter. If you find 10 or more earthworms, you have healthy, biologically active soil.

YOUR GARDEN, YARD & ORCHARD

IMPROVING SOIL CHEMISTRY

A Self-Sustaining Ecosystem

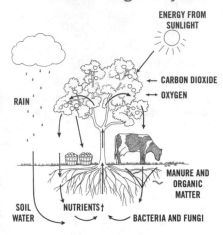

ENERGY FROM SUNLIGHT

CARBON DIOXIDE

OXYGEN

RAIN

MANURE AND ORGANIC MATTER

SOIL WATER

NUTRIENTS↑

BACTERIA AND FUNGI

Best Sources of Organic Matter

Here are some readily available sources of organic material:

- **Compost** (see pages 272–278)
- **Plant residues**, such as the chopped leaves of deciduous trees (run a lawn mower over them), seaweed, apple or grape pomace, sawdust, and straw (these two should be used in moderation, or just in the fall, to give them time to break down)
- **Animal manures**, particularly aged cow, horse, and chicken manure
- **Green manure** (see pages 282-283)

In addition to choosing your source of organic matter, you need to decide how to apply it. One or more of the following methods will work for most sources.

- **Soil amendment.** Mix the material into the soil.
- **Topdressing.** Spread material on top of the soil. Ideally, it should disappear fairly quickly so it's available to plants.
- **Mulch.** Really just a year-round, slow-acting topdressing. Ideally, it should stay around longer so you don't have to replenish it frequently.

—from *Secrets to Great Soil*

pH

When you test for your soil's acidity or alkalinity, you're really measuring the concentration of hydrogen ions. Acidity controls how well nutrients dissolve. In very acidic and alkaline soils, most nutrients dissolve very slowly or not at all. They may form insoluble compounds, locking up nutrients so plants can't use them. That's why it's important to test and correct the pH of your soil before you add fertilizer. By correcting extreme acidity or alkalinity, you can bring more nutrients within plants' reach without adding fertilizer!

Testing Your Soil

You can have your soil professionally tested at a state laboratory. Call your local Cooperative Extension Service for information and prices. Or you can purchase an easy-to-use soil-testing kit from a garden center or catalog. Some measure only pH, but others measure nitrogen, phosphorus, and potassium.

1. Dig several 6-inch-deep holes in different areas of your garden or lawn.

2. Carve a thin vertical slice from the side of each hole and place it in a bucket. Mix the samples together, breaking up clumps and removing pebbles and large pieces of plants.

3. Follow kit directions for the amount of soil and amount of indicator chemical to use. Mix as directed, allow the soil to settle, and compare the test tube to the colored chart in the kit.

Managing Soil pH

Correcting soil acidity or alkalinity may improve your garden more dramatically than any other soil-building effort. Slightly acidic soils (pH 6.3 to 6.8) are best for most plants and soil organisms because they ensure the greatest availability of essential nutrients.

Acidic soil (pH 5.0–6.0). Periodic liming of acidic soil can replace the neutralizing calcium and magnesium that get washed away by rain. Don't add lime unless you need it, though. Overliming causes worse problems than those caused by acidity. Work in abundant organic matter (avoid acidic ingredients such as pine needles and peat moss), especially alkaline nutrient sources such as well-aged manure, bonemeal, rock dusts, and guano. Consider what you're trying to grow, also. If you're growing a food crop that likes acidic soil, such as blueberries or potatoes, you may have no need for lime.

Alkaline soil (pH 7.0 to 8.0). For moderately alkaline soils, apply powdered sulfur to lower the pH. It works in six to eight weeks and lasts six months or more. For a slower but longer-lasting treatment, work in acidic ingredients such as oak leaves, leaf mold, ground bark, aged sawdust, peat moss, pine needles, and pine or cypress bark mulch. While they can take three months to a year to work, their benefits last much longer than those from sulfur.

Nutrients in Your Garden

The major nutrients plants need are nitrogen, phosphorus, potassium, calcium, magnesium, and sulfur. Without them, garden plant growth is likely to be limited. Most soils that are gardened or farmed intensively need periodic resupplies of nitrogen, phosphorus, and potassium. Calcium, magnesium, and sulfur already exist at adequate levels in many soils, and may not need to be applied at all.

Micronutrients are also called trace elements because only a very small amount of each is required for healthy growth. They include iron, boron, manganese, copper, zinc, and molybdenum. You may never have to worry about micronutrients if you routinely add compost or manure, or if you use fish emulsion and/or liquid seaweed as fertilizers from time to time.

Organic Matter: The Key to Balancing Nutrients

Work organic matter into your soil to maintain a steady supply of nutrients, especially nitrogen and potassium. Fresh plant residues and manures supply all nutrients. Well-decomposed forms and humus supply micronutrients and low levels of nitrogen, phosphorus, and sulfur but little calcium, magnesium, or potassium.

—from *Secrets to Great Soil* by Elizabeth P. Stell

Breaking New Ground

If you are gardening a new piece of soil, a soil test will help you determine levels of phosphorus and potassium as well as giving you the lime requirements. Adding rotted manure will correct most deficiencies. Till it in at the rate of one pound per square foot, in both fall and spring.

—from *Grow the Best Tomatoes* by John Page

IDENTIFYING NUTRIENT DEFICIENCIES

Here are a few clues to possible nutritional deficiencies in garden plants, and what to do if you see them.

Nutrient Nitrogen
Symptoms light green leaves, slow growth, slightly smaller size
Treatment Manure, blood meal, cottonseed meal, alfalfa meal, fish meal, and many other soil amendments supply nitrogen.

Nutrient Phosphorus
Symptoms purple coloring on leaves, stems, other unusual places
Treatment Soil that regularly receives compost should not be deficient; eliminate the risk by scattering bone meal or rock phosphate into soil every few years.

Nutrient Potassium
Symptoms thin stems, leaves with scorched edges
Treatment Add compost, manure, other organic soil amendments; or apply granite dust or greensand to soil in fall every few years.

Nutrient Magnesium
Symptoms yellow, red, orange, or purplish splotches on older leaves of plants; leaf tips curl upward
Treatment If soil test indicates problem, correct with dolomitic limestone; until limestone takes effect, spray plants with seaweed or kelp foliar spray; if soil is alkaline, apply compost instead of limestone.

Nutrient Iron
Symptoms pale green or yellowish color on youngest leaves
Treatment Correct soil pH; in alkaline soil, add acidic organic amendments such as rotted leaves and peat moss; add greensand to compost before using it to boost iron content.

Nutrient Manganese
Symptoms yellow color in young leaves, similar to iron deficiency but not as severe, especially in alkaline soil
Treatment Correct soil pH.

Nutrient Boron
Symptoms skin blisters and brown spots inside sweet potatoes, black areas inside beets; stunted growth; twisted, thick deformed leaves
Treatment Use plenty of compost or sprinkle very small amounts (1 teaspoon per 9 square feet) of household borax into soil.

Nutrient Zinc
Symptoms small leaves; older leaves with yellow spots or stripes
Treatment Correct pH or add manure.

COMPOSTING

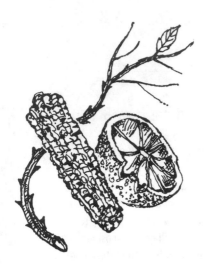

What Compost Does for Your Soil

Compost is the best form of organic matter to add to your soil. It's a mix of organic materials such as grass clippings, garden waste, and kitchen scraps that have decayed into a crumbly, dark mass. A balanced, slow-release source of nutrients, compost can keep soils stocked with all the micronutrients that plants need. It supplies small amounts of major nutrients and helps soil hold onto nutrients and water long enough for plants to use them. It increases the overall health of your garden by suppressing disease organisms in the soil. When sprayed on leaves in the form of compost tea, it can suppress leaf spots, mildews, molds, and other leaf diseases. Compost also encourages beneficial soil organisms, which feed on disease organisms or make nutrients available to plants.

Making and Using Compost

Compost is so simple that you might as well make it yourself instead of buying it. After all, you're just trying to speed up nature's nutrient recycling program, which goes on constantly all around us. There's no need for an elaborate system. Simply piling leaves will do if you're not in a rush. If you don't have deciduous trees, you can make concentrated compost—pure humus—from kitchen scraps with a low-maintenance indoor worm bin.

—from *Secrets to Great Soil*

Materials to Compost

To be composted, a material need only have two characteristics—it must be biodegradable and it must contain things that are usable and available to microorganisms. Here is an incomplete listing of such materials:

Feathers	Hay or straw	Newspapers	Sod
Garbage	Hedge trimmings	Peat moss	Weeds
Grass clippings	Hops (brewery waste)	Pine needles	Wood ashes
Ground stone and shells	Leather waste	Sawdust	
	Leaves	Seaweed (kelp)	

leaves

kitchen scraps

hay

Materials to Avoid

Animal products	Colored paper	Pet droppings	Seeds and pits
Charcoal	Diseased plants	Pet litter	
Coal ash	Pesticides		

—adapted from *Let It Rot!* by Stu Campbell and *The Big Book of Gardening Secrets* by Charles W.G. Smith

---

Carbon-to-Nitrogen Ratio in Compost

As you gather materials, keep in mind the ratio of carbon (C) materials to nitrogen matter (N) in your compost. Scientists have determined that a good ratio of carbon to nitrogen in a compost pile is 25 to 30 parts carbon to 1 part nitrogen, or 30:1 (commonly shortened to "30"). In practical terms, this means most of the materials you add should be carbon materials. A pile with a C:N much higher than 25 or 30 will take a long time to decompose. If the C:N ratio is very low (if there is too much nitrogen), your pile will likely release the excess as smelly ammonia gas.

The C:N ratio need not be exact. In general, add 2 to 3 pounds of nitrogen materials for every 100 pounds of carbon materials. I prefer to put up with a slight odor and keep a small surplus of nitrogen in the pile, just to make sure there is always enough to speed decomposition.

Here are the average C:Ns for some commonly used compostable materials:

alder or ash leaves 25

grass clippings 25

leguminous plants (peas, beans, soybeans) 15

manure with bedding 23

manure 15

oak leaves 50

pine needles 60–100

sawdust 150–500

straw, cornstalks, and cobs 50–100

vegetable trimmings 25

The carbon-to-nitrogen ratio of your compost pile should be 25 or 30 to 1.

—from *Let It Rot!* by Stu Campbell

Fertilizers for Free

In a hurry-up world, the making of leaf mold is largely forgotten. Because leaves have little nitrogen, they decompose slowly and do not heat up as they do if high-nitrogen material is added to them.

The two-year process of decomposition can be hastened by running the leaves through a shredder before piling them. Fence in the pile with wire netting to keep the leaves from spreading back across your lawn. Stamp the pile down. Expect to see it half its original size when the leaves have turned to leaf mold ready for use.

After a year, turn the pile, cutting and mixing it as much as possible. In this stage it can be used as a mulch, and will be welcomed by the earthworms in your garden.

—from *Fertilizers for Free* by Charles Siegchrist

Brewing Compost Tea

Compost slowly and reliably adds nutrients to the garden. But sometimes it is nice to speed things up a bit, as when the summer veggies need a little boost. Enter compost tea. To brew some, place about a bushel of fresh, finished compost in a waterproof garbage can and add water to within about a foot of the top. Cover and allow to brew for a few days in a cool, shady place. Decant into a watering can and pour over the garden for a safe, natural, easily absorbed fertilizer.

—from *The Big Book of Gardening Secrets* by Charles W. G. Smith

Using Compost Activators

Any substance that speeds up decomposition in your compost pile is an activator. Activators generally supply nitrogen, microorganisms, or both. Save money by making your own from the ingredients here. Avoid synthetic fertilizers, which contain no protein and seem to inhibit compost organisms. Activators work best if mixed in thoroughly. If you'll be turning your pile soon, simply spread a thin layer every 6 inches or so. Use only 1 cup of dry meal per layer but up to a 2-inch layer of soil or compost.

Nitrogen/Protein Sources
Alfalfa meal
Blood meal
Dehydrated manure
Fresh grass clippings
Fresh manure
Hoof or horn meal

Microorganism Sources
Compost (the fresher the better)
Fresh or well-aged manure
Healthy, humus-rich soil
Strips of sod

—from *Secrets to Great Soil* by Elizabeth P. Stell

COMPOSTING

Stuart Campbell's book Let It Rot! *is the classic guide to turning household waste into gardener's gold. He is an accomplished gardener, writer, and skier, living in Stowe, Vermont, as well as a compulsive composter, collecting piles of particularly attractive leaves from the side of the road. Stuart is also author of* The Mulch Book *and* The Home Water Supply.

Locating Your Bin or Pile

Place your compost pile as close as possible to the garden, so you don't have to lug or cart materials back and forth over a long distance. Your bin or pile should be near a water source, but don't place it too near the house itself, or directly under dripping eaves or downspouts.

If you live in a cold climate, you'll want the help of the sun's heat to warm your pile, but you'll have to be prepared to add water so it doesn't dry out. In a warmer climate, locate the pile in the shade, where it won't dry out so quickly. If you have the foresight, it would be ideal to locate your pile on a future garden spot, so the nutrients that leach from the pile will be put to good use later.

A fairly standard bit of advice is that the pile should be protected on the north, east, and west sides by some sort of wall, hedge, or container, and that the south side, if possible, should be left open.

—from *Let It Rot!* by Stu Campbell

Building Compost Bins

A compost pile works fine if you have the time and patience to build it carefully, shape it properly, and keep it correctly shaped after you have turned it or added materials. The main advantage of a bin is that you don't have to waste time tapering the pile to prevent it from becoming top-heavy and falling over. The container can be complicated or very simple. Here are two time-tested, effective designs.

The New Zealand Box

The New Zealand box is a bin made of wood. Besides assorted nuts, bolts, and washers, you need:

    6 pieces of 2" x 2" wood, 39 inches long, for uprights

    24 pieces of 1" x 6" wood, 48 inches long for the sides

    1 piece of 2" x 2" wood, 56 inches long for crossbar

Drive the uprights into the ground to a depth of 3 inches. The sides, six boards to a side, should be bolted to the uprights around three sides. Leave a ½-inch gap between each of the side boards to allow air into the pile.

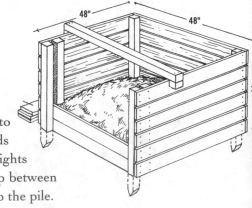

The box has no top and no bottom, and removable front boards. The 1" x 6" front boards are not fastened by bolts, but can be slid in and out as needed to permit access to the pile. The base is 4 feet by 4 feet. It is 3 feet high, and allows air circulation from all sides. To keep the sides of the box from bulging out, you can use a crossbar with blocks on either side. Cut 2-inch blocks off of the 56-inch 2" x 2". This rests, unfastened, on top of the container.

The Circular Bin

To build a circular bin 3½ feet in diameter, you'll need:

12½ feet of 36" wide, 1" poultry wire

4 metal or plastic clips, or copper wire ties

5 four-foot wooden or metal posts to support the poultry wire

Roll out and cut 12½ feet of poultry wire. Roll back 3 to 4 inches at each end of the cut piece to provide a strong, clean edge that will be easy to latch. Set a wire circle in place for the compost pile and secure ends with clips or wire ties. Space wood or metal posts around the perimeter inside the wire circle. Pound posts firmly into the ground while tensing them against the wire to provide support.

The wire provides good aeration, but the edges of the pile may dry out in warm weather. Sprinkle sides and top frequently in summer to keep the pile moist.

Sprinkle the top and sides of the compost with water to keep it moist.

COMPOST TROUBLESHOOTER

You can solve most compost "problems" simply by waiting. Most material will break down eventually. But if you don't want to wait a year or more for nature to take its course, use the remedies below.

Symptom	Cause	Remedy
Pile doesn't heat up, feels dry	Too dry	Add water until materials in center feel evenly moist; in dry climates, water pile and cover with tarp whenever it dries out.
Pile doesn't heat up, feels moist	Not large enough	Make sure pile is 3 feet square and at least 4 feet tall, or wait for cold composting to happen.
Large pile doesn't heat up, feels moist	Not enough nitrogen	Add alfalfa meal, manure, fresh grass clippings, or other nitrogen source and turn pile.
Pile cools off before most material has decomposed	Needs to be turned	Turn pile with garden fork, mixing material in center with outer or undecomposed material.
Pile smells bad, feels soggy or wet	Too wet	Add shredded newspaper, straw, or other dry, carbon-rich material and turn pile; in wet climates, cover pile to keep off rain.
All material doesn't break down	Too much nitrogen or not enough air	Add shredded newspaper, straw, or other carbon-rich material (plus water) and turn pile to aerate.
Matted layer doesn't break down	Too dry or not enough nitrogen; needs mixing	For soil that is too dry, add water until materials in center feel evenly moist; in dry climates, cover pile with tarp and water whenever it dries out. For soils needing nitrogen, add alfalfa meal, manure, fresh grass clippings, or other nitrogen source and turn pile.
Some pieces didn't break down	Pieces too large, too woody, or not biodegradable	Turn pile, breaking up matted layer and mixing with other material. Sift compost.

—from *Secrets to Great Soil*

COMPOSTING

Trench Composting Rotation

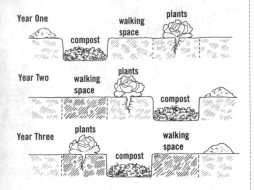

Trenching Tips

- Don't try to dig your trench when the soil is bone dry. It's hard work. Wait until soil is moist—spring or fall, in most areas.
- Don't dig your trench when the soil is wet.
- Where the soil freezes, you'll need a waterproof container filled with dry sand or sawdust to cover kitchen scraps during winter. Spread some soil over top in spring.

Trench Composting

If you don't mind digging, the simplest way to compost is right in the soil. Dig a hole or trench in the ground, fill it with kitchen and/or garden trimmings, and cover with the removed soil. In a few months, even the most stubborn clay will be crumbly, easy to dig, and loaded with earthworms.

Trench composting is perfect if you want to return kitchen and/or garden wastes to the soil but don't want to worry about carbon/nitrogen balance or turning piles. It's an excellent way to improve the soil for a new bed if you can plan six months ahead. If you eventually decide to double-dig or build raised beds, the soil will be much easier to work and will be improved in its structure.

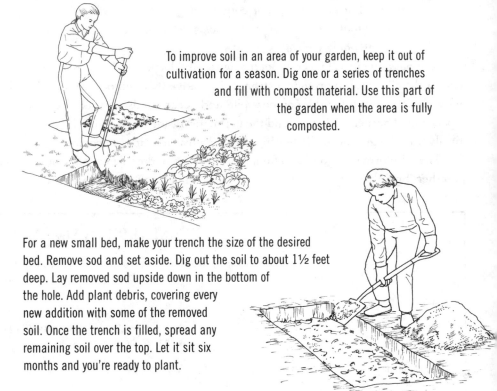

To improve soil in an area of your garden, keep it out of cultivation for a season. Dig one or a series of trenches and fill with compost material. Use this part of the garden when the area is fully composted.

For a new small bed, make your trench the size of the desired bed. Remove sod and set aside. Dig out the soil to about 1½ feet deep. Lay removed sod upside down in the bottom of the hole. Add plant debris, covering every new addition with some of the removed soil. Once the trench is filled, spread any remaining soil over the top. Let it sit six months and you're ready to plant.

Basic Worm Composting

Earthworms live in the soil in our gardens, where they work with microorganisms to digest organic waste, breaking it down into simpler forms and making it more accessible as nutrients to living plants.

Worm composting adapts and confines this process. You build a worm bin, stock it with food that worms will thrive on (your own kitchen and garden wastes), keep it full of bedding, and add worms. These are not the same earthworms you find in the garden, but instead are red worms suited to life in a worm bin.

The worms will leave behind something called vermicompost, a highly concentrated, excellent soil amendment made up of compost and castings. Use this end product on your garden, houseplants, or lawn. You will not only enrich your garden soil and plants, but also dramatically decrease the amount of waste your family contributes to the landfill.

Setting Up the Worm Composting Bins

Many garden supply companies sell bins complete with your first pound of worms. Alternatively, you can set up a simple plastic bin that will work just as well. You will need at least 1 square foot of surface area in the worm bin for each person in the household. And you will need about a pound of worms per person.

1. Use a plastic bin with handles and a matching lid, approximately 1½ x 2 feet and at least 8 inches tall. Using a ½-inch bit, drill 12 holes in the bottom of the bin, 4 to 5 inches apart. Set the bin on a tray, mounted on a couple of foot-long pieces of scrap wood.

2. Place a piece of 24- x 18-inch fiberglass window screening over the bottom of the bin and fill the bin halfway with moistened bedding, such as newspaper strips or chopped leaves. Release about 2 pounds of red wigglers or red worms on top of the bedding.

3. Place the bins in a dry place indoors (in cold northern regions or the blazing-hot Deep South) or in a protected but accessible spot outdoors (in moderate climates).

Worms are sensitive to vibration, so do not put the bin in front of a stereo speaker or near any major appliance. Your worms might try to leave home in search of a more peaceful place.

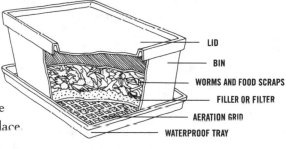

LID
BIN
WORMS AND FOOD SCRAPS
FILLER OR FILTER
AERATION GRID
WATERPROOF TRAY

Feeding

Feed your worms vegetable (or garden) trimmings and/or coffee grounds. Don't add eggshells, fats, oils, meat scraps, or cheese. Peel back bedding to add a couple of pounds of food a week. Leave the bin lid slightly open for ventilation, and open farther if contents get soggy.

Using the Castings

When the material in the bin looks like soil, it's ready for use on your garden or houseplants. Wherever you would use traditional compost or fertilizer, use worm compost instead. Add a scoop to your tomato planting holes, scatter on your lawn before it rains, mix with soil in containers, add a ¼-inch layer to all seed holes or furrows before planting seeds, work liberal amounts into your vegetable garden in spring.

If you harvest your compost in the winter and want to wait till spring to use it, spread it out to dry slightly and then package it in plastic bags to await spring.

—from *Worm Composting* by Joshua D. Nelson

Diet for Worms

Good Foods
- Leaves and grass clippings
- Fruit and vegetable wastes, such as orange and banana peels, apple cores, potato skins, and corn husks
- Animal manures, particularly aged cow, horse, or chicken manure
- Grains, including leftover rice, stale cereal, pasta, and old bread
- Tea bags, coffee filters, and coffee grounds
- Crushed eggshells
- Any garden waste
- Manure of plant-eating animals such as horses and cows

Bad Foods
- Large quantities of meat or fish
- Any oily foods
- Dairy products
- Manure of meat eaters (such as dogs and cats)
- Manure of any animal recently wormed

Buying Worms

One source of worms is your local bait shop, many of which stock red worms for anglers. The other option is garden suppliers—local or mail order. You will be buying your worms by the pound. Don't be alarmed, but a pound of worms is about 1,000 of the little wigglers.

—from *Worm Composting*

COMPOSTING

Using Your Compost

Finished compost can be used anywhere in the garden. It is finished when it develops the sweet, woodsy smell of rich soil and most ingredients have become a crumbly or fluffy, dark brown, soil-like material. Some large or recognizable pieces usually remain, but everything should be a relatively uniform dark brown.

To maximize its benefits, use finished compost within a few months. Like well-aged manure, though, even the oldest compost still improves soil.

Add a handful of finished compost to the bottom of each hole when transplanting seedlings. Add a shovelful for larger plants and heavy feeders such as tomatoes, melons, and squash. Sprinkle finished compost into rows when planting seeds.

You can spread unfinished compost over the garden in fall. It will finish breaking down by spring and may be left on the surface or tilled under. Avoid spreading unfinished compost around vegetables and flowers as a topdressing. To use it as mulch on annual flowers or vegetables, spread a layer of finished compost underneath. You can use unfinished compost alone as a mulch for shrubs and trees.

Compost can be used as a foliar fertilizer in the form of compost tea. (For directions on how to make it, see page 273.) This liquid form of compost can be sprayed on or poured over leaves, or used to water houseplants. Compost tea gives plants a nutrient boost and controls some diseases.

—from *Secrets to Great Soil* by Elizabeth Stell

Mulches

Mulches provide a protective blanket for the soil, and mulching is one of the easiest ways to add organic matter: Spread the material on top of the soil and let earthworms do the tilling for you. Mulching (or its close cousin, top-dressing) is often the only way to supply organic matter to trees, shrubs, berry bushes, and perennials. If these are shallow-rooted, they'll resent any attempt to dig in amendments. As a bonus, mulching greatly reduces watering and weeding chores. Mulches improve the soil in many ways, from adding humus to reducing erosion and encouraging soil organisms.

Organic Mulches

Only organic mulches provide organic matter and nutrients. Organic mulches can be anything you'd put in the compost heap. For mulching, though—unlike composting—the longer something takes to break down, the better.

However, in wet soils and very humid climates, organic mulches can promote some diseases and increase chances of rot. If spread too thickly, they can interfere with the soil's air circulation. Fresh, unweathered, carbon-rich mulches such as sawdust can temporarily tie up enough soil nitrogen to interfere with plant growth. This problem is easily solved by letting them weather until their color fades, or by spreading nitrogen-rich material underneath them.

Inorganic Mulches

Inorganic mulches include black paper, black plastic, gravel, and landscape fabric. These mulches also provide some benefits, such as warming the soil in spring. It's a good idea to spread 1 to 2 inches of compost or aged manure over the soil before using inorganic mulches. Once the mulches are in place, it's hard to replenish soil organic matter.

Topdressings

Mulches that disappear very quickly are more properly called topdressings. The purpose of topdressing is to get organic matter and nutrients into the soil as quickly as possible. Mulches need to stick around a little longer to fulfill their main purpose, which is protecting the soil.

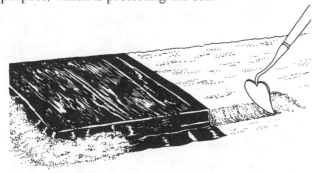

Black plastic mulch evens out the moisture supply, absorbs a lot of heat, and generally speeds things up.

18 Reasons to Mulch

- Keeps soil moist.
- Smothers most weeds.
- Keeps soil soft so that weeds are easy to pull and more rain soaks in.
- Shades soil, reducing heat stress for plants and soil organisms.
- Keeps soil warmer on cold fall nights.
- Prevents sudden swings in soil temperature, increasing winter survival of plants.
- Helps prevent plants from heaving out of soil in winter.
- Reduces wind and water erosion.
- Prevents puddling or crusting from hard rains.
- Reduces or prevents soilborne diseases by keeping rain from splashing soil onto plants.
- Keeps fruits and vegetables clean.
- Minimizes stress for new transplants.

If the mulch is organic, it also:

- Adds organic matter and humus.
- Feeds and encourages earthworms and other soil organisms.
- Conditions soil.
- Slowly adds nutrients to soil.
- Increases retention and availability of nutrients.
- Recycles lawn, garden, and tree trimmings.

—from *Secrets to Great Soil*

STU CAMPBELL ON CHOOSING THE BEST MULCH

While there is no one perfect mulch, there are factors to make one mulch a better choice for a given situation. Specific mulches have advantages and disadvantages. How do you narrow the list? Here are factors to consider.

Availability

The availability of a mulch often determines what the cost will be. What is plentiful and available is probably cheap—in some instances, even free. Check with local municipalities, utility companies, and lumberyards. They may be dying to give away composted leaves or wood chips to someone willing to cart them away. Perhaps there is a processing plant nearby that has buckwheat hulls or peanut shells available.

Ease of Application

We don't want you to be a slave to mulching. If you have an established bed full of trees and shrubs, you probably won't want to slit dozens of holes in landscape fabric or black plastic to cover it. You might not want to hassle with the weight and bulk of crushed stone to mulch a small garden path. Pick a mulch you can handle.

Appearance

Pick a mulch that won't cause people in the neighborhood to whisper behind your back. Try not to offend anyone. Get a peek at what you're thinking of buying, then visualize how it is going to look in your garden. Will those bright red lava rocks go with the rest of the colors in your garden? Black plastic and straw are popular in vegetable gardens, but may not look terribly attractive in the peony bed.

Water Retention/Penetration

You'll want the rainwater to soak down to your plant roots, but perhaps it's not as important when you're mulching a pathway. Assess your situation and choose accordingly. The same is true with air exchange. Plastics won't let air in or out, and this can suffocate plants; however, if your primary concern is weed control, maybe that's acceptable.

Lasting Qualities

In a vegetable garden, you usually turn the mulch into the ground at the end of the season. Chances are you'll want to pick a mulch that decomposes quickly. Conversely, mineral mulches like gravel and crushed stone will last for an incredibly long time with a minimal amount of bother. Remember, fine or chopped mulches rot faster, while coarser mulches tend to hang around longer and demand less maintenance.

Staying Power

You don't want to spend Saturday afternoons chasing your mulch around the yard. If you live on a windy hill, lightweight mulches like straw and buckwheat hulls are unsatisfactory. Paper or plastic mulches will need to be anchored with pegs, stones, or something else. Small, fine bark chips can wash away with the first heavy rainfall on even the slightest incline.

Odor

Manure and poultry litter have their strong points, and smell is often one of them. Grass clippings can also literally raise a stink. Some people even object to the smell of chocolate given off by cocoa hulls. Keep odor in mind when selecting your mulch.

—Stu Campbell is the author of *The Mulch Book, Let It Rot!,* and *The Home Water Supply*

Using Organic Mulches

Prepare the garden before mulching. Remove any weeds and level or smooth the surface.

Spread the mulch evenly, at least 2 inches deep and 1 to 2 inches away from plant stems to promote good air circulation and minimize diseases.

Using Fabric Paper and Plastic Mulches

Spread the material over the garden. For small plants, cut an X in the fabric and gently slide the X over the plants. With large plants, cut a small circle or square large enough to fit around the stem(s).

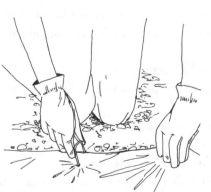

Secure the edges of the material with soil; in windy areas you'll also need a few rocks or U-shaped wire pins.

Cover landscape fabric with an attractive mulch of gravel or bark chips.

Marvelous Mulch Materials

Here is an alphabetical rundown of selected mulches.

Bark
Cocoa hulls
Coffee grounds
Compost
Corncobs and cornstalks
Fabric paper
Grass clippings
Hay
Hops
Leaves
Paper
Peanut hulls
Pine needles
Plastic (polyethylene)
Reflective mulch
Seaweed (kelp)
Stone/gravel
Wood chips

—adapted from *The Mulch Book* by Stu Campbell

GREEN MANURES

Nitrogen Boosters

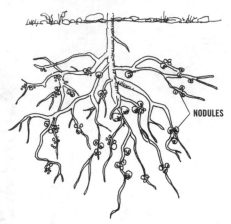

Round nodules that form on the roots of healthy pea and bean plants convert inorganic nitrogen into organic nitrogen the plant can use.

---

20 Common Green-Manure Crops

Legumes
Alfalfa
Alsike clover
Bur clover
Cowpea
Fenugreek
Field peas
Lespedeza
Red clover
Soybeans
Sweet clover
Velvet bean
Vetch

Non-Legumes
Barley
Buckwheat
Brome grass
Oats
Rape
Rye

—from *Fertilizers for Free*

About Green Manures

Green manures are crops grown to be plowed under at an immature stage of development, in order to boost the organic content of the soil. There are two types of crops grown for this purpose—the legumes and the non-legumes.

Legumes are able to form partnerships with certain soil organisms called rhizobia, which absorb nitrogen from the atmosphere. Where the rhizobia attach themselves to the roots of legumes, little nodules form. The nodules help supply the plant with nitrogen by converting inorganic atmospheric nitrogen to organic nitrogen that is used by the plant. The process is known as nitrogen fixation.

Cultivated vegetables that are leguminous include peas, soybeans, and beans. All are among the most nutritious of crops. As cover crops, legumes are valuable because some fix more nitrogen from the atmosphere than they need for themselves. Rather than being soil depleters, legume crops can be soil improvers.

In general, non-legume green manures conserve the soil's supply of nitrogen and organic matter, while a leguminous green-manure crop under favorable conditions will actually increase it.

Growing Cover Crops

Ideally, a home gardener should have two plots. While one is in use for vegetable production, the other can grow soil-improving cover crops. Alternation of the pattern would allow for steady improvement in both plots.

One of the easiest ways to rotate for cover crops is to plant the early produce in a different location within the garden each year. Peas, radishes, and lettuce are all out of the ground relatively early in the gardening season. When harvest of these spring crops is completed, turn under their residue, mix in some compost, level a good seedbed with a rototiller or rake, and plant a green-manure crop.

Sow half the seed in one direction—east and west, for example—then sow the other half north and south. This will help provide even coverage and thus a good stand of plants.

Back to the Soil

Some green-manure crops, such as alfalfa, will give the greatest benefit if left growing more than one year. Others are short-season crops that can be returned to the soil in six weeks.

The decomposition of non-legumes can be hastened by spreading a high-nitrogen fertilizer such as blood meal about two weeks before the crop is to be turned under.

For best results, turn under a green-manure crop when it is actively growing but before it blooms, when it is tender and succulent. Decomposition of the organic matter will be slowed once the plants have become woody.

The green manure can also be harvested with a scythe or string trimmer and used as mulch for vegetables elsewhere in the garden. This practice "spreads the wealth" of your green manure.

—from *Fertilizers for Free* by Charles Sielchrist

Build Mighty Soil with Green Manure

1. Dig up and remove any sod and weeds. Loosen the top few inches of soil. If the soil is poor, amend with organic matter and fertilizer (or choose a green manure that tolerates poor soil). This is a great time to apply a slow-release nutrient source such as granite meal, greensand, rock phosphate, or limestone. Rake the seedbed smooth.

2. Scatter seeds evenly over the entire bed. For large areas, a broadcast seeder is a big help. If you're sowing less than a pound over 1,000 square feet, mix seeds with sand or sifted soil to get even coverage. Rake the bed to cover seeds and tamp down the soil. Spread a light covering of straw or grass clippings to reduce the need to water. (Floating row covers also reduce watering needs.)

3. Cut or mow the crop before tilling. A string trimmer makes quick work of soft, lush growth. For tall crops, make several passes with the trimmer, to chop while you cut. A sickle-bar mower or scythe will cut tougher stems. Before turning under, leave the cut material for a couple of days to wilt.

4. Turn under the cut material and mix into the top few inches of soil. For large areas, use a rototiller (small cultivators work only if material is chopped finely). Vigorous perennials such as winter rye may need to be turned again in a week to stop resprouting. After turning under, leave soil surface rough. The bed should be ready for smoothing and planting in a week or two, or longer if you turned under a large amount of coarse material (full-grown alfalfa) or will be planting seeds after turning under winter rye).

—from *Secrets to Great Soil* by Elizabeth P. Stell

14 GARDEN PESTS & DISEASES

GARDEN MANAGEMENT • COMMON GARDEN INSECTS • PEST REMEDIES • PLANT DISEASES • ANIMAL DETERRENTS

In the early 1960s we discovered a self-published volume titled The Bug Book: Harmless Insect Controls. *The authors, John and Helen Philbrick, were early Bio-Dynamic Method gardeners, helping, in their words, "to turn every farm, every estate, even every back yard garden into a unit complete in itself." Opposing toxic chemicals, they argued that we should get to know "the biters and suckers and crawlers and swoopers." We were proud to become the publishers of their work, and we never looked at a bug the same way again!*

—John & Martha Storey

Healthy plants in healthy soil do not attract insects or disease organisms.

Have you ever noticed that bugs seem to besiege plants already in a weakened state? It's true. Tests confirm that healthy plants tend to stay healthy, while sickly ones are in for a struggle. A plant weakened by disease, transplant shock, improper hardening off, poor nutrition, or insects is an easy target. The plant's color changes, and some bugs pick up on that. It may smell or taste different to an insect.

One tactic aimed at raising "tougher" plants is to water them less. When plants are subject to slight water shortages, they react by developing a tougher outer layer to protect them from loss of moisture. While using plenty of water produces plants that are tender and juicy, slightly underwatered plants may have less-bug-appealing stems, leaves, and other parts. It's unlikely that the human consumer of these garden goods will detect any differences in quality, but to the bugs such differences may be enough to send them buzzing off.

Beneficial insect. A garden insect that attacks and eats other insects that destroy crops

Crop rotation. The practice of moving crops to different locations at each planting, so you are not growing a family of crops in the same place two or more years in a row. This often interrupts the life cycles of harmful disease organisms and/or insects

Emergence time. The time of the year when an insect species first appears

Integrated pest management (IPM). Use of preventive planning to maintain a healthy, balanced garden in which plants thrive

Pesticides. Biological, natural, and synthetic pest controls for use on specified plants. This general term includes insecticides, fungicides, and herbicides

Solarization. Use of a transparent plastic covering placed over garden soil to trap the sun's heat in the soil, thereby killing pests and diseases

Trap crop. A crop planted to attract insects. The crop can be removed or destroyed after it is infested with insects

A First Strategy: Plan Ahead

Sound management practices go a long way in discouraging pests and diseases in your garden. An approach called *integrated pest management* (IPM) combines preventive planning and carefully targeted controls. The idea is to maintain a healthy, balanced environment in your garden, one where pests don't feel welcome and plants thrive.

Rotating Your Crops

Farmers and gardeners have used crop rotation for centuries. By not growing the same crop or family of crops in the same place two or more years in a row, they can control many soilborne diseases and insects. Rotating, or moving crops to different locations at each planting, interrupts the life cycles of harmful organisms.

Insects that lay eggs, pupate, or otherwise overwinter in the soil wake in the spring ready to devour those first tender shoots or roots. They expect to find the same feast before them as last season. By planting a crop from an entirely different family, you can cut them off from their food source. For instance, root maggots waiting for tasty broccoli roots can starve in a healthy pea patch.

Certain pests are more resilient than others, so it is sometimes necessary to plan on *not* using a patch of garden for the same crop for three to five years. This is especially true of cabbage family crops such as broccoli, cauliflower, Brussels sprouts, cabbage, and kale.

Some crops, such as corn, celery, and tomatoes, are considered "heavy feeders" because they demand more soil nutrients than other crops. Your soil, and thus future plantings, will benefit greatly if you alternate such crops with peas, beans, or another legume or cover crop to replenish nitrogen and other nutrients.

—from *The Big Book of Gardening Skills*

Increase Your Garden's Health by Planning Ahead

- Pest control is important at all times, from planting and pruning through harvesting.

- Before applying pest controls, consider what you are after. Any control is far more effective when carefully timed and targeted at a specific problem.

- Spraying or dusting with pesticides is only one part of a pest-control plan and may be insufficient to curb insect and disease problems. Often you can avoid using pesticides if you employ other methods first.

- Preventive measures are usually more effective than spraying after insects and disease have damaged plants. These measures include crop rotation, timing your planting and harvesting around bug emergence, planting resistant varieties, companion planting, and using plant coverings.

GARDEN MANAGEMENT

Soil Solarization: Purify Your Soil in 5 Easy Steps

1. **Prepare the soil.** Pull weeds or old crops. Turn in any soil amendments and rake the surface smooth. Remove any stones or clumps that might raise the plastic and create air pockets, which could cause uneven heating.

2. **Water thoroughly.** This creates 100 percent humidity under the plastic, and the humidity acts with the heat to kill unwanted critters.

3. **Dig a trench.** Make the trench 6 to 8 inches deep all around the bed or plot.

4. **Lay clear plastic.** Lay a sheet 6 to 8 mm thick over the area, overlapping the trench on all sides. Fill the trench back in, weighing down the plastic while pulling it as tight as possible.

5. **Sit back, relax, and wait.** Although cloudy weather will slow things down by cooling the soil under the tarp, a few weeks of sunshine will improve your soil dramatically.

Covering the soil with plastic for several weeks can eliminate many harmful pests.

—from *The Big Book of Gardening Skills*

Covering Your Plants

The use of horticultural fabrics can deter insects, rabbits, and birds; protect against weather extremes, wind, and hail; and exclude airborne weed seeds.

Some coverings are made of spun-bonded polypropylene. They are porous and translucent, allowing air, water, and 70 to 90 percent of the available sunlight to pass through to plants. Though extremely lightweight, these fabrics are strong and tear-resistant. They can be used for several seasons if treated with care. Avoid walking on the coverings. Lift and place them out of the way when cultivating, and store them when not in use.

All plant coverings trap heat. This makes them wonderful season extenders, both by aiding early planting and by protecting crops in the fall. But in spring and summer, they can raise temperatures underneath by 15 to 35 degrees, too much for many plants.

Lay these fabrics over the crop as soon as it goes in the ground. Weight down the edges and ends with soil or boards, so nothing can creep underneath and to prevent the wind from blowing the fabric off. Leave extra headroom for the plants as they grow. The cover can rest on plants with no ill effects or can be draped over them with hoops.

Installing a "floating" row cover

Using the Sun to Control Insects and Diseases

If there were a sure way to destroy virtually every kind of harmful insect egg and larva in your garden soil, would you be interested? How about if the process were easy, cheap, and carried a host of other benefits along with it?

Soil solarization is a simple, five-step process that kills insects, nematodes, harmful fungi, and weed seeds, and eliminates plant diseases. At the same time, helpful microorganisms within the soil apparently benefit, possibly from the lack of competition. Soil that has been solarized allows plants to draw on nutrients, especially nitrogen, calcium, and magnesium, more readily. Seeds germinate more quickly. Plants grow faster and stronger, often maturing earlier with substantially higher yields, than in unsolarized soil.

Solarization works in the same way as a greenhouse. A transparent covering, in this case 6 mm or 8 mm plastic sheeting, traps the sun's heat. After several days of sunshine, soil temperatures rise to as high as 140°F at the soil surface and well over 100°F as far down as 18 inches. It takes four to six weeks of sunny weather to pasteurize the soil. For most of the country, that means spreading plastic somewhere between the end of June and the first of September. To solarize your soil, follow the five easy steps at left.

—from *The Big Book of Gardening Skills*

COMPANION PLANTING WITH HERBS

HERB	COMPANIONS
Basil	Companion to tomatoes; dislikes rue. Repels flies and mosquitoes.
Borage	Companion to tomatoes, squash, and strawberries; deters tomato worm.
Caraway	Plant here and there; loosens soil.
Catnip	Plant in borders; deters flea beetle.
Chamomile	Companion to cabbages and onions.
Chervil	Companion to radishes.
Chives	Companion to carrots.
Dill	Companion to cabbage; dislikes carrots.
Fennel	Most plants dislike it; plant away from gardens.
Flax	Companion to carrots, potatoes; deters potato bug.
Garlic	Plant near roses and raspberries; deters Japanese beetle.
Horseradish	Plant at corners of potato patch; deters potato bug.
Henbit	General insect repellent.
Hyssop	Companion to cabbage and grapes; deters cabbage moth. Dislikes radishes.
Marigolds	Plant throughout garden; it discourages Mexican bean beetles, nematodes, and other insects. The workhorse of companion plants.
Mint	Companion to cabbage and tomatoes; deters white cabbage moth.
Mole plant	Deters moles and mice if planted around garden.
Nasturtium	Companion to radishes, cabbage, and cucurbits; plant under fruit trees. Deters aphids, squash bugs, striped pumpkin beetles.
Petunia	Companion to beans.
Pot marigold	Companion to tomatoes, but plant elsewhere, too. Deters tomato worm, asparagus beetles, and other pests.
Rosemary	Companion to cabbage, beans, carrots, and sage; deters cabbage moth, bean beetles, and carrot fly.
Rue	Companion to roses and raspberries; deters Japanese beetles. Dislikes sweet basil.
Sage	Plant with rosemary, cabbage, and carrots; dislikes cucumbers. Deters cabbage moth, carrot fly.
Southernwood	Companion to cabbage; deters cabbage moth.
Summer savory	Companion to beans and onions; deters bean beetles.
Tansy	Plant under fruit trees; companion to roses and raspberries. Deters flying insects, Japanese beetles, striped cucumber beetles, squash bugs, and ants.
Thyme	Companion to cabbage; deters cabbage worm.
Wormwood	As a border, it keeps animals from the garden.
Yarrow	Plant along borders, paths, and near aromatic herbs; enhances production of essential oils.

—from *Tips for the Lazy Gardener* by Linda Tilgner

Companion Planting

For generations, gardeners have noticed that some plants seem to do better in the presence of others. Part of this happy coexistence is attributed to the ability of certain plants to repel, ward off, or confuse insects. A patchwork garden of staggered plantings helps interrupt the spread of insects. It's easiest for them to go down a neat row of vegetables, one plant after the other.

—from *Carrots Love Tomatoes* by Louse Riotte

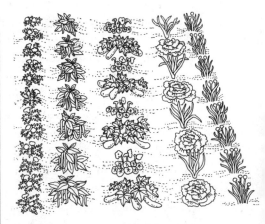

This garden plan shows, left to right, marigolds, green beans, summer squash alternating with nasturtiums, lettuce alternating with onions, and chives.

COMMON GARDEN INSECTS

BARBARA PLEASANT ON GARDEN INSECTS

Living and gardening alongside insects requires that we know who they are and how they live. Many books provide color photographs that can help you discern one bug from another. In addition to identifying insects with your eyes, consider where you find them and what they are doing. Most insects are quite particular where their food supply is concerned and will eat only certain plants. Since very young insects have limited abilities to move about, the adults are careful to lay eggs on or very near plants suitable for their young to eat. Yet the right host plant for an egg or larva may not be the right host for the adult form of the same insect.

How do insects find their host plants? Many are able to "smell" the character of a plant with their feet or antennae, while others look for certain colors, such as the bright orange-yellow of squash blossoms. Still other insects sample whatever plant they happen to land on and then decide whether they have found a good place to feed. By paying close attention to where insects are found, you can often discern their identity.

Another helpful identification factor is when the insect appears. Some pests, like flea beetles, feed most heavily in early spring; others wait to appear in mid-summer or even fall. The time when you first start seeing a certain species is called the emergence time.

Tracking the emergence times of pests that appear year after year in your garden yields excellent information to use in planning a more pest-resistant garden. In many instances, you may be able to schedule plantings so they escape damage entirely. Eggplant set out late, for example, has few problems with flea beetles. If you want to be a good garden manager, keep records of emergence times and pest activities.

Gentle Intervention

When control is called for, gardeners can choose from an assortment of natural, low-impact chemical compounds, as well as a number of homemade concoctions and formulas. Choose the least toxic method that provides an acceptable level of control.

Not all insect control is accomplished by applied substances. Many garden insects are controlled simply by the creation of maximum biological efficiency in the plants themselves. Healthy plants may have a few insects nibbling here or there, but they are not completely devastated. With well-nurtured plants, the damage is barely noticeable and may even strengthen the plants' defenses.

Another kind of insect control is the use of predacious insects to prey upon those that cause trouble. In this sort of "organized mayhem," the insects that eat plants are killed by other insects. Predators might include roving mantises and assassin bugs; larval lady beetles and lacewings, which eat aphids; and the parasitic braconid wasp, which makes its home in or on the bodies of tomato hornworms.

Among the gentlest of pest controls is growing plant varieties that pests do not like. The reasons insects bypass insect-resistant varieties range from the chemical to the physical. In the case of nonbitter cucumbers, cucumber beetles fail to find the chemical compound that signals them to feed.

Plants may also offer physical resistance to insect injury. Many plants defend themselves with leaf hairs sharp enough to stab small insects, or sticky hairs loaded with chemicals that make insects sick. Some vegetables slow down the insects by making them ingest so much plant fiber that they expend too much energy eating.

—Barbara Pleasant is the author of *The Gardener's Bug Book*.

BENEFICIAL INSECTS . . . THE "GOOD GUYS"!

Spined soldier beetles
Attack cabbage loopers, cabbage-worms, Mexican bean beetles

Green lacewings
Larvae attack aphids, spider mites, mealybugs, leafhoppers, thrips, corn earworm, and caterpillar eggs

Predatory mites
Attack pest mites

Ground beetles
Attack caterpillars, cutworms, and other soft-bodied larvae

Mealybug destroyers
Attack mealybugs

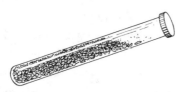

Ichneumon wasps
Attack caterpillars and borers

Braconid wasps
Attack aphids, hornworms, cutworms, cabbageworms, tent caterpillars, and more

Assassin bugs
Attack aphids, caterpillars, Colorado potato beetles, Japanese beetles, leafhoppers, Mexican bean beetles, and more

Ladybugs
Attack aphids, rootworms, whiteflies, chinch bugs, Colorado potato beetles, mealybugs, scales, and spider mites

Trichogramma wasps
Attack cutworms, armyworms, cabbage loopers, hornworms, corn borers, codling moths, fruitworms, leaf-worms, and more

Tachinid flies
Larvae feed on corn borers, cutworms, armyworms, Japanese beetles, Mexican bean beetles, and more

Praying mantids
Prey on aphids, various bee-tles, leafhoppers, flies, caterpillars, and more

—adapted from *Easy Gardening 101* by Pat Stone and *Bugs, Slugs, and Other Thugs* by Rhonda Massingham Hart

YOUR GARDEN, YARD & ORCHARD

COMMON GARDEN INSECTS

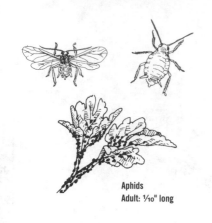

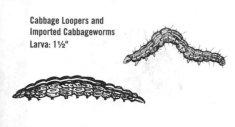

Aphids
Adult: ¹⁄₁₀" long

**Cabbage Loopers and
Imported Cabbageworms**
Larva: 1½"

Colorado Potato Beetle
Adult: Larva: ⅓"

Corn Earworm
Larva: 2"

Cucumber Beetles
Adult: ¼"

Cutworm
Larva: 1½"

Japanese Beetle
Adult: ½"

Fourteen Bugs You Don't Want in the Vegetable Garden

Aphids

Description: Tiny, most under ¹⁄₁₀ inch long. Soft, pear-shaped bodies with two long antennae at tip of head and a pair of tubes. Colors range from translucent green to pearly black, with pink, red, purple, and blue varieties.
Garden targets: Most vegetables and ornamentals are susceptible. Orchard trees may be damaged or stunted.
Damage and signs: Leaves often turn yellow as plant weakens. Leaves of potato plants turn brown and curl. Fruit trees with swollen twigs and branches and covered with white fluff have been taken over by woolly apple aphid.

Cabbage Loopers and Imported Cabbageworms

Description: 1¼ inches. Loopers are green with white stripes, humpback. They loop or inch along. Cabbageworms are paler green with yellow stripe, velvety hairs.
Garden targets: Cabbage, broccoli, cauliflower, kale, kohlrabi, radish, turnip.
Damage and signs: Irregular holes in leaves. May bore into plant heads to feed. Leave green fecal pellets.

Colorado Potato Beetles

Description: ⅓ inch long, hard, round outer shell; wing covers creamy yellow with 10 black stripes; head and thorax decorated with black marks.
Garden targets: Potato, tomato, eggplant, peppers, cabbage, petunia.
Damage and signs: Stripped foliage; also leave black excrement.

Corn Earworms (Tomato Fruitworm or Cotton Bollworm)

Description: 2-inch caterpillar in shades of green, pale yellow, or brown, with light or dark sidewalls.
Garden targets: Corn, tomato, cotton, peppers, eggplant, okra, potato, squash, beans, peas.
Damage and signs: Chew on corn ears and tassels, eat holes in green tomatoes, and eat chunks of new leaves and buds.

Cucumber Beetles

Description: Striped version, ¼ inch, bright yellow with three broad, black stripes and black head; spotted version has 11 large, black spots on wing covers.
Garden targets: Cucumbers, melons, squash, pumpkins. Striped version goes for beans, peas, corn, beets, eggplant, tomato, potato. Spotted likes corn, cucurbits, tomato, eggplant, potato.
Damage and signs: Holes chewed through foliage, flowers, fruits.

Cutworms

Description: 1–1½-inch soft, bristly caterpillars in gray, brown, or black to greenish white and red.
Garden targets: Tender seedlings or transplants. Brassicas, beans, corn, tomatoes, and just about everything else.
Damage and signs: Plants gnawed at the base, may fall over. They leave a telltale ¼- ½-inch tunnel at the base of the plant.

Japanese Beetles

Description: ½ inch long, metallic green with copper-colored wing covers. Bristly white hairs/downy gray hairs.

Garden targets: Rhubarb, corn (silks). Nuts and fruit trees. The grubs like lawns.

Damage and signs: Skeletonized leaves, lacy veins intact.

Mexican Bean Beetles

Description: ¼ inch, rounded. Yellow when young, copper as adults. Wings sprinkled with spots, but no white markings like ladybugs.

Garden targets: Beans, cabbage, kale, collards, mustard greens.

Damage and signs: Skeletonized leaves, lacy veins intact.

Root Maggots

Description: Appear similar to houseflies. Fat, whitish larvae, ⅓ inch and tapered to a pointy head.

Garden targets: Onions, cabbage, broccoli, cauliflower, Brussels sprouts, turnips, radishes, rutabaga.

Damage and signs: Sudden wilting, yellowing in hot spells. Leave scars and tunnels in roots.

Spider Mites

Description: Tiny specks. Color varies with diet, from red to yellow to green.

Garden targets: Strawberries, melons, beans, corn, tomato, eggplant.

Damage and signs: Leaves turn yellow, first along veins; foliage wilts. Angelhair-like webs cling to leaves and stems.

Squash Bugs

Description: 1 inch, dark brown, flat backs, long legs and antennae. Eggs shiny gold when laid, then red-brown, arranged in patterns under leaf veins.

Garden targets: Squash, pumpkin, melon, and cucumber.

Damage and signs: Young plants easily killed; older ones wilt, blacken, and die.

Tomato Hornworms

Description: 4-inch caterpillar, green with seven or eight diagonal white stripes down its sides, shadowed by a row of black dots, has a "false eye" spot. Black tail.

Habits: Chew leaves, moths take flight at night.

Garden targets: Tomatoes, peppers, potato, eggplant, dill.

Damage and signs: Eat large amount of leaves; fecal material like rabbit pellets.

Whiteflies

Description: Tiny, milk white, covered with waxy powder.

Garden targets: Nearly everything in the garden.

Damage and signs: Plants weaken and turn yellow. Fungal growths often accompany their secretions.

Yellow Jackets

Description: Adult wasps are ½ to 1 inch long, bright yellow and black or white and black bands decorating abdomen. Transparent wings.

Habits: Furiously defend their nest. Inactive at night.

Garden targets: Adults lap up pollen and nectar. Will chew up sweet ripe fruit such as strawberries, blueberries, tree fruit, and melons.

Damage and signs: Holes in ripe fruit.

—adapted from *Bugs, Slugs, and Other Thugs* by Rhonda Massingham Hart

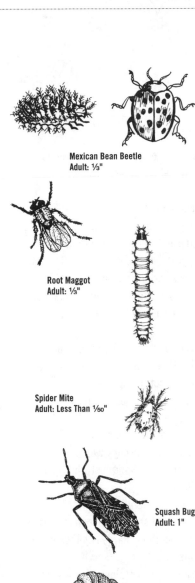

Mexican Bean Beetle
Adult: ⅓"

Root Maggot
Adult: ⅓"

Spider Mite
Adult: Less Than 1/60"

Squash Bug
Adult: 1"

Tomato Hornworm
Larva: 4"

Whitefly
Adult: 1/10"

Yellow Jacket
Adult: ¾"

PEST REMEDIES

Guidelines for Spraying

Here's how to make pesticide use as safe and effective as possible.

1. Read and follow directions. Ask your nursery or Cooperative Extension Service for advice if you are unsure about handling pesticides. If products call for wearing gloves or goggles, do so.
2. Store pesticides in their original containers always locked away from children and pets.
3. Mix only what you can use at one time.
4. Mix wettable powders in a separate container, not the sprayer. Filter the mixture through cheesecloth, then transfer it to the sprayer. This ensures that the powders will not clog the applicator.
5. Don't spray in windy weather. You want the pesticides to land just where you aim them.
6. Clean up carefully when finished. Thoroughly rinse out applicators, wash hands, and throw garden clothes into the wash.
7. Never reuse containers. Dispose of leftovers as indicated on the product's package.

Wear protective clothing, including goggles and gloves, if product instructions call for them.

Sprays and Dusts That Control Insects

One of the major advantages of organic pesticides is that they break down quickly, posing little threat of chemical buildup in soil or plants, or groundwater contamination. Here are a number of organic sprays and dusts that can help you control garden pests.

Spray insecticidal soap directly on foliage.

Soap Sprays

Soap sprays are among the safest of preparations, effective against aphids, mealybugs, spider mites, spittlebugs, stinkbugs, crickets, grasshoppers, and other soft-bodied insects. Mix 3 tablespoons of mild or insecticidal soap to a gallon of water and apply to foliage with a hand sprayer. Most bugs will die within an hour, but the spray degrades quickly, so spraying must be repeated often. Soap sprays can damage some plants such as melons, cucumbers, and African violets. To reduce the chance of leaf damage, use commercial preparations when possible and rinse plants with clear water as soon as pests have died, usually less than 1 hour.

Garlic and Hot Pepper Sprays

These are effective against many insects, as the bugs are sensitive to differences in the smell or taste of their preferred foods. Naturally occurring sulfur compounds in garlic repel many pests, from insects to animals.

Bacillus thuringiensis (Bt)

Bt is a naturally occurring bacterium that infects and destroys leaf-chewing caterpillars. It must be eaten to work, so apply it when pests are feeding. Spray plants thoroughly, including the undersides of leaves. To get the most from Bt, spray when caterpillars are small and most susceptible. Bt breaks down almost immediately and poses no health risk.

Botanical Insecticides

The natural plant derivatives rotenone, pyrethrins, and azadirachtin (neem) are potent bug killers. Buy the purest form and apply according to instructions.

Diatomaceous Earth (DE)

This substance comprises the skeletal remains of microscopic sea creatures called diatoms. The shells contain silica particles that penetrate the bodies of some insects and desiccate others. Dusting after a light rain or mixing the powder into a spray will help ensure that it stays where you put it. Although considered safe, it does irritate some people's lungs. Be sure to buy the diatomaceous earth produced for garden use.

More Earth-Safe Remedies for Insect Problems

Here is a selection of recipes and methods for controlling garden insects—some traditional, some of recent invention.

Aromatic Herbs

The best herbs for making sprayable teas include wormwood, mints, lavender, rosemary, sage, tansy, and southernwood. To make herb sprays with fresh herbs, crush a large bunch of leaves and stems with your hands and place them in a heat-proof container. Pour a quart of boiling water over the herbs, stir well, and allow to cool. Strain through a metal strainer, then through muslin or another fine cloth. Add 2 drops of mild liquid soap and decant the tea into a pump spray bottle. Apply early in the morning.

Collars

Collars are made from paper, cardboard, or metal. They form a barrier that pests are unable to cross. Collars to keep cutworms from felling young vegetable plants are easily made from paper cups with the bottoms removed, or from strips of cardboard stapled into a ring. Place these rings around tomatoes, peppers, and eggplant at transplanting time. Collars made from copper strips are an excellent defense against slugs and snails. To be effective, the collars should be 3 to 4 inches wide.

Cultivation

Many pests spend time in the soil as eggs, larvae, or pupae. When you cultivate the soil, they become dislodged and disoriented, and may be eaten by larger predators or killed by weather conditions at the soil's surface.

Handpicking

Handpicking should be your first line of defense against any pests large enough and slow enough to gather by hand. When picking, take along a jar or can of vegetable oil, very hot water, or a half-and-half mixture of water and rubbing alcohol. Drop the collected bugs into the container. You can also use a hand-held vacuum cleaner to gather bugs.

Milky Spore Disease

Japanese beetles are such a widespread problem in the East that controlling them calls for a large-scale effort. Milky spore disease is a bacterial formulation that kills the grubs as they feed. It also kills the grubs of June beetles. To use, simply spread the powder or granules over your land just before a rain.

Sticky Traps

These are among a gardener's most useful tools. The traps themselves can be homemade, but you will probably want to buy the sticky stuff that snares the bugs. Simply smear it on your traps and you can study, count, and dispose of the bugs you capture.

—from *The Gardener's Bug Book* by Barbara Pleasant

Wormwood contains substances that can be used to create an effective garden herbicide.

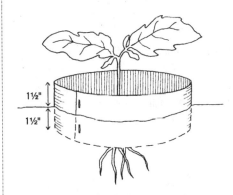

Encircle young seedlings with a 3-inch-wide collar of paper or cardboard to prevent cutworm damage.

PLANT DISEASES

Bacterial leaf spot

Leaf spot fungus affects beets, chard, roses, and tomatoes.
Treatment. Avoid touching foliage when wet. Destroy affected parts. Keep area clean and open. Drench plants with compost tea (see page 273).

Virus disease affects many plants.
Treatment. Plant resistant varieties; control weeds and insects; sterilize tools.

Diseases and Your Garden

There's no such thing as a disease-free garden. Like fleas on a dog, organisms that cause plant disease are always present, waiting for a suitable host to appear. When a disease does develop, there's no single magic formula for getting rid of it. Some understanding of the troublemaker is first required, followed by a logical, organized treatment plan.

—from *The Gardener's Guide to Plant Diseases* by Barbara Pleasant

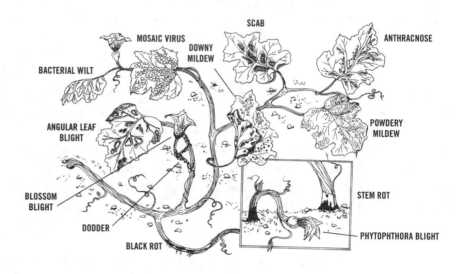

Different diseases have very different effects, as shown on this unfortunate pumpkin plant.

Damping-off fungus affects many plants.
Treatment. Plant in well-drained soil; use sterile potting mix for indoor growing.

Mosaic virus affects beans, cucumbers, melons, peppers, squash, and tomatoes.
Treatment. Plant healthy seeds and resistant varieties. Destroy infected plants. Control weeds. Use insecticidal soap to control aphids.

Getting to Know the Culprits

The organisms that cause plant diseases are living things that enter plant tissues and reproduce.

- **Fungi.** Microscopic organisms that parasitize plants. They may infect roots, stems, or leaves, causing plants to rot, wilt, or develop leaf spots. Fungi begin as seed-like spores that germinate when they come in contact with a suitable host plant. They send tiny threadlike filaments, called hypha, into plants' tissues and soften their cell walls for nutrients.

- **Bacteria.** Much smaller than fungi. They take nutrition from plant cells and multiply quickly and aggressively until cell walls burst. Bacteria force their hosts to accommodate their population explosions by releasing enzymes and toxins as they grow. This activity clogs plants' vascular systems in only a few days, causing them to wilt and die.

- **Mycoplasmas and viruses.** Even smaller than bacteria. Their tiny viral tidbits rob plants of their genetic organization and divert energy to themselves. They may live inside plants all season, never killing them but causing many aberrations in plant growth. Leaves crinkle, twist, or show bubbles of lost color. Insects spread viruses as they feed from plant to plant.

- **Nematodes.** The largest organisms that cause plant diseases. Often called eelworms or roundworms, they resemble microscopic snakes that become plant parasites, living in roots, stems, or leaves. Their eggs survive in soil for many years. They suck plant juices through a needlelike stylet. The holes they make in plants provide entryways for secondary infections.

—from *The Gardener's Guide to Plant Diseases*

Botrytis rot affects berries, lettuce, beans, asparagus, tomatoes, and many flowers, especially tulips.
Treatment. Keep plants thinned; spray with compost tea (see p. 273) or baking soda (1 teaspoon to 1 quart water.)

Healthy-Plant Checklist

At the first encounter with a garden disease, ask yourself questions about how the episode developed. The following checklist should help you identify contributing factors.

- ❏ Is the plant appropriate for your soil type, climate, and growing season? Pushing plants to grow in hostile environments increases their susceptibility.
- ❏ How is the drainage? Waterlogged soils can give rise to root-rot diseases.
- ❏ Are adjoining plants affected, or only isolated plants or leaves? Small problems can often be eliminated by removing the first plants or plant parts to become infected.
- ❏ Did you use seeds or plants that might have carried a disease? Seeds and plants shared among friends may not be safe.
- ❏ What plant grew in the soil before the one having trouble? Was it a host for the same disease?
- ❏ How well can fresh air circulate through the plant? Is tight spacing or neglected pruning causing growth to become too crowded?
- ❏ Are other host plants living nearby?
- ❏ Is the plant old and deserving of an honorable death?
- ❏ Have you seen insects that may have transmitted the disease?
- ❏ Are there resistant varieties that you could plant instead?

—from *The Gardener's Guide to Plant Diseases*

ANIMAL DETERRENTS

Infamous Animal Pests

rabbit

gopher

mole

rat

mouse

vole

Four-Legged Ravagers

In general, a fenced garden fares better than one open to traffic. A fence keeps out the neighbor's dog, your own children, a few rabbits, and cats, but it doesn't stop groundhogs, moles, raccoons, squirrels, deer, or birds. Fences can be expensive and sometimes impractical. See Chapter 27 for more on fences.

It's a good idea to garden in an area for a while to find out just who your enemies are and which plants are most attractive to them. Then you can take steps to repel the culprits and concentrate on protecting specific crops.

Lethal traps and rodenticides are not the only approaches to rabbits and rodents; here are some alternatives.

Rabbits

Rabbits nibble on carrots, peas, beans, lettuce, beets, strawberries, and many flowers, as well as tulip shoots and bark from rose and berry bushes.

Traditional rabbit repellents include wood ashes, crushed limestone, ground hot peppers, ground black pepper, chili powder, and talcum powder scattered on the soil around the plant. Blood meal spread on the soil works, as do mulches of human and dog hair. Interplant garlic, onions, or marigolds with target plants, or use fish emulsion. Because rabbits are timid, you can scare them with dogs, fake snakes or owls, or even with empty glass pop bottles set with the tops poking up. They are afraid of the wind whistling on the bottle tops.

Gophers

Gophers are fond of alfalfa, but almost any plants with roots or bulbs qualify as gopher chow. Gophers are exasperatingly difficult to get rid of. Try planting gopher plant (*Euphorbia lathyris*) which is said to deter gophers and moles. They also dislike daffodils, scilla, and the castor-oil plant. Using newspaper for mulch can turn back surfacing gophers.

Moles

Moles eat grubs, earthworms, insects, and snails rather than plants. Most mole damage is due to their tunneling. Before you decide to eliminate them, be sure they are causing problems. They can be beneficial in devouring pests.

Compacting soil with a heavy roller makes it less appealing to moles. Planting mole plant, also called gopher plant (*Euphorbia lathyris*), may deter moles. Here is a castor-oil mixture you can try: Mix 2 parts castor oil with 1 part liquid detergent. Dilute 2 tablespoons in 1 gallon of water and saturate soil in and around the mound.

Rats, Mice, and Voles

Rats and mice dig up freshly planted seeds, nibble on tender transplants, and taste fruits or berries. Voles ruin field crops like legumes, grains, and potatoes.

General sanitation is a basic requirement for discouraging rodents. Remove sources of food, water, and shelter. This means cleaning up, burning, or deeply burying refuse, properly packaging stored edibles, and excluding rodent entry into or under buildings. They also dislike daffodils, hyacinths, and scilla.

Squirrels and Chipmunks

Gray squirrels take their toll on berries, fruits, corn, just-planted seeds, tender plants or plant parts, and flower bulbs. Chipmunks and ground squirrels excavate the newly sown seeds and happily sample many vegetables, bulbs, flowers, and fruits.

A spray made from pureed and strained hot peppers, in water with a tablespoon or so of liquid soap, is said to keep squirrels away from plants. A resident cat will greatly cut down on squirrel visitors; in fact, cat or dog hair, suspended in pouches or scattered around plants, is sometimes enough to keep them at bay.

squirrel

Woodchucks (Groundhogs)

Woodchucks are general herbivores that make the most of almost any available greenery. They favor succulent plants, plantains, and some grasses. Clovers and legumes are special favorites, but they are also fond of melons and fallen tree fruit. Large mounds of earth may be the first signal that you have these climbing and burrowing animals about.

Remove woodchuck cover, such as tall grass, weeds, woodpiles, and old stumps, to make your garden area less inviting. Plant onions or garlic near burrows or sprinkle ground hot pepper or black pepper near burrow openings. A thoughtfully constructed fence may be your best protection. Build a sturdy fence 3 to 4 feet high, leaving the top 12 to 18 inches unattached. Bend this section outward at an angle of about 65 degrees away from the garden.

—adapted from *Bugs, Slugs, and Other Thugs* by Rhonda Massingham Hart and *SCAT: Pest-Proofing Your Garden* by Ruth Harley

woodchuck

Winning the Battle with Crop-Eating Birds

A little bird-watching during the season will help you determine which crops need protecting from birds. Your purpose is not to get rid of all the birds. The same birds that torment you by pulling up the corn seedlings also gobble up bugs and slugs. The trick is to devise a plan whereby both you and the birds benefit. Here are some thoughts:

- Because wild berries are more attractive to birds than cultivated ones, allow wild plants to grow near your garden.
- Be neat when planting. Avoid dropping seeds on the surface and leaving them uncovered. A crow will spot a loose kernel of corn here and there, then discover the whole row.
- Cover newly planted corn seeds with mulch. When their heads poke through, pull the mulch aside; crows won't be interested any longer.
- Plant corn in a shallow trench and cover with fine-mesh poultry wire.
- Use garden netting over berry bushes and dwarf fruit trees and across strawberry patches. Ordinary nylon net is equally effective.
- Cover bunches of grapes with sections of nylon stockings.
- Stretch a string over a row of ripening strawberries and suspend strips of aluminum foil or aluminum pie plates to dangle in the breeze.

—from *SCAT: Pest-Proofing Your Garden*

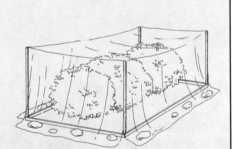

Enclose berry bushes in garden netting.

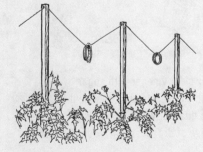

Suspend aluminum pie plates over plants.

ANIMAL DETERRENTS

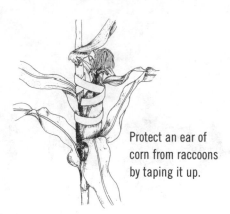

Protect an ear of corn from raccoons by taping it up.

Squash or pumpkin vines and pole beans make natural barriers for corn.

Raiding Raccoons

Raccoons are night raiders pursuing their business under cover of darkness. Extremely intelligent, they can be more than a match for any gardener's wits. Their well-rounded diet includes bugs, snails, crayfish, eggs, and mice as well as garden groceries. Their all-time favorites are corn and melons.

raccoon

Deterrents

The scent of natural enemies will keep many raccoons away. Try leaving your dirty clothes in the corn patch. Other repellents include dusting corn ears and leaves with baby powder, which raccoons apparently detest. Sprinkling ground hot peppers on corn silks or on vulnerable crops also makes them less palatable to raccoons. Finally, consider picking corn just a little early to beat your rivals to the crop.

Raccoon Fencing

Create a living fence by interplanting vine crops (cucumber, pole beans, squash, pumpkin) with your corn.

Raccoons are superb climbers. However, a fence of chicken wire or 2- by 4-inch mesh, 4 feet or more high, with the top 12 to 18 inches left unattached and bent outward, will successfully exclude most raccoons.

Garden Lowlifes: Slugs and Snails

These mollusks are among the most common garden pests. Slugs can grow to several inches in length, and their most prominent feature is one long, muscular foot that extends the length of the body. A snail is a fancy slug. The chief garden targets for slugs and snails are young, tender transplants, leafy vegetables, foliage plants, and flowers.

slug

snail

Because slugs and snails are fond of decaying vegetation, keep your garden as free of dead leaves and debris as possible. They may hide under mulch, so hold off on mulching until plants are well established or temperatures are over 70°F. Some mulches such as eggshells, wood ashes, gravel, and cedar bark form deterrent barriers.

Effective home remedies include interplanting repellent plants such as prostrate rosemary and wormwood. The latter is also effective when made into a tea and sprayed around the base of likely targets. Another potent attack involves spreading powdered ginger around the plants, creating a barrier that slugs and snails will not cross. A 1:1 vinegar and water solution can also be applied directly to plants or slugs.

Home Brew for Slugs

Here are some slug attracters that you can serve in a shallow dish deep enough to drown them when they visit.

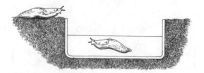

- Mix cider vinegar with sugar.
- Allow fruit peelings to ferment in a quart of water, along with ½ package of dry yeast and ½ cup of beer.

—from *Bugs, Slugs, and Other Thugs*

deer

Deer: Beautiful Browsers

Deer are at once among the most graceful, majestic, and troublesome of wildlife. A deer's year-round diet staples include the leaves, stems, and buds of woody plants. However, their menu is governed by what's available, and they seem eager to try new fare. Deer readily demolish corn, soybeans, small grains, alfalfa, vegetables, and fruit trees. Roses are a special treat.

The surest way to keep deer out of your garden is to prevent them from getting in. Erecting deer fencing is the most reliable method. Use hog-wire fencing and 12-foot fence posts to create a fence that is durable, though expensive. Sink the posts 3 feet deep, spaced every 20 feet, then attach two widths of 4-foot-wide fencing to make an 8-foot-high deer fence, keeping it as snug to the ground as possible.

—from *Bugs, Slugs, and Other Thugs* by Rhonda Massingham Hart

DEER DETERRENTS AT A GLANCE

REPELLENTS

Deterrent	Longevity	Relative Cost	Comments
Soap	Several weeks	Low to moderate	Very easy to use
Hair	Few weeks	Free	Very easy to use
Repellent plants	Indefinite	Low to moderate	Avoid toxic plants
Garlic, rotten egg	Few weeks	Free to low	Smell bad during preparation
Fabric softener	Until hard rain	Moderate	Very easy to use
Mothballs	Few weeks	Moderate to expensive	Avoid fumes, skin contact
Blood meal	Days to few weeks	Moderate	May attract predators
Bone tar oil	Few weeks	Low	Hold your nose
Predator urine	Days to weeks	Free to moderate	Challenging to acquire
Hot pepper spray	Days to weeks	Free to low	Wait at least one week before harvesting
Egg spray	Days to weeks	Free to low	Requires preparation
Soap spray	Days to few weeks	Free to low	Easy to use

OTHER DETERRENTS

Deterrent	Longevity	Relative Cost	Comments
White flags	Weeks	Low	Work only for whitetails
Mechanical gizmos	Weeks	Free to moderate	Easy to use; may require assembly
Floodlights	Weeks	Moderate to expensive	Require installation
Homemade noisemakers	Weeks	Free to moderate	Require assembly
Radios	Weeks	Moderate to expensive	Very easy to use
Deer whistles	Weeks	Moderate to expensive	Questionable effectiveness
Ultrasound	Indefinite	Moderate to expensive	Questionable effectiveness
Monofilament	Days to weeks	Low	Watch where you walk
Electric strand	Weeks	Moderate	May be a hazard to children
Timed sprinklers	Indefinite	Moderate to expensive	Remember when they start!

—from *Deer Proofing Your Yard and Garden* by Rhonda Massingham Hart

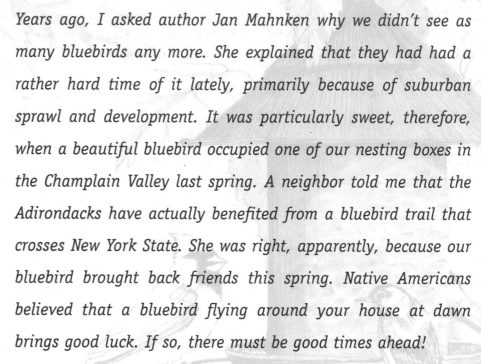

15

BIRDS & BUTTERFLIES

**FEEDING THE BIRDS • GARDENING FOR THE BIRDS
HUMMINGBIRD GARDENS • BUILDING NEST BOXES
BUTTERFLY GARDENS**

Jan Mahnken has loved birds from childhood and has come to know them particularly well on her Massachusetts farm. She is author of Feeding the Birds, Hosting the Birds, *and* The Backyard Bird-Lover's Guide *and has also written for many national magazines.*

Years ago, I asked author Jan Mahnken why we didn't see as many bluebirds any more. She explained that they had had a rather hard time of it lately, primarily because of suburban sprawl and development. It was particularly sweet, therefore, when a beautiful bluebird occupied one of our nesting boxes in the Champlain Valley last spring. A neighbor told me that the Adirondacks have actually benefited from a bluebird trail that crosses New York State. She was right, apparently, because our bluebird brought back friends this spring. Native Americans believed that a bluebird flying around your house at dawn brings good luck. If so, there must be good times ahead!

—John Storey

Probably the best reason to start feeding birds is that you *like* birds. You enjoy having them around for a variety of reasons, mostly aesthetic. Their songs, their squawks, their comments drifting through open windows on a summer day keep you informed of what's going on outside, whether you can see it or not. Loafing on the porch steps after dinner, we watch the swallows darting about the pasture, the hummingbirds visiting petunias, the kingbird sitting motionless on a fence post. The evening grosbeaks, the cardinals, and the blue jays brighten up a winter day when the rest of the world seems somber in black and white and shades of gray.

Wherever you live, you'll find a wide variety of wildlife, and much of that variety comes in bird form. Globally, there are over 8,500 living bird species, 950 of them on our continent. Many are highly visible and relatively easy to attract if we provide food, water, and shelter.

The Bird Food Menu

It's important to shop around for the best prices on bird food, because prices vary widely. If you live near a livestock feed store, you'll discover that prices are cheaper there than at supermarkets or garden centers.

Thistle

Thistle seems expensive, but it's so lightweight that you get a lot of seed per pound. Use it only in feeders designed for it, to avoid waste.

Finches dote on thistle, as do sparrows, chickadees, titmice, towhees, and juncos. Mourning doves also like it, but can't negotiate thistle feeders.

Sunflower Seeds

Sunflower seed is popular with many birds, so it's more economical to buy it in large quantities. Shelled kernels are less messy but close to prohibitive in price. You may decide that if the birds want sunflower kernels, they can jolly well crack the shells themselves.

Among the many birds willing to do so are titmice, grosbeaks, chickadees, nuthatches, towhees, jays, cardinals, and blackbirds. Starlings and sparrows have difficulty cracking the shells, but they eat leftover bits.

Most birds prefer black-oil sunflower seeds.

Cracked Corn

You'll save at least 50 percent by buying cracked corn in bulk at a feed store. One disadvantage of cracked corn is that it spoils quickly in wet weather. Dispose of feed not cleaned up in a short time to avoid sickening the birds.

Birds fond of cracked corn or scratch feed include red-winged blackbirds, red-headed woodpeckers, grackles, blue jays, sparrows, buntings, mourning doves, purple finches, cardinals, crows, and cowbirds.

Suet

"Bird suet" (see next page) is available in supermarkets, butcher shops, and wherever you buy bird food. It is usually inexpensive.

Among the many birds that go for suet are sparrows, grackles, mocking-birds, chickadees, warblers, nuthatches, starlings, thrushes, summer tanagers, Carolina wrens, northern orioles, and blue jays.

Hummingbird Food

The healthiest thing to offer hummingbirds is genuine flower nectar. Grow plants with showy, deep-throated blooms in hot colors (see page 308). Otherwise, they like a concoction of sugar water, where the recommended ratio of sugar to water is 1:4.

Commercial nectar is a high-energy sugar compound simulating flower nectar. An accompanying vitamin supplement has been formulated to counteract deficiencies. Whatever you use, clean your feeders on a regular basis.

—from *The Backyard Bird-Lover's Guide*

More Foods That Birds Like

berries

cheese

cornmeal

fruit

millet

nut meats

oats

peanut butter

pumpkin seeds

raisins

squash seeds

weed seeds

Unhealthy Foods for Birds

dog food

products made with white flour and sugar

—from *The Backyard Bird-Lover's Guide* by Jan Mahnken

FEEDING THE BIRDS

How to Serve Suet

Suet is beef fat, and insect-eating birds like woodpeckers, flickers, nuthatches, orioles, and chickadees love it. You can buy suet in chunks from meat markets or you can prepare your own. Here's how:

Chop up fat trimmings from steak or roast beef, immerse in water in a covered heavy pot, and cook over medium heat. When the fat begins to melt, remove the cover and cook over low heat until most of the fat has melted out and any bubbling stops. Strain the cooked mixture through a sieve into a bowl. Let cool. Skim off the solidified pure fat.

To make suet cakes, pour melted fat into muffin tins or small aluminum pie pans. Chill in the refrigerator until the fat hardens.

To serve, put the suet cakes in a mesh onion bag. Tie the bag shut at the top and hang it from a tree branch.

—from *Everything You Never Learned about Birds*
by Rebecca Rupp

Robin Rounds

Cooked spaghetti
Cheese, cut in strips
Chopped apple
Sprinkling of sand
Suet

Arrange loops of spaghetti in papered muffin tins. Add cheese, apple, and sprinkle with sand. Pour melted suet over mixture and allow to cool. Remove paper and set out at ground level.

Come One, Come All

3 parts sunflower seed
3 parts millet
1 part finely cracked corn
3 parts hempseed
1 part canary seed
Grit

Mix and offer at any level. This healthy mix has vast appeal.

Summer Suet Substitute

1 part flour
3–4 parts yellow cornmeal
Dash of salt
1 part peanut butter
1 part vegetable shortening

Mix dry ingredients and stir into gooey consistency. Spoon into containers. Favored by tanagers, thrushes, and warblers.

Cottage Cheese Salad

Currants, raisins, blueberries, grapes, or mulberries
Cottage cheese

Stir fruit into cottage cheese and set out in shallow containers. Don't set out more than the birds will eat in a day. Better to refill several times a day than to let the salad spoil.

Cardinal Candy

½ part green grapes
½ part blueberries or black cherries
1 part bread crumbs
1 part sunflower seeds
1 part cracked corn
Suet
Sprinkle of sand

Arrange all ingredients except suet and sand on bottom of foil pan. Melt, cool, and remelt suet. Pour over other ingredients. As mixture cools, sprinkle with sand and mix well. Place on ground feeder when cool.

Goldfinch Glory

Suet
Thistle seed
Millet
Hempseed

Pour twice-melted suet over a mixture of the seeds and cool. Place at feeder.

—from *Bird Food Recipes* by Rhonda Massingham Hart

SIX KINDS OF BIRD FEEDERS

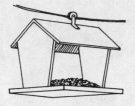

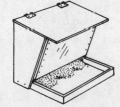

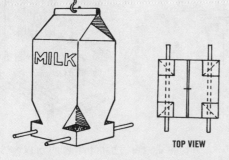

TOP VIEW

Feeder	Description
See-Through	This "food house" makes birds feel right at home, with a roof and four walls. It may have one or more glass panels to provide a closer look. When you attach it to a rope line with a pulley, you can draw the house a bit closer each day to a really good bird-watching vantage point.
Corn	In rural areas or on the fringes of suburbs, shy birds will come out of hiding to feast at your corn feeder. This is a type of feeding shelf. The corn is set on spikes driven upward through a board. Place the shelves under or near hedges, just above the snow line.
Seed and Suet Ball	Mold a mixture of seeds and melted suet into a ball. Let it harden. Place the ball in a loosely knitted twine or yarn sack for support. Do not use wire or other metal—in extreme cold, the moist tongue or eye of the bird could stick to the frosted metal. Hang the ball from the porch or a tree branch.
Hopper	The simple hopper feeder is useful because it holds a large supply of feed and guards it from contamination. The hopper also serves the feed easily and economically.
Window Shield	The window shield is the kind of feeder station most commonly used. It can also be placed on a tree or pole. It is best to put the shelf in a sunny window on a protected side of the house.
Milk Carton	Empty milk cartons, slightly modified, make good bird feeders.

For a milk carton feeder, cut out triangular sections at each corner, 1 inch from the bottom. Place ½-inch dowels through below the cutouts for perches. Place a hook on top and hang from a branch.

—from *Bird Food Recipes*

The Simplest Feeder

Many birds are picnickers: They like to eat on the ground. These birds like a tray or table-type feeder. A table feeder can be as simple as a flat piece of plywood on bricks or a backyard stump. Or you can build a simple table of your own.

A good size for a table feeder is about 2 feet by 3 feet, with legs 6 to 12 inches high. A 3-inch-deep rim around the tabletop is helpful to keep the feed from blowing away. It's also a good idea to have drainage holes at the corners, to keep the feeder from filling up with water.

—from *Everything You Never Learned about Birds*

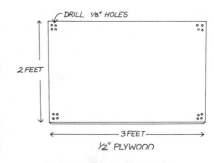

DRILL ⅛" HOLES

2 FEET

3 FEET

½" PLYWOOD

Drill drainage holes at each corner.

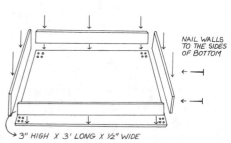

NAIL WALLS TO THE SIDES OF BOTTOM

3" HIGH X 3' LONG X ½" WIDE

Attach a rim to the perimeter of your table to keep seed from blowing off.

FEEDING THE BIRDS

Build a Juice Bottle Bird Feeder

You can recycle that fruit juice bottle by turning it into a bird seed dispenser. Remove the paper label by running hot water over the bottle. Add scrap wood, and you have a functional and nice-looking bird feeder.

Directions

1. Measure and cut all of the wood pieces. Cut the center support to the same diameter as the juice bottle.
2. Position and attach the center to the back, using glue and screws. You may want to predrill the holes with a countersink bit.
3. Place the bottom board against the end of the back board. Place the bottle into position with the rim on the bottom board. Trace a pencil mark around the rim of the bottle, marking its position on the bottom board. Remove the bottle.
4. Remove the bottom board from the back and drill three 1" holes spaced as shown halfway through the bottom board.
5. Glue and screw the bottom and top boards to the ends of the back board.
6. Measure and cut the ¼" wooden dowel into four pieces 2" long.
7. Position one of the perch bars against the side of the bottom board and drill two ¼" holes approximately 1" from each end of and through the perch bar and ½" into the bottom board. Repeat for the other perch bar.
8. Position and glue the ¼" dowels into place on the bottom board. Attach the perch bars to the ¼" wooden dowels with glue. Allow a 1" space between the perch bar and the base.
9. Attach ½" cup hooks to the sides of the center support.
10. Fill the bottle with birdseed and attach it to the feeder, holding it in place with a rubber band or string wrapped around the jar and attached to the cup hooks.
11. Attach the feeder to the side of a building or mount it on a post.

Materials

1 x 6 lumber, pressure-treated,
 36" long
2 pieces 6" x 7½" top and bottom
1 piece 10" long back
2 pieces ¾" x ¾" x 6" perches
1 piece 3½" x 6" center support
¼" wooden dowel, at least 8" long
2 cup hooks ½"
6 screws 1½" Dacrotized
Rubber band or string
Silicone glue
40-ounce juice jar

Tools

Drill with 1" spade bit
Screwdriver
Hammer
Hand saw or saber saw

Trace the rim of the bottle in position on the bottom board, and then drill three 1" holes halfway through the board as shown.

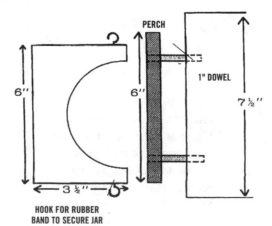

Assemble pieces as shown.

Attach the perch bars to the bottom board with dowels and glue, allowing 1" space.

—from *Birdfeeders, Shelters, and Baths* by Edward A. Baldwin

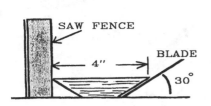

Build a Hexagonal Bird Feeder

This tall and graceful feeder is actually an eight-station feeder. It can be mounted on a post or suspended on a strong chain from a tree limb.

Directions

1. Measure and cut the six sides of the feed chamber from the ¾" pressure-treated plywood. Cut 4" wide with a 30-degree bevel on each side and 16" long.

2. Drill a 1" hole centered into each of the six side boards. If you like, stagger the position of each hole. Drill holes in two boards 5" from the top, two boards 5" from the bottom, and two boards centered. Cut a shallow V slot in the bottom of the two boards with the center hole.

3. Position the boards so that those with like hole placement are opposite each other. Glue all boards together. Hold in position with web clamp, rubber bands, or rope drawn tight around the assembly. Allow to dry.

4. Measure and cut the base and the roof of feeder from ¾" plywood. Center and attach the base and roof pieces to feeder using glue and 1½" screws.

5. Make the perches by drilling 1" holes 1" deep into the center of a 2 x 4 every 3½", then ripping the board down the center and cutting the perches to 3½" lengths with the half hole in the center. Cut to shape using saber or band saw.

6. Drill a countersink hole in the lower center of each perch and attach to the feed chamber sides with a 2" screw. (Position the perches so the top of the hole in the feed chamber is ¼" above the top of the perch.)

7. Measure and cut the three pieces forming the lid and assemble all of the pieces, with smallest on top for handle, using glue and a 2" wood screw.

8. Measure and cut six base rim strips from the 2 x 4 stock and attach to the base using ¾" wire brads and glue. Trim the pieces to fit flush.

9. Decorate the sides of the feeder with painted vines and leaves, or in any manner you like.

Materials

¾" plywood, pressure treated:
1 piece 12¾" hexagon (base)
1 piece 8" hexagon (base of lid)
1 piece 5" hexagon (lid top)
1 piece 2¾" hexagon (lid middle)
6 pieces 4" x 16" (sides)
1 piece 2½" diameter (lid bottom)

2 x 4 lumber, pressure treated:
6 pieces 1¾" x 3½" (perches)
6¼" x 1" x 1" (base rims)

Hardware and miscellaneous:
7 (1½") screws
7 (2") screws
12 wire brads, ¾" galvanized
Silicone glue

Tools

Drill with countersink bit, 1" and 2½" hole cutters
Screwdriver
Hammer
Table saw
Compass
Band saw or saber saw
Web clamp, rubber bands, or rope

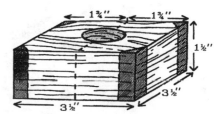

The perches are made from a 2 x 4. Drill 1" holes first, then rip the board down the center. Cut the perches to 3½" lengths, and saw off the sharp corners.

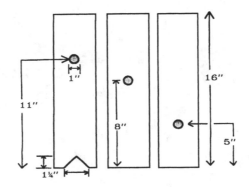

Cut six ⁴⁄₁₆" sides from the plywood, beveling the edges at a 30-degree angle.

Stagger the position of the feeder holes, making two sets of each.

—from *Birdfeeders, Shelters, and Baths*

GARDENING FOR THE BIRDS

house sparrow

blue jay

nuthatch

chickadee

Any property can serve as a sanctuary for birds. "Sanctuary" implies that the yard supplies natural cover, adequate food, and protection from natural enemies. The numbers and species of wild birds you attract will depend on the size of your property as well as its natural features.

It's suggested as a general principle that 8 to 12 percent of your permanent plantings should afford food or protective shelter for birds. Let's begin with the largest and most important of these permanent plantings—trees.

Evergreens

In colder climates especially, evergreens are useful for bird shelter and add color to your yard after the deciduous trees and shrubs are bare.

Pines of whatever variety find favor with practically all birds. Their long, soft needles provide shelter from severe weather, and the cones provide food. Besides those trees identified by the word *pine,* the family includes red cedar, a great favorite with a large number of songbirds. Spruces, firs, and hemlocks also belong to the pine family. Balsam firs attract finches, nuthatches, game birds, grosbeaks, chickadees, and crossbills. Finches are also quite partial to the seeds of spruce trees.

Shade Trees

Many shade trees are a boon to the birds even when they are young and modest in size.

There are over 50 species of oak in the continental United States. Mourning doves, flickers, woodpeckers, jays, nuthatches, and thrashers are among the birds that feed on their acorns.

The American beech, a lovely native tree in the eastern United States, produces nuts eaten by game birds, crows and grackles, jays, woodpeckers, crossbills, grosbeaks, and finches.

The paired, winged fruits of maples are a favorite source of food for evening grosbeaks, purple finches, and pine siskins. The box elder, a maple family member common to the central states, also provides food for evening grosbeaks.

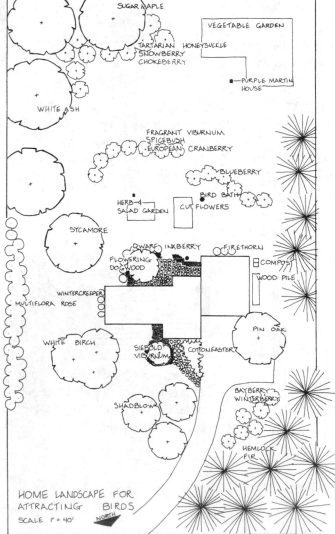

HOME LANDSCAPE FOR ATTRACTING BIRDS
SCALE 1" = 40'
NORTH

SUGAR MAPLE
VEGETABLE GARDEN
TARTARIAN HONEYSUCKLE
SNOWBERRY
CHOKEBERRY
PURPLE MARTIN HOUSE
WHITE ASH
FRAGRANT VIBURNUM
SPICEBUSH
EUROPEAN CRANBERRY
BLUEBERRY
HERB &
SALAD GARDEN
BIRD BATH
CUT FLOWERS
SYCAMORE
DWARF INKBERRY
FIRETHORN
FLOWERING DOGWOOD
COMPOST
WOOD PILE
WINTERCREEPER
MULTIFLORA ROSE
PIN OAK
WHITE BIRCH
SIEBOLD VIBURNUM
COTONEASTER
BAYBERRY
WINTERBERRY
SHADBLOW
HEMLOCK FIR

goldfinch

grosbeak

mourning dove

This yard features trees and shrubs that will provide shelter and nourishment for birds throughout the year.

mockingbird · cardinal · titmouse · bluebird · robin · downy woodpecker · wren

Smaller Trees

Let's move down in size to the birch family. These wonderfully attractive trees produce catkins, green in summer, that turn brown in the fall. Cardinals love them. So do crossbills, finches, grouse, nuthatches, and chickadees.

Black gum, also called tupelo or sour gum, is another medium-size tree. Its fruit attracts bluebirds, catbirds, kingbirds, flickers, mockingbirds, robins, thrashers, and tanagers. Any kind of cherry tree will bring bluebirds, grosbeaks, robins, crows, thrushes, game birds, waxwings, and woodpeckers.

Ornamentals

Whether your garden is large or small, you'll surely want to tuck in one or more smaller ornamental trees. Try catalpa, a small tree of the trumpet creeper family, if it will grow in your climate. Evening grosbeaks think it's wonderful.

Hummingbirds come to the chinaberry tree. Dogwoods are popular with songbirds, and so are magnolias in their various sizes and varieties. Hawthorn fruits look like tiny apples and are eaten by many favorite birds. Locusts appeal to hummingbirds, titmice, chickadees, and game birds. Mountain ash provides food for orioles, evening grosbeaks, bluebirds, and others.

Don't forget crab apples, which are lovely in the spring. If the waxwings discover a variety they like, they'll strip it of its fruit in a couple of days.

Shrubs

The single best way of enticing a variety of birds is to include shrubby hedgerows in the landscape design. In addition to providing shelter, they can offer various kinds of natural food. Common honeysuckle and Hansen's bush cherries are prime examples, as are currants, gooseberries, and wild or cultivated blueberries, if you're willing to share.

You may prefer shrubs that are more decorative than utilitarian. Cotoneaster is a widely grown ornamental shrub whose fruit is enjoyed by bluebirds, robins, waxwings, finches, and mockingbirds. Catbirds and cardinals join the bluebirds in their enthusiasm for autumn and cherry elaeagnus. In its multitudinous forms, euonymus will please bluebirds, warblers, sparrows, and mockingbirds.

—from *The Backyard Bird-Lover's Guide* by Jan Mahnken

Plants Birds Love

Flowers and Herbs
aster
cosmos
evening primrose
forget-me-not
foxglove
lavender
lobelia
marjoram
petunia
poppy
sunflower
thistle
thyme

Trees
alder
beech
birch
oak
poplar
willow

Shrubs
bearberry
dogwood
elderberry
flowering Japanese quince
hawthorn
holly
honeysuckle
juniper
nettle
rose
scarlet firethorn

Vines
bittersweet (invasive)
grape
ivy
trumpet vine

—from *The Backyard Birdhouse Book*
by René and Christyna M. Laubach

HUMMINGBIRD GARDENS

Choose hot-colored flowers with tubular structures, such as foxgloves and bee balm.

Hummingbirds will eagerly visit hanging baskets full of fuchsias.

Perennial Favorites of Hummingbirds

Red-hued varieties of the following perennials attract hummingbirds and supply nectar as well.

beardtongue	garden phlox
bee balm	globe thistle
bellflower	hollyhock
betony	iris, bearded
bouncing bet	larkspur
butterfly weed	lily
campion	loosestrife
carnation	lupine
catmint	pinks
columbine	poppy
coralbells	sage
daylily	sweet William
foxglove	

Designing a Hummingbird Garden

It's true that many hummingbirds have a preference for red flowers, and for a very good reason. They have learned that red flowers frequently have more nectar than others. Ruby-throated hummingbirds have the strongest attraction to red, while this characteristic is less pronounced in many of the western species. However, hummingbirds also feed at pink, orange, purple, yellow, and even white blossoms. In short, there are innumerable tubular-shaped flowers that can justly be called hummingbird flowers.

Obviously, not all flowers that attract hummingbirds will be hardy in your area. But if you're among those lucky enough to live in a zone suitable to a wide range of plant life, your selection will be limited only by personal preference and space considerations.

Choosing Plants

When choosing plants for your hummingbird garden, select varieties with overlapping periods of bloom. You can select combinations of annuals, perennials, flowering shrubs, vines, and even some vegetables and herbs. Plant species that are native to your region, especially wildflowers. These are much better nectar producers than non-native plants and cultivars.

To ensure an adequate supply of nectar at all times, plant a variety of flower producers in sizable numbers of each. Nectar production in some plants can slow or stop altogether when it's too hot, too cold, too wet, or too dry.

Most gardens have a combination of herbaceous perennials and annuals. Although perennials reappear year after year, they bloom for only three or four weeks in any one season, whereas many annuals produce flowers all summer long. Although not every flower in a hummingbird garden needs to be red, a patch of bright red blossoms will be a highly visible sign to hummingbirds that your garden is an excellent source of food.

Laying Out Your Garden

Once you choose hummingbird-attracting plants appropriate for your region, zone, and soil conditions, you're ready to begin breaking ground. Remember that hummingbirds prefer areas with trees and/or shrubs that provide perching locations, sheltering foliage, and protected roosting sites. The ideal hummingbird habitat has about half full sun and one-quarter each of full shade and partial shade.

Group the plants in your garden so the blossoms are easily accessible to hummingbirds, with ample room for hovering and flight maneuvering. Flowers are more visually interesting when they're tiered, with the tallest in back and the shorter ones in front. A tiered design also provides better hummingbird access to all the blossoms.

Don't overlook decks and porches, or even apartment balconies. These are potential hummingbird garden sites. Hummingbirds are fearless creatures that will visit container plants and hanging baskets as often as they do more traditionally embedded flora.

The Life of a Hummingbird

If asked to name the most captivating creatures on our planet, most of us would be hard pressed to top hummingbirds. Their ethereal qualities include:

- *Minute size.* Some species weigh only a fraction of an ounce.
- *Beauty.* Iridescent plumage, courtesy of special feather structures.
- *Aerobatic abilities.* They fly in *any* direction, including backward.
- *Migratory feats.* Some species fly nonstop across the Gulf of Mexico.
- *Appetites.* They eat half their weight in sugar every day.
- *Aggression.* They're fierce protectors of their territories and nests.

Food. Hummingbirds are extremely active creatures with an astonishing metabolic rate that requires high caloric intake of both nectar and insects. This means hundreds of food forays during their waking hours, primarily to flowers.

Water. Hummingbirds need to bathe, and they are resourceful in employing water sources that match their tiny size—such as beads of water left on leaves after a rain, or the fine spray from a waterfall. Hummingbirds prefer moving water and are fond of flying through the spray of lawn sprinklers. Set up a sprinkler for a hummingbird bath, using a nozzle that gives off a continuous fine spray.

Shade and shelter. We think of hummingbirds as being constantly on the wing, but they spend about as much time resting as feeding. Males rest on exposed branches, clotheslines, and TV antennas, but females and immature birds seek the shade and protection of foliage.

Nesting sites. It's doubtful that you'll ever see a hummingbird nest. If you do see one, you may not realize it. The nests are tiny structures 1 to 1½ inches in diameter. They are usually lichen-covered, and are so effectively camouflaged that you would assume a nest is simply a knot on a branch. Hummingbirds nest in deciduous and evergreen trees, anywhere from 4 to 50 feet up.

rufous hummingbird

ruby-throated hummingbird

Anna's hummingbird

Allen's hummingbird

black-chinned hummingbird

—from *Grow a Hummingbird Garden* by Dale Evva Gelfand

Wildflowers for Hummingbirds

It's likely that hummingbird-attracting wildflowers are already established in or near your yard. You can help them thrive by thinning or pruning your trees to let in more light and watering wildflowers during dry spells. See p. 243 for a sample garden plan, and here are some classic hummingbird favorites:

bee balm
buttercup
cardinal flower
evening primrose
fireweed
paintbrush

Eastern Wildflowers
Canada lily
fire pink
impatiens
lily

Western Wildflowers
California fuchsia
California Indian pink
canon delphinium
coast lily
coyote mint
crimson columbine
gentian
grand collomia
hummingbird's trumpet

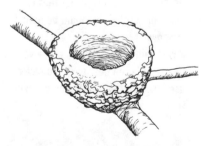

A hummingbird nest, shown here actual size, is thimble-sized, made of lichen, moss, and down, all lashed together with spider silk.

YOUR GARDEN, YARD & ORCHARD

BUILDING NEST BOXES

Tufted titmice (above) and their relatives, bridled and plain titmice, are cavity nesters—birds that nest in holes in trees and will accept nest boxes. The box should have a 4-inch-square floor and a 1½-inch-diameter entrance hole, and it should be placed 5 to 15 feet above the ground.

Nestbox Don'ts

- Never purchase a box with a perch, which will give predators access to the interior.
- Never purchase a nest box that is glued or stapled; it should be nailed or screwed.
- Never paint, stain, or use preservatives inside the nest box, and never use insect spray. The fumes may kill young birds and adults.

Keys to Nest Box Success: Box Design and Location

Watching birds select a nest site, build a nest, and raise young can be a fascinating and exciting experience. It can also provide immense satisfaction to nest box owners, who are doing their part to help restore the natural balance that humanity has disturbed.

Location, Location, Location!

Before you place a nest box, consider whether you have the proper habitat for the type of bird you are trying to attract. Knowing the bird's needs will assist you in placing the box appropriately. Not all cavity nesters will accept housing placed in the middle of a yard or meadow, away from the protective cover of woods and underbrush. Keep in mind that most woodland species favor having shrubs near the nest box. Remember, too, that birds need to find food in the area of your nest box.

Think Like a Bird

Good nest boxes should be made from ¾-inch-thick untreated lumber. If you build one, put the wood's rough surface on the inside to provide footholds for the birds. Cutting a series of horizontal grooves into the wood below the entrance can make it easier for young birds to fledge.

The roofs of nest boxes should be sloping and extend beyond the sides of the box. Depending on the design, the roof should extend 2 to 5 inches beyond the front of the box. This will exclude driving rain, wind, and sun, and will help deter predators. Generally, the sides of the box should extend at least ¼ inch beyond the floor to allow water to drip off.

Make sure the entry hole is large enough to admit the bird you are trying to attract, but small enough to exclude undesirable species. If you are familiar with the birds that frequent the area of the nestbox, you will have a fair idea as to your possible tenants.

Monitoring

If you have left your nest box up over the winter, inspect it in late winter or early spring. If the box has been claimed by small mammals such as mice, don a rubber glove, stand upwind, and remove the contents. Avoid inhaling the dust inside.

You can check the contents of the box occasionally during breeding season, as long as it's not when the eggs are being incubated or the young are just about to fly. They may take off prematurely if disturbed.

—from *The Backyard Birdhouse Book* by René and Christyna M. Laubach

Perches are not recommended for nest boxes.

Build a Bluebird House

Although this birdhouse is designed for bluebirds, it may instead be occupied by tree swallows, wrens, chickadees, or titmice. Attracting *any* native species to your nest box should be considered a success. All native birds have their charm and beauty, and each has a special niche in our ecosystem.

1. Cut this birdhouse from a 6-foot piece of board that is 1 inch thick and 6½ inches wide. In marking for cutting, allow for the kerf, the width of the cut made by your saw—usually about ⅛ of an inch. You'll also need a 3-inch brass hinge, six ¾-inch metal screws, and a handful of 1¾-inch galvanized or aluminum nails.

2. Connect the back and the top of the nest box with a 3-inch brass hinge and six ¾-inch metal screws.

3. Use 1¾-inch galvanized or aluminum nails to assemble your nest box. Be careful that nails do not protrude into nest box cavity.

4. Air vents and drainage holes are essential for the health and comfort of the residents of the box.

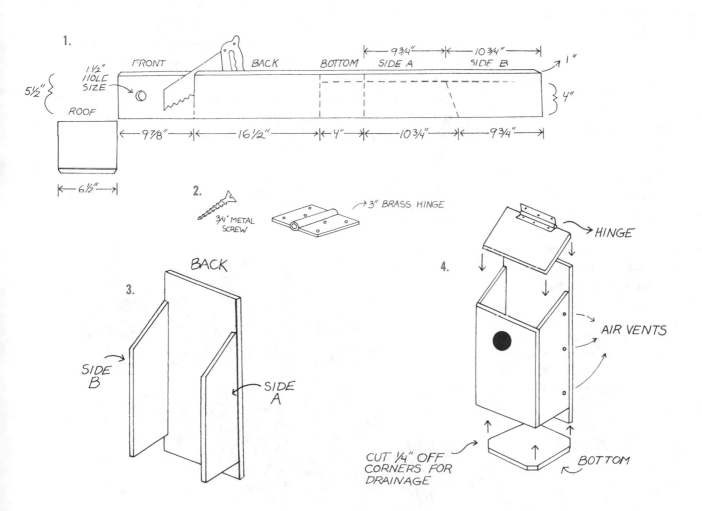

—from *Everything You Never Learned about Birds* by Rebecca Rupp

BUTTERFLY GARDENS

Butterflies are sun worshipers, so plant your butterfly garden in a sunny spot. If you are planting a window garden for butterflies, place it on the south wall of the house.

Although butterflies do need some shade when the sun is scorching, for the most part they spend their time in the sunshine. This is because they need to raise their body temperature to 86° to 104° in order to fly.

Raise Your Own Butterflies

In nature, very few caterpillars survive to become butterflies. If you find a caterpillar, you can try raising it yourself.

1. Place the caterpillar in a glass jar or old aquarium. Cover the container with screening, secured with a rubber band.
2. Supply your caterpillar with plenty of leaves from its host plant (usually the plant where you found it), and a dry twig to climb on to pupate. Remove droppings from the container daily.
3. When the butterfly emerges from its chrysalis, remove the top and set the container outside. The butterfly will need some time to dry its wings and raise its body temperature, but soon it will be airborne.

Grow a Garden for Butterflies

You don't need a large area to have a successful butterfly garden teeming with winged color: You can grow one in a window box, from hanging pots on a terrace or balcony, or from a patch of yard.

Most butterfly flowers are easy to grow and require little care. Mix together host plants and nectar flowers to increase the number of butterfly visitors.

Host plants. The plants on which a butterfly will lay eggs are called host plants. When the eggs hatch, the plant provides the food and shelter the caterpillars need to survive. Some caterpillars will feed on only one specific plant species, while others can feed on many different plants within the same family.

For example, clover is the host plant for many species, including clouded sulphurs, gray hairstreaks, and eastern tailed blues. Check with resources such as the National Audubon Society or any local nature or conservation association, for information about caterpillar plant preferences in your area.

Nectar plants. The plants adult butterflies feed on are called nectar plants. The chart opposite lists annuals and perennials that are popular nectar plants.

Color. Butterflies often prefer purple, pink, yellow, and white, so keep these colors in mind when planning your garden. Because color plays such a vital role in attracting butterflies, plant groups or masses of a plant in one particular color, rather than single plants of different colors. A group of purple coneflower and a mass of white phlox will attract more butterflies than single flowers in each color.

Herbs. Grow your favorite herbs in the butterfly garden, trimming them in rotation so there is always at least one herb in flower. Plant extra dill, parsley, and fennel as host plants for the black swallowtail butterfly.

A butterfly garden in summer with (clockwise from upper left) purple coneflower, lupine, tickseed, Oriental poppy, and butterflyweed.

BUTTERFLY FLOWERS

PLANT	HARDINESS	HEIGHT	BLOOMING SEASON	BLOSSOM COLOR
Aster	Zones 2–9	6 inches–6 feet	spring–late autumn	white, lavender, purple, pink, blue, rose
Baja fairy duster	Zone 10	to 4 feet	midsummer	purple
Bee balm	Zones 4–9	2–4 feet	summer	usually red
Black-eyed Susan	Zones 3–9	2–3 feet	summer	yellow, orange
Coneflower	Zones 3–9	2–4 feet	early summer–autumn	white, red, pink, light purple
Cosmos	Zones 7–10	1–4 feet	late spring–early autumn	pink, red, orange, yellow, white
Dogbane	Zones 3–9	1–4 feet	midsummer	pink, orange, red, purple, white
Eupatorium	Zones 3–8	2–10 feet	midsummer–early autumn	white, purple, lavender
Fleabane	Zones 2–9	4–36 inches	summer–early autumn	pink, purple, white, yellow, orange
French marigold	annual in any zone	6–18 inches	summer–frost	yellow/orange
Gayfeather	Zones 3–10	2–6 feet	summer–early autumn	pink-purple
Globe thistle, small	Zones 3–9	1–3 feet	summer–autumn	blue
Goldenrod	Zones 3–9	6 inches–8 feet	summer–early autumn	yellow
Heliotrope	Zones 9–10	1–4 feet	early spring–early autumn	violet to deep purple
Honesty	Zones 6–9	1–3 feet	summer	purple, white
Impatiens	annual in any zone	12–24 inches	late spring–frost	pink, white
Mexican sunflower	annual in any zone	2–6 feet	midsummer–frost	orange
Milkweed	Zones 3–10	1–6 feet	summer	orange, other
Morning glory	annual in any zone	5–8 feet	summer	blue, purple, rose, white
Mountain mint	Zones 4–8	to 3 feet	summer–frost	white
Pentas	annual in any zone	to 4 feet	early spring–frost	pink, red, lilac, white
Phlox	Zones 3–9	5 inches–4 feet	spring–early autumn	red, pink, purple, white, blue
Pincushion flower	Zones 3–9	6–24 inches	summer–early autumn	purple, pink, white, light blue
Red bird-of-paradise	Zones 10–11	to 10 feet	summer	red, orange, yellow
Red valerian	Zones 4–9	to 3 feet	spring–midsummer	red
Scarlet sage	Zones 8–10	2–3 feet	summer–autumn	red, white
Sunflower	Zones 3–10	3–10 feet	mid summer–mid-autumn	yellow, orange, cream
Sweet William	annual in any zone	6–24 inches	late spring–summer	red, white, violet, pink
Tickseed	Zones 3–10	8–30 inches	summer–early autumn	yellow, orange
Verbena	Zones 3–10	4–24 inches	late spring–frost	pink, white, purple, red
Zinnia	annual in any zone	8–36 inches	summer–frost	light pink, white, red, orange

YOUR GARDEN, YARD & ORCHARD

16

LAWN CARE

INSTALLING A NEW LAWN • TACKLING WEED PROBLEMS
REJUVENATING YOUR LAWN • LAWN ALTERNATIVES

I grew up near New York City, on a 60 x 110' lot. Every lawn was manicured, and when chemical lawn treatment emerged, so did a ready market, seeking "all green, and no weeds." Increasingly, we're learning the value of the natural or untamed lawn. True, it's a treat to run barefoot in your backyard, but letting a lawn go to pasture, creating a wildflower meadow, and introducing patches of ground cover and low-maintenance perennials will create a more interesting environment.

—John Storey

Stuart Franklin believes you can have a lawn that is beautiful and healthy at the same time if you simply understand how grass grows and what it needs to thrive. Stuart's book is called, fittingly, Building a Healthy Lawn. *He lives in western New York State.*

Who says watching grass grow is dull? For anyone who has a lawn, knowing how grass grows and what kind of grass is growing can save a lot of time, effort, and money.

This can be achieved by understanding the watering, fertilizing, and mowing needs of various grasses, as well as the diseases that plague them. Understanding how grass grows can help you work with nature, not against it.

Grasses survive because they are different from many other plants. If other plants are mowed or grazed off almost to the ground, they die. But grasses do not grow from their top ends, as most plants do. That makes all the difference.

Grass grows from a crown that is just above ground level but low enough to escape mowers and grazers. Growing right up from the center of the crown is the leaf sheath, which is wrapped around the stem. As the stem grows, the leaf blades unwrap and grow away from the sheath, forming the foliage that most of us think of as grass.

Since the growth springs from the crown and not the tip, we can cut grass without killing it, as long as we don't cut it too short. Cutting the lawn too short can make your lawn shallow-rooted and subject to drought. This is because the more grass that is allowed to grow above the ground, the larger the root mass that will develop underground.

Cool-season grasses. Grasses that grow best in 60° to 75°F and can survive freezing winters. Grasses go semidormant in areas where summers are hot

Crown. Main growth center for the aboveground portion of a grass plant, located just above the soil surface

Herbicide. Substance used to kill plants

Photosynthesis. The process by which a plant makes carbohydrates (food) and oxygen from sunlight, carbon dioxide, and water. Usually takes place in leaves

Root zone. The top 6 inches of soil below the crown of a lawn

Thatch. A matted layer of dead grass stems, roots, and clippings, that sits on top of the ground, choking out grass

Warm-season grasses. Grasses that grow best in 80° to 95°F. They go dormant in winter, even if temperatures rarely reach freezing

Laying the Groundwork for a New Lawn

The best times to sow a new lawn are spring and fall. In the fall, do not leave it until too late because grass needs a week or more to germinate and six weeks or more to become established.

Careful soil preparation is essential in building a fine lawn. The more care you put into the preparation, the less maintenance you will have in the long run. Here are the basic steps:

- Loosen the soil with a rototiller. Set its blades to cut 6 inches deep, tilling in a crisscross pattern.

- Remove all roots, stones, and other debris, and rake well to remove any remaining debris.

- Give the whole area a fine grading. The easiest way to do this is with an old tire attached to a rope. Let the tire lie flat on its side and draw it over the seedbed several times to level it.

- Water the area well and sprinkle it thoroughly once a day for at least a week. The water settles freshly tilled soil and encourages weed seeds to germinate.

- Three weeks after the first tilling, repeat the tilling, raking, and grading procedure. This not only loosens the soil further, but also kills the young weed seeds that germinated. Do not use an herbicide on the weeds, because it can affect germination of grass seed for a year or more.

- Consider adding new topsoil, either to raise the ground level or to improve soil quality.

- Test the pH of the soil with a soil-testing kit. Soil that tests below 7.0 pH is acid; if the pH is below 5.0, the soil will not sustain a lawn. You can decrease its acidity by adding lime. A rule of thumb is to spread 50 to 80 pounds of lime per 1,000 square feet of lawn, but follow package directions.

- If your soil is extremely heavy and claylike with poor drainage, amend the soil with manure, compost, coarse sand, or very well-rotted sawdust. Or add a new topsoil mulch 2 inches deep over the whole area.

—from *The Big Book of Gardening Skills*

Lawn-Seeding Tips

Grade the lawn area before seeding by dragging an old tire over it.

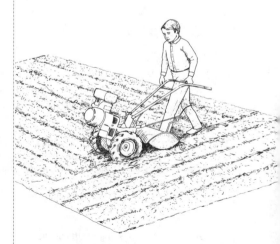

Give the area two tillings, first passing over the area in one direction, then again at right angles to the first tilling.

INSTALLING A NEW LAWN

GRASSES AT A GLANCE

COOL-SEASON GRASSES

Annual Ryegrass
Best for: A nurse grass for permanent cultivars; an excellent cover crop for vegetable gardens.
Appearance: Fine to coarse texture depending on variety; gets clumpy over its season of growth.
Strong points: Dark green color; many varieties heat tolerant.
Weak points: Coarse-bladed varieties tear on mowing.

Chewings Fescue
Best for: Shady areas and mixes.
Appearance: Fine, thin, upright blades.
Strong points: Tolerates close mowing and traffic; requires little fertilizer or water once established.
Weak points: Susceptible to disease in areas with warm, moist summers. Water in early morning to prevent disease problems.

Creeping Fescue (red fescue)
Best for: Blends well with bluegrass in seed mixes.
Appearance: Fine blades; deep green color.
Strong points: Grows well in sun or shade and in a variety of soils.
Weak points: Susceptible to diseases in hot, moist areas. Leaf blades tear easily during mowing.

Hard Fescue
Best for: Low-maintenance areas.
Appearance: A bunch grass with medium green color.
Strong points: Tolerates shade, heat, drought, and many diseases better than other fine-leafed fescues. Also has low fertilizer requirements and is good on poor soils.
Weak points: Slow to get established.

Kentucky Bluegrass
Best for: Sunny areas.
Appearance: Deep green, fine-textured, attractive.
Strong points: Spreads well; forms strong sod. New varieties tolerate drought, close mowing, and are disease resistant.
Weak points: Not for shade; can suffer in heat and may go dormant or die in extreme conditions. Older varieties are high maintenance.

Perennial Ryegrass (turf type)
Best for: Playing fields, high traffic areas.
Appearance: Newer varieties are deeper green than many other grasses.
Strong points: Establishes quickly; new varieties are insect and disease resistant.
Weak points: Winter-kills in cold climates.

Tall Fescue
Best for: Play lawns, high-traffic areas
Appearance: Medium to coarse texture, green year round.
Strong points: Good shade and moderate drought tolerance.
Weak points: Can grow taller than the varieties it is blended with.

WARM-SEASON GRASSES

Bahia Grass
Best for: Coastal areas, sandy soils, areas prone to erosion.
Appearance: Coarse open plants that need frequent mowing.
Strong points: Thick root network helps control erosion, resist drought, and wear well.
Weak points: Not easy to mow; weedy appearance.

Bermuda Grass
Best for: Warm-season lawns.
Appearance: A spreading, coarse- to medium-textured grass that needs frequent mowing.
Strong points: Easy to grow and requires little maintenance.
Weak points: Poor shade tolerance; can be invasive.

Centipede Grass
Best for: Low-maintenance lawns on poor soil.
Appearance: Coarse texture with light green color.
Strong points: Crowds out weeds; needs little mowing.
Weak points: May yellow in low temperatures.

Hybrid or Improved Bermuda Grass
Best for: Soft, fine-textured lawns.
Appearance: Spreading grass with deep green color and fine texture.
Strong points: More attractive; stays green longer than other grasses.
Weak points: Not for shade; requires more watering, fertilizing, and mowing than common Bermuda grass.

St. Augustine Grass
Best for: Shady or coastal areas and places with alkaline soil
Appearance: Thick-bladed; forms dense but rather spongy turf.
Strong points: Grows fast; tolerates shade and salt.
Weak points: Susceptible to St. Augustine grass virus.

Zoysia Grass
Best for: Anywhere a dense, wiry lawn is desired.
Appearance: A very thick, deep green spreading grass.
Strong points: Tolerates heat and drought; resists insects and disease.
Weak points: Slow to establish and turns straw-colored where summers are short and cool.

—adapted from *Down-to-Earth Natural Lawn Care* by Dick Raymond and *Building a Healthy Lawn* by Stuart Franklin

Choosing Seed

There are two major groups of lawn grasses. Cool-season grasses are sold for Canada and the northern two-thirds of the United States. They grow most rapidly in the spring and fall. Warm-season varieties are used in warm areas such as the lower third of the United States and flourish from March through August; in the fall, they turn brown and go dormant.

Local garden centers sell only lawn grass mixtures that are appropriate for your area. The available blends are almost always mixed by a commercial wholesaler, who chooses varieties of seeds that ensure continuous growth. Don't try to mix your own blend; leave it to the experts.

Always purchase a little more seed than seems necessary. More expensive grass seed is always the better buy, because it is almost totally free of weed seeds and the seeds of undesirable grasses.

Sowing Grass Seed

Broadcast lawn seed evenly over the entire area to be seeded. For a regular-size home lawn, use a hand-cranked spreader. This is a spinning disk that throws the seed out in a 5- to 6-foot arc. Crank at a steady speed and walk at a steady pace to ensure an even spread. Touch up the edges with a bit of hand-sowing afterward.

After the seed is sown, walk backward over the area with a garden rake. Rake in and evenly spread the seed as you go. Rake gently and lightly, in a row-by-row pattern, making sure you don't overlap where you have already raked. Do this only once. Raking gives the seeds better contact with the soil, so that germination will be more uniform.

—from *The Big Book of Gardening Skills*

A broadcast spreader has a whirling wheel beneath the seed container, which throws the seed evenly over a wide area. You can use it to spread fertilizer and lime, as well as seed.

SODDING AND SEEDING: PROS AND CONS

PROS

Sod
- Provides an instant green covering
- Establishes itself quickly
- Can be installed anytime during the growing season
- Can be placed on slopes and will not wash away
- Smothers many potential weeds near the soil surface

Seed
- Almost unlimited variety available to match needs
- Less expensive than sod
- Can be sown quickly over large areas
- Will normally grow on its own with no further help after sowing seeds

CONS

Sod
- Higher cost
- Very limited choice of grasses
- May be so matted that it needs aerating
- Might bring in insects, disease, or weeds

Seed
- Demands more time and water
- Subject to weed competition
- Hard to plant on slopes
- Can't be installed between late spring and midsummer
- Usually needs spot-seeding for areas that don't fill in

—from *Building a Healthy Lawn*

Common Lawn-Seeding Mistakes

To help you avoid them, here are the most common mistakes made when establishing a new lawn.

- Applying too little seed
- Using old seed
- Using the wrong type of seed for climate and conditions
- Using inferior bargain seed
- Poor soil preparation

—from *Building a Healthy Lawn* by Stuart Franklin

INSTALLING A NEW LAWN

Laying Sod

The quickest way to convert a piece of bare ground into a lush lawn is to lay down sod. These pre-grown rolls of grass are easy to install. They look good instantly and protect the soil from washing away. Autumn is an excellent time to lay sod, since the grass will have a month or so to take hold before winter's cold halts growth for the season.

Sod is sold in strips 2 to 10 feet long and 1 to 2 feet wide. Because the strips dry out quickly, pick them up or arrange for delivery as near as possible to the day you are going to lay them. In hot weather you'll have to get them down within a day; in cool weather, within two to three days. Keep stored sod strips damp but not saturated.

The strips will be less likely to dry out as you work if you tackle the project on a cool, cloudy day. Before you begin, however, check the site's moisture level. The soil should be just moist enough to crumble in your hand with slight pressure. If it is too wet, wait for it to dry a bit; if it is too dry, sprinkle it thoroughly and start the job the next day.

1. Preparing the ground. Do not expect sod strips simply dropped on top of the ground to grow. You have to prepare the site first. If the soil is covered with heavy weeds or existing lawn, strip it off with a shovel or a sod stripper to make rototilling easier.

Before tilling, broadcast any lime or sulfur needed to adjust the soil pH, then spread a 3-inch layer of organic material such as rotted manure, compost, dampened peat moss, or spent mushroom soil.

Rototill the patch first lengthwise, then crosswise to loosen the soil to a depth of 6 inches. Do not overtill. Your objective is to turn the soil into pea-size granules, not dust.

Next, spread fertilizer on the ground at the rate of 25 pounds per 1,000 square feet. Use a high-phosphorus fertilizer to promote root growth. Then rototill once more to incorporate the fertilizer into the top 3 inches of soil.

Finally, rake the surface smooth, discarding rocks and other debris, and firm the soil by running an empty lawn roller over the surface.

2. Laying the first row. Place the first row of sod along a straight line. If you can, use your driveway or a path as a guide. Otherwise, use a string pulled taut between two stakes.

Unroll each sod strip, taking care to avoid tearing it, and press it firmly into position. Sod will shrink slightly after it has been laid, so don't stretch it as you put it down—especially where edges meet. Don't let it buckle, either. If you are worried about the strips drying out as you work, sprinkle each one with the hose once it's laid.

1. Rototill the lawn area, tilling first in one direction and then again at right angles to the first pass.

2. Unroll the sod strip and press it firmly into position.

3. Laying subsequent rows. Lay a plank on the first row to distribute your weight as you work on the adjacent row. Snug the next row tightly against the first row, allowing for shrinkage. To avoid concentrating breaks in the sod in one area, stagger the joints between the pieces so they do not align with those in the first row.

Continue other rows the same way. When you reach the edge of your new lawn, cut the sod to size with either a sharp spade or a serrated knife such as a bread knife.

4. Finishing touches. When you have covered the ground with sod, go over it lightly with a partially weighted roller to get rid of air pockets and to ensure good contact between the sod and the underlying soil. A roller that is too heavy will damage the sod and ruin the soil structure. Roll first at a right angle to the direction of the strips, then in the same direction as the strips. After rolling, fluff up the grass blades lightly with a bamboo rake.

5. Watering. Do not be lulled into complacency by the sod's established look. The top inch must not dry out while its roots are knitting into the underlying soil.

As soon as you finish rolling and raking, set up a sprinkler and water to a depth of 6 inches. Every sunny, warm day for the next few weeks, water lightly around midday; the developing lawn is most vulnerable to losing moisture then. Pay special attention to sod near pavement; it dries out quickest and may need heavier spot watering. As the sod's roots grow into the soil, approach a normal watering schedule. Keep off the sod as much as possible for the few weeks it takes to establish.

3. Kneeling on a plank, continue to roll out strips of sod, butting each strip tightly against the one next to it.

4. Roll the sod and then fluff it up with a bamboo rake.

5. Water well, and stay off the sod for a few weeks after planting.

—from *Year-Round Gardening Projects,* text by Lee Reich;
illustrations by Elayne Sears

TACKLING WEED PROBLEMS

19 COMMON WEEDS AND THEIR EARTH-SAFE CONTROLS

ANNUAL BLUEGRASS
Characteristics
Shallow-rooted annual
   that sprouts early
How to Control
Mow higher to crowd plants out; aerate soil
   and hand-pull.

BERMUDA GRASS
Characteristics
A narrow-leaf lawn grass that can become
   invasive
How to Control
Dig out clumps and reseed.

BROAD- AND NARROW-LEAVED PLANTAIN
Characteristics
Broadleaf weeds that fill in bare areas
How to Control
Hand-pull; overseed to thicken up lawn; use
   herbicidal soap.

CINQUEFOIL
Characteristics
Broadleaf perennial with leaves that resemble
   strawberry leaves; cinquefoil has five leaves,
   strawberry three
How to Control
Amend soil with organic matter to improve soil
   and thicken turf.

COMMON AND MOUSE-EAR CHICKWEED
Characteristics
Common chickweed is a broadleaf annual that
   prefers shade and cool, moist weather; mouse-
   ear is a perennial that withstands summer heat.
How to Control
Hand-pull plants; mow often; and overseed with
   vigorous, spreading grasses; use herbicidal
   soap.

COMMON PURSLANE
Characteristics
Thick, fleshy leaves; an annual broadleaf that
   looks like a prostrate-growing jade plant
How to Control
Pull individual plants and reseed. Water lawn
   more frequently.

CRABGRASS (HAIRY AND SMOOTH)
Characteristics
Both are grassy, narrowleaf annual weeds;
   low-growing and can't stand shade
How to Control
Mow lawn higher and water less frequently;
   hand-pull where possible and overseed with
   a vigorous, spreading variety.

CREEPING BENT GRASS
Characteristics
A perennial, fine-bladed horizontal-growing grass
   similar to nimblewill and Bermuda grass
How to Control
Keep soil surface dry and the bent grass raked.

DALLIS GRASS
Characteristics
Perennial with light green, wide-bladed leaves
How to Control
Hand-pull where possible; amend soil with
   organic matter and reduce fertilizer in spring.

DANDELION
Characteristics
A perennial, broadleaf weed with yellow flowers
   that turn into white seed puffs
How to Control
Best prevention is a thick, healthy lawn; dig indi-
   vidual plants by hand; mow more frequently.

GROUND IVY
Characteristics
Broadleaf perennial with mint smell and purple
   flowers
How to Control
Hand-pull, and improve soil with applications
   of organic matter; water less frequently.

PROSTRATE KNOTWEED
Characteristics
Broadleaf annual that can form a thick mat; also
   called wine grass
How to Control
Amend soil with organic matter and aerate;
   hand-pull plants when soil is moist.

NIMBLE WILL
Characteristics
Perennial, grassy, shallow-rooted
How to Control
Hand-pull.

SPOTTED SPURGE
Characteristics
Annual broadleaf that tolerates fertile or infertile soil
How to Control
Hand-pull plants when soil is moist.

NUT SEDGE
Characteristics
Perennial with light green, wide-bladed leaves
How to Control
Hand-pull and and improve soil with applications of organic matter.

TALL FESCUE
Characteristics
A coarse perennial grass considered a weed when not wanted in a lawn
How to Control
Keep lawn thick; dig out individual plants.

OXALIS
Characteristics
Perennial, broadleaf plant that resembles clover
How to Control
Improve soil with applications of organic matter.

VERONICA
Characteristics
Broad-leaved, spreading weed with perennial and annual varieties
How to Control
Control by establishing thick turf.

WHITE CLOVER
Characteristics
Broadleaf perennial with white flowers that attract bees
How to Control
Seed with vigorous, spreading varieties and mow shorter.

—adapted from *Building a Healthy Lawn* by Stuart Franklin

YOUR GARDEN, YARD & ORCHARD

REJUVENATING YOUR LAWN

Three Useful Lawn Tools

Aerator. Use to open up the turf for fertilizer, air, and water.

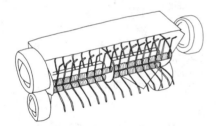

Power rake. Use to break up light cases of thatch.

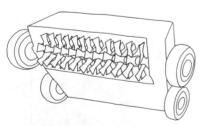

Vertical mower. Metal blades slice through thatch, thin it, and bring it to the surface.

Improving a Problem Lawn

Improving a poorly growing lawn is not as difficult as you might think. Most lawn problems are caused by forgetting to do a few simple things, such as aerating.

Aerating and Improving the Soil

In spring or fall, rent an aerator-spiker from a garden center. This tool takes out little cores of soil about ½ inch in diameter and 2 to 3 inches long.

Next, to benefit the roots, add a topdressing of sand, peat, and some good compost or aged manure. This fills in the holes made when you aerated and improves your soil quality.

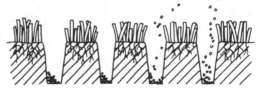

A cross section of aerated lawn

Dethatching the Lawn

Thatch is a layer of dead plant material on the surface of soil. When it builds up more than ¾ inch deep, it slows or even stops the penetration of water, air, and fertilizer into the soil. The lawn begins to show dry, dead patches; when you walk on it, the ground feels springy.

Dethatching should be done every three to four years. You can rent a dethatching machine, which is about the size of a lawn mower and is quite easy to operate. It has 8 to 12 blades that cut through the thatch and bring it to the surface. After the thatch is removed, apply fertilizer and water the lawn daily. The lawn should recover completely in about six weeks.

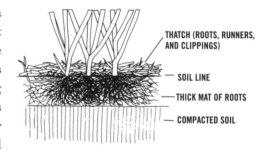

THATCH (ROOTS, RUNNERS, AND CLIPPINGS)

SOIL LINE

THICK MAT OF ROOTS

COMPACTED SOIL

—from *The Big Book of Gardening Skills*

Lawn Diseases

Anything that kills soil life makes a lawn more prone to disease. Is it any wonder that lawns treated with chemical fertilizer need frequent spraying? And, of course, the disease-controlling sprays kill off even more soil life. The only real solution is to bring your lawn into a healthy condition and then keep it that way.

Is It a Disease?

Diagnosing lawn diseases can be tricky. Usually you'll see patches or spots of brown grass, or grass blades that are wilted or coated with some type of growth. Consult a trained professional to identify the problem and offer ways you can control it.

Sometimes spraying soap and water will do the trick. Or perhaps one of the natural products on the market will solve the problem. If the disease is caused by thatch, overly wet soil, compaction, or incorrect pH, you can rectify the problem without directly attacking the disease organism.

Natural Disease Prevention

There are some simple and specific ways to prevent lawn disease from occurring.

- Plant a mixture of grasses rather than just a single variety.
- Plant disease-resistant varieties.
- Avoid overwatering.
- Water the lawn sufficiently.
- Make sure there is a free flow of air by thinning out dense shrub or tree growth to open up your yard.
- Remove thatch.
- Try a soap spray occasionally.

—from *Building a Healthy Lawn* by Stuart Franklin

Spot-Seeding a Lawn

Spot-seed when you need to reestablish small areas of lawn, such as thin and tire-damaged sections.

Prepare the spot. First, pull out the weeds. Then scratch up the soil with a heavy dirt rake or cultivating tool. If there is already some good grass growing, work around it.

Next, mix 1 part sphagnum peat moss or compost with 2 parts good garden soil. Add 1½ cups of balanced organic fertilizer per bushel of soil. Spread this mixture over the bare spot until it is slightly higher than the soil level of the surrounding grass. Gently mix it into the scratched-up soil.

Plant the seeds. Sprinkle on your seed. Fifteen to 20 seeds per square inch is about right. Bury the seed ⅛ to ¼ inch into the soil. Dragging a rake with the tines inverted is a good way to work the seeds deeper. Now gently tamp the soil until it's level with the surrounding soil. Don't compact the soil, because you want water to soak in easily. Now throw some extra seed just to the outside of the spot-seeded area to help the new grass blend in when it grows.

—from *The Big Book of Gardening Skills*

Common Lawn Pests

Healthy soils and lawns are teeming with insect life. Most insects are harmless, some are beneficial, and some can harm your lawn. Here are a few damaging insects.

 Grubs. The most damaging insect is the white grub, which is the larval form of many types of beetles. Grubs destroy grass by chewing the roots off. They move slowly across the lawn, killing each grass plant in their path. If you spot the grubs in time, you can try using a biological control on them. One of the newer controls is a beneficial parasitic nematode that feeds on harmful soil pests. Milky spore powder is a sure control for Japanese beetle grubs and a few others. You can also spread 15 to 20 pounds of diatomaceous earth per 1,000 square feet of lawn up to four times a year.

 Sod webworms. The adult moths lay their eggs in the grass, then the eggs hatch into small caterpillars that chew off the grass. You'll see small dead spots on the lawn by late spring. Control sod webworms by spraying with soap and water every couple of weeks. A parasitic nematode can be used, and the caterpillar-killing bacteria Btk can also be effective. Plant endophytic grass varieties that have genetic defenses against webworms.

 Chinch bugs. Chinch bugs love thatch, and are the greatest enemy of St. Augustine grass. Fight them by fighting thatch. You can try diatomaceous earth or a parasitic nematode, but soap and water every 10 to 14 days is sufficient in most cases. Plant endophytic grass varieties that have genetic defenses against webworms.

—from *Building a Healthy Lawn*

LAWN ALTERNATIVES

Ground Covers: Not Just Another Pretty Grass

A ground cover is a bed of low-growing, spreading, or multiplying plants. These plants fill in areas rapidly and grow under conditions where grassy lawns prove impossible. They also require very little maintenance. But ground covers are not used solely for difficult lawn areas. They are often included in landscape designs as part of beds or foundation plantings. They can also provide erosion protection.

Any plant that tends to spread and isn't too high can be used as a ground cover. You can be imaginative with your choice as long as it will grow under its planting conditions. Lilies, ferns, herbs, flowers, vines, bulbs, and even special grasses can function as ground covers. Small shrubs such as low-growing junipers and euonymous can also function as ground covers by spreading over a slope or bed.

Common Ground Cover Plants

Ajuga, Carpet Bugleweed. Ajuga is found in all but the hottest climates. This 6-inch plant spreads quickly by its roots and produces dark blue flowers. It tolerates both sun and shade.

Bishop's Weed (variegated), **Snow-on-the-Mountain.** A useful ground cover in the North because it is very hardy and grows in both partial sun and shade. The foliage is green with creamy white edges. It grows to 10 inches and spreads rapidly, sending up a white flower stalk in early summer. Plants set 15 inches apart will fill in quickly.

Bluets. Also known as Quaker ladies and innocence, bluets grow in low mats in a variety of conditions. Their small, four-petaled flowers range in color from white to light blue and have a yellow eye. These plants spread slowly into large beds.

Bunchberry. In fall, the bright red bunches of berries and dark green foliage will remind you of holly. In summer, a white flower forms in the center of a cluster of six leaves. Bunchberry likes cool, moist, shady spots and very acid soil rich in humus. Unless you can duplicate its growing conditions, you won't have much luck. But if you can, divide the plants to propagate them.

Candytuft. This 8-inch evergreen is popular because of its clusters of white flowers in May and June. It spreads slowly by aboveground runners, likes sun or shade, and will grow in most of the United States.

Common Violet. This 5- to 8-inch plant grows in sun or shade. Although it can be a nuisance in a lawn, it makes an excellent ground cover that spreads rather quickly and produces pretty flowers. Quite hardy.

Creeping Lilyturf. A beautiful evergreen that grows in mid-Atlantic and southern climates. It has lavender, bell-shaped flowers on spikes up to 15 inches tall. It tolerates sun or shade, heat, salt, drought, and poor soil. Some people use it as a grass because it has similar foliage.

Crown Vetch. Along with bird's-foot trefoil, this is an excellent choice for erosion control on steep banks. It grows in a dense, 2- to 3-foot-high mass of pink flowers in summer. It is grown from seed or from crowns that are set 18 to 24 inches apart.

Dichondra. This is a favorite southern ground cover that does well where temperatures don't drop below 25°F. It forms a thick green carpet of rounded, slightly heart-shaped leaves that can be mowed to about 1½ inches. It is not good in heavily traveled areas.

While attractive, it unfortunately can provide a home for snails, slugs, cutworms, and flea beetles.

English Ivy or Baltic Ivy. A creeping ground cover that can also be a climbing vine, English ivy forms a thick (9-inch), fast-spreading evergreen mat that turns slightly purple in winter. Ivy is very useful on slopes.

Ferns. These versatile plants can 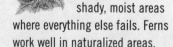 be used as foundation plantings in shady, moist areas where everything else fails. Ferns work well in naturalized areas.

Golden Moneywort, Creeping Charlie. Penny-shaped leaves form along trailing vines, which produce a yellow flower in summer. The plants are vigorous and good for holding banks. The trailing foliage cascades over walls when planted along terraces. Also used in hanging baskets and window boxes, this plant likes sun or partial shade.

Planting Procedures

Before you plant a ground cover, remove any grass from the planting area. To do this, scrape it with a hoe or dig it out, till it under, or cover it.

Prepare a bed 6 to 8 inches deep. If you're competing with tree roots, add soil and organic matter to build up the bed. Mix in at least 2 inches of organic matter. Use aged leaves, clippings, sawdust, compost, manures, and peat moss. If some of the materials aren't sufficiently aged, add a high nitrogen fertilizer to speed up decomposition. Let it work for a couple of weeks before planting.

Build your bed higher than the lawn so it will drain easily, and for aesthetic reasons as well. The smaller the plant, the closer the spacing in the bed. Keep the plants from drying out. A 1- to 2-inch layer of shredded wood mulch will conserve moisture and discourage weed growth.

—from *The Big Book of Gardening Skills*

Hosta.  Hosta grows from a clump and sends up a stalk of bell-shaped flowers that range in color from purple to white, depending upon the variety. They are often used in borders, edgings, and around the base of trees. Partial shade is best. There are varieties with very different leaf colorings, ranging from pale green with ivory to deep blue-green. Plant hostas 2 to 3 feet apart. They are very hardy.

Japanese Spurge. An 8-inch evergreen with dark, glossy leaves, this plant grows in shade or sun in all but the extremely hot and cold sections of North America. It prefers a moist, loose soil and spreads slowly with underground roots and stems to form new plants. Occasional cutting back accelerates spreading. Its white flower spikes are barely noticeable.

Lily of the Valley. 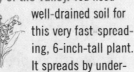 You need well-drained soil for this very fast-spreading, 6-inch-tall plant. It spreads by underground stems and dies back each fall. Each May or June it produces wonderfully scented white, bell-shaped flowers. It grows in sun or shade.

Myrtle or Periwinkle. This is a 4- to 9-inch evergreen with oval leaves along a wiry stem. Its light, violet-blue flowers bloom in late spring and early summer. It spreads by both roots and above-ground runners. It will prevent erosion once established, and it can grow in sun or shade in a slightly moist soil.

Plumbago, Leadwort. This is an adaptable ground cover that grows in sun or shade to about 10 inches. It produces blue flowers from midsummer until frost. Planted 12 to 15 inches apart, it fills in fast with dark green foliage on wiry stems. It should be cut back for the winter.

Sedum, Stonecrop. There are so many sizes and colors of sedum it is hard to believe they are all part of the same genus. They range from gold to bright red and grow from 4 or 5 inches to as tall as 24 inches. These creepers fill in rapidly and like hot, dry weather. Sedum may grow where grass won't. Plant 12 to 24 inches apart in sun or light shade.

Sweet Woodruff. This is a ground cover that smells good and grows in partially shaded, moist areas. It produces white flowers in the spring, traditionally used to make May wine. Set the plants a foot apart or a little closer.

White Clover. This clover produces a small white blossom. When heavily seeded, it makes an attractive and hardy ground cover that will smother anything else. It reseeds itself every year.

Wild Ginger. The leaves of this wildflower are heart-shaped and the stalks are fuzzy, with a brown flower near the ground. It grows very densely to about 8 inches in full shade.

Wild Thyme. This can be seeded over bald areas or transplanted as clumps. It might not take hold in damp or shady spots, but where it does it is tough and needs no mowing. Mowing does produce tiny flowers and it smells good.

—adapted from *Down-to-Earth Natural Lawn Care* by Dick Raymond and *The Big Book of Gardening Skills*

17

BERRIES AND FRUITS

STRAWBERRIES • RASPBERRIES AND BLACKBERRIES
BLUEBERRIES • GRAPES • FRUIT TREES

Our home in the Berkshires came with a dozen mature fruit trees, including apples, cherries, and pears. We lovingly cared for the orchard and gathered fruit in alternate years. One October a freak storm deposited heavy, wet snow on the trees, which still bore their summer leaves. The result was disastrous: The trees froze, snapped, and broke before we could remove the snow. Miraculously, two trees—a pear and an apple—survived. The rest became firewood to heat our home and to add special flavor to our barbecues. Martha's pear tarts and apple cobblers are a tribute to this survival of the fittest. In this chapter we begin with advice from old friends Lewis and Nancy Hill.

—John Storey

As a child Lewis Hill would raid his family's ancient apple orchard on his way home from his country school, and he learned to savor some of the old apple varieties that are rarely grown today. Later he and his wife Nancy began operating Berry Hill, a nursery in northern Vermont that for decades specialized in hardy fruit trees, berry plants, and ornamental shrubs. The Hills are the authors of many acclaimed books, including Fruits and Berries for the Home Garden.

Every spring, the same couple used to come to our nursery to buy vegetable and flower plants. They always looked longingly at the little trees and said, "If only we weren't so old, we would put in a few fruits and berries." They repeated that same line for over 15 years, and I had trouble not pointing out that if they had planted their orchard the first year, they could already have harvested a dozen crops!

The truth is, if you choose the right kinds and give them a suitable place to live and a little attention, fruit trees and berries require no more—and often less—care than other growing things.

You can plant and enjoy your own produce even if you are along in years or you have only a small lot. Dwarf fruit trees begin to bear within two or three years, and many grow to full size within an 8-foot circle. Small fruits can produce big crops within three years, and you can pick everbearing strawberries the first year.

Our orchard and berry patch are small, but each year we put hundreds of packages into the freezer and fill our root cellar as well. We appreciate our orchard and berry patch more each year.

Cane. The woody stem of various berries, grapes, and other plants

Cultivar. A cultivated variety created by cross-pollinating two different plants within a species

Girdle. To remove a strip of material or bark all around a plant, thus cutting off its water and nutrient circulation

Graft. The surgical union of two different plants or trees by attaching a branch (scion) to a rootstock

Runners. Horizontal stems with new plants along their length

Scion. The portion of a grafted plant above the rootstock

Self-fruitful. Describes a plant or variety that can be fertilized by pollen from the same variety

Growing Strawberries

If there is one fruit every homesteader and suburbanite should cultivate it is strawberries. No matter where you live, there is a variety that will thrive in your area. Though they do best in cool, moist regions, they can be grown in hot, dry climates, especially where windbreaks are provided and supplemental watering is possible during July, August, and September.

Selecting the Best-Bet Berries

There are three distinct fruiting habits in strawberries. Summer-bearers produce one large crop of fruit once during the season, usually for about two weeks. Depending on your growing season and region, you can get early-season, mid-season, or late-season bearers. Everbearers produce a crop in the spring, then either produce smaller crops every six weeks or so or produce one more crop in the fall. Alpine strawberries, the closest descendants of wild strawberries, are perennial and often grown as borders or ground covers. Unlike the other types of strawberries, they can be grown from seed and will bear throughout the growing season. Their fruits are small and often intensely flavored.

How They Grow

Strawberries require two years to produce the best fruit. If you set healthy plants in moist soil in a prepared bed in early spring, they will produce new roots in a few days, followed by several new leaves of normal size.

For most varieties, runners begin to emerge in June, forming new plants that take root near the original plant. New runners grow from the new plants, and in this way a succession of new plants is soon growing around the original.

Plants produce blossoms the first year, and these will develop into fruit if not pinched off. Pinching them off will encourage your plants to develop strong root systems and vigorous growth. Your reward will be next season's abundant crop of large, healthy, delicious berries.

In the spring of the fruiting year, buds that developed the previous fall develop into blossoms. The first one to open on a cluster contains the most pistils (female elements) and becomes the largest fruit with the most seeds. The next and later ones become successively smaller fruits.

—from *Grow the Best Strawberries* by Louise Riotte

The Best Strawberries by Region

The following strawberries are renowned for their excellent flavor.

South and Gulf Coast
Tangi (medium to large)

Mid-Atlantic Coast
Pocahontas (medium to large, bright red)
Raritan (medium to large, firm, bright red)
Surecrop (medium to large, dark red)

Northeast
Earliglow (medium to large, deep red)
Red Coat (medium to large, sweet and firm)
Sparkle (medium to large, dark red)

Midwest
Guardian (large, bright red)
Midway (medium to large, dark red, juicy)
Sparkle (medium to large, dark red)

Southern Plains
Cardinal (very large, rich flavor)
Trumpeter (medium to large, bright red)
Pocahontas (medium to large, bright red)

Upper Plains and Rockies
Cyclone (large, bright red)
Dunlap (medium to large, dark red)
Sparkle (medium to large, dark red)
Trumpeter (medium to large, bright red)

Northwest
Hood (very large, dark red)
Totem (medium to large, bright red)

California and the Southwest
Tillikum (small to medium, soft, tart)
Tioga (medium to large, firm, shapely)

STRAWBERRIES

Planting Strawberries

Since your strawberry plants will be growing in the same spot for at least two years, prepare the ground well. The small, shallow-rooted plants will have to receive all their moisture and nourishment from the top few inches of soil.

This soil should be light, rich, slightly acid (pH of 5.5 to 6.0), and full of rich humus (aged manure, compost, or peat) that will hold moisture even during the driest weather. Strawberries grow best in moist soil in full sun.

—from *The Big Book of Gardening Skills*

Step 1. Till soil to a depth of 6 inches, removing weeds and roots. Work 2 inches of organic matter, such as peat moss, compost, or well-rotted manure, into the soil.

Step 2. Strawberry plants usually come in bare-root bundles. Snip the roots to a length of 4 inches before planting, and pull off all but two or three of the youngest leaves on each plant. This will reduce water loss when the plants are in the ground. As you work, keep the plants in a pan with a little water in the bottom and drape a damp cloth over them.

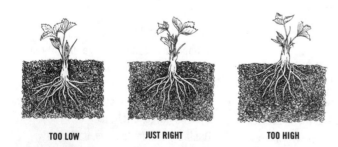

TOO LOW   **JUST RIGHT**   **TOO HIGH**

Step 3. Plant by plunging a trowel straight down into the soil. Pull the handle toward you to open a slit in the ground. Fan out the roots and place them in the opened slit, making sure they don't bend as you set them in. Then set the top of the crown just above the soil line. Any deeper and the crown will rot; any shallower and the roots will dry out. Remove the trowel and firm the soil with the heel of your hand. Give each plant a pint of water to settle the soil.

Step 4. As the plant begins to grow, pinch off all flower buds. Pinch June bearers until flowering ceases in early summer. Pinch everbearers for about three months and then stop and allow subsequent flowers to produce berries.

—from *Gardening Techniques Illustrated*, text by Lee Reich, illustrated by Elayne Sears

Growth, Care, and Harvest

The matted row system is an easy way to grow a large bed of strawberries. Set rows of strawberry plants 12 inches apart. Let the plants put forth as many runners as they can. As the runners form, arrange them in a roughly circular pattern around the mother plant. Once you've achieved strawberry plants every 3 to 4 inches, snip off additional runners so the plants don't become over-crowded. Although this system produces good crops, the berries are smaller than those grown using the double hill system.

The Double Hill System

The double hill system is a versatile method that is also effective in raised beds. To plant this way, begin by removing any runners from the mother plants. Set your plants 10 to 12 inches apart in paired, hilled rows that are themselves 10 to 12 inches apart. Space the pairs of rows 18 inches apart.

A variation on the hill system requires raised beds, usually of timbers, that are 24 inches wide. Fill the beds with sandy loam amended with compost or rotted manure, and adjust the pH to between 6.0 and 6.5. Set plants in twin rows 6 inches from the edge of the timbers and 12 inches apart.

Fertilization

Beginning in the spring of your plants' first year and continuing into fall, water every other week with a low-analysis fertilizer such as fish emulsion. This will normally supply plants with all the nutrients they need. In some soils of the South, East, and Midwest, extra phosphorus is needed. In the Northwest, applications of trace minerals may be required. From their second season on, fertilize the plants at the beginning of the growing season and when blossoms open.

Watering

While the fruit is ripening, strawberries need about 1 inch of water per week. This will produce large, juicy berries. Too much water at this time will yield large fruit that has a watery, diluted flavor. In general, moistening the soil in a way that does not get the leaves wet reduces the spread of foliar diseases.

Cold and Frost Protection

Mulch helps keep moisture in the soil, which protects root systems. It also reduces heaving of soil in late winter and early spring. In areas where the temperatures drop to 0°F without a snow cover, a thick straw mulch can prevent severe damage.

Harvesting

When is it time to pick the berries? As strawberries ripen, the fruit changes color, from white to pink to red. As the color changes, sugars are deposited in the fruit. Berries picked before they are fully ready will not have as much sugar as ripe ones. Pick in the cool of the morning, when the berries are firm.

—adapted from *The Big Book of Gardening Secrets* by Charles W.G. Smith

Strawberry Systems

In the matted row system, arrange runners around the mother plant.

These strawberries are trained to a double hill system.

A circular raised bed is an elegant and practical way to raise strawberries.

RASPBERRIES AND BLACKBERRIES

Raspberries by Region

These berries all have excellent flavor.

South
Bristol (black)
Cumberland (black)
Heritage (everbearing red)
Sunrise (red)

Mid-Atlantic Coast
Fall Gold (everbearing gold)
Jewel (black)
Sentry (red)

Northeast
Allen (black)
August Red (everbearing red)
Heritage (everbearing red)
Latham (red)
Royalty (purple)

Midwest
Black Hawk (black)
Durham (everbearing red)
Jewel (black)

Southern Plains
Indian Summer (everbearing red)
Jewel (black)

Upper Plains and Rockies
Durham (everbearing red)
Latham (red)

Pacific Northwest
Munger (black)
Willamette (red)

Blackberries by Region

Mid-Atlantic and South
Chester (semi-upright)
Comance (upright)

Northeast and Midwest
Chester (semi-upright)
Youngberry (trailing)

Pacific Northwest
Black Satin (semi-upright)
Dirksen (upright)
Marion (semi-upright)

Raspberries and blackberries are prolific, reliable, useful, and long-living. They blossom late, so spring frosts never ruin the crop. The diseases and insects that trouble them are easy to control if you buy virus-free and virus-resistant plants. They need little care and are easy to pick without bending.

Classes of Raspberries

Red raspberries are the most familiar bramble. The reds come in both one-crop and two-crop varieties. The one-crop type bears fruit that matures in mid-summer on canes that have grown the previous season. The canes die within a few weeks after bearing. Two-crop raspberries are often called everbearers. They bear once during the summer and put out an additional crop in fall on canes grown during the current year.

Yellow raspberries are closely related to the reds and vary in color from yellow to pale pink. These are so fragile that they are seldom seen in stores. However, they are ideal for home gardens and many fruit lovers regard the ripe yellow raspberry as the finest fruit in the world.

Black raspberries have an unusual flavor that many people like very much. They differ from red raspberries in that they never produce suckers. Instead, they start new plants when their long canes bend over and touch the soil. The tips form roots and grow into new plants.

Purple raspberries are closely related to the blacks, with a similar flavor and growth habit. Some varieties send up suckers, like reds.

Classes of Blackberries

Blackberries come in three types: the upright, the semi-upright, and the trailing kinds, which are called dewberries. The growth habit of the upright is very similar to that of red raspberries. Dewberries, however, resemble black raspberries in that they don't form suckers. Their vinelike canes trail on the ground unless supported, forming new plants by tip layers. The semi-uprights share some of the characteristics of both.

Hardiness

Many of the red and yellow raspberry cultivars are hardy as far north as Canada. Others have been developed for Zones 5 through 8. Black and purple raspberries are slightly less hardy, although some cultivars are suitable for Zone 3. Most fall-bearing raspberries are winter-hardy, but many of them fail to ripen their second crop before the early frosts of Zones 3 and 4.

Most blackberry cultivars have hardy roots. Their canes are not as hardy as raspberries, though, and are apt to die to the ground over the winter in cold climates. Few nurseries carry the older, hardy kinds anymore, so growers in cold areas may have trouble locating a blackberry that will produce fruit. Trailing blackberries are even more tender. Most are suitable only for Zone 6 and warmer climates.

—from *Fruits and Berries for the Home Garden* by Lewis Hill

Planting a Raspberry Patch

No fruits are tastier or more perishable than perfectly ripe raspberries, a fact that argues for growing them within arm's reach. Get your patch off to a good start by purchasing certified disease-free plants. Those dug from a neighbor's patch may seem economical, but they often carry diseases. Choose a site that has full sun and well-drained soil and is as far as possible from other cultivated or wild raspberries. Don't plant them where you have recently grown eggplants, peppers, potatoes, tomatoes, or strawberries, which are hosts to raspberry diseases. Clear the area of any sod or weeds before you get started.

1. Prepare an area 2 feet wide and as long as the row you intend to plant. Work a few inches of compost, peat moss, or rotted sawdust into the top 12 inches of soil. Of all nutrients, raspberries need nitrogen most, so add a high-nitrogen fertilizer as well. Top the fertilizer with the recommended amount of lime or sulfur necessary to adjust the soil pH to about 6.0.

2. Erect a trellis to keep your plants upright. Set a 4 x 4 cedar post at each end of the row, sunk into the ground at least 2 feet deep and braced. Use 12- to 14-gauge wire, placing one wire five 5 above the ground and the other 2 feet above the ground.

3. Before planting, soak the roots for a couple of hours in a bucket of water. Dig holes 2 to 3 feet apart in the rows. Set each plant in its hole, spread out the roots, and backfill with the loose soil, making sure the crown is just below ground level. Tamp the soil with your fingers. Cut back all canes at ground level, then pour a gallon of water around each plant.

—from *Gardening Techniques Illustrated*, text by Lee Reich, illustrated by Elayne Sears

RASPBERRIES AND BLACKBERRIES

Steps for Success in the Bramble Patch

First Year
Prepare the soil carefully and plant the berries 2 feet apart. If you set out bare-root plants, cut the tops back to 2 inches above the ground after planting, but leave potted plants unpruned. Water both potted and bare-root plants with a liquid fertilizer, then mulch.

Second Year
Spring. Cut back all plants that didn't make a strong showing the previous year to 2 inches above ground level. Add to the mulch, and apply a light helping of plant food.
Fall. Cut tops of plants back so canes are about 4 feet tall. This makes a stiff plant that doesn't fall over in winter. Install a fence or other support.

Third Year and Thereafter
Spring. Add fertilizer and fresh mulch. Trim out any broken canes. Spray with a fungicide if you spot evidence of spur blight or anthracnose.
Early summer. Spray once more with fungicide if any disease appears. Mow or pull out tips or sucker plants growing in the wrong places. Cut off and burn wilted tops. Remove any sick-looking plants.
Late summer. Cut to ground level and remove all canes that bore fruit. Cut out weak canes and thin remaining canes to 6 inches apart.
Late fall. Cut canes back to 4 or 5 feet in height for winter. Tighten wire supports if necessary.

—from *Fruits and Berries for the Home Garden* by Lewis Hill

Care and Harvesting of Brambles

Pruning. To keep your patch productive, cut each dead cane to ground level. You'll recognize the dead ones by their pallid color and brittleness. Insects and disease overwinter in the old canes, so burn them as soon as possible.

As your berry patch ages, more pruning becomes necessary because the plants produce too many new canes each year. Cut off all the weak new canes when you remove the old ones, and thin out the strong, healthy canes if they are closer together than 6 inches.

Keep rows of red and yellow raspberries and upright blackberries no more than 2 feet in width, and those of black or purple raspberries and trailing blackberries no more than a foot and a half wide. This permits easier harvesting and pruning, and also allows better air circulation.

Harvesting. Raspberries ripen a few weeks before blackberries, and the long ripening season of both lets you enjoy fresh picking every day for several weeks. If you want to further extend the season, plant early, mid-season, and fall-bearing raspberry cultivars. Use only small pails for picking raspberries, because too many piled together will crush those on the bottom. Avoid handling the berries any more than necessary, and move freshly picked berries out of the sun as soon as possible.

CONTROLLING BRAMBLE PESTS

Pest	Description	Control
Raspberry cane borers	Small galls appear at the base of a wilted cane. Small white grubs live inside the galls.	Remove and destroy infested canes. Apply rotenone.
Raspberry crown borers	Larvae tunnel into cane bases, stunting growth and sometimes killing the canes. Most common in western states.	Spray with pyrethrins.
Raspberry fruit worms	Small worms feed on the light green receptacle at the berry's center. Infested fruit drops. Most common on red raspberries.	Spray with pyrethrins.
Raspberry sawflies	Foliage eaten by small greenish larvae on the undersides and margins of the leaves. Most common in northern Great Plains and Rocky Mountains.	Spray with neem or pyrethrins.
Spider mites	Barely visible pests produce thin webs on leaf undersides. Foliage appears pale or speckled with tiny yellow spots. Worst in hot, dry weather.	Spray with neem and insecticidal soap.

Raspberry cane borer

Raspberry fruit worm

Raspberry crown borer

Raspberry sawfly

Spider mite

wouldn't be surprised to hear the expression "as American as blueberry pie" sometime soon, because the treat has become one of the most popular desserts in restaurants. Furthermore, blueberries are a North American fruit, while the apple tree is an import.

Three species of blueberries are commonly grown in North American gardens: the hardy lowbush, the popular highbush, and the rabbit-eye, which grow in the southern United States. In addition, crosses between highbush and lowbush blueberries have resulted in several hardy, large-fruiting cultivars.

All types of blueberries do best at in acidic soil pH of 4.5 to 50. If your soil tests from 5.5 to 6.0, mix sphagnum peat moss with the soil around the plants. Cottonseed meal, composted pine needles or oak leaves, or compost made from pine, oak, or hemlock bark also helps acidify the soil. After planting, mulch your plants with pine needles, oak leaves, or shavings from oak, pine, or hemlock to help maintain the soil's acidity.

—from *Fruits and Berries for the Home Garden*

The hardiest of the three types, the **lowbush**, are the blueberries everyone loves to pick from the wild. Wild lowbush blueberries are grown commercially in some northern states, such as Maine. Backyard lowbush blueberries will yield about a pint of berries for each foot of row.

The **highbush** grows 6 to 15 feet high and produces large berries in midsummer and later. It is less hardy than the lowbush, but some cultivars do well in zone 3 when sheltered from the wind. Yields vary widely among the cultivars, but most gardeners can expect 5 to 15 pounds of fruit per bush.

The **rabbit-eye** blueberry cannot stand low winter temperatures, so the plants are suitable only for the southern United States. They need a chilling period, however, so they cannot be grown in tropical climates. Rabbit-eyes grow on drier soils than the highbush kinds will tolerate, but in hot climates most need some type of irrigation. They are very productive, often yielding 20 pounds of fruit per bush.

10 Great Blueberries

Highbush Blueberries

Bluecrop
Fruit: Very large
Ripens: Early to mid-season
Hardiness: Zones 4 to 8

Blueray
Fruit: Very large
Ripens: Early to mid-season
Hardiness: Zones 4 to 8

Earliblue
Fruit: Large
Ripens: Early
Hardiness: Zones 5 to 7

Eliot
Fruit: Medium
Ripens: Late
Hardiness: Zones 4 to 7

Jersey
Fruit: Small to medium
Ripens: Late
Hardiness: Zones 5 to 8

Patriot
Fruit: Medium
Ripens: Mid-season
Hardiness: Zones 3 to 7

Highbush and Lowbush Hybrids

Northblue
Fruit: Medium
Ripens: Mid-season
Hardiness: Zones 3 to 7

Northland
Fruit: Small
Ripens: Mid-season (one week before Northblue)
Hardiness: Zones 3 to 7

Rabbit-Eye Blueberries

Bluebelle
Fruit: Large
Ripens: Early to midsummer
Hardiness: Zones 6 to 10

Brightblue
Fruit: Medium to large
Ripens: Early to midsummer
Hardiness: Zones 6 to 10

BLUEBERRIES

Blueberry Pie Deluxe

We always make this favorite during the berry season and again in the cold months when we have access to a pint of fresh berries. We feel that the delightful texture and flavor that results from the combination of raw and cooked berries makes this pie superior to all others.

¾	cup granulated sugar
3	tablespoons cornstarch
⅛	teaspoon salt
2	cups blueberries (fresh or frozen)
¼	cup water
1	tablespoon butter
1	tablespoon lemon juice
2	cups fresh blueberries
	Baked 9-inch pie shell
	Whipped cream (optional)

Combine the sugar, cornstarch, and salt in a medium-size saucepan. Add the 2 cups of fresh or frozen (thawed) berries and water. Cook over medium heat, stirring constantly, until mixture boils, thickens, and clears. Remove from heat and stir in the butter and lemon juice. Cool.

Place the 2 cups of fresh berries into the pie shell and top with the cooked mixture. Chill. Serve with whipped cream.

Yield: One 9-inch pie

—from *Fruits and Berries for the Home Garden* by Lewis Hill

Planting and Care of Blueberries

Blueberry plants from the nursery come bare-rooted, canned (potted), or balled-and-burlaped. Place bare roots in a trench until ready to plant and mound soil or damp peat moss around them. They can be planted in fall, but spring is best in most areas, on a cloudy afternoon. Plant as soon as the ground can be worked. Prune off any damaged or long roots, any weak or broken wood, and all flower buds, because fruiting the first year may stunt the bush.

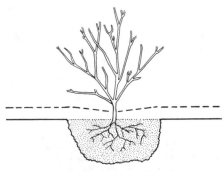

Step 1. Plant your bushes 1 to 2 inches deeper than they were in the nursery and 4 to 6 feet apart in rows spaced 8 to 10 feet apart. In large plantings, do not separate cultivars by more than two rows from others with similar ripening seasons.

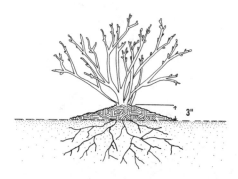

Step 2. After you put a plant in its hole, fill the hole three-fourths full of soil or a 50-50 loam-peat and sand mixture, then flood it with water. After the water seeps out, fill the remainder of the hole and pack it gently with your feet. Water the plant with a starter solution and add a layer of an acidic mulch such as pine needles.

Step 3. If irrigation is necessary, water during the early morning but don't wet the bushes when berries are beginning to ripen. You can use ground flooding or a soaker hose. Apply an inch of water each time.

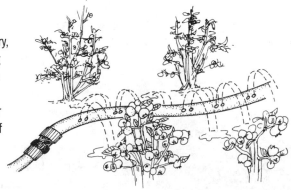

Fertilizing

Fertilize blueberries with blood meal, cottonseed meal, tankage, or well-rotted manure about a month after planting and again in midsummer. Thereafter, fertilize twice a year, at the beginning of bloom and again five to six weeks later. Use combinations of the materials to provide balanced fertilization. Don't use bonemeal or wood ashes, because they tend to sweeten the soil.

—from *The Big Book of Gardening Skills*

Pruning Blueberries

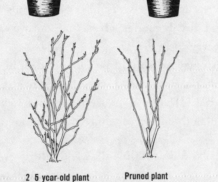

Planting time. Remove all weak, diseased, and broken wood and all flower buds.

Planting time

Pruned plant

After one year. Again prune any diseased or broken wood. Vigorous plants may be allowed to bear up to a pint of fruit (20 to 30 flower buds). Remove any additional buds.

2 5 year-old plant

Pruned plant

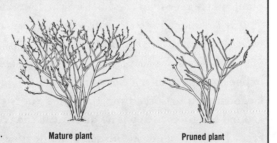

After two to five years. Continue similar pruning. If the plants appear vigorous, do not remove more flower buds than necessary during pruning. The emphasis should be on producing healthy bushes and not on fruit production.

Mature plant

Pruned plant

Older bushes. Blueberry bushes that have been neglected may be rejuvenated through severe pruning. Cut these back to the ground, leaving only short, 2-inch to 3-inch stubs. The whole bush ma be done at once, or half the bush can be done one year and the other half in the following year. By using the one-year method, the entire crop is lost for one season. The two-year method allows the plant to bear a portion of the crop each year.

—from *The Big Book of Gardening Skills*

Controlling Blueberry Pests

Black-Vine Weevils
Adult weevils feed on leaves, cutting small, semicircular notches from leaf margins in early to midsummer. Larvae are whitish grubs that feed on stems and roots near or under soil line.
Control. Wrap base of each stem in plastic wrap painted with Tanglefoot or petroleum jelly to trap adults.

Blueberry Maggots
Small, whitish worms hatch from eggs. Maggots feed on berries, turning them soft. Infested fruit drops before it is fully ripe.
Control. Do not pick berries until fully ripe. Cover bushes with fine netting after fruit set to impede egg-laying.

Cranberry Fruit Worm
Small, greenish caterpillars appear inside webs that hold fruit clusters together.
Control. Hand-pick and destroy infested fruit. Spray plants with pyrethrins after fruit set.

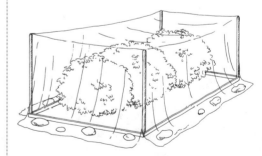

Probably the worst pests where blueberries are concerned are common garden birds. Protect your crop by draping the plants with garden netting, available at garden stores.

GRAPES

The Best Fertilizer for Grapes

The best fertilizer for grapes is well-rotted manure, or compost made with large amounts of strawy manure, applied as a mulch during the growing season. In fall, apply either manure compost or straight, well-rotted manure at the rate of 15 to 20 pounds per 100 square feet. In most cases, no other fertilization is required. Vineyards given this treatment consistently yield up to 30 percent more fruit than those fertilized with commercial preparations.

—from *The Big Book of Gardening Secrets*

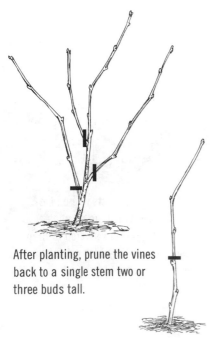

After planting, prune the vines back to a single stem two or three buds tall.

Grapes have the reputation of being fragile and difficult to grow. Many northern gardeners do not even consider trying to grow them, yet some vines will flourish in regions of every state and in several Canadian provinces. A good rule of thumb is that if wild grapes grow in your area, you can grow plump and tasty domestic grapes of some kind.

Grapes need an abundance of heat and sun to grow and to produce. They are one of the last fruit plants to start growth in the spring, and they bloom much later than any of the tree fruits. If you live in one of the cool northern states, plant them in heat pockets whenever possible—spots where buildings, walls, or hills form corners that trap the southern and eastern sun. You can also mulch them with black plastic or crushed rock.

Soil Needs

Grapevines grow in many soil types. Well-drained, deep, fertile loams are excellent, yet grapes thrive on soils containing clay, slate, gravel, shale, and sand. Gravelly, stony soils generally drain well, and they absorb and reflect the sun's warmth, providing heat for the vine bottom.

Very dry, very wet, and very rich soils are bad for grapes. Leaner soils yield comparatively modest crops that mature earlier and have considerable sugar in the berry.

A vineyard should be plowed deeply and well disked, so the soil is thoroughly pulverized and weed-free. These conditions do make erosion a significant risk. If your slope is steep, your local soil conservation service can help you plan the most advantageous contour rows for your vines.

Planting and Supporting Grapevines

In northern areas, grapes should be planted as early in the spring as the soil can be worked. Farther south, the vines can be planted in the autumn. The plants must get established before the long, hot days of summer begin.

Order your grape stock from a nursery as nearby as possible; if you can, pick out and pick up the plants yourself. The best stock is strong, sturdy, one-year-old plants with large, fibrous root systems; two-year-old plants are more expensive and will not bear any sooner. Dig a good hole in worked-up soil, large enough to spread out the vine's roots comfortably. Pack the soil firmly around the roots, leaving no air spaces that could increase the chances of disease. Plant the vines at the same depth they grew in the nursery, then prune them back to a single stem two or three buds tall. If it is early spring and the soil is moist, you need not water. Later in the spring you may want to water the stock well after planting. You will need a trellis.

Space most hybrid cultivars 8 to 10 feet apart in the row, with the rows 10 to 11 feet from each other. Less vigorous vines can be closer together—7 or 8 feet apart in the row. If your grape selection is not self-pollinating, it will need a partner nearby to produce well.

—from *The Big Book of Gardening Skills*

A GALLERY OF GREAT GRAPES

AMERICAN GRAPES

Beta
Hardiness: Zones 3 to 6
Flavor: Tangy, definite wild quality
Fruit: Blue
Quality: Good, medium-size berries
Ripens: Early to mid-Sept.
Best uses: Juice, jelly, wine

Canadice
Hardiness: Zones 5 to 7 (8)
Flavor: Sweet, fruity, with a touch of spice
Fruit: Red
Quality: Excellent, medium-size seedless berries in large clusters
Ripens: Mid-Aug. to late Sept.
Best uses: Eating, juice, jelly, wine

Catawba
Hardiness: Zones 5 to 7 (8) (-10°F)
Flavor: Sweet, rich
Fruit: Copper-red
Quality: Excellent, large to medium-size berries
Ripens: Late Sept. to early Oct.
Best uses: Eating, wine, jelly, juice

Concord
Hardiness: Zones (4) 5 to 8
Flavor: Excellent; sweet and clean grape taste
Fruit: Blue-black
Quality: Excellent, medium-size berries
Ripens: Late Sept. to early Oct.
Best uses: Eating, wine, jelly, juice

Concord Seedless
Hardiness: Zones 5 to 9
Flavor: Excellent; sweet, clean
Fruit: Blue-black
Quality: Excellent, medium-size berries
Ripens: Mid- to late Sept.
Best uses: Eating, pies, jelly, juice, wine

Fredonia
Hardiness: Zones (3) 4 to 9
Flavor: Excellent; sweet and spicy
Fruit: Blue-black
Quality: Excellent, large to medium-size berries
Ripens: Early to mid-Sept.
Best uses: Eating, wine, jelly, juice

Himrod
Hardiness: Zones 5 to 8
Flavor: Excellent; sweet, clean, and delicate
Fruit: Yellow-green
Quality: Excellent, large berries
Ripens: Mid-Aug. to early Sept.
Best uses: Eating, juice, excellent raisins

Niagara
Hardiness: Zones 5 to 7 (8) (-15°F)
Flavor: Delicately sweet, slightly tart, with a subtle wild flavor
Fruit: Green
Quality: Excellent, large berries
Ripens: Late Aug. to mid-Sept.
Best uses: Eating, wine

Reliance
Hardiness: Zones 4 to 8
Flavor: Excellent; very sweet, rich, and fruity
Fruit: Pink
Quality: Excellent, medium-size seedless berries in large clusters
Ripens: Early to mid-Aug.
Best uses: Eating, jelly, juice

Swenson Red
Hardiness: Zones (3) 4 to 7
Flavor: Very sweet
Fruit: Red with blue tinge
Quality: Excellent for fresh use
Ripens: Late Aug. to early Sept.
Best uses: Eating, jelly, juice

MUSCADINE GRAPES

Dixie Red
Hardiness: Zones 7 to 9
Flavor: Well balanced, sweet
Fruit: Pale red
Quality: Excellent, large berries in large clusters
Ripens: Midseason
Best uses: Eating, wine, juice, jelly

Hunt
Hardiness: Zones 7 to 9
Flavor: Very sweet
Fruit: Black
Quality: Very good, large to medium-size, juicy berries
Ripens: Mid-Sept.
Best uses: Eating, wine, juice, jelly

Scuppernong
Hardiness: Zones 7 to 9
Flavor: Variable from very sweet to lightly tart
Fruit: Light bronze-red
Quality: Very good, large, thick-skinned berries
Ripens: Mid-Sept.
Best uses: Eating, wine, juice, jelly

Triumph
Hardiness: Zones 7 to 9
Flavor: Sweet
Fruit: Bronze-green
Quality: Good, medium-size berries
Ripens: Mid- to late Sept.
Best uses: Eating, wine, juice, jelly

Welder
Hardiness: Zones 8 to 9
Flavor: Very sweet
Fruit: Bronze
Quality: Excellent, medium-size berries
Ripens: Early to mid-season
Best uses: Eating, wine, juice, jelly

EUROPEAN GRAPES

Baco Noir
Hardiness: Zones 5 to 7
Flavor: Fruity, light, high acid
Fruit: Blue-black
Quality: Good, small berries in long clusters
Ripens: Late Aug. to early Sept.
Best uses: Wine

Chardonelle
Hardiness: Zones 5 to 8
Flavor: Dry, clean
Fruit: Green
Quality: Excellent, small to medium-size berries
Ripens: Sept.
Best uses: Wine

Foch
Hardiness: Zones 5 to 9
Flavor: Low acid, clean
Fruit: Blue-black
Quality: Good, medium-size berries in long clusters
Ripens: Late Aug.
Best uses: Juice, wine

Thompson Seedless
Hardiness: Zones 7 to 9
Flavor: Very sweet, clean
Fruit: Green to greenish-yellow
Quality: Excellent, medium-size berries in long clusters
Ripens: Aug. to Sept.
Best uses: Eating, wine, jelly, juice, raisins

—from *The Big Book of Gardening Secrets*

GRAPES

Pruning Grapes: The Kniffen System

Pruning is a very important part of grape culture, and one that must not be neglected. Because of the grape's tendency to grow vigorously, a lot of wood must be cut away each year. Grapevines that are overgrown become so dense that the sun cannot reach into the areas where fruit should form. The easiest way for beginners to manage a backyard vineyard is with a two-wire fence using a method called the Kniffen System. With this type of training, each mature vine should produce 12 to 15 pounds (30 to 60 bunches) of grapes per year. If more bunches are produced, remove the surplus before the grapes develop to avoid overbearing and thus weakening the plant. In this way, your vines should go on producing for 50 years or longer.

First Year

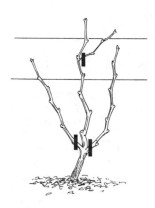

Staple smooth 9- or 10-gauge wire to sturdy posts, and brace the posts with wire to keep horizontal wire from sagging. Center the plant between posts, about 8 feet apart, in rows 8 feet apart.

Cut back bare-root vines after planting so each is only 5 or 6 inches long and contains just two or three fat buds. This encourages root growth. If you planted potted vines, omit this cutting back. Water the vines frequently and allow them to grow freely the first year.

Second Year

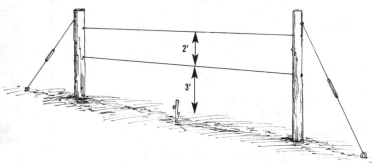

Very early in the spring, before the buds start to swell, cut back the vine to a single stem with no branches. This will encourage faster growth.

During the year, allow four side branches to grow (two in each direction) and train them along the wires. They will grasp the wires with their tendrils. Pinch off all buds that start to grow in other directions.

By the end of the second year, if growth has been good, the space along both wires should be filled. These vines should then bloom and produce a few grapes the third year.

Third Year

During the year, allow only four more canes to grow from buds along the main stem. Train these to grow along the ground parallel to the four on the wires. These four will eventually replace the first four.

In late winter following the third growing season, cut off the canes that produced that year and tie the new canes to the wires. Trim off all excess growth except the four new canes.

The Secrets of Great Homemade Wine

The byword among traveled wine drinkers is that any wine tastes best in the region (and with the regional food) it comes from. If that's true, then homemade wines must taste best when drunk at home. There are not many peak experiences available to us for the dollar or so that our homemade wine costs.

Winemakers say the secret of the wine is the grapes it's made from. The winemaker's role is to protect and preserve the quality of good grapes right into the bottle. Jim Mitchell, of Sakonnet Vineyards in Rhode Island, quotes these maxims:

1. The most important elements of great wine are: first, the grape; second, the climate; third, the soil; and fourth, the skill of the winemaker—in that order.
2. The best wines are made as far north as that grape variety will grow.
3. To produce great wines, the vines must suffer, rather like athletes.

The elements for great wine, then, are the same for the home winemaker as for commercial wineries: The right grape variety in the right climate and soil achieves the right balance of sugar, acid, pH, and flavor components. When all these things come together, the results can be spectacular indeed.

Whatever your property, there is a variety of grape that will produce the most excellent wine possible. Your task, long before the first bottles come to life in your cellar, is to identify that vine.

—from *From Vines to Wines* by Jeff Cox

Vineyard Soil and Grape Quality

All grapes have an affection for gravel, flint, slate, or stony soils. One reason why hillsides are so good for grapes is that erosion has scoured the land to its poorest, stoniest constituents. The best acres are so infertile and stony that a corn farmer wouldn't take them as a gift. But soil that produces great grapes (and fine wines) must offer a number of qualities that help grapes flourish. Here are some characteristics of productive vineyard soil:

- Good soil drainage. This is crucial. Grapes do not like wet feet.
- Soil pH appropriate to the variety.
- Soil depth of at least 30 inches, due to the deep-rooting habits of grapes.
- Proper soil preparation. Loosen, break up, and mix soil layers well below ordinary cultivation depth

---

SUGGESTED WINE GRAPES BY REGION

This list includes white vinifera, red vinifera, white hybrid, red hybrid, and American grapes.

New York State (Finger Lakes and the Hudson River Region). Chardonnay, Riesling; Ravat 51, Cayuga Seyval Blanc; Chancellor, Foch; Delaware.

Southern New Jersey, Eastern Long Island, and Coastal Rhode Island. Chardonnay, Reisling, Sauvignon Blanc, Gewürztraminer; Pinot Noir, Cabernet Sauvignon, Merlot; Seyval Blanc, Vidal 256, Cayuga; Chancellor

Northwestern Pennsylvania. Riesling; Vidal 256, Ravat 51, Seyval Blanc; Chancellor, Chelois, de Chaunac, Foch

Southeastern Pennsylvania. Chardonnay, Riesling, Gewürztraminer, Pinot Noir; Seyval Blanc, Vidal 256, Cayuga; Chancellor, Foch, de Chaunac

Ohio. Gewürztraminer, Chardonnay; Vidal 256, Seyval Blanc; Chambourcin, Foch; Delaware, de Chaunac

Virginia. Chardonnay, Riesling, Sauvignon Blanc, Gewürztraminer; Cabernet Sauvignon, Merlot; Seyval Blanc, Vidal 256, Cayuga, Aurora; Chancellor, Foch, Villard Noir, Chambourcin

Southeast and Gulf States. Due to special conditions, varieties of *Muscadinia rotundifolia* are recommended for this region. They are classified as bronze, black, or white. Bunch grape varieties that will grow in the Southeast include Moored, Alwood, Delaware, Rougeon, and Rosette.

Arkansas. Ravat 51, Verdelet Blanc, Villard Blanc, Seyval Blanc, Vidal 256, Aurora; Villard Noir, Baco Noir, Chancellor; Delaware, Niagara

Oklahoma. Aurora, Rougeo, Delaware, Seyval Blanc, Villard Blanc; muscadines also do well in southern Oklahoma

Texas Hill Country. Chenin Blanc, Colombard, Barbera, Carnelian, Ravat 51

Central Midwest. Vidal 256, Chancellor, Delaware, Aurora, Chelois, Seyval Blanc, Foch, Ravat 51, Baco Noir, de Chaunac

Northern Cold Tier. Seyval Blanc, Aurora, Foch, Millot. Wine grapes that don't require winter protection include St. Croix and Swenson Red (reds) and Kay Gray and Edelweiss (whites)

Arizona–New Mexico. Chardonnay, Sylvaner, Riesling, Zinfandel, Cabernet Sauvignon, Pinot Noir, Ruby Cabernet

Oregon–Southern Washington. Chenin Blanc, Chardonnay, Semillon, Riesling, Sauvignon Blanc, Pinot Noir, Pinot Meunier, Cabernet Sauvignon, Merlot, Malbec, Pinot Blanc

Southwestern Idaho. Sylvaner, Chardonnay, Riesling, Gray Riesling, Gewürztraminer, Pinot Noir, Seyval Blanc, Chelois

British Columbia. Aurora, Okanagan, Riesling, Foch, Chelois

FRUIT TREES

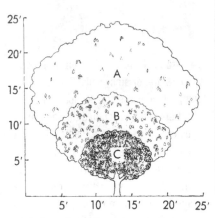

(A) Standard. (B) Semi-dwarf.
(C) Dwarf.

How Big Are They?

The following are approximate diameters of some full-grown fruit trees. When you plant them, allow enough additional room so that you will be able walk through them, and so that light can reach the entire exterior of each tree.

Fruit Tree	Crown Diameter
Apple	
Standard size	25 to 35 feet
Semi-dwarf	15 to 20 feet
Dwarf	7 to 10 feet
Apricot	
Standard	18 feet
Dwarf	8 feet
Peach	
Standard	18 feet
Dwarf	8 feet
Pear	
Standard	18 feet
Dwarf	8 feet
Plum	
Standard	18 feet
Dwarf	8 feet
Quince	12 feet

The Home Orchard

When you are involved in a home orchard that will quite likely last a lifetime or more, you naturally want to do it right. Mistakes made early have a way of coming back to haunt us.

Even if you can't plant everything you want the first year, make a plan so you will have the best possible trees growing in the best possible locations. Give your trees full sun, plenty of room to grow, and well-drained soil.

It helps to sketch the orchard on paper ahead of time. First, measure the area where your orchard will be and match it up to the gridlines of graph paper. Note objects that you will have to work around, such as buildings, large boulders, property lines, walkways, inhospitable neighboring plants, and anything else that might influence your planting decisions.

After you have chosen the number and varieties of trees you want to plant, draw in each tree based on the crown diameter of the mature tree, leaving enough space for them to grow without crowding.

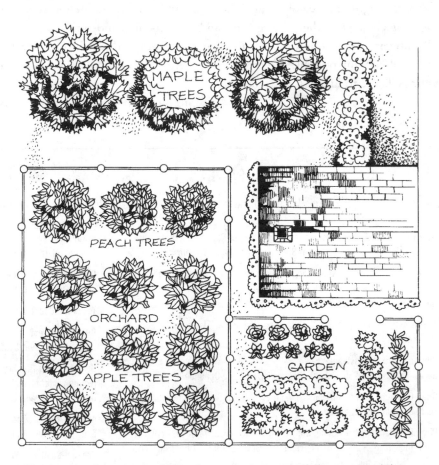

Sketch your entire property, showing house, gardens, and existing trees, and then plan the placement of your orchard. Keep in mind as you sketch which trees need to be near each other for cross-pollination.

—from *The Big Book of Gardening Skills*

Think Small: Planting a Dwarf Fruit Orchard

The fruits produced by dwarf trees are every bit as large and tasty as those on standard-size trees. The basic differences between standard and dwarf trees are in their growth habits. A dwarf fruit tree grows less vigorously than a standard tree, is smaller at maturity, and begins to produce blossoms and fruits at an earlier age, as soon as the second year after planting. There are other advantages as well. In the space needed by four standard-size apple trees, planted 40 x 40 feet, you can plant 30 to 40 dwarf trees without crowding them. This lets you plant early, mid-season, and late-ripening varieties to extend the harvest period. More perfect fruits often grow on dwarf trees, because maintenance is easier. There is no need for ladders: Both pruning and maintenance can be done while standing on firm ground.

Fruit Varieties for Beginning Growers

Zone 3

Apple. Astrachan, Connell, Dolgo Crab, Duchess, Peach Apple, Prairie Spy, Quinte, Wealthy, Yellow Transparent

Peach. None

Pear. Golden Spice, Luscious, Mendall, Parker, Patten

Plum. La Crescent, Pipestone, Redcoat, Waneta

Plum cherry. Compass, Sapalta

Sour cherry. Meteor, North Star

Sweet cherry. None

Zone 4

Growers in this zone should be able to grow everything listed for Zone 3 plus:

Apple. Cortland, Imperial, Lobo, Lodi, McIntosh, Northwest Greening, Regent

Cherry. Richmond

Peach. Reliance (in favored spots)

Pear. Flemish Beauty, Kieffer, Seckel

Plum. Greengage, Monitor, Stanley

Sweet cherry. None

Zone 5

Growers in this zone should be able to grow everything listed for Zones 3 and 4 plus:

Apple. Delicious, Empire, Gravenstein, Northern Spy, Prima, Priscilla, Rhode Island Greening, Yellow Delicious

Peach. Stark Frost King, Stark Sure Crop, Sunapee

Plum. Burbank, Damson, Earliblue, Italian, Santa Rosa, Shiro

Sour cherry. Montmorency

Sweet cherry. Bing, the Dukes, Stella, Windsor

Zones 6 to 8

Many varieties that will grow in the colder zones will also do well here, but certain kinds of fruits developed especially for the colder climates may not be satisfactory for these zones.

Apple. Grimes, Golden, Rome, Stayman, and Winesap should all do well here. Apples that grow best in Zone 3, including those of the McIntosh family, are not recommended.

Cherry. All should do well.

Peach. Candor, Elberta, Halehaven, Madison, Redhaven

Pear. Anjou, Bartlett, Bosc, Clapp Favorite

Plum. Most should do well.

—from *The Big Book of Gardening Skills*

FRUIT TREES

Planting a Fruit Tree in Three Simple Steps

Quick root development is important for any newly planted tree, so plant early in the season, as soon as the soil has dried enough to crumble easily in your hand. A tree planted this spring will reward you with bushels of luscious fruit in the years to come, the first crop in some cases appearing as soon as next summer.

Step 1. Soak bare roots in a bucketful of water for a few hours to plump them up. Before planting, trim back long or frayed roots to just a few inches.

If the tree is branched, choose three or four healthy branches starting 2 feet above ground level and shorten them to just a few inches. Each one should end in an outward-pointing bud. Then cut away any other branches and cut off the top of the trunk just above the uppermost branch. If the tree is not branched, simply cut the trunk back to 3 feet high.

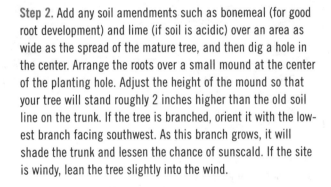

Step 2. Add any soil amendments such as bonemeal (for good root development) and lime (if soil is acidic) over an area as wide as the spread of the mature tree, and then dig a hole in the center. Arrange the roots over a small mound at the center of the planting hole. Adjust the height of the mound so that your tree will stand roughly 2 inches higher than the old soil line on the trunk. If the tree is branched, orient it with the lowest branch facing southwest. As this branch grows, it will shade the trunk and lessen the chance of sunscald. If the site is windy, lean the tree slightly into the wind.

Step 3. As you fill the hole, bounce the tree up and down slightly to settle the soil among the roots. After you've filled in the hole, construct a soil dike around the base of the tree to form a catch basin for water—2 feet out from the trunk in all directions should be sufficient. Spread compost or manure over the catch basin and then a layer of straw or leaf mulch. Drench the soil to settle the tree into place.

Water generously once a week through August. Be sure to weed the catch basin diligently, as weeds will compete with the tree for nutrients and water.

—from *Gardening Techniques Illustrated*, text by Lee Reich, illustrated by Elayne Sears

Grafting Fruit Trees

Grafting is the method most often used in propagating fruit trees. It is simply the joining of two different plants by surgery. Anyone can do it, but only plants that are closely related can be successfully grafted together.

Grafting is a fast method to start large numbers of trees of the same cultivar. It allows the orchardist to choose from a variety of rootstocks that will determine whether the tree will be dwarf, semi-dwarf, or full-size. Grafting can also determine the age at which a tree will begin to bear, and how well it will adapt to your soil and climate.

Cleft Grafting

For a home gardener, cleft grafting is a practical and easy type of grafting. You can use it to graft small trees or to graft new cultivars on the limbs of large trees, a process known as "top working."

The best time to cleft graft is in early spring, just as leaf buds are beginning to turn green. Sap is flowing at that time, so scions are less likely to dry out before they begin to grow. To perform the grafting, you'll need a high-quality, sharp knife and some grafting tape, wax, or tree compound. Choose a tree or limb ½ inch to 2 inches in diameter for best results. Then follow these steps:

1. Cut off the tree you're using for the rootstock a few inches above the ground or, if you are doing a branch on a larger tree, cut the branch off wherever you want to put the graft. Make the cut as smooth as possible.

2. With a sharp knife or grafting tool, split this cut end in the middle about ¾ to 1½ inches deep, depending on the size of the branch. Avoid cutting too deep.

3. Prepare the scion. Cut a piece from the branch of the fruit tree you want to propagate. A scion from 2 to 5 inches long with no more than 2 or 3 buds is about the right size. It should be the same diameter or slightly smaller than the limb or stem it is to be grafted upon. Never let your scions dry out before the operation.

4. After splitting the rootstock, sharpen the cut base end of the scion into a wedge (not a point), using the sharp knife so the edges will be smooth. Don't drop the scion or allow the cut edges to touch anything that could infect it—not even your fingers.

5. Pry open the split part of the rootstock with your knife and slide the wedge-shaped scion down into it. Since your scion and rootstock are not likely to be exactly the same diameter, carefully align the cambiums (green layers under the bark) of both on one side. This is necessary so that sap can flow from the rootstock to the scion.

6. When the scion is solidly in place, cover the wound to keep air from drying it out. Regular grafting wax is the conventional way of sealing the wound. However, many prefer to use a commercial tree compound, or to wrap the juncture with strips of rubber electrical tape. Plastic electrical tape is not as good because it constricts growth.

Grafting Simplified

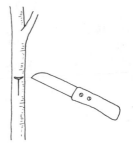

Step 1. Cut a T-shaped incision as low as possible in the tree to be budded.

Step 2. Cut a small, shield-shaped piece that includes a fat bud and a leaf stem.

Step 3. Pull open the flaps of the T and insert the shield-shaped piece, holding it by the leaf stem.

Step 4. Close the flaps and tie the bud tightly in place.

FRUIT TREES

Pruning a Fruit Tree in Four Steps

A tree that has reached its mature size and is yielding fruit requires regular pruning to stay healthy and productive. Although you'll remove some fruit buds and, hence, potential fruits as you prune, the quality of those that remain will be better. In addition, pruning maintains a balance between fruiting and nonfruiting growth. After you prune, the tree will respond with a flush of leafy shoots that provide new bearing wood and nourish developing fruits.

The best time to prune a tree is from late fall until its blossoms open in spring. Where winters are severely cold, wait until after midwinter to avoid cold damage in the cut area.

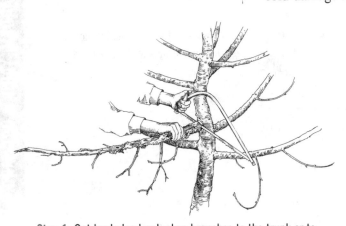

Step 1. Cut back dead or broken branches to the trunk or to healthy buds. Then check twigs or branches for evidence of disease, such as dark, sunken lesions or the black specks of fungal spores. Cut off infected wood 6 inches (15 cm) back from the diseased area.

Step 2. Remove large limbs at their origin or shorten them back to small, healthy side branches. First shorten the branch to about a foot, then undercut the branch slightly before sawing it from above. Finally, saw off the stub, leaving a slight collar to promote good healing.

Step 3. Take out most of the water sprouts, or suckers—overly vigorous, vertical branches that produce only a few, poor-quality fruits and shade the interior of the tree—at their bases. If there are many water sprouts, leave a few to protect the tree from sunscald. In addition, shorten branches that droop downward, and remove any twiggy branches growing from the undersides of limbs.

Step 4. Only on apple and pear trees, thin crowded spurs—the fat, stubby growths on which these trees bear most of their fruit. Cut them back to strong buds. If they are crowded, remove a few so that fruit will be evenly distributed, but not crammed, along the branches.

—from *Year-Round Gardening Projects,*
text by Lee Reich; illustrated by Elayne Sears

Encouraging Pollination

Nearly all fruit trees do better with a mate. Although a few are self-fertile, which means that a single tree can bear fruit by itself, most need what is known as cross-pollination and require a partner nearby. In order to cross-pollinate each other, the trees must be in the same family group. Apples cannot pollinate pears, nor can pears pollinate plums. You therefore need at least two different varieties of each species of the fruit tree you plant.

Most ornamentals, vegetables, and fruit trees are pollinated by insects—primarily bees. As a rule, bees should not be forced to fly more than 500 to 600 feet to bring about the mating of two blossoms.

When only one kind of fruit tree is blooming and there is no suitable partner blossoming anywhere in the neighborhood, here's what we do. We drive across town to an abandoned farm, where a big, ancient pear tree always blossoms at the same time as ours. We cut off a few branches, bring them home, and put them in a bucket of water under our pear tree. The bees take over from there.

When bees are scarce, we sometimes pollinate a few of our fruit trees ourselves. We take a small artist's paintbrush and gently dust the pollen from the flowers into a teacup. Then we brush it carefully onto the blossoms of an adjoining tree.

If you do this, mark the limbs to show which ones you have treated. Or, if you have the energy, you can pollinate the entire tree. It takes only a short time to pollinate a small orchard of dwarf trees, since you need to dust only one bloom in a cluster.

Harvest Time in the Orchard

How can you tell when a fruit is ripe? Most varieties of tree fruits fall from the tree soon after ripening, so the fruit is ready as soon as it will separate from the branch with an easy twist. Most fruits change color as they ripen. If you are in doubt about the ripeness of an apple or pear, cut one open. If the seeds are dark brown, the fruit is ready to be picked. Only pears, a few varieties of peaches, and winter apples that finish ripening in storage should be picked before they are tree ripened.

Pick on a dry day, if possible. If the fruit is wet, it may quickly begin to spoil. Put the fruit in a cool place as soon as possible after you pick it.

Ordinary plastic pails are satisfactory for picking cherries and plums. For apricots, peaches, nectarines, pears, and apples, we prefer the bags used by commercial growers. They hang like knapsacks on the front and are easy to use, even when you are working from a ladder. You can dump the fruit into baskets without bruising it or removing the bag.

Pick each fruit by hand, and never club or shake it from the tree. Bend the fruit upward and twist it gently. If it is ripe, the stem will separate easily from the tree and stay on the fruit. Never pull out the stem, for it will leave a hole where rot will develop.

—from *Fruits and Berries for the Home Garden* by Lewis Hill

Pollination Requirements of Fruit Trees

Apples. Two or more different cultivars are recommended for pollination. If several apples belonging to the same family group are planted together, plant another cultivar nearby.

Peaches. Many peach cultivars are self-fertile, but several of the most popular kinds are not. Mikado, J.H. Hale, and Elberta are among those that need a mate. It is a good idea to plant two different cultivars for insurance.

Pears. Two or more different cultivars are recommended for good crops. A third kind is needed if you plant Bartlett and Seckel together.

Plums. There are several families of plums, and two different cultivars within the same family are necessary for pollination.

Sour cherries. Sour cherries are one of the few fruits that nearly always self-pollinate well, so one tree is all you need.

Sweet cherries. Two or more different cultivars are necessary. Sour cherries are not good pollinators for sweet cherries because they often bloom at different times.

—from *Fruits and Berries for the Home Garden*

FRUIT TREES

The Trick's in the Thinning

Here's a trick little used by home gardeners that could make you the envy of your neighbors: If you want your tree to produce its best fruit and bear big crops every year, simply thin the little fruits as soon as they reach marble size. The tree's strength and energy will then be diverted to the remaining fruits, which will grow much larger.

Peaches, apples, pears, and the large fruited plums all benefit from trimming, but don't bother to thin cherries, crab apples, the small canning pears, or small fruited plums. How many should you pluck off? We like to leave only one fruit in a cluster and about 6 or 7 inches between each fruit.

Painful as it is to throw away perfectly good apples, pears, and peaches, you won't mind doing it after you see how much bigger and better the fruit is, and when you find that you actually have more bushels of usable fruit than you would have picked otherwise.

—from *Fruits and Berries for the Home Garden* by Lewis Hill

Organic Pest and Disease Controls

Because of concern for the health and environmental side effects of agricultural sprays, many alternatives to dangerous chemicals have become popular. The first and simplest thing to do when you see an unwelcome bug in your orchard is to hand-pick it. It's easy, and it usually has no harmful side effects.

Traps and Bands

A trap can be a jar or cup containing molasses and water, vinegar, or even beer, depending on the pest you're after. Place the trap in the neighborhood of the bug, monitor it carefully, remove and destroy captured insects, and replenish the lure as needed.

A band can be as simple as a folded strip of fabric tied around a tree. When crawling insects get caught in the fabric, remove and destroy them. Check bands frequently; if neglected, they can end up harboring pests. Other bands can be made of tar building paper painted with sticky material such as petroleum jelly or molasses, which stops crawling insects in their tracks. Sticky commercial products have been developed for this purpose.

Botanical Insecticides

Various plant parts are used in manufacturing insecticides. Though most botanical preparations are relatively safe, always follow label directions.

Effective mixtures can also be made from herbs and plants that you may have in your house or garden. Insects normally avoid strong-scented herbs such as parsley, tansy, garlic, and hot red peppers. You can prepare a spray by grinding the leaves, adding a little soap and water, letting the mixture steep, and then straining. The mash can be buried in the garden to enrich the soil while discouraging soilborne pests.

Rotenone and pyrethrin are derived from plants and are commonly used in commercial insecticides, because they kill a large range of insects. They wash off easily and have a relatively low toxicity, which is both good and bad, because it means they need to be applied frequently to be useful. However, they are harmful to bees and should be used after bees have returned to the hive for the evening. Rotenone is also extremely harmful to fish.

Sabadilla usually comes in dust form and is good against many types of beetles, webworms, army worms, codling moths, grasshoppers, and aphids. It is relatively nontoxic to humans and wildlife. However, some people have an allergic reaction to it, and it is toxic to honeybees.

Dormant Oil Sprays

Organic gardeners use dormant oil sprays to control the first infestations of many pests. Dormant oil spray can be bought ready to mix at many garden supply stores or can be prepared at home by mixing 2 quarts light motor oil with 1 pound fish oil soap or ½ cup liquid detergent. Mix 1 part of this mixture with 20 parts of water as needed. Use at once after mixing it with water, because the oil and water will separate if stored. Use dormant oils on the trunks and branches of trees early in the spring before any growth starts.

Other Sprays

Commercially produced insecticidal soaps are effective against many pests. Even a spray of water mixed with a small amount of soapflakes can clean away aphids, whiteflies, and other insects.

Bacillus thuringiensis (Bt) is a bacterium that sickens chewing insects like caterpillars and other wormlike larva. Bugs swallow the disease organism along with bites of your leaves. *Bacillus popilliae* (milky spore disease) is useful against Japanese beetle grubs and other ground-dwelling pests.

Abrasive Substances

Scratchy materials can be effective when applied in dust form to surfaces that insects frequent. These generally have no toxic side effects.

Diatomaceous earth is made from needle-sharp fragments of seashells and fossils. When spread on leaves, fruit, and branches, it scrapes and pierces the bellies of cutworms, grubs, and caterpillars. Even if they are not killed by these wounds, the scratchy material will repel them.

—from *The Big Book of Gardening Skills*

COMMON FRUIT TREE INSECTS

Insects	Enemy of	Attacks
Aphid	All fruit trees, especially apple	Leaves, fruits
Apple maggot	Apple	Fruits
Borer	All fruits, especially peach	Trunks
Cherry fruit fly	Cherry	Fruits
Codling moth	Apple, pear	Fruits, leaves
Curculio	All fruits except pear	Fruits
Mites	Apple, peach, plum, nectarine	Fruits, leaves
Oriental fruit moth	Peach, apricot, plum	Leaves, fruits
Pear psylla	Pear	Leaves
San José scale	All fruits	Trunks, twigs, fruits, leaves
Tent caterpillar	All fruits	Leaves

Aphid • Apple maggot • Borer • Cherry fruit fly • Codling moth • Curculio • Mite • Pear psylla • San José scale • Tent caterpillar

---

Spray Schedule for Most Home Orchards

Since trees bloom at different times, the first four sprayings may occur at irregular intervals, according to the flowering period of specific trees. After the fourth spraying, you can spray the whole orchard at one time. To coordinate, you can allow 7 to 12 days between petal fall and summer sprays. Dormant oil spray can be used for the first spray. After that, use orchard spray or your choice of organic sprays.

- **Dormant spray.** Use when tips of buds are swelling but before they begin to turn green.
- **Bud spray.** Use when leaf buds are just beginning to open.
- **Pink spray.** Use when blossom buds show pink and are nearly ready to burst open.
- **Petal-fall spray.** Use when nearly all petals are off the tree.
- **Summer sprays.** Two or more additional sprays may be needed in some areas and in some years. If so, they may be continued at intervals of 10 to 12 days until two weeks before harvesting begins.

—from *The Big Book of Gardening Skills*

18

ARBORS AND TRELLISES

BUILD A LOUNGING ARBOR • CREATE A ROSE ARBOR
TRELLISING VINING CROPS • BUILD A BENTWOOD TRELLIS

This will be the year for new projects on our farm, most involving the yard and gardens. For years we have grown our pole beans on tepee trellises, saving room in the garden, avoiding back strain, and creating fun hiding places for the grandkids. Now we want to add some more beauty and have chosen natural trellis designs to build ourselves, using saplings from our woods. We envision the garden gate accented with an arbor of morning glories and a sitting area with bountiful, trellised grapevines providing shade and ready-made snacks. Jim Long begins this chapter by evoking the essence of summer. A selection of easy-to-build projects follows.

—*John & Martha Storey*

Jim Long grew up loving the shapes of arching tree limbs weighted down by snow or heavy with ripening fruit. He started experimenting with bentwood projects when he was six years old, bending vines and limber saplings into objects for his mother's garden. Trellises were his favorite project. "The great part about making bentwood structures," he says in his book Making Bentwood Trellises, *"is that you are not trying to achieve a perfect, finished look. The unique curves and characteristics of the branches you select are part of the rustic charm." See page 356 for one of Jim's projects.*

When I think of an arbor, what comes to mind is the grape arbors of my childhood. These were usually simple affairs, comprising several tall posts set into the ground and connected at the top with crosspieces. They were finished with rails or rafters across the top. Grapes were trained to grow up the posts and then over the top. It was a convenient method for growing that fruit, making it easy to prune the vines in early spring. In late summer, the bunches of grapes hung down beneath the leaves, where picking was an easy chore.

I remember my family sitting on chairs under the arbor, sipping lemonade with mint leaves, the ice cubes clinking on the glasses and the mint giving off a fresh, soothing aroma. Back in those days, before air-conditioning was common, the arbor was a pleasant place to spend a hot summer afternoon. Neighbor ladies would sit under the arbor, too, sewing and gossiping about the goings-on in our little town. Mothers would bring their babies and put them down on a blanket to play.

Today's arbors are smaller, used less as an outdoor room than as a place to stop for a minute to sip a drink or rest on a bench.

An Arbor for Lounging

The arbor can be constructed as a permanent structure with the posts set in concrete or anchored to concrete pads or piers. It can also be made portable, so it can be moved if you change your landscaping.

The structure should be made of a long-lasting and moisture-resistant material such as pressure-treated wood. Use galvanized nails to fasten the structure together. This will prevent staining problems and provide a durable construction.

Driving Stakes

Once you've determined the location of the arbor, drive two stakes to mark the position of the back posts. Measure and drive two stakes for the front posts as well. Be certain the posts are positioned correctly, so the arbor will be square. Once the stakes are in place, you can measure diagonally between them to determine squareness. If the diagonal measurements are not the same, the layout is not square. Move the stakes until the measurements are the same.

Setting the Posts

With the stakes in place, dig the holes for the posts. The interior height of the arbor is a matter of preference. The project shown is 6 feet, 2 inches from the ground to the underside of the top strips and 5 feet, 8½ inches from the ground to the bottom edges of the front and rear rafters. I suggest 8-foot posts for a permanent structure and 6-foot posts for a portable structure. In cold areas of the country that have a deep frost line, talk with a trusted builder, lumberyard, or your Extension agent to determine how deep you should embed your posts. If you prefer a higher clearance beneath the arbor, you'll need to purchase 10-foot poles in order to provide 7 feet of clearance to the tops of the poles, assuming a 2-foot embedment.

Materials List

4	posts, 4 x 4 x 72" for portable unit; 4 x 4 x 96" for permanent unit
2	lower end supports, 2 x 4 x 44"
2	upper end rafter supports, 2 x 4 x 47"
1	lower back support, 2 x 4 x 84"
2	spacers, 2 x 4 x 34½ ", cut to fit
2	rafters, 2 x 6 x 96"
9	top strips, 2 x 2 x 54"
3	back seat boards, 2 x 6 x 84"
4	seat boards, 2 x 6 x 77"
1	back lattice panel, 4 x 7'
2	end lattice panels, 37 x 57"

Tools for the Job
Hammer ■ Square ■ Level
Handsaw or portable electric saw
Table saw, radial arm saw, or
portable circular saw ■ Saber saw
Sawhorses

YOUR GARDEN, YARD & ORCHARD

This arbor can provide support for climbing plants such as grapes, wisteria, clematis, and climbing roses. It also gives you a pleasant, shady resting spot in your garden or backyard.

—from *64 Yard and Garden Projects You Can Build Yourself* by Monte Burch

BUILD A LOUNGING ARBOR

Set the posts in the holes, plumb both ways, and temporarily brace with 2 x 4s to hold the posts in position. Make sure they are square by running a string line around the outside edge and using a square on the string to check for squareness. Don't worry about having all posts level across the top, but make sure their top ends are at least the proper distance above the ground.

Embed the posts in concrete. You may wish to stop the concrete a few inches below ground level and finish filling with topsoil for a better appearance. You may want to add gravel or other materials such as bark mulch to the inside of the arbor to cut down on mowing problems.

Once the concrete has set, measure up to the correct height on the post on the highest ground level (if your ground is not level). Mark this post, then use a long level and straight board to mark this same level position on the other posts. Use a square to mark around each post at this level. Cut off each post at this height using a handsaw or portable electric saw.

Cutting Supports and Crosspieces

Cut the upper rafter supports to length and fasten them to the inside top of the end posts with 16d galvanized nails. The rafter supports should be positioned 3½ inches below the post tops and protrude past each post by 1½ inches. Trim the front and back rafters to the proper length. Enlarge the squared drawing pattern for the ends and cut to shape with a heavy-duty saber saw. Fasten these rafters on the front and back with 16d galvanized nails, positioning them down on the previously installed inside rafter supports.

Saw the lower inside crosspieces to the correct length and attach to the inside of the end posts with their top edges approximately 16 inches above ground level with 16d galvanized nails. When cutting the lower back support piece to length, remember that it extends to the outside edge of the back posts. Fasten in place with its upper edge flush with the upper edge of the two end supports and hammer 16d galvanized nails into both the posts and the lower side supports.

Making the Seat Boards

Cut the back seat boards to length and nail them in place, spacing them ½ inch above the lower back 2 x 4 support and ½ inch apart. The 2 x 4 spacers must be cut and fit between the back rafter and the top back

Rear and Side Elevations

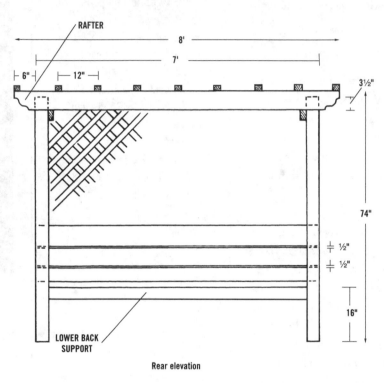

Rear elevation

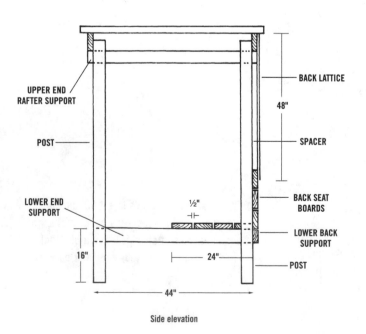

Side elevation

seat board and nailed to the back of the back posts with 16d galvanized nails. Saw the seat boards to proper length and fasten to the lower side supports using 16d galvanized nails, which should also be spaced ½ inch apart.

Using a table saw or a portable circular saw with a ripping guide attachment, rip 2 × 6s into 2 × 2s (1½ inches by 1½ inches) to create the top strips. Attach the top strips on the front and back rafters with 16d galvanized nails.

Latticework

The back and sides are covered with pressure-treated latticework, which comes in 4 × 8 sheets and can be difficult to handle and cut. The sheets can split or break quite easily until installed. Store them by leaning them against a flat, smooth surface.

Here's how you can cut them them to fit. Position a pair of sawhorses about 6 feet apart, then place four wooden "waste" strips at least 8 feet long across the sawhorses. These will support the panels. Measure the panels for the cuts and mark across them using a long straightedge such as a 4-foot level. Cut the panels to size using a portable electric circular saw with the blade set so it passes through the latticework without entering the support strips too deeply. If you don't use the support strips, the lattice will bend and fall, break off in pieces, or catch the saw blade and cause a dangerous kickback situation. Even with supports, watch closely so that the front of the saw shoe doesn't slide under and catch on the diagonal strips as you push it forward. Don't push the saw too quickly.

First cut the back latticework panel to fit lengthwise. It doesn't have to be ripped to fit horizontally. Fasten the latticework to the back rafter and top seat board using 4d galvanized nails along each edge to secure it solidly. Carefully measure between the end posts for one panel. Measure across and between the posts at both their top and bottom to be certain you cut the panel small enough to fit in place properly. Cut and fit one panel, then cut and fit the opposite panel. Anchor both panels with 4d galvanized nails along the top and bottom strips.

Finishing Touches

Using the portable circular saw and a rip guide, rip 1-inch-thick pieces for the outside front and back panel supports. An easier method is to simply purchase a treated 1 × 4 and rip it into 1-inch-wide strips. Cut these support pieces to the proper length and fasten them on the inside of the posts up against the panel; make sure you don't push the panels out of place. Nail the support pieces to the posts using 8d nails spaced 6 inches apart. Then fasten the panels to these support strips with 4d galvanized nails driven from the inside.

Your arbor can be stained, painted, or simply given a coat of protective finish. Then it's time to grab some cushions and crawl in for a nap!

—from *64 Yard and Garden Projects You Can Build Yourself*
by Monte Burch

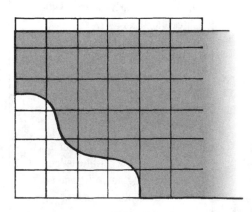

Pattern for ends of rafters (1 square = 1")

CREATE A ROSE ARBOR

A rose arbor is a traditional garden fixture that can provide enjoyment for years.

Materials List

4   posts, 4 x 4" x 8'
8   arch pieces, 2 x 6 x 19", cut to fit
2   upper side crosspieces, 2 x 4 x 28"
3   upper arch crosspieces, 2 x 4 x 28"
2   lower side crosspieces, 2 x 4 x 24"
8   upper and lower horizontal lattice
    cleats, ¾ x ¾ x 22 ½"
8   vertical lattice cleats, ¾ x ¾ x 63"
2   treated lattice panels,
    23 ¾ x 62 ½"
4   angle braces, 4 x 4"

Tools for the Job
Heavy-duty saber saw or band saw
Compass ■ Straightedge
Doweling jig ■ Hammer
Carpenter's square or
combination square
Handsaw ■ Portable circular saw
Protractor ■ Level
Resorcinol glue

Climbing Roses

In truth there is no such thing as a climbing rose, for no rose possesses tendrils enabling it to cling by itself to a vertical surface. But certain roses grow extra-long canes, and such plants can be truly stunning when tied to trellises, arbors, walls, fences, or other structures. Here are some tips to keep them in beautiful health:

■ **Tie as you go.** Tie the canes with 8- to 10-inch lengths of string or strips of cloth. First tie the string tightly around the support, then loop it around the cane and tie very loosely.
■ **Let canes grow outward.** Roses bloom best on horizontal, not vertical, canes.
■ **Prune lightly in spring.** Climbers produce their best blooms on the youngest wood. As spring begins, trim back each stem so as to leave three or four bud eyes. Trim back the longest canes by about a third to keep them in bounds. Cut on the diagonal.
■ **Remove blooms as they fade.** Cut just above a stem with five small leaflets.
■ **Cut away old wood.** Remove any canes with hard, treelike bark.

See chapter 11 for more on roses.

An Arbor for Roses

A rose arbor can stand alone or be joined to a fence and gate. This project is fairly simple to build. Each arch is constructed of four 2 x 6s doweled together.

Assembling the Arch

To shape the 2 x 6s, draw a full-size pattern on a big piece of cardboard such as a large refrigerator box. A big compass is quite useful for this task, but you can make a temporary compass with a piece of string, a pencil, and a nail or tape to anchor it to the cardboard.

Using a straightedge, measure out and draw a line at the bottom of your cardboard equal to the total desired distance from one outer edge of the arch to the other. A 48-inch arch is shown in the illustration. Position the point of the compass (or the nail attached to the piece of string) at the center of this baseline. Extend the pencil arm to the outer radius point (half the total base length) for your desired arch. Keeping the center point still, trace the outer arch from one end of the baseline to the other. Then position the pencil arm at the inner radius point of your arch (5½" in from outer point) and trace this arch. Divide the arch into four 45-degree angles by measuring with a protractor (see drawing of front elevation). These four sections are cut separately and then joined by dowels. Use this arch pattern to trace and cut light arch pieces (four for each arch), using a saber or band saw.

Use a doweling jig to bore holes in the ends of the arch pieces. Then coat each dowel and the mating ends of the pieces with resorcinol glue. Force glue into the dowel holes as well. Then tap the dowels into one piece and tap the second piece to the first. Assemble the halves of each arch first, then join them together. The completed assembly can be clamped with long pipe or bar clamps with a 2 x 4 straightedge across the bottom of the arch.

Once assembled, measure the distance between the bottom ends of the arches. This will be the exact distance your posts must be set. You need to create the arches first to handle any discrepancies created in the spacing.

Setting the Posts

Lay out the post spacing and dig the holes. Set the posts in the holes and embed them in concrete, making sure they are exactly plumb in all directions. Measure again to ensure that the arches will fit the posts properly. Don't worry about the height of the posts at this time beyond confirming that they are more than high enough.

Once the concrete sets, mark the desired post height on one post and use either a long level or a level placed on a straight 2 X 4 to mark the correct height on the remaining posts. With a carpenter's or combination square, mark around all four sides of the posts at this measurement. Then cut the posts to the correct height with a handsaw or large portable circular saw.

Cutting the Crosspieces

Cut the lower side crosspieces and fasten them by toenailing in place or, better yet, with 5-inch lag bolts through the posts into the ends of the crosspieces.

Next, cut the 2 X 4 upper side crosspieces and fasten them down on the posts with galvanized nails driven through the crosspieces into the post tops. Note that the crosspieces are cut short so the arches will fit down over the front and back of the posts.

Anchoring the Arch

With the upper side crosspieces in place, position the front arch and fasten 3-inch lag bolts or 16d nails through the arch bottoms into the ends of the 2 X 4s. Anchor the back arch in the same manner. You will probably need to brace the upper ends of the arches until the remaining braces are installed. These braces consist of 2 X 4s placed between the arches and anchored on their front and back with lag bolts or nails. Angle braces can also be screwed on the inside of each arch corner to further strengthen and anchor the assembly.

Cut four vertical and four horizontal lattice cleats for inside ends by ripping them to size from 1-inch-thick stock using a portable circular saw with ripping guide or a table saw. Fasten two cleats to the inside of the posts and two to the upper and lower side crosspieces on both ends with galvanized 8d nails. Cut the lattice panels to the correct size and insert them behind the inside cleats. Thin stock like latticework will sometimes split when you hammer nails into it. Preboring holes with a bit slightly smaller than your nails prevents the problem. Cut the vertical and horizontal cleats for the outside and fasten on the outside lattice to hold the lattice panels securely in position. You can now stain, seal, or paint as desired.

The arbor is designed to support a climbing rose bush on each side. Dig the holes according to the instructions that come with the rose or refer to the section in chapter 11 on roses and plant accordingly. It's a good idea to use a mulch around the plants to help retain moisture and keep down weeds.

—from *64 Yard and Garden Projects You Can Build Yourself* by Monte Burch

Side and Front Elevations

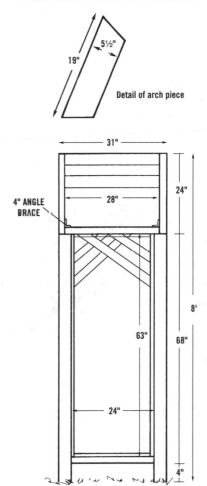

Detail of arch piece

Side elevation

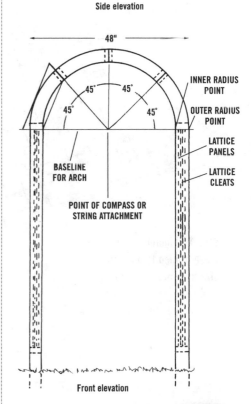

Front elevation

TRELLISING VINING CROPS

Step 1: Concrete reinforcing mesh mailed to an A-frame of 2 x 3s makes an ideal trellis for melons. Situate the trellis to face south.

Trellising Melons and Other Vining Crops

Training melons to grow on a trellis, a technique often used in Asian gardens, is a good solution to the problem of melon sprawl. Trellising encourages the vines to climb rather than sprawl, increasing the surface area available to other plants in a small garden. Growing melons on a trellis also simplifies harvesting. Also, the improved air circulation helps keep the vines healthier and free of that fungal scourge powdery mildew (see chapter 14). The system described here can be used to grow all sorts of vining crops—cucumbers, squashes, even pumpkins.

1. Site the trellis. An A-frame structure of wooden 2 x 3s (5 cm by 7.6 cm) and concrete reinforcing mesh is sturdy, cheap, and easy to build. Make it about 4 feet (1.2 m) tall, and tailor its length to your garden. A 60-degree angle between legs and frame is optimal for exposure to sunlight and ease of harvesting. Drive the legs 1 foot (30 cm) into the ground to anchor them firmly.

The more heat and light the vines receive, the better the harvest, so site the trellis as you would a solar collector. The trellis ought to face south, so run it from east to west along the northern end of your garden, where it won't block the sun from other crops. (The strip of shaded earth underneath the trellis is ideal for a summer crop of leaf lettuce, by the way.)

2. Plant. The first week of June is melon-planting time in my area of New York State (USDA Zone 6), though I start the seedlings in peat pots around the first of May. Since melons are greedy feeders, plant them out in a row of specially enriched soil. Dig a trench 1 foot (30 cm) deep and 2 feet (.6 m) wide along the front of the trellis. Line the bottom with 6 inches (15 cm) of well-rotted horse or cow manure and several handfuls of bonemeal; then replace the excavated soil.

Don't set this heat-loving plant out in soils cooler than 80°F (27°C). Covering the mound with a piece of black plastic mulch will warm the soil to the temperature melons prefer.

Plant the seedlings at 2-foot (.6 m) intervals, using a knife to make slits through the plastic for planting holes. Water them in (through the slits) with a soluble fertilizer high in root-promoting phosphorus. During their first weeks of growth, cover the young plants with a floating row cover to protect them from marauding cucumber beetles.

3. Train. Train the vines up the wire while they are young and soft, and keep an eye on them—the earlier you redirect runaway vines, the better. As they age, vines become more brittle and may snap if you try to move them. Fasten the new growth in place with ties of soft yarn or strips of old nylon stockings, not wires. To avoid compacting your carefully prepared soil, stand on a scrap of lumber while you work around your trellis.

4. Secure the fruits. Because a melon stem will not support the weight of the maturing melons, you must give each fruit extra support. As the melons grow, they will hang down behind the trellis. When the melons are about the size of golf balls, cradle them in a strip of old nylon stocking (some gardeners prefer old onion sacks) and tie both ends of this improvised sling securely to the back of the trellis. The melons will grow into these pockets, and harvesting is simply a matter of releasing them when they are ripe.

—from Year-Round Gardening Projects, text by Thomas Christopher; illustrated by Elayne Sears

Step 2: Cover the soil with black plastic and plant melon seedlings 2 feet apart.

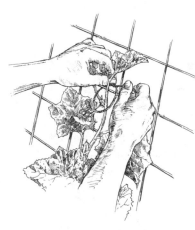

Step 3: Train the vines when they are young.

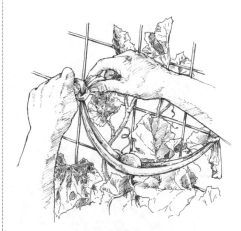

Step 4: Support young melons with a cradle made of old nylon stockings.

BUILD A BENTWOOD TRELLIS

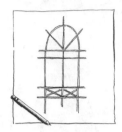

Step 1: Sketch your design.

Step 3: Lay out the side uprights.

Steps 4 and 5: Attach the lower and upper crosspieces.

Steps 6 and 7: Secure the joints with wire and then bend down nail ends.

Step 8: Bend the uprights into an arch.

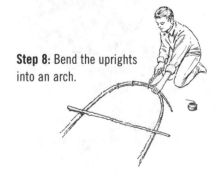

This trellis has a finished height of 7 to 8 feet, large enough for clematis or scarlet runner beans.

1. Planning the design. Before you start, make a sketch of what you want your trellis to look like.

2. Gathering the wood. Using your sketch, make a checklist of all the pieces of wood you will need to gather. Note which ones need to be flexible and which ones are straight crosspieces. (For an 8' finished height, side uprights should be 12 to 14' long to allow for sufficient bending.) Then gather the wood you need, checking to make sure the pieces intended to be flexible will indeed bend. Cut a few extra pieces just in case.

3. Laying out the side uprights. Using your sketch as a reference, lay the two side uprights parallel to each other on a worktable or other firm, flat surface. Place them about 24" apart, with the thicker ends even with the near end of the table.

4. Attaching the lower crosspiece. Lay a crosspiece across the two uprights about 16" from the end of the uprights. Center this piece so that about 12" extends beyond each side. Don't worry about cutting off the excess at this point. Nail the crosspiece in place with nails long enough to go all the way through the crosspiece and most or all of the way through the upright.

5. Attaching the upper crosspiece. Lay the second crosspiece across the uprights, about 40" to 45" from the lower crosspiece. Adjust all the pieces as needed to get the whole structure square, with the crosspieces at right angles to the uprights. When you have the second crosspiece positioned, nail it in place at both joints. Be sure to get it as square as possible. If the crosspieces do not look symmetrical with the uprights, it is easy at this point to pull out the nails, reposition the pieces, and nail again.

6. Securing the joints. With pliers and tie wire, secure the four nailed joints. Cut off a piece of wire about 6" long and go around the joint, catching both pieces of wood. Twist the wire with the pliers until it is as tight as possible. Cut off some of the excess wire and bend the rest out of the way. The wood will shrink about 25 percent in two weeks, so you will probably need to retighten or rewire these joints at that point.

7. Bending down the nails. Turn over the entire trellis rectangle and hammer down any nail ends that may be sticking out the back. Then return the trellis to the "front" side.

8. Bending the uprights into an arch. If any step of the trellis project is going to be difficult, this is the one. Either ask for some help holding the pieces as you bend them; or bend one piece of the small end of the upright over and temporarily tie it, then bend the other one over and secure the two together.

Tip: Drive a nail through the two side uprights into the work surface. This gives you some leverage as you bend the uprights and keeps the trellis from flopping around on the table.

Readjust the arch if necessary and wire it securely into position. Wire the two bent pieces together about every 8" around the arch, twisting the wire tightly to secure it. Your basic structure is finished.

9. Attaching the center upright. With the trellis lying flat on the table, crosspieces down, position the center upright in the middle, with about 6" of the thicker end extending below the bottom crosspiece. Don't worry about how much of the top end extends beyond the arch. Nail the upright into position at each crosspiece, but don't nail into the arch, as nailing may split the bent wood. Instead, wire the joint where the upright crosses the arch.

10. Attaching additional crosspieces. Turn the trellis over and position an additional crosspiece 6" above the lower one. Nail it to the uprights and wire the joints securely.

Position the last crosspiece 6" below the upper crosspiece, then nail and wire it in place. Turn the trellis over and bend over any nail points sticking out the back. Leave the trellis face down.

11. Attaching the lattice pieces. Beginning with the thinner end of one of your decorative pieces, cut a piece long enough to fit diagonally across one of the rectangles formed by the two bottom crosspieces and the middle upright. Nail it in place, then trim off any excess with hand pruners.

Cut another piece of equal length from the same branch, place it diagonally across the rectangle to form an X, and nail it in place. Repeat the process to form an X in the other rectangle on the other side of the center upright.

12. Attaching the fan pieces. Turn the trellis over, with the crosspieces facing up. Cut two decorative pieces about 3' long. Position the bottom of one end at the intersection of the top crosspiece and the center upright, with the limb extending up at about a 45-degree angle across one side of the arch. Hide the bottom end behind the center upright and nail it in place. Place the other limb in the same position on the other side of the arch. Nail it in place. Securely wire the upper ends of the limbs to the arch. Do not nail into the arch.

13. Trimming and finishing. Trim off the ends of all the crosspieces to leave about 12" extending over each side upright. Trim the fan pieces and center upright to leave about 18" (or whatever length is visually pleasing to you) extending beyond the arch. If you want to embellish the design, you can add more latticework or other decorative pieces.

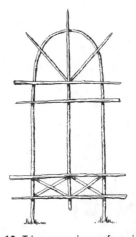

Step 13: Embellish the design with more decorative pieces, if desired.

—from *Making Bentwood Trellises, Arbors, Gates, and Fences* by Jim Long

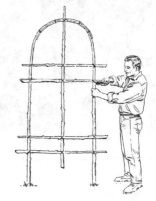

Step 10: Position an additional crosspiece 6" below the upper crosspiece.

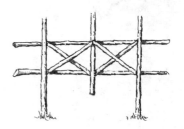

Step 11: Attach diagonals between the bottom and middle rectangles.

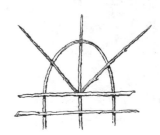

Step 12: Attach decorative fan pieces.

Step 13: Trim crosspieces, fan pieces, and center upright.

19

GREENHOUSES

GREENHOUSE CHOICES • SETTING UP A GREENHOUSE
GROWING IN A GREENHOUSE • TROUBLESHOOTING

I'll admit that the reason we decided to install a passive solar greenhouse was the manufacturer's headline on the brochure, "Enjoy the aroma of fresh basil in February!" This was quite a promise at a time when the powerfully aromatic herb wasn't generally available in supermarkets. We bought a good kit, but getting it installed and functioning properly was more of a job than we thought. We found ourselves coming home at lunchtime to water or rotate plants during hot weather to keep them from wilting. And there's nothing quite like a whitefly infestation! But oh, the aroma of basil in February! This chapter begins with advice from Sandie Shores, who grows fresh-cut herbs through the frigid Minnesota winters.

—John Storey

To be most efficient, writes Sandie Shores, author of Growing and Selling Fresh-Cut Herbs, *a greenhouse's length should be twice its width. The covering for the greenhouse, called glazing, is usually glass or rigid plastic. The roof should be slanted for maximum light transmission; otherwise, the plants will lean toward the sun.*

A greenhouse gives you the opportunity to control the weather. Frost, rain, storms, and winter are not a problem for the greenhouse-grown plant. You can control the environment and provide exactly what the plants need for optimal growth, no longer at the mercy of Mother Nature.

A greenhouse can be used to start plants early for transplanting outdoors, to extend the growing season, or to grow herbs year-round. If you grow herbs or other plants commercially, you will eventually want a greenhouse. As plants grow, they need plenty of space and light. Without proper light the plants become leggy and the growth soft. Better-quality plants result by using a greenhouse to prepare them for transplanting outdoors.

If you want to grow plants all year, you will need heating, ventilation equipment, and artificial lighting, which can be expensive. As a year-round grower in Minnesota, I can testify to this. It is, however, a glorious sensation after trudging through snow and cold wind to step into a warm, humid, green environment. Instant summer!

GREENHOUSE CHOICES

Although most people envision freestanding buildings, greenhouses come in a variety of shapes and sizes. Large-scale growers may have huge glassed-in buildings, but the amateur horticulturist can build or purchase a small, freestanding backyard greenhouse, constructed with aluminum frame and glazed with plastic or polycarbonate. Regardless of the size of your greenhouse, plant cultivation should follow similar guidelines (see next pages).

Which Greenhouse Is For You?

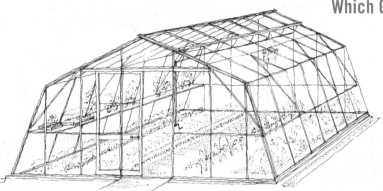

Traditional greenhouses are freestanding glass enclosures. This "Dutch" greenhouse has splayed sides, which are good for structural rigidity and increased ground planting areas.

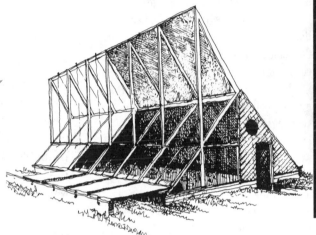

Window-box greenhouses can provide a small growing area attached to almost any building.

A wide-span A-frame solar greenhouse can be designed with reflecting shutters rigged to an external pulley system. This kind of shutter must be braced strongly to withstand high winds.

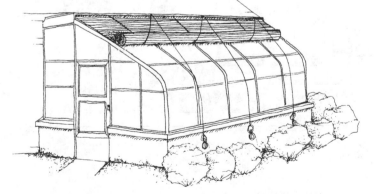

Lean-to greenhouses attach to the south side of a building and may double as a sunroom with roll-up shades to regulate light and heat.

Window greenhouses can be integrated into the design of a home and become functional yet attractive, ideal for plants and plant lovers, and visually interesting from both inside and outside.

—from The Big Book of Gardening Skills

SETTING UP A GREENHOUSE

Of Benches and Beds

Inside your greenhouse you can grow plants in containers, raised beds, beds in the ground, or a combination of these. Convenience and efficiency are the main considerations.

Most growers will want some bench area for potted plants and flats of seedlings. Place these on the north side or end of the greenhouse where they won't shade the growing beds. Space-saving hanging baskets can be used for low-growing plants such as thymes, pansies, and nasturtiums. Hang the baskets just above head height to prevent bumping into them. These, too, are best hung on the north side to prevent shading of the growing beds.

The beds or benches should be accessible from at least three sides. If they are wider than 4 feet, you may have trouble reaching the plants on the inside. Allow enough space between the beds or benches for easy passage and turning around, usually 2 to 3 feet. The main aisle (or aisles) should be wider to allow people and equipment to move around.

Choosing a Site for a Greenhouse

The location for your greenhouse is critical. Even if you never plan to have another greenhouse, do choose a site that would accommodate more than one. Allow at least twice as much room as you think you will need. Here are some other considerations:

Sunlight. Pick a site that receives unobstructed sunlight, especially from the south. Keep in mind that the track of the sun is lower during winter.

Flat terrain. Your site should be solid and level, free from hills and ridges, although a hill on the north side could be valuable protection from the cold north winds of winter.

Drainage. The greenhouse should sit at least 1 foot higher than the surrounding area. Determine where the water will run in the event of large amounts of rain or spring floods.

Snow. If your region receives snow, be sure to leave enough space around the greenhouse for its removal. Snow slides off the greenhouse and large banks of snow can build up around the base, pressing into the sides or blocking sun.

Access. Consider your site in relation to utilities. You will need water and probably electricity available at the site. It's helpful to have a driveway directly to your greenhouse, if you should have materials delivered. You will also need to know the location of buried cables and gas lines before construction begins.

—from *Growing and Selling Fresh-Cut Herbs* by Sandie Shores

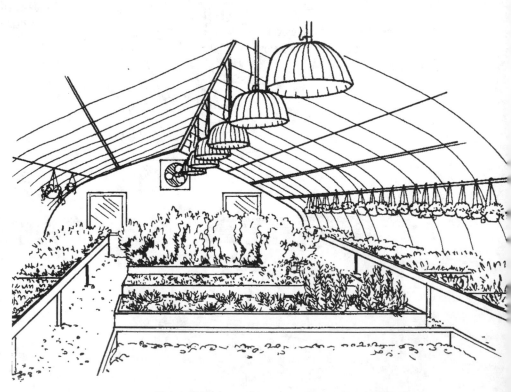

Make efficient use of your greenhouse space with beds, benches, and hanging pots that are all easily accessible.

Herbs in the Greenhouse

Rich, heavy soil is not necessary for growing herbs, but good drainage is critical. Most herbs don't like "wet feet" and will grow poorly in heavy, wet soil. A soil mix that is too heavy holds too much water and doesn't allow enough oxygen to reach the plant roots.

The soil mix for greenhouse raised beds should be light enough to dry out completely within four or five days in the high-humidity conditions during the cool months. It also must be heavy enough for the roots to support large plants without pulling out of the soil. Good soil drainage is achieved by incorporating amendments into the soil. Ideal components are:

- Sterilized topsoil to provide nourishment and stability
- Peat moss to loosen the soil, hold water, and bind it together when wet
- Perlite (crushed volcanic rock) to aerate and provide good drainage
- Sand and fine gravel (pea rock) to provide good drainage
- Compost to offer soil nutrients and suppress disease

Managing Microclimates

Every greenhouse has several microclimates. Some areas are colder, hotter, sunnier, or more shaded than others. Conditions and temperature can vary greatly even on the same side of the greenhouse.

Next to the glazing on the south side of the greenhouse will be the hottest during a sunny day but the coolest at night. The north side of the greenhouse is cooler and receives less light.

You can take advantage of these microclimates because not all herbs favor the same growing conditions. Basil, for instance, likes sun and heat; mint prefers cooler conditions.

—from *Growing and Selling Fresh-Cut Herbs*

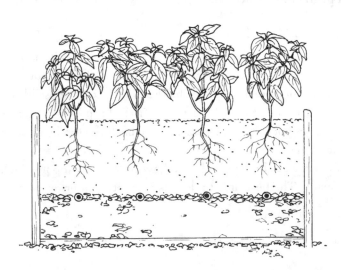

The bottom of this raised bed is lined with gravel for drainage. Soil-heating pipes or PVC can be placed below, above, or within the gravel before you add the soil mix. Fill the rest of the bed with soil mix to a couple of inches from the top.

In Stormy Weather

Storms of all kinds strike fear in the hearts of greenhouse growers everywhere, but there are steps you can take to minimize damage.

Strong winds can cause severe damage to greenhouses of all types. All greenhouses should be able to withstand 80 mph gusts if they are built to code. Make sure the area around the greenhouse is free of debris that could blow around and through the poly glazing. Check metal chimney pipes to make sure they are properly secured.

All doors, windows, louvers, and vents should be closed tightly. If wind is allowed to enter the greenhouse, it creates more wind inside. With double-poly houses, strong winds create a lifting effect and the greenhouse actually rises and sways with the gusts. Make sure the poly is fastened securely to the baseboards and end walls, and slightly increase the air pressure between the poly layers to keep them taut.

If electrical power is lost, your plants can suffer from temperature extremes or from water deprivation. If you are dependent on your greenhouse for food or livelihood, consider investing in a gas-powered electric generator that will start automatically after a power outage.

GROWING IN A GREENHOUSE

Six Tender Perennials for Greenhouses

Begonia
Cactus
Cineraria
Fuchsia
Gardenia
Orchid

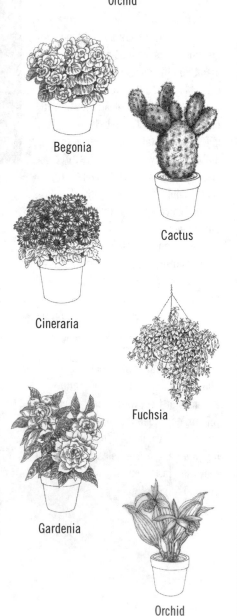

Begonia

Cactus

Cineraria

Fuchsia

Gardenia

Orchid

Tender Perennials

Tender perennials are the most common greenhouse subjects. These include most common houseplants, but also many flowering plants that could not stand the dry heat of an ordinary house. They are grown for the beauty of either their flowers or their foliage. Almost any attractive, hardy garden plants can also be brought indoors to bloom a few weeks early. You'll be able to enjoy them indoors, and the blooms will be protected from the ravages of the weather.

Keeping Greenhouse Plants Comfortable

Most ornamental plants will grow well in a commercial mix or a homemade mixture of 2 parts loam to 1 part peat to 1 part sharp sand. Seeds can be started in the same mix with some extra peat and sand. Cuttings do best in half peat and half sharp sand or in pure vermiculite.

Plants will often stop blooming or look unhappy if temperatures are too cool. If tender plants get frozen, spraying them with cold water before the sun hits them will sometimes save them.

Generally, foliage plants prefer, or at least accept, indirect light. Ideally, this means a northern exposure with plenty of sky light and no direct sun, but partial shade cast by other plants or a place at the back of a greenhouse with a solid roof will do almost as well.

Most flowering plants need lots of sunshine. (African violets, begonias, and impatiens are the major exceptions to this rule.) They will continue to grow with less light but will get long and spindly and will soon stop flowering.

Keeping leaves clean will increase photosynthesis as well as make the plants more attractive. Wipe the leaves with a damp cloth whenever they begin to look dusty. Avoid hard water, which will leave lime spots. A solution of half water and half skim milk will give the leaves a good shine. Large plants can be put outside in a gentle rain or even be given a shower to clean them off.

Repotting for Good Health

Extra-large specimens need big pots, but don't put small plants into large pots. Wait till the roots have used up the available soil, then pot into the next size pot. If that is not convenient, just shake as much soil as possible off the root ball, cut off a quarter to a third of the roots with a sharp knife, and repot it with fresh soil in a clean pot of the same size. Prune back the top by about one quarter at the same time.

Most plants need to be repotted or to have at least the top few inches of soil replaced annually. The best time to do this is in late winter or early spring.

Annuals and Bedding Plants

In general, annuals and bedding plants are started in flats in the greenhouse to be planted out of doors in summer. Most of them, however, can also be sown in late summer or fall to bloom indoors in winter or spring if sufficient light and heat can be given. If winter-flowering or indoor varieties are available, use them for forcing indoors in winter.

Here are some tips on starting seeds in your greenhouse.

1. Use ordinary potting mix with a bit of extra peat and sharp sand; or try the recipe at right.

2. Sow the seed of annuals thinly and shallowly.

3. If the type of seed you are planting needs light for germination, just press it gently into the surface of the soil. Otherwise, cover it with a thin layer of fine peat or soil.

4. Cover the seed box with plastic or glass to retain humidity until the seeds have sprouted, then remove the cover and allow air to circulate.

5. Most annuals germinate in about two weeks. Bottom heat will speed them up by a few days.

6. Transplant or thin your seedlings as soon as the leaves touch. Pinch out the growing tip to encourage branching.

7. Gradually harden off those that are to be planted outside.

8. Annuals are usually planted out two or three weeks after the last possible date of frost in your area.

Homemade Potting Soil

- Five parts leaf mold or vegetable-based compost (manure composts may contain disease
- Four parts good topsoil
- Two parts sharp sand

Mix together thoroughly.

—from *Easy Gardening 101* by Pat Stone

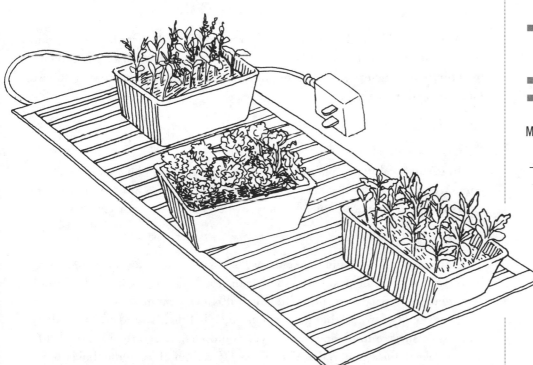

Providing bottom heat is one of the best ways to ensure good germination. Purchase a propagation mat from a garden center or mail-order company.

GROWING IN A GREENHOUSE

Storing and Forcing Bulbs

Hardy bulbs, like crocus, hyacinth, narcissus, and tulip, need a cold, dark rooting period. They can be forced to flower at any time of the year if they are first given a cold period. Some people put pots of bulbs in the refrigerator in August or September to be sure of flowers by December. For later blooming, bulbs are better left outside under a pile of leaves or straw once the weather turns chilly. You can buy specially preconditioned bulbs that need less time in the dark, so they will bloom earlier.

When the bulbs are well rooted and the leaves are 1 to 1½ inches tall, the base of the leaves should be fat with the emerging bud. At this point they are ready to come into the light, but some can be left for several weeks longer to give a succession of blooms.

Give some shade for the first week indoors as the white leaves green up, then full sun at 45 to 50° F. After a few more weeks you can increase the temperature to 60° F to speed them up, but never let them get really warm until the buds have opened. Even then, cold will prolong the flowers' life.

Forced crocus bulbs

Vegetables in the Greenhouse

Just like garden plantings, virtually all greenhouse vegetables require full sun for optimal growth. But those that are grown for their leaves or roots rather than for their fruit will usually grow moderately well, though more slowly, when partially in the shade. Winter vegetables should be well advanced by mid-autumn. They will stay in good condition but won't make much more growth in the depths of winter.

Soil

Most vegetables are grown in the standard soil mix of 2 parts loam to 1 part peat and 1 part sand. The depth of soil needed depends on the final size of the plant and whether most of its growth takes place aboveground or below-ground (carrots will obviously need deeper soil than will lettuce, even though they take up less room aboveground). Generally, 10 to 16 inches is sufficient, with a 2-inch to 4-inch layer of gravel or other free-draining material below.

Starting Seeds

Most vegetable seeds will germinate at 50 to 60° F, though they will sprout sooner with more heat. A few plants absolutely require more heat to germinate, including corn, cucumbers, eggplant, melons, okra, peppers, pumpkins, squash (summer and winter), and tomatoes.

Bulbs in the Greenhouse

In general, cultivated plants grown from bulbs, corms, and tubers will not come true from seeds. If you have extra space in the greenhouse, it is fun to experiment, but you are unlikely to improve on the parent variety.

Soil

Any good, free-draining greenhouse soil is suitable for growing hardy bulbs. Equal parts of peat, sand, and loam (or compost) is a good mixture. Many bulbs can be grown successfully in bulb fiber, peat moss with some charcoal, or even plain gravel, but they will use up all of their stored energy and are unlikely to survive to bloom another year outdoors. They are also more difficult to stake in these materials. When flowers fade, cut off only the flower head, leaving the green stalk to help feed the bulb for next year.

Greenhouse Pest and Disease Problems

Your greenhouse provides good growing conditions for plants. It can also be a haven for many insects and diseases because their natural enemies are excluded. In an enclosed space, sprays and other cures that are effective in the garden may not be practical. A well-run greenhouse is much less susceptible to problems, so prevention is the best defense.

To Avoid Problems

- Good ventilation discourages insects and prevents fungal diseases that thrive in stagnant, moist air.
- Clean up dead leaves, litter, and old pots that might harbor insect eggs and fungus spores.
- Check plants frequently for aphids and other small insects that cause injury and spread disease.
- Once a year, disinfect the glass and surface areas with 10 percent bleach solution to kill growing fungi. Remove or cover plants that might be injured by drips or splashes. Cleaning the glass will also improve lighting and decrease the chance of condensation dripping on plants.
- Use only clean pots for repotting. Scrub and sterilize pots before reuse. Old clay pots should be soaked and scraped clean of any mineral crust that might keep air and water from passing through the clay.
- Use pasteurized soil for starting seeds and cuttings.
- When bringing in potted plants from outdoors, set the pots in water to the rim and soak them overnight to drown any insects in the soil.
- Do not handle plants when they are wet, because diseases are transferred more easily then.

When Problems Occur

- If you have the space, quarantine unhealthy plants away from your healthy specimens.
- Destroy badly infested or diseased plants before the problem spreads.
- After handling plants, especially after inspecting unhealthy plants for problems, wash your hands and any tools you used before touching other plants.
- For aphids and other small insects, often a good shower of water is enough to dislodge them.
- On a small scale, hand-pick and destroy larger insects.

Lizards in the Greenhouse

One expert gardener whose greenhouse is heated year-round introduced a pair of anoles—a type of arboreal lizard of the genus *Anolis*. These brightly colored, 4-inch-long lizards devour insects and change color the way chameleons do. The only drawback was that the anoles were so efficient in eating insects that she had to purchase crickets to supplement their diet. But her greenhouse was completely free of insect problems.

Whitefly

Greenhouse Whitefly

Greenhouse whiteflies are a common problem, along with sweet potato whitefly. These insects prefer warm temperatures and become more inactive as the temperature drops. They cannot survive freezing.

The best control is exclusion through screening. Avoid wearing yellow clothing because whiteflies are attracted to yellow and will hitch a ride into the greenhouse on a yellow shirt.

If possible, allow the greenhouse to freeze during the winter. An alternative is to remove all plants for a week during the summer and close the greenhouse tightly. Adult whiteflies will die after a week without food.

Whiteflies are susceptible to some botanical sprays, including pyrethrum, rotenone, ryania, tobacco, neem, insecticidal soap, and oil sprays. They will quickly build up a resistance to these agents, however, except for the oil spray.

There are also some biological controls available, such as the tiny beneficial wasp *Encarsia formosa* and a small black lady beetle called *Delphastus pusillus*.

—from *Growing and Selling Fresh-Cut Herbs* by Sandie Shores

SHEDS AND MORE

GARDEN SHED • STORAGE SHED • TOOLSHED
TREE HOUSE

Early on in corporate publishing, it was never clear to me how decisions got made. I'd leave a meeting thinking one thing and come back to discover another. When I joined the entrepreneur Lyman Wood, Garden Way founder, decision making became much clearer. If Lyman didn't like the way a meeting was going in his log cabin, he'd call a break, and suggest to one or two of his errant managers that they "take a walk." Invariably, they'd wind up out behind the woodshed. Returning, they'd have had a change of heart. So the woodshed, in addition to keeping hardwoods dry for corporate fires, also served as a setting for avoiding them.

—John Storey

For many gardeners, a shed can solve a myriad of problems. It's a place to store all the untidy rubbish that helps make a great garden: used seed flats, bags of peat moss and steer manure, hoses, bamboo poles, and fabric row covers. If situated close to the garden, it's a place to keep your hoes, spades, and trowels so they won't rust but will still be near at hand. A shed with a large enough entrance and a ramp can store small machines such as tillers and lawn mowers, along with their paraphernalia of fuel and extra parts. And a south-facing shed wall can even provide a warm backdrop for trellising heat-loving crops like cucumbers or flowering vines like morning glories.

Make sure you locate your shed on a level spot with good drainage. And check with local building regulations before beginning construction. Some communities have certain restrictions on the size structure that can be built.

Counterboring. A technique used to sink the head of a bolt or screw below the
level of the surrounding wood

Gusset. A plate or bracket used in building to strengthen an angle

Purlin. A horizontal beam in a roof

Toenailing. Driving a nail at an angle through one piece of wood into another

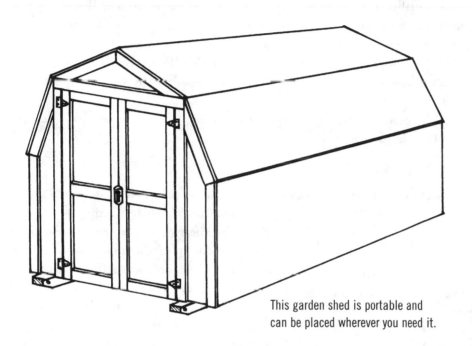

This garden shed is portable and
can be placed wherever you need it.

A Portable Garden Shed

Garden sheds are often practical additions to homes in the suburbs and
countryside. Sheds can be used to store garden tractors, lawn mowers, tillers,
rakes, hoes, and all your other garden and lawn tools. Sheds can be a focal
point of a backyard or garden setting.

This shed has a gambrel roof, which makes it more attractive and provides
more headroom. Although the gambrel design appears somewhat complicated,
it's really an easy project, even for the first-timer.

Because it is constructed on skids, the shed is portable. If you don't like
where you've put the shed, simply slide it to another location. By building on
skids, you also eliminate footings, foundations, and other expensive permanent
supports.

Beginning Construction

1. The shed rests on 4 x 6 skids, so start by cutting the skids to 13-foot lengths.
Cut the fronts and backs on a 45-degree bevel so they don't dig in when the
structure is pulled or moved. Bore a ¾-inch hole in each end at the front and
back. Loops of #9 wire are fastened in each of these holes for a hook-up to a
chain you can use to move the building.

Materials List

Base
2 Skids, 4" x 6" x 13'
2 Floor joists (front and rear),
   2" x 6" x 8'
2 Side headers, 2" x 6" x 11'9"
5 Inside floor joists, 2" x 6" x 7'9"
3 Sheets ¾" plywood 4' x 8'

Back
4 Short studs, 2" x 4" x 45"
3 Long studs, 2" x 4" x 79¾"
1 Bottom plate, 2" x 4" x 8'
2 Center plates, 2" x 4" x 23¼"
2 Upper plates, 2" x 4" x 51"

Sides
14 Studs, 2" x 4" x 3'9"
2   Bottom plates, 2" x 4" x 11'5"
2   Upper side plates, 2" x 4" x 11'5"

Front
6   Short studs, 2" x 4" x 45"
2   Long studs, 2" x 4" x 79¼"
2   Bottom plates, 2" x 4" x 24"
2   Center plates, 2" x 4" x 22¼"
2   Door headers, 2" x 4" x 51"
1   Upper girder, 2" x 6" x 12'
14 Rafters (A), 2" x 4" x 42", cut to fit
14 Rafters (B), 2" x 4" x 29", cut to fit
12 Top braces, 2" x 4" x 24", cut to fit
24 ⅜ plywood truss plates: 6" x 12"
12 ⅜ plywood truss plates: 7¼" x 30"
12 sheets siding
94 linear feet trim, 1" x 4"

Door
4   Uprights, 2" x 2" x 80½"
6   Crosspieces, 2" x 2" x 20½"
12 Lag screws, ⅜" x 8"
    Door hardware and hinges

Roof
200 square feet of shingles

— from *64 Yard and Garden Projects You
Can Build Yourself* by Monte Burch

GARDEN SHED

2. Position the skids on a smooth surface, spacing them 8 feet apart. Cut the front and rear floor joists and anchor them with 8-inch lag screws in counterbored holes down through the top into the skids. Saw the side headers and anchor them with lag screws into the skids as well, adding more lag screws through the floor joists into each header. It's extremely important to make sure the structure is square at this point. Use a carpenter's square to achieve squareness initially, then measure diagonally from corner to corner. If the diagonal measurements are the same, the structure is square. If not, shift the corners until the measurements are correct.

3. Once the unit is square, position the inside floor joists between the side headers, spaced every two feet on center, and nail solidly with 16d galvanized nails.

4. Position the ¾-inch plywood floor sheets in place and fasten to the headers and floor joists with 8d ring-shank nails.

The Front End

5. Construct the front end by cutting the pieces to size, then shaping and fastening them together on the plywood platform. Start by cutting the bottom plate. Cut the two long studs and the short outside studs, plus the short center plates. Lay all of these on the platform along with the bottom plate. Note that the bottom plate is cut full length; the opening for the door is cut after the frame is erected.

6. Cut the two 2 x 4s to form the door header that fits over the door uprights. Nail them together to create a doubled header and put in position.

7. With these pieces in place, begin nailing them together with 16d nails. Drive nails through the bottom plate into the door uprights and the outer studs. Hammer through the center plates into the upper ends of the outer studs, then fasten the opposite ends in the proper position with nails through the door uprights. Cut the short "cripple" studs on either side of the door uprights and attach.

8. The door header isn't as thick as the width of the 2 x 4s, so use shims to hold it up flush with the outside edge of the 2 x 4s and toenail the header in position.

9. Cut two of the lower front rafters (A) to shape and fasten them to the center plates and the headers by toenailing.

10. Cut the upper front rafters (B) to size

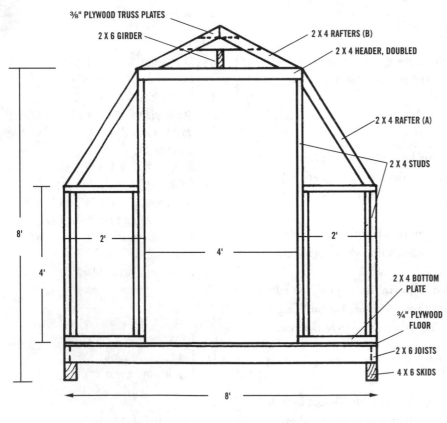

Front Elevation

and shape and cut a ⅜-inch plywood gusset. Nail and glue this with resorcinol glue to the backside of the rafter pairs at the top, then toenail the upper rafter assembly to the top of the door headers.

11. Stand the assembled front up on the floor platform and plumb it using a level. Check to be sure it is square with a carpenter's square as well, unless you're sure the floor platform is absolutely level. Next, brace the assembly in place with 2 × 4s nailed to the side studs and back to the side headers.

Rear and Side Frames

12. Assemble the rear frame in the same manner as the front except for the upper section on top of the studs, which utilizes two plates or 2 × 4s laid flat. Nail the lower in place first and then the upper plate on top of it.

13. The side frames are assembled by cutting a bottom and top plate and the studs to size and shape, then nailing all of them together on the floor platform. Stand the assembly up and nail the outer end studs on front and back into the studs of the side frames and the bottom plate through the flooring and into the side headers.

14. Cut the 2 × 6 upper "girder" and fasten it on top of the front header and rear upper plate by toenailing. Short blocks of wood can also be nailed on either side of it to help provide more strength.

Inside Rafters

15. The inside rafters are actually trusses created by cutting the rafters to the proper shapes and angles as shown in the drawing and fastening them together with ⅜-inch plywood gussets on both sides of each joint. Assemble one truss, then use it as a pattern to assemble the others. You can even stack the pieces on it and fasten them together to ensure that all trusses are assembled in the same manner.

16. With a helper, lift the first interior truss and put it down on the girder. Toenail the ends of the truss to the upper top plates and the plywood gussets to the top girder. Install the remaining trusses in the same manner.

17. With all trusses assembled, cut the brace pieces that run between the trusses and attach them.

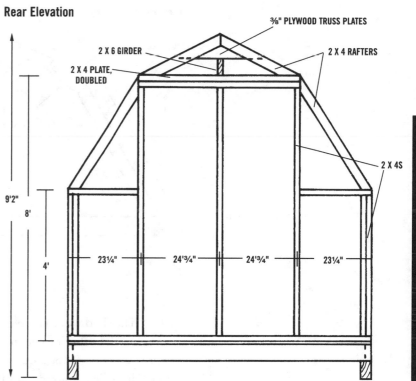

Rear Elevation

⅜" PLYWOOD TRUSS PLATES
2 X 6 GIRDER
2 X 4 PLATE, DOUBLED
2 X 4 RAFTERS
2 X 4S
9'2"
8'
4'
23¼" 24'¾" 24'¾" 23¼"
8'

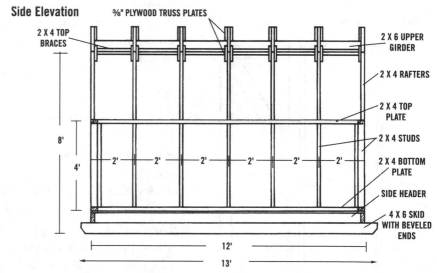

Side Elevation

⅜" PLYWOOD TRUSS PLATES
2 X 4 TOP BRACES
2 X 6 UPPER GIRDER
2 X 4 RAFTERS
2 X 4 TOP PLATE
2 X 4 STUDS
2 X 4 BOTTOM PLATE
SIDE HEADER
4 X 6 SKID WITH BEVELED ENDS
8'
4'
2' 2' 2' 2' 2' 2'
12'
13'

GARDEN SHED

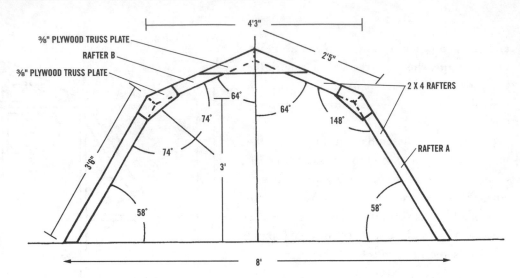

Truss Elevation

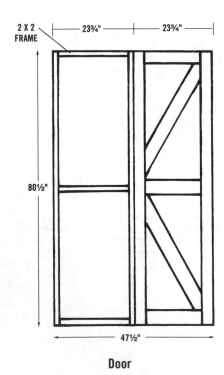

Door

The Walls

18. The shed walls can be covered with metal, solid siding, hardboard siding, or plywood. Prefinished hardboard siding or prefinished plywood are both excellent choices for a quickly covered building. Cut the siding pieces and fasten with 4d galvanized nails into the studs and upper and lower plates. The siding should drop down below the flooring to the bottom edge of the side headers and come up flush with the top edge of the upper plate on the sides.

19. Once the siding has been installed, you can add decorative trim. It's a good idea to paint these in a color that contrasts with the siding. Cut the trim to fit first, paint it, and then fasten with galvanized 4d nails.

The Roof

20. The roof can be metal if you prefer, in which case horizontal purlins are nailed over the rafters. The metal roofing is nailed to the purlins with roofing nails with neoprene washers.

21. In most cases, the roof will have a wood decking with shingles. Create the deck with ½-inch plywood sheathing. Cut the pieces to the correct size and nail them to the rafters, starting at the bottom rafters and using 6d ring-shank nails. Note that the bottom ends should protrude past the wood siding on the walls about 1 inch. Then cut the upper sheathing pieces and nail them in place in the same manner, but remember the sheathing protrudes out flush with the upper trim boards on each end.

22. The next step is to apply asphalt or fiberglass shingles to the roof.

Finishing Touches

23. Create the double door by nailing plywood siding cut from the door opening to a 2 x 2 frame as shown. You can nail the (prepainted) decorative trim boards over the door facing.

24. Hang the doors with decorative strap hinges and then install a latch that can be locked from the outside with a padlock.

—from *64 Yard and Garden Projects You Can Build Yourself* by Monte Burch

This portable, free-standing storage building has 2 X 4 framing, but treated and embedded 4 X 4 posts might be used at the corners if you want to add more stability and anchor the building permanently. Here's how to build the structure as shown:

1. Begin by framing the walls with 2 X 4s. These are doubled at the door to provide enough surface for the hinges. In the back wall, the 2 X 4 studs extend up to the rafters and ridge board.

2. Fasten the four walls together by nailing horizontal 2 X 4 girts at base, midpoint and top.

3. Fasten ridge board to top of block in front and to extended 2 X 4 stud in rear wall.

4. Cut rafter ends at required angles and nail to ridge board and top wall pieces. Install purlins.

5. Frame doors, using two 2 X 4s to accommodate hinges.

6. Paint or stain framing.

7. Apply panels or covering.

8. Hang doors and install door hardware. Add door stop at bottom by toe-nailing 2 X 4 to door frame; face the 4-inch side to the ground.

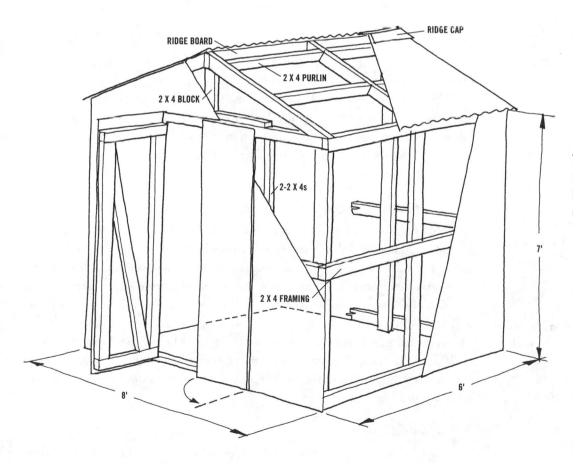

RIDGE BOARD · RIDGE CAP · 2 X 4 PURLIN · 2 X 4 BLOCK · 2-2 X 4s · 2 X 4 FRAMING · 8' · 6' · 7'

This small storage building has 2 x 4 framing throughout. If you wish to add stability, use 4 x 4s for corner posts.

— from *Building Small Barns, Sheds, and Shelters* by Monte Burch

TOOLSHED

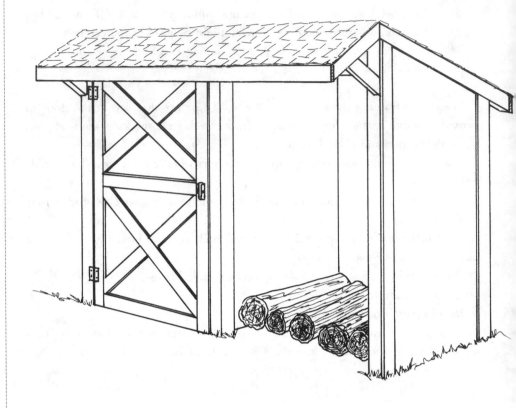

Materials List

3	Posts, 4" x 4" x 10' - 12'
3	Posts, 4" x 4" x 8' - 10' *(depending upon frost line)*
1	Front upper girt, 2" x 4" x 8'
1	Front lower girt, 2" x 4" x 7'9"
3	Rear girts, 2" x 4" x 8'
6	Side girts, 2" x 4" x 34½"
6	Inside side girts, 2" x 4 x 34½"
3	Inside back girts, 2" x 4" x 3'9"
3	Floor supporting girts, 2" x 4" x 41½"
1	Floor, ¾" plywood x 41½" x 4'
2	Center and left front trim strips, 1" x 5" x 6'8"
1	Left upper front trim strip, 1" x 5" x 16"
1	Right lower front trim strip, 1" x 7¼" x 6'8"
1	Right upper front trim strip, 1" x 7¼" x 16"
2	Top plates, 2" x 4" x 8'
5	Rear rafters, 2" x 4" x 5'3"
5	Front rafters, 2" x 4" x 2'3"
5	Gussets, ½" plywood x 6" x 12"
2	Side front braces, 2" x 4" x 25", cut to fit
2	Fascia boards, 1" x 4" x 8'
8	Siding sheets, 4' x 8' sheets plywood or prefinished hardboard Door framing, 22 linear feet of 2 x 2s Door trim, 40 linear feet of 1 x 4s
3	Roof decking, ⅜" x 4' x 8' sheets 64 square feet of shingles Hardware, door hinges, and latch

*—from 64 Yard and Garden Projects
You Can Build Yourself by Monte Burch*

Tip: Use pressure-treated lumber for posts and girts that contact the ground.

Tool Storage Center

This storage center holds firewood as well as rakes, hoes, a push mower, and all the other assorted gear needed for caring for your lawn and garden. It has an enclosed side for tools and an open area for wood storage. It is a permanent structure utilizing pole building techniques that are easy even for a beginning carpenter.

Beginning Construction

Start by determining the exact site for the building and marking the post locations. Make sure the posts will not interfere with utility lines or underground cables. To lay out the building, measure the approximate distance for each of the four corners according to the plans, and drive stakes at the rough location of each post center. Remember, the post centers will be approximately 3 inches inside the perimeter of the building. To ensure that the building is square, measure diagonally from stake to stake. The diagonal measurements should be the same. If they are not, move the stakes until the diagonal measurements are equal and the proper measurements for the sides, front, and back are still maintained.

Setting Posts

Dig the holes for the posts. A local Extension agent can tell you how deep you need to dig. Allow for the depth of the post embedment plus 4 inches for a layer of gravel or concrete. The holes should be twice the width of the posts. The posts can be set in concrete or (in most parts of the country) tamped earth and gravel, depending on your local soil conditions. Concrete lasts the longest, but gravel and tamped earth will often suffice for a building of this size.

To set the posts in concrete, pour a 4-inch punch pad in the bottom of each hole and let cure for 24 hours before setting the posts.

Position the posts using 2 x 4 braces to hold them in the proper location and keep them plumb. A long carpenter's level can plumb them in both directions (their two outer sides). Again, measure the diagonals to check for squareness.

For the small amount of concrete used for this project you can use premixed concrete that comes in a bag with sand and gravel. Simply add water and pour the mixture in the hole around the braced and supported posts. Round the concrete up around the posts and smooth it down so water will run away from the posts.

Tamped-earth posts are erected in much the same manner, except that a layer of gravel is placed in the hole before the posts are positioned in place and plumbed. Next, a layer of earth and then a layer of gravel are shoveled in the hole around the posts and tamped solidly. Then another layer of soil and another of gravel are added and tamped. This process is repeated until the hole is filled and the post anchored solidly in place.

Use a straightedge such as a long 2 x 4 and a level to mark across from the shortest rear post and cut the other rear posts to the correct height using a handsaw or portable electric saw. Do the same for the front posts.

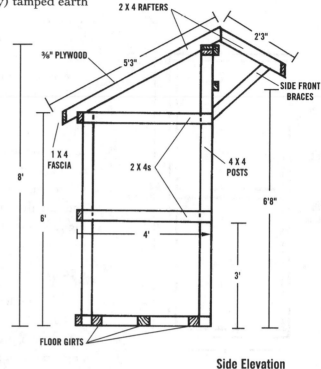

Side Elevation

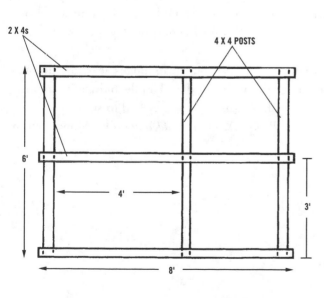

Rear Elevation

Front Elevation

Floor, Roof, and Wall Supports

Cut the short side horizontal girts and nail them to the posts enclosing the tool storage area on both the outside and inside walls. Then cut and nail the long rear horizontal girts across the rear posts with 16d nails. Saw and fasten the top plate for the front wall, nailing the front top girt and the post fronts to it. Cut the bottom floor supporting girts and attach one in front, one in back, and one in the center.

The rafters supporting the cantilevered roof are actually trusses formed by gluing and nailing plywood gussets to the eave joints of the two rafters. Cut the rafters to the proper length, cut a notch in both the lower and upper ends of the long rafters, and join the rafters together to create the trusses. Position a rafter truss on one end of the building and nail it securely through the notch and into the back top girt and the top plate with 16d nails. Fasten the remaining rafters in the same manner. Nail the fascia boards on the front edges of the rear and front rafters. Finally, nail the side front roof braces in position.

Siding

The building can be covered with any number of siding types. The simplest and fastest siding is probably either prefinished hardboard siding such as masonite or plywood siding such as Georgia Pacific Ply-Bead, which gives the appearance of tongue-and-groove planking.

Start covering the building by fastening back pieces in place first, then the ends. Make sure you get the first sheet plumb so the second sheet will fit properly. Nail the inside sheets in the same manner. Cut outside trim pieces to cover the rough edges of the siding and to fill the open area at the front post. Use the narrower trim stock for the other areas or make all the trim wider if you desire.

Cover the rafters with 3/8-inch plywood sheathing nailed with 3d or 4d ring-shank nails. Shingle the roof to match existing architecture.

The door is a 2 x 2 frame made by ripping the 2 x 2s from 2 x 4 stock with a portable circular saw with a ripping guide or a table saw. Nail plywood siding to the frame before ripping trim strips for the outside edges of the front of the door.

You can hang the door with butt hinges, but strap hinges are more decorative. Then add a hasp and padlock as well as a door handle and you're in business. If you are not using prefinished siding, paint the shed to suit.

—from *64 Yard and Garden Projects You Can Build Yourself* by Monte Burch

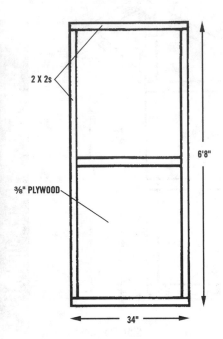

2 X 2s

3/8" PLYWOOD

6'8"

34"

Back of Door

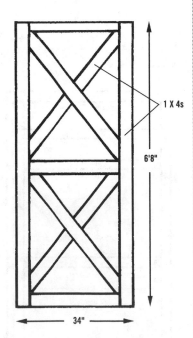

1 X 4s

6'8"

34"

Front of Door

A Triangular Tree House

This particular tree house does not require the use of tree branches for its support. Instead, the hut is cantilevered off the tree trunk with the help of braces and cables. The structure's triangular shape gives it greater strength.

You will need a tall ladder to build this structure and to enter it when you are finished. Hide the ladder in the woods to keep out unwelcome guests when you are not using it.

—from *Rustic Retreats* by Jeanie and David Stiles

TREE HOUSE

Jeanie and David Stiles have been called America's First Couple of Do-It-Yourself Building Projects. Together they have written 14 books on woodworking, which have sold more than 300,000 copies, including Rustic Retreats and Garden Retreats.

Materials List

The lengths given for beams and braces are approximate.
They can vary depending on the size of the tree.

Part	Quantity	Description
Platform frame		
Bottom side beams	2	8' 2 x 8
Crossbeams	3	2 x 8 approx. 8', 5', and 3' in length
Rear brace	1	3' 2 x 6
Front support braces	2	6' 2 x 6
Cabin		
Floor	1½ panels	¾" exterior plywood
Top side beams	2	8' 2 x 8
Crossbeams	3	2 x 8 approx. 8', 5', and 3' in length
Wall studs	10	7' 2 x 4
Siding		Rough slab lumber
Roof	1½ panels	¾" exterior plywood
Roof trim	2	8' 1 x 2
Other materials	2	Turnbuckles
	2	¾" x 4" lag screws
	2	½" x 7" bolts with washers
	2	½" x 3" bolts with washers
		¼" steel cable, 20' long
		1½"-diameter steel pipe as long as the diameter of the tree
		Roll roofing
		4" galvanized nails
		Other assorted nails and screws

— from *Rustic Retreats* by David and Jeanie Stiles

Platform Framing

1. Throw a rope over a branch, high up in the tree. Attach the loose end of the rope to one end of a 2 x 8 side beam and use the other end of the rope to hoist up the beam. Drive a pivot nail in the center of the beam where it joins the tree.

2. Pull on the loose end of the rope to level the beam and drive in four 4"-long, galvanized nails or screws.

3. Attach a 2 x 6 support brace to the side beam and the tree to help hold the beam in place.

4. Attach the second side beam to the other side of the tree, using the same technique.

5. Join the two side beams together in three places with 2 x 8 crossbeams. Attach the middle crossbeam first, nailing each end to the side beams. The three crossbeams are approximately 3', 5', and 8' long, but the lengths vary according to the thickness of your tree. If you are working alone, use temporary supports to help hold the crossbeams in place as you're nailing them to the side beams.

6. Bolt a 2 x 6 rear brace between the two side beams and nail the top to the tree.

7. For additional strength, thread a ¼" suspension cable through a 1½"-diameter iron pipe, the same length as the width of the tree. Rest the pipe on two ⅜" x 4" lag screws, screwed into the tree 7' above the platform. Attach each end of the cable to the side beams.

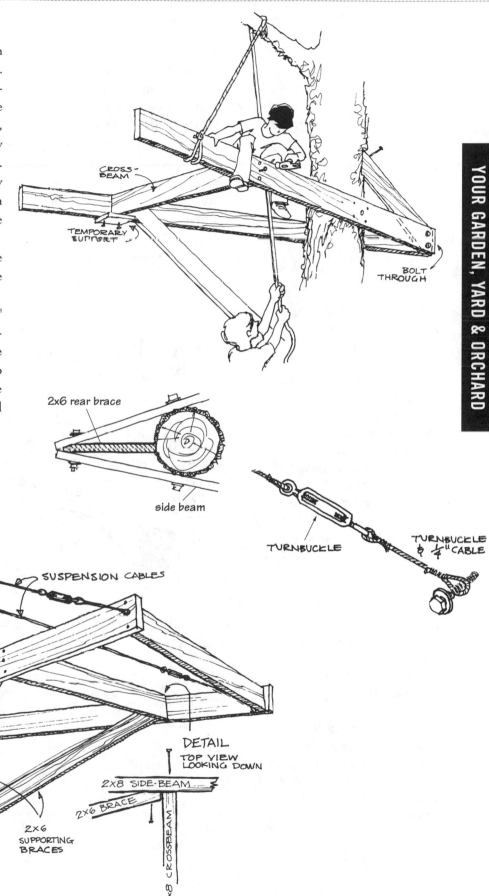

CROSS-BEAM

TEMPORARY SUPPORT

BOLT THROUGH

2x6 rear brace

side beam

TURNBUCKLE

TURNBUCKLE & ¼" CABLE

IRON PIPE

SUSPENSION CABLES

TWO ⅜"x4" LAG SCREWS TO HOLD PIPE IN PLACE

2x6 rear brace

2x4 STEP

2x6 SUPPORTING BRACES

DETAIL

TOP VIEW LOOKING DOWN

2x8 SIDE-BEAM

2x6 BRACE

2x8 CROSSBEAM

TREE HOUSE

Cabin

1. Build a ¾" exterior-plywood floor with a trap door, hinged to open in.

2. Install top side beams, slanting toward the rear of the tree house to shed rain, and 2 x 4 corner posts (attached inside the side beams).

3. Frame the roof the same as the floor platform, except on a slant, and cover it with plywood and roll roofing. Fold the roll roofing over the edges of the plywood and nail it to a 1 x 2 piece of roof trim.

4. Frame the sides and front with 2 x 4s, spaced 16" apart, and cover with slabs, overlapping them from the bottom up. (Slabs are the unused portion of a tree after they are cut up at the sawmill. You can often get them for free.)

5. Add 2 x 6 steps. Cut wedge-shaped blocks to level and support the steps, and nail them to the braces.

—from *Rustic Retreats* by Jeanie and David Stiles

Don't Go Out on a Limb: More Tree House Tips

- If possible, make the first platform within arm's reach from the ground, or at least within reach of a stepladder.
- Use a safety harness and make sure the rope from the harness is attached to a strong branch.
- Provide strong handles at the top of ladders and inside doorways to make climbing in and out of your tree house safer and easier.
- If you plan to use your tree house for several years, make sure the tree you build in is strong and sound.
- Allow for flexibility in the joints, so the tree can grow and move with the wind.
- Use only galvanized nails. Unprotected nails will rust away in three years.
- For framing tree houses, galvanized deck screws are more practical to use than nails. They hold better and can be removed if you need to modify your hut.
- For attaching beams, use ½-inch diameter, galvanized hex-head lag screws with washers rather than relying on several little nails. A socket wrench is very handy for putting lag screws into wood.

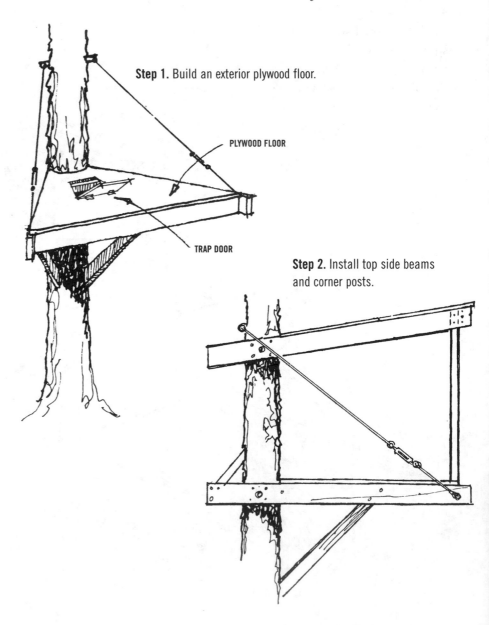

Step 1. Build an exterior plywood floor.

PLYWOOD FLOOR

TRAP DOOR

Step 2. Install top side beams and corner posts.

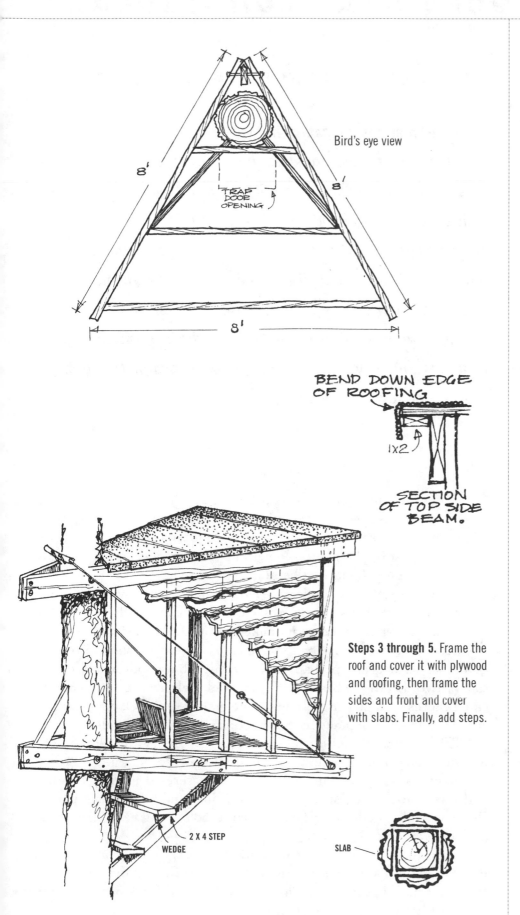

Bird's eye view

8'

8'

8'

TRAP
DOOR
OPENING

BEND DOWN EDGE
OF ROOFING

1x2

SECTION
OF TOP SIDE
BEAM.

Steps 3 through 5. Frame the
roof and cover it with plywood
and roofing, then frame the
sides and front and cover
with slabs. Finally, add steps.

16"

2 X 4 STEP

WEDGE

SLAB

Still More Tree House Tips

- Materials particularly suitable
  for tree house construction are
  synthetic rope (not manila), steel
  cable, and forked branches (for
  braces).
- You can nail or screw into large
  trees without causing much damage, but never cut the bark all the
  way around the tree.
- Don't worry if the frame of your tree
  house is not square. It is more
  important to make sure it is level.
- Use 2 x 6 braces where support is
  needed and branches do not exist.
- Check with your local lumber yard
  for knot-free scrap wood or ask a
  local builder for scrap wood from
  a new house site.
- Take advantage of what the tree
  offers in the way of natural supports. Never design your tree hut
  first and then try to find a tree
  that fits.

— from *Rustic Retreats* by
Jeanie and David Stiles

21 TOOLS AND TECHNIQUES

I've never met anyone as ingenious with tools as Dick Raymond. Dissatisfied with the standard hoe because of its width, he developed a "finger hoe," literally the size of your index finger, with an extra-long handle to save your back. Anxious to thin his seedlings without picking them by hand, he invented the "in row weeder," somewhat like a steel rake, but with much finer tines. When word got out about these tools, Dick got thousands of orders without advertising. "I build them for myself," Dick wrote his unhappy followers. His fellow innovator Monte Burch shares tool advice in this chapter.

—John Storey

With the right tools, you can do anything. With the wrong tools, even the simplest jobs can be tough. Remember that sometimes the wrong tool isn't cheaply made or badly designed—sometimes the wrong tool is simply inappropriate for the task at hand.

Fortunately, you can undertake even major projects without a shop full of expensive tools. Most jobs can be handled with hand tools, although a few power tools can make the process easier and faster. If you don't already own the tools you need, I suggest you start with a few quality hand tools and perhaps an economical but good-quality power tool or two. Learn the basics with the hand tools, so the more complicated chores with power tools will come more readily. Of course, some specialized tools can make particular jobs a great deal simpler.

The basic hand-tool kit should contain a hammer, handsaw, tape measure, carpenter's square, combination square, block plane, wood chisel, pliers, several standard and Phillips screwdrivers, push drill and bits, 4-foot level, string line, chalk line, and carpenter's pencil. Purchase only good-quality, name-brand tools. With care, they'll last a lifetime and more

Good tools require less effort and, more importantly, are safer to use. Sharp tools are also safer and much more efficient than dull ones. It is important to remember that a tool designed for a particular job is probably the best tool for that job.

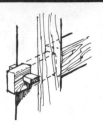

Handsaws

Handsaws come in two basic varieties: crosscut saws and rip saws. Crosscut saws are made for cutting across the grain of the wood, while rip saws are designed for ripping, which is cutting with the grain. A crosscut saw can be used for both chores, but it won't rip as easily as a ripping saw.

Handsaws are available with different numbers of teeth per inch (tpi). The fewer the teeth per inch, the faster and rougher the saw will cut. For most rough-cut exterior work, and especially for use with pressure-treated wood, a saw with 6 to 8 tpi is excellent. This should be a good, sturdy saw, preferably hollow or taper ground. If you're doing more finished work, you'll want a saw with more teeth to the inch.

Three Handy Squares

In order to assure that projects fit together properly, you'll need a few types of squares. The oldest and most basic type is the carpenter's square. These are available in aluminum or steel. They are 16 by 24 inches, and are L-shaped. Carpenter's squares are particularly useful with larger projects.

The combination square is much smaller. Its 12-inch blade has a central groove that allows a triangular body to slide along the length of the blade. Combination squares are most useful to mark cuts on smaller boards. Because there is a 45-degree angle on the body, you can also use this square to mark 45-degree cuts.

A T-bevel square is necessary for determining and marking angles. It most commonly has a steel head with a wooden arm. Because T-bevel squares can be adjusted to any angle, they can be used with protractors to set exact angles or match existing ones.

Levels

You'll probably need several levels. The first is a standard, 2-foot aluminum  model—the kind you should own if you purchase only one. This can be used for most construction work; however, a 3- or 4-foot level is essential for many chores. Naturally, the longer levels are more expensive.

Use a string level to set a level line between corners of a building, or as a guide for installing concrete blocks. A combination plumb bob/chalk line is useful for marking cut lines and determining the plumbness of corners or walls. Keep several lengths of string on hand. Mason's line is preferred because of its strength and durability.

—from *64 Yard and Garden Projects You Can Build Yourself*
and *Building Small Barns, Sheds, and Shelters* by Monte Burch

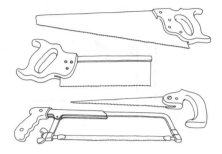

Hand tools, top to bottom: handsaw, tenon saw, keyhole saw, and hacksaw

Cutting with Hand Tools

Cuts made with handsaws are often rougher than those made with power tools. After making each cut, hold your square against the side of the board and the cut edge to determine whether the cut is square. Then hold the square across the edge to make sure the cut is not slanted one way or the other. If the cut is not square, you can often remedy it by sanding with a block of wood and sandpaper. Or you may have to recut the piece.

When a project requires several pieces with the same dimensions, it's a good idea to cut all the pieces at the same time. But don't saw all the pieces for a project before you begin. You'll often find small discrepancies between your actual measurements and the plans, so it's usually better to measure as you go along by comparing the plans and the pieces already cut to ensure that the pieces fit snugly and properly. Sand the edges of project pieces before joining them together and you'll remove any splintering.

BASIC HAND TOOLS

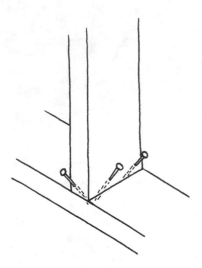

How to Toenail a Board

Sometimes you will need to nail one piece, often a stud, between other pieces that have already been fastened. Toenailing is the best way to handle such situations. Basically, toenailing is driving a nail at an angle through one piece of stock into another.

Toenailing is one of the hardest things for a beginning carpenter to learn, because it involves holding one piece of wood in place while starting a nail and driving it in at an angle. To toenail a stud, first start an 8d nail about 1½ inches from the bottom at approximately a 60-degree angle. Position the stud on the plate and gently but firmly drive the nail into the stud until the nail contacts the plate. If the stud moves, reposition it and then sink the nail fully into the stud and plate. Once you have completed the first toenail, the others are much easier to nail since the stud is secured.

Tip: To start the nail off right, drill a pilot hole at the proper angle in the top board.

Best Hammers for the Job

Hammers are very personal. I have a number of 12-ounce claw hammers I've accumulated over the years, some of which I inherited and some of which I picked up at auctions and farm sales. I often find myself picking up one particular hammer for a job because the balance and fit seems to suit me better than any of the others just then. When shopping for a hammer, it's a good idea to feel the heft of several different ones; you can even ask the salesperson to let you swing it solidly on a surface to feel how it responds.

The best all-around choice is a standard 16-ounce hammer. It's an all-purpose workhorse you can use on most projects. When you're framing with stock 2 inches or more thick, building wooden fences, or working on larger projects, a framing hammer is a better choice than a 16-ounce hammer. Framing hammers are available in 20- and 22-ounce weights. After a day of driving large 16d nails, you'll appreciate the heavier hammer's weight and balance. Framing hammers also have straight claws that provide more leverage and make it easier to pull or remove nails.

Using the proper hammer for the job is important. Hitting the nail squarely on the head with a smooth, even swing is equally important. Don't try to drive the nail down with a few hard licks; use easygoing swings and allow the weight of the hammer to drive the nail. Nails should be driven snugly into the wood, but not so hard that you dent or damage the wood surface and break the wood into splinters.

Use enough nails to firmly hold a project together, and check to make sure the nails don't protrude through the back side, which in the case of fencing and gates will often be a problem. If nails do protrude, hammer or bend the nails over, clinching them down flat against the wood surface.

Sometimes it's hard to know what a particular nail looks like or what it's for. This illustration should help.

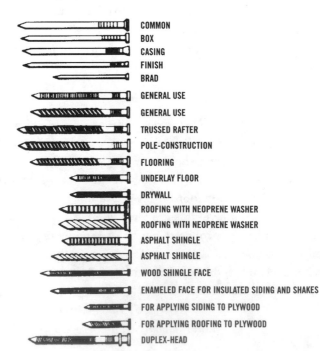

COMMON
BOX
CASING
FINISH
BRAD
GENERAL USE
GENERAL USE
TRUSSED RAFTER
POLE-CONSTRUCTION
FLOORING
UNDERLAY FLOOR
DRYWALL
ROOFING WITH NEOPRENE WASHER
ROOFING WITH NEOPRENE WASHER
ASPHALT SHINGLE
ASPHALT SHINGLE
WOOD SHINGLE FACE
ENAMELED FACE FOR INSULATED SIDING AND SHAKES
FOR APPLYING SIDING TO PLYWOOD
FOR APPLYING ROOFING TO PLYWOOD
DUPLEX-HEAD

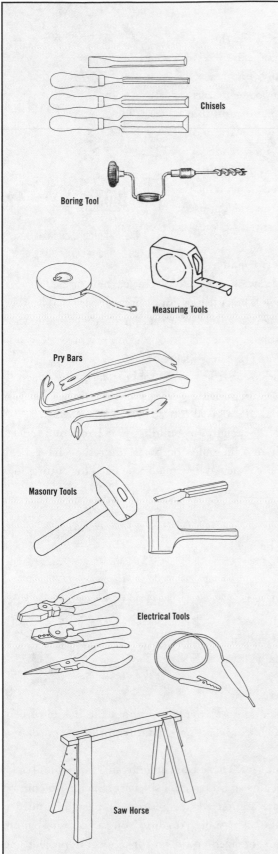

Chisels

Boring Tool

Measuring Tools

Pry Bars

Masonry Tools

Electrical Tools

Saw Horse

The Well-Equipped Toolbox

There are many other useful hand tools. The primary ones are listed below, but some, such as post-hole diggers, are for specific jobs and may not be what you need. Simply select the tools that suit your needs and construction methods.

- **Chisels.** These are indispensable for many woodworking chores. For notching studs and cutting mortises and tenons, you will want several chisels of different widths. Avoid cheap sets. They can't be easily sharpened, won't hold an edge, and are simply dangerous.
- **Plane.** You may need a plane to smooth down wood for a joint.
- **Boring tools.** These are needed to install bolts and hinges, and sometimes for cutting mortises. A good brace and bits are invaluable. Make sure the brace is double acting so you can use it in tight corners. The bits should be large, high-quality auger bits.
- **Measuring tools.** The first and probably most important measuring tool is a good steel measuring tape. You may want a 12-foot tape for in-shop use and small projects, and a larger 25-foot tape for larger projects. A 100-foot tape ruler can be handy for laying out barns and extensive fencing.
- **Pry bars.** A nail puller called a cat's saw is essential for removing nails from wood. Another good tool for this task is a pry bar. For prying nailed boards loose, you may also want a 3-foot crowbar with a double-angle claw on one end.
- **Masonry tools.** Tools for working with concrete include a float for smoothing off foundation tops, a trowel for applying mortar, and an edger for rounding corners to prevent chipping. A hammer and cold chisel are needed for cutting concrete blocks.
- **Electrical tools.** Get a good pair of lineman's pliers for installing wiring. They should have insulated handles and be large enough so you can easily cut through plastic-sheathed cables. A pair of needle-nose pliers will also come in handy for bending wire leads. A combination stripper-crimper can save a great deal of time when stripping wire ends for connections. In my opinion, the plier type is much better than the knife style. Make sure all your screwdrivers have insulated handles, and that you have at least one large screwdriver with a long handle. A small power-testing light enables you to determine when a wire is "hot."
- **Plumbing tools.** You will need a pipe cutter, flux, solder, and a propane torch for installing copper pipe. A pair of large pump pliers and leather gloves are useful for holding hot pipes. In addition, a 10-inch crescent wrench and a 10-inch pipe wrench are necessary for working with threaded joints or old galvanized pipe.
- **Saw horses.** Two good saw horses will help you support material to be cut and lay out rafters. You can make these with scrap wood or lumber.

—from *64 Yard and Garden Projects You Can Build Yourself* and *Building Small Barns, Sheds, and Shelters* by Monte Burch

POWER EQUIPMENT

How to Counterbore

Counterboring is a technique used to sink the head of a bolt or screw below the level of the surrounding wood, which may be important, for example, when one piece of wood must cover another piece of wood where there is a bolt.

To counterbore, first bore a hole large enough to accommodate the bolt head and a wrench to tighten it. Drill the hole to the depth of the bolt head. Then extend the hole with a smaller bit to accommodate the rest of the bolt.

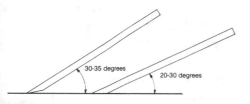

Keeping Tools Sharp

Sharp woodworking tools are a necessity if you are going to work efficiently and skillfully. Circular-saw blades and hand-saws are best taken to a professional sharpener. However, you can sharpen chisels and plane blades in your shop or on the job very easily.

You'll need a grinding stone and some lightweight oil. When sharpening a chisel, first grind the bevel, then hone the cutting edge to make it razor sharp.

To grind the bevel, place the chisel or plane blade on an oiled stone with the beveled edge down and at an angle of 20 to 30 degrees. Keeping the angle constant, move the blade back and forth with short, easy strokes until the nicks are gone from the cutting edge.

Hone the blade by increasing the grinding angle to 30 to 35 degrees and moving the blade in a figure-eight pattern across the stone. The blade should now be sharp enough to slice a piece of paper.

Power Sawing

A portable circular saw is probably the single most important power tool you can own. It can crosscut, rip, or bevel any number of materials, including wood, composite materials, and (with special blades) metal. Portable circular saws are available in a wide variety of sizes, ranging from a small 6½-inch blade up to 10-inch commercial versions. A 6½-inch blade cuts 2 inches at a 45-degree angle, which is all that's necessary for most projects. Choose a heavy-duty, double-insulated saw to protect against shock.

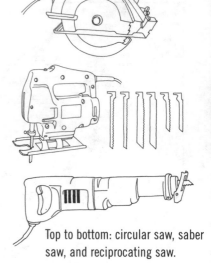

Top to bottom: circular saw, saber saw, and reciprocating saw.

Choosing the correct blade to match the chore is important with circular saws. I generally prefer carbide-tipped blades, in spite of their added cost. If you'll be cutting a lot of pressure-treated lumber, you will need a saw blade designed specifically for that purpose. A combination crosscut/rip blade is quite suitable in general, although you might wish to add a smoother-cutting blade for more "finished" projects.

Hole cutting is best done with a saber saw. This tool can also handle scroll-work and other curved designs. A reciprocating saw is a heavy-duty saber saw that can cut through any material. It's a great tool for remodeling work.

Another essential power tool, especially for building pole barns and fences, is a chain saw. You can use it to trim poles or posts after they have been installed. A chain saw mounted on a special jig can also be used for cutting logs into boards.

Drills and Bits

A portable electric drill can be used for many tasks besides boring holes.

Power drills are compared by their maximum bit sizes, rather than by horsepower. Bit sizes range from ¼ inch to ½ inch. A ⅜-inch portable drill is perfectly adequate for practically any project.

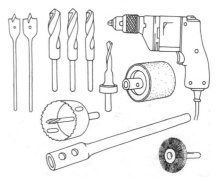

Cordless models are an excellent choice because they can be taken almost anyplace without the hassle of providing electricity at the site, which can be an important factor in the garden or the back-forty.

Most people purchase bits in sets. These can range from a large number of bits to smaller sets of half a dozen or so bits in a plastic case. Small sets contain the commonly used sizes, and are a good way of getting the basic bits needed for most projects. Just be sure the bits are high quality. You can purchase more expensive specialty bits in the exact sizes you need for a specific project and add them to your tool chest gradually. In addition to regular drill bits, consider buying a set of blade or paddle bits for larger boring jobs.

Special Tools for Special Jobs

Some tools have only a limited use. In some cases, you may be able to rent or borrow these tools. In other cases, you may need them often enough to warrant buying them. Here is a list of specialty tools and their functions:

BELT SANDER

- **Sander.** Some projects, such as furniture, need careful sanding. This can be done most cheaply with a block of wood and different grades of sandpaper. However, you can speed up the job by using a power sander. A belt sander is used for rough work. Finish pad sanders are good for smoothing up to obtain a final finish. Quality belt sanders are usually about 1¼ horsepower.

- **Router.** A handheld router and bits are necessary for routing decorative grooves and completing other decorative tasks. A good-quality router will generally provide about 2 horsepower.

- **Power fasteners.** When it comes to big jobs, power fasteners can really save time and labor. These include power nailers and automatic screwdriver fastening systems. Because these tools are designed for contractors, they are generally expensive.

POWER FASTENER

- **Dowelling jig.** A dowelling jig is used to join together pieces of wood. It is quite simple to operate and assures a strong and accurate joint.

- **Stationary power tools.** The use of these tools speeds up the process of cutting and shaping wood. However, they are costly and require a workshop. A table or radial arm saw is a good first choice if you can afford only one stationary power tool. It can be used for ripping, crosscutting, and (with accessories) other cutting and shaping chores. A band saw is handy for cutting curved pieces. A drill press is useful for precise boring jobs, and there are multipurpose tools available that combine a table saw, sander, lathe, drill press, and other tools in one unit.

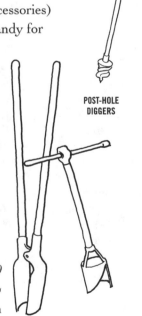

POST-HOLE DIGGERS

- **Post-hole digger.** There are various types of post-hole diggers. For digging fencepost holes or holes for foundation piers, use a digger that has two handles and a pair of clam-type blades. Another type of digger has a motor that drives an auger. If you're going to be digging a lot of holes, you may prefer a power digger.

—from 64 Yard and Garden Projects You Can Build Yourself and Building Small Barns, Sheds, and Shelters by Monte Burch

Tip:

Be sure to read and fully understand the instructions that come with the tools.

Tool Safety

Both beginning and experienced woodworkers need to think carefully about safety practices. Handsaws, drill bits, and portable electric and stationary power tool blades, bits, and cutters are all sharp. They can do a great deal of damage, even when they are standing still.

Always keep a first-aid kit with antiseptic and wound wraps in your shop or close at hand. You might as well add a pair of tweezers, too. Sooner or later, you're going to get a splinter.

Use hammers only for their job. Carpentry hammers are not made for striking other metal objects such as chisels, bolt heads, and screwdrivers. Chips can fly off the head of a hammer and injure you or someone else.

Anytime you're working with sharp cutting tools or hammering, you need eye protection such as safety goggles. When using portable electric cutting or boring tools, ear protection is also necessary. When sanding or cutting treated work, wear a sanding or dust mask. Steel-toed boots are good to have when you drop heavy posts on your feet. When working with any power tools, wear comfortable clothes but avoid loose, floppy clothing that can be caught in the tools and cause injury.

Most of today's double-insulated power tools can be safely operated in ordinary outdoor situations, but avoid running them in a rainstorm or in an extremely wet situation. If at all possible, use a ground-fault interrupter when you plug the tools in.

YOUR GARDEN, YARD & ORCHARD

ILLUSTRATION CREDITS

All-America Selections: 216 (petunia, salvia, zinnia)

Nancy Anisfield: 334, 335 (box)

Cathy Baker: 66 (top), 69 (top), 239 (aphid, beetles, mite, thrips), 269 (screen), 289 (ground beetle, Ichneumon wasp, ladybug), 290 (aphid, cabbage worm, cucumber beetle, Japanese beetle), 291 (bean beetle, root maggot), 323 (chinch bug, grub), 347 (aphid, fruit fly, codling moth, scale, tent caterpillar)

Kathy Bray: 68 (left), 253, 256 (right), 260

Sarah Brill: 201 (right), 204 (basil, catmint), 207 (lavender, lemon balm), 209 (watercress, woodruff), 325 (thyme)

Jane Clark Brown: 2 (screen), 4 (screen)

Carolyn Bucha: 24 (top), 25, 271 (screen)

Monte Burch: 350, 353, 367, 368, 369, 370, 372, 373, 374, 382 (bottom)

Monte and Joan Burch: 6 (center), 23

Rick Daskam: 132, 133, 134, 135, 264, 356, 357

Jeffrey Domm: 302, 303 (top and bottom right), 311 (top)

Beverly Duncan: 199 (top), 202 (bottom), 204 (chamomile), 206 (feverfew), 215 (bottom right), 223 (bottom left), 289 (predatory mite), 292 (bottom), 294 (bottom, sidebar), 295, 360, 361 (bottom)

Judy Eliason: 22, 171 (left), 172 (left), 173 (top), 175 (bottom), 177 (center), 180, 181, 183 (bottom), 188 (top), 189 (center),191 (top), 214 (center, bottom), 215 (top), 216 (aster, cosmos, snapdragon, sweetpea), 217 (top), 220 (top, center), 223 (top and right), 226 (left center), 239 (beetles, borer, leafhopper), 247 (left), 248, 249, 251, 289 (assassin bug, brachonid wasp, lacewing, ladybug, mantis, mealybug destroyer, soldier bug, tachnid fly, trichogramma wasp), 290 (cabbage looper, potato beetle, earworm, cucumber beetle, cutworm), 291 (root maggot, spider mite, squash bug, hornworm, whitefly, yellow jacket), 296, 297 (squirrel, woodchuck), 298 (top right and left, lower right), 299, 332 (cane borer, crown borer, sawfly), 347 (apple maggot, borer, curculio, pear psylla)

Brigita Fuhrmann: 8 (lower right), 9 (top), 10, 11, 20, 85 (top), 87, 88, 127, 130, 131 (top, bottom), 136, 137 (top), 151, 153 (bottom), 163 (center), 169 (right center and bottom right), 199 (bottom), 200 (top), 202 (top), 203 (top), 204 (costmary), 206 (box), 207 (hyssop, marjoram), 208 (parsley, sage), 209 (tarragon), 213, 218, 219, 221 (bottom), 222, 229 (tulip), 250, 274 (top), 277, 287, 329 (center), 363 (left), 380, 381 (right and bottom), 382 (top and left), 383, 384 (top and bottom right), 385 (top and center)

Chuck Galey: 176

Susan Gliss: 61 (bottom), 63, 65 (bottom left), 69 (bottom), 72

Kay Gough: 248 (screen)

Kathryn Hard: 6 (bottom), 54 (bottom)

Keith Heiberling: 183 (top)

Millie Holderread: 471

Nancy Hull: 167

Michael Jager: 77

Charles Joslin: 70 (left), 153 (top), 204 (bay, burnet, chives), 205 (dill), 206 (fennel, garlic), 207 (horehound, lemon verbena, lovage, mint), 208 (oregano, pennyroyal, rosemary, rue), 209 (geranium, sorrel, thyme), 215 (bottom left), 293 (top), 325 (woodruff), 361 (screen)

Carl Kirkpatrick: 18 (bottom), 20, 168 (left center), 262, 263, 265 (bottom)

Kimberlee Knauf: 300, 301 306 (birds), 307, 309 (birds), 310, 311 (plans)

John M. Knight: 6 (top)

Alison Kolesar: 49, 50, 52, 53, 54 (top), 55, 56, 57, 58, 83 (bottom), 84, 89, 89, 90, 91, 101, 102, 103, 104, 105, 106, 107, 108, 109, 110, 111, 113, 116, 117, 118, 119, 120, 121, 122, 123, 128, 168 (right), 169 (top left, center, left), 172 (right), 173 (right), 174 (left), 184, 186 (box), 205 (echinacea), 216 (impatiens), 231, 268 (bottom), 269 (left), 270, 272 (box), 273 (sidebar), 274 (bottom), 276, 277, 278, 279, 286 (right), 292 (top), 293 (bottom), 297 (box), 298 (bottom left), 303 (box), 308, 309 (lower right), 312 (top right and left), 313, 315, 317, 320, 321,

322, 323 (sod webworm), 324 (ivy), 325 (sedum), 343 (right), 362 (screen), 383

Mallory Lake: 216 (sunflower), 224, 225, 228 (allium, caladium, calla, crocus, dahlia, gloriosa lily, gladiolus, grape hyacinth, windflower), 229 (begonia, hyacinth, lily of-the-Nile, Peruvian lily, ranunculus, snowdrops, star of Bethlehem, trout lily, aconite), 324 (bishop's weed, bugleweed, candytuft, lily turf), 325 (ginger, hosta, Japanese spurge, lily-of-the-valley, periwinkle, plumbago)

Susan B. Langsten: 171 (right), 194 (bottom), 269 (sidebar), 281, 282, 283, 286 (left), 294 (right top), 298 (top, center left)

Jean Loewer: 272 (box right, screen, sidebar)

Jerri Long and Ev Harlow: 304, 305 (bottom)

Charles McRaven and Chandis Ingenthron: 16 (screen), 19

Doug Merrilees and Ralph Scott: 17

Randy Mosher: 154, 155, 383 (brace)

Douglas Paisley: 7 (top and center), 24 (left), 67, 70 (right), 71 (bottom), 73, 143, 161, 188 (bottom), 190 (kale), 191 (mustard), 268 (box), 305 (top right)

Ann Poole: 178 (center, left), 179, 191 (melon), 348, 352

Louise Riotte: 216 (calendula, nasturtium, pansy), 234 (left and screen), 237 (screen), 256 (left), 257, 332 (fruit worm, spider mite)

Paula Savastano: iv, vi, ix, 28

Ralph Scott: 38, 39, 327, 329 (bottom)

Hyla Scudder: 244, 245, 324 (bluets, bunchberry)

Elayne Sears: 38 (screen), 55 (screen), 163 (top), 166, 169 (top right), 174 (right), 177 (top and bottom), 178 (bottom), 186 (bottom), 187, 188 (center), 191 (bottom), 192 (top and bottom), 193, 194 (top), 195, 196, 197, 216 (morning glory), 217 (center), 220 (bottom), 221 (top and center), 226, 227, 228 (amaryllis, daffodil, freesia), 229 (gladiolus, iris, lily), 230, 232, 233, 234 (right), 235 (top and bottom), 236, 237, 238, 240, 242, 243, 246, 247 (right), 254, 255, 258, 259, 261, 263 (screen), 264 (screen), 265 (top), 273 (bottom), 275, 280 (screen), 312 (bottom), 314, 316, 318, 319, 323 (top right), 324 (fern), 328, 329 (top), 331, 332 (screen), 336, 338, 340 (screen), 341 (screen), 342, 346, 354, 355, 362 (plants), 363 (right), 364

David Stiles: 375, 376, 377, 378, 379, 381 (box)

Russell Stockman: 68 (right)

Sue Storey: 189 (top)

Robert Strimban: 138, 139, 140 (right), 141

David Sylvester: 163 (bottom), 358

Laura Tedeschi: 200 (bottom), 201 (left), 324 (violet)

Joan E. Thomson: 115

Bob Vogel: 29, 31, 32, 33, 34, 35, 36 (bottom), 37, 40, 46 (bottom), 71 (top), 76, 83 (top), 85 (right and bottom), 86, 273 (top), 371, 384 (left), 385 (bottom)

RESOURCES

Here are some companies with products and/or information that will help you live a more self-reliant, independent life. These listings are up-to-date as we print this book, but web sites and offers change frequently.

BOOKS AND INFORMATION

Storey Books
210 Mass MoCA Way
North Adams, MA 01247
(413) 346-2100
fax: (413) 346-2199
www.storey.com
how-to books for country living, gardening, crafts, birds, cooking, do-it-yourself, animals, horses, pets, natural health, beauty

American Nurseryman Publishing
77 W. Washington St. Suite 2100
Chicago, IL 60602-2904
(800) 621-5727
fax: (312) 782-3232
books@amerinursery.com
www.amerinursery.com
mail-order horticultural books, videos, and software; free catalog

A Country Bookstore
HC78, Box 1105
Zanoni, MO 65784
(417) 261-2610
genegerue@ruralize.com
www.ruralize.com/country
 bookstore.html
country book reviews by Gene GeRue

B4UBUILD.COM bookstore
(877) 273-6175
www.b4ubuild.com/books
books for the country home do-it-yourself person; mail order and retail books on plumbing, water systems and home care; online catalog only

Back Forty Books
26328 Locust Grove Rd.
Creola, OH 45622
(740) 596-4379
fax: (740) 596-3079
locustgrove@ohiohills.com
www.back40books.com
mail-order and retail books on agriculture, native ways, and health

Backwoods Home Magazine
P.O. Box 712
Gold Beach, OR 97444
(800) 835-2418
fax: (541) 247-8600
editor@backwoodshome.com
backwoodshome.com
writings on personal independence, survival tips, gardening and building

Builders Booksource
1817 4th St.
Berkeley, CA 94710
(800) 843-2028
fax: (510) 845-7051
service@buildersbooksite.com
www.buildersbooksite.com
mail-order and retail books on architecture, design, and construction; free newsletter

Cambium Books
(800) 238-7724
www.cambiumbooks.com
authentic information for woodworkers, furniture makers and much more; free catalog

Countryside and Small Stock Journal
W11564 Hwy. 64
Withee, WI 54498
(715) 785-7979
fax: (715) 785-7414
csymag@midway.tds.net
www.countrysidemag.com
writings on country living and livestock

Dan's Garden Shop Bookstore
5821 Woodwinds Cir.
Frederick, MD 21703
(301) 662-3572
sales@dansgardenshop.com
www.dansgardenshop.com/garan
 dcounli.html
gardening books; online catalog

The Environmental Magazine
P.O. Box 5098
Westport, CT 06881
(800) 854-5559
fax: (203) 866-0602
info@emagazine.com
www.emagazine.com
writings on issues concerning the environment; free trial issue

Eureka Gardening Collection
P.O. Box 7611
Asheville, NC 28802
(828) 236-2222
fax: (828) 236-2226
bloom@gardeneureka.com
www.gardeneureka.com
gardening titles related to irises and daylilies; online newsletter

Homebuilding Manuals

(800) 205-1050

www.homebuildingmanual.com

manuals on home inspection and managing the building of your home; online catalog only

Home Planners, Inc.

3275 W. Ina Rd.

Suite 110

Tucson, AZ 85741

books: (800) 322-6797

blueprints: (800) 521-6797

fax: (800) 224-6699

customerservice@eplans.com

www.homeplanners.com

mail-order books and residential blueprints; free catalog

Mother Earth News

1053 SW 42nd St.

Topeka, KS 66609-1265

to subscribe: (800) 234-3368

books: (800) 888-9098

fax: (515) 262-6165

askmother@motherearthnews.com

www.motherearthnews.com

writings on country living and do-it-yourself projects

Taylor Publishing

P.O. Box 375

Cutten, CA 95534

(888) 441-1632

fax: (775) 845-9772

tms@northcoast.com

www.dirtcheapbuilder.com

mail-order books on natural building and sustainable living; catalog $1

CHAT ROOMS AND FORUMS

About Birding

http://birding.about.com

chat room, forums, relevant links, how-to's, and answers to just about any question; free newsletter

Build Talk Network

www.buildtalk.com/talk

gardening, home repair and do-it-yourself projects around the house; forums include "home and garden" and "home remodeling"

Craft Express

http://soapmaking.chatboard.org

chat board for soap makers

DoitYourself.com

http://doityourself.com

forums, chat room and lots of how-to information; free newsletter

Herbs and Garden Things

55 Springdale St.

St. John's, Newfoundland

Canada, A1C5B2

(709) 726-3271

info@talkherbs.net

www.talkherbs.net

online discussion forum inviting visitors to ask questions and share herbal recipes, tips and experiences; news and online shopping

Homeownernet

http://www.homeownernet.com/chat/index.html

chat rooms and message boards for home improvement, lawn and garden, home interior and real estate

iVillage

www.ivillage.com/home/chat

women's network for sharing ideas and knowledge for gardening, home improvement and repairs

Log Home Listers

www.loghomelists.com/chat room.asp

share information and learn about building your own log home

The Mining Company's Home Repair Online

http://homerepair.miningco.com/mpchat.htm

question and answer bulletin board and chat room on home repair

Remodel Online

www.remodelonline.com

forums, books, classifieds, free e-mail, house plans and information about remodeling your home

The Wildlife Garden

http://forums.gardenweb.com/forums/wildlife

forum and message board for creating gardens hospitable to wildlife

EXTENSION AGENTS

Texas A&M Horticulture Newsletter

202 Horticulture Science Bldg.

College Station, TX 77843-2133

RESOURCES

(979) 845-0627
http://stephenville.tamu.edu/~nroe/newsletter/n599.htm
information about home landscapes and ornamentals

United States Department of Agriculture Home and Garden Bulletin

www.hoptechno.com/book26.htm
information on starting up and growing vegetables in a home garden

University of Florida

http://edis.ifas.ufl.edu/BODY_UW120
learn how to deal with roof rats and other pests that attack fruit trees

University of Kentucky at Lexington

University of Kentucky
College of Agriculture
Lexington, KY 40546-0091
(859) 257-2758
www.ca.uky.edu/agcollege/plant
  pathology/PPAExten/ppaext.html

educational materials and diagnostic support on diseases of crops, landscape plants and other plants

University of Maryland Cooperative Extension Service

Knapp Hall, P.O. Box 6031
Morgantown, WV 26506-6031
(304) 293-4221
www.agnr.umd.edu/ces/home
  gardenyard.html
information about grounds and gardens, home maintenance, pest control and soils

ONLINE RESOURCES

The Aquatic Critter

5009 Nolensville Rd.
Nashville, TN 37211
(615) 832-4541
www.aquaticcritter.com
information about ponds such as winterizing your pond, pond plants, pond medication, pond planning, tips about good pond care

Build Advice

donna.shearing@buildadvice.com
www.buildadvice.com
free home improvement resource for extending, modernizing or refurbishing your home; free online newsletter

The Chamomile Times

Jackie@chamomiletimes.com
www.chamomiletimes.com
informative Web site about growing and using herbs; book reviews, recipes and links to other herbal sites; free online newsletters

DoItYourself.com

http://doityourself.com/electric
information and supplies for home electric lighting and repair; free online newsletter

Garden Guides

gardenguides@gardenguides.com
www.gardenguides.com
information on herbs, vegetables, flowers and seasonal gardens; free newsletter and bulletin board; general gardening links, plus shopping and catalog links

Home Time Projects

www.hometime.com
advice on installing hardwood floors, decks, framing, garages, home maintenance and electrical; tools and safety; recommended manufacturers list; forum groups

Hometips

don@hometips.com
www.hometips.com
help with home improvement, remodeling, home repair, decorating and major purchases of appliances and other home products; free online advice

The Kitchen and Bath Network

www.kitchenet.com
multiple listings of manufacturers, associations with free information, merchants, resources and other services

Martha Stewart Living

P.O. Box 60001
Tampa, FL 33660-0001
(800) 950-7130
fax: (813) 979-6685
www.marthastewart.com
information on cooking, gardening, kids, crafts, books and more

The Money Pit

(888) MONEY PIT
www.888moneypit.com
home improvement radio and online program; tune in online each Friday at 4 p.m. or e-mail them via their Web site

National Wildlife Federation

www.nwf.org/habitats/backyard/
  beyondbasics/hints/frogpond.cfm
*free biweekly e-newsletter; pond care
information; free newsletters*

NW Gardening

2438 Wickstrom Pl. SW, #1
Seattle, WA 98116
(206) 938-3130
mariem@nwgardening.com
www.nwgardening.com/index.html
*tips on garden design, winterizing,
pruning; recommended reading*

Organic Shopping Mall

ads@organicshoppingmall.com
www.organicshoppingmall.com
*links to organic farm vendors, gro-
cers and vineyards; cookbooks, clubs,
organizations and other helpful tips*

RepairClinic.com, Inc.

47440 Michigan Ave., Suite 100
Canton, MI 48188
(800) 269-2609
www.repairclinic.com
appliance parts and free repair help

SOS Mole Trappers

5309 Palisades Dr.
Cincinnati, OH 45238
(513) 922-4419
fax: (503) 210-7831
sosmole@yahoo.com
www.moletrapper.com
*supplies, information and assistance
with mole control*

PRODUCTS AND SUPPLIES

A.M. Leonard

241 Fox Dr.
Piqua, OH 45356
(800) 543-8955
fax: (800) 433-0633
www.amleo.com
*mail-order horticulture tools and
supplies; free catalog*

Acres USA

P.O. Box 91299
Austin, TX 78709-1299
(800) 355-5313
fax: (512) 892-4448
info@acres.com
www.acresusa.com
*mail-order newspapers and books on
ecology and sustainable agriculture;
free catalog*

Advance Solar, Hydro, Wind, Power Co.

P.O. Box 23
Capella, CA 95418
(707) 485-0588
advance@advancepower.net
www.advancepower.net
*high-quality, low-cost energy
systems and components; online
catalog only*

American Forest Famous & Historic Trees

8701 Old Kings Rd.
Jacksonville, FL 32219
(800) 320-8733
info@historictrees.org
www.historictrees.org
*recognizing trees for their historic
stature and growing direct-offspring*

*historic trees for schools, communi-
ties and homes; free catalog*

Articles

P.O. Box 80
Underwood, IA 51576-0080
(800) 589-8500
fax: (800) 600-3964
www.articles.com
home decorations; free catalog

Audubon Workshop

5100 Schenley Pl.
Lawrenceburg, IN 47025
(812) 537-3583
fax: (812) 537-5108
http://audubonworkshop.com
*supplies, equipment and information
for the wild bird lover; free catalog*

Bountiful Gardens

18001 Shafer Ranch Rd.
Willits, CA 95490
(707) 459-6410
fax: (707) 459-1925
bountiful@sonic.net
www.bountifulgardens.org
*gardening lessons and mail-order
seeds, books, and supplies; free catalog*

Casual Living

5401 Hangar Ct.
P.O. Box 31273
Tampa, FL 33631-3273
(800) 652-2948
www.CasualLivingUSA.com
*unique home décor, kitchenware and
apparel; free catalog*

Country Home Products

Meigs Rd.
P. O. Box 25

Vergennes, VT 05491
(800) 687-6575
fax: (802) 877-1213
specialmkts@countryhome
  products.com
www.countryhomeproducts.com
products for lawn, garden, tool sheds and general outdoors

Cumberland General Store

1 Hwy. 68
Crossville, TN 38555
(800) 334-4640
fax: (931) 456-1211
info@cumberlandgeneral.com
www.cumberlandgeneral.com
mail-order and retail turn-of-the-century reproductions; catalog $4

Dripworks

190 Sanhedrin Circle
Willits, CA 95490-8753
(800) 616-8321
fax: (707) 459-9645
dripwrks@pacific.net
www.dripworksusa.com
mail-order drip irrigation systems and design service; free catalog

Excalibur Products

6083 Tower Inn Rd.
Sacramento, CA 95824
(800) 875-4254
fax: (916) 381-4256
mail-order versatile, high-quality dehydrators; free catalog

From Nature With Love

258 Longstreet Ave.
Bronx, NY 10465
(888) 376-6695
fax: (718) 842-6620

www.from-nature-with-love.
  com/soap
soap-making, candle-making and potpourri supplies and bath accessories; online catalog only

Gardener's Supply Company

128 Intervale Rd.
Burlington, VT 05401
(888) 833-1412
fax: (800) 551-6712
info@gardeners.com
www.gardeners.com
seed starting supplies and garden furniture, flower supports and greenhouses; free catalog

Gardens Alive

5100 Schenley Place
Lawrenceburg, IN 47025
(812) 537-8650
fax: (812) 537-5108
www.gardensalive.com
environmental friendly products for all types of gardens; free catalog and e-mail newsletter

Garrett Wade

161 Avenue of the Americas
New York, NY 10013
(800) 221-2942
mail@garrettwade.com
www.garrettwade.com
hand tools, power tools, finishing products, hardware, books, and home and living products; free catalog

Good Time Stove Company

Box 306 Route 112
Goshen, MA 01032-0306
(888) 282-7506
fax: (413) 268-9284

www.goodtimestove.com/htm/
  pot_belly_stoves.html
vintage American potbelly stoves, kitchen ranges and heating stoves; free video and catalog

Gourmet Mushrooms

P.O. Box 515 IP
Graton, CA 95444
(800) 789-9121
fax: (707) 823-9091
gourmet@gmushrooms.com
www.gmushrooms.com
mail-order mushrooms and mushroom products; free catalog

Happy Valley Ranch

16577 West 327th St.
Paola, KS 66071
(913) 849-3103
fax: (913) 849-3104
hvrinfo@happyvalleyranch.com
www.happyvalleyranch.com
mail-order cider presses; free catalog

Hard to Find Tools

17 Riverside St.
Nashua, NH 03062
(800) 926-7000
fax: (573)581-7361
www.brookstone.com
practical, problem-solving products for smart solutions to common problems indoors and out; free catalog

Hardware Accents

135 Dynex Dr.
Pewaukee, WI 53072
(262) 695-8838
fax: (262) 695-8841
msveley@execpc.com
www.store.yahoo.com/hardware
  accents

decorative hardware featuring cabinet knobs, pulls and handles; free catalog

HardwareSource.com

840 Fifth Ave.
San Diego, CA 92101-6189
(877) 944-6437
fax: (619) 232-6527
info@HardwareSource.com
www.HardwareSource.com
specializing in hinges; free catalog

Harmony Farm Supply

3244 Gravenstein Hwy. N.
P.O. Box 460
Sebastopol, CA 95472
(707) 823-9125
fax: (707) 823-1734
info@harmonyfarm.com
www.harmonyfarm.com
mail-order and retail organic gardening and farm supplies; free catalog

Harris Seeds

P.O. Box 24966
Rochester, NY 14624
(800) 514-4441
fax: (877) 892-9197
www.harrisseeds.com
mail-order and retail commercial and home garden supplies; free catalog

Herbal Accents

8663 Magnolia Ave., Suite G
Santee, CA 92071
(619) 562-2650
fax: (619) 562-5414
Herbal@herbalaccents.com
www.herbalaccents.com
soap-making supplies, essential oils, fragrance oils, carrier oils, vegetable oils and toiletries-making supplies

Heirloom Seeds

Box 245
W. Elizabeth, PA 15088-0245
phone and fax: (412) 384-0852
mail@heirloomseeds.com
www.heirloomseeds.com
mail-order old-fashioned flower herb and vegetable seeds

Home Again Home Again

18160 Hwy. 281 N. Suite 108-234
San Antonio, TX 78232
(210) 490-1498
fax: (210) 495-0564
leslie@homeagainhomeagain.com
www.homeagainhomeagain.com
decorative accessories for home, cottage or cabin; online catalog only

The Home Marketplace

4510 Edison Ave.
Colorado Springs, CO 80915-4127
(800) 356-3876
help@thehomemarketplace.com
www.TheHomeMarketplace.com

kitchen and home specialty items; free catalog

Home Trends

1450 Lyell Ave.
Rochester, NY 14606
(800) 810-2340
fax: (716) 458-9245
customerservice@hometrends catalog.com
www.hometrendscatalog.com
mail-order home cleaning supplies; free catalog

Jade Mountain Inc.

P.O. Box 4616
Boulder, CO 80306
(800) 442-1972
fax: (303) 222-3599
service@jademountain.com
www.jademountain.com
mail-order and retail sustainable/ renewable energy systems; catalog $7

Johnny's Selected Seeds

Foss Hill Rd.
RR1, Box 2580
Albion, ME 04910-9731
(207) 437-9294
fax: (800) 437-4301
staff@johnnyseeds.com
www.johnnyseeds.com
mail-order and retail seeds and garden accessories; free catalog

Lee Valley Tools, Ltd.

P.O. Box 1780
Ogdensburg, NY 13669-6780
(US) (800) 871-8158
(Can) (800) 267-8767
US fax: (800) 513-7885
Can fax: (800) 668-1807
customerservice@leevalley.com
www.leevalley.com
mail-order woodworking and gardening supplies; free catalog

Lehman Hardware

One Lehman Circle
P.O. Box 41
Kidron, OH 44636-0041
(330) 857-5757
fax: (330) 857-5785
info@lehmans.com
www.lehmans.com
mail-order and retail old-fashioned home supplies; catalog $3

RESOURCES

Leslie Geddes-Brown Catalog Company
Columbine Press
42 Canonbury Sq.
London, England N1 2AW
(020) 7704 9173
fax: (020) 7704 1509
mediasales@LeslieGeddes
  Brown.com
www.lesliegeddesbrown.com
several catalogs to choose from including home and bath decorations, gardening and gifts; free catalogs

Linen Spot
1832 East Votaw Rd.
Apopka, FL 32703
(407) 247-1370
fax: (352)735-2347
www.linenspot.com
bedding, window treatments and bathroom; online catalog only

Little Wonder—Mantis
Division of Schiller-Pfeiffer Inc.
1028 Street Rd.
Southampton, PA 18966
(800) 366-6268
fax: (215) 357-1071
www.mantisgardentools.com

mail-order and retail garden supplies; free catalog

Lynden House International, Inc.
5527-137 Ave.
Edmonton, Alberta
Canada T5L 3L4
(780) 448-1994
fax: (780) 448-0086
www.lyndenhouse.net
candle-making and soap-making supplies; online catalog only

Major Surplus & Survival
435 W. Alondra Blvd.
Gardena, CA 90248
(800) 441-8855
fax: (310) 324-6909
www.majorsurplusnsurvival.com
mail-order supplies for self-reliant living; free catalog

Marasco's Craft King
12750 W. Capitol Dr.
Brookfield, WI 53005
(800) 373-3434
fax: (262) 781-3779
craft@happyhobby.com
www.craftking.com
craft suppliers for every type of crafter; online catalog only

Mellinger's Inc.
2310 W. South Range Rd.
N. Lima, OH 44452
(800) 321-7444
fax: (330) 549-3716
mellgarden@aol.com
www.mellingers.com
mail-order and retail seeds, plants, and garden supplies; free catalog

Miller Farms
14501 South Ave.
Delhi, CA 95315
(209) 668-1937
fax: (209) 667-8105
webmaster@babysbreath.com
www.babysbreath.com
air-dried and glycerin-dried baby's breath for crafts; online catalog

mybackyard.com, Inc.
1501 N. Broadway, Suite 320
Walnut Creek, CA 94596

(888) 830-6930
info@mybackyard.com
www.mybackyard.com
gardening, herbs, do-it-yourself country crafts and garden art; tips for the gardener, the cook, and country living; online catalog only

Nichols Garden Nursery
1190 Old Salem Rd. NE
Albany, OR 97321-4880
(800) 422-3985
fax: (800) 231-5306
www.gardennursery.com
mail-order and retail seeds, herbs, and garden supplies; free catalog

Northern Tool Company
P.O. 1219
Burnsville, MN 55337-0219
(800) 222-5381
www.northerntool.com
quality tools and equipment for the home, yard and country life; free catalog

Oriental Trading Company
P.O. Box 3407
Omaha, NE 68103-0407
(800) 228-2269
fax: (800) 327-8904
www.orientaltrading.com
easy-to-do craft projects; free catalog

Pacific Yurts
77456 Highway 99 S
Cottage Grove, OR 97424
(800) 944-0240
fax: (541) 942-0508
pacyurts@yurts.com
www.yurts.com

mail-order and retail recreational living structures; free brochure and price list

The Paragon

89 Tom Harvey Rd.
Westerly, RI 92891
(800) 657-3934
fax: (800) 227-3690
customerservice@paragongifts.com
www.paragongifts.com
personalized gifts and items for the animal lover, the home buyer and everyone in the family; free catalog

Park Seed Company

1 Parkton Ave.
Greenwood, SC 29649
(800) 213-0076
fax: (864) 941-4206
info@parkseed.com
www.parkseed.com
mail-order and retail seeds, plants, and garden accessories; free catalog

Peaceful Valley Farm Supply

P.O. Box 2209
Grass Valley, CA 95945
(888) 784-1722
fax: (530) 272-4794
www.groworganic.com
mail-order organic farming supplies; free catalog

Pinetree Garden Seeds Box

P.O. Box 300
New Gloucester, ME 04260
(207) 926-3400
fax: (888) 527-3337
superseeds@supperseeds.com
www.superseeds.com
mail-order and retail seeds, garden supplies, and books; free catalog

Plow and Hearth

P.O. Box 6000
Madison, VA 22727-1600
(800) 627-1712
fax: (800) 843-2509
www.plowhearth.com
products for country living; free catalog

Plumbing Supply

994 E. 20th St., Suite Y
Chico, CA 95928-6712
(530) 891-8521
fax: (530) 891-8521
Sales@PlumbingSupply.com
www.plumbingsupply.com
large selection of plumbing products at low overhead prices; online catalog

Ready-Made Resources

5069 New Highway 68
Madisonville, TN 37354
(800) 627-3809
fax: (423) 420-0194
robert@readymaderesources.com
www.readymaderesources.com
off-the-grid and preparedness supplies; catalog $5

Real Goods

360 Interlocken Blvd., Suite 300
Broomfield, CO 80021-3440
(800) 762-7325
fax: (800) 508-2342
realgood@realgoods.com
www.realgoods.com
products for ecological and solar living; free catalog

Restoration Hardware

104 Challenger Dr.
Portland, TN 37148-1703
(800) 762-1005
fax: (615) 325-1398
www.restorationhardware.com
furniture, lighting, garden, home and hardware; free catalog

Roofing Wholesale Company

1918 West Grant St.
Phoenix, AZ 85009
(800) 528-4532
fax: (601) 256-0932
sales@rwc.org
www.rwc.org
everything for your roofing, stucco, and flooring needs; online catalog

Sancor

140-30 Milner Ave.
Scarborough, ON M1S 3R3
Canada
(US) (800) 387-5126
(Can) (800) 387-5245
fax: (416) 299-3124
info@envirolet.com
www.envirolet.com
mail-order and retail composting toilets; free catalog

Sax Arts and Crafts

2405 South Calhoun Rd.
New Berlin, WI 53151
(800) 558-6696
fax: (800) 328-4729
info@saxarts.com
www.saxarts.com
arts and craft supplies; free catalog

Seeds of Change

P.O. Box 15700
Santa Fe, NM 87506
(888) 762-7333
gardener@seedsofchange.com
www.seedsofchange.com
mail-order seeds; free catalog

RESOURCES

Select Seeds

180 Stickney Hill Rd.
Union, CT 06076
(860) 684-9310
fax: (800) 653-3304
info@selectseeds.com
www.selectseeds.com
*mail-order antique and heirloom
seeds; free catalog*

R.H. Shumway's Seeds

P.O. Box 1
Graniteville, SC 29829
(803) 663-9771
fax: (888) 437-2733
www.rhshumway.com
*mail-order heirloom vegetable seeds;
free catalog*

Smith and Hawken

P.O. Box 431
Milwaukee, WI 53201-0431
(800) 776-3336
fax: (414) 259-2330
www.SmithandHawken.com
*home decorating, yard art, gardening
tools, clothing and furniture; free
catalog*

Stokes Seeds

P.O. Box 548
Buffalo, NY 14240-0548
(800) 396-9238
fax: (888) 834-3334
www.stokeseeds.com
*mail-order seeds and garden sup-
plies; free catalog*

Stokes Seeds

P.O. Box 10
St. Catharine's, Ontario Canada
  L2R 6R6

(905) 688-4300
www.stokeseeds.com
*mail-order seeds and garden sup-
plies; free catalog*

Sturbridge Yankee Workshop

90 Blueberry Rd.
Portland, ME 04102
(800) 231-8060
fax: (207)774-7809
www.sturbridgeyankee.com
*home decorations and collectibles;
free catalog*

Sun Coast Soaps and Supplies

45311 28th St. E.
Lancaster, CA 93534
(661) 946-2655
fax: (661) 946-3155
SunCstCo@aol.com
www.suncoastsoaps.com
*supplies for the soapmaker; online
catalog only*

Sun-Mar Corporation

600 Main St.
Tonawanda, NY 14150
(800) 461-2461
fax: (905) 332-1315
compost@sun-mar.com
www.sun-mar.com
*mail-order and retail composting toi-
lets; free catalog*

Sundance Supply

P.O. Box 225
Olga, WA 98279
(800) 776-2534
fax: (800)-775-4479
info@sundancesupply.com
www.sundancesupply.com

*free plans for building attached and
freestanding greenhouses; greenhouses, sunrooms, pool enclosures and
misting equipment; online catalog*

Survival Center

P.O. Box 234
McKenna, WA 98558
(800) 321-2900
fax: (360) 458-6868
sales@survivalcenter.com
www.survivalcenter.com
*mail-order and retail family pre-
paredness supplies; catalog $2*

Territorial Seed Company

P.O. Box 158
Cottage Grove, OR 97424
(541) 942-9547
fax: (888) 657-3131
tertrl@territorial-seed.com
www.territorial-seed.com
*mail-order and retail garden sup-
plies, seeds, plants, and books*

Design Toscano, Inc.

1645 Greenleaf Ave.
Elk Grove Village, IL 60007
(800) 525-0733
www.DesignToscano.com
*historical European reproductions
for home and garden; free catalog*

Touch of Class

709 West 12th St.
Huntingburg, IN 47542-8915
(800) 457-7456
fax: (812) 683-5921
www.touchofclasscatalog.com
decorations for the home and office

Touch Stone
10 Georgian Ct.
Ridgely, MD 21685
(800) 800-962-6890
fax: (800) 759-8477
www.touchstonecatalog.com
elegant but practical home and garden décor; free catalog

Traditions at Home
3224 E. Douglas
Witchataw, KS 67208
(800) 350-2180
fax: (316) 684-2315
info@traditionsathome.com
www.traditionsathome.com
unique gifts and home décor

W. Atlee Burpee Company
300 Park Ave.
Warminster, PA 18974
(800) 888-1447
fax: (800) 487-5530
burpeecs@surfnetwork.net
www.burpee.com
mail-order and retail seeds and bulbs; free catalog

Waterford Irish Stoves, Inc.
6988 Venture St.
Delta, BC V4G 1H4
Canada
(604) 946-4188
fax: (604) 946-0479
rokum@regency-fire.com
www.waterfordstoves.com
manufacture wood stoves

Wildwood Designs
P.O. Box 676
Richland Center, WI 53581
(800) 470-9090
fax: (608) 647-3066
www.wildwooddesigns.com
variety of scrollsaw fretwork patterns and supplies, including scrollsaw blades, lumber and clock components for woodworkers

Wood Classics, Inc.
20 Osprey Ln.
Gardiner, NY 12525
(845) 255-7871
www.woodclassics.com
teak garden furniture, trellises and accessories for the outdoors

Woodstock Soapstone Company
66 Airpark Rd.
West Lebanon, NH 03784
(800) 866-4344
fax: (603) 298-5958
info@woodstove.com
www.woodstove.com
wood stoves and gas fireplaces

Yale Ogron Windows and Doors
671 W. 18th St.
Hialeah, FL 33010-2480
(305) 887-2646
fax: (305) 883-1309
www.yaleogron.com/catalog.html
doors and windows since 1958; free catalog

Ye Olde Soap Shoppe
15602 Olde Hwy 80
Flinn Springs, CA 92021
(800) 390-9969
www.soapmaking.com/soaps up.htm
soap-making supplies free catalog

INDEX

The term "(def.)" indicates that a definition appears on that page.

A

AC, 83 (def.), 92, 93, 96
Achillea, 224
Acidic soil, 270
Adirondack chair, 26–27
Aerating lawns, 322
A-frame trellises, 179
African marigold, 216
Air-drying plants, 248–49
Ajuga, 324
Alkaline soil, 270
Allium, 227, 228
Aluminum windows, 120
Amaryllis, 228
Amperage, 83 (def.), 84
Animal deterrents, 296–99
Annual phlox, 241, 244
Annuals, 213 (def.), 213–17, 363
Ants, 153
Aphids, 239, 290
Apple(s)
  cider vinegar, 125 (def.), 150–51
  trees, 340–47
Aquatic plants, 253 (def.)
Arbors and trellises, 348–57
  bentwood trellis, 356–57
  lounging arbor, 349–51
  rose arbor, 352–53
  trellising vining crops, 354–55
Arrangements, flower, 213, 247
Arranger's Garden, 246–47
Asbestos and health, 8
Ashlar, 18 (def.)
Asparagus
  growing, 186
  harvesting, 180
Assassin bugs, 289
Aster, 216, 247, 313
Astilbe, 224
Attics, 11, 78
Augers, 57
Axes, 68

B

Baby blue-eyes, 241, 244
Bacillus popilliae (milky spore disease), 293, 347
Bacillus thuringiensis (Bt), 292, 347

Bahia grass, 316
Ball (toilet), replacing, 55
Baltic ivy, 324
Bare-root rose planting, 236
Barrett, Patti, 144
Basements, 11
Basil, 176, 180, 204, 287
Bathroom cleaning, 145
Bay (bay laurel), 204
Beans
  companions, 160
  growing, 159, 186
  rotation, 161
  seed saving, 185
Bedding plants, 363
Bee Gardens, 211
Beetles, 239
Beets
  companions, 160
  growing, 159, 187
  rotation, 161
  seed saving, 185
Beneficial insects, 285 (def.), 289
Bent willow furniture, 132
Bentwood trellis, 356–57
Bermuda grass, 316, 320
Berries, 326–35.
  blackberries, 330–32
  black raspberries, 330
  blueberries, 333–35
  fertilizing, 329, 335, 336
  harvesting, 329, 332
  mulching, 329
  pests and diseases, 332, 335
  pruning, 332, 335, 344
  raspberries, 330–32
  strawberries, 327–29
  watering, 329
Bible leaf, 204
Biblical Gardens, 210
Bird feeders, 303–5
Birds, 300–311
  birdfeed, 301–2
  bird feeders, 303–5
  bluebird house, 311
  gardening for, 306–9
  hummingbird gardens, 243, 308–9
  nest boxes, 310–11

as pests, 297
  suet, 301, 302
Bishop's weed, 324
Blackberries
  growing, 330–32
  pests, 332
Black-eyed Susan, 241, 244, 313
Black polyethylene mulch, 169, 279, 281
Black raspberries, 330
Blackspot, 239
Black-vine weevils, 335
Blanketflower, 241, 244
Block flooring, 101
Blueberries. *See also* Berries
  growing, 333–35
  Pie Deluxe, 334
Bluebird house, 311
Blue-eyed grass, 241, 244
Blue flax, 241, 244
Bluegrass, 316, 320
Bluets, 324
Bog gardening, 253 (def.), 256–57, 260
Bored wells, 31, 32
Borers, 239
Boron for soil, 271
Botanical pesticides, 292
Botrytis rot, 295
Braconid wasps, 289
Braiding garlic, 206
Brambles. See Berries; Blackberries; Raspberries
Brassicas, 159
Brick homes, 7
Brick patios, 24, 25
Broccoli
  growing, 159, 176, 187
  harvesting, 181
  seed saving, 185
Broth, herbal, 201
Brussels sprouts
  growing, 159, 187
  seed saving, 185
Bt (Bacillus thuringiensis), 292, 347
Btu, 61 (def.)
Bubel, Mike and Nancy, 182

Buddleia, 233
Building a home, 12–15
Bulbs, 226–30, 364
Bunchberry, 324
Burch, Monte, 22
Burnet, 204
Bush roses, 235
Bushway, Stephen, 64
Butterfly gardens, 243, 312, 313
Butterfly weed, 241, 244
Byers, Dorie, 200

C

Cabbage
  companions, 160
  growing, 159, 176, 187
  seed saving, 185
Cabbage loopers, 290
Cages, vegetable, 179
Caladium, 228
Calcium in water, 46
Calendar lampshade, 141
Calendula, 176, 216, 247
California poppy, 241, 244
Calla lily, 228
Campbell, Stuart, 274
Candytuft, 324
Cane, 327 (def.), 331, 332
Cane borers, 332
Carbon filters, 42
Carbon-to-nitrogen ration in compost, 272–73
Carpet bugleweed, 324
Carpeting, 110–11, 147, 151
Carrots
  companions, 160
  growing, 159, 188
  rotation, 161
  seed saving, 185
Cartridge faucets, 52
Castings, worm, 277
Caterpillars, 239
Catmint (catnip), 204, 287
Cats, 518–19
Cauliflower
  companions, 160
Cauliflower (continued)
  growing, 159, 176, 188
  rotation, 161
  seed saving, 185

Ceiling
  lights, 86
  inspecting, 10
  repairs, 118–19
Cellars
  inspecting, 11
  root, 180–83
Centipede grass, 316
Centrifugal pumps, 34–35, 36
Ceramic tile, 108–9
Cesspools, 51
Chaenomeles, 233
Chain saws, 70
Chairs
  Adirondack, 26–27
  ladder-back, 134–35
Chamomile, 204, 287
Chickens
  water for, 44
Chickweed, 320
Chiffon cleaning, 148
Children's flower gardens, 217
Chinch bugs, 323
Chintz cleaning, 148
Chipmunks, 297
Chives, 176, 199, 204, 287
Chlorides in water, 46
Chlorination, 43
Chrysanthemum, 224, 247
Cinquefoil, 320
Circuit breaker, 83 (def.), 84
Circuits, blown, 84, 98
Cisterns, 41
Clay soil, 268
Cleaning. See Housekeeping
Cleft grafting, 343
Climbing roses, 235, 352
Clover, 321, 325
Coal for heating, 61, 72
Cold and Flu Garden, 200
Cold frames, 169
Collards, 176, 188
Collectors (solar panels), 76
Colorado columbine, 241, 244
Colorado potato beetles, 290
Comforters, cleaning, 148
Companion planting, 160, 287
Composting, 272–78
Concrete patios, 24, 25
Concrete walks, 21

Connections, electrical, 86–87
Construction (home), 12–15
Containers
  for flowers, 217
  for herbs, 211
  for vegetables, 170–71
Contaminants (water), removing, 46–47
Convertible stoves, 62
Cooling homes, 81
Cool-season
  grasses, 315 (def.), 316
  vegetables, 166
Coping, 18 (def.)
Cord (wood), 61 (def.), 69
Cord repairs, 91
Coreopsis, 224
Corn
  companions, 160
  growing, 159, 189
  seed saving, 185
Corn earworms, 290
Cornus, 233
Cosmos, 176, 216, 241, 244, 313
Costmary, 204
Cotton cleaning, 148
Counterboring, 367 (def.)
Country homes, 2–15. See also Decorating; Electricity; Heating homes; Home improvements; Housekeeping; Plumbing; Tools; Water supply
  building a home, 12–15
  inspecting, 8–11
  land for, 2–5
  types of, 6–7
Courses, 18 (def.)
Cover crops, 282
Covering plants, 286
Crabgrass, 320
Cranberry fruit worm, 335
Creeping bent grass, 320
Creeping Charlie, 324
Creeping lilyturf, 324
Creosote buildup, 65
Crocus, 227, 228
Crops
  cover, 282
  rotation, 161, 285, 285 (def.)
  trap, 285 (def.)
  vine, 159, 354–55

Crown, 314, 315 (def.)
Crown borers, 332
Crown imperial, 227, 228
Crown vetch, 324
Cucumber beetles, 290
Cucumbers
  companions, 160
  growing, 159, 167, 189
  seed saving, 185
Cultivar, 327 (def.), 336
Cupboard, 136–37
Curtains
  swag, 125 (def.)
  tab, 130–31
Cut-Flower Garden, 243
Cuts, infusion, 201
Cutting back, 221
Cutworms, 290

Daffodil, 227, 228, 247
Dahlia, 228, 230, 247
Dallis grass, 320
Damping-off, 294
Dandelions, 320
Daphne, 233
Daylily, 224
DC, 83 (def.), 92, 93, 96
Dead-bolt locks, 123
Deadheading, 213 (def.), 215, 220, 232
Decker, Phillip J. and T. Newell, 48
Decks, 22–23
Decorating, 124–43. See also Home improvements
  furniture renovation, 138–43
  lampshade, calendar, 141
  moldings, 137
  with plants, 127
  re-upholstery, 141
  stenciling walls, 125 (def.), 128–29
  tab curtains, 130–31
  tips, 124–27
Deer deterrents, 299
DE (diatomaceous earth) filters, 42, 292
Delphinium, 224
Desiccants for drying, 213 (def.), 250
Detail sanders, 142
Dethatching, 322
Dewberries, 330
Diatomaceous earth (DE), 42, 292

Dichondra, 324
Diesel generators, 97
Dill, 176, 205, 287
Dill Pickles, 458–59
Dimmer switches, 89
Disbudding, 221
Diseases, plant, 294–95
Dividing perennials, 223
Dodt, Colleen, 150
Dogtooth violet, 229
Doorknobs, 122
Doors
  inspecting, 10–11
  repairs, 122–23
  weatherizing, 80, 81
Dormant oil sprays, 346
DOT cylinders, 73
Double-digging, 171
Double hill system, 329
Dowelling jig, 541, 385
Downdraft stoves, 62
Dowsers, 29
Drains, clogged, 56–57
Drawdown, 29 (def.)
Drills and bits, 384
Drum sanders, 102, 103
Drying
  flowers, 250
  herbs, 202
Dry walls, 18 (def.)
Dusting, 144
Dusts for pests, 292–93
Dwarf fruit orchard, 341

Early-Spring Woodland Garden, 242
Earth-friendlier toilets, 54
Earthworms, 269, 276–77
Eastern columbine, 241, 244
Easy and Fragrant Kitchen Border, 200
Echinacea, 205, 225
Edgers for sanding, 102, 103
Edgings for perennials, 222–23
Eggplant
  companions, 160
  growing, 159, 176, 189
  seed saving, 185
Eggs, 410–12, 413
Ejector (jet) pumps, 35–36
Elastic storage cells, 41
Electricity, 82–99
  assessing system, 84–85
  boosting system, 88

circuits, blown, 84, 98
connections, 86–87
cord repairs, 91
in emergencies, 99
generators, fossil-fuel, 97
inspecting, 10
light fixtures, 90–91, 98
needs, determining, 95
new work, installing, 85
outlets, replacing, 90
photovoltaics, 92–95
plugs, replacing, 90
repairing, 90–91
rewiring, 85, 86–89
solar, 92–95
switches, replacing, 88–89
understanding, 82–83
wind power, 95, 96
Electric sanders, 142
Embankment ponds, 38–39
Emergence time of pests,
   285 (def.), 288
Emergencies
   power outages, 99
   water in, 45
English ivy, 324
Erosion chlorinators, 43
Essential oils, 125 (def.),
   151, 153
Evergreens
   for birds, 306
   shrubs, 233
Excavated ponds, 38

Fabric cleaning, 148–49
Felling trees, 70
Fence trellises, 179
Fennel, 206, 287
Ferns, 324
Fertilizing
   berries and fruits, 329,
      335, 336
   by composting, 213 (def.),
      272–78
   flowers, 215, 227, 237
Fescue, 316, 321
Feverfew, 206
Filtration systems, 42–43
Fire-building, 66
Fireplaces and woodstoves,
   62–65
Fir trees, 526
First-Aid Garden, 201
Fish
   cleaning, 423
   for ponds, 257

Flagstone paths, 20
Flagstone patios, 24, 25
Fleas, 153, 518-19
Flooring
   carpeting, 110–11, 147, 151
   cleaning, 147, 151
   hardwood, 102–5
   inspecting, 11
   insulating, 78
   squeaky, 104
   vinyl, 106–7
Floribunda roses, 235, 237
Flow, in water systems 29
Flower gardens, 212–51. See
   also specific flowers
   air-drying plants, 248–49
   annuals, 213 (def.),
      213–17, 363
   arrangements, 213, 247
   Arranger's Garden, 246–47
   arranging tips, 213
   bare-root rose planting, 236
   bulbs, 226–30, 364
   for butterflies, 243, 312–13
   for children, 217
   in containers, 217
   Cut-Flower Garden, 243
   cutting back, 221
   deadheading, 213 (def.),
      215, 220, 232
   disbudding, 221
   dividing perennials, 223
   drying with desiccants, 213
      (def.), 250
   Early-Spring Woodland
      Garden, 242
   edgings for perennials,
      222–23
   fertilizing, 215, 227, 237
   grasses, native, 240
   ground cover, 213 (def.),
      243
   Hummingbird Garden,
      243, 308–9
   mulching, 215, 227
   perennials, 213 (def.),
      218–25, 226, 362
   pinching back, 221
   pressing flowers, 250, 251
   pruning, 215, 232, 237
   Rock Garden, 243
   roses, 234–38, 239, 247
   shrubs, 231–32, 233, 307
   spring-flowering bulbs,
      226–27
   staking, 222

summer-flowering bulbs,
   230
   watering, 215, 227
   wildflowers, 240–45, 309,
      313
   winterizing roses, 238
   Xeriscape Garden, 242
Flu and Cold Garden, 200
Flue, 62–63, 64, 65
Fluoride in water, 46
Footings, 18 (def.), 19
Foundation, weatherizing, 80
Fragrance Gardens, 210
Fragrant and Easy Kitchen
   Border, 200
Franklin, Stuart, 314
Freesia, 228
Frost dates, 170
Frozen pipes, 59
Fruit trees (orchards)
   dwarf fruit orchard, 341
   grafting fruit trees, 317
      (def.), 343
   growing, 340–47
   harvesting, 345
   pests and diseases, 346–47
   pollination, 345
   pruning, 344
Fruit worms, 332
Fuelwood, 68–70
Fungi in plants, 295
Furniture
   Adirondack chair, 26–27
   bent willow, 132
   cleaning, 146
   ladder-back chair, 134–35
   outdoor, 26–27
   renovation, 138–43
Fuse, 83, 84

Gardening. See Arbors and
   trellises; Berries and
   fruits; Birds and butterflies; Flower gardens;
   Greenhouses; Herb gar-
   dens; Lawn care; Pests
   and diseases; Sheds; Soil
   improvement; Vegetable
   gardens; Water and rock
   gardens
Garden sheds, 367–70
Garlic, 206, 287, 443
Garlic sprays for pests, 292
Gas for heating, 73
Gasket, 120, 121
Gasoline generators, 97

Gayfeather, 241, 245, 313
Generators, fossil-fuel, 97
Germination, 172
GFCI (ground fault circuit
   interrupter), 83, 84
Gladiolus, 228, 230, 247
Gloriosa lily, 228
Golden moneywort, 324
Gophers, 296
Grafting fruit trees, 327
Grandiflora roses, 235
Grape hyacinth, 227, 228
Grapes
   growing, 336–39
   Kniffen pruning system,
      338
   wine making, 339
Grass
   cool-season, 315, 316
   farming, 524–25
   native, 240
   warm-season, 315, 316
Gravity tanks, 41
Gravity Water Systems, 76,
   77
Greasy stains, 149
Grecian windflower, 228
Greenhouses, 358–65
   for annuals, 363
   for bedding plants, 363
   for bulbs, 364
   for herbs, 361
   for perennials, 362
   pests and diseases, 365
   potting soil, 363
   site for, 360
   types of, 359
   for vegetables, 364
Green lacewings, 289
Green manures, 282–83
Ground beetles, 289
Ground covers
   flowering, 213 (def.), 243
   herb, 210
   for lawns, 324–25
   roses, 235
Ground fault circuit interrupter (GFCI), 83, 84
Groundhogs, 297
Ground ivy, 320
Groundwater, 29 (def.), 30,
   37, 46
Grubs, 323
Guntlow, Pauline, 124

Half-hardy annuals, 215
Hammers, 382
Handpicking pests, 293
Hand sanding, 142
Handsaws, 381
Hand tools, 381-382
Hardening off, 174
Hard water, 46
Hardwood floors, 102–5
Hardy annuals, 215
Harvest, preserving, 428–43
  berries and fruits, 329,
    332, 345
  flowers, 250–51
  herbs, 202
  vegetables, 180–83
Head, 29 (def.)
Heating homes, 60–81
  with coal, 61, 72
  cooling in summer, 81
  costs, cutting, 81
  doors, weatherizing, 80
  fire-building, 66
  fuelwood, 68–70
  with gas, 73
  inspecting system, 10
  insulating, 78–81
  passive solar design, 74–75
  pellet stoves, 67
  solar domestic hot water
    heating, 76–77
  with solar energy, 74–77
  stacks, cleaning, 65
  weatherproofing, 78–81
  window heat loss, 79
  with wood, 61, 66–71
  woodsheds, 70–71
  woodstoves and fireplaces,
    62–65
Heldmann, Carl, 12
Herbal
  Soap Ball, 199
  teas, 201
  Wreath, 203
Herbal vinegar
  for cleaning, 150–51
  making, 205
Herb gardens, 198–211. See
  also specific herbs
  Bee Gardens, 211
  Biblical Gardens, 210
  broth, 201
  Cold and Flu Garden, 200
  Container Gardens, 211
  cuts and scrapes infusion,
    201

drying herbs, 202
Easy and Fragrant Kitchen
  Border, 200
First-Aid Garden, 201
Fragrance Gardens, 210
  ground covers, 210, 213
  harvesting and storing, 202
Herbal Soap Ball, 199
  herbal vinegars, 205
Herbal Wreath, 203
Partial Shade Gardens, 210
Potpourri Gardens, 211
Rock Gardens, 210
Salad Gardens, 210
Shakespeare Gardens, 211
  starting with, 198–99
Tea Gardens, 211
Herbicides, 315 (def.)
Herb(s)
  companion planting for
    pest control, 287
  greenhouses for, 361
  for moth control, 152
  for pest control, 293
Heritage roses, 235
Herrick, Lyn, 50, 100
Highbush blueberries, 333
High-yield gardening, 177
Hill, Cherry, 496
Hill, Lewis and Nancy, 326
Home improvements,
  100–123. See also
    Decorating; Electricity;
    Heating homes;
    Plumbing
  carpeting, 110–11, 147,
    151
  ceiling repairs, 10, 118–19
  ceramic tile, 108–9
  dead-bolt locks, 123
  door repairs, 10–11, 122–23
  glazing compound, replac-
    ing, 120
  hardwood floors, 102–5
  loose boards, 103
  molding, removing, 102
  painting, 112–13
  plaster wall repairs, 118
  refinishing wood floors,
    104–5
  sanding wood floors, 102–3
  screen repairs, 121
  sheetrock repairs, 119
  squeaky floors, 104
  stripping wood floors, 103
  vinyl flooring, 106–7

wallpapering, 114–17, 146
wall repairs, 10, 118–19
window repairs, 10–11,
  120–21
wooden flooring, 100–105
Horehound, 207
Horseradish, 190, 287
Hosta, 225, 325
Hot caps, 169
Hot Pepper Jelly, 193
Hot water systems, 76–77
Housekeeping, 144–55
  bathrooms, 145
  dusting, 144
  with essential oils, 125
    (def.), 151, 153
  fabrics, 148–49
  furniture, 146
  with herbal vinegar,
    150–51
  kitchens, 144–45
  laundry, 148–49
  milk-based soap, 154–55
  mirrors, 146
  moth control with herbs,
    152
  and pests, 153
  rugs, 147
  Shepherd's Pride, 155
  soapmaking, 154–55
  wallpaper cleaning, 146
  windows, 147
Hummingbirds, 301
  gardens for 243, 307–9
Humus, 267 (def.), 328
Hyacinth, 227, 229
Hybrid tea roses, 235, 237
Hydrangeas, 233
Hyssop, 207, 287

Ichneumon wasps, 289
Impatiens, 216, 313
Impounded water, 39
Indoors, sowing seeds,
  172–73
Insects. See Pests and
  diseases
Inspecting
  homes, 8–11
  plumbing, 10, 48–50
Insulating
  homes, 78–81
  pipes, 58
Iris, 225, 229, 247, 256
Iron for soil, 271
Iron in water, 46

Ivy, 320, 324

Jacobs, Betty E.M., 248
Jamb, 101 (def.), 106, 122
Japanese
  beetles, 290–91
  rock gardens, 264
  spurge, 325
Jerusalem artichokes, 190
Jet (ejector) pumps, 35–36
Jetted wells, 32–33
Joists, 101 (def.), 104

Kale
  growing, 159, 176, 190
  rotation, 161
  seed saving, 185
Kitchen
  Border, Easy and
    Fragrant, 200
  cleaning, 144–45
  design, 383
  inspecting, 10
Kniffen pruning system, 338

Lace cleaning, 148
Ladder, quilt, 133
Ladder-back chair, 134–35
Ladybugs, 289
Lampshade, calendar, 141
Lance-leaved coreopsis, 241,
  245
Land, finding, 2–5
Landscaping, 16–27. See also
  Arbors and trellises;
  Gardening; Lawn care;
  Sheds; Soil improve-
  ment; Water supply
  concrete walk, 21
  decks, 22–23
  flagstone path, 20
  furniture, outdoor, 26–27
  patios, 24–25
  stonescaping, 16–19
  stone wall, 18–19
  walks and paths, 20–25
Latex paints, 112
Laundry, 148–49
Lavender, 207
Lawn care, 314–25
  aerating, 322
  cool-season grasses, 316
  dethatching, 322
  diseases, 322–23
  ground covers, 210,
    213 (def.), 243, 324–25

installing new lawn, 314–19
pests, 323
seeding lawns, 317, 323
sod, laying, 317, 318–19
warm-season grasses, 316
weeds, 320–21
Leaching system, 51
Lead and health, 8
Leadwort, 325
Leafhoppers, 239
Leaf spot, 294
Leafy greens, 159
Leeks, 176,185, 190
Legumes, 159, 267, 282
Lemon balm, 207
Lemon verbena, 207
Lettuce
  companions, 160
  growing, 159, 176, 190–91
  rotation, 161
  seed saving, 185
Light fixtures, 90–91, 98
Lilac (*syringa*), 233
Lily, 229, 230, 247
Lily of the Nile, 229
Lily of the valley, 325
Linen cleaning, 148
Liquified-petroleum gas
  (LP gas), 73, 97
Lizards, 365
Llamas, 483
Loam, 267 (def.), 268
Locks, dead-bolt, 123
Log homes, 6
Long, Jim, 348
Lounging arbor, 349–51
Loose boards, repair of, 103
Lovage, 207
Lowbush blueberries, 333
Low-e glass, 61 (def.), 75
LP gas (liquified-petroleum
  gas), 73, 97
Lye, 125 (def.), 154, 155

M
Macunovich, Janet, 222
Maggots, 335
Magnesium for soil, 271
Magnesium in water, 46
Mahnken, Jan, 300
Manganese for soil, 271
Manganese in water, 46
Marigold, African, 216
Marjoram, 176, 207
McKenzie, James, 138
McRaven, Charles, 16
Mealybug destroyers, 289

Melons, 159–60, 185, 191
Metals in water, 46–47
Mexican bean beetles, 291
Mexican hat, 241, 245
Mice deterrents, 296
Microclimates, 163, 361
Midges, rose, 239
Milk-based soap, 154–55
Milk freezing, 403
Milky spore disease (*Bacillus
  popilliae*), 293, 347
Miniature roses, 235
Mint, 207, 287
Mirror cleaning, 146
Moldings, 102, 137
Mole deterrents, 296
Morning glory, 216, 313
Mosaic virus, 294
Moths, 152
Mulching
  berries and fruits, 329
  flowers, 215, 227
  soil, 279–81
  types of mulch, 169, 279, 281
  vegetables, 168–69
Mustard, 191, 456
Mycoplasmas, 295
Myrtle, 325

N
Nasturtium, 216, 287
Native plants, 253, 260
Nematodes, 295
Nest boxes, 310–11
New England aster, 241, 245
Newton, Hardie, 212
New Zealand Box, 274–75
Nightshade family, 159
Nimble will, 321
Nitrates in water, 46
Nitrogen fixation, 267 (def.),
  282
Nitrogen for soil, 271
Nut sedge, 321

O
Off the grid. *See also* Solar
  energy
  earth-friendlier toilets, 54
  generators, 97
  liquified-petroleum gas
    (LP gas), 73, 97
  thermal electric stoves, 67
Okra, 185, 191
Onions
  companions, 160
  growing, 159, 176, 192
  rotation, 161

seed saving, 185
Oregano, 208
Organic matter for soil, 267,
  268, 270–71
Ornamental trees for birds,
  307
Oster, Maggie, 150
Outdoors, sowing seeds,
  174–75, 317
Outlets, replacing, 90
Oven cleaning, 144
Oxalis, 321

P
Painting, 112–13
Pansy, 216
Parsley
  companions, 160
  growing, 208
  seed saving, 185
Parsnips
  growing, 159, 192–93
  seed saving, 185
Pasqueflower, 241, 245
Passive solar design, 74–75
Paths and walks, 20–25
Patios, 24–25
Peach trees, 340–45
Pear trees, 340–45
Peas
  companions, 160
  growing, 159, 193
  rotation, 161
  seed saving, 185
Peat moss, 171
Pectin, 429 (def.), 447
Pellet stoves, 67
Pennyroyal, 208
Peony, 225, 247
Peppers
  companions, 160
  growing, 159, 176, 193
  seed saving, 185
Pepper sprays for pests, 292
Perennials, 218–25, 226, 362
Periwinkle, 325
Perlite, 171
Peruvian lily, 229
Pesticides, 285, 292
Pests and diseases, 284–99
  animal deterrents, 296–99
  ants, 153
  aphids, 239, 290
  assassin bugs, 289
  bacteria, 295
  beetles, 239
  beneficial insects, 285

(def.), 289
  birds, 297
  blackspot, 239
  black-vine weevils, 335
  borers, 239
  botrytis rot, 295
  braconid wasps, 289
  cabbage loopers, 290
  cane borers, 332
  caterpillars, 239
  chinch bugs, 323
  Colorado potato beetles,
    290
  and companion planting
    with herbs, 287
  corn earworms, 290
  and covering plants, 286
  cranberry fruit worm, 335
  crown borers, 332
  cucumber beetles, 290
  cutworms, 290
  damping-off, 294
  deer, 299
  diseases, 294–95
  emergence time of pests,
    285 (def.), 288
  fleas, 153
  of fruits and berries, 332,
    335, 346–47
  fruit worms, 332
  fungi, 295
  gophers, 296
  in greenhouses, 365
  green lacewings, 289
  ground beetles, 289
  groundhogs, 297
  grubs, 323
  ichneumon wasps, 289
  Japanese beetles, 290–91
  ladybugs, 289
  lawn diseases, 322–23
  in lawns, 322–23
  leafhoppers, 239
  leaf spot, 294
  lizards, 365
  maggots, 335
  mealybug destroyers, 289
  Mexican bean beetles, 291
Pests and diseases
  (continued)
  mice, 296
  midges, rose, 239
  moles, 296
  Mosaic virus, 294
  moths, 152
  mycoplasmas, 295

nematodes, 295
pesticides, 292
powdery mildew, 239
praying mantids, 289
predatory mites, 289
rabbits, 296
raccoons, 298
rats, 296
roaches, 153
root maggots, 291
of roses, 239
and rotating crops, 161,
    285
rust, 239
sawflies, 332
silverfish, 153
slugs and snails, 298
sod webworms, 323
and soil solarization, 286
spider mites, 239, 291, 332
spined soldier beetles, 289
sprays and dusts for,
    292–93, 346–47
squash bugs, 291
squirrels and chipmunks,
    297
tachinid flies, 289
thrips, 239
tomato hornworms, 291
trichogramma wasps, 289
viruses, 294, 295
voles, 296
whiteflies, 291, 365
woodchucks, 297
worms, 239
yellow jackets, 291
Petunia, 176, 216, 287
Phlox, 225, 313
pH of soil, 270, 315
Phosphorus for soil, 271
Photosynthesis, 315 (def.)
Photovoltaics, 92–94
Pinching back, 221
Pipes, water, 49, 58–59
Piston (reciprocating)
    pumps, 34
Plantain, 320
Plants. *See also* specific plants
    decorating with, 127
Plaster wall repairs, 118
Plastic pipes, 59
Plugs, electric, replacing, 90
Plumbago, 325
Plumbing, 48–59
    ball, replacing, 55
    drains, clogged, 56–57

faucets, leaky, 51–53
frozen pipes, thawing, 59
inspecting, 10, 48–50
insulating pipes, 58
pipes, 49, 58–59
plastic pipes, 59
septic systems, 9, 51
toilets, 54–55
water, turning off, 50
Pole-built homes, 6
Pollination, 345
Ponds, 38–39, 252–55
Pool gardens, 253–55
Positive displacement
    pumps, 43
Posts, setting
    fence, 510
    shed, 372–73
Potassium for soil, 271
Potatoes
    growing, 159, 194
    rotation, 161
    seed saving, 185
Potentilla, 233
Potpourri Gardens, 211
Potting soil, 363
Powdery mildew, 239
Power sawing, 70, 540
Praying mantids, 289
Predatory mites, 289
Pressing flowers, 250, 251
Pressure tanks, 41
Propane
    generators, 97
    liquified-petroleum gas, 73
Prostrate knotweed, 320
Pruning
    annuals, 215
    berries, 332, 335
    fruit trees, 344
    grapes (Kniffen system),
        338
    hybrid tea rose, 237
    perennials, 220–21
    shrubs, 232
PSI, 29 (def.)
Pumpkins
    growing, 159, 194, 195
    seed saving, 185
    shell bowl from, 395
Pumps, water, 9, 34–36, 257
Purlin, 367 (def.), 371
Purple coneflower, 241, 245
Purple raspberries, 330
Purslane, 320

Quilt ladder, 133

Rabbit-eye blueberries, 333
Rabbits
    deterrents, 296
Raccoons, 298
Radishes, 159–61, 185, 195
Radium in water, 47
Radon and health, 8, 47
Raised beds, 162–63
Ranunculus, 229, 230
Raspberries
    growing, 330–32
    pests, 332
Rat deterrents, 296
Red raspberries, 330
Refinishing
    furniture, 142–43
    wood floors, 104–5
Relishes, 428, 459
Rennet, 399
Repairs. *See* Home improve-
    ments
Retaining walls, 18 (def.)
Reupholstery, 141
Rewiring, 85, 86–89
Rhododendron, 233
Rhubarb, 195
Riotte, Louise, 160, 252
Roaches, 153
Robinson, David, 28
Robinson, Ed and Carolyn,
    4, 382
Rock gardens, 210, 243, 253,
    261–65
Roof inspecting, 8
Root
    cellars, 180–83, 429
    maggots, 291
    vegetables, 159, 181
    zone, 314, 315 (def.)
Rosemary, 187, 208
Roses
    arbor, 352–53
    for arrangements, 247
    growing, 234–38
    pests and diseases, 239
Rotation, crop, 161, 285
Rotor (windwheel), 96
Routers, 385
Row covers, 168
Row planting, 164–65
Rue, 208, 287
Rugs, 110–11, 147, 151

Runners, 327, 329
Rust, 239
Rutabagas, 185, 196
R-value, 61 (def.), 78
Ryegrass, 316

Sage, 160, 208, 287
Salad Gardens, 210
Salvia, 216
Sand filters, 42
Sand for drying flowers, 250
Sanding, 385
    furniture, 142, 143
    wood floors, 102–3
Sandy soil, 268
Sawflies, 332
Saws
    chain saws, 70
    handsaws, 381
    power sawing, 384
Scarecrows, 176
Scarifying seeds, 173
Scented geraniums, 209
Scion, 327 (def.), 343
Scrapes, infusion, 201
Screen repairs, 121
Sealing for hardwood floors,
    104
Season extenders, 168–70
Sedum, 225, 325
Seeding lawns, 317, 323
Seeds
    growing from, 170–77, 317
    saving, 184, 185
Septic systems, 9, 51
Shade gardens, 210
Shakespeare Gardens, 211
Sharpening tools, 68, 384
Sheds, 366–79
    garden, 367–70
    storage, 371
    tool, 372–74
    tree houses, 375–79
    wood, 70–71
Sheetrock repairs, 119
Shelton, Jay, 60
Shepherd's Pride, 155
Shrub roses, 235
Shrubs, 231–32, 233, 307
Shutoff valve, 49, 50
Silica gel for drying flowers,
    250
Sillcock, 29 (def.)
Silverfish, 153
Sink augers, 57
Sink cleaning, 145

Slugs, 298
Snails, 298
Snapdragon, 176, 216
Snowdrop, 227, 229
Snow-on-the-mountain, 324
Soap Ball, Herbal, 199
Soapmaking, 154–55
Soap sprays for pests, 292
Sod, laying, 317, 318–19
Sod webworms, 323
Soil improvement, 266–83
  carbon-to-nitrogen ration
    in compost, 272–73
  by composting, 213 (def.),
    272–78
  and earthworms, 269,
    276–77
  by green manures, 282–83
  by mulching, 215, 227,
    279–81
  New Zealand Box, 274–75
  nutrients, 271
  organic matter for, 267,
    268, 270–71
  and organisms, 269
  pH of, 270, 315
  solarization for pests, 286
Soil improvement
    (continued)
  structure of, 268
  subsoil, 267
  texture of, 268
  tips, 4, 267
  by trench composting,
    276
  by worm composting,
    276–77
Solar energy
  for electricity, 92–95
  for heating, 74–77
  for heating water, 76–77
Solar gain, 61 (def.), 74
Sorrel, 209
Soups, 384–85
Sphagnum moss, 171
Spider mites, 239, 291,
  332
Spiderwort, 241, 245
Spinach
  companions, 160
  growing, 159, 196
  seed saving, 185
Spined soldier beetles, 289
Spirea, 233
Splitting wood, 69
Spotted spurge, 321

Sprays for pests, 292–93,
  346–47
Spring-flowering bulbs,
  226–27
Springs for water, 4, 37
Spruce trees, 527
Squash
  companions, 160
  growing, 159, 176, 196
  seed saving, 185
Squash bugs, 291
Squeaky floors, 104
Squirrels, 297
St. Augustine grass, 316
Stacks, cleaning, 65
Stain cleaning, 149
Staining
  furniture, 143
  hardwood floors, 104
Staking plants, 178, 197,
  222
Star of Bethlehem, 229
Stell, Elizabeth P., 266
Stenciling walls, 128–29
Sticky drawers, 138–39
Sticky traps for pests, 293
Stiles, Jeanie and David,
  376
Stonecrop, 325
Stone homes, 6–7
Stonescaping, 16–19
Stone walls, 18–19
Storage sheds, 371
Storm doors, 80
Storm windows, 79
Stoves
  pellet, 67
  woodstoves for heat, 62–65
Strawberries
  growing, 327–29
Stripping
  furniture, 140–41
  wood floors, 103
Subflooring, 100, 106, 110
Submersible pumps, 35, 36,
  257
Subsoil, 267
Succession planting, 161
Suet, 301, 302
Sulfates in water, 46
Summer-flowering bulbs,
  230
Sunflower, 216, 313
Sweet pea, 216
Sweet potatoes, 196–97
Sweet-scented gladiolus, 229

Sweet woodruff, 209, 325
Swept area, 83 (def.), 96
Switches, replacing, 88–89

Tab curtains, 130–31
Tachinid flies, 289
Tarragon, 209
Tea Gardens, 211
Teas, herbal, 201
Tender annuals, 215
Tepee trellises, 178
Thatch, 315 (def.), 322
Thermal
  electric stoves, 67
  mass, 61 (def.), 75
Three-way switches, 89
Three-wire extension cords,
  90
Thrips, 239
Thyme, 209, 287
Tile, ceramic, 108–9
Tincture, echinacea, 205
Toenailing, 367 (def.), 368,
  369
Toilets, 54–55
Tomatoes
  companions, 160
  growing, 159, 176, 177, 197
  rotation, 161
  seed saving, 185
Tomato hornworms, 291
Tools, 380-385
  axes, 68
  chain saws, 70
  dowelling jig, 385
  drills and bits, 384
  hammers, 382
  handsaws, 381
  hand tools, 381-383
  levels, 381
  nails, 382
  post-hole diggers, 385
  power fasteners, 385
  power sawing, 384
  routers, 385
  sanders, 385
  sharpening, 384
  squares, 381
  toolbox, 383
Toolsheds, 372–74
Topdressings, 279
Transplanting, 173
Trap crop, 285 (def.)
Tree houses, 375–79
Tree roses, 235

Trees
  for birds, 306, 307
  felling, 70
Trellises and arbors, 348–57
Trellising vining crops,
  354–55
Trench composting, 276
Trichogramma wasps, 289
Trout lily, 229
Tuberous begonia, 229
Tulip, 227, 229, 247
Turnips, 159, 185, 197

UF wires, 85
Underground homes, 7
Underlayment, 100, 101

Vapor barrier, 61, 78, 79
Varnishing hardwood floors,
  105
Vegetable gardens, 158–97.
  A-frame trellises, 179
  cages, 179
  cold frames, 169
  companion planting, 160,
    287
  cool-season vegetables, 166
  double-digging, 171
  fence trellises, 179
  frost dates, 170
  germination, 172
  greenhouses for, 364
  hardening off, 174
  harvesting and storage,
    180–83
  high-yield gardening, 177
  hot caps, 169
  microclimates, 163
  mulches, 168–69
  phenology, 167
  planning, 158–65
  raised beds, 162–63
  root cellars, 180–83
  root vegetables, 159, 181
  rotation practices, 161,
    285, 285 (def.)
  row covers, 168
  scarecrows, 176
Vegetable gardens
    (continued)
  season extenders, 168–70
  seeds, growing from,
    170–77
  seed saving, 184, 185
  sowing seeds, 172–75
  staking, 178, 197

succession planting, 161
tepee trellises, 178
tips, 162
transplanting, 173
trellising, 178–79
warm-season vegetables, 166–67
wide row planting, 164–65
Veneer repairs, 139
Vermicompost, 267 (def.)
Vermiculite, 171
Veronica, 321
Vertical plant growing, 178–79
Viburnum, 233
Vine crops, 159, 354–55
Vinegar, distilled white, 125
Vinegar, herbal
  for cleaning, 150–51
  making, 205
Vinyl flooring, 106–7
Violet, 324
Viruses, plant, 294, 295
Vole deterrents, 296

Walks and paths, 20–25
Wall boxes, 86
Wall-O-Water hot cap, 169
Wallpaper, 114–17, 146
Walls
  inspecting, 10
  insulating, 78
  repairs, 118–19
  stenciling, 128–29
  stone, 18–19
Warm-season
  grasses, 315, 316
  vegetables, 166–67
Water.
  hammer, 49

heating, solar domestic, 76–77
  pressure, 49
  table, 29 (def.)
  turning off, 50
Water gardens, 252–65
  bog gardening, 253 (def.), 256–57, 260
  fish for ponds, 257
  plants for, 260, 263–65
  pool gardens, 253–55
  waterfalls, 257
  water lily planting, 253, 258–59
Watercress, 209
Waterfalls, 257
Water-flow-activated chlorinators, 43
Watering
  berries and fruits, 329
  flowers, 215, 227
Water lily, 253, 258–59
Water supply, 28–47. See also Plumbing
  bored wells, 31, 32
  centrifugal pumps, 34–35, 36
  chlorination, 43
  contaminants, removing, 46–47
  distribution system, 40–41
  dowsers, 29
  drilled wells, 31, 33
  driven wells, 33
  dug wells, 30–31
  embankment ponds, 38–39
  in emergencies, 45
  excavated ponds, 38
  filtration systems, 42–43
  freeze protection, 41
  jet (ejector) pumps, 35–36

jetted or washed wells, 32–33
  needs, determining, 32
  ponds for, 38–39
  pumps, 9, 34–36, 257
  quality, 42–45
  reciprocating (piston) pumps, 34
  reserves, 41
  solutions, short-term, 45
  sources for, 28–29
  springs for, 4, 37
  submersible pumps, 35, 36, 257
  testing quality, 44
  wells for, 4, 28, 30–33
Watt, 83 (def.), 84
Waxing hardwood floors, 105
Weatherproofing homes, 78–81
Weeds, 320–21
Weep holes, 18 (def.)
Wells for water, 4, 28, 30–33
White clover, 321, 325
Whiteflies, 291, 365
White vinegar, 150–51
Whitner, Jan Kowalczewski, 262
Wide row planting, 164–65
Wild bergamot, 241, 245
Wildflowers, 240–45, 309, 313
Wild ginger, 325
Wild thyme, 325
Willow furniture, 132
Windows
  cleaning, 147
  heat loss, 79
  inspecting, 10–11
  repairs, 120–21

wallpapering around, 117
Wind power, 95, 96
Windwheel (rotor), 96
Wine making, 339
Winter aconite, 229
Winterizing roses, 238
Wiring, electrical, 85, 86–89
Woodchucks, 297
Wood floor refinishing, 102–5
Wood for heating, 61, 66–71
Wood-frame homes, 6
Woodsheds, 70–71
Woodstoves
  cooking on, 387
  for home heating, 62–65
Wool cleaning, 148
Wool farming, 535
Working dogs, 516
Worms
  composting, 276–77
  as pests, 239
  for soil, 269
Wreaths
  herbal, 203
Wythes, 18 (def.)

Xeriscape Garden, 242

Yards. See Gardening; Landscaping; Lawn care
Yellow jackets, 291
Yellow raspberries, 330

Zen dry landscapes, 264
Zinc for soil, 271
Zinnia, 176, 216, 247, 313
Zoysia grass, 316

HARDINESS ZONE MAP

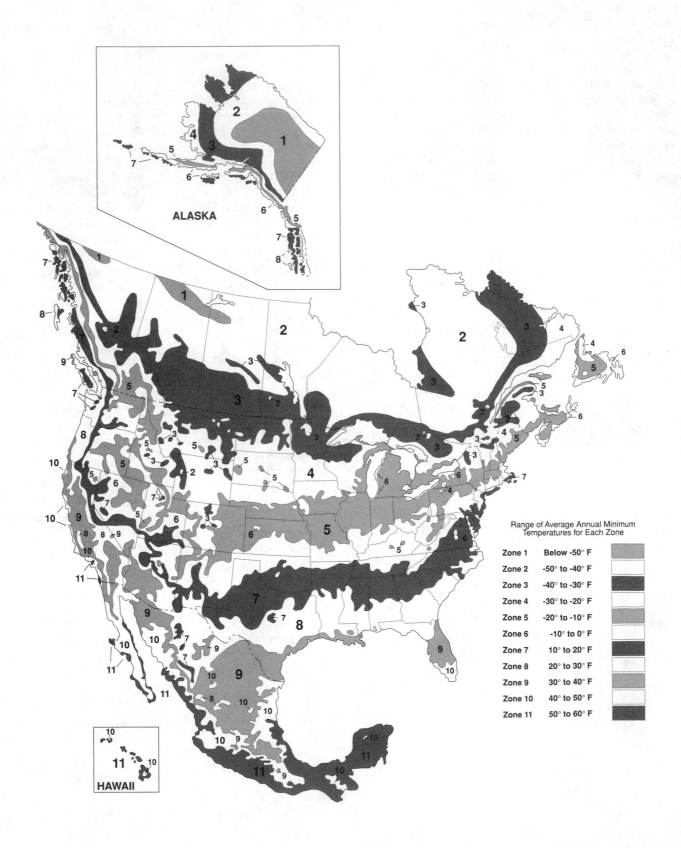

ALASKA

HAWAII

Range of Average Annual Minimum
Temperatures for Each Zone

Zone 1	Below -50° F
Zone 2	-50° to -40° F
Zone 3	-40° to -30° F
Zone 4	-30° to -20° F
Zone 5	-20° to -10° F
Zone 6	-10° to 0° F
Zone 7	10° to 20° F
Zone 8	20° to 30° F
Zone 9	30° to 40° F
Zone 10	40° to 50° F
Zone 11	50° to 60° F